MW01295174

Marc Stevens'
Government: Indicted

Believing in government is the worship of psychopaths. Ridding the world of the *idea* that governments are legitimate.

Showing there's no rational basis for government

Written by Marc Stevens; Edited by Marc Stevens, MRW and Denny Jackson; anarchy illustration by Michael of www.EndlessUnlimited.com, turtles by Kelly Coldren

Dedication

This book is dedicated to my wonderful wife who stuck through the years after my book *Adventures in Legal Land.*

Acknowledgements

First to my co-host on the **No State Project** radio show, JT; his support has been as valuable as it's been unwavering.   Calvin has been a tremendous support with the website and production of the podcast. Ian Freeman for his support of the NSP on his network LRN. To NonEntity and MRW for their help editing this book. All those men and women who freely chose to work with me since *Adventures*; I've not only had the opportunity to help you folks, but I've also been able to use our experiences to help others through the radio show, website and this book; Ernest Hancock for having me on his radio show when no one else would; John Stadmiller of RBN for putting the **No State Project** on the air; my boy Chris Case, Greg, Bill Bochynski, Armando, Denny, Kim, Vin James, Keith O'Brien, Keith in Melbourne, Sam in New Zealand, Mark, Tharrin, Dave, Poppy, Denis and too many others to list here who strive to bring about a voluntary society living consistent with the non-aggression principle. And to Brian, Mark and JT for the sand sculpture on the cover http://www.sandiegosand.com/.

As with *Adventures in Legal Land*, there's no protection from the criminal cartel known as the United States government i.e., no copyright on my work. We all stand on the shoulders of those who went before us; so it's laughable to claim these are purely original ideas and that men with guns should be used to stop others from using and copying this material. I do ask that if you see the value of my work and you copy and distribute it, then credit is given and some donation provided so I can continue working towards bringing about a voluntary society.

November 2013, Mesa, Arizona
March 2015, Mesa, Arizona

"PERHAPS the sentiments contained in the following pages, are not YET sufficiently fashionable to procure them general favor; a long habit of not thinking a thing WRONG, gives it a superficial appearance of being RIGHT, and raises at first a formidable outcry in defence of custom. But the tumult soon subsides. Time makes more converts than reason." <u>Common Sense</u>, Thomas Paine (emphasis in original).

Table of Contents

Primum non nocere
First do no harm

Preface

The concept of government is a castle made of sand. It seems to be solid, but that's to be expected when we are forced, from childhood until we're adults, to believe that. We're conditioned by those calling themselves government that the concept is so rational, so important, that society would collapse if not put into action. But it's complete nonsense, the concept falls apart under any critical analysis. It's fraud on a foundation of violence. The concept falls apart just by not using the words government and state. It's amazing people still buy into it.

Graft, bribes, no-bid contracts, murder and cover-ups are not a perversion of political systems; they are an integral part of it and the natural result. I'm thinking of Dick Cheney shooting a man in the face without any police investigation. It reminds me of those ridiculous warnings on some foods. You pick up a bag of peanuts, there is a health warning: product contains peanuts. You think so? Really? Why would a bag of peanuts have a warning there are peanuts inside?

Unfortunately, there are many times we need to point out the obvious. It's evidence people are programmed to not be able to process observable facts right in front of them. It's called confirmation bias http://en.wikipedia.org/wiki/Confirmation_bias.

People will tend to see what they are conditioned to see, and a lot of money and effort is spent every year making sure the obvious is not seen by the masses. An example is most people are oblivious to the fact they are owned by the top of society's hierarchy-though only the ones calling themselves governments openly admit to this ownership.

Don't believe we have owners? Claim to be stateless or *res nullius* and see what happens when you don't have approved ID.

I've asked prosecutors what facts they rely on their code is applicable to my client, and they tell me because the code says so. When I tell them that's circular, some have then accused me of talking in circles. Is it because they really don't see the obvious, or are they assuming I'm still just stupid? It's probably a bit of both. Either way some days it's tough playing Captain Obvious all the time, especially with people who hold doctorate degrees.

Despite the observable evidence the people are forced to support governments under threat of jail, most think they are consenting and governments are public servants. One prosecutor insisted he was a public servant doing the will of the people. Those same people you forcibly take your salary from? Those same people you will have thrown in jail if they don't pay you? You steal from them so you can do their will? Got it, sounds legit.

You have what appears to be a majority of people who see peaceful people growing plants as criminals and the dozen crazed men with machine guns breaking into their house in the middle of the night as the good guys. Or viewing a peaceful man offering silver coins to a willing market as a terrorist, but the men and women forcing millions of people to use their credit/debt as money as honorable.

Judges coerce a dozen strangers to participate in the prosecution of someone they've never met before. They sit there as dozens of witnesses are coerced into testifying to things that are irrelevant, and the judge, knowing the testimony is irrelevant, denies every single objection without explanation. He also denies all cross-examination into essential elements of the prosecutor's charges.

This insanity is tolerated by twelve adults. How and why is that possible? The twelve should stand up, give the lawyers the finger and go back to living their lives. Why do we not hear about at least one of the twelve standing up and at least questioning the judge? One word: Coercion. Not one of the twelve has had the guts to question this lawyer yet and the longer it goes on the less courage they'll have-especially when they think they are probably standing alone. They are afraid of the judge and what the others of the group will think. Two powerful forces.

> "There is only one evil worse than violence, and that is cowardice." Mahatma Gandhi

Who's going to question the violent lawyer who forced everyone to be there in the first place? They didn't say a word to him/her about being coerced to show up that day. They didn't say a word when the judge refused any discussion on jurisdiction, the applicability of the law and the prosecutor's complete lack of evidence for elements of the crime. This is a typical tax prosecution by the way. They sit there and watch while almost every relevant question from the defendant is refused and they either know the defendant is being railroaded or if they don't they're incompetent to sit as a juror.

They just let it happen and it's not just the jurors, defendants and their lawyers if they have one are usually just as afraid of judges. I can't tell you how many times I've heard people talking about not getting the judge upset. It makes you question why some people call themselves liberty activists. Why are they activists?

For me it's because liberty is exhilarating; it's when we're truly alive. Those who love life and hold it sacred also love liberty because that is when and how life is truly expressed. You can see this with a great artist like Miles Davis when they enter the "zone." This is a celebration of life. To me, the noblest thing we can do with our precious little time here on earth is to ease another's pain.

I believe all life is precious. If we believe in liberty, we should ask ourselves why. Why is it so important to have liberty? Why is liberty so important anyway?

This is a personal issue of course, and will dictate how we go about trying to achieve a voluntary society. If we want a society based on liberty, because we say we see aggression as destructive to life, then we need to start with ourselves and purge the aggression from our personalities.

When it comes right down to it, all we can do is change ourselves. Anger about the control others want to exert is merely an expression of our own issues with controlling others. The world does not conform to what we think it should be, so we get angry. We want them to change - they should not believe that way, why can't they just voluntarily interact with us? Why can't everyone around me accept my beliefs? Maybe a bit of authoritarian attitude is being picked up on by those around us?

That's a control issue for us. Speaking for myself, this caused me much grief until I finally accepted we can't change someone else's behavior, only our own. We can talk about liberty just like politicians looking for votes, but talking about non-violence and being non-violent are not the same thing.

We need to be non-violent and be an example, a positive example where others will want to change themselves. People need a reason to change their behavior and that's why we need to be a positive model for that change. People have to see their behavior may be a problem first, and that's not an easy task.

If the average person sees an overweight activist without a shirt on in public, berating a cop who is arresting another activist, they may see the cop as being the wrongdoer, but they probably won't sympathize with the message of the activist. It's a simple concept: Know your audience. If the point is to expose those acting as government as the criminals they are to the mainstream of society, then our behavior must be favorable/acceptable to them, be consistent with the end. Anti-social behavior is not acceptable by anyone and just calling yourself an activist and protesting or engaging in civil disobedience does not excuse the behavior anymore than a bureaucrat saying he/she is just doing their job.

If we engage in the same kind of behavior as the criminals, the audience won't empathize with us and if there is no empathy, there probably won't be any social change. Berating cops: "How do you live with yourself?!" is not consistent with building a community. Yeah, there will be some who may be motivated to activism, but probably not the mainstream we are trying to eventually reach.

It comes down to knowing your audience, who you are trying to reach and providing a message that will not only interest them, but hopefully inspire them to look into the information further.

We only get one chance with life; I think we need to make it count and actually live it for ourselves. The way the world is now we tend to live our lives for the benefit of people we will never meet who couldn't care less about us. When we die there are always more consumers coming up to replace us who will give their lives for the wealthy elite's bottom line.

Just as lawyers look at us as another house, boat and car, Madison Avenue types and politicians view us as mindless animals to be farmed.

Looking at how people in the US behave on Black Friday it's no surprise the elite see us as animals.

The fact there are still elections makes it easy to see why they do it to us: because we let them. Life is apparently not important to most. Being alive yes; but living life? Not so much.

I've long said we're all anarchists/voluntaryists because we all share a common principle: <u>we don't want to be attacked</u>. That is, with the exception of Crazy Joe Davola, but you have to allow for him. <u>http://www.youtube.com/watch?v=uov9d-nqyFY</u>.

Primum non nocere, first do no harm. That's as difficult as this needs to get; it's our starting and ending point. This simple principle should govern our behavior. For most of us it does. The problem is when it comes to the government concept, we give a small percentage of the world's population a free pass on this principle: do no harm...unless you are a government, then it's good. We not only allow predators to violate this basic principle, we cooperate with them making it possible to control the overwhelming majority of us.

All sorts of excuses are given of course, but that doesn't make it any less real. I'd like to shorten a quote from Howard Zinn, as it seems to be more effective as just:

> "There is no flag large enough to cover the shame of killing innocent people..."

Unfortunately, most bureaucrats I've spoken with don't believe they are attacking us when using threats and actual violence against us. I had Mary with the east Mesa justice court tell me straight out she didn't think it was dishonest to force people to pay a fine the day it was imposed even though the law permitted thirty days. She justified it by saying the same day is within thirty days. Yeah, but so is twenty-nine. So I couldn't help but ask: "Mary, are you this dishonest in your private life?" She didn't like that and she walked away.

And such dishonesty is not just at some little traffic court, it's only a fraction of the overall dishonesty that permeates the gangs of killers, thieves, and liars we call governments. But it shows the lies are not limited to just the psychopaths at the top or just the elected politicians, it's an integral part of the system.

> "Our lives begin to end the day we become silent about things that matter." Martin Luther King, Jr.

Paying taxes is the moral equivalent of driving your children to a pedophile's house. If that offends anyone, then ask yourself why. When we pay taxes we enable politicians to pay for cops and agents to terrorize us into further compliance so they can buy weapons of mass destruction and kill people by the thousands, and to build massive spy networks such as the FBI's latest facial recognition network.

10

It's the moral equivalent because even statist apologists in the media complain every day about how those called governments spend the money forcibly taken from us. Whatever political affiliation one of them has, they complain about governments and what they're doing. But, do they do anything about it? If you talk about abolishing governments they'll start defending them.

If you're offended, then good. Maybe you'll take the time to look at the evidence before you dismiss the rest of this book. Because as long as you hold as a core value that no one should aggress against you, then the only logical position you can take on governments is they are immoral and must be abolished. If you know it's wrong to kill people in order to provide them services, then my pointing it out should not offend you. Any offense should be towards those people who do believe forcing people to pay for services is somehow virtuous and honorable.

There's a motto in science: "Let the data speak, whatever the data say." This is a scary proposition for most people, even libertarians who claim to know about the evils of governments. It's one of the reasons I don't participate in debates, such as anarchy and minarchy. If you see virtue in coercing people to pay you, there is nothing to debate.

The facts tell the story - those calling themselves governments are criminals for no other reason than because they coerce us to pay them. Those are the facts everyone.

A lot of writers will make a big deal about their qualifications, like George Costanza http://www.youtube.com/watch?v=cKUvKE3bQlY, I will do the opposite; I will showcase my lack of approved training and credentials. I have no formal legal training; I've never worked for anyone with formal legal training and I don't have a college degree from a government approved school. I don't work for a government agency and receive no federal grants for education. My work has never, to my knowledge, been published in any academic or professional journals, even if just for criticism.

My point? I don't need the above to see the truth about governments and neither do you. We've been taught many things and led to believe they are so complicated that they're best left to the experts, or authorities. When it comes to government and the law, it's not complicated if one just looks at the facts. But those same authorities have a vested interest in our not examining their system and asking probing questions. Yes, part of it is because attorneys don't like us to find out no one needs a doctorate degree to understand it, but it also has to do with people withdrawing their support. Once people see governments for what they are viz., killers, thieves and liars, they tend to withdraw their already reluctant support.

You see the same thing with nutrition. We're supposed to leave our health to the so-called experts. Let's remember the simple truth Jack LaLanne taught: "If man made it, don't eat it." No, only licensed (taxed, controlled) professionals are allowed to give nutritional advice right? What nonsense: if we just stick to what Jack taught we'd enjoy far better health than we'd get from paying a PhD nutritionist for a few hours of consultation and advice. I'll even go on record that it's the most valuable

Also → The guy growing weed is peaceful while the armed guys storming his house, breaking down his door w/guns are supposed to be the good guys? OPPOSITE nutritional advice you can get and you don't have to pay for a government mandated degree and license.

Whatever knowledge I pass on in this book is primarily from more than a decade of personal experience with politicians and bureaucrats. After the Kimberly Clarke call was posted in January 2011, I spent five days a week for months on end resolving tax issues. Believe it or not it wasn't much fun.

I draw from personal experiences and none of the names have been changed this time around. For example, Jeff Thompson is a lawyer prosecuting people in Utah. John Webb is a lawyer with the prosecutor's office in Keene, New Hampshire.

I invite all to verify what I present herein, take nothing at face value and investigate everything. If you doubt politicians have no facts proving their constitutions and laws apply, then call them up yourself and hold them to the facts. No one has to take my word for anything; the facts speak for themselves once you open your mind and drop the political perceptions interfering with the processing of the facts.

Jeff Thompson, when pressed about the facts the Utah constitution and code were applicable to my friend James, was finally clear when I kept pressing for his evidence the laws applied to James: "Because the people said so." That's your legal standard of proof Jeff-the people said so? The code is applicable because an abstraction called "the people" ostensibly "said so." If you investigate, you'll notice lawyers and bureaucrats have a serious problem conflating opinions as facts. It's as if they don't understand the difference between the two or think we don't.

Anyone can call these politicians and bureaucrats up and ask for the facts their code is applicable or what they mean when they claim jurisdiction over you, and you'll get the same results. Call them in California, Toronto, Bristol, Melbourne or Auckland-it doesn't matter because when you look at the facts, political laws only apply because some very violent people "said so." Doesn't matter where they are.

This is where I see where the effectiveness of the **No State Project** lies - we are participating in questioning the foundation of lies all governments stand on. We're actually doing something, not just talking about it and complaining. While some may criticize saying we're just having traffic tickets thrown out, that ignores how dangerous going into court really is and that we're challenging the basis of governments themselves. But this is not limited to only the courts; we do this with tax agents and prosecutors-anyone who claim to be a government.

I had a county attorney named Ben Pearlman, who, when he couldn't prove the laws of the state of Colorado applied to my client, made a comment about the system collapsing. I said, "Great, your system is built on a foundation of violence, you have no voluntary support and it should collapse." Of course he disagreed; he wasn't able to accept the true violent nature of his job.

If you're new to this material, there is nothing stopping you from calling a politician and asking them questions. Challenging the very existence of the state with tax agents is pretty effective at convincing people there is at least something very wrong here.

12

One tax agent named "Mr. Bean", when asked what facts he relied on to prove the constitution was applicable, stated, "I don't have any facts at all." He seemed very upset when I connected this to the sacred code he thought applied to everyone. To start to tear apart his perception of the world, I just had to point out that if there are no facts proving the constitution was applicable, it follows that the code, derived from the constitution, was not applicable. You could hear the stress in his voice.

Again, this is very simple and anyone can and should call politicians and ask them what facts they rely on. Investigate everything and verify it for yourself. In other words, do not accept anything just because it came from a so-called "authority." Confront city councils publicly in their meetings and watch the blank stares.

Under the psychology section I write about mind control; notice the rage when you bring these issues up and ask yourself: why? Is that not proof of mind control? What else explains such automatic responses?

If you tell someone 1+1=4, do they get upset and offended? Then why the rage when told police are not there to protect them?

It's more than just asserting something inaccurate, it's much more. We're talking about things that are obviously consistent with the facts. The anger comes into play when those facts contradict someone's perception of the world. We'll see later that *perceptions* are more important than facts, so do not be so quick to dismiss the idea of mind control. The more automatic/mechanical responses you personally witness the more you'll understand why I talk about mind control.

What follows is an indictment of the concept of government. Unlike a typical indictment from a government-in actuality lawyers-this indictment will focus on the damage caused by the concept of government, the psychological and economic reasons such damage is caused. I will also lay out the supporting facts, something you won't see in a typical tax evasion indictment.

This indictment is not against any one particular man or woman, or group of them, but only a concept. For it's this concept, accepted and acted on by billions, that's the real problem. The concept is:

When men and women call themselves a government it's perfectly legitimate for them to steal, kill and lie.

Basic principles of morality (do no harm) just don't apply to ordinary people when called a government. The rest is just public relations to distract us from this insane idea. This includes anything that makes us feel compelled to obey until the law is changed, that there is any obligation to cooperate with people calling themselves a government. Put this way there's no reason to continue writing this book and doing a radio show (I'm sure there are many people who wish I did stop here). The problem is; it's not that simple; the PR (public relations) used by those who support "government" is extremely effective and getting better as technology advances.

What is the PR? Anything regarding it being legitimate to steal, kill and lie if you call yourself a government is PR. Any excuse, theory or ideology whose purpose is to convince you governments are legitimate or necessary is PR. Imagine that - a necessary evil - now that's effective PR. Any rapist or robber could claim that.

And that's more proof of the effectiveness of the mind control employed. Imagine that government, long held to be evil, is permitted because for some unexplained or undisclosed reason it's necessary. Ever question exactly whom this evil is necessary for? Just how much of reality and our own deeply held principles do we have to suppress to accept such a ridiculous premise? This was accepted by no less than Thomas Paine:

> "Society in every state is a blessing, but government even in its best state is but a necessary evil; in its worst state an intolerable one; for when we suffer, or are exposed to the same miseries BY A GOVERNMENT, which we might expect in a country WITHOUT GOVERNMENT, **our calamity is heightened by reflecting that we furnish the means by which we suffer**." *Common Sense*, Thomas Paine (bold emphasis mine).

But you have to have some respect for a man who published *this* in 1776 America:

> "A French bastard landing with an armed banditti, and establishing himself king of England against the consent of the natives, is in plain terms a very paltry rascally original. It certainly hath no divinity in it."

This necessary evil claim is nonsense even if attributed to Thomas Paine-another example of the appeal to authority fallacy.

Necessary for whom, the enslaved Africans? The native Americans who lost lands they had inhabited for millenniums? The whites that were not given huge land grants from George? The issue of necessary depends on whom you're asking. It's completely subjective with no basis in fact; that's why there has to be such a facade of public relations fictions. Who will stand up from the crowd and question the founding fathers?

You have to ignore the fact that protection of life, liberty and property can be provided on a voluntary basis. It's not necessary to kill people in order to protect them. Did I really just write that? Start talking to people, you won't believe how many people will tell you it is necessary to kill people to provide roads, let alone protection. They won't use those words, but they will justify governments as being necessary.

When people use the phrase necessary evil, they are deleting the violence from their experience. But why is this essential part so consistently deleted?

I can only wonder if Mr. Paine recognized the American founding fathers as also using armed banditti to establish themselves. He notices that the people do furnish the means by which they suffer though. He had to recognize the great mass of the people on the eastern seaboard of North

America did not give any kind of individual consent to those white men acting as a government. Even then, despite all the jingoistic propaganda, their particular protection of life, liberty, and the pursuit of happiness was still provided at the barrel of a gun, same as the **"French bastard" who established "himself king of England"**.

It really is not possible to take seriously slave owners who wrote about all men being created equal, they didn't even believe all the pasty white folk were equal, only those who owned a certain amount of property, and they didn't have a choice whether they wanted the founders' services. And let's not forget whom these patriots got their lands from – the descendants of that same "French bastard" possibly? They had no problem getting land grants and other royal privileges from George, did they?

Not even all the rich white people were considered equal; women had no political voice in government. Always look at someone's actions, not their speeches, to know their character.

It is fascinating to watch how ignorant people are to how destructive the government concept is, just oblivious; at least until their door is busted down and dog shot dead.

An example of the damage caused by the government concept and hierarchy happened at the hospital where my wife works. A marine and career cop about fifty-four was in the hospital and had surgery. His nurse and doctor had told him he needed to move, to walk around to aid in his recovery. Not only did he refuse to move, he was nasty to the nurse and wanted her fired. He didn't want to move on anyone's orders; though I'm guessing he would if his police captain ordered him.

This guy was willing to endanger his life, at least hinder his recovery, because he could not take directions from a nurse. She was lower on the food chain. She didn't order him, she was giving him directions for improving his health. Why would someone put his life in such danger?

Do you think Hitler, Stalin, Pol Pot and Mao accomplished mass murder on their own? How *did* they accomplish such mass murder?

A *concept.* There was a concept they used so that millions of others carried out their orders. It's that concept that is the subject of this indictment.

What about the so-called founding fathers in the United States? These were guys, mostly slave owners, who if they were insulted had to get their honor back. And how did they get their honor back? By killing someone. Maybe that's the basis of calling politicians honorable. It's their intention to kill you for something as petty as a perceived insult. While some may claim that was a different time, it was custom. Does that make it any less violent? What about the ancient cultures who killed children to please the gods? That was custom; still barbaric even if deemed a custom.

What cultures did the founders admire and emulate; who did they look to for a model of how they thought society should be structured? Greece and Rome: two ancient cultures based on violence - war and slavery was the MO. Of course Benjamin Franklin and his fellow masons also adopted much of the Masonic system as well.

All hold allegiance as an essential part of the hierarchical structure of society. That is, allegiance to the psychos called government, not allegiance of the psychos to the people they pretend to serve. This allegiance is very important psychologically and will be addressed later.

Autonomy of every individual is what a healthy, peaceful society should be based on. Is that my opinion? Of course, but is there a better alternative? If not respect for autonomy, then we only have varying degrees of what we have now: societies based on violence. If we're to talk about whether there should be governments, then any discussion has to center on whether the means of government is consistent with the end and there is only one legitimate end: the protection of each individual's autonomy. Any deviation, however slight, from this is going to be, by definition, violent.

The simple question here, for those interested in honest investigation, is this:

Do we want a society based on freedom/autonomy or one based on violence/slavery?

There really is no gray area here; you either believe in personal autonomy or you don't. As we'll see, the society based on violence, what we have now, has profound psychological effects that could take generations to recover from after the structure itself finally collapses. Though I do hope the structure collapses because enough people see it for what it is and stop cooperating.

Do we want a society consistent with our core principles, or one in direct contravention of the simplest rule of human interaction? Do no harm is as easy as we can make it.

For those who like the way things are now, please stop giving lip service to concepts of freedom and liberty. At least be honest about the situation. One radio show host, Ian Punnet on Coast to Coast Live, when confronted with facts he was not free, justified it by stating he was more than happy to trade his freedom for governments. Really? Is the trauma bond to governments really so strong that a man can cling so desperately, despite all evidence those same governments are actually the most dangerous group of people he is likely to encounter in his life?

Apparently so, and he has a microphone reaching millions and sponsors filling his bank accounts. And it's not just *his* freedom he's willing to trade, but everyone else's too. That's because for most people freedom is not nearly as important as being perceived as being right. They think the way they see the world is the only correct way, this is doubly true for Americans.

And it's precisely because we do all see the world differently is why there should be freedom, not slavery, regardless of the PR used to cover it up.

I'll repeat myself: All we want to do is change the *manner* in which these services, by men/women called governments, are provided. Why is this so difficult for people to see and accept? You don't kill people in order to protect them. We talk about being evolved and enlightened and yet

16

people still accept the idea that it is morally justified to take life, liberty, and property in order to protect life, liberty, and property?

16 March 2013 there was a first for the **No State Project** - a prosecutor joined me as a guest. His name is Eric and he was very open with us. He agreed with us that a core principle was the personal autonomy for everyone. Yet, he also stated there has to be a government, even though he agreed that forcing people to pay violates the very personal autonomy we both held in such high regard. To his credit he does agree he's maintaining a contradiction and called it "Orwellian", but could not drop it. His bias as a prosecutor is probably a big reason why.

He could not accept that the same services could be provided to the market on a voluntary basis which would really respect everyone's autonomy. But he's not alone and the resistance to dropping one's support for the concept of government is discussed in detail later.

The root of the problem is the ideas and concepts in your head; they are what cause you to behave the way you do. Those concepts, your model of the world, are why you get an internal struggle when you read or hear the facts presented in this book and on my radio show. Not only is our model of the world not consistent with the real world, but we all maintain contradictory maps and thoughts.

That's a compelling reason why we should not have governments. It's precisely because everyone doesn't agree; freedom/liberty is about choice; tyranny begins by the restriction of choice, it's that simple. All the PR does is work to limit choices, either by outright denial or by providing only false choices such as labor or conservative, right or left.

But consider this, those are not *your* thoughts; you heard and learned them from others. As children we model our parents, teachers and others; those patterns of thought become mere habits we don't even notice. We mistake those habits for actual thinking.

Those concepts and ideas are not yours and let's take this further: how many original thoughts have you had in your life? This isn't a personal attack; we all build on the ideas of those who came before us, so we shouldn't feel depressed or that we're less of a person (or heaven forbid less of an *American*). Well, if you're a bureaucrat or politician, then yes, you should feel you're less of a person.

A lot of my work is based on putting what I learned from Lysander Spooner into action. Those familiar with Spooner will immediately recognize this when they hear me challenging jurisdiction.

So even if you're a groundbreaking inventor or scientist, you're still building on the ideas you learned from others. Someone like Galileo, often called the father of modern science, advanced what he learned from others, such as Copernicus. We're all standing on someone else's shoulders; so don't cling so tightly to what you think are your ideas. At least don't cling so desperately as some radio show hosts do. The less you cling to concepts you think are yours the less you find yourself getting into heated disagreements.

If you honestly investigate this, you'll also see how the concept of intellectual property just falls apart. How the whole notice of copyrights and patents are ridiculous, as if it is somehow moral to use force to protect

17

ideas. All right, you wrote a novel - how original is the story anyway? How much of the garbage put out by Hollywood is original? Oh, you have a three-act structure and a character arc, how original. Sorry that's an infringement. What about music? Sounds like you're playing a I-IV-V blues; that's an infringement, you need permission.

Are your ideas worth the use of force against other people?

Real searchers of truth-those who love truth and figuring out how things work and why-encourage vigorous challenges to their ideas and theories. That's how we find the truth: multiple minds, coming from different perspectives, examining, testing and attempting to find every weak point in as many different contexts as possible, to find and exploit any and all flaws to either improve on the idea or theory, bringing it closer to self evident truth, or to forever cast the theory into the dustbin of history. One example is the idea of royalty the Brit's still seem to hold on to for some reason.

Another example is slavery. While most people will profess overt slavery, such as Africans working in cotton fields, is repulsive and not to be tolerated, they see nothing wrong with the less overt slavery of citizens to governments and people forced to be jurors in court. The average person doesn't even see jury duty as a form of slavery, but as a civic duty or privilege or some other equally empty political platitude. The underlying facts are ignored and many, especially Americans, will refuse to accept it.

It's the same dynamic though-only the degree of control is different. Yes, slaves had a place to sleep and food as long as the owner was happy with the slaves' performance, and citizens have a place to sleep as long as the master is happy with the citizen's performance.

Reputations should be based on one's adherence to the pursuit of truth-a fluid, dynamic process-not to the creation and strict adherence to a theory and certainly not to some authority figure. We should never try to get the facts to fit our theories and opinions, especially when interacting with others:

> *"Facts are stubborn things; and whatever may be our wishes, our inclinations, or the dictates of our passion, they cannot alter the state of facts and evidence."* John Adams.

Wise counsel is: "By their fruits ye shall know them." If you want to know who's being honest, look for those encouraging challenges and open investigation. Those who resist investigation, at the least, are not confident in their position. More than likely, they're hiding something, such as the Bush administration resisting investigation into the attacks of 11 September 2001. Think George wanted to be asked why thirty-nine minutes (according to NORAD, his administration) elapsed before any responsive action was taken when there were hijacked aircrafts?

Now, more than ten years later we'll probably never know. But grow a plant, trade raw milk, or sell lemonade and harm no one and see what happens to you. Disobey the whims of politicians and you'll see their wrath, but not when three-thousand people are killed.

For more examples of politicians running from the facts and honest investigation, listen to the many phone calls I've posted with IRS agents and their lawyers: http://marcstevens.net/cos. I've had IRS agents hang up on me for asking simple questions such as, "Aren't only taxpayers required to file tax returns?" I had one hang up on me for asking, "Are these hearings only available for taxpayers or are they available for non-taxpayers also?" I get hung up on a lot. If you start questioning them about the evidence they rely on, then you'll get hung up on also.

Honest people aren't afraid of investigation and challenges to their claims/opinions/theories; cowards, liars and conmen are. They don't want to be exposed. Pretty basic stuff right? I also point out the obvious a lot.

Maybe that's why loyalty oaths are so common with politicians and lawyers; they take oaths,not to protect the people they steal from, but to protect the system they use to steal. Those known as the mafia have their *omerta*, and the police have their own, called the "blue wall of silence" or as I call it, the blue wall of cowardice.

You'll notice this in the oath taken in England by judges:

> "I, _____, do solemnly sincerely and truly declare and affirm that I will be faithful and bear true allegiance to Her Majesty Queen Elizabeth the Second Her Heirs and Successors according to Law."

There is a second oath and again, nothing about protection:

> "I, _____, do swear by Almighty God that I will well and truly serve our Sovereign Lady Queen Elizabeth the Second in the office of _____, and I will do right to all manner of people after the laws and usages of this realm, without fear or favour, affection or ill will."

The fact that governments are not there to protect you is even more blatant in the United States as the oath is to protect and defend the constitution, not the people. I cannot believe they inadvertently forgot to put "to protect the people" into their laws and in all these years never corrected it. The alleged purpose is to protect the people and that's not in the oath? Probably just a subtle cue to the bureaucrat's unconscious mind that he/she is not there to protect the victims of the government concept.

Cover-ups and politics go hand in hand because politics is all about covering up the truth. The truth is there are no Citizens, States, Commonwealths, Kings, Queens, Presidents etc. They're all lies to divert your attention. This book exposes it and no amount of spin can change that. Remember, *facts can be very stubborn.*

It's not that people don't see and understand (at least on a deep level) governments are the problem; it's the paralyzing fear when you discuss abolishing government and replacing those killers, thieves and liars with no one. Why the fear and can we help overcome it?

Why are people so afraid of not cooperating with people who are lying and stealing from them? The same people who would have no problem shooting someone breaking into their home wouldn't think of not filing a tax return or not paying taxes. People will go faster than the posted speed limit, not come to a full stop at a stop sign, but they generally won't refuse to file a tax return or hire someone without withholding taxes from their checks. Why?

This requires no violence; just non-cooperation and building a free society. We just need our means to be consistent with the end, a free, peaceful society. Yet, it scares the crap out of people to even think of trading with the market without permission.

People ignore the law every day; ever notice they tend to ignore those laws the psychos profit from? If people complied with the traffic laws the way they comply with the tax code then you'd see a dramatic increase in traffic fines to make up the difference because so few tickets would get written.

Either that or the bureaucrats would keep lowering the speed limit and creating more violations and make it impossible to not violate some law. It would be interesting to see just how low bureaucrats would set a speed limit if there was near 100% compliance. I'm certain the psychopaths in New York would lower the limit on the Long Island Expressway to fifteen mph if they had to in order to still give speeding tickets.

But why the invisible line in the sand? Why do people ignore some laws but not others? There is more chance of being caught speeding than not filing a tax return. Maybe that's one of the reasons why they use the lure of a refund.

It's more than just not wanting to going to jail, it's also *herd mentality*. While this is discussed in detail later, it's probably because people don't want to be perceived as different from their friends and neighbors. Everyone else ostensibly files a tax return, so I probably should. This happens even in the face of zero evidence proving anyone is required to file a tax return or pay taxes. Social pressure plays a huge role in this.

It's also interesting to note the account of the five monkeys. The story goes five monkeys are put in a cage and bananas are put on top of a ladder. When a monkey would go for the banana, all the monkeys were sprayed with cold water. To avoid being sprayed again, the monkeys would stop any monkey from going up the ladder. This happened even after all five monkeys were replaced, one at time, until none of the original monkeys were left. This has long been used as a corporate tool about just doing things because "that's the way it's always been done." This is an example of mental habits instead of actual thinking.

It's similar to the crab mentality: put a single crab in a bucket and he will easily get out, but put a bunch of crabs in together, and if one tries to get out, the others pull him back in. I can't help but think of my friend Larken Rose here http://larkenrose.com.

Larken was prosecuted for willful failure to file a tax return, meaning he supposedly knew he was required but didn't. However, the judge stated he knew Larken was sincere in his belief he was not required to file.

He was still convicted and sent to live in a cage. The twelve crabs had to keep Larken from climbing out of that bucket.

I know someone who was convicted of willful failure to file despite the fact she filed returns for the years in question. The law is about punishing people who are non-compliant with the demand to file a return; it's not about filing a return deemed correct by some unknown IRS employee. Again the obvious: filing even a frivolous return does not mean a return was not filed. There's a separate penalty for that. This didn't matter to the prosecuting lawyers, agents and the twelve people (crabs) sitting as a jury.

So what kind of concepts do people have to have in their heads that cause them to initiate violence, even kill others who are no danger to them? This is where hierarchy comes in. A pecking order of authority on a foundation of aggression and lies will do nicely as history and contemporary society proves. This hierarchy comes from the government concept itself. There are two main classes: owners and slaves, or leaders and followers. We have those who issue the orders and those who obey them.

Within the class who gives orders, there are varying degrees called a pecking order. The higher on the pecking order, the fewer orders one is given. The opposite is also true; the lower one is, the fewer orders one gives. The hierarchy is kept in place partly because we are taught to be obedient, to be law-abiding, regardless of the rationale behind the law.

The lower one is on the political pecking order the more direct aggression is employed. These bureaucrats, such as cops, because they blindly follow orders, expect our unquestioned compliance. And they know why people comply with them. While those higher on the pecking order talk about law, the grunts with the boots on the ground only know coercion, so do as they order or suffer swift and immediate punishment. This is not a new way for such to look at the world; it was old when this was attributed to Gnaeus Pompeius Magnus, who allegedly said, "Stop quoting laws to us, we carry swords!" Given what we know about this psychopath, it's entirely reasonable he said that, or something very close.

That is the mindset though, and anyone who has ever interacted with and questioned the lower rung bureaucrats knows first-hand that the laws mean nothing to them. Their perceptions do not permit those lower than them questioning them, right or wrong, only those higher up may do that.

Cicero remarked about this, "When arms speak, laws are silent." Ever deal with the IRS, CRA or just some cop intent on taking your property? I think a better way to say it is: When arms speak, principles of right and wrong are silent.

> "But the maxim applies, *quod non apparet non est*. The fact not appearing is presumed not to exist." The Clara, 102 US 200. (Emphasis in original) http://supreme.justia.com/cases/federal/us/102/200/case.html.

And there's evidence every time you speak to the IRS or go into court. These people just don't care about the law if it gets in their way. Governments are built on violence; why would a judge, who has no voluntary support, care about a law written by some dead lawyers if it gets in his way? If the law is contrary to his/her nature, what do you think is going to prevail?

Like most people, they believe their map of the world, built from the government concept with its hierarchy, is absolutely correct, so there is little chance of changing their minds easily.

The concept, being imposed by violence and lies, is kept in place by violence and lies. This is obvious; think about any family or friends who work in the war industry such as Raytheon. Then think about this quote attributed to John Hawkwood. He allegedly said in response to two friars saying something about god giving him peace:

> "God take away your alms. For as you live by charity, so do I by war, and to me it is as genuine a vocation as yours...Do you not know that I live by war, and that peace would be my undoing?"

True or not, it accurately depicts the mindset of those who profit from war and enslaving most of the earth's inhabitants.

This mindset, this economic model, is still prevalent today. I know someone who shocked me when he told me he invested in Halliburton. *Halliburton?* But you're one of the most anti-war guys I know, how could you do that? He tried to justify it. All I could say was he was profiting from the killing of innocent people and that won't change regardless of how you justify it.

All governments profit from war, but what about the private sector? Who provides the support for the war machine? Private individuals such as those collectively known as Halliburton, Lockheed-Martin, The Carlyle Group, McDonnell-Douglas, Raytheon, and many others. Are the stockholders of such companies going to really be interested in peace?

What a sick model; get your victims involved by giving them a substantial economic interest in war and you polarize populations. You make them accomplices in mass murder and economic destruction by exploiting a pervasive personality flaw: the draw of easy money, profit without effort. Well, there is effort to ignoring exactly how the money was acquired. So many people are attracted to get rich quick schemes because there is no work required; it's the promise of something for nothing. That's one hell of a drug! Look at Las Vegas to confirm this. It may be sick, but it's also very effective at keeping people from withdrawing their cooperation.

How can the average person, even if they see how violent the system is, withdraw support when so much of their life is dependent upon those called government? How many people are willing to live consistent with their principles, even take some baby steps towards it? At least to Americans, not voting because you see it's a rigged game is too difficult to contemplate. It's justified with nonsense such as: "If you don't vote you can't complain, you have to work within the system to change it," and other silly platitudes.

Government bonds are a great example. They are sold as an almost risk-free investment: buy government bonds, they will always pay out. Why? It doesn't matter what the bond is used to pay for, whether roads or a library. What's important is how the bonds are funded and they are always paid for by forcibly taking money from an unwilling society. Government bonds are a lien on all the men and women in the area; it's part of their slavery if only for a short period of time. When someone buys a bond, are they thinking they are engaging in a system of theft, and also profiting from it?

When you get a government bond, you are endorsing human farming, slavery. You are providing a gang of killers, thieves, and liars with funding and support to kill innocent people, but also enabling them to pay professional psychopaths to steal from your family, friends, and neighbors so you can make a few percentage points of interest.

Look at the support system for the war machine, commonly called the military-industrial complex. I cannot dedicate the space necessary to really detail what this entails. Suffice to say, there are millions of people who are involved working with companies such as McDonnell-Douglas who rely on that paycheck or stock dividends to support themselves and their lifestyle. I would presume for most involved it is their sole resource for supporting their family. They have to be aware that war is good for their family's lifestyle. I doubt we're going to find too many anti-war people working for Halliburton.

So if we are anti-war, how are such people going to respond? Will they see it as an attack on them and their family? I think so. What about someone who is relying on a pension from Lockheed-Martin and owns stock? Think they want to hear the war on terror is a PR stunt? Endless war means economic security for them and their family. They'll naturally defend genocide just as a traumatized wife defends the bastard who beats her regularly. He has convinced the victim he loves her and is the only one who can take care of her.

That is exactly what governments do and you can hear the victims themselves when you talk about abolishing governments: "But who'll build the roads!? Who will protect us from the terrorists?" Most people can't even conceive of protection and roads being provided without coercion because they believe the psychopaths when they tell them only they, the government, can do that.

They believe this despite not only no evidence to support it, but in spite of governments telling them there is no duty to protect them. Money is a hell of a drug and statism is a hell of a religion.

While statism may be a form of religion, there are two very big differences from this and traditional religions. First, all government support is compulsory. At one time there was coerced support of religion (churches), but that is not the norm now.

Second, and very important, while parts of some religious teachings require belief in things without evidence (faith), statism is the opposite. Statism requires belief despite evidence to the contrary. With statism, you don't ignore the lack of evidence; you have to ignore overwhelming, in-your-face evidence.

So while some atheists say religious people cling to comforting lies, so too does the atheist.

This is an issue I've had with objectivists and other non-religious people who claim religious people are delusional and believe fairy tales. They claim to base their lives on evidence - what can be proven - and reject appeals to authority (rightfully so) and the concept of faith. Yet they will argue, despite overwhelming empirical evidence, there are states, citizens and nations. This is an instance where one can prove a negative (i.e., there are no states, citizens or nations). I know from personal experience that not all objectivists and atheists reject the idea of states just as not all religious people are statists. Anarchists/voluntaryists can be religious, non-religious and agnostic.

There are many religious people who easily see through the falsehood of states and citizens because it's demonstrably false while so-called empiricists readily accept the lies despite all evidence to the contrary. This is not a matter of who is worse, only to point out we all tend to have our way of seeing the world. And even those who claim to be empirically based, while bashing religious people, just as dogmatically hang on to their own false concepts.

Even scientists admit they fall into the trap of authority: "But science students accept theories on the authority of teacher and text, not because of evidence." Scientific Revolutions, Kuhn, page 80.

What I want to do, to borrow a phrase, is to strike the root, not the branches of organized violence. Have religious organizations been responsible for incalculable human suffering and mass murder? Absolutely, there is no doubt. One need only look at the last thousand years of European history to confirm that. In the last hundred years though, there have been hundreds of millions of murders by leaders who were not religious or using a god as an excuse for their mass murder. The constant, though, is the concept of states and governments. That is far more important in my view. It's about treating the cause, not putting Band-Aids on a sucking chest wound.

As far as murders, plunder, and torture based on the ideas of a book, the Communist Manifesto, for the years it has been published, certainly at least rivals the Bible for the same time period, if not surpassing it. Looking at atheism or theism as the problem is to go a step or two beyond the root; it ignores the actual mechanism psychopaths use to commit crimes against entire communities and continents.

And there is no merit to the claim that religious people are more likely to be statists, as there are plenty of atheists that are believers and supporters of states. Some very prominent atheists are tenured professors at state schools. Look to their funding and you can easily explain why some people, while claiming to be driven by the evidence, turn a blind eye to the evidence.

Governments have almost always been the tool of mass slavery, mass murder, plunder and genocide, whether by a religious organization or not. Why were the popes able to slaughter, torture, enslave and plunder so

24

many? How did the feudal lords maintain control over huge tracts of land?

The false concepts of governments are the constant: the tools necessary for such murderous actions. Like the saying attributed to Carlos Marcello, you don't cut off the tail, you cut off the head. Without government (the head), violent religious and secular organizations (the tail) are essentially neutered. Strike the root...

So whatever the tail may be, whether banks, labor unions or religious organizations, without governments, and enough people who accept such programming, those organizations are powerless to conduct reigns of terror and mass murder. Their message, or PR, is neutralized and ineffective in bringing about their real objective: control.

Governments have misused many things such as psychology and physics. That doesn't mean we seek to rid the world of either one. It was scientists using physics that deliberately created the atom bomb and provided the equipment necessary to murder over a hundred thousand people instantly; that doesn't mean physics is evil or even responsible. I want to remove the concepts that permit their misuse.

The rationale that built the war machine is what I am indicting in this book. If we destroy the rationale that built the hierarchy-the machine of mass murder and robbery-then we destroy the means for it to continue to happen and be built back again.

In the hallway of the hotel hosting the 2009 Liberty Forum in Nashua, New Hampshire, someone asked me to the effect, "You say politics is just a PR scam and a few people pulling the strings from behind the scenes know it's a scam, but what if it's not true? What if there is no wealthy elite running the show?"

This really struck me; I hadn't really considered it before. What if it were true, we really were doing it to ourselves? But is that possible? I think so. Most people apparently buy into the PR (nations, citizens, constitutions, political democracy etc.), though most see politicians as crooks. Even popular right-wing talk show hosts have admitted they believe government is a "necessary evil". It reminds me of the "respect the office, not the man" crap we've all heard. While it is possible, how probable is it?

While it's certainly thought provoking, it's ultimately irrelevant to bringing about a voluntary society and the factual grounds proving governments are nothing more than men and women providing services on a pay-or-get-shot basis. It doesn't explain why seemingly normal men and women are willing to kill others who don't appear to obey them.

If true, it's certainly a great human tragedy, especially when the big picture is seen. People calling themselves governments have not hidden much from those they control or farm. All one has to do is some research and they can find it out for themselves. Politicians have preserved some truth in their sacred writ, their law books, for all to read. As I've mentioned before, it's not some esoteric knowledge known only by a few that must be revealed by those who control the masses, it's simple observable facts. Given this, the politicians have to know the truth; they know they're not in office to protect the people they steal from.

We don't need admissions from politicians that they are not here to protect us; we can observe the manner in which they behave. But, it certainly makes it easier to convince some of their victims when it comes directly from the politicians' own filthy mouths.

However, there are people who, for whatever reason, refuse to believe governments are not here to protect the people they steal from. Some have been radio show hosts who argued incessantly with me on the air as if it were my opinion. I had one host in California hang up on me during a live show because he was so offended by this information. I guess he forgot we had spoken about it when I first called him to book the show.

There is something stopping people from believing or acting on what the facts tell them. There may also be something making it difficult or impossible to mentally process the information.

And as you sit with this book in your hands, what will you do with the information? Is there a part of you refusing to accept the truth? Is there a part that refuses to act or not act on what you know is true/correct? Remember the crabs in a bucket.

Most likely that part was created by outside manipulators; those people who have an interest in you believing you're a pretended citizen of a pretended nation, or acting as if you are. It's an accepted part of human psychology; we are influenced by the barrage of media today, whether we admit it or not, and maybe not being able to admit it is just another part of the programming? I'm sure my European friends would agree Americans are definitely programmed to believe Americans are the only holders of truth and light in this world, and nothing of any value exists outside of the United States, except traveling Americans.

What more evidence does one need to prove governments are not here to protect than the fact support is coerced? These people will imprison you and take all your property if you don't pay them. Do you really need any more evidence than that to know they're not here to protect you? That should be the only evidence needed, anything more is just silly:

> *OK, convince me governments are not here to protect me!*
> Sure, support is coerced - pay or go to jail.
> *That's no evidence; show me the law!*
> [Face palm] No problem; there are statutes and court cases such as *Warren v. District of Columbia*, 444 A.2d. 1, that state explicitly the government has no duty to protect you.
> *Liberal, activist judges! That's no evidence!*
> There are laws such as section 845 from the California government code.
> *What do you expect from California, the liberal coast?! That doesn't apply anywhere else!*
> *Every* supreme court, including the United States Supreme Court, and foreign courts have all held there is no duty to protect.
> *You're an idiot Marc.* [This is called moving the goal posts.]

Those who continue resisting the truth at this point are the people this book is primarily written for. Such people are not as interested in evidence; they are interested in keeping their current view of the world intact and not straying from the tribe. If that strikes a nerve with you, then good. Decide to look at the facts and verify everything for yourself; it's a pretty big step in rejecting the concept of authority. And it's not easy when you live in an authoritarian society like the United States or England. It's very difficult to question what you think everyone else thinks is true.

It's to break apart from the herd and think for yourself and it's always discouraged by those claiming to represent the collective. You'll be referred to as the fringe and hear specious arguments: "Do you know how outside the mainstream that thinking is?" It's always with a condescending tone of scorn that tends to accompany that logical fallacy *argumentum ad populum*. Watch cable "news" channels and you'll hear that one anytime someone dares to speak the truth. As we'll see throughout this book when dealing with bureaucrats, it's all about opinions and groupthink; so the argument from popularity fallacy is going to be common. So if you find yourself doing that, remember it's your opinion. And what's more important-what you *think* everyone else believes or the observable, verifiable facts?

It's not easy to question what most people seem to take as absolute truth; there is social pressure because no one wants to be mocked and go against the tribe. I'm used to it now; I expect it. When dealing with bureaucrats I embrace it because I know I'm closer to getting an admission there are no facts. I know the bureaucrat is on the ropes when they ask: "What evidence do you have the code is not applicable?" They're ready for a knockout punch.

But what's important to me are the facts; what's really going on? Who really wants to be that little kid who breaks from the pack and points out the obvious, that guy has no clothes, or that castle is made of sand? I do; and I want to point out the obvious.

To change; you need to place the truth over the perceived comforts of the herd. You get used to being mocked and you consider the source and avoid such people. We can't reach everyone and don't need to. Consider how much people like Sean Hannity or Jeremy Paxman have invested in this perverse concept.

Think about the enormous amount of social and economic pressure they are under to not only never question the government concept, but to continue to vigorously defend it. We'll see later people will lie about the facts right in front of them, such as the length of a line. If people will lie about something as trivial as the length of a line, then why would we not expect the same behavior with those in the media who have built their careers on the government concept? See, no backroom conspiracy necessary. It's easily explained with social pressure to conform.

This is why I go into the psychological effects of the concept and practice of government in detail as part of this indictment. The psychological trauma and effects are dramatic and far-reaching; this may be what led Stanley Milgram to investigate how/why the German people (as if they should be singled out when so many other governments are just as violent) could do or allow what happened before and during WWII. I can only speculate why he focused on the Germans though and the government concept in general. Maybe it had to do with who funded his studies, or it was an innocent oversight, but I doubt that.

The same with Zimbardo's prison experiment. Their experiments were all funded by governments; so it's irrational to think they would want the stolen money used to undermine the very concept keeping them near the top of the current hierarchy. Would Milgram or other researchers really bite the hands that feed them? It happens occasionally, but I have not seen it with psychological studies.

So while I do cite the results of those experiments, there is still some healthy skepticism because of how they were funded. Milgram was at Yale, Zimbardo at Stanford; so it's reasonable to question the funding. It just seems that those who are heavily invested and rely on the government concept are not going to fund projects that would undermine the legitimacy of the concept. Self-preservation explains that well enough.

Do we really think we're going to see government employees openly attacking the very concept that permits them to do their studies, research and experiments? I don't see many tenured professors calling for the abolition of governments.

Those with an open mind, willing to let the facts speak no matter what the facts say, will come to the same conclusion as those calling themselves anarchist, voluntaryist, agorist or whatever word is being used today: the concept of government is irrational, self-contradictory and all governments should be abolished for no other reason than:

The means are inconsistent with the end

That should be all that needs to be said. That is the indictment of the concept right there; that's it. I can't make it any simpler or shorter. However, there's been a tremendous amount of energy expended to convince us of the exact opposite or to not even question the concept of government itself.

No one can seriously doubt for a moment there isn't a steady campaign extolling the virtues of the concept of government. We're continually led to believe that without government there will be chaos and mayhem, the destruction of society; but they're all lies of course. One only needs to look at the constant warfare around the world as evidence.

There are those who readily accept the evils of the concept of government, but refuse to discuss abolishing governments by using the political excuse it's a "necessary evil". You also get the support of the "lesser of the two evils" rationale for continuing to vote. For some reason, explained in part later, these people will never discuss why the same services, provided on a voluntary basis, are not preferable to ones provided by coercion.

No, when we discuss a rational, proven alternative to the pretended "necessary evil" we're called nut jobs or "conspiracy theorists". But *this* garbage is supposed to be rational:

We need to be protected from evil people in the world, so we'll put them in control over us.

Because only evil/immoral people would want to control other people. This is basic stuff here; so you can see the necessity for massive public relations to distract attention away.

This indictment will show not only why the concept is nonsensical, but also the incalculable physical, economic and psychological damage caused by those empowered by the concept of government.

As I've said before: mankind will not socially evolve until the concept of government is rejected by enough people that governments start to collapse worldwide. The first step to social evolution though, is to see governments for what they are: killers, thieves and liars. The second is to stop making excuses and act consistent with our principles and the evidence before us.

To paraphrase Paul: it's time to put childish things away and grow up.

Introduction

"It requires a very unusual mind to undertake the analysis of the obvious." Alfred North Whitehead

It's been ten years since my first book, **Adventures in Legal Land**, was released. Since then, I've done hundreds of radio shows and started my own radio show, The **No State Project**. I've been privileged to communicate with thousands of people, whether in person, on the phone, radio or over the interwebs. Hosting my own radio show allows me access to some people I would otherwise never have the opportunity to meet and speak with.

Regular listeners to my radio show know getting politicians and bureaucrats to come on The **No State Project** is no easy task. It's no surprise, just look at the name of the show. Most politicians and bureaucrats are not willing to discuss basic issues, such as why there are governments.

In some cases, I just said too much. Such was the case with a former United States Attorney now in private practice in Los Angeles. I had mentioned that to have standing in any federal court a plaintiff must plead the violation of a legal right and damage. The former US attorney agreed. Not being satisfied and moving to book him as a guest, I used the IRS as an example; when the IRS files a complaint to enforce a summons, there are no allegations a legal right was violated or of any damage. Although he reluctantly agreed there would be no standing and the court may not proceed or a "judgment would be void," he decided he was no longer interested in doing my show. Yes, I have learned to keep my mouth shut…well, to a point.

My opinion is he probably wasn't comfortable knowing hundreds or even thousands of complaints were filed under his name when there was no standing. That's a lot of guilt.

Most politicians and bureaucrats don't want to discuss why there are governments because in my experience, they don't know. That's tantamount to a doctor not knowing why humans have lungs or sending a battalion of Marines into the field without telling them the mission. The media relations sergeant for the Seattle police department got very angry when I asked him. He didn't think he needed to know why the government was established in order to do his job as a cop. Try to imagine a plumber who doesn't know what plumbers are supposed to do. Such a plumber would probably need to use force to get people to do business with him.

And it's not just politicians-the majority of people don't know why there are governments. If most people did know why there are governments, then it would be extremely difficult to maintain a government.

People would see through scams such as the drug war and traffic courts. We could probably bring about a voluntary society doing nothing more than educating people on the stated reason for having government. Think about it; imagine how difficult it would be to teach children about the reason for government with the mechanics of taxation:

Well children, everyone in 1776 decided they should have people protect them and their property. They all agreed to have a group of people to protect them and call them the new American government.

Teacher, I have a question. Do you mean everyone in 1776 living on the eastern seaboard agreed to have a government?

Yes Timmy, that's correct, the state is everyone.

So children like us had to agree?

Well no Timmy, children aren't old enough. Voting age was twenty-one at the time.

So it wasn't everyone. What about women? When you said everyone, did it include women?

No Timmy, women couldn't vote until 1920.

But women had to pay taxes?

Yes.

But they couldn't vote, why not?

Because that's what the law of the United States was at the time.

So not everyone agreed, it was against some people's will?

No, that would be tyranny. Everyone had to consent and they did.

But you said the state was everyone, how did they get record of their consent?

Because they lived there and didn't move when the government was created.

So the British soldiers consented?

British soldiers? Why of course not, why would you think British soldiers consented?

Because they were there and didn't leave in 1776 when the new government was created. I had no idea the Hessians consented. Were the governments obligated to protect the British soldiers?

No, the American government was fighting against them. Why would you think the government was obligated to protect them?

Because they were part of the state; you said you agreed to be part of the state when you lived in the area and didn't leave when the government was created.

But they weren't part of the state.

Why not?

Because they didn't consent.

Yes they did consent, they didn't leave like you said. Did they pay taxes?

No, I wouldn't think so.

But if they didn't leave, and that was their consent to the government, then why didn't they have to pay taxes?

31

Because they were the enemy of freedom and liberty, they weren't part of the state.
I'm confused. You said everyone was the state, and that those who weren't allowed to vote consented to the state by not leaving the area. Why weren't the British soldiers part of the state?
That's silly. I can't imagine the British soldiers putting their guns down to vote on the new government.
But you said voting isn't necessary for consent, only not leaving the area.
Yes, but there was a vote on the constitution.
There wasn't a constitution in 1776. But why would there have to be an election for the approval of the constitution if consent is based on where you live?
Because people have a right to vote and American government is by consent unlike the barbarians in Europe.
I think I'm starting to understand: those who have the right to vote and choose to support the constitution, even if they are outvoted, they still consent because they voted. But, if they don't have the right to vote, or chose not to, then they still consent if they didn't move?
Yes, that's right.
So whether you actually consent or not, the people called government act as if you've consented? How is that different than how the barbarians do things in Europe?
Uh…What does that have to do with consent for protection though?
So if I want to have a business protecting people, then all I have to do is set the business up and those people in the area who don't move away are automatically my customers and must pay me or I can take their property by force?
No of course not, that's silly, you'd be a criminal for doing that.
Why though? I don't understand.
Because not everyone agreed to have your services.
So, my company's policy is the same as the American government's - children and women don't have to agree.
Timmy, please see the principal now.
Teacher, what's the difference between a business and government? Aren't they both just people?
"Shut up! I order you to be quiet!"

I've spoken to cops and asked them and they claim to "work for the government," but can't tell me what it is. I don't blame you if you think that's surreal. Imagine not knowing what you work for; how's that for mind control? Try it yourself. Just start asking people, especially those who are complaining about governments, what a government is. Don't be surprised by the initial blank stare.

Just as I discuss later, the more specific you have someone get by asking questions, the weaker their position becomes, if based on lies, fabrications, or appeals to authority.

So you work for the government Mr. Police Officer?
Yes I do.
What do you mean by government?

32

Well, you know, the system of laws and government.
That's kinda circular, and the system of laws makes no sense to me. Do know what the government is factually?
Well, it's, you know, it's a system of laws and courts.
No, I don't know and you didn't answer my question, do you know what government is factually?
Well yes of course, I ought to, I work for the government, I should know.
Sure. Are you a government though, or part of one? Can we get that specific?
I'm not the government; I only work for the government.
Is your boss the government?
No, he works for the government too.
What about the entire police force, is that the government?

He/she is in trouble if they get desperate and claim they work for the people. But all support is coerced, so that doesn't sound like you work for them, and if that's true, then where does government come into play? Claiming to work for the people doesn't tell us what the government is. I just ask, "So you don't work for the government?" They tend to get pretty upset by that.

Do you think it's just a coincidence most people don't know what a government is or what the purpose is for having government? I don't think so. I write that, because from experience, when I do raise it in the context of a court proceeding, the systemic refusal to recognize it leads me to believe those people acting as government don't want it known and openly discussed. Why else the constant refusal to recognize and be consistent with the stated purpose of government? If they were interested in administering justice, then they'd be willing to be consistent with the object of their pretended establishment. However, it's naïve to think constitutions and laws are anything but public relations tools because the evidence proves otherwise.

That's one of the motives for writing this book-to educate, to change perceptions: so when you hear or read *government* you don't think of some abstraction, but individual men and women. When you look at a cop you'll know you're face to face with a government. This book proves once and for all government (men and women providing services on a compulsory basis) is not some necessary evil or necessary for anything; except of course mass murder, world-wide plunder and organized deception.

One goal in writing this book is that no one who reads this book will ever support the government concept again. And I don't mean, "getting back to the constitution." I mean no government at all (what we call government anyway, because there are no governments now). My first book *Adventures in Legal Land* did not accomplish that. Many people read *Adventures* and still believe government can be reformed or limited by such things as political voting and activism. It didn't always break the thought process causing one to believe a legitimate government could exist.

33

Unlike *Adventures*, I'm providing material for helping with bureaucratic attacks with this book. There are chapters dealing with such attacks and how I responded. I also discuss why and the results.

I've also put together a cross-reference to the same laws in Australia, Canada, England and New Zealand http://marcstevens.net/articles/standing-cross-reference.html.

The cross-reference is not exhaustive, though it's sufficient. Keep in mind there are no magic words (at least I'm not aware of them) to get bureaucrats to stop attacking (well, maybe some well-timed Masonic distress symbols). Most of the phrases are very similar though; it's all the same because it comes from the same source and is the same scam.

It's no surprise the public relations are practically identical in most cases. People in Australia, Canada, England and New Zealand have used my scripts in court, asking the same questions we Yanks ask here in the states and have gotten the same inane responses and blank stares. I'm still waiting for someone to report a bureaucrat got so upset during a hearing that he/she had a spontaneous nosebleed.

It's even easier in England, Canada, Australia and New Zealand to show the "judge" represents the alleged plaintiff. All you need to do is show up with the loyalty oath: "I, _____, do swear by Almighty God that I will well and truly serve our Sovereign Lady Queen Elizabeth the Second..." The "Queen" is the bloody plaintiff! That's a textbook conflict of interest, mate.

I know people who have raised this issue in England and yes, the English bureaucrats tend to be just as violent and evasive as their North American counterparts. Not once have any of them been able to explain exactly how someone can get a fair trial when there is a conflict of interest. I ask, "So you're not a fair, impartial, independent decision maker?" Not surprising either is that none of them have been willing to let the matter be decided when there is a conflict of interest between the defendant and the decision maker. Just so long as the conflict of interest is to their advantage they have no issue with it. Who said they make it up as they go?

I had a hearing officer agree he was an independent decision maker after he claimed he was appearing on behalf of the commissioner. I asked him to explain how he could be independent of the commissioner he was appearing for. He had nothing and was desperate to "move on."

You already decided to change by reading this book. But, most of us go through life just accepting the reality that's handed to us. Even worse, as you'll find out, most people accept a reality because they mistakenly believe that's what everyone else believes. Now that's a tragedy. Think about that for a while - it's really a striking concept, almost surreal. For me it's both incredibly inspiring and discouraging. The support system, to me, seems so flimsy just one event at the right time, will collapse the entire matrix permitting the farm to continue.

Some start to question and our model of the world starts to go through revisions and our perception of reality starts to more closely resemble the world. This book will radically speed up that process.

Typical response: this can't be true, it requires too many participants. leave your emotions out of a critical analysis of the facts. Do your beliefs negate the facts? Just because you may think, "This can't be true, it requires too many participants to keep their mouths shut," doesn't make the facts disappear. Such a response is emotional and overrides the rational part of our brains. Don't ignore the facts; look at what can be objectively observed and proven. Does such a belief make taxes any less compulsory?

It also flies in the face of historical facts, doesn't it? Consider the "Manhattan Project" or CIA operations such as MK-Ultra; there were thousands of participants and yet they stayed secret for many years. When people did speak out about them the media and governments vilified them as tin-foil hat-wearing nut jobs.

The Manhattan Project alone included about a hundred and thirty thousand (130,000) people. I guess it never happened. Too many people to keep their mouths shut. How silly is that, especially when people do leak the info, no one believes it anyway?

Just how many people have to be involved before something can't be kept a secret? Maybe 130,001 was just one too many. Can you imagine just how pissed off that one physicist must have been to be left out?

The Manhattan Project involved approximately 130,000 people from three different national governments and resulted in the instant death of over 220,000 people. By contrast, 9/11 resulted in the death of a few thousand.

Exactly how many government operations are classified TOP SECRET? Does the belief "it requires too many people to keep their mouths shut" mean those secret operations don't go on every day? There are many more intelligence agencies in the US government than the CIA and NSA; can you name them all?

The belief "it requires too many participants" holds no water to anyone claiming to be rational to any degree. It's only an excuse to ignore the facts and impose our precious beliefs instead.

When such an excuse arises, it's the fragile ego (or that part of our unconscious mind we label the ego) coming to the rescue to protect the conscious mind from being overwhelmed by something deemed so horrible it may not be able to accept it. But is it really so difficult to accept men kill other men? The history of mankind is murder; and yes, mass murder and genocide. The names of only two of the many wars in Europe paint a pretty good picture: the Hundred Years' War and Thirty Years' War.

Get over it; even Rush Limbaugh admits it. Rush actually admitted in December 2009, "Public service is a get rich quick scheme by theft." But that admission hasn't stopped him from cheerleading for the concept of government every day. It keeps the sponsors happy.

Pretty much every action taken by government is an attack upon the innocent. The very existence of government is unimpeachable evidence of violent domination of the many by the few and is textbook terrorism. There are over forty thousand military raids on American homes every year, swarms of men with machine guns going after plants. The evidence of governments killing their own people just in the last one hundred years would fill volumes. The evidence is so overwhelming I don't need to present much.

Here is but one example of governments engaged in conspiracies; these are some of the few that are caught and actually put on trial. So the idea that there are no government conspiracies flies in the face of tons of evidence:

> "In all of my years as a supervisory assistant district attorney, chief of the criminal division at the U.S. Attorney's Office, and almost 20 years on the federal bench, I have neither imagined nor heard of a more treacherous or despicable conduct by law enforcement officers than that which was described today.
>
> "You, and others like you, through an **elaborate conspiracy** of deceit and obstruction, have caused an inordinate degree of mental anguish and pain to those injured at the Danziger Bridge and their families, the families of those who were shot and killed, and Lance Madison, who was wrongly accused.
>
> "You have compounded the damage caused by Hurricane Katrina in an immeasurable way. You and others should know that *but for* your cooperation, you would be facing the prospect of a more severe sentence of imprisonment.
>
> "Your conduct was an aberration. You have disgraced your badge and caused damage to the credibility and morale of honest, hard-working law enforcement officers who place their lives on the line on a daily basis." US District Judge Lance Africk Eastern District of Louisiana (emphasis mine).
>
> http://www.wwltv.com/news/Judge-Treacherous-and-despicable-conduct-87342487.html   March   31,   2010.
> http://www.laed.uscourts.gov/200th/judges/africk.php

And don't let any media personalities or politicians trick or discourage you when they label this book as some kind of conspiracy theory. This book does not contain a conspiracy theory. I just lay out the evidence-facts anyone can verify for themselves: support for governments is compulsory. No theory needed.

Any excuse, especially those emotionally driven, that tries to negate the facts, is just that, an excuse; the facts do not change. Our maps of the world change every day though. Every day we learn or absorb something, right or wrong, our perception of the world changes, even if just slightly and there's nothing we can do about it. We can either be conscious of it, or be oblivious. Either way, your "world" is changing. I think it's better to be aware of the process.

That's what I want to do with this book. So if anything I present in this book creates an internal conflict with you, then verify the information.

Then do one better-call a politician or local bureaucrat and ask him what evidence he has anyone voluntarily supports governments. If you get an answer, then ask him why taxes-the support of the government-are compulsory. If people really want and support the government, then support, the paying of taxes, would be voluntary. Don't take my word for anything; verify, verify and then verify it again because the truth can withstand investigation. What do the facts tell you?

There's something a man attacked by the IRS knows: he's experienced true government. No amount of spin and insults from slick radio and television show hosts can change what he has experienced. The radio show host is probably not speaking from personal knowledge. Those who have personal knowledge of being attacked by the IRS will not be making excuses for the abuse they know is true.

If you doubt what is presented in this book, then I urge you to experience politicians first-hand. Then call into my radio show.

I also want to point out, unlike *Adventures in Legal land*, even though I do not accept the idea of a state, citizen, government, constitution etc., I will not be putting those words in quotes to always show the concept itself is being challenged.

Part One: Indictment

"Words can be weapons..." attributed to Oliver Holmes

Indictment explained. What will be shown, as opposed to most political indictments, is causation. For each element, legal, economic and psychological, I will show the facts proving causation. This is usually simple-basically cause and effect, act and result: what did A cause? There are court decisions where they actually talk about real crimes, the act and the result, such as with the *corpus delecti*.

I'm not claiming causation is always very simple, only in the general sense; there are very complicated situations such as medical issues. However, we'll see in most government prosecutions, the issue of causation is not a complicated matter. For real crimes *mala in se*, yes; government cash cows i.e., *mala prohibita*: "Wrong only as forbidden by positive law." *Ballentine's Law Dictionary*, page 767) not a chance. *Mala prohibita* by definition doesn't involve causation.

If you read a typical indictment, say for drug possession or tax evasion, there's never any mention of causation; the defendant is not accused of causing anything. Obviously there's no need then to show causation. Yes, he/she is accused of doing something, but not causing anything. Does anyone really think it's just a coincidence courts can only hear a cause or cause of action? A right is a legal claim and what do tyrants use as an excuse if you file a complaint against them? That's right "Failure to state a claim [cause] for which relief can be granted."

I've had bureaucrats tell me clients are not accused of any wrongdoing, they're accused of non-compliance. That's what bureaucrats are after, not protecting people, but control. They want to control behavior and they will kill you to get compliance.

It's just basic common sense there has to be some result caused by a wrongdoer for there to be a cause and cause of action. And courts are limited to only causes. You'd think somewhere down the line they would have stopped using the phrase cause of action so it would be easier to prosecute non-crimes such as growing poppies.

If you look at a real crime, such as manslaughter, there is a **chain of causation**, a series of events leading to the death of a man or woman. An example would be:

Man A drinks beer for several hours.
Man A gets into his car and drives down Main St.
Man B is riding his bike down 5th Ave towards Main.
Man A does not hit his brakes.

Man A's car hits Man B.
Man B is killed.

It's a way of reconstructing the act and acts leading to the crime; it's how we explain what happened, why and who is responsible. There is a common sense legal standard called "but for"; *but for* the actions of A, B would not be dead. We don't need to be a genius to know the *but for* principle is relevant only with real crimes. Unlike with politicians and those who profit from the current system, defining a crime is pretty easy. Those who profit from crimes have a vested interest in keeping the definition as vague as possible. Of course, those interested in truth strive for as precise a definition as possible.

Any act where there is no need for the *but for* test and chain of causation, is no crime. Of course, the even simpler principle or maxim is: A crime is any involuntary human interaction. Given the public relations in place already, all I am doing is restating the obvious. *Mala prohibita* crimes are not crimes *but for* the opinion of a politician. Ask a cop on cross-examination and they'll agree.

This is why a factual timeline is so important in resolving disputes and problems. It's one of the first things I usually request from people I do consultations with. This is not limited to only disputes where the local tyrant is involved; it's very effective regardless of who is involved in the dispute.

A friend called me in a panic because someone was claiming a right to his property. I told him to write this guy and tell him you want to resolve this matter without the courts. He was to ask this guy to provide him with a factual timeline showing exactly where, when, why and how the rights to the property were acquired. This is preferably by affidavit. Once he provided the factual timeline, my friend would give up the keys and walk away.

He never heard from the guy again about it. I've asked tax agents to do the same thing: provide a factual timeline, by affidavit, of exactly where, when, why and how the government acquired a right to the property in question. I've never gotten such a timeline.

The timeline will contain a chain of causation and the facts necessary to properly determine any *but for* tests. If the timeline doesn't, then it's pretty obvious there are no facts to support the accusation. I doubt anyone could construct a factual timeline to prove someone has taxable income. Well, it's beyond *any* doubt. No timeline could show a connection between the constitution/law and anyone, at least no one alive today.

As I go about this, remember, my interest here is not in pointing out the individual men and women responsible for the damage caused by the government concept, but the concept itself. As far as I can tell, every bureaucrat and politician has blood on his hands, as do the rest of us, for letting them get away with their countless crimes every day.

"No one raindrop feels responsible for the flood." Anonymous

The concept of government is what creates the context necessary for people to act and cause the actual trauma and damage. It's the rationale/concept that creates the context, as we'll see in the psychological part, that has such a dramatic effect on people.

Don't think for a moment that perceptions, when talking about crimes, are irrelevant. There is no need for me to actually have a gun to be guilty of armed robbery; all that's necessary is for me to act in a manner that's intended to make everyone in the bank believe I have a gun and that I will harm them. It's the perceptions of the victims that are important. Look at self-defense killings; was the victim's belief his life was in imminent danger reasonable?

This is a pet defense of cops isn't it? The cop reasonably believed his life was in danger, so he choked a man in a wheelchair [this really happened in Phoenix, Arizona]. There's supposed to be an investigation into the facts to see if the situation/context, would lead a reasonable person to believe their life was in immediate jeopardy.

This is our *but for* test though: *But for* the concept of government, you would not have people cooperating in their own enslavement, enabling a small minority to control a vast majority. There would be no large scale wars *but for* governments as wars are fought by governments to take control of resources.

This reconstruction is not about opinions, it's about the evidence-empirical, verifiable facts. The opinions are drawn from the facts, which usually speak for themselves. If the facts show someone, let's say George, knowingly sent men into a dangerous situation and did so under false pretenses, and those men were killed, what opinion would you draw from those facts? Most would agree the facts prove that *but for* George's acts, the men would not have died. George did not pull the trigger of the gun that killed the men, however, if not for, or *but for*, his deception, the men would not have been in that dangerous situation.

So the facts, through a chain of causation, prove George caused the death of the men; they would not have been killed *but for* George having deceived them. To me, that's the end. We just need the facts; who really needs to draw an opinion from that? For sake of demonstration, what opinion do you draw from these facts? Most would agree, even prosecutors, it was premeditated murder, and if he planned the act with others, most would agree it was a conspiracy to commit murder. In fact, the most famous prosecutor in the world, Vincent Bugliosi, wrote a book about it. He also did many talk shows about the indictment of George W. Bush for murder. (I always enjoy watching them eat one of their own.)

Look at this from a tax indictment against Mike in Idaho. Read through it-I've only included one "count"-and see if you can find anything about causation. The *but for* legal standard is never applied to *mala prohibita* crimes because they're not real crimes. They are just acts politicians criminalize for control and to provide the pretense for stealing more money.

40

THOMAS E. MOSS, IDAHO BAR NO. 1058
UNITED STATES ATTORNEY
TRACI J. WHELAN
ASSISTANT UNITED STATES ATTORNEY
DISTRICT OF IDAHO
6450 N. MINERAL DRIVE
COEUR D'ALENE, IDAHO 83815
TELEPHONE: (208) 667-6568

U.S. COURTS

APR 1 4 2010

Rcvd_____Filed_____Time_____
ELIZABETH A. SMITH
CLERK, DISTRICT OF IDAHO

LORI A. HENDRICKSON
JENNIFER R. LARAIA
TRIAL ATTORNEYS
U.S. DEPARTMENT OF JUSTICE, TAX DIVISION
601 D STREET NW, 7TH FLOOR
WASHINGTON, D.C. 20004
TELEPHONE: (202) 514-2174

IN THE UNITED STATES DISTRICT COURT FOR THE DISTRICT OF IDAHO

UNITED STATES OF AMERICA,)	Case No. **CR 10-0089 ·N EJL**
)	
Plaintiff,)	**INDICTMENT**
vs.)	
)	26 U.S.C. §§ 7201 and 7203
MICHAEL GEORGE FITZPATRICK,)	
)	
Defendant.)	
)	

The Grand Jury charges that:

Introductory Allegations

At all relevant times to this Indictment:

1.   MICHAEL FITZPATRICK is a United States citizen who resided in Kent, Washington,

Sandpoint, Idaho and Hope, Idaho.

2.   During 1997, MICHAEL FITZPATRICK purchased Investt Acura Cal S.A. (IACSA), a

Costa Rican company, and listed himself and his wife as agents. MICHAEL FITZPATRICK

Indictment – 1

41

opened bank accounts in the name of IACSA which he used continuously from 1997 through 2003.

3.   Beginning no later than 2002, MICHAEL FITZPATRICK began marketing and selling products that purportedly allowed individuals to completely eliminate credit card debt and other types of debt. MICHAEL FITZPATRICK used the internet to market and sell these products. MICHAEL FITZPATRICK also used agents to market and sell the debt elimination products.

4.   On or about May 2, 2003, Dynamic Solutions, Inc. (DSI) was formed. DSI was a corporation formed in the state of Washington. MICHAEL FITZPATRICK was listed as the President of DSI. MICHAEL FITZPATRICK primarily operated this business from his residence in Idaho. MICHAEL FITZPATRICK used DSI to market and sell debt elimination products.

5.   On or about December 30, 2003, NAES, Inc. (NAES) was formed. NAES was a corporation formed in the state of Nevada. MICHAEL FITZPATRICK primarily operated this business from his residence in Idaho. MICHAEL FITZPATRICK used NAES to market and sell debt elimination products.

COUNT ONE

Evasion of Income Tax
26 U.S.C. § 7201

The Grand Jury repeats and realleges each of the Introductory Allegations contained in paragraphs 1 to 5 above.

From January 1, 2003 through at least April 15, 2004, MICHAEL FITZPATRICK, in the District of Idaho and elsewhere, did willfully attempt to evade and defeat income tax due and owing by him to the United States of America, by failing to file a 2003 individual income tax

Indictment – 2

return, Form 1040, on or before April 15, 2004, as required by law, to any proper officer of the Internal Revenue Service, failing to pay to the Internal Revenue Service the income tax due and owing, and committing the following affirmative acts of evasion, among others, knowing the likely effect of each of which would be to mislead or conceal his true and correct income and taxes due thereon from the proper officers of the United States of America by:

    1.   issuing and causing to be issued payments to third parties for personal expenses from bank accounts he controlled and which were held under the names of businesses and nominees;

    2.   moving, participating in the movement of, and causing funds to be sent to accounts outside of the United States over which he had dominion and control, in order to conceal and disguise the existence and ownership of the funds;

    3.   paying and causing to be paid personal expenses with funds outside the United States, in order to conceal and disguise his ownership and control of the funds;

    4.   purchasing and holding a vehicle in the name of a nominee entity, for the purpose of concealing and disguising his ownership of the property.

All in violation of Title 26, United States Code, Section 7201.

COUNT TWO

Evasion of Income Tax
26 U.S.C. § 7201

The Grand Jury repeats and realleges each of the Introductory Allegations contained in paragraphs 1 to 5 above.

From January 1, 2004 through at least April 15, 2005, MICHAEL FITZPATRICK, in the District of Idaho and elsewhere, did willfully attempt to evade and defeat income tax due and

Indictment – 3

The same holds true for any so-called "victimless crime." There is never any accusation of injury or damage and it's not a crime or cause without it. According to the PR, the purpose of the courts is to redress or correct a wrong. Yet, millions are prosecuted every year for not putting a seatbelt on or for growing plants.

If there is no chain of causation there is no crime. Can't make it much plainer than that. Without a *but for* test, act and result, there is no cause of action, no case and it follows, no crime.

Again, the public relations justifying governments is that they are to protect rights, yet why don't most people bring this up in court? It can't be because lawyers don't know this; we're all taught this in school, at least here in the so-called United States. We all learn about the Declaration of Independence of July 4, 1776, so they do know it. For some reason it's not discussed and it could be as simple as custom, not a concerted effort to keep it out of the courts.

I'd like to think that it was true, that courts are to protect rights, though my experience doesn't support this. Bring up the single stated purpose of government, viz., to protect and maintain individual rights, and the state lawyers will object and mock you as if you are spewing gibberish. They act as if you're retarded for even suggesting it. Don't believe me? Try it for yourself in court. Then you can call into the radio show and confirm it, again. I get the mocking all the time; it's my signal I'm presenting the inconvenient truth.

Until some state attorney or judge is open about why they react the way they do regarding the purpose of government, we can only speculate based on the facts before us:

1. They make billions from fines levied against people who've injured no one;
2. The courts (governments) are limited to protecting rights;
3. They mock the very suggestion the courts are limited to protecting rights and refuse to take mandatory judicial notice (itself a crime) of the law stating so;
4. They continue making billions from fines levied against people who've injured no one.

See how self-evident facts tend to be? That's pretty strong evidence the people running the courts are deliberately not applying their sacred writ. Who really needs an opinion? It's so easy to see what's going on just using the facts.

Another example is with taxes. There are anti-injunctive tax laws denying courts jurisdiction to hear cases where people want to stop the taking of their property under the guise of a tax. Despite there being well-known and established exceptions [Calfarm Ins. Co. v. Deukmejian (1989) 48 Cal.3d 805 , 258 Cal.Rptr. 161; 771 P.2d 1247, http://scocal.stanford.edu/opinion/calfarm-ins-co-v-deukmejian-31141, Western Oil & Gas Assn. v. State Board of Equalization (1987) 44 Cal.3d 208 [242 Cal.Rptr. 334, 745 P.2d 1360 http://scocal.stanford.edu/opinion/western-oil-gas-assn-v-state-bd-equalization-28520, Enochs v. Williams Packing Co. (1962) 370 U.S. 1, 7 (8 L.Ed.2d 292, 82 S.Ct. 1125 http://supreme.justia.com/cases/federal/us/370/1/case.html#7)are just such cases], we have never been able to get a judge to acknowledge them. We've used requests for mandatory judicial notice and not one judge has ever complied. Why the systemic refusal to take mandatory judicial notice of law? The facts really tend to speak for themselves.

The billions of dollars involved are one hell of a motive and more than enough to make a very strong circumstantial case for fraud, kidnapping and false imprisonment. It's circumstantial only because no further investigation is included, that's all we have and it's plenty to convince rational people beyond a reasonable doubt that the people running the courts are committing fraud on an almost unimaginable scale.

Money is certainly a motive for the worst of real crimes, even murder; and as the amount of money goes up, so does the motive. So it's reasonable to conclude the reason bureaucrats don't talk about the purpose of government is because it would cost them billions and they are committing, at the least, fraud and extortion. What other rational explanation is there for the absolute institutional refusal to acknowledge the single legitimate purpose of government? If there is a legitimate reason, then judges would calmly articulate it, not burst into a fit of rage and threaten you with contempt of court.

They cannot claim ignorance, especially when it's presented to them and shown to be the law. Ignorance does not explain the refusal to take mandatory judicial notice. There is no other rational explanation. They are being deceptive. Bureaucrats know that in traffic, tax, and drug proceedings there is no case and no jurisdiction and yet they prosecute anyway. Why? Money and control. If millions are a motive for murder, then it's no-brainer for lesser crimes of fraud.

The three main elements of crimes are: intent, means and opportunity. Since they are all code violations, the applicability of the code is the single most important, but will be discussed in detail later.

Let's look at **intent**. The purpose of traffic courts is definitely not justice; it's to take as much money from the people as possible. Proof? All support is compulsory. Those interested in justice do not force people to pay them. Justice requires it to be voluntary; justice begins with respect for each other's autonomy. If someone initiates force, their intent is to injure. That should be a maxim.

Additional evidence is the absolute refusal to take notice of the claimed purpose of government. If justice was the intent they would not refuse to take mandatory judicial notice of the purpose of government. If their intent was consistent with the purpose of government, then they would proudly display that in the courtrooms alongside the flags. Better yet, it should be on a placard on the front of the bench.

Further evidence is the judges' systemic, automatic relieving prosecutors of their burden of proof on jurisdiction-coming into the hearing/trial insisting the laws apply without any evidence.

Think about this; judicial notice is not discretionary, it's mandatory for a judge (rule 201(d) of the federal rules of evidence http://www.law.cornell.edu/rules/fre/rule_602).

Even if we excuse those traffic courts where the rules of evidence do not apply, rules of justice, fairness and due process still do. For what purpose would judges refuse to acknowledge the purpose of their job?

There's no reasonable explanation to refuse to acknowledge the law, and no reasonable doubt. These judges are purposely refusing to acknowledge the law in order to take money away from people. They are knowingly taking money by force and under false pretenses.

That is the same with the concept of government. We know, beyond any doubt, the intent of government is not protection and justice. The evidence is **taxation**; support is always coerced-pay or get shot or stuck in a cage. What is the intent though?

It's obvious: control over others, taking money under false pretenses. (I'll admit, not every bureaucrat may be knowingly taking the property under false pretenses.) While the law may state "ignorance of the law is no excuse," especially for bureaucrats and bankers, there is no such claim for ignorance of the facts. How could a bureaucrat not know they do everything by coercion and not permission? They, like many of their victims, have to be ignoring the gun in the room because they do know the proceedings do not involve permission. What bureaucrat or politician asks for permission?

The rule lawyers like to quote is applicable here also, they know, or are reckless in not knowing, they are taking money by force and under false pretenses. They must know they do not rely on consent; they never ask for permission. Like typical narcissists, they crave attention and need to constantly have their grandiose view of themselves fed. What facts do I rely on? That's easy; I've personally spoken with hundreds of bureaucrats -professional parasites-five days a week for the past decade and have posted many calls on the website where you can hear them come unglued when questioned.

All I have to do is claim their opinions are arbitrary and they immediately jump to the defense of their facade of legitimacy. They refuse to accept their opinions are groundless, that they operate by assumption and custom without any factual support. This goes to their mindset and proves they know they are making things up as they go along; there are no facts to support their opinions. With first degree murder and other serious crimes, such behavior is called "with malice aforethought."

I have had dozens of bureaucrats admit there were no facts and they were not qualified to claim anyone is a taxpayer with taxable income and, like Daniel with the California FTB, laugh while saying, "There doesn't need to be evidence." Didn't matter that a few minutes earlier he agreed that a lack of evidence was grounds to abate an assessment.

The simple, direct questions quickly undo their false impression of facade. All I have to do is ask:

Beyond your opinion, what facts do you rely on proving your laws apply to me just because I'm physically in California?

Just answering, "you're here," doesn't answer the question; there are no dots connected. It does not factually connect the law, whatever it is, to me or anyone else. I can impose more leverage on the economic predator by first asking if his opinion is based on facts. Then just ask for the facts I already know don't exist. The need to maintain the facade necessitates the taking of positions that are untenable. It really is easier to just play it straight. But that would mean they could not control others; they'd have to bring their services to the market like normal people.

Knowing they are going to always commit to an untenable position because it squares with their public relations, makes it easier to expose them. We really only set the stage for them to expose themselves. Asking if I'm entitled to a fair hearing is one example, as is the presumption of innocence. The reality is that we're *not* entitled to a fair hearing; if we were then they would not be forcing us to participate in the first place.

The fact they do not ask for permission or cooperation is evidence of malice and reckless disregard for the autonomy of others. Children understand this, yet this fact is lost on most adults. Most will choose to ignore what the facts tell them and simply cower, with their tails between their legs, hoping the police or tax psychopaths will just leave them alone.

We do not even need to add in the aggression used to get people to comply with governments to prove intent beyond a reasonable doubt. The violent support does, in my opinion, move it from beyond a reasonable doubt to beyond any doubt. People who refuse to respect you as an autonomous adult are not intent on protecting you.

As "enlightened" a society as we're supposed to be, you would think that would be a self-evident truth. It is, but there are just too many layers of PR and severe social pressure keeping most people from speaking this truth.

Means. The means to steal under false pretenses forms the structure of the system, together with some serious mind control. Criminal liability is not confined to just the ones giving the orders though. Remember the chain of causation, the bureaucrat can be just a link in the chain and still be liable. Again, when describing liability or culpability, we can rely on: "should have known or was reckless in not knowing."

Those punishing us when we haven't caused any injury, must know (or are reckless in not knowing) their own PR, that governments have one stated legitimate purpose: the protection of rights. They should know that unless we have violated someone's rights, they have no legal justification interfering in our lives.

Of course, if they really gave it any serious thought, they'd realize the means of government are completely at odds with the ostensible end. The proper course of action would then be to promptly quit these jobs and begin living peaceful productive lives, while apologizing for all the damage they have inflicted on their victims.

This tends to make it easier to articulate probable cause, doesn't it? In the United States, police are required to have probable cause or reasonable articulable suspicion (RAS) of criminal activity. I would say that if questioned publicly, most cops outside of the United States would agree they may not arbitrarily interfere with people's lives, even if it is not part of the sacred writ.

Generally, there are considered to be rights to life, liberty and property. If a cop is acting pursuant to the constitution when he interferes with someone's life, then he should be able to easily articulate why, and should at least be able to identify the person's actions as having violated, or are in the process of violating, someone's life, liberty, or property. Most of the time these violations are not abstract, they leave empirical evidence behind. Remember: *act* and *result*. The result tends to leave evidence.

In other words, even if acting pursuant to the constitution, the cop would probably not be the one initiating force. However, with victimless crimes, the cops are always the ones initiating the force, i.e., committing the actual crime. The cops are doing an act which under the same circumstances would be a crime if we, the little people, did it. The courts then continue the assault.

It's the same when cops tase people; it's about non-compliance, not because someone is being violent. I've been told a number of times my client is not charged with any wrongdoing, but with non-compliance. Anyone paying attention to the facts, to what is really happening, should not fail to see the obvious: those people calling themselves governments are into control, not respecting individual autonomy. They are into

47

protecting those coercing us to keep governments in business.

Every cop on the street has the means to kill us, and rob us. They drive around our neighborhoods in cars paid for with money stolen from us; track us on computers our money paid for. They tase and shoot us with guns bought with money forcibly taken from us. Through the use of mind controlling PR, all cops have to do is to flash some lights to get most people to stop their cars. Yes, most of us know the cops will increase their aggression to get what they want, but the fact most people stop with just the flashing lights does not negate the violence or threatened violence involved in the situation.

Every IRS agent has the means to shut down entire businesses without so much as a signed order; it just requires a phone call and a form letter. Why?

Because of the structure; we've been programmed, and from that is massive social pressure to comply. Banks have entire departments just to process and comply with IRS summonses. A summons is just a piece of paper signed by someone who is incapable or willing to provide services to the market on a voluntary basis. Yet, people don't look at the facts, they comply every day out of fear of what that predator can and will do to them if they don't jump when barked at.

People in business will blindly obey the tax psychopaths despite overwhelming evidence what they are doing is wrong and hurting one of their own employees. I'm working with someone where the IRS has hit him with a double levy, the same account, despite the fact the IRS stole enough with the first levy to cover the "assessments." The company cries there is nothing they can do but comply until the IRS or a judge tells them to stop.

People are so afraid of the IRS that I cannot get most companies to give a statement that the information, such as 1099's and other tax forms, is only provided out of fear of the IRS. I have worked with someone who did get such a statement from the company-and I know this is going to be hard to believe-but the IRS retaliated and attacked the company. I know, it's *so unlike* the IRS to retaliate; who would believe it?

That is a good list of means so far; the victims are accomplices to the crimes against their fellow victims. The predators cannot accomplish everything on their own; they need their victims to help, to have the herd attack themselves. Why else would companies have legal immunity from any kind of action for damages they cause if they comply with an order to steal on behalf of those called government?

If you didn't already know, if the company you work for, or your bank/credit union, takes your money and gives it to the tax psychopaths and you are damaged, then you have no recourse to hold them accountable. Yes, do our dirty work and in return we won't put you in jail, take your business, and our victims will not be able to hold you accountable. That's a pretty big carrot there and it's based on fear, the mother of cruelty.

That fear provides the means necessary to get the victims to be accomplices and the means for governments to commit their crimes. Such complacency then leads from means to opportunity.

Opportunity. Opportunity is there every day; look at traffic court judges. Each day cops are on the street giving out tickets. Most people just play along and participate, even if they complain about it. Yes, the victims do provide the criminals with opportunity because they maintain the fictions - they cooperate.

I spoke to a traffic court clerk in Los Angeles, California and asked why a cop who wrote a ticket, who did not show up in court for the hearing did not get charged with failure to appear. She said the cop is not just a defendant (such as my client, we're the little people), but a witness in many cases, he's really busy writing tickets. I told them he shouldn't be giving out frivolous tickets and wasting people's time. If we blew off a subpoena the judge would immediately issue a warrant for our arrest. It's good to be the king, or at least one of the king's men.

There are computers spitting out threatening form letters every day that are mailed to people who comply out of fear. All a tax agent has to do is send a fax to a business ordering them to send our money to them and they comply.

Actus reus. This means a guilty act, and can be proven by the actions and statements of judges. It's not that they politely disagree when they ignore the very law they claim to administer, they always seem to have anger problems. There are typically threats of jail if we challenge their sacred cows such as jurisdiction. It typically goes something like this:

> Sorry Sir, I don't really understand all this complex legal stuff, but I intend on pleading guilty, I just have a few questions.
> *I'm happy to help you, what are your questions my good man?*
> Well, before I can ask you a question, would you please take judicial notice the sole purpose of government is protecting individual rights?
> *What did you just say?*
> I asked if you would take judicial notice the sole purpose of government is protecting individual rights.
> *You little jerk, think you're smart, eh? You ask any more questions like that and I'll hold you in contempt. What are those, internet questions?*

That's a real answer by the way. People have reported to me that when they went to court and asked judges tough questions, the lawyers have tried to dismiss the question with the wave of a hand claiming, "That's an internet question." They act as if that's a reason to not answer relevant questions.

> Can I see your license and registration, peon?
> *Sorry, that's an internet question. I think I remember hearing that in a cop show on TV also.*

Can you imagine being a witness in a murder trial and being asked:

"Is the killer in this courtroom today?" And you respond with: "Sorry, that's an internet question" or better, "Come on Clarence, that's a *Law and Order* question, this isn't *Matlock* either, Perry Mason." That should be our response in a tax audit:

> *Did you receive income from Acme Inc., during the year 2010?*
> That's an internet question.

One need only look at judges who sit on cases where taxation is an issue to see the extreme punishment they dish out for daring to challenge a tax assessment. In the US tax court, you can be punished up to $25,000 for raising an argument the judge disagrees with. In fact, I have seen people sanctioned thousands for arguments they didn't raise.

The almost complete disconnect in communication with tax agents can only be by design. Either that or most tax agents are illiterate. But if they are all illiterate, that doesn't stop the courts from protecting them and rubber stamping their nonsense.

To prove this, we request a hearing with the IRS on grounds there are no witnesses and no evidence to support the assessment. This is based on observation and from speaking with the agents themselves. We are denied a hearing with a form letter stating we only raised frivolous arguments. If this happens to you, do what I do: call the agent and kindly ask them to identify the alleged argument. You shouldn't be surprised when they can't. Evidentiary challenges have never been held to be frivolous. You may be wrong, there may actually be evidence, but the challenge and issue is not a frivolous argument.

I've had lawyers during cross-examination tell me they did not understand this question: "Factually, what is the state?" If they are literate, they understand the question. What they are doing is using that as an excuse to protect the witness from having to answer; a good ol' fashioned stall tactic. I told them I don't care if they understand the question; does the witness I'm cross-examining understand? If the witness doesn't understand, then I can ask if they are literate and know what the state is.

Think about that-lawyers claiming they don't understand the question. They'll insist I'm within the state, that they represent the state; but what the state is factually...suddenly they don't understand basic English. And **I'm** the one playing games! Is this a stupid legal tactic taught in law school?

> *"Ok, if you get someone who asks questions, calling you on your lies, just fake stupidity. You can't be expected to answer a question you don't understand."*
> "Won't we just come across as idiots?"
> *"No, you're a doctor of law, doctors aren't idiots."*

Judges are spin masters; their job is to make excuses for the crimes regularly done by the cartel and those who work with the cartel. If someone challenges the forcible taking of their property, the judge's job is

50

to make it look good. Watch out for people who are judges, or used to be. Some could get a rape victim to feel responsible for the rape.

An example is *US v. Shunk*, 881 F.2d 917, on pages 918-919, they wrote:

> "An analysis of **every crime** reveals three component parts — (1) the occurrence of the specific kind of **injury** or loss (as in homicide, a dead person; in arson, a burnt house; in larceny, property missing), (2) somebody's criminality as the source of the loss (in contrast, *e.g.*, to an accident), and (3) the accused's identity as the doer of the crime. Wigmore on Evidence § 2072 (Chadbourn rev. 1978); *accord*, McCormick on Evidence § 145 (3d Ed.1984). The first two of these elements are what constitutes the concept of corpus delicti." (Emphasis mine)

Then, on the next page, the same lawyers wrote:

> "We do, however, recognize that the corpus delicti concept **is not relevant to a crime such as the present one** where there is no tangible injury or loss and the crime cannot be found to have been committed without reference to a specific defendant." (Emphasis mine)

I'm sorry, I thought "every" meant every or all. See how they spin things? This must have caused them some concern. On one hand there are hundreds of years worth of rulings: the *corpus delecti, the crime itself,* requires injury; on the other hand, they need to justify a criminal proceeding without one. Yes, it's an adversary proceeding without an adversary. What do they do to resolve it? *It doesn't apply.* It's supposedly "not relevant". That's all they have, no attempt to even spin it beyond their say-so; they just deny it applies.

Every single time someone files the motion template I have available and the grounds for denial are given, the only thing the judge offers is: "It doesn't apply here." They can't offer any legal citations of course. I would ask, "Really, it doesn't apply, that's actually a legal defense now? Can you provide facts and cite for me the law that gives this court an exception to a requirement that applies to every single court in the United States?"

Warning: Do NOT hold your breath waiting for a legal citation. Use that defense on the judge against your ticket:

> Sorry Clarence, this ticket doesn't apply to me.
> *Really, and what's the legal basis for that?*
> Well, I guess I'll threaten you with contempt and act like a child until you throw the ticket out.
> *I'm very impressed young man. Have you ever sat as a judge?*

That is also the basis of immunity from action. When a government claims he/she is immune from suit, it does not deny the tort, it only denies courts jurisdiction: Yeah, I damaged you, but I was smart enough to do it as a government and we don't allow you little people to hold us accountable through our own courts. We may be unwilling to provide the market services on a voluntary basis, but we're not stupid.

Yes, the old legal defense: "That doesn't apply here." Too bad that doesn't hold for us little people:

> You're charging me with a violation of your statute?
> *Yes.*
> Sorry, that doesn't apply to me.
> *Good to know; sorry to have bothered you mate. Would you like me to sanction this cop for your trouble responding to his frivolous complaint?*

Additional evidence for the *actus reus* is the compulsory support for government. What more do you need for a criminal act than terrorizing people to pay you?

Most people are blinded to the facts by the word government. Never lose sight of the fact we'd be considered criminals if we acted in the same manner as those called government.

Look at the facts, pay attention to what they do, not what they say.

There are no governments-there are only men and women calling themselves governments. There are also their victims who have not looked at the facts and just blindly accept these predators as governments. There are only individual men and women. The words or labels attached do not change the facts.

The concept of government is that **it's just fine to kill people to provide services, as long as it's done under the name of government**. That's really as far as we can break it down. Normal people understand this, though most people are too blinded by politics to see it clearly. Others have a serious investment in the concept, whether economic or perhaps otherwise, such as having a father or son die in the military or working as a cop.

While most people tend to reject the idea of mind control, I think it looks pretty obvious here. Why else would people think mass robbery is good when you do nothing more than use the word government as justification? I've spoken with many people pretending to be a government who believe taking property by force is not stealing if the taking is done under the label of government. We expect them to say that; they are profiting from it. But their victims also go along with it!

Most people are disassociated from the real violent nature of government, which is by design, and that's why they can desperately cling to the idea and cheerlead for a new owner - I mean new leader - every two years. The violence of the DEA or IRS is too far removed for them to care; it's not until the DEA barges into their home with hot machine guns that they stand up and notice. Well, if they're not shot dead first. These predators go after children with machine guns. Look up Elian Gonzales if you're unaware.

This is why it's so effective to question bureaucrats about the nature of government; people can see for themselves the true nature. We need to stop the disassociation, bring the violence front and center, and never take focus off it. People need to see the horrific psychological and economic damage caused by the government concept and that it does affect them directly. This will make it more difficult to ignore.

It's why asking, "*Excepting physical violence, factually what is your jurisdiction over me?*" is so effective. It's all violence. If they want to deny it's violence, then I can ask, "So if I walked out of this court right now you won't retaliate in any way? I can just leave and you won't bother me anymore?"

What are the psychological effects and damage caused by the government concept? There is the pecking order (hierarchy) that is at least a two tier pecking order established when people accept other people as a government. The hierarchy comes directly from the concept it is somehow moral to use violence against peaceful people if you are called a government. The rules such as "do no harm" don't apply, so you have a separate class; one controls the other.

The idea of slavery is made acceptable because it's not recognized as slavery. The people forced to pay for a government are forced to pay a certain amount of their time to support the people called government. Governments are rightly seen as not having to work for the support, they get paid regardless of performance, which causes contempt and breeds animosity between the two groups. Look at people who have to deal with the bureaucrats at the Department of Motor Vehicles; they typically have nothing but contempt for each other.

Those acting as a government are a class elevated above those forced to pay. We all know about the "us & them" attitude held by cops. I've worked with enough tax agents to know the "us & them" attitude is very widespread and not limited to cops.

We know being able to dominate others without personal responsibility to the victim will cause the one dominating to become sadistic. With just that, we can see how it would be on a larger scale such as we have every day in every society or community.

It's through the use of mind control, the use of words to change our perceptions - that ordinary people called governments can dominate us. They have conditioned people to ignore the facts right in front of them; to believe the judge who issues a warrant for your arrest is independent of the prosecutor and police; that he's fair and impartial. They give themselves a presumption of fairness. You have to see where I'm going with this. These facts paint a clear picture.

The formula is clear and is easily identified with most, if not all, proceedings with bureaucrats. It forms the foundation for understanding how to deal with these professional predators. The facts are set forth as follows:

A forces B to answer C's complaint

All the PR is to cover up these facts; we hear lies, such as a judge being independent and impartial. How do we know they are lies? That's easy; the facts are represented by the formula. For example:

Judge forces defendant to answer prosecutor's complaint.

These facts cannot be reasonably disputed. If a judge or prosecutor claims the judge is not forcing me to respond to the prosecutor's complaint, then I ask if there are any consequences if I choose to walk away and not participate. Of course I'll be threatened with arrest. At the least there will be a judgment whereby state goons will then feel justified to attack and murder me.

To anyone with the capability of rational thought, the obvious is clear: A cannot be independent when forcing B to answer C's complaint. These facts don't change because some lawyer claims the opposite: *You little jerk, of course I'm independent. Why? Because I said so.*

Collections of words called constitutions, rules of court and canons claiming that judges-who are paid by the plaintiff state-have an oath to the plaintiff state and sit underneath a flag of the state-are independent, are *just words*. They do not change the fact the judge is forcing me to answer a lawyer's complaint. It doesn't change the fact he's going to punish me at the request of another state lawyer.

Adding to these facts is a simple model to follow. Regardless of the distraction and evasion techniques being used, we should always be going from the abstract (the vague) to the specific:

Vague ==> Specific

As we separate the facts from the fictions, we're just asking questions to keep the attacker from staying vague. If they are permitted to stay vague, then we're not going to be able to resolve anything in our favor; they'll be comfortable insisting they, judges and bureaucrats, are independent. That is so vague, it ignores the facts.

An example is when a judge insists he's not forcing me to do anything, rather the court is. What do you say to such nonsense? They are evading the issue and deflecting our attention. I would ask, "You and the court are not the same thing? What is the court then, Sir? Is it some incorporeal being you are taking orders from? Are you hearing voices from this alleged court? It comes down to: Is this alleged court acting independently of you? Is it man-made or natural? Is it sentient, like Skynet?

You may also hear long-winded explanations about the three independent branches of government. They are only empty political platitudes, there's no substance behind the words. They may as well say: It is what it is.

It's a gaslighting technique because they are so arrogant and condescending when they tell you, as if you're the idiot for not buying such flimsy PR. Remember, politics is about distraction and evasion, keeping your attention away from the machine guns under all that paperwork. Even most psychopaths probably don't want everyone to know they are just criminals with titles-it's bad PR.

Using the word "court" is classic evasion; it's so easy to see when they're not screaming at us. The tactic is using a pseudonym in place of himself because they don't look so good when you expose their aggression. So it makes sense to ask if that is what he/she is doing, "Sir, is the phrase 'the court' a pseudonym you use?" The other lawyer is using the state as a pseudonym and the judge, if he's being careful, will use "the court."

It's really embarrassing when you ask, "Is that court that you referred to a court of the plaintiff state-the same plaintiff state the prosecutor claims as a dba or pseudonym? Just who is this court you keep referring to be acting on behalf of?"

But therein lies yet another problem: Isn't the prosecutor also an officer of the court, the same court the judge is claiming is forcing me to participate? Is the judge admitting to taking orders from the same court the prosecutor is acting on behalf of?

Simply ask the judge who is giving the orders, him or the court? The more you discuss the matter with them, the less credibility they have on the issue. So you won't actually use your name when you issue orders and warrants? Most political issues, in and out of court, cannot withstand scrutiny.

Exactly who or what are the jurors acting on behalf of? We know the narcissistic lawyer with the black dress is forcing them under threat of jail to participate, and he claims to be the court. The court is one of the three branches of the government of the plaintiff state. Obviously the jurors are acting on behalf of the plaintiff state. Again, how is that fair and independent? Can it just be assumed the jurors don't realize they're actually acting on behalf of a party to the proceedings? Do they have to realize this before there can be a significant issue of fairness and bias?

Look at him, with his stupid orange jumpsuit, thinking he's better than us. No judge or jury would let me get away with not paying my fair share; I'm not letting him either. No one else is going to feel sorry for this jerk. He's not on our team.

Look at how people are with sports teams; they usually tend to favor the team closest to them. I followed the NY Giants as a kid. Why? For no other reason than they were also from New York. There was what seemed an automatic bias against those other teams, *especially* the 49ers. I think it's fairly reasonable to speculate there aren't many Kiwis cheering for and supporting the Australian football teams when they play against New Zealand.

At the last Olympics, most people in the US tended to support the US athletes and made comments such as, "We've got the most gold medals again!" No, you didn't. Michael Phelps got the medals, not us.

I doubt the collective mind set-that psychology-is lost on jurors. They don't walk in and leave their habits at the door. Things just don't work that way. I wish they did, but facts are pretty stubborn things and we know people just don't drop habits easily. At least if you're a rational adult you know better.

Just as the cops have that disgraceful 'us and them' attitude, the same thing is present in court. We can be sitting there and the jurors are acting on behalf of the plaintiff state in an *adversary* proceeding. There are two separate teams; it's only natural for there to be collective bias with jurors: it's us against the schmuck in the jumpsuit. We're not on the same team, like when we see someone else pulled over by a cop: "Better him than me" is the common attitude.

But that is part of the PR supporting government: divide and conquer, get the slaves to fight amongst themselves. *Even if we give them a pass* saying there is no conscious bias, on an unconscious level the judge and jury know they are not only on the same team, they know the idiot in the jumpsuit is on the *other* team. As long as there is that unconscious influence on behavior, then it doesn't matter, the negative effect on their behavior is what counts especially since the proceedings are supposed to be fair.

Whether the tribal or herd mentality was used deliberately by those who designed the system or not, the effect is all that's important. Who cares if there's evidence or not of the designers sitting down and plotting: You know, the herd mentality can really be used to our advantage with juries; we force people in and have them act on behalf of the plaintiff state…

What's important is being able to prove there is a definite influence on behavior that *causes* people to act in a certain predicable way: Does A *cause* B? Putting people on opposing teams will cause a change in behavior, and that's without adding in any violence. Ever play a friendly game of baseball with guys who fail to recognize that the dream is long over, that there are no professional scouts watching them? There is no excuse for dropping a pop fly; they'll kill you before forgiving you for allowing that base.

Now imagine adding a healthy dose of violence into the mix: "But the judge ordered us, he made us take an oath to follow his instructions!" The underlying violence of court proceedings can only make the splitting up into opposing teams worse. Are we to believe a bad situation is not going to be made worse when there are threats of violence added? Sorry, I don't buy it.

Another example of them staying vague is when I've asked tax agents for the facts they rely on proving jurisdiction or that my client is obligated to register with an agency. They will say they are following their procedure. That's non-responsive and predictably vague. We want them to be specific, so I ask: "OK, is your procedure arbitrary or based on facts?" But even point out that is not responsive. "Yes or no, do you rely on facts proving you have jurisdiction over me?"

…don't give a responsive answer and provide facts, it doesn't …hey spit out, they are being evasive and vague. Just stay on …ng how to respond is easy when you know the model they

56

are working from, and if you are aware of whether or not you get a responsive answer.

They can try to turn the tables and take control of the flow of the conversation by putting the burden on us and getting us to help them: "Doesn't your client have a business in New Hampshire?" Not relevant or responsive; what facts do you rely on proving you have jurisdiction over my client?

When I asked an IRS agent in August 2012 about the facts he relies on proving the code was applicable, he responded with: "I am not going to go there." He also tried to get me to believe his department is not allowed to discuss the facts. Really? A policy forbidding employees from discussing the facts? Think I can get a copy of that policy? It should come as no surprise the agent's name was Mr. Weed.

If we assume this is a real policy, what type of people would work at a job where there was a policy forbidding them from discussing facts? Makes you think hallucinations are an essential part of the job.

> Welcome to the IRS. We permit you to do unimaginable damage to peaceful strangers, but you're forbidden from discussing the facts. You'll get your guns after your free lobotomy.

"Words are, of course, the most powerful drug used by mankind." Rudyard Kipling

Chapter One – Part 1

The beginning of wisdom is to call things by their right names.
-Chinese Proverb

<u>What is Government?</u> Looking at the facts, we see why there are no governments. As shown later, a state is supposed to be:

> "**state**...People, territory, and government considered in combination. Texas v White, (US) 7 Wall 700..."
> *Ballentine's Law Dictionary*, page 1210.

<u>Empirical evidence tells us government is men and women.</u> The facts separating them from others are they pretend to be protectors of life and property and provide those services to the market on a compulsory basis: you pay or you get shot. Those are the irrefutable facts, and no amount of spin will change that. Taxes are compulsory; it's so obvious even the politicians have to admit it:

> "**tax.** A forced <u>burden</u>, charge, exaction, imposition, or contribution...for the support of the government...51 Am J1st Tax § 3." *Ballentine's Law Dictionary*, page 1255.

These facts are the basis of why the concept is immoral and irrational; not the *type* of government, such as communist or democracy. All governments rest on the same violent foundation i.e., violent support commonly called taxation. Taxation is factually the taking of property without consent, the same thing as stealing or robbery:

> "**robbery**...The gist of the offense of robbery both at common law and under the Illinois statute is the force or intimidation employed in taking from the person of another, and against his will, property belonging to him or in his care, custody, or control. People v. Casey, 399 Ill 374, 77 NE2d 812...An intent to deprive an owner of his property and to convert it to the use and benefit of the accused is an essential element of the offense of robbery. People v Gallegos, 130 Col 232, 274 P2d 608..." *Ballentine's Law Dictionary*, page 1123.

This is really the be-all-end-all of political discussion. Claiming, "not everyone will pay" is just an excuse and doesn't make taxation any less robbery. Evidence that politicians know it's wrong to provide services on a compulsory basis are all their statutes classifying as crimes the taking of property by force without being a government, such as theft, robbery, extortion and racketeering.

We should do some wordsmithing of our own: from now on it's not robbery, it's *private taxation* mate.

Look at what they're doing, not what they're saying. There are always conflicting messages, and we're constantly bombarded with them. As shown later, a constant barrage of incongruent messages is a good way to teach someone to be schizophrenic. At the very least, you'll have someone who will have trouble making sense of the messages they're receiving.

I always ask:

Should a service or product be provided at the barrel of a gun?

This cuts through the PR and usually puts people in a double bind. Every now and then I get a smart aleck who says yes because they know I'm talking about government and they don't want to admit they are voluntaryists.

So I say really? Then give me your address so I can send you a thousand copies of my book and you better make sure you pay, or else! They may not openly admit it, but their generalization has been challenged and seeds of doubt have been sown.

If you're dealing with honest people, not affected by social pressure, this is really the only question you need to ask people to convince them governments should be abolished.

When you examine the different types of government, you'll see they're all essentially the same; the only real difference is the perceived level of aggression employed. We'll look at the facts regarding different types of governments: we'll examine republican, democracy, dictatorship, monarch, communist, and socialist. For republican or democracy we'll use the United States; for dictatorship we'll use North Korea; for monarch we'll use Sweden; China for communist; Cuba for socialist.

When comparing governments, there are common characteristics. All governments depend on taxation to exist. So, a common factor with governments is they all operate on a pay-or-get-shot basis. In that regard, all governments are equally brutal, even those with so-called constitutions. Remember, the Chinese psychos use a constitution also.

No government permits elections where the people are able to choose whether they want government or not. That's really the only important element to look at though. No one wants governments, as they all rely on compulsory support. Look at the following elements that are identical regardless of the "system" of government:

	Men & women Providing services	Pay or get shot basis	Elections	No choice whether there's a government	Constitution
United States (r)	X	X	X	X	X
North Korea (d)	X	X	X	X	X
Sweden (m)	X	X	X	X	X
China (c)	X	X	X	X	X
Cuba (s)	X	X	X	X	X

While there are many differences, when you look at these factual similarities it's the pay-or-get-shot basis of doing business that's really what's important. Killing people and caging them under the guise of protecting them is the problem. That's the true nature of all government and puts everything they say and do into question. Even the most benevolent group of people calling themselves a government still rely on violence to be in business. What governments do is always more important than what they say.

Each leader of the so-called countries listed above is paid in the same way; the only disagreement seems to be what they do with the stolen money. Funny enough, they all seem to build roads. Instead of seeing that the pay-or-get-shot basis is absolutely immoral, people are caught up with what the criminals are doing once they're paid. Unfortunately, it doesn't dawn on enough people to just stop paying the criminals. Take Nancy Reagan's advice: just say no [to paying taxes and supporting gangs called governments].

The Chinese governments are correctly seen as the antithesis of freedom and liberty while the United States is seem as a beacon of freedom and liberty (at least to Americans); but both governments are imposed and supported in exactly the same manner. The men pretending to be the Chinese and United States governments are just as willing to use aggression against their alleged customers. Both use violence for the same purpose.

Yes, there are varying degrees of violence, but the degree of violence doesn't really make them any different. It's sort of like a rapist who uses a knife instead of a gun. What's the real difference between a serial killer who has killed ten people as opposed to a serial killer who only killed seven? They're both killers; neither is the moral superior to the other, and I'd rather not be around either one. Isn't that the basis of the "lesser of two evils" platitude though? People know voting's nothing more than choosing a guy they believe will do less damage than the other one running.

I've said it before; I prefer to live in Arizona because, for the most part, the criminals called government leave my family alone. The aggression is much less than other places. So yes, I prefer this brand of tyranny over what's available in China. That doesn't mean I should be "grateful" for the somewhat limited imposition of my liberty and not seek to diminish that aggression even more.

The most significant constant is the pay-or-get-shot manner in which all governments are imposed and maintained. That's why the Chinese psychos have no problem with brutal atrocities such as Tiananmen Square, the American gangsters with Waco or the British nut jobs with Bloody Sunday. Well, it may not be fair to compare the Brits with the Chinese or the Americans, as I'm sure the soldiers who shot those unarmed men and women didn't miss their tea on 30 January 1972 in Derry, Ireland. How many of the world's problems wouldn't be here if the English government stayed in England?

It's also why all the problems associated with governments will continue until enough people stop accepting the program and they are

60

abolished. Every problem associated with governments exists because the foundation is immoral and irrational. The concept of government is that it's moral to kill people to protect them. It's obvious that governments will act consistent with their nature: violent and deceptive. What is irrational is thinking it can be reformed.

Factually, government is men and women providing services on a violent basis to pretended customers. More accurate, it is one man controlling another man without his freely given consent. Everything else is public relations; it's all distraction. So governments are men and women providing services on a compulsory basis; why then do people accept them and keep paying every year?

So who is the government? We can see it is men and women calling themselves that and other names, such as president, senator, policeman, judge, clerk etc.

Where is the government? These are the same people as above calling themselves the state and they are everywhere. They drive around in cars bought with the money they steal from us; sit in cubicles in buildings we paid for; they live in our neighborhoods and their children may go to the same schools.

When is there government? Any time people accept the concept that other people are authorities and can order people around just because they anoint themselves as government. It's a very powerful word.

Why government? Because due to conditioning, a fear of critical thinking and analysis, and social pressure from asking probing questions, the great majority just comply. They participate in their own slavery while waving the flag and sending their kids to die for Halliburton's corporate bottom line.

How are there governments? Through massive, incessant propaganda, from the time we are kids, being conditioned to think it is somehow civilized to kill, steal and lie in order to protect an unwilling population. A population sold a lie that fictions and herds are better than truth and individual autonomy.

If you doubt this and are skeptical (and that's good), then be scientific about it, put what you may call my theory to the test. If you believe those people called governments are benevolent individuals who really care for you, want to protect you and not see you harmed, then take the tax plate off your car and see how you get treated. Go to court and address the lawyer with the robe by his/her *first* name. Tell the local tax thugs you're not interested in having them take your money any longer. Then report to me how nice they were to you.

What's stopping you from quoting Howard Beal and telling those who don't lower themselves to our level and ask permission when confronting us, that you're a human being dammit, and your life has value? https://www.youtube.com/watch?v=WINDtlPXmmE

Because it's a truth we all know: The how and why of government is fear. We know they are violent psychopaths; that's how and why they still infest our communities.

61

Asking six questions (who, what, where, when, why & how) is really all we need to know this; we've all had plenty of experience to know it's true.

Did you know politicians can stop their wars anytime they want? History proves this and it's not just based on the technology of today.

In the Archaic Age of Greece, from 776 BCE on to about 339 AD, all wars were stopped for the Olympic games. I know, hard to believe, the games were considered more important than killing other Greeks. So, every four years, the Greeks stopped killing each other long enough to watch naked men wrestle. The Greeks, so admired by the Romans, were so civilized they never caught on to the idea that not killing each other just for the sake of not killing each other was also a really good idea.

A more recent example is the Christmas Armistice during World War I, 24 December 1914, lasting in some places until 1 January 1915. This is profound and what I believe one of the most important historical events in recorded history. Its importance cannot be overstated.

It started when German soldiers lit candles and sang carols in their trenches. The British, not to be outdone, followed suit. What happened next is one of the most dramatic examples of spontaneous order I've ever heard about: men from both sides started walking out and in what was called, "No man's land" exchanged gifts and sang together. It just may be the biggest middle finger given to The MAN ever.

These men, who were earlier that day trying to kill other, walked out and exchanged gifts of food, cigarettes and alcohol. How does one then go back to killing again the next morning?

This is evidence there is hope for us; despite all the conditioning, these men stopped the senseless killing and gave each other gifts. If they, in the trenches of WWI, can resist the conditioning and behave as mature adults, then certainly there's a chance the world can also.

If these men, trained to kill indiscriminately, with the "enemy" actively engaged in killing them, can stop and have empathy (become human again), then it's possible for us to live without asking permission and engaging a caste system. They didn't ask their "superiors" for permission; they found that human part of them, if only briefly, and they acted as men and they lived.

In the face of unspeakable horror, without statutes, orders and politicians, these pretended enemies stopped following orders and instead enjoyed the holiday. It was the religious soldiers who saw through statist madness. That's one hell of a contradictory model, that without laws and politicians, there will be chaos and mayhem. The politicians were reportedly enraged and took steps to try and ensure something like that did not happen again. Can't have peace in the middle of a war, can we? What fun would that be? We'd have to slow production at the munitions factories. And we know you don't dare minimize the demand for war. The pigs who control the world won't sit still for that.

How much easier is it for us to offer services/products to the market without submitting to unproductive parasites, than for those in the trenches that Christmas in 1914? Seen in that light, selling turkeys without a license doesn't seem like a radical an idea.

It also shows we can and should treat bureaucrats as we want to be treated. The fictions between those two groups, counted on by the pigs who treated them as farm animals, were temporarily broken. For a few days, they refused to accept the program and this enraged the psychopaths who were in charge. One of my favorite lines from *Dr. Strangelove* is, "Gentlemen, you can't fight in here, this is the war room!"

What would have happened if from that day forward soldiers refused to accept the fictions? Word was bound to get out to the other men fighting; they could have stopped the war themselves. Of course the generals couldn't have that, peace only comes when the politicians order it. The evidence is there proving it. But it also proves the politicians are not ultimately in control; the people are, and this is evidence the conditioning can be overcome and the victims can reclaim their lives and walk off the farm.

What triggered the breakdown of the program though? Something touched them and they saw past the fictions. They did not see English and Germans, they saw other men; men who though they were trying to kill each other that same morning, forgot about why, realizing that other guy over there is no different from them.

The Black Panthers and drafted black soldiers had a popular slogan about Vietnam: "No Vietnamese Ever Called Me Nigger." Muhammad Ali, who was prosecuted for refusing to comply with the draft, is also quoted as saying it. (Remember, when the US government fought racism in Europe during WWII, they sent the soldiers overseas in segregated ships.)

Does it take the absolute horrors of war to break the programming though? Of course not; if it did mankind would be doomed to live as farm animals.

The word government is a public relations word, it's mind control; it diverts attention away from what's really happening (violent control) and provides a perception of legitimacy for the violence perpetrated by men and women against their victims. It creates perceptions where the attacker is viewed as the innocent victim and the victim the criminal.

Just look at what happened in Waco, Texas in 1993 for a good example. A gang of men and women initiated the use of physical violence against men, women and children at Mount Carmel in Waco, Texas in 1993. When you take the label government away it's clear whom the real criminals were. This is why governments will claim immunity for their crimes, as if the opinion they are acting on behalf of their victims i.e., we the people, actually makes it so.

We've all been conditioned to believe: when men and women interact with others, if any are labeled a *government*, fundamental rules of human interaction (for some unexplained reason) just don't apply. By rules, I mean commonly accepted behaviors for individual men, women and children. A good example is: aggression and initiating force is wrong. As we'll see, these expectations, our maps of the world, govern how we will behave and respond to others.

You can already see where society, as individual men, women and children, are being set up for serious psychological problems from these two incongruent messages:

1. Attacking others is bad.
2. Attacking others is good if you're called a government.

How are we supposed to process this information? Will a part of the message be processed and another part deleted? I believe the evidence shows the violence part is not deleted, that most people are accepting the "violence is good" part, and not always the rest. Evidence shows the majority of people accept these contradictory ideas.

Another example: Christians and Jews will usually cite the Bible regarding "Thou shalt not steal." Exodus 20:15. Most would agree this applies to every individual man, woman and child. However, for some reason, this commandment from god does not apply to those same men and women when acting as a government. Why? And if you suggest it does, then you are attacked as some kind of radical or anti-government nut.

For many Christians, one need not look further than Romans 13 for the excuse. But what about those of the Jewish faith? Certainly no credibility is given to the writings of Paul as an authority applicable to the Jews. Why then do so many of the Jewish faith believe stealing by those called government is not against the commandment and immoral? Do they believe it's not stealing when property is taken by force when the thief call himself a government?

Why isn't the obvious contradiction noticed between "Thou shalt not steal" and "For this cause pay ye tribute [taxes]…"? You really can't get much easier than "Thou shalt not steal" and yet most people do not understand, or refuse to accept, that government is nothing more than men stealing from other men under the guise of protection. Even a child can recognize you don't steal from those you seek to protect.

And keep in mind; if Romans 13 is supposed to be taken literally, then there can be no wars. Talk about an internal conflict. There's no distinction between which governments are allegedly ordained by god and those that are not. Why then were Hitler and his followers resisted?

How insane is it that men and women, forcing themselves on others, are ordained by god? A popular Christian belief is freewill or agency; that god cannot, and will not, force us to do certain things. So god will never force us to do something, but I'm to believe he is personally deputizing mere men to do it for him? What about the maxim of law then? "**Nemo potest facere per alium quod per se non potest**…No one can do through another that which he cannot do by himself." *Ballentine's Law Dictionary*, page 844. Come to think of it, that sums up exactly why the concept of government is ridiculous:

Q: Why should governments be abolished?
A: Nemo potest facere per alium quod per se non potest

It's silly to think governments are ordained by god. God is love; yet, god would ordain one government to attack another government? Rubbish, what nonsense. "Let the data speak, whatever the data say."

Why would god ordain men to control, deceive and kill other men under the guise of protecting them? I know god is supposed to be mysterious, but I don't buy the PR governments are ordained of god. Are governments supposed to be like prophets? Maybe if spelled profits, then it makes sense.

Look at the so-called revolutionary war, that's a great example of this craziness. If governments are ordained by god, then ol' Georgey boy was king of England and his colonies. Why should the founding fathers have complained? These good Christians complained and rebelled against a minister of god:

> "For rulers are not a terror to good works, but to the evil...
> For he is a minister of God to thee for good...Wherefore ye
> must needs be subject, not only for wrath, but also for
> conscience sake. For this cause pay ye tribute also: for they
> are God's ministers, attending continually upon this very
> thing." Romans 13:3-6.

The revolution was about "no taxation without representation" right? They want us to believe it was a revolt against paying tribute to George. How does this square with the so-called Christian belief kings are God's ministers and should not be resisted? And yet it's a Christian nation? What a silly notion when you compare the facts with the public relations.

And if this is true: "Where the spirit of the Lord is there is liberty." 2 Corinth 17, then why would there be governments taking away that same liberty?

Why would a professed Christian object to any acts of government when Romans 13:2 mandates: "Whosoever therefore resisteth the power, resisteth the ordinance of God: and they that resist shall receive to themselves damnation." Sounds pretty serious to me. Would that include going to court for a trial? Are you not supposed to resist a cop's claim you were growing illegal plants?

On what grounds did the American government resist Saddam Hussein? Wasn't Saddam, an elected official, one of god's ministers? Are we really supposed to believe god told George W. Bush (god's minister) to attack Saddam, another one of god's ministers? This is what GWB is quoted as saying:

> "I am driven with a mission from God. God would tell me,
> 'George go and fight these terrorists in Afghanistan'. And I
> did. And then God would tell me 'George, go and end the
> tyranny in Iraq'. And I did. And now, again, I feel God's
> words coming to me, 'Go get the Palestinians their state and
> get the Israelis their security, and get peace in the Middle
> East'. And, by God, I'm gonna do it."

I don't know about you, but I don't need any more evidence to know I'm listening to a raving lunatic or a lying psychopath. Two more examples are from daddy Bush https://www.youtube.com/watch?v=tgCeFXeuE4U and Sarah Palin https://www.youtube.com/watch?v=NnGSk6N0Ugg&feature=related.

Ever in the military? Really want to feel like a pawn? Consider this: god supposedly ordained both George Bush and Saddam Hussein, according to Romans 13 that is. If both are "God's ministers", then god anointed and was directing both of them. And if you're in the military, then you're stuck in the middle of these two ministers of god. Who do you fight for and why? And why would god direct a war be fought between two of his own ministers?

Also, there are plenty of atheists and non-believers around who believe government is legitimate and when governments take property by force it's not stealing; the Bible is probably not the source of their conditioning. Atheists know it's wrong to take property by force, yet how many believe it's not stealing when you call yourself a government?

Are there constants though? Of course; and where are we conditioned about government but in government-run schools and through mass media? Statism is a religion and it's taught in government schools for a reason: to condition us from the time we are five years old to at least sixteen to believe the concepts of states, nations and citizens are real things. If not believe them, to act as if we do.

The media (print, radio & television) today basically serves two functions for governments: 1) as a public relations arm of governments and 2) distraction. The media always portrays government as a wonderful organization and concept while distracting the masses from government mass murders with a constant bombardment of fluff such as which celebrities are sleeping with who and the newest resident in rehab. I'm not claiming this is necessarily by design by the media industry, though we cannot ignore historical facts such as Project Mockingbird. The people in the media industry are victims of the trauma inflicted by governments just as the average person is (this is described in detail later in the psychology chapter).

If you doubt this, try to get on as a guest or as a caller on a mainstream show. You'll be cut off before you get to say Lysander Spooner; and even if you do get to say it, there's a several second delay and the audience will probably never hear it. Again, I'm not alleging there's a conspiracy among media owners, producers and hosts to keep the truth out of the media; that's the genius of this religion called statism. The victims do it on their own; no central planning necessary. There is definitely evidence of collusion.

The owners of the Federal Reserve Bank don't have to call anyone to keep me or Larken Rose off the air, the members of the church called the state do it on their own. They do it automatically because that's what they've been programmed to do.

A good example of this is Art Bell whose Coast to Coast AM show is a top rated nighttime show with several hundred AM/FM radio affiliates. Art told one of his producers I would "definitely never be on [his] show"; the reason being I talk about the "granddaddy of conspiracy theories." Here is one of the most successful radio show hosts, whose show was built primarily on conspiracy theories, not wanting to have me on. And unlike most of the guests talking about conspiracies he has on regularly, I easily prove the government hoax.

Art is probably like most others in the business and belongs to the church called the state. Members of this church have no problem passionately discussing government corruption and even talking about starting wars on false pretenses and government-sponsored genocide. But, mention abolishing government and that same passion is now directed against you.

Don't believe me? Call any mainstream radio show and find out first-hand. This is because statists-atheist and theists alike-believe the concepts of states and government are part of who they are. That is why the actors involved are scapegoated; to protect the fragile ego. As we'll see later, no conspiracy is necessary because of groupthink. Art Bell is part of the herd and he's not going to discuss ideas he does not believe the herd holds or will accept.

Obviously, understanding the word government is critically important to undoing the mind control it has over us. It includes the cult of authority. When one refers to a government actor as an authority, this is PR for a man willing to kill anyone who doesn't follow his orders.

Cops, judges and other people acting as governments are certainly not authorities on healthy, normal social interaction. Their model of the world is based on a pecking order.

It may be is a deliberate substitution of words, using authority for expert. This is done with the word anarchy, obviously; most using anarchy-literally, "no ruler" is a synonym for chaos, violence and mayhem.

In summary, a government is one man controlling another man without the latter's freely given consent. Or, men and women providing services on a compulsory basis.

Look at the control words have over us: people think, because it's been said so often, that it's "our" or "your" government. Well how many are honest enough to admit something of "theirs" or their family and friends, is bad? How about downright immoral and the cause of genocide, economic destruction, slavery and environmental disaster?

What facts would even suggest it's *your* government, that you have any choice or control? Most likely, like me, you've never had, and never will have, any personal contact, however slight, with any of the people who appear to be at the top of the political pecking order. Even if the services were provided voluntarily, it would still be no more ours than Acme is ours because we shop there.

Using "your" and "our" at least implies some kind of control, and not the myth of collective control; I mean individual control. The coerced support and compliance from those called government are the men and

67

women exercising control, so the facts just don't support that it's our or your government. As I'll show later, the facts are not what most people follow when it comes to government; behaviors are dictated by their perceptions. Even otherwise brilliant scientists seem to overlook this. This may be in part to the favors so many scientists get from the criminals called government.

The gangsters steal from the community and then give out favors for scientific experiments and research. Pretty much guarantees you have all the latest technology to continue stealing and killing those at the bottom of the pecking order.

It certainly makes sense that you would want to neutralize groups of people who are generally skeptical by nature and tend to ask lots of questions. So you buy off the scientific class; they depend on money stolen from the people for research, experiments and equipment, of course. How many scientists teach? There are many who are heavily dependent on the government concept, and that will ensure they do not bite the hand that feeds them.

So whether verbalized or not, conscious or not, it's reasonable, as evidence shows, that scientists don't openly question the concept of government, and instead support them, because their perception is: How bad can the concept of government be when we get millions in grants? If there's any questioning about these violent gangs of criminals, then it's not directed at the concept of government, but at the policies and the actors. It's the few bad apples nonsense no self-respecting scientist would accept in another context.

The verbal attacks on religion and religious organizations for the stifling of scientific advancement (I agree religious organizations did greatly inhibit scientific advancement) always seems to give a pass to the fact it was the government concept itself that provided the perceptions causing a change in behavior so the atrocities could be carried out. Why is the chain of causation always truncated? Why isn't the government concept at least equally vilified by scientists as the religious concepts are?

The consistent avoidance of the concept of government itself as the cause is because people who are professors at government universities are not going to attack their own livelihood. That's easy to figure out; it's no different than a judge who profits from putting peaceful people into cages. Their interest in the truth does not extend as far as they proclaim. So while atheists proudly assert religious people are blind to the truth, they can be just as blind.

We all tend to have blind spots; it's not to our advantage to attack each other because of it. Those who are farming us probably laugh at all of us when we attack each other. The old divide and conquer routine. Keep the slaves fighting among themselves.

You hear all the time, "The people here in California, by being here, consent to the government." If it were not for fear and heavy-duty mind control, most people would laugh at such a statement; it's just ridiculous. It's like a rapist defending his attack, "She just laid there, mate."

68

If people consent, then taxation would not be compulsory. It really is that simple: consent and coercion are opposites. They're opposites, unless you ignore the facts and only focus on the opinions. This mindset crosses all facets of society. It doesn't matter if one believes in gods or rejects the concept completely.

I've had one attorney for a tax agency tell me the people have agreed to be forced to pay. Yes, I laughed when she said that; I couldn't help it, it was one of the silliest things I've ever heard an adult say when trying to be serious. Talk about being desperate to maintain legitimacy. We agree to be forced. Yeah, as if we're participating in some S&M ritual. Sadly, this is probably not far from the truth.

I had an IRS agent tell me it's not force because we're all forced, no exceptions. So when is force not force? When applied to everyone. If you didn't know why those called governments need guns, then that should clear up a but for you.

You can also ask them: Since we know taxation is compulsory, beyond your opinion, are there any facts to prove people have consented?

As we'll see later in the psychology chapter, people will work desperately to make the facts conform to their map of the world. In this attorney's world, governments are good and don't use coercion; so to reconcile the obvious compulsory basis of government with her perceptions, she makes up silly excuses such as: "people agree to be forced". Sounds a little schizophrenic to me.

This is how we can know judges in traffic court come into court having already judged us guilty. Because the opinion comes first, the facts and what happens at the trial have to then conform.

An example is a Maryland tax hearing. Despite all of his claims to the contrary, the hearing officer already prejudged Denis to be a taxpayer. Everything then had to conform to his opinion and be twisted to fit. Even if the tax agent, under oath, admitted to not being qualified to do an assessment and determine Denis is a taxpayer, the hearing officer had to refuse to strike the assessment because the opinion Denis is a taxpayer would be unsupported. And it was admittedly unsupported; that didn't matter because it did not conform to the opinion Denis was a taxpayer. Appearances are important.

His perception my client is a taxpayer dictates his experience and he will either not be able to process the incongruent evidence, or he will just refuse to accept it. That's all his model of the world will permit. It's the old *reductio ad absurdum* fallacy Dan Evans used with me. It's not the proper use though. With statists like Dan Evans, if they disagree with the logical conclusion, then no investigation is necessary of the supporting facts. It's really just using a Latin phrase to condemn without looking at the evidence. It doesn't even matter what the starting point is with your proof, they will not want to get into any discussion where they may agree with any part of what you are presenting. This is exploited later with the request for judicial notice in court.

This is why it's so important to ensure the concept of *not* being a taxpayer-just the possibility-is part of the agent's model. We need to discuss it with them prior to any discussion of the facts and the process of vacating an assessment when not dealing with a taxpayer. When the mind is shut to any possibility, then rational discussion is not possible. We'd better be flexible in our communication or we may not meet our objectives.

If the agent's model doesn't permit the idea someone may not be a taxpayer, then we're going to have a very difficult time getting it thrown out on that premise. They will probably agree there needs to be evidence proving I'm a taxpayer, then at least we've got a generalization that includes there may not be evidence, at least not evidence the agent can provide.

This is why bureaucrats impulsively turn things upside down: What facts do you have proving the constitution does not apply? I've had lawyers ask me this despite having several agents already admitting they had no facts proving the code was applicable.

> The agent who did the assessments admitted he didn't have evidence the code applied.
> *Okay, but still, what facts do you have the code doesn't apply?*
> Again, the agent who did the assessments admitted he didn't have evidence.
> *That's not relevant, what facts do you have the code doesn't apply?*
> As a lawyer you know the burden is on the one making the claim?
> *Yes, but what facts do you have the code doesn't apply?*
> Are you drunk or stupid?

This is what happens when people think their opinions are real things outside their heads. When you use guns to effect behavior, then you don't need facts and a logical position; the gun does the convincing for you. People tend to respond to threats.

Those same people using the gun to compel behaviors then convince themselves it was the opinion that convinced people to act or not act a certain way. The gun is conveniently deleted from the experience.

An example is how bureaucrats so completely delude themselves into thinking people pay taxes because they believe they are required to, that they agree to be forced to pay. I go into more detail later, though anyone familiar with tax evasion prosecutions knows the prior acts of paying taxes is used as circumstantial evidence the defendant knew he/she had a legitimate obligation to pay taxes. No, they were responding to a threat. The circumstantial evidence is tortured to fit the opinion; the latter is direct evidence and doesn't need to be twisted. We all know which evidence is stronger.

Speaking of twisted, I love this reasoning. This is from one of many computer-generated form letters from the FTB:

> "The term resident is defined to ensure that every person who is physically present in California for other than a transitory purpose and thereby receives the benefits and protections of its laws and government, contributes to the support of the state (*Whittel v. Franchise Tax Board* (1964) 231 Cal.App.2d 278, 285)." FTB PASS 2190 (REV 02-2008).

70

First, this is only the opinion of a lawyer, probably long dead by now; and it's just a variation of the chicken or the egg dilemma. To really understand this, we have to know that governments are men and women, that states are dba's, and that their laws are just opinions. Let's break this down, layman's terms:

> *We can take your property by force because we previously took your property by force to provide benefits.*

Strong position there, a real moral high ground. Where did the money come from to support the government who made all those laws and allegedly provides benefits and protections? Here's where the chicken and egg come in.

The facts show there were/are people in California. Factually, governments are people. The people exist, and then they are supposed to establish governments. The people of a community are first. Then there are people calling themselves governments, who have no voluntary support; whose laws and benefits (not protection) are forced on everyone in the community whether you want them or not. Nothing gets done without stealing money from an unwilling community first. Then, they rationalize present and future robberies with the previous robberies.

Only psychopaths and criminals would justify robbery today on their past robberies.

Notice here there's a clear distinction made between California and the state. They wrote about being "physically in California" and to support the "state" regarding "benefits and protections" of their laws and governments. Yet, if you bring up the obvious differences between California and the State of California, their thought process shuts down faster than they can say frivolous.

This does not provide any facts though beyond: "because we said so." One opinion supports another opinion. The problem for us is that politicians think the more an opinion is quoted, the more valid it is. Rationally, we keep examining the facts, and if they continue to support the conclusion/opinion, then the conclusion is strengthened. With government predators, their opinions become more valid the more times they are repeated.

In the context of the naked moron parading around as if he was an emperor, it would play out like this:

> *The emperor has wonderful new clothes!*
> Yes, the emperor has wonderful new clothes!
> *I agree they are fantastic!*
> But he's actually not wearing clothes.
> *That's frivolous, the courts have consistently held the emperor does have wonderful clothes.*
> But he's paying you.
> *The emperor has wonderful new clothes!*

71

More distractions

"words are weapons..." Attributed to Oliver Holmes

Since the government concept holds it is legitimate/acceptable to threaten, kill, rob and lie if you do it under the guise of being a government, it requires many other supporting concepts to divert our attention away from the actual violence. The diverting concepts help delete the violence from our generalizations. Once deleted from our generalizations or model of the world, then our behaviors will be governed by that, instead of the actual *deep structure* as described in transformational grammar, a big influence on NLP:

> **Men and women calling themselves governments pretend to protect life, liberty and property by threatening to take away your life, liberty and property.**

The supporting concepts enable the deleting of most of the experience, so all that most people know is what is left, the deliberately vague *surface structure*:

Governments protect life, liberty and property.

This is the generalization people have about governments. They also add to this the idea that only governments can protect life, liberty and property. Nice sales pitch, isn't it? If this was not the case, if people had a more accurate model, then I believe most people would not accept the program and governments would collapse as not enough would cooperate.

Below is a short list with explanation of this very effective mind control.

The word government, like the rest we'll examine below, is a mere symbol to represent our world and experiences. Words are only tools to convey ideas to others. There should be precision so the people we are communicating with will better understand us, so we're all on the same page. As shown later in more detail, these make up our maps of the world. As with all of our maps, we generalize, delete and distort the representations based on factors such as awareness and prior learning and expectations:

> *"Generalization* is the process by which elements or pieces of a person's model become detached from their original experience and come to represent the entire category of which the experience is an example. Our ability to generalize is essential to coping with the world. For example, it is useful for us to be able to generalize from the experience of being burned when we touch a hot stove to a rule that hot stoves are not to be touched. But to generalize this experience to a

72

perception that stoves are dangerous and, therefore, to refuse to be in the same room with one is to limit unnecessarily our movement in the world." *The Structure of Magic*, Vol. 1, Richard Bandler & John Grinder, page 14.

When we think of government, we don't think of people such as George Bush, Tony Blair or Julia Gillard. We'll think instead of things like offices, courts, prisons, laws; a system that's for fighting wars and building roads. As shown above by Bandler & Grinder, actual elements have "become detached from [the] original experience." The coercive nature-how the means oppose the stated end-is dropped from the generalization. While this has devastating effects worldwide, it's very beneficial to people pretending to be governments or profiting therefrom.

With experience, our maps and generalizations can be updated, for better or worse. My experiences changed my generalization of governments from governments being a gang of killers, thieves and liars, to being men and women providing services at the barrel of a gun, to being only a concept where it's acceptable to kill people to provide them services.

What is troubling is that when part of an experience is deleted from our experience and not part of our map of the world, there is a very strong tendency to continue rejecting such part. This is equally applicable to religious and non-religious alike. As we'll see later, there can be resistance, an inability to process facts inconsistent with our maps.

Each one of the following words is itself a generalization and governs how we experience and respond to the world. Some things have been deleted from the real world experience (facts) and some have been distorted. As shown later, these generalizations are the basis for our expectations, and those expectations are critical to how we perceive facts and events. Our perceptions will dictate our responses and behavior. Some people cannot even process experiences incongruent with their perceptions and expectations. This is some serious psychological stuff here. People are far more mechanical than we realize or like to admit.

The denial we are mechanical is usually evidence of mechanical behavior. So much emphasis is put on freedom, free will and choice; but how much free will and choice do we really exercise? How much of our behavior and experience is dictated by our past conditioning?

I think you'd be surprised to find out how much our choices are limited, how much our generalizations limit our freedom and experiences. So much of our conditioning was done without any conscious effort and knowledge on our parts. There is so much we're unaware of, it certainly makes a good case that we really aren't exercising real free will because we either don't have access to the whole truth, or cannot process evidence inconsistent with our maps of the world.

That's why the following words, when objectively examined and questioned, cause cognitive dissonance with so many people. They can't accept that the PR and the facts are so incongruent. Why admit that deeply held beliefs are wrong? What is more important is for people to think they're always right.

The following words are the most popular supporting symbols for the government concept. I'll apply basic questions, as mentioned in *Adventures*, the six wise men Kipling wrote about: **who, what, where, when, why** and **how**. What is distressing to people is how simple this is. It's more difficult to accept the facts than to investigate them because you have to accept you were tricked by something so flimsy. Add to that the intense social pressure we may feel by misjudging how others will accept us if we are questioning sacred cows.

This is where the trivium is so valuable. No preconceived notions; just look at the facts, ask questions, identify and finally explain. Then repeat as often as necessary until there is a high level of certainty. Fortunately for me, this stuff is really easy to identify and explain.

    State. Governments only exist with so-called states. Part of the legitimacy of governments is they are the duly appointed agents acting on behalf of the state. So what is a state?

A so-called state is very important to maintaining the government concept. I won't make a distinction here between nation, country, Commonwealth or city because they are all the same concept. Even politicians make a distinction, at least part of the time, between geography and politics.

An example from Keene, New Hampshire is from the city charter, which tells you what the city is supposed to be:

> "The inhabitants of the City of Keene shall continue to be a **body politic** and **corporate** under the name of the "City of Keene," hereinafter sometimes referred to as "the City,"" (emphasis mine).

This is political magic where people and land become a fiction. When someone is alleged to be within the City of Keene, the words don't match; the map does not match the territory. The words "within the City of Keene" do not mean a physical location; they refer to a "body politic and corporate". And we know a corporation is a fiction.

A lawyer named Michael Detmer provides more evidence of this in a response he filed into a Las Vegas court:

> "CITY OF LAS VEGAS, Plaintiff...**CITY'S OPPOSITION TO MOTION TO DISMISS**...NOW COMES the City of Las Vegas...by and through its Attorney...City is aware that suppression...City is aware that its duty of disclosure...The City recognizes...The City respectfully submits...The City is not obligated to conduct..."

Call me crazy, but I'm pretty certain geographic landmasses are still incapable of being "aware", let alone having duties and obligations. It's scary enough thinking about computers becoming aware, but downright terrifying if they're aware and working together with the ground. Are

Michael Detmer and these other prosecutors the slaves of the computer-geographic military complex?

Are these lawyers under the impression the ground is talking to and directing them? "Thank you, sir, SIR, do not start with me, just do not start with me."

In the so-called "Realm", this distinction is also made. In Australia, there's a written instrument called a constitution wherein men calling themselves a parliament wrote about a Commonwealth, see clause one. In the definitions, clause four, section 5, there is mention of States and colonies. Notice similar words to the United States constitution are used:

> "WHEREAS the people of New South Wales, Victoria, South Australia, Queensland, and Tasmania, humbly relying on the blessing of Almighty God [no atheists on the continent?], have agreed to unite in one indissoluble Federal Commonwealth under the Crown of the United Kingdom of Great Britain and Ireland, and under the Constitution hereby established…"

First, notice a Commonwealth is not a geographic area, but people that have allegedly "agreed to unite." Any evidence the people living in Australia voluntarily agreed to such? None provided and apparently not required: Government means no evidence required. I know the English may claim Australians wouldn't understand evidence if given to them, but that opinion isn't a substitute for evidence.

I imagine this did not include atheists, as no atheist believes in Almighty God. Maybe more atheists would believe in god if god would bless us by protecting us from governments? It's reasonable to assume the Almighty God being referred to here may be the concept of government itself. There are certainly atheists who worship that particular god.

Exactly who were these alleged people living in New South Wales anyway? As put so well by Lysander Spooner, even if those people did have an agreement amongst themselves, it only applied to them as they had no ability to obligate anyone other than themselves. Maybe this Almighty God bound everyone?

And what about that adjective about these people being humble? Do humble people force others to pay for services they may not want?

In Canada it seems no pretense is made it's from the people; but it's still clear a province is political, not geographic:

> "Whereas the Provinces of Canada, Nova Scotia, and New Brunswick have expressed their Desire to be federally united into One Dominion under the Crown of the United Kingdom of Great Britain and Ireland, with a Constitution similar in Principle to that of the United Kingdom…" Canadian Constitution 1867.

I'd have to consult a geologist to know if Canada, the landmass, was expressing desires back in 1867; but I doubt it. We know pretended states, provinces or commonwealths are not geographic, they're political as shown above in the quoted section of the Australian constitution, the organic law (meaning it's supposed to be really, really important). This is explicitly admitted in the following citation from the United States Supreme Court, specifically from some really long-winded bloke named John Blair, Jr., coincidently (?) also a *Grand Master of Freemasons* in Virginia:

"A distinction was taken at the bar between a *State* and *the people which comprise that State*. It is a distinction I am not capable of comprehending. By a *State* forming a Republic (speaking of it as a *moral person*) I do not mean the Legislature of the State, the Executive of the State, or the Judiciary, but *all the citizens which comprise that State, and are, if I may express myself, integral parts of it; all together forming a body politic*. The great distinction between Monarchies and Republics (at least our Republics) in general is, that in the former the monarch is considered as the sovereign, and each individual of his nation as subject to him, though in some countries with many important special limitations: This, I say, is generally the case, for it has not been so universally. But in a Republic, all the citizens, as such, are equal, and no citizen can rightfully exercise any authority over another, but in virtue of a power constitutionally given by the whole community, and such authority when exercised, is in effect by the whole community which forms such body politic. In such governments, therefore, the sovereignty resides in them not as so many distinct individuals, but in their political capacity only. Thus A. B. C. and D. citizens of *Pennsylvania*, and as such, *together with all the citizens of Pennsylvania*, share in the sovereignty of the State. Suppose a State to consist of exactly of the number of 100,000 citizens, and it were practicable for all of them to assemble at one time and in one place, and that 99,999 did actually assemble: The State would not in fact be assembled. Why? Because the state is in fact comprised of *all* the citizens, not *a part* only, however large that part may be, and one is wanting." *Penhallow v. Doane*, 3 Dallas (US) 54, 93 (1795) (emphasis in original). http://supreme.justia.com/cases/federal/us/3/54/case.html

Wow, eerily recalling *Soylent Green*, the State is people. https://www.youtube.com/watch?v=8Sp-VFBbjpE
That's quite the metaphor; makes one think of cannibalism, doesn't it? Ayn Rand wrote of that in *Atlas Shrugged*. That's how governments operate, they're parasites, they feed off their victims. There are many other examples where the obvious is admitted: "There cannot be a nation without a people." *Minor v. Happersett*, 88 U.S. 162, 165 (1874).

Next time you're in court and you hear a man or woman claiming to represent the state or province, then you know they are claiming to be standing in place of "all the citizens." You also know when he or his comrades claim you are within the state, the commonwealth or province they are really claiming you're actually a citizen, part of the alleged body politic. Just reference the constitutions to see what they are talking about.

It's people, not the continent. This has nothing to do with your physical or geographic location; it has to do with you and the pretended relationship with a group of criminals calling themselves government. So when people snarl at you, "If you don't like the US, then leave!" you can show them why it doesn't matter where you go; it's not about your physical location:

> "While it appears that the petitioner removed his residence to France in the year 1924, it is undisputed that he was, and continued to be, a citizen of the United States. He continued to owe allegiance to the United States. **By virtue of the obligations of citizenship, the United States retained its authority over him, and he was bound by its laws made applicable to him in a foreign country**. Thus, although resident abroad, the petitioner remained subject to the taxing power of the United States. Cook v. Tait, 265 U.S. 47, 54, 56 S., 44 S. Ct. 444. For disobedience to its laws through conduct abroad, he was subject to punishment in the courts of the United States." *Blackmer v. United States*, 284 U.S. 421, 436 (1932) (emphasis mine).

> "The jurisdiction of the United States over its absent citizen, so far as the binding effect of its legislation is concerned, is a jurisdiction **in personam**, as he is personally bound to take notice of the laws that are applicable to him and to obey them." *Blackmer v. United States*, 284 U.S. 421, 438 (emphasis mine).

I hope the physical location nonsense has been put to rest. Also, the psychos called the United States government stripped any pretense it's based on a relationship with such garbage titled section 877 of the United States tax code (26 USC § 877). This is the authority to continue taxing you for ten years after canceling citizenship and you're living outside the United States. That's right, no physical location, no relationship, no benefits and privileges, just naked aggression. That contradicts the following legal authority doesn't it?

> "That test is whether property was taken without due process of law, or if paraphrase we must, whether the taxing power exerted by the state bears fiscal relation to protection, opportunities and benefits given by the state. The simple controlling question is whether the state had given anything

for which it can ask return." *Wisconsin v. J. C. Penney Co.*, 311 U.S. 435, 444.

The psychopaths called the US government just don't care about even a pretense of legitimacy. How else could someone who lived in Australia, never a US citizen, be charged with violating US codes? That's exactly what happened to Hew Raymond Griffiths http://en.wikipedia.org/wiki/Hew_Raymond_Griffiths. He was charged with violating the US code. What was the pretense the code was applicable though? Do your own research and see if the valiant lawyers presented any facts proving the code applied to someone in Australia. Don't hold your breath though.

How and why is the whim of 535 men and women called Congress applicable to a bloke in Australia? Because some lawyers said so, that's why.

To quote an old friend: "**under all that paperwork is a gun.**" We all know this and yet continue to dance around it and make it easier for the tyrants to keep hidden. The purpose of asking a bureaucrat about evidence is to prove all they have is an opinion and a gun to back it up. Bureaucrats don't always like you to see the gun in the room, they usually believe they're the good guys. It's why they get so agitated when you ask for evidence. Don't make it easier for them. Always stick to the facts; don't continue deleting those facts from your map of the world. It's all about the gun.

All you are doing is having them verify their procedures and opinions. You're asking questions to bring into the open the means of government are not consistent with the stated end. If charged with not wearing a seatbelt, then the questions are designed to show the charge is not consistent with the stated end of government, to protect individual rights. After it's admitted you haven't been accused of violating anyone's rights, then the aggression is stripped bare for all to see. All they want is our obedience and money. With every question it gets easier to see that gun in the room.

Think of it this way: only three pieces of paper are covering that gun, each question you ask is removing one piece of paper. When you get to the gun, most of the time even the agent admits there's no evidence against you. But he still may not drop the attack; he may be driven to attack even more aggressively.

What you are doing is putting the agent into a double-bind situation: damned if he does, damned if he doesn't. It's perceived as a no-win situation and can be very stressful. It's really no different when people are confronted with the truth of government and still pay taxes. They know they are paying not only for their own enslavement, but also for the mass destruction in the Middle-East and in other parts of the world they cannot pronounce or find on a map.

This is not a comfortable place to be in and doesn't make the task of getting the bureaucrat to drop his attack any easier. He must believe that dropping the assessment or ticket is consistent with his model of the world, not an attack against it. This is why if you can scapegoat someone, or something, consistent with their map of the world, we stand a much better chance of getting the attack dropped. One way is to either have an agent admit they are not qualified or declared incompetent. Their map of the world requires a competent witness and evidence. Throwing out an assessment made by an unqualified agent leaves their model intact and doesn't cause as much emotional distress.

Another is purposely getting a judge to deny cross-examination because their map does not permit the taking of property without a fair trial. Denial of a fair trial leaves the model intact and they can be perceived as the good guys administering justice.

During a cross-examination with a Texas health department employee in Sept. 2010, I had the agent admit presence within the State of Texas was necessary for there to be a violation. He also agreed the regulations in question only applied in the State of Texas. Basic stuff, right? Must be easy to prove. After all, everyone knows there is a State of Texas.

When I asked what the State was factually, his lawyers each claimed they did not understand the question. It's no surprise they refused any kind of answer from the witness. The cross-examination was stopped when I started asking for the facts relied on proving the regulations were applicable. This was not even necessary as the agent was not permitted to testify to what the State was.

Of course they understood the question and were only protecting their witness. More important, they were protecting their model of the world. If states really existed, then you would not see such consistent refusals to address what they are factually.

That's the essence of the idea of a sacred cow; the person's false personality, or ego, is attached to the concept and any attack is seen as personal and must be avoided.

But let's allow for the possibility they really did not understand the question. Besides the obvious question: Are they literate? Everything these lawyers do is supposed to be on behalf of the state, and they admit they don't understand the question: What is the state factually? I suggest that if they really didn't understand the question, they don't know what the state is or is supposed to be; and because that conflicted with their generalization the law was applicable to everyone, they had to dodge any attempts to investigate what the state is. That would explain why they would not even let me try to rephrase the question so they could understand better.

Had there been a shred of honesty with the three of them, they would have dropped the attack. If they don't know what a state is, then their entire case collapses.

Imposing themselves on others is more important to them than honestly investigating what the state is because they had already admitted their laws and regulations only applied within the state. Challenging that stereotype/generalization calls into question the veracity of their model where they have the right/authority to control others through using those laws and regulations.

It's natural for people to resist investigation into anything tied to their personality, their persona or mask. Not many people want to be confronted with evidence that part of who they think they are is based on myths, lies and distortions. The intimacy that the government concept has psychologically within people is critical to its continued existence. This is explored in depth later.

But for now, these supporting concepts, or memes, are like the monster in the movie Alien that attached itself to Kane's (John Hurt) face. When the crew tried to get it off, like a snake, it constricted itself tighter around Kane's neck. The more we have invested in these concepts, the tighter we cling to them and the more we will resist anything that tends to conflict.

Try convincing an uber republican, who loves the military and police, that he/she is a dedicated socialist and you'll see what I mean. They will get very upset and start making personal attacks against you. Because the best defense when confronted with the truth is an emotional outburst; just ask a traffic court judge. You're bringing two conflicting generalizations together, a double bind, and they won't like it at all. They probably won't have the integrity or emotional/psychological coping skills to drop or re-examine one of their generalizations, so it's better to just cry like a baby and tell you to move to Somalia if you don't like it.

But this is both good and bad. Just as false concepts and distortions of the world can be a part of our personality that we cling tenaciously to, so it also is with true concepts and models that are closer to the truth, such as all human action should be voluntary. Once the government concept is broken, people will cling to voluntaryism just as persistently as the government concept they cling to now.

This model is better because the same rules apply to all, individuals as well as the group and between groups.

Let's examine testimony from those who actively do business as a state; the people who unfortunately still command respect as some kind of experts. Prosecutors, such as John Webb in New Hampshire, claim to stand in place of these fictions called states. John Webb actually signs court documents as the STATE OF NEW HAMPSHIRE. He refuses to discuss what he means by this though. Big surprise. Peter Heed, John's boss (until his DUI http://www.nashuatelegraph.com/news/991146-469/former-ag-peter-heed-pleads-guilty-to.html), also refused to discuss the issue.

Stephen B. McGrady is another one, and he claims to represent the State of Indiana. I'll quote directly from a court response he filed into the Fountain Traffic court; you can decide for yourself if the State of Indiana he is writing about is a geographic area or not:

"Comes now Plaintiff, the State of Indiana, by Stephen B. McGrady...violated the legal rights of the *State of Indiana*...on behalf of the State...the State of Indiana's legal right to enforce traffic tickets...Indiana, like other states, has opted to create...the state requires...The State's right to regulate...the

State has the legal right...The State of Indiana will still have to prove its case..."

Remember, signing a court document means you are certifying the contents are factually and legally accurate; Federal Rules of Civil Procedure rule 11 is proof of this. Each jurisdiction appears to have a similar certification requirement.

Prosecutors are certifying the state has legal rights and can build and maintain roads. Certify is a good word to use here of course. It should go without saying that geographic areas can't appear in court, let alone build and maintain roads. These same prosecutors are supposed to prove beyond or by a preponderance of evidence our presence within the same plaintiff state to get a valid conviction. Do I really need to point out this is just not possible? But they get away with this every day. Most people just let it go, and lawyers certainly give prosecutors and judges a free pass with this issue.

These lawyers are claiming a man/woman is or was *within the plaintiff* on a certain day. Is it a rape case? Yes, but the defendant is the one getting gang raped. These honorable lawyers will not even discuss what they mean by the state they believe they are representing. How then could they prove my presence within the same state?

Anyone who has been to court knows the other lawyer representing this fictional state gives the prosecutor a free pass on this. Isn't presence with the state an element of the crime? No worries, mate; no need to prove every element of the crime here.

To further beat this long dead horse, I'll end this part of examination of the word state and cite from the New Hampshire constitution where they spell out what the state is supposed to be:

> "Article 1. [Name of Body Politic.] The people inhabiting the territory formerly called the province of New Hampshire, do hereby solemnly and mutually agree with each other, to form themselves into a free, sovereign and independent body-politic, or state, by the name of the State of New Hampshire."
> Part 2, article 1.

That should settle the matter. States are fictions. But with the above in mind, let's ask some basic questions about, let's say, a situation where you get a letter wherein there are claims you owe the state money. Each general question includes many specific questions to narrow down what we're supposed to be talking about. I ask agents directly, "What idea are you trying to convey to me when you use the word state?"

You'll notice these also lend themselves to cross-examination questions to cops and agents making claims against us. We know their claims are subterfuge to cover up their violence, and their rules require witnesses to have personal first-hand knowledge of the facts. So if someone claims you are within their state, then start asking questions to test their competency and get them to verify their wild claims.

81

Who is the state? Despite claims you and I are the state, who exactly is the state? We can ask the agents at the office where the letter came from: Are you the state? I personally don't get responsive answers; they don't give me any facts.

The simple identification of people, such as Julia Gillard, helps to break down the power of the fiction. You can't fight city hall, but you can certainly question this claim you owe Julia or George. You're saying Julia is the state and I owe her money?

What are the names of those who comprise this so-called state? Is this the same state you think I'm in? Was it voluntary? That last one will give them fits because now they're forced to make the distinction between the geographic state and the political one.

What is the state? Shown above, a state is supposed to be either a political body or a certain geographic area, such as either the state of Australia or the continent of Australia. Is the state a fiction, is it man-made? Factually what is it? Are there different states depending on the context you're referring to?

Where is the state? I like: Where was the State of New York on 3 July 1776? It is commonly accepted there was no State of New York prior to 4 July 1776, just as there was no Commonwealth of Australia prior to 1 January 1901. This starts to get us closer to identifying with certainty who and what the state really is.

When did the state come into existence? This includes when they acquired jurisdiction over me. This really does end discussion the state is physical, as shown above. So we know the state is man-made; what exactly is it and when are you claiming they acquired jurisdiction over me? What facts do you base that on?

Why a state? Because if they don't lie, steal and kill us, there will be mayhem. Worse, who would build the roads?

How did the state come about and how does it apply to me, if at all? This opens up a pretty big can of worms if they even try to explain. How these fictions come about is typically some psychopaths pretending to act on behalf of others in the community; just say there is a new state.

Since the state factually is nothing more than the say-so of politicians, what facts are there it applies to me? In other words, how does a pseudonym apply to me? We can demonstrate the phrase "The State of New Hampshire" is a pseudonym, a dba? How does that apply to me?

The same applies to "subdivisions" called cities, villages, counties and boroughs.

Not only are cities created by "law" as presented in *Adventures*, if you needed further proof, look no further than the case of New Rome, Ohio. This "city" was "dissolved" in 2004 by the stroke of a pen http://en.wikipedia.org/wiki/New_Rome,_Ohio . That's right, an attorney named David Cain, with a black robe, "dissolved" an entire "city" by signing his name to a piece of paper on August 9, 2004.

The "city" of New Rome was notorious for being a speed trap; most of the money to pay for the police and other government workers came from traffic tickets. Other examples of cities not being geographic are:

Helgi Johanneson, attorney general, wrote: "As of November 1, 1971, the city of Werner, North Dakota, was dissolved as an incorporated city." http://209.85.173.132/search? q=cache:IWmYGsSFgBoJ:www.ag.nd.gov/Opinions/1971/71-39.pdf+city+dissolved+incorporated&hl=en&ct=clnk&cd=3&gl=us&client =firefox-a

In Japan, we see that "provinces" are "dissolved", such as "Futoru - dissolved April 1, 1955" according to wikipedia http://en.wikipedia.org/wiki/Former_Provinces_of_Hokkaid%C5%8D

In Canada, "1969 - (Jan. 1st) Carleton County dissolved. Regional Municipality of Ottawa-Carleton replaces it." http://www.gloucesterhistory.com/history.html

And recently the city of Pacific in Washington http://www.king5.com/news/City-of-Pacific-prepares-to-disincorporate-176367761.html I like where they write: "The 103 year old city of Pacific would cease being a city."

Citizen. This one is huge and does more to create a strong emotional bond to politicians/abusers than the other political mind control words. If you really want a demonstration of its effectiveness, put the word *American* in front of it. Be forewarned though, it comes with an extra strong dose of arrogance.

This word causes division and sets people apart from others, very effective in controlling people and getting them afraid of others. If you want citizens to disparage/attack other citizens of the same nation, then you just need to divide them up further, using words such as liberal and conservative. The Romans used the word to get foreigners to kill people for them. Remember, with psychopaths it's divide and conquer; it makes their jobs easier. The Asch conformity experiment discussed later explains why it is so effective.

This also creates a hierarchy, which is essential to causing a loss of empathy and a general sense of resentment. You see this with fraternity hazing programs. The freshmen who get abused resent the abuse and then turn around and not only abuse new freshmen when they move up in the hierarchy, but they tend to look forward to when they are able to dish out the abuse.

The hazing can also be used later as leverage; there's a good reason they are a humiliating ritual. Look what those sick Skull & Bones people at Yale do. These disgusting rituals can later be used against the politician, who probably doesn't want it publicly revealed they laid naked in a coffin, among other things.

When a politician is outed in the media for some "indiscretion," it's probably because they were not keeping to the party line. A good example is Eliot Spitzer, the former head of the criminal syndicate called the New York State government. He was-at least by the public perception-going after Wall Street firms, and suddenly in March 2008, just a few months before the housing bubble burst, Eliot's fondness of high-priced hookers was reported in the media. There is also the British MP who was critical of Murdock's News Corp and was suddenly outed as a homosexual.

There are so many examples, it would take several volumes to cover them, and we'll never know the full extent of the depravity of politicians and bureaucrats. It does explain why the "blue wall of silence" is so strong; corruption tends to build a pretty strong bond, self-preservation being the motive, of course. The criminals have the goods on each other.

It's pretty well established that groups like the FBI, CIA, NSA have dirt on many people, especially those considered political enemies. John Lennon is a good example.

There is also a notable pattern, together with "incompetence", of government agencies not cooperating when it may involve one of their own. Three glaring examples are: the Manson family, the Zodiac killer and the mother of alleged incompetence and non-cooperation, 9/11.

An official excuse, part of the official conspiracy theory for 9/11, was a lack of cooperation between intelligence agencies such as the CIA and FBI. Really? So how many lost their jobs and were prosecuted? I seem to remember it's a crime to willfully engage in behavior that results in the harm or death of another man, woman or child.

Not one member of the agencies whose alleged non-cooperation and incompetence with 9/11 was prosecuted or lost a day's pay. But, that doesn't stop the Feds from million dollar investigations of people selling raw milk. The cops can bust kids for selling lemonade, but not share information regarding piles of dead bodies turning up all over the place.

The .22 used in the Tate-LaBianca murders in August 1969 was in police custody for weeks, yet not given to prosecutors. When the man who found the gun called the police about it, an agent told him they didn't know about it and it was probably destroyed. Maybe if they said it was in a bag of pot they would have shown appropriate interest in a gun used to kill people.

The hierarchy with citizens is blatant; all you need to do is look at the facts, not the slogans. The citizen is subject to the control/jurisdiction of the government, and support is compulsory. Yes, there are incongruent messages because the PR is that governments are public servants and work for the people. This flies in the face of the compulsory support of all governments.

You also have implied hierarchies; an example is the absolute immunity for the cult of the black robe. These anti-social lawyers gave themselves absolute, unqualified immunity for what they do on their wooden thrones. The theory is that without personal responsibility for their actions, they will be more honest. Really, and how's that working out for you? Do you see judges applying this immunity to other professions?

Keep in mind that immunity doesn't deny the claim, it is just like a child yelling ha, ha, ha, you can't touch me. This is an example where one lawyer is extending the lawyer-made absolute immunity to another lawyer. This makes more sense when we realize most judges are *former* prosecutors; the defendants are *current* prosecutors at the time of the complaint:

> "Martinez remains entitled to absolute immunity even if he acted "**maliciously, wantonly or negligently**." Morrison v. City of Baton Rouge, 761 F.2d 242, 248 (5th Cir.1985). Because Martinez is absolutely immune from suit, he is immune from damages as well. See Disraeli v. Rotunda, 489 F.3d 628, 631 (5th Cir. 2007) (noting that **absolute immunity denies all remedies to an individual**); Hulsey v. Owens, 63 F.3d 354, 356 (5th Cir. 1994) (holding that absolute immunity is immunity from suit rather than simply a defense against liability)." *Rodriguez v. Lewis, Martinez*, No. 10-20484 201, 5th Cir. Ct. of appeals. (emphasis mine)/

Go ahead and do things harmful things, your fellow lawyers will fall over themselves protecting you. I would say such a license to behave maliciously is going to come in handy for those who *grant* such protection. The opening scene of the Godfather dramatizes this:

> "Good. Someday, and that day may never come, I'll call upon you to do a service for me. But until that day–accept this justice as a gift on my daughter's wedding day." Vito Corleone.

There is also a scene in The Godfather II where the "family" sets up a senator who is most grateful for the "help" covering up a murder they committed. They make the senator think he killed a prostitute, they cover it up and, of course, all that was left was their "friendship."

Can you see better now why apologists will also ask about the roads when discussing the violent nature of government? Why almost every time you are talking about abolishing government people will focus on the roads? Even those who complain about taxes will desperately cling to their abusers claiming, "It's okay, I get a nice refund every year."

So even before really examining the psychological aspects in detail, we can already see a recipe for disaster. We can see the cause of these *friendships* and relations built on a pecking order. And this pecking order, of which citizenship is a part, cannot be reformed. It can only be replaced and never brought back or mimicked.

After all, there's an ancient maxim describing this: "Protection draws to it subjection, subjection, protection." And as quoted by the lawyers of the supreme court:

> "**Protectio trahit subjectionem, et subjectio protectionem**...
> Protection draws to itself allegiance, and allegiance, protection. United States v. Wong Kim Ark, 169 US 649, 655..." *Ballentine's Law Dictionary*, page 1014.

And your history teachers told you patronage was dead; the United States is somehow different, so much better than the "royal" patronage

85

system in Europe. Dare I write the immunity of these lawyers, who hold the key to indictments, the grand jury, is a vast conspiracy? The bottom feeders are bound to those higher up the pecking order because they are actively permitting them to commit their crimes. It's an old sales pitch: give someone something for free, a free pass, and they'll feel obligated to return the favor. I know this may be tough to believe, but psychopaths don't just give favors out of the goodness of their black hearts. There is also a maxim for this that has been codified in some places such as California:

> "He who takes the benefit must bear the burden."
> California Civil Code § 3521.

We know it's admitted the property stolen by police and prosecutors, enabled of course by their co-conspirators called legislators, (drug laws being a clear benefit to those henchmen on the bottom: the cops are the first ones to a drug bust, no other witnesses, who knows how much money and drugs were really there? Gonna take the word of a drug dealer over a cop's?) under the guise of forfeiture, stay with those who are doing the stealing. So there is a huge incentive and motive to just steal the property and threaten prosecution to get the hapless victim to back off. This is accomplished with the help of the so-called defense lawyers who clearly aid in the prosecution. It's an old story; old, but tragic nonetheless.

Unfortunately, I have direct, personal knowledge of this. I work with people who have had thousands of dollars worth of FRNs (Federal Reserve Notes) and other property forcibly taken from them by police. Sometimes, there are no drugs involved; they just happened to have been stopped with large amounts of cash on them.

If they are bailed out and have an attorney, then the pressure is poured on by *both* attorneys. And you thought attorneys that you pay are looking out for your best interest? Both will say the same thing. All the defense lawyer will do is repeat what the prosecutor tells him, and it usually is:

> If you don't take a deal, they will aggressively prosecute
> and go for the max and you will not only lose and go to
> prison, it will cost you a small fortune to pay for me to
> not defend you.

I heard a call someone made to a public defender who was defending her. He advised her that the best thing to do was waive the prelim and just file a motion to dismiss. When she decided not to waive the prelim, because even the lawyer admitted the charges could be kicked out, the lawyer ratcheted up the fear. He said that while the judge has the discretion to do that, he could also *add* charges if he bound her over for trial. Really? So the judge is now going to also charge someone personally? Talk about evidence the judge and prosecutor are working together.

Each defense lawyer I have spoken to has always maintained there is no getting a drug charge thrown out. Despite evidence to the contrary, they just keep beating the same drum. It's good for business: keep the fear level high, disengage rational thought and get a predictable emotional response. Well, keep the fear level elevated at least as long as the victim or their family has money to give the lawyer.

Why are these defense lawyers so confident you will get convicted if you go to trial? Maybe they know they are not very effective litigators, or maybe they are really just playing the fear card so they can make five to ten thousand bucks making a deal with fellow lawyers?

And therein lies a major problem regarding the favors between lawyers, bureaucrats and politicians, as stated above, "He who takes the benefit must bear the burden." They're going to want that favor returned. So let's look at a good example where there are $millions involved at the local level. Money is one hell of a motivator to kill and otherwise harm others; that's too well established to reasonably question.

You have drug cops, who we know are involved in the possession, distribution and sale of drugs. The forfeiture laws prove the money, when reported by the police, stays with the police and prosecutors. Forfeitures are all *off budget*.

If a cop is accused, who is going to prosecute? That's right, the prosecutors who are working the drug war with the cops. It's not without evidence that judges are corrupt and take payoffs from cops and prosecutors-that's a lot of benefits; benefits that come with burdens. Those burdens can include throwing complaints out against the cops and extending immunity to prosecutors if anything comes through against them.

A recent example is of a prosecutor from Texas being indicted. Cameron County District Attorney Armando Villalobos is accused of bribery in a case connected to another lawyer named Abel Limas. Abel was a state judge who pled guilty to taking bribes in return for judicial favors. http://www.chron.com/news/article/Attorney-Texas-DA-arrested-in-judge-bribery-case-3539898.php?utm_source=twitterfeed&utm_medium=twitter

Jason Phillabaum was a prosecutor indicted for altering grand jury indictments http://www.local12.com/news/local/story/Ex-Butler-County-Prosecutor-Accused-of-Tampering/wvuVXgM--kmXree091Fr4A.cspx?rss=30

Giuliano Mignini, the Florence, Italy prosecutor in the Amanda Knox trial was convicted in 2010 of numerous crimes, including illegal wiretapping. http://www.westseattleherald.com/2010/01/31/news/amanda-knox-head-prosecutor-charged-abuse-power

Myrl Serra, another prosecutor, pled guilty to several crimes, including extortion. His sentence? Two months in jail. Yes, two *months*. I would love to be able to investigate the connections between the sentencing judge, prosecutors and the honorable Myrl. http://blogs.denverpost.com/crime/2012/01/26/colorado-district-attorney-myrl-serra/3584/ You get years for pot possession, and this lawyer only gets two months? Really?

Doug Godbee, a Tennessee prosecutor, was indicted on felony misconduct charges because he promised leniency in exchange for sex from women he was prosecuting. http://www.abajournal.com/news/article/ex-prosecutor_indicted_in_sex-for-leniency_case_charged_with_official_misco/

A prosecutor fabricating evidence in a murder trial: http://austin.ynn.com/content/top_stories/291543/warrant-issued-for-prosecutorial-misconduct--judge-anderson-turns-himself-in-to-wilco-jail This is one where he was caught. I would say fabricating evidence in a murder trial is pretty serious; I doubt this was his first and only time.

Though misconduct may be enough to get a complaint kicked out and get a prosecutor put in jail, there is no responsibility to the victim. This lack of personal accountability just emboldens the criminal. Below are cases where the courts have given immunity to prosecutors for committing crimes that would get those lower on the political order very long prison sentences:

> "The question presented is whether a judge and prosecutor are immune from damages in a civil rights action charging them with **conspiracy to predetermine the outcome of judicial proceedings**. We conclude that the judge and prosecutor are immune." *Ashelman v. Pope*, 793 F.2d 1072 (1986) (Emphasis mine).

> "This Court, in interpreting Imbler, has agreed that prosecutorial immunity extends to a prosecutor's actions in "initiating and pursuing a criminal prosecution and in presenting the state's case . . . . [E]ven where the prosecutor **knowingly used perjured testimony**, deliberately withheld exculpatory information, or failed to make full disclosure of all facts."" *Henzel v. Gerstein*, 608 F. 2d 654 (1979) (emphasis mine). see *Imbler v. Pachtman*, 424 U.S. 409 (1976).

Yes, these former prosecutors, pretending to protect life, liberty and property, extend immunity to current prosecutors when they "knowingly used perjured testimony" and caused people to be severely damaged. Let me point out the obvious here: perjury is usually a *felony*, as well as kidnapping and perverting the course of justice. Most places, including Arizona, it's a felony. If you don't think giving psychopaths immunity for felonies is going to cause problems, you really need to wake up and start thinking. Those prosecutors owe those judges for these favors.

So what happens when there is evidence of a corrupt judge? If there are charges brought by a prosecutor, then his/her fellow judges can quash indictments or extend immunity. Occasionally there is a prosecution; already mentioned was the "kids for cash" scandal http://en.wikipedia.org/wiki/Kids_forcash_scandal. I think some investigation would reveal the abuse of those kids went way beyond a false imprisonment; there very well may be a Sandusky element there.

All the money made from the drug war is going to continually strengthen and reinforce bonds with those and their system. Lawyers who have provided the structure-the laws-for the cops and everyone else to reap such enormous profits. This explains why there are so few prosecutions against judges. A few are below:

James "Jay" Taylor, a former judge indicted on theft charges http://www2.tricities.com/news/2012/may/31/former-hawkins-co-judge-indicted-davidson-co-ar-1956202/.

Samuel B. Kent was a federal judge sentenced to thirty-three months in prison "for lying to investigators about sexually abusing two female employees." http://en.wikipedia.org/wiki/Samuel_B._Kent. He was also impeached.

Walter Louis Nixon, Jr., a federal judge was impeached and convicted for lying to a grand jury. http://en.wikipedia.org/wiki/Walter_Nixon.

Phil Fitzgerald, a former judge indicted for misappropriation of funds http://news92fm.com/241920/former-liberty-county-judge-phil-fitzgerald-cleared-for-now/.

Suzanne Wooten, a judge in Texas indicted for being "engaged in organized criminal activity." http://dfw.cbslocal.com/2010/10/15/collin-county-judge-indicted-for-bribery/.

Karl Prohl, another judge in Texas indicted on theft charges. http://www.dallasjustice.com/dallascriminallawyerblog/another-texas-district-judge-indicted-on-felony-charges-and-jailed-on-friday http://exposecorruptcourts.blogspot.com/2012/05/judge-indicted-for-campaign-false.html.

G. Thomas Porteous, a federal judge was impeached and convicted of kickbacks and lying to the FBI and other government investigators.

Robert F. Collins was the first federal judge convicted, among other things, for taking bribes. From who you ask? A *drug* smuggler. See, there was a reason this book was not finished until this year; I needed some more evidence regarding the drug war. http://community.seattletimes.nwsource.com/archive/?date=19910630&slug=1291915.

Back to prosecutors. As a prosecutor, part of the job description admittedly includes acting "maliciously, wantonly or negligently" and "knowingly us[ing] perjured testimony". If it didn't, then there would be no immunity from liability for acts done while on the job: "Martinez was acting within the scope of his employment as a prosecutor".

Obviously we cannot expect justice and good faith from people who have no voluntary support and whose job description includes acting maliciously. That would be a good question to ask a prosecutor:

Sir, why does your job include being malicious and negligent?
I couldn't get in the door to do my job otherwise.

89

Why do these lawyers get a free pass for being malicious and negligent? Could you imagine such a pass given to doctors?

My qualifications? I received a medical degree from Yale, malicious negligence courtesy of Wash. DC.

I doubt all those malpractice lawyers would accept doctors giving *themselves* immunity for malicious and negligent acts. But lawyers should have it? How about auto mechanics? I know one from Long Island who decided to drive a customer's Corvette to lunch. Instead, he lost control and had an accident.

Sorry about your car, sir, but I'm blameless even when I'm malicious and negligent.

What kind of justification is there to be malicious when the job description is supposed to be administering justice? "Justice in all cases shall be administered openly…" Arizona constitution article II § 11.

There should be no pass given. Present the *Rodriguez v. Lewis, Martinez* opinion to these lawyers and ask them about it, "Sir, do you think you're immune from malicious and negligent acts towards me? Mr. Judge, would you extend this lawyer such immunity? Have you acted this way towards me already?"

And since most judges are former prosecutors, what kind of disposition are they going to have towards us? They've done a job for years that includes being malicious; I'm betting that's not going to stop.

It's the same with cops; they are legally allowed to lie as a part of their job. It's one thing to lie, but to have it part of the job? This is from the opinion cited as a basis that cops may lie on the job:

> "The fact that the police misrepresented the statements that
> Rawls had made is, while relevant, insufficient, in our view,
> to make this otherwise voluntary confession inadmissible."
> *Frazier v. Cupp*, 394 U.S. 731 (1969)

Talk about coercion and social pressure-combine the lies with the constant barrage from cops and your own lawyer that if you go to trial you will lose, and people will confess to things they haven't done. And let's not forget the element of overt torture added to this. Chicago is not an isolated example http://chicagotorture.org/history/.

There is a huge issue here: cops and prosecutors have no respect for human life; proof is that they cannot understand how traumatic it can be to lose what little control we have over our lives and be at the mercy of cops.

People plead guilty and settle all the time; that doesn't mean they did anything wrong or what they were accused of. Look at Joe Arpiao in Phoenix as an example if you still think politicians are an authority. Joe's subordinates have killed people *on video* and when lawsuits have been filed, the suits were settled. What does Joe do? He gets on TV and says despite the settlement his men did nothing wrong.

People make a cost-benefit analysis and decide it's much cheaper and easier to cop a plea to something you didn't do to avoid a costly trial and risk being falsely convicted. And that makes sense when the prosecutors have immunity to knowingly use false testimony.

None of the psychological factors are taken into account when the lawyers determined if the confessions are voluntary or not. Imagine being in a police station, separated from family and friends and being practically tortured, excuse me, having "enhanced" interrogations, and then the cops lie to you about what someone else is saying. Imagine the cops, after interrogating you for ten hours, are now telling you your best friend has already confessed and implicated you. If you were sitting in your living room and hearing this, that would be bad enough, but you're in a police station.

After this you're forced in front of a judge:

> You have violent control over me and are making decisions affecting my life and I cannot hold you personally accountable for any damage you do to me?
> *Yes, that's right.*
> And you're telling me you're going to be fair?
> *That's right.*
> And this has nothing to do with my consent?
> *No, my jurisdiction is not based on your consent.*
> So your jurisdiction is violent control with no personal responsibility; so now what's your motive for being fair again?

Maybe it's just me, but is it rational thinking someone who takes violent control over your life is going to be fair towards you? You have to really delete much of your observable reality to create such a perception. The fact this is done by the majority of people is evidence there is mind control, or control over people's perceptions. If you doubt this, then you are really blind to the facts.

Reasonable questions when you get a traffic ticket or an indictment for possession of certain plants are:

At what point in these proceedings will you start being fair?

I know from personal experience that just challenging jurisdiction is as offensive to judges as if you kicked their kittens. It really seems to be a trigger or psychological anchor for rage to question a lawyer's control over you, a natural response from a petty control freak. I think challenging their perception of jurisdiction is more offensive to them. Why the zero tolerance; how was the anchor developed? I'm betting it's so traumatic an experience it only takes one experience to anchor; it's like a phobia. It may only take one experience, one person to challenge them publicly on their wooden thrones.

91

The reason it's a trigger is because the actual control, the underlying violence, cannot survive any kind of serious investigation; and they seem to know it. To be challenged in public in front of people who see you as a legal expert, and not be able to meet that challenge is going to be pretty embarrassing. As we'll see later, this challenge to a psychopath's grandiose view of themselves triggers rage, their main coping skill. Why else do they all have such a short fuse with the issue of jurisdiction? They consistently ignore their own law requiring them to presume there is no jurisdiction, except when one of the little people files against them of course. Then it's another free pass judges give prosecutors every day.

The evidence strongly suggests the judges know full well they are sitting on a cheap throne of lies. Why else a small army to carry out your orders? How many honest, peaceful people do you know with a crew of unthinking, armed automatons? If you haven't heard the insulting: "I'm just doing my job" then listen to some calls I have on the website.

And I think it's a good idea and effective strategy to not hide the gun in the room. I see no rational purpose to giving the lawyer with the robe a pass regarding his position and purpose in the proceedings. He should be questioned regarding his acquisition of control over me and his complete lack of responsibility for his actions.

This goes right to the heart of the nature and cause of the charges and proceedings. If they admit we are entitled to be informed so we may adequately defend ourselves, then this is an essential challenge and line of questioning. Those who force themselves on me do not deserve a pass; it's my life that's being affected, so it's in my best interest to make it as difficult as possible for them to hide it. Everyone in that room should be made aware of it and encouraged to also challenge this anti-social lawyer.

This hierarchy is going to cause such reactions in the lawyers though; how could it not? The judge is literally looking down on everyone. Everyone is there out of fear. I know from personal experience the fear cops have of these lawyers. I've told them I want a judge arrested for disturbing the peace, threatening and intimidation and they get that glazed over look in their eyes. They then give me the scripted response I've heard dozens of times, "I can't touch him; the judge can do whatever he wants."

The immunity judges gave themselves has made it much worse than with cops or IRS agents. Neither are easy to hold accountable in the courts, but at least the remedy is there and people have "won" cases against them in court. Not so with judges. Except for the CEO's of each state, the next highest level of immunity from a judge is for prosecutors. Again, this is where lawyers gave themselves immunity. Prosecutors have immunity, but not blanket absolute immunity, qualified immunity. It's still extremely rare for a prosecutor to be held accountable by his victims.

Prosecutors know these special favors they enjoy come from their fellow lawyers sitting as judges. The technical phrase for this is: prosecutors know which side of their bread is buttered. They know if they have a complaint filed against them, it'll be one of these special lawyers who will extend them immunity for any malicious and negligent acts against victims the judges force into proceedings.

92

Look at these facts; tell me they don't reek of-well, you be the judge: The judges force us to participate and answer the prosecutor's complaint. If the prosecutor damages us, even *maliciously*, the judge extend immunity to the prosecutor. Judges work together with the cops and prosecutors and they give themselves immunity. As the importance is always under appreciated, I have to repeat: *lawyers gave themselves immunity.* Exactly how is that not evidence of collusion? Reminds me of the ancient maxim: Don't bite the hand that feeds you.

The facts speak for themselves; that's why there has to be so much spin explaining them away. It's why there is such a violent reaction when you ask a judge the nature of his/her relationship to the cop and prosecutor. When just a relevant question triggers such a consistent violent reaction, regardless of the geographic location, I think we're touching a nerve-a serious weak spot that should be exploited if we want them to leave us alone.

Someone recently asked me about this. He had spoken with a judge about his forcing him to answer the prosecutor's complaint; he asked: How was that not a conflict of interest? The judge is reported as saying that's the way things work. He was stumped on how to respond. Why do people just accept what these crooks say, as if they had any credibility at all? Why not just challenge the statement? It's just a political platitude, the judge may as well say, "It is what it is." Think judges would accept stupid platitudes as a defense?

> *You've been charged with possession of marijuana. How do you plead?*
> Well, what are you going to do when life hands you lemons? Make lemonade and if it's god's will.
> *Well said young man. Have you considered law school?*
> Everything happens for a reason, and it is what it is.
> *Brilliant, just brilliant! You have a gift there; you remind me of myself.*

A childish statement like the one the judge gave should not be accepted for a moment as an answer. Think about it for a second; don't you agree it's unacceptable? If a judge said that to me, after rolling my eyes, I'd say: I know that's how it's done; I'm asking you how you can force me to answer his complaint and there not be a conflict of interest.

It's very difficult for me not to be sarcastic when I speak with judges, prosecutors and tax agents and get such non-responsive statements: Oh really, that's how it's done? Well what are you doing to do? I know that's how it's done; I can observe that, your oh-so-subtle threats of violence didn't escape me. I'm questioning that and want you to explain this apparent contradiction.

I recently got this line from an agent in New Hampshire when I asked if there were facts my client was required to register with him:

> *This is the procedure.*
> Alright, is the procedure based on facts?
> *I don't understand; where are you going with this?*

93

(Yes, I facepalmed) You may have a procedure, but there are no facts proving my client is required to register?

Then I got accused of "twisting" his words and being "condescending". It's the ol' switch the facts for procedure ploy. It's just a dodge; if they dealt with facts then they'd just present them. We know they have no facts. Facts are so far removed from their day-to-day operations, they'll routinely ask: where are you going with this? We should start doing that with them:

Can I see your license and registration?
Where are you going with this?

Why didn't you file a return?
Where are you going with this?
Well, why didn't you file a return?
Whoa, don't twist my words.

And they don't have to understand their own procedures; everything is so broken down and distributed among the bureaucracy that they can be honest when they say they don't understand. With a hierarchy, they can always pass the buck and deny responsibility.

Anyone familiar with human psychology and sociology will see a guaranteed recipe for disaster with the hierarchy created with citizens and political offices where there is no accountability to those lower on the scale. We can see this played out to such a degree that even the mainstream media reports on some of the examples of judicial crimes. Taking personal responsibility away from people, especially in a hierarchy, will always result in callous abuse. Well, maybe not always; if we use experiments such as the Milgram experiment mentioned later as a guide, then we can say sixty to ninety-one percent of the time there will be abuse.

As shown in *Cook v. Tait*, 265 US 47 (1924), citizenship is a "relationship"; it was also shown in:

"An Act relating to Australian Citizenship" from 1948:

> "Australian **citizenship** represents formal **membership** of the community of the Commonwealth of Australia; and Australian citizenship is a **common bond**, involving **reciprocal rights and obligations**, uniting all Australians, while respecting their diversity; and
>
> Persons granted Australian citizenship enjoy these rights and undertake to accept these obligations
>   by **pledging loyalty** to Australia and its people, and
>   by sharing their **democratic beliefs**, and
>   by respecting their rights and liberties, and

by upholding and obeying the laws of Australia..."
(Emphasis   mine)
http://www.comlaw.gov.au/Details/C2006C00317.

How do you respect others' rights while "upholding and obeying the laws?" Notice the similarity with American law, the: "reciprocal rights and obligations." The United States Supreme court has held for over two hundred years: "Taxation and protection are reciprocal," *Union Refrigerator Transit Company v. Kentucky*, 199 U.S. 194.
Look at the similarity to the American 14th amendment:

> "All persons born or naturalized in the United States, and subject to the jurisdiction thereof, are citizens of the United States and of the State wherein they reside."

> "a person born in Australia after the commencement of this Act shall be an Australian citizen." *An Act relating to Australian Citizenship*" *from 1948*, part III, division 1, 10(1).

Just how does an infant pledge loyalty anyway? Does a statement from 1948 create some kind of loyalty pledge for someone born in Brisbane today? I would say yes, but only in the minds of the insane. Unlike the insane, I don't think politicians believe this stuff about allegiance and protection. Their actions prove they at least don't take it seriously. We already know they acknowledge there is no duty to protect.
The following was written by a 1955 Citizenship Convention in Australia. It's from a paper titled *Notes on the Responsibilities and Privileges of Australian Citizenship* and gives a clear picture of this so-called "citizenship." I like how the first part is reminiscent of the Roman standard:

> "For the Commonwealth, allegiance was always the most significant element of citizenship in Australia; indeed it was the very basis of citizenship. This is clear throughout the history of naturalisation policy, and the Commonwealth's various pronouncements on the meaning of citizenship. During times of perceived threat or war, the question of allegiance was explicitly at the fore of Commonwealth policy. Aliens and citizens alike were appraised and treated around various beliefs about allegiance. **Ultimately, the meaning of allegiance was revealed as a willingness to serve the state in time of war**. Allegiance aside, the sum of the paraphernalia on the duties of citizenship amounted to little more than obeying the law (something not limited to citizens in any case) and voting at elections (which was dealt with in the

95

previous section) even though voting was compulsory from the 1920s." (emphasis mine)

Remember all that crap about civilizing the native savages the British government spewed? Who are the real savages here? As history has shown, one may be "enlightened" and highly educated and be a savage. The meaning of allegiance is nothing more than a willingness to kill on demand, no personal discretion though, mate.

> G'day Mate, welcome to Australia. Are you willing to kill people in Iraq who pose no danger to you whatsoever?

> Geez Bruce, I know god told George Bush to invade, but I just wanted to have a barbie, some bevies, a few snags and surf. Hey is that Kevin Bloody Wilson, mate?

The curse and blessing of language is we have abstract concepts-words that have no physical referent. The concepts only exist in language, not experience or reality. The word citizen, like the other words, at first glance appears to have a connection to reality, to men, women and children - but this is clearly false when we investigate evidence for this alleged relationship.

I explained this in detail in *Adventures in Legal Land*, so I won't go into much detail here. Suffice to say, **there are no citizens because there is no relationship**; no reciprocal obligations of allegiance and protection between citizens and the governments. Violence has a way of negating such things.

Constitution. Just like the United States constitution, the Australian constitution is paper and ink, and the words on it are not binding on anyone. It's no more magic parchment than this book. Reading this book does not create any kind of allegiance or willingness to kill on my orders. It's as if most people need to be convinced to protect their family. Not all of us are pacifists. But what if you are? Let's say you're a Quaker or Mennonite, does that preclude one from being a Citizen in Australia?

The word Constitution is used to convince people of many things, chief among them, that violent gangs of men and women will keep their violence within the limits of words on a piece of paper. They don't have enough respect to deal with you as equals and voluntarily, but words on a piece of paper they'll respect?

Why would governments respect anyone allowing themselves to be controlled, to be used as their slaves? Would you respect someone who let you turn them into a farm animal? Does a farm animal deserve it? Now imagine how the farmer perceives his chattel when that chattel attacks someone pointing out the truth? I'm thinking of those radio show hosts that attacked me for pointing out there are no states and citizens. I've been attacked for pointing out the master has no duty to protect anyone.

Constitution is a powerful word for distraction; instead of resisting the violence or not complying with some law, the farm animals bitch and

96

complain about a law or policy being unconstitutional and not authorized by the prisoners. Because it says "We the People of the United States..." the prisoners believe it came from them; that the prisoners, according to the PR, delegated the authority to the prison guards. Unfortunately, the act of submission could be perceived as delegating authority.

Fact is, no one today was alive when the words were put on the parchment, and even if they were, it doesn't matter. Just because I write: "We the People of the Planet Earth" and follow it up with what I call a constitution, is no evidence it applies to anyone. I'm sure if I wrote a constitution and put the words "every politician had to pay me a tax every year" they would laugh at me, as they should. They'd laugh because they know what constitutions are. Unfortunately, too many people still don't know what a constitution is. My evidence? There are still politicians; that's my evidence. When enough people do realize what they are, there are going to be a lot of laughs directed at politicians.

You need to stop thinking in terms of "rights" to really understand this. It's wrong to think:

> "Writing something on a piece of paper does not give
> you the *right* to control me."

Tyrants want/need their victims to believe constitutions, mere pieces of paper, give them a right to control (govern) you. How would the psychopath convince you of this if he didn't use the word right? Go ahead and try it for yourself; how would you phrase it without using the word right?

You could say, "I'm able to control you because of the constitution" or, "Because of the constitution, I can control you."

How so?
Because the constitution says I can control you.
What is the constitution?
I don't know...that's irrelevant!

It quickly becomes apparent how important words are when you take key words and phrases out. Try coming up with convincing PR without using the words government, constitution and right. Get into a tyrant's head and think like them. The more political mind control words you leave out, the more difficult it is to convince people.

Do politicians have a right to protect you? Think about that for a moment. Rights, in the legal world, are not unilateral; there is always a corresponding legal duty. If I have a legal right to liberty, then there is a corresponding legal duty to not violate that right held by others. You'll notice that a cause action is a violation of a legal right and a breach of a known legal duty.

So if we have a duty to allow psychopaths to steal our property, there must be a corresponding right for the psychopath to steal our property. And that's what they believe, although they use tax instead of stealing.

Law. There seems to be more reverence for political laws than for religious texts. Talk about gross generalizations and false paradigms. If people could actually love their neighbor as themselves or have even a little bit of empathy, this would be a much better world to live in. Unfortunately, blind obedience to politicians is still the norm.

This three-letter word is the reason or excuse for untold horrors. Want to justify the worst behaviors and paralyze any opposition? Just say the action is the law. Want to get people to give you half of their time, money and energy? Tell them it's the law.

I've already discussed this in *Adventures in Legal Land*, so I won't go into much detail here. **A law is just on opinion backed by a gun.** What's important are the facts: a bunch of men and women called politicians get together and take a count regarding how they want to further control others. If they get enough support, the new way to control others is dubbed the "law." All that means is:

Men with guns now have a new pretext to kill us.

The machine can grind up more victims. That's really all a political law is: a justification for killing us. Well to be fair, it's also a justification for stealing from us.

As with all political words, what it does is change our perceptions; changing perceptions causes changes in behavior. Instead of letting simple notions of right and wrong learned by the time we're five dictate our behavior, we surrender the decision to politicians. And are politicians the type of people we should be modeling?

Such people are either aggressive narcissists or plain ol' psychopaths. Maybe I'm just being silly, but our behavior should not be dictated by people lacking empathy and doing business on a pay-or-get-shot basis. I really doubt if we did a poll asking if politicians are the type of people we should model our lives on, if anyone would say yes. During election cycles, it is typical of politicians running on a platform for not being a politician. Even politicians don't want to be viewed as politicians; the other guy running is the rotten politician, I'm here to save you from the evil Washington insider.

Politicians-especially those who are also lawyers-are uniformly despised and rejected as human beings, let alone as role models. The nature of the politician must be deleted from our generalization of the law. If not outright deleted, it is distorted to an acceptable degree. If it weren't, most people would rightly reject their rules (laws) without a second thought. We know it's wrong to initiate force and hurt others; we don't need psychopaths dictating proper behavior to us.

A group of professional parasites can impose rules on everyone within the range of their guns because they have been successful in getting their victims to separate their will from the final product. They do this with a stage act and call it by a fancy word: legislation. Legislation sounds much better than: making up rules to control others and reap huge profits.

Every time I hear that word I can't help but roll my eyes; it's an anchored response.

As stated, politicians have succeeded in convincing enough people there is an "office of the president" that is somehow separate from the man they see acting as president. That's some trick. Try doing that yourself. It'll be a fun exercise in futility; you'll quickly learn why politicians have armies of unthinking henchmen on the payroll. You'll always hear cops excuse their criminal acts by saying they're just doing their jobs. No thought, no discretion, just following orders. In the military, not following an order is a crime. That means it's a crime to exercise critical thought when told to do something by someone higher on the political pecking order.

This is no different than convincing people there is a corporate person separate and distinct from the people who comprise the corporation. It's getting people to accept fiction after fiction after fiction. Now the fictions will dictate someone's reality instead of the actual facts being presented to them. And when those fictions are challenged, they tighten up and there will be resistance to the truth.

Whenever you hear about the law from now on, you'll know it's just a pretext to stealing and killing peaceful people. The person using this pretext has no evidence to back up his accusation. What they are trying to do is divert your attention away from what's really happening.

And just a few questions are all it takes to verify they are fictions. This is why it's so effective when questioning bureaucrats on the application of the law. All they may know are the words making up the law; they read it and there are words that it applies to all residents of the state. But they cannot discuss what the law is and the facts connecting it to me. So what you are getting at by asking questions is the law is applicable because the law says so. In other words, because some politicians said so.

Why are you a resident of the state because you live in Toronto, or Arizona? Because the law (politician) said so.

Fortunately, for the PR to be accepted by most of the people, the politicians had to make false promises of justice and due process. That's where the rules of evidence come from, that they are supposed to be fair and not make arbitrary claims and accusations. We can use their PR against them to set up double-binds, expose the fictions and get tickets and assessments dropped.

Politicians and bureaucrats make things up as they go, so it's really easy to put them into a double bind.

Let's look at the history of the parliaments and where these laws come from. Even in Greece, the councils were made up of very wealthy people who were also slave owners. Was that a coincidence? Hardly; they were doing only what came natural: dictating the behavior of others. The fact they owned other people as property is evidence of the type of people they were; they were anti-social, they were psychopaths. The Spartans were just extreme examples of this.

We need not be anthropologists to understand parliaments were not, and are not now, interested in freedom and justice. The purpose of a parliament-slave owners making up their own compulsory rules-was to maintain the social and economic position of both the parliament and those wealthy psychopaths whose tools parliaments are. It was to make sure the social elite stayed the social elite. The same social structure was brought to North America.

The original English parliament was composed of the wealthy feudal barons; today they are called the House of Lords and House of Commons. How do these so-called lords get things done? Well, we know how they got their Magna Carta sealed, don't we? Same as any other law; under threat of death at Runneymede in England. After John sealed the Magna Carta under threat of death, the barons did what any rational psychopaths would have done; they pledged their loyalty or fealty to John.

Agree to this John or we shall slay thee!
Ok then, sounds good, mate, where shall I affix my seal?
Oh great and benevolent king John, we swear unto thee our unbreakable allegiance... again. And we swear this time, and this time we *really* mean it, we will be thy loyal servants. Well, unless of course you violate the Magna Carta we just forced thee to seal. Just go ahead and read clause sixty-one again my lord. Long live the king!

You would think it would be the other way around: the king swearing allegiance to the barons. But in politics everything is backwards and upside down. Maybe it's me, I've lived in North America all my life, and the monarchy system just doesn't make sense. When you really examine it, the whole system-pyramid shaped, or vertical in structure-works bass-ackwards. The ones with the real power-the people who allow the ones on top to rule-are the ones who pledge allegiance and subject themselves.

What happened with John and the barons is just a small model of the world. But why didn't the barons just dispose of the king and take charge of the entire English farm themselves? It had to dawn on them; it's the nature of politics to be drawn to the top. Maybe it was because they saw how vulnerable the psychopath at the top really was and thought: It's not really *that* good to be the king. These animals could be threatening me with their silly Magna Carta next time.

John as the king was supposed to be the sovereign, the ruler over the barons who had pledged their allegiance; and yet they were forcing him to submit? Reminds me of the PR in the united states where "We the People" are supposed to be sovereign, yet the *sine qua non* of citizenship, like in Australia, is allegiance or obedience, meaning of course, submission.

It makes one wonder if they could have gotten away with it had news traveled faster back then. We know there were people in the sixteenth century who did know how things worked; we have the *Discourse on Voluntary Servitude* by Etienne de la Boetie as proof. I imagine the common folk, the peasants of the day, may have seen what happened at Runnymede as a model to be used against the local lords.

S'cuse us, mate, seeing how we outnumber thee at least a hundred to one...

The wealthy elite in the United States and Canada got title to huge tracts of already inhabited lands the same way as most feudal barons: a "royal" grant from the king. Herr Washington and Patrick Henry were no exception. How did they enforce such ownership against the rest of the people, even those who were already living on the land for countless generations? At the barrel of a gun. Washington had no voluntary support when president, and Patrick Henry didn't as governor of Virginia.

It was the same thing in eighteenth-century North America as it was in Europe. Probably no surprise because of all the damn Europeans. A few people controlled the land and forced the rest to pay them rent. Land was further controlled and taxed by the tools we call government.

I think it's safe to assume most would consider one man owning North America, especially since it was already inhabited by millions, as the ranting of the insane. That's how I look at it though, and if I claimed to own a continent, you no doubt would consider me a nut job. I've been considered a nut for far less.

Not so crazy though if I had a violent scheme ensuring you and your family would profit from it in perpetuity. Your family, by grant from me, would own a part of North America and you could then charge others rent to live on and work the land. If anyone did not pay, then you could have the local goons violently remove them from your property and then get new tenants.

This feudal system should sound familiar because the same system is still at work today. And it will continue as long as the victims cooperate by providing the psychopaths with their money/property so the psychopaths can keep paying unthinking squads of soldiers.

Now you could argue that because of the Europeans taking over, the standard of living improved dramatically, leading to the Industrial Revolution and of course the technology for me to do a radio show from a computer in a hotel. But not only does that assume there could have been no Industrial Revolution without the genocide of the American Indians and complete theft of their lands, but also assumes the hundreds of millions of people butchered by that same technology in the last one-hundred and fifty years made for a better society than that of the native Americans.

Yes, the drive to kill more people more efficiently has lead to many technological advances, but I still don't see that as the only way to advance science and improve society.

If there is one thing wealthy white Europeans have a really good track record at, it's devising or funding better and better ways to kill people, especially poor non-whites. Their wealthy American progeny seem to have perfected mass murder and plunder. While we know drug use is prevalent with wealthy, pasty white kids and their parents, when was the last time you heard of a drug sweep in Beverly Hills or Belle Terre?

Do an internet search of "Beverly Hills no knock drug raid" and compare to "Detroit no knock drug raid" for some interesting reading. There's plenty of evidence the wealthy partake of illegal drugs, so why are the drug warriors not doing no-knock drug raids in Beverly Hills?

The following from John Locke describes the real situation with a so-called citizen to someone claiming to be a government:

> "17. And hence it is **he who attempts to get another man into his absolute power does thereby put himself into a state of war with him**. It being to be understood as a declaration of a design upon his life. **For I have reason to conclude that he who would get me into his power without my consent would use me as he pleased when he had got me there, and destroy me too when he had a fancy to it**; for nobody can desire to have me in his absolute power, unless it be so to compel me by force to that which is against the right of my freedom i.e. **make me a slave**. To be free from such force is the only security of my preservation, and reason bids me look on him as my enemy to my preservation, who would take away that freedom which is the fence to it. So that he who make an attempt to enslave me thereby puts himself into a state of war with me." *Second Treatise of Government*, John Locke (Emphasis mine).

How could such clarity of thought then somehow justify government at all? It's almost as if John Locke was a closet anarchist; sounds more like Lysander Spooner, doesn't it? Was Locke afraid of retaliation from the "Crown" at the time?

The first sentence is an indictment itself against all so-called governments. As long as support is compulsory, there is an ongoing state of war between individuals who are rightly to be seen as enemies.

Politics, like public relations/advertising, is about controlling perceptions. You don't need direct physical control over people if you control their perceptions. No one needs to overtly control people if they can effectively control people's perceptions. That is where the words and phrases discussed above come in. You didn't defend yourself against a man who initiated physical violence against you; no you attacked a duly authorized agent in the administration of official duties.

On a different level, you didn't freely trade with your community; you didn't pay your fair share. As long as the perception is only people called government can protect you, then any perceived opposition is seen as an attack on the only people who can protect you. No wonder there is an emotional response to voluntaryism.

So, even with an empiricist such as John Locke, you see diversion or deletion of facts; Locke was a proponent of the social contract theory. Yet, he didn't see (from my readings of his works) the apparent lack of evidence of such a contract or agreement. How does one not take into account the compulsory nature of all government support? It really is the only way to theorize there is a social contract. How else can you harmonize coercion with consent?

As long as the citizen has no choice-comply or die-then citizen is just another word for slave.

Closely examine any political words, and you'll see the same thing. An example is from Utah. Look at the following "legalistic gibberish" from the Utah Enabling Act:

> "That perfect toleration of religious sentiment shall be secured, and that no inhabitant of said State shall ever be molested in person or property on account of his or her mode of religious worship; *Provided*, That polygamous or plural marriages are forever prohibited."

The people who wrote this had to know it was contradictory. Plural marriages were at that time a religious matter with members of the L.D.S. church, who settled and built most of the communities in Utah. Polygamy has been around for thousands of years and is practiced in many communities around the world.

This is the same as saying: Perfect toleration of religious sentiment, *provided* there are no Jews and Muslims. I always liked the quote from Ford: "Any customer can have a car painted any color that he wants so long as it is black."

Whatever our opinion on the matter, it certainly doesn't violate anyone's life, liberty or pursuit of happiness when freely consenting adults engage in the practice. You can see how silly this Enabling Act was when you read the following clause:

> "The constitution shall be republican in form...and not be repugnant to the Constitution of the United States and the principles of the Declaration of Independence."
> Section 3.

Remember that line from the Declaration? I mean the one about the purpose of government to "Secure...Life, Liberty, and the Pursuit of Happiness." Do you think the writers of the Enabling Act asked themselves how freely consenting adults entering into a marriage was a crime? Where's the *corpus delecti*? This includes typical marriages between consenting adult men and women. That's what it means when a license is required; it is a crime to do it without the license.

What about the argument the United States is a Christian nation, based on Judeo-Christian values? What about Abraham, Isaac and Jacob?

Doesn't the Bible state Abraham, Isaac and Jacob were all polygamists? Would these self-proclaimed Christians jail their patriarchs?

Of course, when dealing with killers, thieves and liars there's always going to be such contradictions. Yes, perfect religious tolerance, *except* for

103

polygamy. And let's not forget the peyote used for sacrament by some religious groups.

For those unfamiliar: peyote is a cactus that grows in southwestern North America and has hallucinogenic properties, such as mescaline. Native Americans have long used it as a religious sacrament. I've known people who have used it and they do not treat it lightly. It's not used in a recreational manner; it's taken as seriously as Catholics take the wine in their sacrament. Even if it's used recreationally, that's no one's business except the people using it.

A simple comparison between the words and the actions will bring out the contradictions. Never look at just the words if you want the truth. Look at the actions first, then compare to the words. Always look at the story the facts are telling, not the story the politician is spewing.

Chapter Two

"If a psychiatric and scientific inquiry were to be made upon our rulers, mankind would be appalled." Alfred Korbzyski

Prepare to be appalled.

The Psychology of Control
The psychological case against government

"We are so befuddled by language that we cannot think straight." Steps to an Ecology of Mind, Gregory Bateson, page 202.

Here is really the heart of this indictment against the concept of government; the concept causes changes in our behavior. These changes make overt conspiracies unnecessary; it's a self-replicating program. It's kept in place by trauma bonds and extreme social pressure.

I don't expect you to take anything here as the truth either. Just like the radio show, verify everything for yourself. Speak to people about abolishing government and watch the reactions you'll get. Call a politician and ask if there are facts proving the laws of the state apply to you. After they laugh at you and say of course the laws apply to you, you follow up with, "What facts do you rely on to prove that?" Notice the response; it'll be the same or very similar to what I report here and on the radio show every week.

I had a manager with the criminal investigation division (CID) of the IRS say my question asking for facts the laws applied was a "stupid argument." Aside from the silly diversion tactic he used, is it really stupid to ask for the facts? I started the call by asking two questions: Are there facts proving you have jurisdiction and the laws apply to my client? He said: "Yes and yes." When I asked the agent about the specific facts, he said he would defer to his manager. It was his way of refusing to answer.

The manager absolutely refused to discuss the facts he claimed he had. He seemed like a decent guy when we started, and he didn't raise his voice or get abusive with us. He just would not, or could not, get specific with me about the facts. Obviously, he was speaking too soon when he said yes.

For him, as with every other bureaucrat I've spoken with, the word law was so heavily a part of his map of the world, his perceptions and behaviors, that he could not permit any kind of challenge. The word "law" excuses everything he does on the job, right or wrong-it's the law and he's always right. It's just a word though.

Yeah, just a word, but the impact words have on our experience and behavior cannot be overstated. So much of our interaction with bureaucrats comes down to words. I was speaking with a bureaucrat recently about jurisdiction; I wanted the facts proving the bureaucrat had jurisdiction over a client. She actually asked me what I meant by the word jurisdiction. I'm thinking quickly here: is this a trap?

I figured since bureaucrats insist they always have jurisdiction over us, they're making the claim. I just asked her, with slight derision in my voice: You don't know what *you* mean by jurisdiction? She backed off that really fast and didn't want to talk about jurisdiction for some reason.

Words and actions don't always match. While that is stating the "blatantly bloody obvious," how many people call politicians and bureaucrats out on it? The fact they are still farming us is evidence not too many are doing it. Governments are given a free pass most of the time. There are several reasons why, and I'll discuss them in detail further on in this chapter.

What it usually comes down to is *fear*. Some of the fear may be from not being able to see through the flimsy tactics bureaucrats use to avoid being exposed. They start to mock, and because people worry others will scorn them, they don't even bother asking the judge who they represent. Then there is the real threat of a psychopath lawyer screaming and having you thrown in a cage. Because asking questions should be met with swift violence.

It's the disconnect between the words and actions, though that's the reason why the world operates the way it does...and its undoing. Of course the words and actions don't match; it's why judges have psychotic episodes when you point it out in their sacred courtrooms. If you want to see it for yourself, then question the high priest while he's sitting on wooden throne.

Incongruent messages bombarding us every day for years are affecting our behavior. How could they not? Incongruent messages with constant trauma, always being in a state of fear, will affect us. Bateson wrote, "If schizophrenia be a modification or distortion of the learning process..." *Ecology*, page 190. Looks like politicians have been using just such a process to stay in the higher parts of the hierarchy, to purposely distort our learning process.

We don't have to use the word schizophrenic, just demonstrate the fact we are constantly confronted with incongruent messages and threats. Anyone paying attention can see this is the method of operation for governments. These two factors cause a change in behavior; it's been studied for years and the effects replicated.

When we investigate the facts and question the constant incongruent messages coupled with fear, it's the only logical conclusion. E.g., governments are by consent while support is coerced. A more dramatic example is when the tanks were demolishing the house at Mt. Carmel in Waco, Texas in 1993 while they announced, "This is not an attack!"

How are we to process the inconsistent messages? We know we have no individual choice; our consent as an individual is non-existent. So how do we deal with this very obvious attack on our minds and bodies? How is any anger or discontent expressed? By voting in elections? As a juror? Not a good time to be on trial for disobedience.

Studies and experiments have shown, depending on the stress, we may not be able to process the inconsistent messages, such as when the facts are at odds with our perceptions. In the experiments, people tended to respond with high levels of frustration, a similar reaction as a cop or judge who is questioned about their jurisdiction. Being questioned goes against their perceptions as authorities, so they get upset because they cannot cope. How could they when their model of the world does not allow for it? The animals are not supposed to ask questions, certainly not questions the authority cannot answer.

Bateson asked the question many will ask regarding this information: "If this family [society] is schizophrenic, how does it happen that all the siblings are not diagnosable as schizophrenic patients?" *Ecology*, page 191. Why assume the rest of the family doesn't have problems? If schizophrenia is a distortion of the learning process, then why assume others do not have an issue? The evidence is overwhelming that many people have problems processing messages; politicians bank on it.

An example of this evidence is that Americans think they are free to travel, as long as they have a compulsory license. It doesn't seem to faze them. The facts show they are only traveling by permission and they just don't grasp it; they think they are free.

Bateson also states, "There is room for only one boss." *Ecology*, page 191. I believe there are varying degrees, and as mentioned by Bateson, there is a *hierarchy* to society, which probably tempers things so there isn't a complete psychotic collapse. He provides a great explanation about how our present society can function by describing how a family, a microcosm of society, can function:

> "Anybody watching the trans-actions which occur between the members of a family containing an identified schizophrenic will perceive immediately that the symptomatic behavior of the identified patient fits with this environment and, indeed, promotes in the other members those characteristics which evoke the schizophrenic behavior." *Ecology*, page 191.

Members of society are promoting "those characteristics which evoke the schizophrenic behavior" by not questioning the inconsistent messages. By standing idly by, because of fear and social pressure, members of society-victims of this perverted concept-perpetuate and enable more of the damaging behavior. We look to others to see how they are responding, and what they will do.

In this way, the abuse continues unabated and the people get less and less resistant to ideas and actions challenging the underlying concepts. Fortunately, we can still teach people and show them there is no state, government or citizens.

I'd like to see one man/woman on a jury refuse to accept incongruent messages, to stand up to judges and refuse to cooperate in the abuse of peaceful people. It may just take one to break from the program for the rest to know it's okay to do the right thing.

When talking about creating schizophrenic behavior, or distorting the learning process, Bateson gives the model used to get people to accept the government concept:

"Double bind experiences must recur *ad nauseam.* The problem is to construct a model which will necessarily *cycle* to recreate these patterned sequences over and over again." *Ecology*, page 177.

And that happens every day. There's no escaping the government concept; it's all pervasive for most of us.

"Double bind situations are created by and within the psychotherapeutic setting and the hospital milieu...we would assume that whenever the system is organized for hospital purposes and it is announced to the patient that the actions are for his benefit, then the schizophrenogenic situation is being perpetuated." *Ecology*, page 169.

"The organism is then faced with the dilemma either of being wrong in the primary context or of being right for the wrong reasons or in the wrong way. This is the so-called double bind. We are investigating the hypothesis that schizophrenic communication is learned and be-comes habitual as a result of continual traumata of this kind. That is all there is to it." *Ecology*, page 182.

Compare this with the government concept-two conflicting messages: We're here to protect you; now pay or get shot. The evidence proves that the concept of government, even when just pretending, causes serious psychological trauma. Can you imagine a concept so dangerous there's trauma caused even when only pretending? It's similar as participating as an actor in a play and becoming the character, adopting the personality. That is actually a problem with such method actors, the Stanislavski method.

This has not only been seen with actors (Heath Ledger being an example), but with scientific studies such as the Stanford Prison Experiment http://www.prisonexp.org/. Just playing a part-*pretending* to be a bureaucrat-can cause significant changes in personality and behaviors.

Think of a judge when he puts on that black dress and walks into the court and everyone stands up in fear. People in court are maintaining fictions, and that causes a certain amount of anxiety; we've all felt it. But I can have lunch with a friend of mine who's a judge and there's no anxiety, and the main reason is neither one of us has to maintain *those* fictions; we're just two friends having a meal. We can talk about law, the immorality of government, even abolishing it, and there are no threats, no harsh words or even raising our voices. If I call him by his first name he's not going to start raging about having me thrown in jail for contempt. (Though I doubt he's the type to do that in court).

If we were both in court, how and if we maintained the fictions will largely dictate our behavior towards each other. It's silly to even suggest otherwise; present situations together with our prior experiences that shaped our current view of the world will control our behavior. Again, our map of the world, our perceptions/generalizations in any given situation, dictates our behavior.

But the politicians and bureaucrats are just playing parts, and those parts become very real to them; their map of the world is real to them. So when you call a judge by his first name, it shakes them up because it's not consistent with their map, so they must immediately start making things conform.

This is accomplished with the only thing they have: violence. If they start screaming and making threats, then he's suddenly "Your Honor" again, not just Timmy. To cause a psychotic break, the cops would also have to treat him as just Timmy and not carry out his orders. If that happened, then he wouldn't even be Timmy, just the crazy douche bag in Courtroom 4.

I've seen where cops were bewildered by a judge's tantrum to a point where they just stood there in shock; I thought the guy was going to have a stroke. Part of me was really pushing for it.

Keep in mind, the map is not the territory, and we constantly update our maps. Let's at least be more conscious about it from now on; because, unfortunately, our perceptions are more important than the evidence right in front of us.

> *"Are you going to believe me, or what you see with your own eyes?"* Groucho Marx (or any politician looking to control you and your property)

This is where I'll lay out how the concept of government causes trauma and effects behavior. It's the situations created by the concept that is a main causal element in people's behavior. The structure of society itself, vertical or pyramid shaped, as opposed to horizontal, is what contributes to the anti-social behavior and general apathy towards others. Horizontal just means there is no hierarchy; no structure where one controls another without mutually voluntary consent.

It doesn't matter what the actual intention of those imposing and maintaining the structure is, criminal responsibility is really on the concept itself, not the actors. However, as with crimes such as involuntary manslaughter, intent does not excuse the perpetrators. There is also negligence and the phrase, "knew or was reckless in not knowing," prosecutors like to use against us. Those causing the damage are still responsible for their actions; they know full well the consequences of their actions. We know this because they have laws in place to punish the same acts if done by those lower on the hierarchy.

Bureaucrats and politicians know they are criminals, whether they want to admit it or not. I've asked if I provided my services and collected money in the same way as governments, would they consider me a criminal? They usually refuse to answer because the question is "offensive." No, the way they're doing business is offensive, not my question.

This is about the concept, not pointing the finger of blame at any one man or group of men. I will show how governments are antithetical to the very thing their PR claims they protect: life. The concept itself is fatally flawed, irrational and cannot be reformed or improved on in any way. When you take away the offending element-compulsory support–you completely destroy the concept itself.

This is about tearing down the vertical structure of society, the rationale that built it; once that's done, the *context* changes and the relationships change as a result. When relationships change, behavior and responses change as well. Those inclined to anti-social behavior don't have the structure to facilitate their destructive behaviors.

Just as serial killers don't usually go around killing everyone they encounter, it depends on the situation. When the rationale creating the context causing the anti-social behavior is gone, there will be a drop in the level of anti-social or psychopathic behavior. Change the cause and you change the effects.

If a society is no longer based on violence, it will be less violent. Not exactly rocket science.

Just as stopping the Stanford Prison Experiment changed the behavior of the participants, the rationale that caused the anti-social behavior is taken away or not accepted and acted on. This obviously causes changes in the behavior. There are contemporary examples such as the Amish. The Amish do not have a vertical structure to their communities; they are horizontal and are probably the most peaceful communities in North America. The peaceful society they enjoy is the natural effect of not basing your society on violence.

This should be as simple as asking:

Should society be based on violence?

It really is that simple, and see how impersonal and objective it is? As we'll see, all the psychological trauma and mind control makes it very difficult to discuss this in such basic terms. Even if, notwithstanding the constant war and economic ruin, having a violent hierarchy is a working model, is this what we really want? Why can't protection of life, liberty and property be provided on a voluntary basis? Why not protect life, liberty and property in a manner consistent with protecting life, liberty and property? What is the problem with only changing the *manner* in which certain services are paid: voluntarily instead of violently? Easy: protecting life, liberty and property is not the objective of governments.

What you have with the government concept is backwards: perceptions are what matter, not the observable facts. I had an agent with the Washington state department of revenue tell me being arrested was a voluntary act. She had already admitted that using violence to provide services was always wrong. When I pointed out the people she worked with used violence to get people to pay for services-you pay or go to jail-she immediately disagreed and stated that an arrest can be gentle and non-violent. Yes, but the same can be said about an armed robbery or some rapes; they're nonetheless violent. Double binds are not fun to be in.

110

I had to tell her that rational discussion was over. If she did not believe being arrested, put in jail and having all your property forcibly taken was violent, then we could not speak any longer.

We're afraid to point out the truth, and even more afraid to act on that truth. These mere services are tied to our very identity and there is a very strong emotional bond to the concepts whether people want to admit them or not. They're all demonstrably false, but there is still a bond nonetheless. Even empiricists have problems letting go. This bond is so strong, that when combined with our perceptions, it's almost insurmountable. By mistaking mental habits for actual thinking, they can inhibit the mental processing of facts right in front of us:

> "We do not attack our minds, *suspect our* minds. All our mental habits are to us not habits, but truths. They are quite right to us. There can be no other point of view. We cannot see them as habits. This is a tragedy. So we cannot see that so many things we keep on *minding* so much are due to invisible mental habits. Of course we have to worry, of course we have to think that this is impossible." *Psychological Commentaries of Guirdjeff and Ouspenky*, Maurice Nicoll, vol. 2, (emphasis in original)

I spoke with an IRS agent named Ryan who could not stop referring to my client as a taxpayer. He apologized saying it was habitual. No kidding, he couldn't stop it. He got very offended when I said that instead of critically examining the evidence or lack of it, he did things habitually without any real thought or investigation. Yes, killing the messenger is a great way to communicate.

It's very painful for most to face the truth; that we don't know it all and may be mistaken. Real science and investigation into the truth admits no real certainty, only that these are the facts as we know at this point. Not so with most people though, certainty rules the day, absolute, unerring certainty.

Americans are particularly subject to this, it's a part of the culture. It's taught the US is the greatest nation on earth, the most innovative, the most free, the most charitable, my country right or wrong, etc. No need to bother with facts, that's not the object of jingoism. When confronted with the truth you run head first into the need to be right. Maslow forgot one of the dearest needs in his hierarchy: the need to be right.

This has been reported recently as the "argumentative theory of reasoning" as if this is a recent phenomenon. http://www.nytimes.com/2011/06/15/arts/people-argue-just-to-win-scholars-assert.html?pagewanted=all.

It is argued that reasoning was a social function that developed as a way of convincing others and to know when someone is trying to put something over on us. Then, somewhere down the line, it became more important to be right than to investigate the facts. Zen Buddhists have described the need to be right as a sickness of the mind for over two thousand years.

111

Given the current state of the world, I would say the evidence proves the need to be right is at the top of the hierarchy, as people will sacrifice everything below for it. Look at those parents who pretend their children died in Iraq fighting for our freedom. Their priority list might would look like this:

The need to be right
Self-actualization
Esteem
Love/belonging
Safety
Physiological

The fact that people like Pat Tillman sacrifice themselves for politicians is evidence the need to be right is more important than the other five, as not much thought was given to safety.

How many are prepared to face the truth about the American founding fathers? Americans dance around the fact that many of the founders were slave owners and traders. In fact, history shows that may have been the least of the anti-social behavior of the American Hitler, Andrew Jackson, whose wrath against the English was only exceeded by his murderous contempt for the Cherokee people. Jackson even had cannons turned on his own men. The guy was a raging psychopath-and that's from historical references-and yet he's still hailed as some kind of hero.

How many founders gave up their royal land grants? It was not only good to be the king, but also good to be some of those rich few who courted and received his favors. They certainly did nothing to change the structure of the society.

No amount of evidence proving that politicians and bureaucrats are gangs of killers, thieves and liars seems to change people's perceptions of governments. I'm convinced that if politicians came right out and declared themselves the owners of the American people, that most Americans, though angry, would still go about complying, paying taxes and voting. "We've gotta vote this guy out or he'll destroy the country with European socialism."

Right after the politicians made their statements, Americans would just change the channel to watch Jersey Shore or some other mindless trash.

Talk about incongruent messages: slavery in the land of liberty and freedom? How was that reconciled? And don't talk about freedom when there were so many restrictions on owning property by non-whites. Women and poor whites could not vote for decades.

As mentioned, most mistake mere mental habits as actually thinking. It's easy for us to see habits and automatic/reflexive actions when it comes to physical activities, but not mental ones. We repeat actions, such as driving a car or something athletic, until it becomes automatic. For such types of actions, it needs to become automatic and drop out of consciousness. But what effect does this have on our thinking and behaviors? The effects are devastating and can be seen all around us. They are a main subject of this book.

The government concept puts people to sleep. This was satirized on the Simpsons, "Lisa, the whole reason we have elected officials is so we don't have to think all the time." Why else do people do things they normally would not do when told to do so by an authority figure? They don't have to think of the consequences because they don't have any responsibility. It's the same with a judge when he's confronted by one of us little people who has the nerve to step out of the line and question the process. Imagine the reaction of a lawyer acting as a judge when asked by one of his cattle, "Sir, what is the nature of your relationship to this prosecutor?"

The judge doesn't ever think about the consequences of his psychotic rages because there won't be any. He/she has absolute, irresponsible dominion of others and the victims cannot legally hold him accountable. Absolute immunity works that way. Only those higher up on the pecking order are allowed to hold judges and prosecutors to any accountability; not us the little people.

If there are any consequences, it's only the strengthening of the trauma bond the victims have to him and the concept of government. I've seen the horror in people's eyes when they spoke to me after I've spoken to a judge, "I can't believe the way you spoke to the judge." Why, what sets them apart from us? Maybe the institutionalized psychopathy and a battery of men willing to kill on orders? That's a good point.

A phobia is an automatic process. A phobia has been described as a one time learning process; one particular event caused an automatic, unconscious pattern of response. Every time the event is repeated, such as seeing a spider, the person will go through the same program mentally and have the same response.

Unlike most other patterns, most phobias are easy for us to notice; mental ones, not so much. They are to an informed observer though. Look at the response you get from people when you mention abolishing governments because the means are destructive to the ends. If you've tried to discuss this with people you've experienced the challenge. Overcoming it seems almost impossible. It is impossible with some.

I've had liberty activists make personal attacks against me as a "snake oil salesman" and other equally baseless attacks. For some people-even self-professed voluntaryists-there is still a habit of having to control other people's behavior and beliefs.

The hateful things they say when you don't hold the same beliefs is evidence that while they may understand on a superficial level that control over another is wrong, and they may never physically attack another man, the mental habit persists on a deep level and the violence is expressed as rage and hateful rants on the interwebs. Anger is rooted in not getting your way, the perception that people should be just the way you want them to be. You think people should act and believe the way you think, and if they don't, then your only way to cope is to be like a child and get mad.

There is no critical analysis of what I present, such as asking a judge whom he/she represents, why I ask it, or why we get the responses we do. The rationale is never examined, it's just ridiculed, "I think that's silly and that's enough to prove you're an idiot, Marc." It's about proving I'm an idiot or scammer, not critical examination of the particular issue. The anger is because they think their map of the world is somehow more accurate than mine or another's who has investigated and seen the merit in asking such a question as it guts the fiction the judge is independent.

I can be a jerk from Long Island even while putting forth the proposition 2+2=4; the two are not necessarily related. The equation is accurate and verifiable independent of me. But the habit of having to control other people's beliefs does not take the equation or position into account - it's about control over behavior. It's very transparent and a character flaw that's caused by the hierarchy of the government concept.

An example of the difficulty and sheer effort to overcome these habits can be shown with an athletic example that's plagued me, and there have been many. Remember, both thinking and athletic performance are neural based.

I love Olympic weightlifting and gymnastics. Both involve very high levels of skill to be able to perform. Perfecting a snatch, at least for me, can be a lifelong process. Try holding a handstand on the rings and you'll notice how much skill is required just to get into it, let alone hold it for more than a few seconds.

Strength is not the only thing required for both sports; there's power, skill, balance and flexibility. You may have brutal strength to do an inverted cross on the still rings, but if you don't have high levels of balance, then good luck and let me know how that works out for you.

The Olympic snatch is deceptive in that you can learn the skill well enough to be able to do the lift, or look like you're doing it right. That is, you can get the barbell locked out over your head in one motion, then stand up, without really performing it correctly. Just watch high school football players lifting to confirm. The problem may not become apparent until you start using more weight than your skill will permit or you cannot continue making progress.

One thing I did was train the power snatch for about a year. Unlike the full snatch, you only drop into a half or quarter squat to catch the barbell. This became automatic, and with such a lift it has to be done that way if you're going to be any good at the sport. This is the benefit of having a coach though, when I started finally training the full snatch, I would still only drop into a half squat.

It drove me crazy and took over a year to break the habit. No matter how much I focused on it, because of the nature of the lift, I could not stop it without a tremendous amount of time and energy. It's also kind of a double-edged sword because the more I did it wrong, the stronger the neural pattern became. It was a very slow process.

To really understand, you need to go through something like it yourself. You're standing there, and it's as if you're fighting your own unconscious processes. Your body just doesn't do what your conscious mind is telling it to do. You find out really fast who's really in control.

114

I would grab the bar and visualize dropping into a full squat; do the first pull, reach my knees and explode into the second pull, fully extend, then still only drop into a half-squat. I was performing a fairly good power snatch, so it looked and felt right. Someone familiar with the lift would watch and not see much wrong. Because it looked and felt correct, it made it more difficult to correct, as it was only the depth of the squat.

No matter how much effort I put in, it was a very long process to overcome this prior conditioning. It's as if you're fighting yourself and it's very frustrating since you think you're spinning your wheels. You can go months without any noticeable progress.

But I was conscious of it, I could see it, I could video record it. I was very aware of what I was doing. What about mental habits where we're not aware of the process? How do we go about changing that and how difficult can that be? Apparently, it's much more difficult than correcting an Olympic lift or a handstand.

Even when aware of it, the process is automatic and our brains seem to resist the change. Just like with the Olympic lifts, just wanting to do it differently was not nearly enough; even putting in effort every day was not enough for any real change in the short term. It took at least as long to correct as it took to learn.

I don't think it takes as long to change a mental pattern. With NLP, a phobia pattern can be stopped within a few minutes; I have personal experience with this. What we have to do is become aware of it; acknowledge the fact we're not thinking so much as going through a habitual pattern or process.

You want to keep this in mind as we go through the psychological studies and experiments. When you're discussing politics/voluntary society with a statist, some of the "resistance" is due to patterns/habits of thinking.

The evidence proves the overwhelming majority of crimes committed worldwide are directly or indirectly caused by the government concept. This is true even when we exclude taxation and all forms of direct government aggression; the concept causes general anti-social behavior and a lack of empathy towards others. This lack of empathy, a necessary quality for serial crime, is caused directly by this hierarchal structure.

A hierarchy by nature is about levels-superiors and inferiors, classes, or a caste system. The reasoning behind divide and conquer is keeping the sheep fighting among themselves. This is easily accomplished with a hierarchy. The lower classes will always tend to hate the rich-the haves and have-nots. It's pretty old. It breeds contempt on each level for each other. This contempt is expressed in many ways. Look at the flash mobs taking place in the United States.

We don't know exactly how such large communities of people really would be, because they have never had the chance to live without the hierarchy and control. Their behavior is dictated and caused, to a large degree, by the hierarchy. I am not excusing the behavior-people still have a choice-just providing an explanation of the causes of that behavior.

Science proves that removing the situation, changing the context, will change behavior dramatically. In the last part of this book I'll address getting rid of the hierarchy. Below I'll present the evidence, proving beyond a reasonable doubt, the government concept is the cause of most of the crime and trauma in the world.

The concept plays out like this:

* Government concept
* Hierarchy of authority
* Acceptance of coercion as moral/normal
* General lack of empathy
* debility, dependence, dread
* immobilizing fear
* habitual mental processes, automatic and unconscious

Government apologists never address the psychology of governing or being government. This is understandable; why would anyone want to discuss how their heroes are anti-social, sociopathic, narcissistic or psychopaths? If government advocates discuss government crimes, such as torture, rape and murder, it's always seen as a few-bad-apples scenario. Government apologists never look at the *concept* of government itself as having anything to do with the problem.

How do I know this? Because the cure is always the same: more government, more of what has *created* the problem. The facts show Reagan did not believe his own rhetoric: "Government is not the solution to our problem, government is the problem." Yet, twenty plus years later you have self-professed "small government" republicans talking about being Reagan conservatives as if Reagan did anything to make governments exercise less aggression. This is technically referred to as "putting one's head in the sand."

Even when government is admitted to be the problem, such as with the democratically elected Hitler, then only the *form* of government is the culprit, not the immoral and irrational concept of government itself. Today, the boogeyman is again "fascism," a form of government.

What's unusual is the basic nature of government is so well known, there are jokes made about it on a regular basis. One example is from *Seinfeld* where Kramer is accused of being a serial killer. Jerry and George are in a police car getting a ride to the station and are asking the cops questions. One asks if the cops can drive on the wrong side of the road and one cop answers, "We can do whatever we want." It's funny because it accurately describes the beliefs and attitudes of government.

The following medical definition describes politicians extremely well:

> "People with a narcissistic personality have a sense of superiority and an exaggerated belief in their own value or importance, which is what psychiatrists call "grandiosity." People with this personality type may be extremely sensitive to failure, defeat, or criticism and, when confronted by a

116

failure to fulfill their high opinion of themselves, can easily become enraged or severely depressed. Because they believe themselves to be superior in their relationships with other people, they expect to be admired and often suspect that others envy them. They feel they're entitled to have their needs attended to without waiting, so they exploit others, whose needs are deemed to be less important. Their behavior is usually offensive to others, who view them as being self-centered, arrogant, or selfish." *The Merck Manual of Medical Information*, page 427.

It's so obvious now, that even the *LA Times* has had articles about politicians being psychopaths:

"While many political leaders will deny the assessment regarding their similarities with serial killers and other career criminals, it is part of a psychopathic profile that may be used in assessing the behaviors of many officials and lawmakers at all levels of government." *LA Times*, quoting Jim Kouri of the FBI's behavioral analysis unit, June 15, 2009.

Kind of ironic one bureaucrat is calling other bureaucrats psychopaths. This Jim Kouri has apparently never questioned *how he gets paid*. If he did, then he might agree with the small change I'd make with his profile:

"...it is part of a psychopathic profile that may be used in assessing the behaviors of [all] officials and lawmakers at all levels of government."

What's important is that the concept/structure of society with a government causes significant trauma on all sides; not just to those on the government side causing direct trauma to the victims. This concept is also the cause of trauma between victims. The world really is in a constant traumatized state with one generation traumatizing the next. It's a self-perpetuating idea, each part of it adding to and strengthening the other.

The most effective thing keeping governments in place is *fear*, but not just fear about government retaliation, also the perceived judgment of friends and family if one refuses to cooperate with anti-social parasites called governments. When we are put into a state of fear, the rational part of our brains tends to shut down and emotion takes over. This is not the best way to make decisions.

People are too scared to either point out the emperor has no clothes, or the elephant in the room. People are immobilized by fear of what they imagine the herd may think of them.

Fear of what others may think of us may do more to immobilize us than fear of government retaliation. People have no trouble speeding because they know most people also speed; they believe their friends and neighbors won't condemn them for going a few miles an hour over the posted limit. But this works both ways. The social pressure, not political law, is what keeps most people from speeding to a point of endangering others. This same social pressure is also what will be at work in a voluntary society; same as now because that is more responsible for why the overwhelming majority of people interact voluntarily. It's not the law that keeps most people from being violent, it's because most people have empathy and want to be a respected member of society.

In addition, this fear is built upon a lack of empathy. The two feed off and strengthen each other. Think of apathy as an accelerant. People may act, despite fear, if they have empathy towards the victims. But, people can easily justify their lack of action or non-cooperation with tyrants when they have no empathy. They just don't care about the victims, so why take any personal interest, let alone any personal risk? Too far outside our little monkey sphere or Dunbar number I guess. Let's hear it for divide and conquer. It's the basis of the famous quote from to Martin Niemöller:

> First they came for the communists,
> and I didn't speak out because I wasn't a communist.
>
> Then they came for the trade unionists,
> and I didn't speak out because I wasn't a trade unionist.
>
> Then they came for the Jews,
> and I didn't speak out because I wasn't a Jew.
>
> Then they came for me
> and there was no one left to speak out for me.

The government concept and its resulting vertical structure of society causes a general apathy, it fragments society. It restricts choice, and freedom is about choice. The fewer choices, whether by force, deception, or both, diminishes freedom. Throw in false choices such as political elections and we really start to have problems. People are divided into right and left; if you disagree with Barack Obama, you must be a pasty white republican. If you dislike George Bush, you have to be a tree hugging liberal.

Empathy is so powerful, it can even overcome what was considered for a long time to be the strongest human drive, the drive for self-preservation. There are countless examples where people have saved others without any thought for their own safety. This is significant and reason for great hope humanity will not continue on its crash-course of self-destruction. It's this hope that drives me to finish this book.

What's lacking is empathy; the government concept is anti-empathy, it causes division and general lack of empathy. The average person acts as if they don't care at all about anyone but themselves. That is the government concept with its built-in hierarchy at work.

When one perceives they are above or over another, that will cause them to see and subsequently treat the other as less human. It's the beginning of apathy. We're not an equal to speak with-no, we're subordinates to give orders to. That's what bureaucrats do: they take orders and then give orders. They're not a group known for being intellectual giants. Life is not about cooperation to bureaucrats and politicians; it's about subjection and control, that's how things are done. It's also the only choice available. It's either done through violence covered by lies or it cannot be done. Remember, without governments, who will build the roads?

The evidence proving this is so overwhelming it's beyond any doubt. I dare say if it's not a self-evident truth, it will be now with this book. If you doubt the truth of this, just go out and start acting as if you are an authority over others. Observe what happens. If you do, it's probably best if you wear a helmet.

This is why in the military, all classes (vertical, pyramid structure) are separated; the officers do not fraternize with the NCOs and the NCO's do not fraternize with the privates. The role of master-slave must be preserved because it's essential to controlling behavior. Those in the military will tell you that is how it has to be. Military men know familiarity breeds contempt for authority.

I remember how odd it was when my platoon sergeant at Ft. Gordon, Georgia came into the weight room and worked in with us when we were benching. I would hardly have taken orders from some guy who worked in with us in the weight room; after all, he was just another guy training. But out of the weight room you didn't dare call him Bibbs. It was a different context and different fictions at play.

This has been ridiculed many times. One of my favorite examples is from the television show *Friends* where Joey starts working at the museum with Ross. The tour guides, wearing blue jackets, do not sit at the same tables at lunch as the paleontologists, wearing white lab coats.

http://www.youtube.com/watch?v=br-jIhnbkYc

There is also a scene in the movie Patch Adams where the doctors went to a butcher's convention with their white coats.

As we'll see later, Stanley Milgram's 1963 experiment on obedience to authority proved what influence just a white lab coat contributes to people's behavior. What does that say about the thought process of people when a white coat can so drastically change behavior for the worst? Maybe congress should ban white lab coats! No, knowing how those psychos are, congress would more likely adopt the lab coat as a uniform. Instead of the black man-dress, judges could also use the lab coat. What would the results be if the experimenters wore the black dress?

It's been observed that people will not give up a false model (paradigm) of the world, even when they know it's false, until there's another alternative that appears at least as successful:

> "These hint what our later examination of paradigm rejection will disclose more fully: once it has achieved the status of paradigm, a scientific theory is declared invalid only if an alternative candidate is available to take its place...The decision to reject one paradigm is always simultaneously the

119

decision to accept another, and the judgment leading to that decision involves the comparison of both paradigms with nature *and* with each other." *The Structure of Scientific Revolutions*, 3rd Ed., Thomas Kuhn, page 77.

This is partly because the model has served the man/woman to a degree and has been proven to be a working model; at least one working to an acceptable degree. It doesn't work one hundred percent of the time, but it does seem to get the job done. It's also just a well-established habit.

Looking at the government model (coercive support and brutal violence is fine when done by people labeled government), there is evidence the model/paradigm partly works e.g., there are courts, jails, unemployment checks and of course, the most important of all, lots of roads. Despite all the death and destruction that come only as a result of having governments, it's apparently worth it to have roads to travel on. Talk about deleting a major portion of your experience from consciousness! Yes, people are walking around fast asleep, not really conscious at all.

The two most admired ancient societies, Greece and Rome, would be considered successful by most. Especially Rome since they had all those roads. They are so revered in Western culture it requires no proof here as it is so obvious.

Those models appeared to work, each for hundreds of years and there were many innovations during that time. But in what manner did they work and from what perspective? What did the people in Carthage think about Roman society? What about the average Roman?

What about the cost to benefit ratio? Like today, were the roads worth the price of constant warfare and a foundation of slavery? Eventually, even the Romans ran out of foreign "terrorists" to preemptively strike, plunder and enslave. They could only preemptively attack Carthage so many times.

Did they even provide a stable society? I would argue any society based on slavery and constant war is anything but stable. There were decades of civil wars in Rome, in addition to the foreign wars and rebellions. I have always been amazed at how such societies were still able to feed themselves. Someone was being productive, but it certainly wasn't the governments and armies.

Look at American society from 1789 through 1865; it was based on two forms of slavery, overt and covert. Overtly in the form of non-white slaves and covertly through the government concept (i.e., citizenship, taxation and regulation). The center of the Industrial Revolution was based on slavery and provided a working model. Even white folks weren't spared at least temporary slavery when it came to the all-important roads. Who would have thought that white Americans were used as slaves to build roads. I guess such inconvenient truths were left out of the history books.

Just because they "worked" doesn't mean they are good models. Because a model seems to work doesn't mean it should be used. Rape may result in pregnancy; but that doesn't mean it's a good way to start a family.

Another example is China. It appears to work right? The communist government even owns a pretty good share of the US government. Is it something we want to emulate?

There are other models though. We already have a working, proven model, we all use it every day, and we all use it, even politicians use it part of the time:

> Human interaction should be voluntary – the initiation
> of force is wrong.

We can prove even politicians know it's wrong to initiate force (including those in China, Iran etc.) because they have laws punishing those who do initiate force and injure others. To justify their existence, they pass laws making the very ways they do business illegal when not done with the government label.

What we are working towards is breaking the generalization this paradigm does not apply to the facts when we change the labels i.e., public and private. The paradigm shift is: The initiation of force is wrong regardless of the man/woman doing it.

> **Paradigm**: Killing people to protect them is good/moral
> when done by people called government, and only
> government can protect people and build roads.

There is great difficultly teaching this because as Kuhn pointed out, "But science students accept theories on the authority of teacher and text, not because of evidence." *Revolutions*, page 80.

Sounds like he's describing a cult of personality, doesn't it? And he's referring to science students; how much more applicable when talking about students in general? Now add the compulsory basis of education, and the swearing of allegiance every morning; you have kids learning theories and fictions based on authority, not evidence. This is nowhere more evident than with the government concept, and it is continuously taught until it becomes a habit, not an actual intellectual process.

That learning is backwards. The evidence, if ever introduced, must conform to the theory or opinion of the authority figure instead of the opinion being drawn from the facts. Examples of this can be seen every day in traffic court and with the IRS. The traffic court judge already has you guilty before you walk in the door, and everything he does must conform to that. That's why you get such ridiculous statements such as there can be a conflict of interest and still be a fair trial, even after they admit you can't get a fair trial when there is a conflict of interest.

We know they have you guilty before you walk in because they've told us. I've asked if the judge was under the impression the constitution and laws of the plaintiff applied to me, and without hesitation they have said yes. They have never met me before, they know nothing about me, but they are so certain their laws apply that they tolerate no challenge to their opinion.

Opinions are what count with bureaucrats. That's also why it's so easy to put them into a double bind. It's a sense of self-importance, a power over reality and others; they know how things are and no amount of evidence is going to change their sacred opinions.

Breaking this generalization is described by Kuhn, who quotes Herbert Butterfield:

> "One perceptive historian, viewing a classic case of a science's reorientation by paradigm change, recently described it as "picking up the other end of the stick," a process that involves "handling the same bundle of data as before, but placing them in a new system of relations with one another by giving them a different framework." *Revolutions*, page 85.

We're interested in just building on a very useful generalization we pick up as children: initiating force against others is wrong. If it's wrong for us as individuals, then it's wrong for all of us. But being conditioned to accept this contradictory model (government) for thousands of years, there is intense resistance to any change. We'll explore the contributing factors to this resistance in depth later.

We're only talking about not accepting violent, anti-social behavior regardless of any label attached to the perp. I've mentioned this before. All we're doing is changing the *manner* in which the services are paid, a manner consistent with the alleged end of government. So why such resistance?

This resistance is recognized in the Declaration of Independence of 1776:

> "...all experience hath shewn that mankind are more disposed to suffer, while evils are sufferable, than to right themselves by abolishing the forms to which they are accustomed."

Seems this particular behavioral flaw has not gone unnoticed by those who wish to farm mankind. Evidence shows it's exploited every day. Can't usually argue with the facts. Sad thing is, not only will people continue engaging in a system that causes tremendous damage, but like drug addicts they will *increase* their activity and often do so recklessly. Black Friday in the United States is a dismal example of this. Seems no amount of economic devastation can stop Americans from getting into further debt.

Science explains this as a "shopper's high." Dopamine, a neurotransmitter that helps control the pleasure part of our brains, is released, caused by anticipation of getting something, especially since it is immediate gratification and it is-for the time, for the moment-for nothing. Gregory Berns, a neuroscientist at Emory University wrote:

"Dopamine is all about the hunt and the anticipation. It is released as you conjure up in your mind the thought of this purchase and anticipate how it will look and how you will use it."

Certainly explains why the banking/debt system has been able to addict so many people. People are getting high by getting into debt.

Dopamine explains addiction to debt, but it doesn't explain it all. Would you continue drinking poison until someone brought you a glass of water? Maybe you would if you were in a room with a hundred other people and you thought they were also happily drinking poison.

Just looking at the job government has done proves they're a failure at their only professed purpose, which of course is nothing more than a very effective sales pitch. The facts also prove governments do the *opposite* of their purpose and are the worst threat to our life, liberty and property. But, because there is some evidence available, e.g., roads, prisons etc., people continue to cling to even a contradictory model. That model of the world must be providing the man/woman something they value more than another model.

Dopamine also explains why bureaucrats seem to enjoy attacking people. There's certainly a hunt and anticipation. Bureaucrats are predators; their job is all about hunting and stealing people's energy and time.

I can't tell you how many people I've spoken to that admit all human interactions should be voluntary but then can't accept the idea of society without government because they don't know exactly how the roads will be built etc.

This is the same as saying that although you agree with the basic principles of mathematics (i.e., addition, subtraction) you reject the entire field because you don't understand calculus and statistics.

So the world should be plagued with economic devastation, slavery and non-stop wars because a majority of people refuse to think for themselves?

Apparently.

Examples may be given with science-astronomy is a good example. Here, concepts evolved over centuries due to the complexity and lack of technology to verify the concept or paradigm. The great scientists' theories and concepts were not widely accepted by their contemporaries. But while concepts such as thermodynamics are complex, the concept of government certainly isn't. It's not rocket science, and no one needs to understand thermodynamics to understand the concept of government.

Because it's so easy to understand, those who have an interest in government work very hard to ensure most people are not taught why there is government and what a government is. While five-year-olds are taught in school to be good citizens, they're not taught what a citizen really is. And with good reason: to keep a scam going you can't have the victims asking questions and discussing such issues. The ruthless pursuit of truth is the enemy of statism, and therefore not permitted in school. That is why schools are controlled by governments.

The difficulty with learning new things *intellectually* lies in our conditioning, and *emotionally* in our investment in the concepts (learning by *experience* is always the more effective way to learn).

We are usually taught the story of Santa Claus when we are very young, and yet we universally drop such a belief as a child. We see a television show or see a parent dressed as Santa or we hear it from someone else. There's not too much pain involved because the same people who gave us presents will continue to give us presents. There isn't such a loss of emotional satisfaction that way. There would be if we found out there was no Santa and the gifts stopped also.

Contemporaries of men such as Kepler, just as people today, had, among other things, their professional reputation as authorities in their field to protect. The need to be right, to avoid the embarrassment of being incorrect, is apparently more powerful than learning the truth. This is especially ironic with those professing to be scientists. I've had self-professed empiricists tell me no amount of evidence could convince them of life after death of the body. Really? Again, perceptions and generalizations are more important than the facts.

The fear of not being right has different aspects, including the thoughts of losing all one has achieved.

The more we have invested in a belief system, the harder it is to break the belief. Does it make sense now why violent psychopaths force parents to put their children in their government schools? There's no need to get into explanations about how home schooled children are better educated than children forced to go to government schools. The issue to focus on is the coercion. If government schools provided a valuable service, there would be no need to force parents to send their children to them. That should end that discussion.

Consider this: the concepts in this book are far more popular than the concept of government. No one voluntarily supports government, but everyone with this book reads it voluntarily. As anarchists we have more actual supporters than all the governments in the world combined.

There is emotional and intellectual investment with conditioning. The intellectual feeds the emotional, the part that rules our behavior; the emotional part overrides our rational mind. Someone learns a particular "hidden" knowledge or gets schooling that the average man or woman doesn't possess feels superior to the unwashed masses. Doctors and attorneys are two examples that come to mind, although brain surgeons are entitled to feel superior to attorneys. Well, we're all entitled to feel superior to attorneys. People involved in the banking industry are the same way. If you want to see the wrath of someone in the banking business, just point out that banks don't make loans, it's just paper for paper, two fives for a ten.

I've seen first-hand the extreme emotional responses from attorneys when they realize I just played them, using their own laws and admissions against them. They can't stand it and act like children. Their image of being a god on a wooden throne four feet off the floor has been damaged in their mind; the unwashed masses may start to see them as less of an authority. More important, the attorney may start seeing himself as less of a god among men. Most narcissists do. That's quite an internal conflict brewing there, and his loyal subjects are watching; whom is the attorney going to lash out at? I'd prefer if it were the cop and his prosecutor buddy, but we all know who the target of his anger will usually be.

The emotional response is the result of numerous things going on internally such as I just mentioned. There is also the ego (false personality) damage because I played him and I didn't need a hundred thousand dollar doctorate degree to do it. That has to be humiliating. I know if there was someone I had nothing but disdain for and saw them as an idiot (this is how judges look at us...well, me anyway) and they owned me in front of people who respected me, I'd feel humiliated.

I think the old saying "He who represents himself has a fool for a client" was intended to keep people like us from humiliating judges. Attorneys have told me they wouldn't do what I do in court, not because it lacks merit, but because they don't want to enrage the judge. Many people I've helped have backed off from asking very effective questions in court out of fear of what they think the judge may do to them. I get emails all the time from people who are being attacked by bureaucrats and although they know how effective it is asking the judge whom he represents, they don't ask out of fear. And yes, it's a legitimate fear. There's no paranoia when going to a court!

There's also shame, a very powerful emotion and used very wisely by those who control us. You'll really ramp up the humiliation when you do this with a narcissist or full-blown psychopath. Their world is built on the fiction they are in control and are the best and brightest in any given room. I cover this in more depth in the chapter on damage control; suffice to say here: this explains why you can infuriate a judge by doing nothing more than referring to them by their first name. They instantly come unglued because with just a few words you've torn down their grandiose facade.

So, what to do when confronted with someone who destroys parts of your map of the world? Adults update their map, pick themselves up and move on. Children, and adults with the coping skills of a child, start screaming and attacking the messenger as a way of discrediting the messenger.

What is sad is the temper tantrum is not a substitute for the truth; it's only a way to maintain control over behavior. It's just a sign the individual is not getting his way; the world is not congruent with their perceptions of how the world should be. Instead of acting consistently with reality, they lash out to get everyone else to conform. It's a typical control freak who never learned the map is not the territory and never developed an adult personality, instead believing everyone should conform to their view of the world. I guess they missed that simple observation about the path of least resistance.

There are people who are impressed when a judge flies into a screaming rage and thinks he's honorable and that it's a rational way to have a discussion in court. I know because lawyers have watched me in court and they thought I was the foolish one. Here I ask if I'm presumed innocent of every element of the alleged crime, and the judge starts raging, turns red in the face, and I'm the one the lawyers laugh at and call an idiot. Maybe I'd get some respect from them if I went to court with a man-dress on and screamed like a child. Well, it's not as if I've ever craved respect from lawyers. I feel sad for those who do.

The problem with people supporting governments lies primarily in our conditioning and can be explained with well-established psychological principles and observations. We'll see it's our expectations that primarily dictate our responses. Those expectations shape our perceptions, and when you understand that, you'll understand how and why it is so easy to control people's behaviors, especially for those who control the media and education.

I mentioned earlier the emotional response people have when you show them the law governments are not here to protect them, "Police officers have no affirmative statutory duty to do anything." *Souza v. City of Antioch*, 62 Cal.Rptr.2d 909.

Why does this seem to automatically trigger an angry response, but saying 1+1 is 3 doesn't? Because it probably hit a nerve. They know it's true and feel helpless. Paralyzed by the truth, after all it's the law, they project that anger at me because they know I'm not the violent one; it's much safer to scream at me than to direct any anger or even non-compliance towards the men and women violently dominating them.

When we are taught about government and law as children, always remember the trauma when first forced to leave mommy and daddy and put into government schools for the day. I don't think the child even needs to be aware at the conscious level they are being forced away their parents.

We are taught in the United States that the police are "hometown heroes," that they are here to protect us, that they selflessly put their lives in danger to protect us. Police are elevated to a higher social status. They are valiantly portrayed in the media, and there are much harsher penalties for people who kill cops, as opposed to one of the unwashed masses like us. It's a caste system at work, and it's not necessary for it to be noticed at the conscious level. In fact, as we'll see later, this effect from a caste system will still manifest even when we are only pretending.

We are taught that the government, in a democracy, is us. We are the government; we put the cops in place to protect us and we pay their salaries and pensions. Forget that this flies in the face of observable reality: if the government were truly us, then support would not be compulsory. Pretty much all the lies about government can be shown by this one observation.

That is how the trauma creates and reinforces the bond to the abuser: the money is taken by force, always under threat of jail and guilt about paying our fair share, and then the abuser promises to protect, because no one else can. This is textbook trauma bonding explored in detail later. Remember how the Native Americans accused the Euro-trash of speaking with forked tongues?

And what about this abstraction "us"? It's the same as saying "we." It reminds me of Tonto: "What you mean *we* Kemosabi?" I remember

126

saying as a kid, "We? Are you speaking French or is there a mouse in your pocket?" Stop with this *we* crap.

This collective mindset is a form of mind control. It blinds you from the fact you and I are as individual men and women. It's a fiction that I'm part of an abstraction called "us" or "We the People."

We are always told we must have a small group of people violently dominating us or we'll sink into anarchy, mayhem and chaos. Only these psychopaths called government can protect us; in fact, the sky will fall without government to protect and lead us. Government cannot survive without taxes, we cannot survive without government:

> "But taxes are the life-blood of government, and their prompt and certain availability an imperious need." *Bull v. United States*, 295 U.S. 247; 55 S. Ct. 695; 79 L. Ed. 1421 (1935).

This idea is constantly reinforced. You'll get notices from tax agencies about all the good things done with taxes, e.g., infrastructure, social security, aid to Israel, tsunami relief, etc. You then have two political parties relentlessly arguing about what the booty should be used for: conservatives argue the booty should go to law enforcement and the military, and liberals argue it should be for welfare and other social programs.

We fall for this and start arguing with one of the sides, even campaigning for the lesser of the two evils so the booty will be spent wisely. We also vote, which again reinforces the bond caused by the trauma of being controlled, manipulated, lied to, threatened and robbed. It reinforces the idea that we are somehow connected to the abusers; after all, we voted for the president and congress.

Let's compare this frank admission from John Marshall, a supreme court attorney and famous Mason, to the *Bull* quote above:

> "That the power to tax involves the power to destroy;" *McCulloch v. Maryland*, 4 Wheat. (17 U.S.) 316, 4 L.Ed. 579 (1819).

> "But taxes are the life-blood of government, and their prompt and certain availability an imperious need." *Bull v. United States*, 295 U.S. 247, 259; 55 S. Ct. 695; 79 L. Ed. 1421 (1935).

Let me get this straight: the "life-blood of government" is the "power to destroy." Nice admission; always good to see the occasional honesty from a gang of madmen.

This is a very popular admission about the nature of government. It's one of a few times Marshall was stating the obvious and not spinning the truth. I was tempted to write that he used a little spin when he wrote "involves," but that is probably a matter of perception. Taxation, the forcible taking of property, also includes mind control or PR to make it more efficient. If we consider the PR as a way to destroy, then he was right on the money and maybe ahead of his time.

Can you imagine the pitch for government if they used these terms?

> *OK, stay with me, you're gonna love this, stay with me OK?*
> OK.
> *We have a service of protecting you, where you have no choice, and the way this service is provided involves the power to destroy you.*
> OK, wait...What?!
> *I said stay with me, okay?*

Consent of the governed? We consented to support these people with a means that also involves the power to destroy us? So these services are so valuable and so in demand they can only be provided by a power to destroy us? And we consented to this?! *Stay with me here.*

Amazingly, most people accept the "lesser-of-the-two-evils" standard. I heard a caller to a radio show in southern California say they were voting for the guy who they thought would hurt them less than the other guys. And that's exactly what that idea means. The politicians' purpose is to hurt you, and voting for the one likely to hurt you less is perceived as some sacred rite and privilege.

When you separate from that mindset and examine it, the only rational conclusion is that the whole premise is crazy. People know this from personal experience. They witnessed first-hand how congress and Obama passed a law making the buying of insurance compulsory despite overwhelming opposition. The average person seems to have nothing but well-deserved contempt for politicians, yet they continue to support them and cooperate.

And that's what is so incredible to watch. The solution is easy: non-violent, non-cooperation, make them irrelevant. Three hundred million people don't want compulsory insurance, and yet, despite having no respect whatsoever for these few hundred politicians, they still feel some kind of moral duty to obey them.

In this chapter we'll examine the powerful psychological elements at play. Why is there such an emotional bond to a group of psychopaths? Why the compulsion to just keep complying with these predators?

What affect does lying as a regular part of your job have on you? Constantly being deceptive has to affect you. Just the stress from having to constantly support the lies can wear on you and lead to substance abuse.

Look at lawyers-they are a good example of a profession where lying is a part of the job. (As they climb the political pecking order, the lies and damage inflicted get worse; the worse the damage inflicted, the more immunity they get). A president or prime minister can order the murder of thousands of people and instead of being put in prison, say that only "history" can judge them.

Lawyers are obligated to argue zealously on behalf of a client whether they believe the argument or not. Many lawyers have told me they were taught to argue both sides of a dispute while in law school. *DeShaney v. Winnebago County*, 489 U.S. 189 (1989) is one of those used.

This may be another reason why lawyers generally look upon non-lawyers with disdain when we are in court; we can actually argue or present what we believe. The facts tell me the judge is forcing me to answer the cop's complaint. The judge is not fair, impartial and independent, and I'm going to ask questions to expose that. I have no allegiance to their system.

Lawyers have to zealously argue in favor of things they do not personally agree with. What honest man or woman would do that? Yes, people lie for money every day, but lawyers are claiming to be aiding in the administration of justice. If you're stuck in a criminal proceeding with a lawyer assigned to assist you and you have a falling out, the assigned judge does not always let them leave. There are times when the lawyer is stuck and has to still defend and raise issues he/she may not agree with; they're being forced to by another lawyer. Judges will limit defenses, especially in drug war persecutions, so the lawyer may be stuck arguing points they don't believe in.

What happens is your core beliefs have to be set aside for a good portion of your life. It has to become a habit after a while. In other situations it's easier to take a position based on perceived social pressure, rather than what you believe or what the facts tell you. Your beliefs take a back seat to what is expedient in whatever situation you are in. This is also why I have always said a lawyer's reality is dictated by what other lawyers say.

Imagine trying to get a job and during the interview they ask you if you can lie convincingly. That would be a big clue: in order to work there, you have to leave your core beliefs, as well as your spine, at the door. If the police were honest when they did the application process, they would ask:

- Are you willing to kick the snot out of someone who questions your authority?
- **Are your communication skills so weak you need to taser people to get them to cooperate with you**?
- Do you have a need to control others?
- **Do you see other people as your slaves to do what you want, the moment you order them**?

Become a cop today!

Lawyers can justify this any way they want-that everyone is entitled to a defense etc. But I think justice, or whatever we're doing, should always be about the truth, a search for the facts. If someone is damaged, then those who caused the damage should make them whole. No immunity, just causation based on facts. Instead, it's about arguing and contention to keep money going into the system.

129

This is not just about lawyers. What about self-professed Christians who work for people making weapons of war, the tools of genocide? How do you square "Thou shalt not kill" with making bombs? But I'm just an accountant, and even if I don't work here, they're still going to make bombs. Yes, "Thou shalt not kill," unless of course other people will just do it anyway. Can we be surprised at the state of things today, why nothing seems to change? Regardless of silly elections, the *same policies* are carried out. It's the same today as it was two hundred years ago: the same process; the *same rationale* is always going to produce the same results, only today technology is better for carrying that out. In 1776, the mail was controlled by the psychopaths, today, the internet is controlled. It's always the same *process*, though sometimes with different content. As long as the process stays the same you'll get the same results, regardless of the content.

Each candidate believes and acts as if it's justified and moral to kill you to provide you their services. How could anything they do be any different from the last administration (regime)? When you start with violence, it's no surprise you continue getting more violence in the form of ObamaCare, indefinite detention, extraordinary rendition, institutional torture, drone strikes, etc.

The lawyers comprising the court system not only believe the same, but have been conditioned to zealously argue in favor of the psychopaths' laws regardless if they agree with them or not. As shown later, bureaucrats maintain a strict "It's not up to me to determine if it's right or wrong" policy. Being a bureaucrat is all about violence and letting other people dictate to you what is right and wrong.

Why else do you think judges and cops get so angry when you question them? The hierarchy maintains that what is right and wrong must come from those above you on the pecking order. This is played out every day, as even the written law only means what the lawyer with the robe on says it means.

You have a system infested with violent people with guns who are unable or unwilling to determine for themselves what is right and wrong. That's not the best combination. Any extant empathy or interest in the truth is going to be subordinate to that hierarchy. It's obviously habitual. Who is going to speak up? There's a reason there are only token whistleblower protections.

And it's not just lawyers who lie as part of their job; it's all bureaucrats and politicians. Cops are permitted to lie to get confessions. Those who tell lies not sanctioned by the code and procedure are called "Brady cops" after a court opinion called *Brady v. Maryland*, 373 U.S. 83 (1963), also *Strickler v. Greene*, 527 U. S. 263, 296 (1999), 514 U.S. 419.

So why do people passionately support government despite the fact they are admittedly not here for protection and commit horrendous criminal acts as a regular course of business? You show someone the law which states governments have no duty to protect and they argue governments are the only ones who can protect us. They usually follow up with undeniable logic, "You're a nut!" Keep this in mind when discussing why government is not necessary. Understanding why they think and feel the way they do will help them more in the long run than just arguing with them.

I spoke with a self-professed libertarian in Phoenix the night of the 2006 Arizona elections. We had been speaking about 9/11 and he said he could not accept the idea the American government would either plan and carry-out an attack on Americans, or know about it and let it happen. The idea of the American government (people coercing others to pay them) killing Americans was unacceptable. I said Americans kill Americans every day; isn't government just American men and women? Look at an arrest warrant. It authorizes the use of deadly force against an American in order to bring him or her into a certain building.

Consider the murders at Kent State in Ohio on Monday, 4 May 1970, or the Civil War where American governments slaughtered hundreds of thousands of Americans. Other examples are a law on the books for one hundred thirty-seven years, and the Utah War. In 1838, Lilburn Boggs, pretending to be the governor of the State of Missouri, issued an order to "exterminate" members of the Church of Jesus Christ, which included their children. This was considered to be law, and made it legal to kill members of that church. Buchanan's Blunder (The Utah War) was a dispute between Mormon settlers in Utah and the United States federal government, from 1857 to 1858,.

Civil war is another example of government going after its own people. People forget, because it's purposely avoided in the history books, that Americans kill other Americans by the boatload all the time, even during the War for Independence from 1775-1783. I have to admit I was ignorant of this obvious fact for many years; that war was not just between the Americans and the British. There were plenty of Americans who sided with the British, the Loyalist and Tories. The Tories fought the Whigs in a bloody civil war. There were atrocities on both sides.

Then, just as now, there was massive "collateral damage" to non-combatants by both American and British soldiers. The idea that men and women who coerce others to pay them would not also kill their victims is irrational at best. You have to deliberately ignore the facts right before your eyes; it's self-delusion.

You hear radio show hosts every day ranting and complaining bitterly about government: the waste, the corruption, the lives destroyed. Yet mention abolishing government and that same passion will now be used to vehemently defend government. You'd think you had suggested killing and eating their children.

Why does the mention of abolishing government-something people complain about bitterly-elicit such an automatic, polarized response?

Despite tremendous evidence, people still revere and defend the government concept. And there's a scientific reason why, it's called trauma bonding or Stockholm Syndrome; and when we know and understand this, then we can begin to break the psychological grip the concept of government holds on us.

What brilliant propaganda: you convince people they are being protected (not controlled and robbed) and you have your victims attack anyone who tells them the truth.

The bond is further exploited with nonsense that we, the victims, are the government. That is, any abuse is being done to ourselves, any debt owed is to ourselves. You hear that about the pretended federal debt, that we actually owe it to ourselves. Yeah, if by "ourselves" you mean the owners of the Federal Reserve and the Chinese psychopaths known as the Chinese Communist Party.

Admitting that government is a tragic mistake would require some humility and that humility just isn't easy to come by. It's much easier to just sit back and allow it to keep happening.

Just ask the average person to prove there's a state or that they're a Citizen, and the response is almost always emotional. They'll call you crazy and suggest you're on drugs. If the existence of states and citizens is so easily proven, then why not step to the plate and take a few moments to present the evidence?

Someone posted my article *"Is the United States a Christian Nation?"* on a biblical forum. Other forum members made personal attacks against the poster and me. This is a response:

> "Dude, listen to yourself! Are you high?!? I'm pretty sure that the U.S of A is a nation. For example, you have a national sport. How could you possibly have a national sport if you're not a nation?"

Nice reasoning: having a national sport means there is a nation. I guess there was no nation until there was a national sport? That's the solution for the problems in the Middle East: the Palestinians just need to start a baseball league.

It didn't matter that I presented a logical position with verifiable facts; I have to be "high" to even suggest there is no "nation."

Let's look into the personality flaws of politicians and bureaucrats and we'll see why they're attracted to jobs involving violent domination with no personal responsibility. Below is a medical description of the average politician and bureaucrat:

> "**Antisocial Personality** People with an antisocial personality (previously called psychopathic or sociopathic personality), most of whom are male, show callous disregard for the rights and feelings of others. They exploit others for material gain or personal gratification (unlike narcissistic people who think they are better than others). Characteristically, such people act out their conflicts impulsively and irresponsibly. They tolerate frustration poorly, and sometimes they are hostile and violent. Despite the problems or harm they cause others by their anti-social behaviors, they typically don't feel remorse or guilt. Rather, they glibly rationalize their

132

behavior or blame it on others. Dishonesty and deceit permeate their relationships. Frustration and punishment rarely cause them to modify their behaviors." *Merck Manual of Medical Information*, Home Edition, page 427.

These are the personality traits associated with aggressive narcissism (I like to just use the word psychopath). Try not to think of cops and politicians when you read the list:

- Glibness/superficial charm
- Grandiose sense of self-worth
- Pathological lying
- Cunning/manipulative
- Lack of remorse or guilt
- Emotionally shallow
- Callous/lack of empathy
- Failure to accept responsibility for own actions

These personality flaws describe almost every single traffic court judge I've ever encountered. I've gotten thousands of reports from people telling me the same thing. Those judges who don't scream in a fit of anger still lied without a hint of shame and didn't think there was anything wrong with violently dominating others.

Critics of mine know this is true. It's why they say you'll go to jail if you ask a judge whom he represents. Anyone who has gone to court knows from personal experience judges are psychopaths. They are not authorities, they are criminals. And they are very protective of their perceived authority.

Impersonating a police officer is a pretty serious crime, but it's not a crime to impersonate a plumber...What's the rationale? I say it's the radical psychological effect seeing a police uniform has on a person and what the victims are willing to do for a perceived authority. And therein lies the distinction between pretended authorities and real authorities, in a legitimate sense. A plumber is an authority on plumbing. They're experts on how plumbing works, how to troubleshoot and how to fix plumbing problems. The distinction being the plumber is not someone who is perceived to be a man who controls us and gives us orders.

Cops are certainly not authorities on providing protection to the people, even though they bust into *thousands* of American homes every year, armed with machine guns. When they're really needed-such as with the Columbine massacre in 1999–they do this: hide outside until after the shooters have killed themselves. (The grave yard scene at the end of the movie *Drowning Mona* more accurately shows how cops really respond to dangerous situations.)

Don't buy the excuse they didn't want to endanger the kids; those drug warriors don't ever seem to be concerned about anyone's safety when they think people may be growing certain types of plants in their

133

homes. Maybe they would have rushed in had an anonymous caller reported to the police the shooters were carrying a few ounces of pot.

So here is the difference: a real authority has a voluntary relationship with us; we seek them out for their expertise, and we're free to accept it or not, whereas a political authority is just a flimsy cover for violence. It requires no consent, and the relationship is anything but voluntary. It seems as though an authority is just a political word for master or slave owner. There is an undeniable intent and motive to control the life of another when we're talking about political authority. A real authority, say someone who is an expert in physics, is not trying to control our behavior. I think the word authority should go the same way as anarchy: reworked and synonymous with owner and psychopath.

Political authority is a willingness to threaten and inflict violence to get people to act the way you want them to. After all, Mao Zedong spoke the truth a few times, "Political power grows out of the barrel of a gun." And just as true, "Politics is war without bloodshed, while war is politics with bloodshed."

So when someone claims to be an authority, he does not intend on asking your permission for anything. He/she is either unable or unwilling to treat you as an equal; they will bark orders fully expecting you to obey. And why do people obey such authority? Habit only partly explains it. I think it's mostly from fear, and that fear has multiple facets; which may tend to support and reinforce the initial fear of retaliation. As we'll see below, the fear may not be in regards to the tyrant's violence, but from the victim's own misjudgment on how his/her peers will respond.

Now that's tragic: people may be more afraid of being judged by friends and family than retaliation by governments. These people don't seem to have any personal convictions apart from "what will others think?"

Max Skousen wrote about people worshipping the "god of what others will think." He knew what he was talking about. It's probably the most popular god being worshipped out there, and is responsible for most of the horrors being committed today. That's a god even atheists can get behind and worship!

We're usually dead wrong about how others really judge us. They probably agree with us, but they're also making judgments about how the crowd is going to judge them; we can't underestimate the power of social pressure.

But psychopaths certainly don't underestimate the power of social pressure; they know how to manipulate others. Lying is second nature to them. They have to cover up their true purpose and motives. Telling people you are going to be their owner generally doesn't go over well, so the psychopath lies and convinces his victim that he is there to protect them.

But all those conflicting messages are causing problems. *But for* these conflicting messages there could be no governments. Without governments, there could be no large-scale wars and economic devastation.

134

The problems confronting the people of the world are not necessarily individual men and women, it's the *beliefs* held by the people of the world. Those beliefs influence people whose actions enable other people, called governments, to do what they do. Our actions are based primarily on our programming, our beliefs. They seem perfectly natural because it's largely an unconscious process.

Significantly, we are very often greatly mistaken in our assumptions what others believe. The mistaken belief we can read other people's minds is a major psychological impediment to change.

We all make models of the world; it's how we interact with the real world. But we only use maps, mere representations. Alfred Korzybski wrote, "the map is not the territory," in 1931 and his work was influential on many, including the creators of NLP, neuro-linguistic programming, Richard Bandler and John Grinder:

> "The most pervasive paradox of the human condition which we see is that the processes which allow us to survive, grow, change, and experience joy are the same processes which allow us to maintain **an impoverished model of the world** - our ability to manipulate - symbols, that is, to create - models. So the processes which allow us to accomplish the most extraordinary and unique human activities are the same processes which block our further growth if we **commit the error of mistaking the model for the reality**. We can identify three general mechanisms by which we do this: Generalization, Deletion, and Distortion." *The Structure of Magic*, Vol. 1, Richard Bandler and John Grinder, page 14 (emphasis mine).

We can see how these maps are really just generalizations; every generalization will either delete or distort our perception of the territory. Anyone who has ever spoken with a tax agent will experience firsthand someone mistaking the map for the territory; they actually believe or act as if their opinions are real-not a mere representation of reality or their perception, but reality itself. To a tax agent, there is no distinction. This is why they tend to be so adamant about the veracity of their opinion that you're a taxpayer, and they usually cannot admit to the possibility of being incorrect. Their model of the world is they are always correct and we're the ones who make mistakes.

I've had tax agents insist my client being a taxpayer is an issue of fact, not a legal opinion. When asked to prove the client is a taxpayer using just those facts and no citations to the law, they get very upset and start yelling.

When you call someone's bluff and they didn't realize it was a bluff, they tend to get upset. Some of you may need to experience this for yourself to understand just how real bureaucrats think their opinions are. Call a tax agent and see for yourself. I've got plenty examples on my website from tax agents who insist their perceptions are real. They believe there are states, taxpayers and taxable income. They are unable to distinguish between the abstract and the concrete.

I had a tax lawyer with the California franchise tax board tell me the application of law was an issue of fact, not opinion. She insisted "Appellant is a Taxpayer that has Taxable Income" was a statement of fact, not an opinion. It's tough to stay professional and focused when someone is trying to put this garbage over on you. I asked if the application of the law involved making an opinion and she said no, it was a statement of fact. I asked what facts do you rely on the law is applicable, and she just insisted it was a fact the law was applicable. But, beyond your say-so, what facts do you rely on? She could not answer; there are no facts. It's always just the say-so of a politician.

There's even a formal name for this in psychology: it's called *reification*. Reification is where opinions-abstract concepts-are treated as real things. The whole of politics can be summed up as **forced reification**. We're forced to act as if abstract political ideas are real (e.g., nations, cities, states, citizens, presidents, jurisdiction, etc.) If we don't, then politicians ramp up the violence until we do comply.

This is also described as:

> "There is an error; but it is merely the accidental error of mistaking the abstract for the concrete. It is an example of what I will call the 'Fallacy of Misplaced Concreteness'." *Science and the Modern World*, Alfred North Whitehead, page 51.

It's been long recognized as a fallacy, yet this fallacious way of thinking/behaving forms the structure of our society. We maintain lots of fictions as if they're real. Some fictions are generally beneficial and some not; sometimes we're aware of the fictions. Many times people are willing to kill us to maintain them. The effects of these fictions (misperceived concreteness) exist regardless of our consciousness of their fictional nature.

When you question someone who is treating abstractions as real, you'll get very defensive, though non-responsive, answers. I got this from a Ms. Garret with the IRS on 2 July 2012 when I asked about facts a client was a taxpayer with taxable income:

> "I don't have to discuss the facts I rely on!"

Oh, but you are allowed to hide them from me? Most adults, and certainly anyone older than seven, will recognize the agent's statement as a dodge. That's why they need guns, "Under all that paperwork is a gun."

The history of Europe is a record of what a small number of psychopaths were willing to do to maintain mass reifications; fictions that kept them at the top of the food chain. The history of Rome is no different-it's essentially a history of the most powerful psychopaths.

I like how Bateson puts it:

> "First, it is appropriate to indicate the matter of Theory of Logical Types; the theory asserts that no class can, in formal logical or mathematical discourse, be a member of itself; that a class of classes cannot be one of the classes which are its

members' that a name is not the thing named; that "John Bateson" is the class of which that boy is the unique member; and so forth. These assertions may seem trivial and even obvious, but we shall see later that it is not at all unusual for the theorists of behavioral science to commit errors which are precisely analogous to the error of classifying the name with the thing named—**eating the menu case instead of the dinner**—an error of *logical typing*." *Steps to an Ecology of Mind*, Gregory Bateson, page 205 (bold emphasis mine, italics in original).

And that's what statists and government apologists do; they eat the menu instead of the dinner. They insist their abstractions are real and any challenge is automatically frivolous. Cops will kill peaceful people to maintain their fictions.

Here's a sick irony: bureaucrats in black robes threaten people with psychological exams for having the nerve to question the bureaucrat's reification. Someone I've worked with was threatened with having her infant taken from her because she questioned whether an *undisclosed* complaint presented a valid cause of action. This lawyer actually stated he doubted she was a good parent because she questioned whether there was a cause of action. I think we can agree the one who needs the examination is the violent lawyer.

But it's precisely this reification that's so important for creating the context necessary to farm people with minimum violence. This causes people to not only submit to the control, but to also embrace it and defend it. The social pressure from the other farm animals makes resistance to the control almost impossible. We see this played out every day where there is news where one of the cattle stands up and does not comply. While the psychopaths attack the one who takes a stand, the media and public jump on the bandwagon and attack also. The public will blame the victim.

This is why there's so much wordsmithing in politics. For centuries, Latin was used because, as a dead language, the words were not subject to incessant redefining. Not anymore. Politicians just redefine words to mean what they want, and then act as if their mere words are magically converted to something physical and tangible. But interpretation itself is a pass for application; it's just distraction from the fact the opinions of politicians and lawyers apply to no one. It helps when they pay people-men and women who are willing to kill others-to also act as if their political abstractions are concrete. They're willing to kill you because they're not aware they are killing for an abstract concept and don't see the schizophrenic nature of their behavior:

> "**schizophrenia**...A mental disorder, not necessarily an impairment of intelligence, characterized by **hallucinations, indifference**, and **delusions of omnipotence** and **persecution**. Not necessarily insanity constituting a defense in an action for divorce. 24 Am J2d Div & S § 409." *Ballentine's Law Dictionary*, page 1142 (emphasis mine).

137

"Hallucinations, indifference, and delusions of omnipotence"-sounds pretty much like almost every cop, judge and tax agent I've ever dealt with in my life. The facts make a very strong case we live in a schizophrenic world by design. The structure of our societies is built on a foundation of violence, slavery, and schizophrenia. Who can seriously argue our world is not based on fictions kept in place by threats of violence? Look at the evidence, it proves beyond doubt this is true. Below is a common and conflicting message:

We're here to protect you–Pay or we'll put you in jail.

I already went through the most common examples of reification, (e.g., citizen, state) and how they influence and cause certain behavior. Jurisdiction is one of the worst examples. People willing to act as cops are an absolutely essential element to human farming; they are the main ones enabling politicians to control millions of other people.

Cops are men and women willing to kill people who don't stop their car fast enough. I'm not making this up, we all know this is true. It's why we stop when those lights come on. This psychopathic behavior is the direct result *caused* by their beliefs, because they believe:

1. The victim is a citizen within the state–reification/hallucination
2. The victim is subject to his control/jurisdiction–indifference/lack of empathy
3. The cop has a right to strict, unquestioning obedience–delusion of omnipotence
4. The victim's disobedience is a personal offense to the cop–delusion of persecution

It's mass reification, *causing* indifference. Indifference then causes feelings/thoughts of superiority, and, in extreme cases, omnipotence that leads inevitably to delusions of persecution. Just think of Stalin's purges or any Roman emperors killing of a family member who may inherit the throne. Though I hardly read the entire work, Hume's *The History of England* makes a pretty good case for not having government, though he doesn't say it directly. Just the history of violence around the English "Crown" and hereditary succession would make Albert "Mad Hatter" Anastasia vomit in horror.

And yes, I can prove the belief to unquestioning obedience element. The lawyers called the Indiana Supreme Court again held there is no right to resist a police officer. Even if the cop is committing a crime against you, you have no right to resist. They claim that, somehow, knowing you can resist cops committing crimes will *cause* an increase in violence against cops. Evidence of this increased violence? None. But you should know already; facts are not important to lawyers.

How many times have you heard politicians and government apologists insisting that bad laws and illegal orders from bureaucrats

138

should be complied with until they are changed? I think it's an accurate assumption most people do not like the IRS and paying taxes. Most people I've had contact with think it's best to comply and work to get the law changed, or get an illegal order struck down by the courts. How's that been working out for you?

There's an unmistakable pattern we'll see here, and it's put into action and directly *caused* by the government concept. What other commonly held belief will cause people to kill their own kids and siblings? This is the pattern causing such violence:

- Reification/hallucinations-
- Indifference/lack of empathy-
- Delusions of omnipotence-
- Delusions of persecution-"us and *them*" attitude
- Violent domination with no responsibility
- Violence - willingness to kill peaceful people

Keep this in mind when we're examining the psychological studies and experiments later in this chapter. They are a common theme and hinge on reification. The government concept is reification; it's dependent on people accepting abstract concepts as real. This sets a horrible chain of events into motion even when everyone is only pretending. What else can you expect when you start with a fiction? *But for* the concept of jurisdiction, no man would be able to stop an entire business with only scribbles on a piece of paper.

The problem is when abstract concepts are used to control behavior. Your internal alarms should go crazy with only the suggestion someone is trying to control your behavior, to limit your choices. This is especially important when those same people are discouraging any independent verification of the concepts being put forth-the old authority routine. Someone trying to limit your choices is trying to control your behavior. The political right-left shtick is one of the most common examples.

If I'm telling the truth, then I present facts and invite/encourage independent investigation and confirmation so you have more choices available to you to choose from, not less. I'm not looking to control your behavior. I'm not interested in being right, or getting people to believe me; just in having you to look at the facts and let the facts speak for themselves:

> Do the facts you can *observe* and confirm prove to you the people called government represent and protect you?

I doubt anyone can read that question without laughing; at least that nervous laugh when you hate to admit the truth. And there is a general apprehension to investigating these facts because politicians can and do retaliate; people know how violent politicians are.

I've had many people say they fear challenging the cult of the black robe because they dread being thrown in jail when the lawyer launches into a rage because he/she was questioned. What do you think will happen if you ask a traffic court judge whom he/she represents? Ask a tax agent who insists they have jurisdiction over you, "Excepting your say-so, what facts are there proving how and why you acquired this jurisdiction over me?"

I know first-hand there is a general policy to not speak to the media about how courts operate; many court employees have told me this directly. This seems to be fairly universal as I've been told this by court employees in Australia, Canada, and England. Why would anyone who claims to openly administer justice refuse all inquiry into how they work? Let the facts speak for themselves:

1. Judges claim to be administering justice-
2. Unwritten policy to never speak about how the courts function.

The above facts can be easily verified by anyone. Some court administrators have claimed there has to be judicial independence, but that doesn't explain why there's a policy to never answer questions about how the courts function. Answering questions about general court procedure in no way takes away from any alleged independence. The same goes for the nonsense about not speaking about ongoing cases; the police say that too. The facts prove they speak about ongoing cases all the time. It's also misdirection, because I've called about general court procedures.

The problem–and the evidence bears this out–is that judges know there's a complete disconnect between what the law requires and what they do in practice: the policy does not match the practice. They don't want to ever have their own words used against them by their victims. An example is where John Webb, a prosecutor in Keene, New Hampshire, wrote a response to my paperwork and claimed I did not have standing to complain because I did not allege any personal injury. Sound familiar? Now his own paperwork can be used against him.

This disconnect is why they refuse any confrontation dealing with it when I'm outside their building. They don't have any immediate violence at their disposal to avoid its discussion. The use of violence in person keeps the perception in place that he/she is some kind of authority figure– crazy, yes, but an authority nonetheless. If I'm on the phone with a lawyer in Melbourne, Australia, there's nothing the lawyer can do to stop the questioning except hang up the phone. Big deal–anyone can hang up on me; it's in no way exclusive to narcissists acting as governments. Getting hung up on is almost a trademark at this point anyway.

His threats are meaningless without any way to carry them out. That's the nice thing about using the phone to investigate–all these psychopaths can do is cry like babies. I've even told them when they ask why I don't come down to the court, "Because I'm out of range of your guns, that's why." I tell them while I've done it in person many times, it's just too dangerous and I don't get any answers anyway.

This is also the case with trials when judges refuse to give grounds for their decisions. The evidence strongly suggests this refusal is to make it very difficult, if not impossible, to embarrass the same lawyer later. If the lawyer gave specific grounds for denying a motion to dismiss, such as claiming standing doesn't require an injury pled, then this frivolous ruling could be used against him later.

Let's say you wanted to sue that same judge for misconduct. You file a complaint and can attach his own order as an exhibit in anticipation of his motion to dismiss. Why stop there? You could file against whomever you wanted for anything; there is no requirement for standing in his court, so file against the guy pretending to be governor.

It's why they tend to suggest you do some legal research. It's polite misdirection:

Pay no attention to the man in the black robe, only look at what they write in those law books.

I tell them I know what the law says. I'm interested in talking about how the judges are acting in court—the disconnect between the law and practice. Facts have no place in the courts...but schizophrenic, conflicting messages do!

Because the psychopath's map of the world includes a generalization they are never wrong (evidence of this is: *any challenge* is automatically labeled frivolous and gibberish by them). When they're in situations where this generalization is seriously challenged, they become flustered and fearful; they don't have the coping skills, as their world view doesn't permit opposing views. Being wrong, even this one time, affects their precious generalization. If they're wrong that I'm a taxpayer, then what else are they wrong about? If someone has a well-ingrained model or paradigm, then how could they have any coping skills dealing with a situation that seems to violate their model?

Without adult coping skills, they tend to quickly revert to the behavior of a child: they get angry and start yelling when put into a double-bind situation—a double-bind being where they're confronted with their conflicting generalizations. While government apologists have claimed the questions are silly (they're not), that does not change the fact the judge is acting like a child.

Gregory Bateson and others have written about the distress schizophrenics feel when put into such a double bind. This distress is not limited to alleged schizophrenics. I would say most people are going to be very uncomfortable being put into a double bind, especially in public. It must be pretty distressing for a judge to be in a double bind in front of a packed courtroom and they cannot talk their way out of it. They have a pretty flimsy facade to maintain.

Bateson wrote that such double binds may cause schizophrenic behavior:

"That is, there is never "a message" singly, but in actual communication always two or more related messages, of

141

different levels and often conveyed by different channels—voice, tone, movement, context, and so on. These messages may be widely incongruent and thus exert very different and conflicting influences." *A Note on the Double Bind—1962*, Gregory Bateson, Don D. Jackson, Jay Haley, John H. Weakland, page 155.

An example of this was presented in *Adventures* regarding how governments do business. The PR is they are protecting life, liberty and property, but the service is provided in direct contravention of that because support is coerced. How could the people of such a society not exhibit schizophrenic behaviors?

Just as a child does not have to be able to articulate incongruent communication for it to cause a change in behavior, neither does the average person have to consciously notice the incongruence. It will affect their behavior whether they're aware of it or not.

If people wanted governments or the services they claim to provide, they would not be forcing themselves to pay. After all, we're all told governments are us. Where are the facts to prove this? You can claim the people can get rid of government whenever they want, but that is just as misleading as claiming we are the government. There is no group known as "We the People" as a real organized group; it's as much a fiction as states and nations. We are the government in the same way we are Al Capone's gang.

What's important to focus on is the *individual* man, woman and child when regarding the abolition of government. When we do so, we easily see that for the individual there is really not much we can do.

How crazy is the claim:

We are the government and we agreed to force ourselves to support it.

It's tough to make sense of that last sentence, and I can't believe I had to write it. Looks like good instructions for creating a malevolent schizophrenic, no?

The claim doesn't make sense, because I didn't delete the "to force ourselves" phrase, the part of the real message politicians and bureaucrats leave out. Normal people cannot make sense of that sentence because it is blatantly contradictory. But even if that part is intentionally left out, on some level, people know the message is incongruent because taxation (support for governments) is coerced. We all know we individually have no choice in whether there is a government or not.

Look at political elections, a good example of a double bind: damned if you do, damned if you don't. Two false choices are given, and even if there is one who seems to be different than the rest, such as Ron Paul, there is a constant media barrage to convince you they are unelectable.

We learn as babies that if we cried, we generally got our way. Anyone who has been to a traffic court and questioned a judge has seen this same behavior. If the judge is not getting their way and needs to maintain their model, in their world the way to do that is to get angry: "You're not doing what I want. You must not have heard me, so I'll raise my voice."

Judges, like any bureaucrat, believe they must be in control of others. That's the nature of the job. If you present a challenge to this generalization, such as asking for evidence proving jurisdiction, they will get very angry with you if you persist in trying to get an answer. Judges must maintain a perception they're a fair, impartial decision maker, and that's just not possible if he has to answer my question. If they can't keep control and maintain the fiction, they get angry or frustrated. He's a baby who isn't getting what he wants. Remember, the irresponsible control of others is the primary motivation people have in being a bureaucrat and getting involved in politics. They don't want that to be made public.

A very important study on perceptions was done in 1949 with altered playing cards. It is a great example of what happens when facts don't match perceptions. People were shown and asked to identity playing cards. Some of the cards were altered from typical cards. For example, a spade card was red instead of black, and a heart card black instead of red. The results are not surprising to anyone who has tried to convince a statist that government should be abolished:

> "Our major conclusion is simply a reaffirmation of the general statement that **perceptual organization is powerfully determined by** *expectations* **built upon past commerce with the environment. When such expectations are violated by the environment, the perceiver's behavior can be described as** *resistance* **to the recognition of the unexpected or incongruous**. The resistance manifests itself in subtle and complex but nevertheless distinguishable perceptual responses. Among the perceptual processes which implement this resistance are (1) the dominance of one principle of organization which prevents the appearance of incongruity and (2) a form of "partial assimilation to expectancy" which we have called compromise. When these responses fail and when correct recognition does not occur, what results may best be described as perceptual disruption. Correct recognition itself results when inappropriate expectancies are discarded after failure of confirmation." *On the Perception of Incongruity: A Paradigm*, Jerome S. Bruner and Leo Postman (1949) Harvard University p. 222-223 (emphasis mine)

Those familiar with NLP would disagree with the resistance label, though most voluntaryists have seen this resistance to observable facts when we discuss the violent nature of politicians. It might be more accurate to say there may be a mental inability to accept the facts right before their eyes. Not unlike with classic Stockholm Syndrome, there may actually be an inability to process the facts.

My position is that *but for* the government concept, people would be able to process the facts right in front of them: psychopaths are coercing payment, and they are willing to kill us under the guise of protecting us. The government concept works to blind people to these facts.

A very perceptive observation was made by P.D. Ouespensky when asked, Why are relationships difficult? He is reported as saying:

> "They are so difficult because two entirely invented people, two entirely pretence people, try to come together." *Psychological Commentaries on the Teaching of Gurdjieff and Ouspensky*, Maurice Nicholl, Vol 2 page 734.

The pretense is built on our maps of world, our many perceptions. These perceptions are shaped by our prior conditioning. These include roles and attitudes we are taught and model in childhood. My wife insists I'm playing a role when I'm on the radio, on either my show or as a guest on someone else's show. Of course, I believe I'm just being myself and don't think I act any differently. I've accused others of that, such as the big syndicated talk shows, because what they say and seem to believe just doesn't convince me they are genuine.

As we'll see with the Stanford Prison Experiment, it's not necessary that people are aware that the map is not the territory–that their entire personality may be fake, or "entirely invented"–for the fictions to cause behavioral problems. And there is evidence proving quite a bit of one's personality is based on lies or public relations. These include citizens, residents, cities, states, countries, presidents, mayors and, of course, jurisdiction and authority.

It's not easy to confront the truth that our personalities, who we think we are-may all be a pretense, all lies. And that is the effectiveness of this mind control. It's perception management. Generalizations and perceptions govern our expectations, and those expectations will generally override the facts before us.

Don't believe the facts right in front of your eyes; no the perception that the United States is the greatest nation on earth is more important. Look at torture. Despite all the pictures, victim accounts and even an official CIA torture manual, there are those who still claim the US government doesn't torture:

> "We are America! I don't give a rat's ass if it helps! We Are America! We do not f***ing torture! We don't do it!" Shepard Smith, *Fox News*
> http://www.youtube.com/watch?v=IG2VF4a0LWs

Torture by those acting as government is such a common practice, even the attorneys in robes, United States federal judges, don't bother trying to spin the facts:

> "It is now **common knowledge** that in the early to mid-1980s Chicago Police Commander Jon Burge and many officers working under him **regularly engaged in the physical abuse and torture of prisoners** to extract confessions. Both internal

police accounts and numerous lawsuits and appeals brought by suspects alleging such abuse substantiate that those beatings and other means of torture occurred as an **established practice**, not just on an isolated basis." *U.S. ex rel. Maxwell v. Gilmore*, 37 F. Supp.2d 1078 (Emphasis mine).

Search the internet for police torture and you'll be busy for months. Yet, despite the mountains of empirical, verifiable evidence, the voices in the media are: "We are America! I don't give a rat's ass if it helps! We Are America! We do not f***ing torture!" Sorry Shep, the evidence is so loud I can't hear a word you're saying. Even when typical American republicans I've spoken to begrudgingly accept the fact American governments do torture, they downplay it and justify it by claiming the "enemy" does much worse.

Blindness to the facts is everywhere. Millions of people believe they are Citizens and there are nations, states, and governments. That's all demonstrably false after any honest investigation into the facts.

Look at the example I gave regarding my friend who is a judge. We all maintain fictions, and those fictions will dictate what role we play in certain contexts. Our fictions/perceptions also dictate our attitudes. Why do people continue paying politicians to torture, plunder and wage aggressive wars? There seems to be no limit to the number of scandals and crimes politicians can commit; the people who enable them will not stand up as adults and stop cooperating with them.

While it's easy to see how phony politicians are, most people are reluctant to see their own phoniness. Why do anything about the phony politician when we may be just as fake?

Because their invented personalities and fictions dictate that, to be a good American or Canadian, etc., one must be law-abiding even if the politicians are murderous barbarians. The pretense that one must work within the system and wait two to four years to vote in the lesser-of-the-two-evils contest only works to keep the system grinding away its victims. It's complete nonsense, but very effective public relations.

That is one of the reasons the control is so hard to break–the fictions make up a significant part of one's perceived (false) personality. There are people claiming to be republicans who cannot tell you why. I've asked many. All they seem to be able to muster are personal attacks against "those democrats" and how they are ruining this great country. Ask someone claiming to be a democrat and they'll tell you pretty much the opposite. They cannot tell you in one sentence why they belong to a particular party, there are no core governing principles.

If they do mention liberty, then it's only the same lip service they've heard from politicians since they were kids. So no matter what evidence you present statists (though most tend to avoid the term as it is correctly seen as the equivalent to authoritarian) any facts that contradict their perceptions will be dismissed or spun away.

That is a common tactic for you to watch for when dealing with an authoritarian. They will always dismiss the facts in favor of their opinions. I was publicly accused of never having helped anyone with felonies. I provided the evidence, a link to an archived show where Randy from Idaho called in to report he went to a preliminary hearing for a felony and got the complaint kicked out on his own without a lawyer to help. When confronted with this evidence, my accuser dismissed it, stating it was not an example from Texas. Even liberty activists can move the goal posts.

Sometimes it's the accuser's perceptions blinding them to the facts, or sometimes they are just being a jerk trying to save face publicly. Either way, it is only a ploy to disregard the facts.

Bruner and Postman discuss four ways people deal with incongruities:

1. Dominance;
2. Compromise;
3. Disruption; and
4. Recognition.

Dominance is the primary response of bureaucrats. Dominance is described by Bruner & Postman as "a 'perceptual denial' of the incongruous elements in the stimulus pattern." (page 213).

A good example is a talk I had with an IRS agent named Laura Gomez in the Austin, Texas office.

She admits she knows nothing about witnesses and evidence. So I point out the obvious: all she has is her legal opinion regarding the code, that she is engaged in blind enforcement. Predictably, she doesn't take it well,

"It is not blind enforcement, sir!"

I remind her she admittedly doesn't know anything about witnesses and evidence, that besides her opinion she has nothing. I ask her to explain how that's not blind enforcement. Ms. Gomez, even more upset now, ends the call by hanging up on us. Instead of trying to explain, she did the standard IRS response: she hung up the phone. Facts are very stubborn, but I guess they don't survive the end of the phone call.

Another example is a telephone "hearing" with the IRS. I ask if my client is entitled to a fair hearing, and agent Fineman said yes. I ask if my client can get a fair trial if there is a conflict of interest, and he said no. I asked whom he represents, and he immediately got upset and said he works for the IRS, but is independent and there is no conflict of interest.

I tell him I did not allege there was a conflict of interest, I'm just asking questions about it, and ask him if he works for the IRS, the same agency making claims against my client. He says yes, he works for the same agency. So I ask, "Can you please explain how you can work for the same agency and it not be a conflict of interest?"

Instead of answering, he launches into a tirade aboutCongress passing laws, he's doing his job, he has authority, and we should take it up with Congress. I point out that none of that explains how he can work for the same agency and be independent. Of course he refuses to discuss the matter and threatens to end the pretended hearing.

What's most important is the *expectation*, not the facts. (That's also the basis of lots of humor.) That's why it's important to ask bureaucrats if they maintain an objective standard of proof. We're separating the expectation from the evidence, and putting more weight into what the facts tell us, as opposed to the expectation or prejudgment. This usually causes a less-than-professional response. I believe it's because they are so arrogant from being in control, higher on the political pecking order, and they don't like to be challenged. And make no mistake, asking them if they maintain an objective standard of proof is a challenge to the way they operate; it really cuts through their facade of legitimacy and they can't stand it.

When your world is based on perceptions/opinions only, you don't want anyone bringing up anything as frivolous as being objective. Facts? Facts are for anti-Americans and other tinfoil hat-wearing terrorists.

Do you hold an objective standard of proof?
Why do you hate America so much, Marc?
Good point. How much should I pay you?

And this response is not limited to only one group of people, such as bureaucrats. This is true even of atheists who claim empirical evidence governs their beliefs. A few atheists have been candid enough to tell me no amount of evidence could convince them of the survival of consciousness after the death of the body.

Another example is a common atheist belief that all religious people are incapable of *any* rational thought. They happily ignore evidence such as Isaac Newton and Philo T. Farnsworth, both religious men of science. Instead of being more accurate, that all people hold both rational and irrational beliefs, they take the irrational all-or-nothing view, "We think religious beliefs are wholly irrational; therefore, if you are religious, you are incapable of any rational thought." Again, the perception rules over the evidence.

It's the same *process* as the religious people they criticize, just different *content*.

Getting back to the study; **Compromise** is described as

"...one in which the resultant perception embodies elements of both the expected attribute and the attribute provided by stimulation. Compromise reactions are, of course, limited to certain types of stimulus situations where a "perceptual middle ground" exists between the expectancy and the stimulus contradicting the expectancy." Bruner & Postman, page 215.

A common example of this is when you speak with someone who agrees it's wrong to use violence to provide services, and then they argue: "What about the roads?" or "Yeah, I agree with you if it only involves small numbers of people, but when you're dealing with lots of people, voluntary won't work."

147

So when we reach an arbitrary number of people, as determined by you, we need to become psychopaths or put them in charge? That's the only way? Sounds like a great plan. 2000+ years of constant warfare hasn't convinced you otherwise yet? Yes, psychopathic control over everyone really is the best way to build roads!

I usually ask why mutual consent and respect for autonomy won't work over large areas, and the problem is, many people cannot think of large areas without the political concepts, "Anarchy is fine for a small area like a city, but not a whole country." They can't easily separate geographic North America from the political concepts of Canada, Mexico and the United States.

It should be obvious why mixing two contradictory concepts will cause a problem for someone. Even when you point out that there are no countries and nations, they fail to see how decentralized everything would be in a voluntary society. I'm sure we'll hear people saying: "Oh no, we have to work together and cooperate!?" How primitive.

Disruption is "a gross failure of the subject to organize the perceptual field at a level of efficiency usually associated with a given viewing condition." (Bruner & Postman, page 218). This basically means the person cannot make sense of the incongruent information they are presented with. It's so outside the content of their expectations, they cannot resolve the conflict. They cannot look at simple facts and identify them.

I've seen this many times where a bureaucrat will admit they can't communicate with me. If you've listened to my calls with tax agents, you'll notice a connection with the following reaction from a participant in Bruner & Postman's study:

> "I can't make the suit out, whatever it is. It didn't even look like a card that time. I don't know what color it is now or whether it's a spade or heart. I'm not even sure now what a spade looks like! My God!"

While this is extreme when dealing with playing cards, it's very typical when a bureaucrat is confronted with the facts. Because the facts tend to conflict with their expectations, they cannot identify in any meaningful way with the facts before them. Go back and read the quote again from Shepard Smith; watch the video to really see this in action.

This is why bureaucrats, when confronted with undeniable truth there is no evidence to support their opinions, rant about their authority, as if that's a substitute for facts. It's amazingly consistent, crosses imaginary political lines, and immediately precedes the slamming down of the phone or threats of contempt.

Of course, sticking their heads in the sand is another method they use; they just refuse to discuss the matter.

I can't tell you how many times I've asked a bureaucrat what facts they rely on proving they have jurisdiction, or that my client's a taxpayer, and they tell me they don't understand what I'm saying. While I allow that some are just being difficult and trying to deflect the attention away from themselves, a lot of them seem genuine; they just don't know about things like evidence because it's not a part of their job.

I had one tell me the decision to attack my client was their procedure. Alright; is it based on facts or is it arbitrary? They stutter a bit and say they don't understand why I'm asking for facts; it's their procedure.

The significance of the Bruner & Postman study was showing the importance our expectations play in how we respond to others. This is essential in understanding why the government concept is so damaging and the resistance people exhibit to change. It's a scientific study showing that people cling more to their maps of the world than to evidence right in front of them. Many can't even process facts incongruent with their expectations; the facts must conform to the opinion, instead of the opinion conforming to the facts. Call into a mainstream radio show and suggest the means of government is opposed to their stated purpose and see what happens. If they understand what you're talking about, then you'll probably be dropped quickly.

Mainstream talk radio and television shows are not about truth; they're about keeping the sponsors happy and taking sides on the latest political news. Each side attacks the other for the purpose of getting people engaged with the system. It serves to reinforce perceptions that governments are absolutely necessary for our very survival.

These expectations, carefully instilled from an early age, together with fear, are the cause of so much death and destruction in the world. When we understand this, it will come as no surprise why the average man/woman, especially those in the media, exhibit extreme hostility to observable facts showing governments are just men and women violently controlling others. In fact, Bandler & Grinder have repeatedly stated:

> "In NLP we have a principle that says "There is no resistance; there are only incompetent [communicators]" I mean that literally. I do not believe there is resistance…There's no resistance if you utilize every response…To be an effective communicator, all you have to do is respond appropriately to whatever spontaneously happens." *TRANCE-formations*, Richard Bandler & John Grinder, page 172.

Knowing this, we can work on improving our own communication skills to deal more effectively with people acting as governments. It's why I say we must meet the bureaucrat at their map of the world; there has to be overlap so we can have a rational discussion. They live by delusions of authority, so we need to accept that and figure out how to *utilize* that to get the attack stopped.

We ask if the agent has the authority to stop an attack, and if not, we need to speak to the one who does. If they have the authority to stop an attack, then it logically follows there are attacks that are improper. It naturally leads to what the grounds are to stop an attack. We're focused on his perceived authority to stop an attack; there is no resistance if we stay within his/her map of the world.

What comes to mind immediately is compulsory education. This is the main institution indoctrinating us as children to be good citizens and subject to the state. We're not taught or encouraged to be responsible, autonomous adults, but instead to be unquestioning law-abiding citizens. They are not the same thing, not even close. Being law abiding only means submission to the whims of politicians without any personal discretion. We're not to have our own principles of right and wrong, things we learn usually before we are six, but to dismiss that in favor of how politicians want us to behave.

Instead of governing ourselves by basic principles such as "Do no harm," it's replaced by a generalization, "Is this legal?" So instead of not harming others, you get the attitude that everything is justified if it's legal, such as dumping toxic waste into a river. Why worry about dumping chemicals into a river in India when it's legal to dump a certain amount? Add immunity from lawsuit into the mix, and anyone with half a brain can see there will be disasters. The Bhopal disaster is one of many.

With **do no harm** there's certainty, whereas with legal/illegal there is very little certainty because what is legal today can be illegal tomorrow, depending on how the lawyers feel that day. The dangerous part of the generalization is that we must not rely on ourselves, but defer to politicians, pretended authorities.

Uncertainty's ugly companion is usually fear. Fear always tends to be right there when we're uncertain, almost by design by the owners of society. Why would our owners want things to be clear? No, the generalizations are usually vague, except for the threats of violence for disobedience–those are clear.

These expectations or generalizations can be changed or modified. One way is to challenge one generalization with another one someone holds. When an atheist insists religious people are incapable of rational thought, mention Newton. The facts conflict with the stereotype. Another example of this happened when I spoke with an IRS agent on the phone. The agent said, "Everyone who receives money is taxpayer and has to file a return." So assuming she would be offended by certain stereotypes, I responded with, "Yeah, and all Sicilians like me are in the Mafia and the Irish are all drunks." This did the trick; she had to reconcile conflicting generalizations. She understood how erroneous generalizations/stereotypes could be. She then had no problem admitting she was not qualified to determine my client was a taxpayer. Her map of the world changed enough to permit it.

Another generalization held by tax agents is the mere statement you are a taxpayer is evidence you actually are a taxpayer. That's serious reification there. I spoke to an agent in Ogden, Utah, and who, like the agent in Winnipeg (Wendi Ornyiak), told me when the IRS says you are a taxpayer, that's evidence you're a taxpayer. I asked, "So it comes down to 'because you said so?'" And you thought evidence was part of the program.

The corollary generalization is any disagreement with the government is frivolous. We can break this generalization somewhat just by asking, "Is the opinion I'm a taxpayer irrefutable?" They also think they provide due process with their administrative hearings, so if their opinions were irrefutable, that would moot their hearings and court proceedings. Also, if they've already agreed they have authority to abate an assessment, it logically follows assessments are not always accurate.

We're all maintaining conflicting generalizations and will go about our day as usual if no one calls them into question. By asking an IRS agent if their opinions are irrefutable, we're putting the agent into a double bind. This is typically described as emotionally distressing and it's easily understood why. We're seriously challenging someone's perception of the world, so it's no surprise judges and tax agents get upset. These are the two generalizations creating the double bind:

1. Any disagreement with the opinion/presumption one is a taxpayer is frivolous.
2. IRS opinions/presumptions are not irrefutable

If people have problems identifying playing cards because they are incongruent with their expectations, then how much more difficult is it for a government agent to make sense of incongruent facts? Their families depend on political lies; they're deeply invested in them. I've done this for years with tax agents; there are plenty of examples of emotional distress when they are put into this double bind.

Another one is asking, "Since all taxation is compulsory, is there any evidence governments have any voluntary support?"

This is an epic double bind and really requires some actual thought by the bureaucrat or politician. There's no way out of this one, there's no spin. They desperately need to keep up the perception governments are by consent, but when you confront them with this question, it always causes distress. It just isn't feasible to reconcile coerced payment with consent. Because of the instant distress, they won't even answer the question, which is a standard yes/no question. I haven't even asked for the evidence yet, and I've already established bad faith and concealment.

Another double bind with tax agents is when you ask if they have authority to abate an assessment. Because authority is so important, they will claim they have it, or direct me to the agent who does. If there is authority to abate, then there are grounds to abate, including an erroneous assessment. It follows that the opinions are not irrefutable. Why would an agent have authority to do the impossible?

In court this is done by using the judge's and prosecutor's nonsense against them. Examples are when a judge denies something on nothing more than his opinion, "That doesn't apply *here*!" and when they insist on taking the testimony of a cop they declared incompetent to testify.

Another is with a tax return. You ask if your voluntary signature is required for a valid return. They'll say yes. Then you ask if the signature is considered voluntary if done under threat of jail. JT gets the credit for this double-bind, as he is the first one I know of doing this with a jury summons.

I like it when a cop stops you and you ask if you're under arrest. He says no, so I answer, "So I'm free to go? Thanks." The cop will usually start getting upset and say no, I'm not free to go. "Well, then, am I under arrest or am I free to go?" Oh no, I'm losing control, let's say hello to Mr. Taser and his partner, Mr. Glock.

The PR usually conflicts with the actions, so it's usually easy to put the agent in a double bind.

There are so many examples of these conflicting messages, all one has to do is look at the public relations and compare it with the facts. If people want others to provide services, such as protection, then what does that have to do with controlling the person? But this is how governments operate, it's admitted openly:

> "From the beginning of our constitutional system *control over the person* at the place of his domicile and his *duty there*, common to all citizens, to contribute to the support of government have been deemed to afford an adequate constitutional basis for imposing on him a tax on the use and enjoyment of rights in intangibles measured by their value." *Curry v. McCanless*, 307 U.S. 357, 366 (emphasis added).

Isn't it incredible how they talk about the citizen's duty, while governments have no corresponding duty? Don't get me wrong, such opinions are unnecessary; we can see for ourselves the way governments interact with us.

But people turn a blind eye to it. Despite governments offering no reason for having to control people in order to protect them, people just accept the conflicting messages, probably figuring since others are not openly questioning it that it must be okay. The violence is deleted from the generalization people have about government. It's always a part of the reality–the real world experience people have with those acting as a government–but this particular part is almost uniformly deleted from the model.

I know this is true from experience. There's the lawyer working for the Franchise Tax Board in California who insisted when she, the government, forces people to do something, it's not threat, duress and coercion. She argued that threat, duress and coercion are not threat, duress and coercion when *she* does it. When asked to explain how it was different factually, she was predictably unable to do so. She still insisted it was more than just the word government added, but couldn't explain why because her model of the world did not permit it. It was not even a possibility as that part of her experience has been consistently deleted.

It's understandable why, as with most people, the violence is always deleted from the generalization: it would conflict with our other models. We learn as children it's wrong to initiate force against others, if only because we don't want it done to ourselves. You cannot reconcile the means with the end: if government is supposed to be about protecting life, liberty and property, then it must respect that and be voluntary. If really by consent, then support would not be coerced. So the violence is conveniently deleted from the equation.

But the double binds are always there, a constant barrage hitting us every day; it's non-stop. This doesn't have to be by design to have the disastrous effects described above:

> "double bind experiences must recur *ad nauseam*. The problem is to construct a model which will necessarily *cycle* to recreate these patterned sequences over and over again."
> *Ecology*, page 177 (Emphasis in original).

Not a problem for those who have a vested interest in the current structure of society. The model providing the incessant double binds is the government concept. The model presents people with conflicting messages *ad nauseam*, just look at typical political speeches, especially when politicians want votes. Examples are:

- You're free to travel: you can't travel without a license;
- You're free to earn a living: you can't trade without a license;
- You're free to get married: you can't marry without a license;
- You're free to educate your children: but only with permission from bureaucrats;
- Perfect religious toleration: no polygamy, no peyote sacrament;
- Governments are by consent: support (taxation) is compulsory;
- Theft is wrong: taxes (theft) are what we pay for civilized society;
- No one is above the law: absolute judicial immunity, executive privilege;
- You own your property: need permission for improvements;
- You have freedom of speech: as long as you're in a free speech zone;
- Slavery is bad: slavery is good to build roads, wage wars, and administer courts.

You get the point. This isn't a matter of whether we think building roads using slavery is moral or not; it's about the effects of constantly confronting people with contradictory messages. Whether it's moral or not, or ethical or not, is a matter of subjective opinion, but the effects *caused* by the conflicting information are observable facts. As far as it being moral, I'm reasonably certain that if faced with the choice of autonomy or slavery for *themselves*, bureaucrats would pick their personal autonomy every time. They just can't extend that to everyone else.

The effects of the double binds will in turn continually affect and intensify the effects of the other behaviors described below, such as the Stockholm Syndrome, peer pressure, groupthink, etc. Each will feed off the other. The results are seen every day where billions are controlled by millions. Look at elections: people keep participating instead of seeing how such cooperation only leads to more control, more wars, more destruction.

People seem to look at things in isolation, as if the war in Vietnam is not related to every other war the psychopaths called the US government have waged. It's the same playbook. Just as Bank of America laundering 378 billion for Mexican drug cartels is related to Fast and Furious and the Iran-Contra scandal.

They are all inter-related and connected to each other. It's how governments operate, and it's not based on any particular individual such as Blair, Bush or Gillard. It's the same model and it will always produce the same results.

These are the scientific/psychological reasons why mentioning the abolition of government elicits such strong emotional responses. Below, I'm going to put them all together. The first is the Stockholm Syndrome (or Helsinki Syndrome for us *Die Hard* fans). Keep the above in mind about expectations and models of the world as you read.

Many people are already familiar with this, though the average person doesn't put it together with the traumatic bond created by the psychopaths called government. Below are six common symptoms associated with Stockholm Syndrome quoted from Joseph M. Carver, Ph.D., a clinical psychologist in Ohio. All six are clearly seen with people who are not only conditioned to believe governments are legitimate, but also resist any suggestions government should be abolished:

1. "Positive feelings by the victim toward the abuser/controller"
2. "Negative feelings by the victim toward family, friends, or authorities trying to rescue/support them or win their release"
3. "Support of the abuser's reasons and behaviors"
4. "Positive feelings by the abuser toward the victim"
5. "Supportive behaviors by the victim, at times helping the abuser"
6. "Inability to engage in behaviors that may assist in their release or detachment"

I must point out these six symptoms are also present in people who see through the government hoax, though, as we'll see later, they cannot, or may not, openly admit it.

1. Governments (people) are controllers, as govern means control. As shown above, this is freely acknowledged in the law e.g., "control over the person" *Curry v. McCanless*, 307 U.S. 357, 366. They are certainly abusers, as all support is compulsory-pay or go to jail. Evidence of "positive feelings by the victim towards" the controller is easy to prove-it's called patriotism. Despite the abuse governments dish out, the victims remain patriotic and continue paying taxes and voting.

Even when politicians are driving society to economic ruin with controls and "quantitative easing," the masses continue cooperating. Despite 10%+ unemployment and political spending skyrocketing, the majority of people continue to provide their cooperation and support the old "my country, right or wrong" garbage. It's more accurate to say, "My politicians, right or wrong."

2. We can see negative feelings by the victims towards those of us pointing out that governments are the problem and should be abolished. Call into a mainstream radio show and suggest government should be abolished and you'll see this in action. Just suggest there should be no more coercing people to pay and watch what you thought were mature adults explode. You can suggest it casually to friends or family and get the same emotional reaction I've seen so many times.

If you know religious people, suggest ending compulsory support for government. You'll quickly see just how much love they have for their neighbor.

3. Support for the abuser's behaviors is seen every day and certainly in every election. Americans should remember the nonsense when Bill Clinton was being impeached: "respect the office, not the man" and similar platitudes. People continue to pay taxes even when the actions of that government violate the victim's deepest-held beliefs. Another example is when people look at some ostensible benefit of government, such as roads and libraries. Yes, kill thousands of people in Iraq, it's fine, just look at our library!

Another example when you mention support is compulsory is the "free-rider" excuse. People know taking property by force is wrong, but they rationalize it; they even sit on juries and convict someone like Larken Rose, who had the guts to stand up to the abusers. Twelve people agreed to put Larken in prison for the crime of not mailing a piece of paper.

It's mind-boggling how any professed Christian, Jew, or Muslim can justify any cooperation with governments. A core belief is supposed to be "Thou shalt not steal," and yet they continue to cooperate with governments, enabling them to steal on a global basis. Then such theft is used to wage non-stop wars all over the world. Well, those parts of the world not inhabited by rich white people.

4. Positive feelings are expressed by the abuser (government) in many ways towards the victims. You hear the PR the government governs by the consent of the governed, and does the will of the people. At least in the United States, in the tax return packets, you'll see statements and charts about all the wonderful services governments provide with the money stolen from the people. You'll also hear Canadian politicians rambling about how fantastic the healthcare system is.

5. The supportive behaviors by the victim, as stated, are paying taxes and voting. The victims not only enable their controllers, they actively cooperate. This includes getting a driver's license or complying with any bureaucratic whim, such as only accepting government credit in trade for commodities. People actually wait for and pay bureaucrats to get permission to make improvements on their own property. They even thank the petty tyrant if he gives them a permit to put a shed in their own backyard.

Another supportive behavior is teaching children it's a good thing to be a cop or a soldier. Parents raise their children to grow up to want to violently dominate and kill others; it's sickening when you think about it.

155

Granted, they don't put it in real terms such as, "Honey, when you grow up, you'll want to dominate other people and use a gun to get them to comply with your orders. Don't be a loser taking orders, be the one giving them."

6. Most people have an inability to stop supporting government. There's a paralyzing fear of not paying taxes or renouncing citizenship-a relationship that doesn't even exist. People will put others at risk by texting while driving, but not think twice about paying taxes, regardless of how much they complain about government waste or illegal wars.

I've spoken to plenty of people since releasing *Adventures in Legal Land* and have seen the fear in their faces when I suggest they stop cooperating with people called governments. The fear is from both internal and external forces; there is a real risk of death from peacefully not cooperating with politicians. The threats are pretty much everywhere we go, so being unable to stop supporting the abusers—people called governments-is very real and understandable. We do need to exercise sound judgment when deciding to engage in living without permission from the masters.

Always keep in mind that politicians do not ask us to comply with their whims, it's always an order backed by a threat of violence.

It's not only an issue of fear, but a practical issue. It really isn't possible to live in a community or society without supporting governments to some degree. Even for those who may not be fearful about withdrawing support, there is the reality that those called government have infected every aspect of our lives. Pretty much everything involves government to some degree.

All sales taxes support governments, and trading with any business that is licensed supports the psychopaths. It is argued that we're free to leave the plantation anytime we want. *Really?* And with what exactly? You have to use government-permitted money or you're a domestic terrorist, and you need government permission with a passport and other ID. Then you need the permission of the other group of psychopaths to stay at your travel destination.

Most sports are intertwined with governments-from taxes, regulations, and the building of stadiums. Education is almost completely dominated by governments. How much scientific research is done privately without any government grants and no licenses? I hate the thought of someone like Neil DeGrasse Tyson being a bureaucrat on the public dole. He hosts a show on PBS and is the director of the Hayden Planetarium, a government-owned business. Does this influence his perceptions? Well, he supports NASA, so the evidence is there.

Philip Zimbardo and Stanley Milgram were professors, Zimbardo at Stanford and Milgram at Yale. Now we can speculate about the Yale and Stanford connections and the funding, but consider the fact someone has what is perceived as a prestigious career; are they going to start challenging the very system paying for their lifestyle?

It has always fascinated me that Zimbardo never, to my knowledge, ever applied what he learned from his prison experiment to the concept of government. If a schmuck from Long Island like me could see it right away, how could Zimbardo not?

So even those people who profess to be governed by what is observable and provable-a "worldview…free of supernatural and mystical elements"-such as the Brights-may not question and investigate the government concept. There's a technical phrase for this: not crapping where you eat. Is a tenured professor going to publicly claim the government concept is immoral-that governments, which he/she is a part of, are just killers, thieves and liars? If they do they won't have a job for long.

All we can do is minimize our support of governments; it touches all our lives. Depending on the degree it can be crippling. It can be like the despair Ray had at the beginning of *Ghostbusters*:

> "Personally, I liked the university. They gave us money and facilities; we didn't have to produce anything! You've never been out of college! You don't know what it's like out there! I've worked in the private sector. They expect results."

Dr. Carver states **four conditions** are the **foundation for developing Stockholm Syndrome**: "These four situations can be found in hostage, severe abuse, and abusive relationships:

> * The presence of a perceived threat to one's physical or psychological survival and the belief that the abuser would carry out the threat.
> * The presence of a perceived small kindness from the abuser to the victim.
> * Isolation from perspectives other than those of the abuser.
> * The perceived inability to escape the situation."

All four symptoms are present in the government-citizen relationship.

The first is easy: pay us (taxes) or go to jail. Even when people admit there's no factual basis for paying taxes, they pay just to avoid the threatened violence of politicians and bureaucrats. You also see increased tax prosecutions and audits in the first few months of the year as a way to encourage "voluntary compliance."

While taxes are taken year-round, there is generally one time of the year for the perceived act of kindness: the tax refund. It's amazing that despite all the complaining about paying taxes and government waste, people see the refund as a benefit, a treat from the benevolent slave masters. People even fool themselves into thinking the withholding is a good thing because they see it as a savings they would have already spent. Some people really do see an upside to armed robbery.

The threats are not limited to only overt taxation; there are the ever-present threats from local regulators, and laws and ordinances too voluminous to mention. Almost everything requires permission, and every command is backed by a gun.

The isolation from other perspectives covers some more ground. First, there is the obvious compulsory education. All a child tends to get

157

are the approved materials-even in private schools-and in most home schooling the subject matter is big on government legitimacy. In the US, the supremacy of the American system over all others is constantly stressed.

It's always taught that anarchy, an absence of government (rulers), is chaos and mayhem, that anarchists are people who want to violently overthrow governments. This is further compounded by laws such as the Alien and Sedition Acts in the United States. The Sedition Act of 1918 made it a crime to "willfully utter, print, write or publish any disloyal, profane, scurrilous, or abusive language about the form of government of the United States." Disloyal language about the form of government? I guess it's a good thing sedition requires there be states and citizens, or some would call my radio show and this book sedition.

When you make it a crime to speak or write anything "disloyal" about the government of the United States, that's certainly a great effort to isolate the victims of government from other perspectives.

Of course, sedition laws are not limited to the United States. I haven't verified it, but we can be fairly certain every government has such laws. In Australia, there is:

(a) to bring the Sovereign into hatred or contempt;
(d) to excite disaffection against the Government or Constitution of the Commonwealth or against either House of the Parliament of the Commonwealth;
(f) to excite Her Majesty's subjects to attempt to procure the alteration, otherwise than by lawful means, of any matter in the Commonwealth established by law of the Commonwealth; or
(g) to promote feelings of ill-will and hostility between different classes of Her Majesty's subjects so as to endanger the peace, order or good government of the Commonwealth;"

Look at subsections (d) and (f) in particular. Talking about the true nature of government, pointing out the coercive support and admissions governments have no duty to protect, is considered a crime. I think they call that "chilling" free speech. It's only logical a gang of criminals would not want their victims to know the truth; they may be disaffected, start thinking for themselves and stop cooperating in their own enslavement. As we've seen, it's very effective to change someone's expectations and perceptions, so the psychopaths make it a crime to investigate and ask critical questions about the government concept.

Knowing, or just thinking, you'll be ostracized by the masses for being a thinker/anarchist is another way people are kept from other perspectives. It doesn't help when it's considered a crime to campaign against the paying of taxes. The motive for sedition laws is not relevant for an indictment; the intent is obviously to "chill" any open investigation and discussion on the true violent nature of governments.

This is why even some liberty activists will say, "I'm not advocating the violation of any laws." *Really*? That's not an activist who's going to be effective at any kind of real social change.

There's no place to go to escape governments, so it does seem that we are unable to escape the situation. All you are doing if you move is to swap one set of abusers/controllers for another. If you move from New York to Arizona as I did, you will likely suffer less institutionalized abuse, but you'll still suffer abuse. Instead of being beaten six days a week, you're only beaten four.

We even have sayings supporting this criminalization of critical thought such as: "You can't beat city hall" and "death and taxes." These can only help make the situation seem inescapable. Under United States law, you can be hounded for taxes for ten years after leaving.

Just as I've mentioned before, Dr. Carver also talks about the investment in the abusive relationship that helps determine the **strength of the bond the abuse creates,** depending on the amount of the investment. The six types of investment are:

* Emotional Investment
* Social Investment
* Family Investments
* Financial Investment
* Lifestyle Investment
* Intimacy Investment

Governments work very hard to foster an emotional investment in the concept of government. A lot of these are cultural anchors we've spoken about before on the show, such as founding myths, the Washington monument, the flag and national anthems. We all know someone who claims the national anthem makes them cry.

We're continually reminded of the "sacrifice" others made for our freedom, those who came before us and gave their lives so we can live in freedom. We have Veterans' Day and Memorial Day in the US and Rememberance Day and Armistice Day in England, Canada, Australia and New Zealand.

Social investment includes compulsory education. Think about how much time and energy is expended with involvement in government: radio, newspapers, television and elections. Most of the news you hear is about politics; every major news and talk show is devoted almost entirely to government. Ninety percent of the syndicated talk radio shows are about politics. If you're involved in collegiate and professional sports, there is always government involvement; governments run all the colleges and steal the money to pay for most sports stadiums.

How much of your own life has been spent talking about government and who to vote for and what laws should be passed? Government is an ever-present part of our daily lives.

Except in extremely limited circumstances, travel involves government to some degree. Getting a driver's license is a rite of passage and major social event in a teenager's life. But if we must have permission to travel, there is no free movement.

Family investments include the military. It's an old story: I went into the military because dad was in with his brothers, grandpa was in the

Corps, etc., Lt. Dan from *Forrest Gump* is an example. Combine that with a family member who was killed "in the line of duty," and you have some serious family/emotional investment. It's not easy to reject the false premise of government if a close family member was killed or missing in action. It's not easy accepting your father or brother died in vain for a narcissist in Washington, D.C. or London.

Financially, governments really have us; it's pretty much complete dependence. Gone are the days when there were privately minted gold and silver coins competing in the market. No, there is no real monetary system; we are forced to use a credit/debt system. In the United States, we must use the Federal Reserve Note. In Europe you're forced to use the Euro. The Federal Reserve Note isn't even a real note, as it is not redeemable for anything; it's just a piece of paper and ink.

Most of us pay some kind of taxes; we think the roads and school exist only because we "gave our fair share."

What part of your lifestyle is not invaded by government? It's all-pervasive. If you're a medical doctor, you had two decades of compulsory education in government schools. You may have had a government grant or loan to pay for it. You then have to maintain a license to be permitted to work. If you fish or hunt, you need to ask a bureaucrat for permission. You may own your business, but at the same time you ask permission to do so. You must trade only for government-enforced credit/debt and you'd better send your financial information the tax bureaucrats or you will go to jail and lose everything you worked for. Whatever your level of success, governments are involved to some degree.

This includes any kind of government-backed mortgage, most student loans and small business loans. Anything involving the credit system is government controlled.

Intimacy is not limited to only one-on-one personal relationships. There are plenty of examples where governments are involved in such relationships. A good one is the gay marriage issue.

If one wants to get married, then you must get permission first. As Dr. Carver points out, this includes *emotional* intimacy and the abuser using that emotional intimacy against the victim. This is usually done by other victims; if one of the victims talks about not paying taxes, the other victims attack them as un-American and tax cheats. This is explained by several psychological theories such as the "spiral of silence" put forth by Elisabeth Noelle-Neumann.

This theory holds that someone is less likely to speak out on an issue if they feel their position is at odds with what they think the majority of people think; there's a fear of negativity from the majority. I discuss this in greater detail later as it relates to the Asch Conformity Experiment.

There is usually no evidence of what the majority really thinks. What we can be certain about, though, is each of the majority does not want anyone aggressing against them; they agree with the non-aggression principle. Sadly, they don't express that beyond themselves and apply it to the concept of government.

We can only speculate on what the majority really believe because of the fear people have that their position may be different from the rest.

160

That's why it's so effective to stick to the non-aggression principle; we can always get some agreement, an overlap in our maps of the world. We can then work out from there.

The combination of abuse and kindness is also described as "trauma bonding." This is basis of Battered Wife Syndrome as well as Stockholm Syndrome which are really the same thing. "Svali", a survivor of "both ritual abuse and governmental mind control," wrote:

> "This is the traumatic underpinning of all cult programming that I have seen: a combination of abuse and kindness; terror and rescue; degradation and praise." *Trauma Bonding: The Pull to the Perpetrator* Oct 12, 2000 - © Svali http://www.shieldofaith.org/resources/library/article.asp?s=7&i=195

This is a constant theme with these government psychopaths. Look at what Oliver Wendell Holmes is famous for inadvertently admitting about the trauma-rescue of being robbed:

> "Taxes are what we pay for civilized society..." *Compania General de Tabacos de Filipinas v. Collector of Internal Revenue*, 275 U.S. 87, 100 (1927).

We rob you, but we protect you and no one else can. We lie, steal from you and control you in thousands of ways, but we build roads, libraries and sports stadiums. Yes, we steal your money before you get your check, but we gladly give some back if you'll file a return. Sacrifice your children to fight our wars and we'll pay for your education and give you a pension. It's amazing how Holmes equates a system of slavery with a civilized society. I guess it's a matter of perception: when you are the beneficiary of the system, things look civilized from your wooden throne.

Do you see it? Holmes admitted the terror-rescue of ritual abuse above; it doesn't matter if he and his associates are aware of it, the results are what are important:

> **Terror**: pay us or get shot or be put in jail;
> **Rescue**: governments protect us and build roads.

Governments and their apologists insist that if they don't steal from us and control every aspect of our lives, there'll be chaos, mayhem, human sacrifice, dogs and cats living together, mass hysteria, etc. We must submit ourselves to their irresponsible domination; they must abuse us to save us from abusing each other. There is the constant, never-ending theme of terror and rescue. It's also one ginormous double bind: we coerce you to protect you from coercion. Wasn't that the theme of *Monsters, Inc.*? "We scare because we care."

Can anyone seriously doubt there isn't trauma caused by governments (men and women) constantly stealing and abusing under the pretext of protecting us?

Here's an example from Canada. This is part of a form letter sent to someone I was helping; the tax agency sent him a form letter telling him to file a tax return. He sent a letter asking about witnesses and evidence he was required to file a tax return and he got another form letter back that had in part, the **terror** part first:

> "People are indeed prosecuted, convicted, and penalized for failure to file. They can be fined from $1000 to $25,000 for each offence, sentenced up to 12 months imprisonment..."

The very next paragraph had the **rescue/reward**:

> "From another *perspective*, it is important to remember that the taxes collected by the federal government are used to maintain Canada's infrastructure and to support Canada's social and benefit programs." (Emphasis mine)

They steal because they care. People tend to focus on the reward; that perspective then causes a problem processing the facts right in front of them, the threats of severe punishment for not paying. Focusing on the reward makes it easier to delude oneself and disassociate from the violent threats ever-present with these psychopaths. Living under constant threats is not healthy, and anyone who says otherwise is lying to protect his interests in the current hierarchy.

It really is quite amazing to speak to tax agents who seem to actually believe people consent to having others (governments) forcibly take their property and provide such programs. I love the blank stare you get when you mention that if people really did agree, then taxation wouldn't be compulsory. It's as if there is no conscious awareness that support is entirely coerced. From experience, most people who think governments are legitimate organizations refuse to accept that support is coerced. Perceptions rule over the evidence.

I mentioned support is compulsory to the tax agent who sent the above to my client, and she defended it by saying if she accepted services from a company and then didn't pay, she would expect collection. It didn't matter to her that payment was compulsory whether you wanted the service or not. She was doing her best to reconcile the facts with her model of the world. I don't think she would have convinced anyone.

While we must allow for the possibility there is a coincidence with the relentless terror-rescue, we cannot get away from the psychological damage from it. Whether by design or accident, the result is the same and that's all that matters here: cause and effect. Does A *cause* B? It seems obvious to me that even if initially by accident, the politicians have picked up on how effective it really is.

The fact politicians admit there is no duty to protect us is pretty strong evidence there is no coincidence. Someone interested in protecting

162

you will not coerce you to pay them. Does this really need to be pointed out? Are people so politically conditioned this needs to be continually brought up? Looking around, the answer is yes.

This bond is strengthened with very high-profile criminal cases, especially when a non-government-sponsored killer is convicted. It gives people the false impression the government is protecting them and the paradigm is a valid working model. Look at such examples as the Scott Peterson case or Ted Bundy. These give false justification for having governments, and you get emotional responses: Do you want people like Ted Bundy and Jeffery Dahmer out there? (The police actually gave Dahmer his last victim back to him after the child had escaped.) Even criminologists admit there are lots of times the capture of a serial killer is not due to police work, but due to mistakes made by the killers.

This is an attempt to guilt the person away from the evidence right in from of them. Governments have to punish some real crimes because if they didn't maintain a minimum appearance, then the masses would easily see through their ruse of protection. The people may even take the drastic measure of withdrawing support and stop paying taxes.

While Casey Anthony is prosecuted, the heads of Goldman Sachs and J.P. Morgan live the high life uninterrupted. Looking just at the numbers (of corpses), which group of psychopaths would you prefer to be among us?

A	B
Ted Bundy	Mao Zedong
Jeffery Dahmer	Adolf Hitler
John Gotti	Josef Stalin
Henry Lee Lucas	Harry Truman

It was interesting when I went to the Tempe city court and had to go through a security checkpoint. I asked, "Who the hell are you guys so afraid of?" The security guard, a former FBI agent, said, "You know, terrorists, anarchists." I had to ask him: how many wars in the last century were waged by anarchists? He got a blank look and I told him the obvious, "Oh that's right, *none*; they were all waged by republicans and democrats." And they're worried about anarchists-the non-violent ones; people who don't believe in rulers. Politicians always fear peaceful people who dare to think and question things because they are a threat to their jobs and pensions.

Before I present more psychological support, I want to quote Dr. Carver again on Stockholm Syndrome:

> "The combination of "Stockholm Syndrome" and "cognitive dissonance" produces a victim who firmly believes the relationship is not only acceptable, but also desperately needed for their survival. The victim feels they would mentally collapse if the relationship ended. In long-term relationships, the victims have invested everything and

163

placed "all their eggs in one basket". **The relationship now decides their level of self-esteem, self-worth, and emotional health.**" (Emphasis mine)

Please re-read the last sentence a few times. It doesn't matter what the intent is of those pretending to be governments, what's important is the context created, the nature of the relationship and the resulting trauma to the victims. If you listen to my interview on Coast to Coast with Ian Punnet, you'll vividly experience the behavior exhibited that Dr. Carver is describing. Just start talking about abolishing government to your friends and you'll see the same thing.

First Ian defends governments by saying he doesn't feel there is any infringement on his freedom. Presented with facts proving the opposite, Ian changes his tune and states he doesn't mind infringements on his liberty when it's to protect him and his property. He then makes personal attacks when I point out governments have openly admitted to not having any obligation to protect anyone. Instead of attacking the ones coercing him and his family, he attacks me. It's utter nonsense and he sounds like a battered wife defending the scumbag beating her every time he gets drunk. But he's got the affiliates and huge sponsors because he supports the current structure/hierarchy, which provides the sponsors the best markets.

This is more clearly demonstrated with Americans; the American identity is particularly strong. So strong that the mere suggestion to an American of expatriation will make them recoil in horror, as if you are somehow less a man/woman if not labeled American. Their identity and self-worth is tied directly to the idea of being American, regardless of the fact they possess none of the qualities typically characterized as American. What's important is the label and the sense they belong to this abstract group of people also labeled American.

The US Supreme Court, spinning attention away from the compulsory nature of taxation, talks about this master-slave relationship as the basis of the power to tax:

> "[t]he basis of the power to tax [power to destroy] was not and cannot be made dependent upon the situs of the property in all cases, it being in or out of the United States, nor was not and cannot be made dependent upon the domicile of the citizen, that being in or out of the United States, but upon **his relation** [terror-rescue] **as citizen to the United States and the relation of the latter to him as citizen.**" *Cook v. Tait*, 265 U.S. 47, 56 (1924) (emphasis mine).

Remember what Dr. Carver wrote about the abusive relationship above. Keep this aspect of the relationship in mind as we go through more of the psychological impact of the government concept and resulting structure.

Fear is the underlying emotion here, it's the single most important reason governments are still farming us today. The experiments done by the CIA and other military agencies on human behavior and mind control bear this out. The object and result of the government concept is to create an immobilizing fear in the victim to ensure an acceptable level of compliance.

Experiments done by psychopaths such as Orval Hobart Mowrer prove the anticipation of punishment was more powerful than the actual punishment. We've already seen how/why these *expectations* are so important to perceptions and then behaviors. It was found, through experiments with electric shock, that keeping a subject in a state of anticipation-not knowing when the pain would come-was more effective in controlling behavior than if the subject knew when the punishment was coming. When the pain did come, it was almost welcomed and the subject was somewhat relieved.

Keeping someone in a constant state of anxiety makes it easier to control them. You are controlling their expectations and thus controlling their behaviors. When you add in almost complete dependency on the one creating that state, you can see why the victim forms an attachment. You can also get a clear picture on why the fear immobilizes people. Their imaginary expectation of punishment is far more powerful than any real risk.

This is explained in the CIA manual KUBARK (http://www.gwu.edu/~nsarchiv/NSAEBB/NSAEBB122/) on how to break people and control them. It details the three D's used: debility, dependency, and dread. The CIA manual was written after studies were done to learn why the communists had been able to so effectively break prisoners of war and get them to cooperate and switch allegiances.

Maybe they just noticed what the government concept was already doing to people and just started applying the same techniques to each individual. Seems obvious on hindsight anyway.

I was in grade school in the late 70's. This was during the so-called "Cold War" and I remember the *constant* threat of nuclear war, mushroom clouds; basically the end of the world. It scared the crap out of me. We used to have drills where we'd have to get under our desk. Yeah, of course we questioned how that little desk was going to help us survive an attack. Maybe instead of Reagan's "Star Wars" system, they should have just built a huge desk to cover North America.

Don't you think it's a bit traumatic to have kids constantly reminded they could be annihilated at any moment? I'd say so; that kept me afraid even years later as I approached eighteen. The Shoreham, Long Island nuclear plant was shut down by then, but I still could not drive past it without an anchored feeling of dread.

Look at military conscription. Now they have the "Selective Service." If you go into a post office in the United States you'll see posters telling eighteen-year-old men to "Do the right thing" and register with the government. You sign up...or you go to jail. Aside from the obvious slavery/involuntary servitude, what about the trauma caused? Knowing

165

you have to register and will possibly be sent to kill or be killed by strangers somewhere that you've never heard of certainly can cause continued anxiety. At least it did for me.

These 3 D's: **debility, dependency,** and **dread,** have always been a part of the government concept, even if not by design. We see it with the Stanford Prison Experiment and the Milgram Experiment. What other intent is there when support is compulsory? The fact coercion is being used is direct evidence of intent to control behavior. Don't let your opinions/expectations take away from the facts. An honest investigation into the facts must start with as few prejudgments as possible.

The 3 D's have to be by design; it's used to get compliance from the victims. Those interested in voluntary cooperation and protecting people do not use coercion and the 3 D's.

You'll notice a constant with each of these three elements of the government concept: they each cause a weakening of our individuality; they do not empower the individual. Quite the opposite, they are geared towards de-individuation, lumping each individual in with an abstract concept called the state. There was de-individuation within thirty-six hours in the Stanford Prison Experiment. Each one used is an attack on individual autonomy.

Debility. Debility, from the Latin *debile,* means weak; it's also defined as a loss of strength. The government concept, if accepted, takes away from the importance of the individual. The group is more important. Even more important than the group are the psychopaths claiming to represent the group. They are the ones with the underground facilities ready for if and when they decide to blow up portions of the earth.

We can't marry without permission, we can't move about without permission, can't support ourselves without permission, etc. Practically everything we do depends on some degree of permission. We may not even trade without using government-approved mediums. If we don't use the Federal Reserve credit/debt system we are considered "domestic terrorists" even though there is no violence involved.

In the United States, children have their lemonade stands shut down and get fined $500. Yes, you need permission to sell lemonade in the Land of the Free and Home of the Brave. The land of opportunity, as long as you grease the right palms.

We constantly hear, "What can one man do," "You can't fight city hall," and "death and taxes." We're told change can only happen by participating in the political process, or don't take the law into your own hands. This is calculated to make us feel weak, that as just one man or woman we are not effective enough to help bring about any meaningful change. You'll notice sedition laws do not apply to peaceful protests and using the political system to bring about change. Of course not, neither one empowers the individual.

This happens even though we know it's nonsense; but that's the politically engineered expectation. There are so many examples of just one person helping bring about major change: Gandhi, Rosa Parks and Martin

166

Luther King, Jr. are just a few. Even the "Don't tase me bro!" and "Don't touch my junk" guys got tremendous media coverage. True, major change didn't come about from either of these guys, but they are an example of how anyone can make headlines.

We're not going to feel too strong and empowered when we have to ask permission for everything; you constantly feel like someone's bitch. It's no surprise a nickname for government is the "nanny state" because we're treated like children.   The concept of *parens patriae* ("**parens patriae**...The parent of the country." *Ballentine's Law Dictionary*, page 911), still exists today. For the United States, you have "Founding Fathers" and in other places the *pater patriae*, the father of the country or fatherland. Motherland is still used in places like England.

Being subject to another's control (jurisdiction) is the opposite of freedom and autonomy. The government concept, even the American one, is admittedly about control, "From the beginning of our constitutional system *control over the person* at the place of his domicile..." *Curry v. McCanless*, 307 U.S. 357, 366 (emphasis mine).

Being controlled causes debility in people. We always feel shackled, always feeling weak like a child having to ask permission from others who are usually inferior to us in ability. This is a real cause of anxiety and frustration. And tyrants don't care about protests:

> "Let them march all they want, as long as they continue to pay their taxes." Attributed to Alexander Haig.

We feel fear of what others will think because we misjudge how others think, and that fear makes us weaker. The resulting debility is exactly what the psychopaths want.   The victim may not like his enslavement, but he's too afraid to do anything about it.

Fear is one of the worst causes of debility, it immobilizes people. It creates a vicious circle within people as the debility is fueled by fear, which then causes more of a weakening/debility.

And reading the news just makes it worse. We read about the Amish being attacked and silver dealers going to jail while Wall Street crooks such as Goldman Sachs, Wachovia and JP Morgan get bailouts and small fines for their monstrous crimes. Wachovia bank was caught laundering 378 *billion* dollars for Mexican drug cartels and no one was prosecuted (who knows what they have not been caught doing?). Bernard von Nothaus sells silver to a willing market and is prosecuted and convicted.

It works this way, each a cause for the next:

- Perception of how others will judge us-
- causes fear, so we-
- knowingly adopt a false premise, and act as if we believe.

Now it makes sense why political democracy is hailed as a virtue, why politicians talk about the fifty-one percent they think support them.

167

Why use fear? Because politicians know fear motivates people; it causes them to do what they otherwise would not do, as shown by the Milgram experiment.

"Fear is the parent of cruelty." James Anthony Froude

Dependency. The debility is increased and made worse with dependency. The three D's are each interrelated and interdependent, each making the others stronger.

Again, we need permission to do just about everything. People are so afraid of the psychos called government that all they accept in trade (for now) at most stores is credit/debt from the Federal Reserve. How many people will build an extension on a house they think they own without first getting permission from the local bureaucrats?

There is almost total dependency on governments for trade, especially with the necessities of life such as food and shelter. How many people in the last seventy years have bought a house or car without government-imposed debt? The credit/debt system has infected almost every part of the world's economies. That's why a global recession started in 2008. Since then we've seen massive credit bailouts of governments in Europe. It's almost impossible to live in society without engaging in the credit/debt system to a degree.

We saw the increase in the armed attacks against people selling raw milk in 2010, which culminated with a yearlong sting operation and raid of the Amish in April 2011 for the crime of selling milk to a willing market.

Education is also almost entirely dependent on government. Compulsory education laws make even home schooling something requiring permission and constant control. Private schools must get permission and almost every college is just another government bureaucracy. Even private colleges must have permission to operate.

Think about self-defense. In places such as Australia, there is a ban on ownership of firearms. This obviously makes people dependent on the public criminals (governments) to protect them from the private criminals.

Extreme examples of dependency on governments are the aftermath of hurricane Katrina in August 2005. Thousands of people were doing nothing but waiting for governments to help.

And this dependency does not go unnoticed by the pigs running the farm; they continually throw it in our faces about the roads and other services provided by force. This naturally makes one feel a bit guilty. After all, we do use the roads and they need to be maintained.

If we're already feeling weak because we need permission to do everything, how does it make one feel to have to be so dependent on the very people causing the debility? See how and why the government concept immobilizes the masses? We can already see how such dependency increases the debility, which in turn makes people more dependent on governments.

This is proven when you discuss with someone the truth of government and they cannot refute that compulsory support is immoral and governments should be abolished. They will immediately get defensive and defiantly ask what voluntaryists/anarchists have heard thousands of times: "But who'll build the roads?" People are so debilitated and dependent on governments, they cannot *think* for a few minutes about how roads will be built, as if the average person has any idea of the real mechanisms of planning, engineering, funding, and building roads.

To further show the dependency on governments, brought about in part by the stealing of trillions of "dollars" from the market every year, look at this article:
http://theeconomiccollapseblog.com/archives/the-federal-government-hands-out-money-to-128-million-americans-every-month
The one hundred twenty-eight million getting government handouts does not include everything either.

Those are not good numbers when you're supposed to have a fair and impartial jury. Doesn't make me too confident a jury is not going to be stacked with people who believe in blind obedience to authority. If you're being prosecuted for disobedience to authority it's stacked against you by design.

Dread.   While there may not be absolute dependency on governments for trade, there is tremendous dread when not using government credit as people like Ann Tompkins have called us domestic terrorists.

Ms. Tompkins is a United States attorney who was in charge of the prosecution of Bernard von NotHaus for selling silver coins to a willing market. Ms. Tompkins got a lot of attention when she made the following statement in April 2011:

> "Attempts to undermine the legitimate currency of this country are simply a unique form of domestic terrorism...While these forms of anti-government activities do not involve violence, they are every bit as insidious and represent a clear and present danger to the economic stability of this country...We are determined to meet these threats through infiltration, disruption and dismantling of organizations which seek to challenge the legitimacy of our democratic form of government."

Nice! In Anne's world, terrorism doesn't have to involve any actual terror. Who wants to be labeled a domestic terrorist? Just the idea you can be accused of being a terrorist for freely trading is going to cause feelings of dread. (Mr. NotHaus informed me that this was a position the FBI had taken, so it did not originate with Ms. Thompkins.)

These threats are intended to discourage or "chill" free trade. What other intended effect is there but to cause feelings of dread among anyone who trades without using the Federal Reserve credit system? She admits there's no violence involved, and then threatens everyone involved in non-violent trade with violence. Look how specific she was, she mentions

169

infiltration without shame. Most people are aware of how such people operate with their "agent provocateurs."

One of the most famous examples is from the United States called COINTELPRO (Counter Intelligence Program), where federal agents posed as violent radicals to discredit groups and movements deemed dangerous to the status quo.

In fact, "false flag operations" are now part of common language. There is a recent example where an Indiana prosecutor suggested Wisconsin Governor Scott Walker stage an attack to then blame it on the worker's union. Carlos F. Lam emailed Scott Walker that the union protests were: "a good opportunity for what's called a 'false flag' operation." He also wrote:

> "If you could employ an associate who pretends to be sympathetic to the unions' cause to physically attack you (or even use a firearm against you), you could discredit the unions..."

This is a state attorney in the United States, not some gangster in Eastern Europe. History shows this is not an isolated incident. False flag is a common phrase now thanks to people exposing operations such as COINTELPRO.

2011 was a particularly violent year, due in part to the catastrophe of the credit system. We've seen increased aggression against people selling milk, health food stores, and even lemonade stands being shut down. There are also attacks against people for having gardens in their yards.

Western civilization is being raped and burned to the ground, and small farms are being investigated. The constant threat of punishment certainly fills the masses with dread; we know we could be prosecuted for dancing in public, while people like Dick Cheney get away with *shooting a man in the face*. And you didn't think a caste system exists in the United States?

When you're out driving and a cop gets in your rear-view mirror what's your first thought? How do you feel? I think the word *dread* nails it. It's not: Oh look, happy days indeed, mate, the Man's got behind us. You feel as safe as I do now?

I know I'm looking for the best place to turn off that road and get the hell away from them. Sorry, let him ruin someone else's day. I've wasted enough time in court fighting against bogus tickets.

Ever get a letter from the IRS, CRA or other government tax agency? In Australia, I'd be thinking, "Oh, what's the commissioner hallucinated this time?" I work helping people with tax issues, and I get that sinking feeling of dread when they mail letters to me and I'm not even the subject of the attack. But you never know, as many times as I've been threatened.

At least with the Patriot Act there is less dread of agents raiding your house and terrorizing you; no the sneak and peek provisions take most of that stress away. What convenience: you leave for a few hours, government agents come into your home, do a thorough search, download your hard drives and leave without bothering you with a search warrant and invasive questions. You never have to know they were there. And don't worry about your neighbors bothering you with any reports, because if they notice, the agents will kindly let them know they are not to bother you with such trivialities, unless they want a one-way ticket to Guantanamo Bay.

Pretty much every aspect of government is a rich source of dread for the masses. There is also the relentless news of bailouts and credit defaults. There is never a shortage of dread when governments are around. It's what they do.

Those are the three D's-debility, dependency and dread-the CIA wrote about using to control people. Deep feelings of dread are caused by the violent nature of government and feed off the dependency caused by that violence. Weak-minded people, such as lawyers with robes, tend to see most things as a threat and will not do anything to help themselves.

Coercion [taxation]
causes:

Debility
Dependence
Dread

It's easy to see how each one leads to and in turn strengthens the other. The more coercion, the weaker the individual feels. The weaker the individual is, the more dependent they are, especially when the aggressor gives rewards with the terror. Any thought of not complying will create feelings of dread; the victim is well aware of the psychopath's violent nature and also doesn't want to be rejected by the crowd.

The three D's each help strengthen the trauma bond between the victims and the aggressors; they are integral parts of the Stockholm Syndrome. It's clearly seen in both the Milgram and Stanford Prison experiments. As stated earlier:

Expectations govern our responses.

The next experiment adds more to the social aspect, the part where other victims contribute to the strength of the bond. Never underestimate the power of the social element.

The Asch Conformity Experiment, and similar experiments and theories are pretty scary when you examine them and apply them to everyday life. These will further help explain why it's so difficult to break the bond people have to the concept of government. We have billions of victims suffering from Stockholm Syndrome, who each believe everyone else sees the world as they do. Is there proof? No, nothing beyond the way they act; they all continue to pay taxes, vote and otherwise cooperate with their slave masters. But that is not proof of what they really believe.

Solomon Asch conducted his famous experiment in 1953. What he did was have subjects take a test with others who were privy to the experiment. Those in on the experiment would purposely answer incorrectly. The experiment was to study how social pressure would affect a person's answers.

What happened supported the long-known bandwagon effect. While most have heard and instantly recognize the bandwagon effect, the Asch Conformity Experiment is lesser known.

(I don't know about parents outside the US, but parents I knew as a kid were fond of retorting, "If your friends were jumping off the Brooklyn Bridge would you jump too?")

The results were no surprise: the larger the number of people giving a wrong answer, the greater the number of test subjects knowingly giving a wrong answer. (Does majority vote (democracy) still seem like a good now?) It was based on what the subject thought the majority believed. But, if the answers were not given out publicly, people were much more inclined to give the answer they knew was correct.

Of course, we may never know the motives or how genuine the person giving an answer is. The test subjects had no idea the ones in on the experiment were not sincere. As mentioned above, apart from actions, we don't really know the motivation. But not being a part of the pack can create significant social pressure, real or imagined. The desire to belong is apparently stronger than our sense of right or wrong. This makes the collective perception of the government concept particularly damaging.

This was explained by two psychologists in 1931, Daniel Katz and Floyd H. Allport. They wrote "pluralistic ignorance" is "a situation where a majority of group members privately reject a norm, but assume (incorrectly) that most others accept it..." *Student Attitudes*, Syracuse, N.Y., Craftsman. Others have described it as a situation where, "no one believes, but everyone thinks that everyone believes." Centola, Damon, Robb Willer, and Michael Macy. 2005. *The Emperor's Dilemma: A Computational Model of Self-Enforcing Norms*, American Journal of Sociology 110:1009.

This helps describe why governments are still in place: no one really believes it's necessary or moral to force people to pay for protection, but most people think everyone else believes it's necessary. It helps explain why those who advocate freedom are attacked by those with a vested interest in government as "fringe and dangerous extremists" who live in "compounds," not homes.

We have the trauma bond together with a need to belong to a pack, to reject any views perceived not to be held by the rest of the pack. That's pretty powerful stuff, and we can see it in action every time we talk to the average person about abolishing government. I've heard it from radio show hosts dozens of times: "Do you know how far outside the mainstream thought that is?" One plus one is two, regardless of the number of people who believe it. At one time, DVD's were outside the mainstream-so what? Truth does not rely on a consensus, and anyone telling you that it does is a liar and playing you for a fool.

This is why the phrase "the fringe" is so often used, especially when talking about abolishing government. You have the victim of government trauma, who may not even believe government has any legitimacy at all, but thinks the majority of the pack does, so they vehemently defend their abusers. You've heard the excuses before about the roads and protection. They look at the ostensible benefits and rewards the abuser provides instead of addressing the abuse.

Even if the victim is inclined to speak out about the abuse, or even contemplate non-cooperation with government psychopaths (in what is often described as "bystander apathy") the victim may look at what others are doing as a gauge of what they should do. So, if others act, then the victim will also act. But if others don't (because they are all thinking the same thing: "I'm not going to the only one!"), then the victim probably won't act either.

There is great hope in this, though. What it means is that if there's but one brave soul in the crowd or jury, the rest may then be inclined to join in, the bandwagon effect takes over. One day, non-compliance with the tax laws will be considered a moral act by the average person.

When this is all put together with the Stanford Prison and Milgram experiments, the behavior of statists is understandable and highly predictable. It should scare the crap out of everyone. This is science, everyone, it's not speculation; it is replicated, observable science. You can experience this for yourself if you're not convinced.

Governments are structured to not only attract the worst of society, but it's a context that brings out the absolute worst in otherwise good people. All rational, peaceful and productive people should be advocating non-cooperation with the psychopaths at every opportunity.

That's a pretty bad combination. If you're not a psycho when you first become a government, don't worry, you will be. But hey, it's only sixty-seven to ninety-one percent of them, right?

The Stanford Prison Experiment was scheduled to be a two-week experiment in 1971 that was terminated after only six days. The idea was to run a pretend prison, with half of the participants pretending to be prisoners and the other half prison guards. What could go wrong?

Whatever the stated intentions were in 1971, the context simulated a **master-slave relationship**: one group pretending to be under the control of the other-the government concept with its hierarchy. But unlike with the government concept, all involved knew they were pretending and could leave at any time.

Dr. Zimbardo stated the experiment had to be stopped because about a third of the participants pretending to be prison guards had become sadistic. That's right, pretending to be a prison guard for as little as six days can make seemingly normal people get sexually aroused by hurting others. Let's repeat that: *sexually aroused* by inflicting pain on others. While the 33% may seem low, especially when you compare that to the sixty-seven percent for the Milgram Experiment, you have to consider this was for only six days and they were *pretending*. It's reasonable, with the findings in Milgram and replications, the number would be much higher if continued for even a few weeks. What about years? What about those who are not pretending?

Just using thirty-three percent means a full one third of all politicians and bureaucrats have "genuine sadistic tendencies," to quote Dr.

Zimbardo. These people get a kick out of abusing you. Looks like politics is not really just about money? Starting to understand why these people are not too keen on dropping their attack against you?

Why would we support a system that not only attracts psychopaths, but also *creates* them? Add to that these people don't personally pay for their acts of aggression (wars etc.) and have no personal accountability, and we really have a monster. Does it now make sense they have to give themselves titles such as Honorable?

Barry Cooper, a former drug cop, testified on **The No State Project** about the adrenaline rush cops have going on a big drug bust. He admitted, as other cops have, the rush is highly addictive. Being a cop then gives these junkies practically unlimited opportunities to get a fix. I'll discuss later how experts have noticed the profession most admired by serial killers is a police officer. Ya think? What a surprise: killers admire a profession based on irresponsible, violent domination.

So we're dealing with a structure where people are on a pecking order, and when those higher up are dealing with someone lower, there is a rush-a hit of adrenaline or even dopamine-they get from the domination, the thrill of the attack.

Think about that: the concept is physically and psychologically addictive to those involved. *But for* the government concept, they would not be able to dominate others with no personal responsibility. This isn't even taking into account the economic advantages. When put together, we get a pretty good idea why there is so much resistance to concepts of freedom, autonomy, and yes, anarchy. Those who want to rule you are probably not going to like the idea of no rulers.

The other side is also true; those conditioned to be ruled will not take to the idea of no rulers.

Another result was what is called "de-individuation" was occurring within thirty-six hours. De-individuation is the technical term for groupthink. It's described as "loss of self awareness and of individual accountability in a group." It's the inability to identify oneself as an individual, only as part of a group. Think about how Americans are. How difficult is it for someone pretending to be an American Citizen for thirty years to accept empirical proof there are no citizens? This collective is not limited to groups such as medical doctors; it's seen almost every day in police brutality cases with the "blue wall of silence."

With the blue wall of silence, police will not cooperate and will actively cover up crimes committed by fellow cops. Obviously, there are varying degrees of such bonds depending on the group. A cop will easily cooperate with a prosecutor when covering up the shooting of an innocent man, but stonewall the same prosecutor if he/she turns their attention to evidence the cop's partner shot an innocent man.

De-individuation explains the conformity experiments, why people give wrong answers. It's difficult to go against the herd.

Zimbardo's experiment included the following elements to create a context to bring out sadistic behaviors and to modify pre-existing sadism. It's a how-to guide for creating psychopaths and anti-social behavior, and each one is an essential part of the government concept:

- De-individuation
- Anonymity
- Dehumanization
- Role-playing and social modeling
- Moral disengagement
- Group camaraderie and emergent norms
- Power differentials between guards and prisoners
- The evil of inaction: passivity of the "good guards"
- In a new context where institutional power is pitted against the individual will to resist

Think of tax agents such as the California franchise tax board and the IRS: tax agents use pseudonyms and employee numbers; there is almost complete de-individuation and anonymity. It's not Donna Eley, doing it; it's the IRS and congress. This woman seemed to believe the crap she was shoveling, that it was not her taking my client's property, it was the government. This madness is demonstrated in the movie *Happy Gilmore* where the tax agent claims *he's* not taking grandma's house.
https://www.youtube.com/watch?v=Bc3gXnhSy4E
Yes, they use false names by law and the excuse is it's because they receive so many death threats. But regardless of even a benign reason, the results are still the same and that's what is important. What does the structure/concept cause? It directly causes a loss of any sense of responsibility for one's actions. It's not the psychopath with the gun, it's the state!

There is **dehumanization,** as you're not Frank Rizzo, you're a taxpayer with an identifying number. I have spoken with some agents who seemed unable to address someone by name; no matter how many times I objected and said his name is Frank (or Mary, or Bill) they still called them "taxpayer." Some just couldn't do it and would refer to them as "my client." But using the word client only contributes to the dehumanization because of the anonymity.

The "**role-playing and social modeling**" is fairly obvious, and it's one of the reasons I recommend not taking fictions into court and other situations with bureaucrats. At least go in knowing they are fictions.

An example is calling a lawyer in a black robe Your Honor or judge/justice. I recommend addressing them as sir or ma'am. Calling them by their first name tends to freak them out; they're typically not used to having their fictions threatened and don't have the coping skills of an adult to deal with the offence. So unless you're looking to use their fits of fury for your benefit, you probably should not call them by their first name.

Calling them Your Honor, in my experience, will change your behavior and your responses to them. This was proven by Dr. Zimbardo. Your communication is going to be affected, so it helps instead to address them as an equal. It has helped me and many others who have reported to me they were able to stay more focused and calm during court proceedings. I always tell people to treat the situation no differently than when talking to me. There's no anxiety when we speak; people are quite comfortable asking me to explain myself. If I make a comment about something and they don't understand, they just question me. It's usually different with lawyers because they're afraid of getting the judge upset.

We see there is a **moral disengagement** because things are looked at not as right and wrong, but twisted into legal and illegal, lawful or unlawful. This is particularly relevant when addressing a jury, whether in a *voir dire* (preliminary examination) or in opening and closing statements.

We almost instinctively know, starting when we are toddlers, that taking property by force is wrong. We're later taught by politicians it's not wrong when done lawfully (remember schizophrenia is about constant, contradictory messages):

> "A. A person commits theft if, without lawful authority, such person knowingly:
> 1. Controls property of another with the intent to deprive him of such property..." Arizona Revised Statutes 13-1802.

Interestingly, this is not found in the robbery statute in Queensland, Australia, but it is in the extortion statute:

> "169. (1) A person must not, without reasonable or probable cause, make an unlawful demand with intent—
>
> (a) to gain a benefit for anyone; or
> (b) to cause a detriment to anyone.
> Maximum penalty—life imprisonment."

Otherwise, all tax agents could be arrested. It's a nice thought though. I'm sure there is a legal exception somewhere else in the law for robbery.

Moral disengagement and openly contradictory messages are throughout their laws and codes. This is the same as saying: "Do as I say, not as I do." I asked a cop in Scottsdale, Arizona a simple question: "If we did business in the same manner as governments, forcing people to pay us, would you consider us criminals?" He immediately got upset, saying it was "offensive," and ordered me to leave.

Do you see a problem with someone's moral choices and perceptions when given such contradictory messages? Basic principles of right and wrong do not come into play, only what their superiors have told them is acceptable. Regardless of whatever personal convictions the cop or judge may have, while on the job they will not act consistently with them; the perceptions learned on the job are paramount.

The same afternoon we were speaking to another Scottsdale cop who said something about how important freedom of choice was. Turns out it's not as important as his job. I mentioned we have no freedom of choice to pay for governments or not; we pay or go to jail. He agreed there was no choice, but he wouldn't put us in jail. Yeah, not without a warrant or an order from his associates; had the judge ordered us arrested for contempt he would have complied immediately.

You could tell this particular cop was troubled by the contradictory messages and ideas he held. Unlike his co-worker behind the bulletproof glass, he was interested in discussing the issues.

What kinds of people are morally disengaged and potentially schizophrenic in that they have serious issues distinguishing fact from fiction? Is that a healthy society? If that's the base, can we really be surprised when innocent people-even children selling lemonade-are regularly attacked?

With anonymity also comes a change in appearance. This has been shown to have dramatic effects on the severity of the trauma and abuse inflicted. Zimbardo calls this the Lord of the Flies effect. He describes it as:

- The power of anonymity, of loss of personal identity,
- To dis-inhibit repressed actions; violence and sexuality
- Behaving in any way permissible in new situations
- Transfer from cognitive to situational control of behavior

We can see each one with governments, especially with the people who actually carry out the politicians' orders, such as tax agents. Tax agents are virtually **anonymous**; we don't know their real names, as they use pseudonyms. Having control over others in society is usually only permitted when they are on the job, so that is certainly behaving in a different way because of a new situation. Add sovereign immunity and a complete lack of responsibility and you'll see a transfer from cognitive (right and wrong) to situational control over behavior (legal and illegal).

There is a scene in the movie *Die Hard* that captures this when the FBI agent wants the city power grid shut down. The power company worker doesn't want to do it and asks about authority. The agent doesn't say, "By my authority, because I said so." That wouldn't get him too far. No, instead he snaps, "How about the United States f***ing government!" His word as just some pockmarked-face loser means nothing, but the abstract "United States f***ing government" carries a bit more weight.

Such behavior may seem acceptable to governments, but it should cease to be for us, the victims. We should live by simple principles of right and wrong. If we did, then the government concept loses its power and people would not cooperate anymore. The government concept requires us to surrender our core principles of right and wrong. That should be sending up red flags that there's a serious problem with the concept.

The "**Group camaraderie and emergent norms**" is obvious. There is overwhelming evidence of this on both sides. With government actors, we all know of the blue wall of silence. The camaraderie is also expressed in the courts. It's why in the courts judges are usually prosecutors first. In the tax court, they are usually IRS or treasury lawyers. Evidence these judges are just rubber-stamps is the systemic refusal to ackn is an exception to the anti-injunctive tax act as held in *En(Packing Co.*, 370 U.S. 1.

This group camaraderie is also proven by the judge-created judicial immunity. This is where judges created this doctrine out of thin air to protect themselves from their legions of victims. These same lawyers who want to control everyone else in the community-even people who wash people's hair-decided they can "self regulate" themselves. The most reviled profession-next to politicians-thinks they are special and regulate themselves.

On the other side, we've seen blind patriotism such as "My country, right or wrong." Look at the super patriotism exhibited by many Americans after 911 or at least they were acting as if they were part of a group.

There was the murder of Balbir Singh on September 15, 2001, by Frank Roque for no other reason than he was angry that Muslims attacked "our way of life."

So when you think Arab Muslims have attacked, the only rational thing to do as an American is to kill a Sikh from India! Groupthink is a wonderful thing, isn't it? With similar non sequitur reasoning, because Muslims allegedly from Saudi Arabia carried out the attacks, you should invade and brutally occupy *Afghanistan*.

The "**Power differentials**" are an integral part in the hierarchy of the government concept. Countless times people have told me I can't call judges by their first name. Really? That's evidence to me there are power differentials at play. The political system itself is a structure of power differentials, e.g., federal (supreme), state and then local. The great mass of the people are at the very bottom of the power differentials.

Also consider how resistant judges are to answering simple questions. Most will refuse, because they are the ones in control; they claim jurisdiction and have a small battery of armed men to carry out their will. Why should they answer questions from an inferior? We're lower on the food chain; we don't get to question the king's men.

How could aggressive domination with no personal responsibility and armed men to carry out your whims not change one's behavior?

Other examples are easy to see such as police and military with officers and non-commissioned officers and the varying ranks. You have the courts with superior, appellate, and supreme courts.

And the unwashed masses-where are we in all this? We're at the bottom of this power differential, at least that's how most act. It definitely causes us to act differently. Instead of just ignoring politicians, we continue to pay for our own enslavement and vote as if that will change anything. *But for* the concept with its hierarchy, many would not cooperate with those people labeled government.

I've seen the **evil of inaction** and agents' "passivity" many times. Excuses are always made for the machine to continue grinding us up. An example of this is John McDonald, a magistrate in Toronto, Canada. He told Keith he knew the traffic ticket did not present a valid cause of action and that he should dismiss, but he wasn't going to do it. It was a year later when another lawyer in the appellate court finally threw the ticket out. Old McDonald was not going to be the kid pointing out the emperor had no clothes; he was too low on the pecking order.

The Tempe police sergeant I spoke with after my parking ticket was kicked out is another example. He didn't know what a valid cause of action was before I told him. Despite knowing there is no cause of action with most traffic tickets, he does nothing to stop his employees from giving out tickets. And why should he? He's close to retirement and those tickets are probably used to help fund those pensions. Yes, hanging on in quiet desperation, is not just the English way, is it?

Such people can claim to be in government employment to "protect and serve," but the facts tell a different story. Where are the Frank Serpicos?

Where's the integrity and guts? People call cops heroes; why? Do you think "hero" when the cops get behind you when you're driving down the street? Trust your gut people.

Where are the cops willing to stand up to organized violence? Despite their lip service to protection and enforcing the law, they are just as paralyzed by the structure as anyone. That's the nature of the structure the concept of government builds. It has built-in self-preservation elements.

How many videos are on the internets where crowds of people just watch uniformed psychopaths (cops) abusing others? It's sick to watch them. Though there are exceptions, such as what looks like a European football game where the audience did not sit by idly,
    https://www.youtube.com/watch?v=cj275JIZh7I
The overwhelming majority of the time people just stand there and let it happen.

For the same reason the adults in the emperor story don't say anything, the cops, when they know there are other cops committing crimes, don't say anything. Peer pressure's a hell of a drug. I don't know which is more powerful: the rush from dominating others or the group camaraderie. I'm pretty sure the power of the group camaraderie is an anchored response (adrenaline/dopamine rush) from dominating others.

The "**institutional power…pitted against the individual will to resist**" is easy to see. What do you think about personally engaging in civil disobedience-non-violent, non-cooperation with the psychopaths called government? Are you willing to grow hemp, travel around without a tax tag on your car, not file a tax return, not collect sales tax, etc.? If not, then why?

It's a no brainer; you're probably thinking about that line from *Die Hard* again: "How about the United States f***ing government!" Do your own investigation: ask friends and family if they'd be willing to not comply with politicians. After they have their anxiety attack, ask them why they had that reaction.

Governments steal $trillions so they have resources to attack us. I've been stalked by a psycho cop who I had admit on the stand in court he was stalking me. The only reason he admitted it was because the judge was furious and ordered him to answer during my cross. To say he was

179

raging about it is quite the understatement. I was legitimately concerned for my safety leaving the building that day. I walked home that day-much less opportunity for Jimmy to stop me for something. Yeah, that's his name, and it also upset him when I called him that. Jimmy insisted I address him as "Officer."

People hear lines from attorneys that a good defense will cost fifty to one hundred thousand dollars for serious government attacks, even when not accused of causing any harm. Why would it cost someone fifty grand to point out the government was created to protect rights, and the complaint makes no allegations of injury and damage? How do you justify so much money when the prosecutor has no evidence the code applies or when government witnesses can be impeached by asking as few as two questions?

It should be self-evident that a structure based on collective fictions is going to be antithetical to the individual. Those with a vested interest in that structure are going to do and say what they need to keep their victims from standing up for themselves.

In California, a criminal prosecution is done in the name of "THE PEOPLE OF THE STATE OF CALIFORNIA." Pretty intimidating that way, instead of it being just a few anti-social lawyers attacking you, it's the millions of people in California against you. False perceptions are a helluva drug.

Feeding on the previous characteristics, we see examples of such "institutional power pitted against the individual" on the government side —against those acting as governments. They're pretty intimate with the institutional power that can be exerted against them. Think of how Stalin's officers and henchmen must have felt about those wonderful purges.

Frank Serpico is a good example of what happens to official whistleblowers in the United States-they can get shot. Thomas Drake is a recent example, he blew the whistle on the NSA. Bradley Manning was tortured for nine months for the murders he revealed to WikiLeaks. That took guts. How many whistleblowers were "fragged" in Vietnam? Was Pat Tilman shot by his own men, a victim of intentional "friendly fire"? Why else lie about the circumstances of his killing?

Look at the many derogatory terms for whistleblower such as weasel, snitch, fink, and the more contemporary: prick.

I've spoken to many bureaucrats about this. I have examples on the website. A good example is where a lawyer acting as a judge gives an opinion, and someone in collections goes about enforcing the opinion. I've been told that even with overwhelming evidence that the lawyer's opinion is wrong and will harm an innocent man/woman, the bureaucrat will still carry out the order. They will tell you-without any hint of shame-their job is not to determine if the opinion is right or wrong, just to carry it out. They, like cops, are not supposed to exercise any discretion, just follow orders. In most cases, they will not just ignore evidence, they will refuse to even look at it.

Evidence is not important to those acting as a government, only opinions-their opinions. They would rather blindly carry out the opinions of a lawyer than even look at the evidence. In most cases, I never get to present the evidence a lawyer acting as a judge is a criminal because the bureaucrats don't care to investigate. I tell them I have evidence a judge is committing crimes, and they hang up the phone faster than you can say "accessory after the fact."

So I've asked bureaucrats if their sense of right or wrong is part of the job, or do they leave that at the door when they get to work. They again say their job is to just carry out the lawyer's opinions, not to question whether it is right or wrong. They tell me point blank their job is to carry out orders without discretion.

What I like to ask is: **Do you exhibit this same anti-social behavior when you're not on the job?**

Erica Hughes with the Enhanced Collection division of the Marin county court system in California told me they presume the lawyer is correct and will not investigate or even consider they may be wrong-that even if the evidence proved a judge was wrong, she would still carry out the order to the harm of someone else.

She told me to appeal the decision and let the courts decide if the lawyer is wrong. If they agree, then they will reverse the order/opinion and there will be no "enhanced collections." It didn't faze her in the least when I pointed out the clerks will not process the appeal. The clerks, just as those in collections, are the lawyers' accomplices in damaging people. She didn't care that the judges and clerks are criminals; it made no difference to her and her co-workers.

The more familiar you are with the people who comprise these systems, the easier it is to see how the concepts-the structure of the system itself-are the problem. It's institutional power against the individual, regardless of your place on the pecking order.

These concepts *cause* people to lose whatever empathy they may have and enable them to then commit harmful acts to others; harmful acts they would never do off the job. Keep the above in mind when we go through Phillip Zimbardo's ten examples of how to create evil in good people:

1. Ideology to justify any means -> good ends
2. Small first step, minor action
3. Successively increase small actions
4. Seemingly "just authority" in charge
5. Compassionate leader changes gradually to become an authoritarian monster
6. Rules are vague, changing
7. Situation re-labels actors/actions
8. Provide social models of compliance
9. Allow verbal dissent, but insist on behavioral compliance
10. Make exiting difficult

All ten of these examples are part of the government concept. Look at the political ideology that taking property by force is stealing unless done by a politician. With the government concept, the means are justified even

181

though contradictory to the stated end. This is said with a straight face, by the way.

Even if the bureaucrat is honest enough to admit their actions are damaging innocent people, they can shrug it off because their perception is that it's not *them* that's the problem-it's the system, state or government. I know this from years of personal experience. Bureaucrats have told me this and if you call them, they'll probably admit to you also.

Another very popular phrase with politicians is "duly elected" or "duly constituted" as a way to justify the violence initiated against peaceful people.

We see number five after every election. Look at the "change" Barack Obama spoke of: he continued every Bush policy and increased them, such as military actions. He attacked Libya in 2011 without even a pretense of legal authority. He claims to be able to assassinate at his own discretion, and has now openly admitted to holding Americans indefinitely without trial.

And what is verbal dissent if one may not *act* on one's beliefs? Complain all you want, as long as you comply with the masters' orders.

During the Bush Regime, there were "free speech zones", which means all the other areas were not free speech zones. Go ahead and protest and criticize, just do it over *there* where we don't have to see and hear you. And keep paying taxes and cooperating.

There is no exit from the dominance of political psychopaths; they are everywhere. All you can do is trade one master for another, and you need permission to do that. These control freaks don't like it when the slaves start thinking for themselves. By making it impossible to exit, they ensure the resulting anxiety will paralyze the slaves from doing any more than just complaining.

One way is to instill terror into those who do go about trying to change the vertical structure of society is with undercover agents, provocateurs. COINTELPRO and the CIA's CHOAS are only two historical example of this. They targeted the leaders of the civil rights movements. It is beyond any reasonable doubt that Frederic Hampton, member of the Black Panther Party, was murdered by Chicago police. Richard Nixon also had the FBI attack John Lennon, as if this anti-war icon was a threat to national security. Well he was, if by national security you mean Nixon's popularity with the industrial war machine.

What this also does is divert attention away from the cause-the ideology-and instead points to the effects. People see the cops as the problem, or others, such as congress. They are a problem, but they are the natural result of the structure created by the concept. The structure provides the means for the cops to do what they do; it's more than just providing psychos with guns. And it's organization and immunity. The Supreme Court admitted in the Dred Scott opinion:

> "The Constitution of the United States recognises slaves as property, and pledges the Federal Government to protect it."
> *Scott v. Sandford*, 60 U.S. 19 How. 393, 395 (1856).

But for the government concept, there could not be such institutionalized power against individual men and women. Cops (and all bureaucrats and politicians) take a meaningless oath to preserve, protect, and defend the constitution, not the people whom they force to live under it. There are plenty of court opinions affirming the constitution does not obligate or even pledge governments to protect anyone. The constitution, as the Supreme Court held, is pledged to protect the vertical structure of society, the enslavement of the masses.

This is why non-cooperation with politicians is so important to bringing about change, and why politicians use terror to keep people compliant. The more people peacefully refuse to cooperate, the more violence politicians have to use, and this just reveals their true intentions.

The Milgram Experiment was conducted in 1961 by Stanley Milgram. Milgram was studying the reasons why people in Nazi Germany committed the acts they did. How could seemingly normal people commit such atrocious acts against other people?

The actual subjects of the experiment were unaware they were the subjects. Instead, they were told they would be assisting in an experiment about methods of learning. They were to administer progressively higher electrical shocks to people in another room. The one in the other room was asked a question and if he got it wrong, the subject would administer the electrical shock. Each time the jolt would be higher, and the subject was told that past a certain point the person being asked the questions could be hurt or killed by the shock.

Milgram told them they had to administer the shock, and that he, Milgram, with the white lab coat, was the authority and was responsible. While most did protest and some did stop, a shocking sixty-seven percent continued to administer the shock "knowing" it could injure the other person.

The one being asked the questions was an actor and was not really being hurt, but the subjects didn't know that. This experiment has been replicated many times; most recently in France, where a reality show was staged for a documentary called *The Game of Death*.

http://www.youtube.com/watch?v=eYHRq7oMnZQ.

When television was added to the experiment, the percentage of participants who continued to shock the target shot up to eighty percent.

With Milgram, the subjects couldn't see the person being shocked; this helped make it easier for the subject to inflict the pain. The further removed from the victim, the easier it is to inflict the pain. That explains the difference between WWII vets, the ones on the line and those who were in planes. The ones on the front lines don't talk about the war much, as opposed to those in planes who often talk very freely about it.

This is also why tax agents act so callously towards us. They are in their little cubicle shut off from the world and almost never have to see their victims. We're only names on a piece of paper, not real people.

When we just look at the results of these two experiments-Stanford Prison and Milgram-the effects are obvious and should repulse you. They really are the only experiments we should have to reference to start a worldwide movement of non-cooperation with the psychopaths running this farm called earth.

When pretending to be a government, not only will at least sixty-seven percent traumatize the innocent because of some perceived authority, but they will also begin to enjoy it after only a few days. Most are going to be getting an adrenaline rush from hurting others. (Are you familiar with the phrase "adrenaline junky"?) And like any other junky, the amount of the drug needed to keep getting a "fix" will steadily increase. Is this the reason for climbing the political pecking order? The higher on the pecking order the more people you can traumatize. Seems logical to me.

The government structure provides the means and protection for psychopaths and sadists to get a fix at our expense, and then cover-up their crimes and hinder investigations. All of this trauma and abuse is being done with money they steal from us. We enable these anti-social adrenaline junky control freaks to get their daily fix.

I don't want to be accused of being overly dramatic, however, it cannot be overstated that the government concept is so detrimental to society that **we should not even pretend with it**. Think about that: it's so dangerous that we'll see the effects even when everyone is only acting. What other activity will traumatize you and others when you are only pretending?

Even engaging in an activity such as boxing training does not lead to the psychological trauma and sadism experienced when people pretend to be governments and citizens.

Earlier we saw the LA Times reported that politicians share many traits with serial killers. Imagine my surprise when I read the following from a very well-known FBI profiler:

> "The three most common motives of serial rapists and murderers turn out to be domination, manipulation, and control. When you consider that most of these guys are angry, ineffectual losers who feel they've been given the shaft by life, and that most of them have experienced some sort of physical or emotional abuse, as Ed Kemper had, it isn't surprising that one of their main fantasy occupations is police officer." *Mind Hunter*, John Douglas and Mark Olshaker, page 105.

Not surprising when you know basic human psychology. The authors also point out these "losers" tend to be police junkies, not only preoccupied with them, but often hanging around police bars to be around cops. It's not a surprise that serial killers would be obsessed with cops; cops and most politicians have a license to be a psychopath. They are considered heroes for exhibiting the same behaviors as serial killers. Of course they want to be around cops, they have the same personality flaws.

Look at the motives this profiler points out and try not to think of cops and judges: "domination, manipulation, and control." If you ever wondered why traffic court judges are so easily enraged, now you know.

When we ask relevant questions, such as, "Whom do you represent?" we are undermining their "domination, manipulation, and control" of us and others in the courtroom. Not having normal adult coping skills, they start screaming and threatening their perceived enemy, us.

Being a politician or petty bureaucrat satisfies each of these three most common motives of psychopaths. The government concept provides the structure and immunity they need to brutalize with impunity.

The structure itself attracts the worst of society and gives an otherwise "ineffectual loser" the platform and means to be an effectual loser. Nice job.

The author also points out how the chase-the getting away with the crimes-is a thrill the psychopath lives for. They feed off the thrill of *not getting caught*. How does this play out with adrenaline junkies working as drug warriors with immunity? This is sick stuff, the stuff of nightmares. There is a double thrill: the actual raid itself and the effect of doing it without being stopped or punished.

In *Mind Hunter*, author John Douglas talks about serial killers who taunt the public, such as the Zodiac killer; it becomes part of the thrill of killing. Psychopaths and sadists enjoy instilling fear into their victims, especially entire populations, the draw of government must be irresistible to the budding psychopath. Giving people with psychopathic tendencies a responsibility-free position doesn't sound like such a good idea, does it?

What the author of *Mind Hunter* doesn't investigate is: how many of these "angry, ineffectual losers who feel they've been given the shaft by life" actually *become* cops or other government enforcers? We already know if you don't start as a psychopath, then becoming a bureaucrat or politician will certainly set you on the path. If you already have those tendencies, it's a structure virtually insuring you'll excel at it. I'd love to speak to Douglas about this topic.

While I don't disagree with the characteristics Douglas presents as the behaviors of psychopaths and serial killers, he never seems to address the obvious parallel to agents of the FBI such as himself. Is it deliberate, are facts too painful to confront? How can someone who works for the FBI for decades not notice the behavior of those all around him? Isn't Douglas supposed to be an expert on human behavior? Then why the disconnect? It reminds me of how governments are portrayed in the movies and on television; there may be rogue agents, but the government is predictably the good guy.

The evidence does not support an innocent ignorance on the part of FBI profilers. He obviously has knowledge of human behavior and cannot claim ignorance of how his salary and pension are provided. I also don't think he and others deserve a pass regarding the Milgram and Stanford Prison experiments.

It stands to reason Douglas is aware of the psychopathic tendencies and behaviors of his associates, and just as police, prosecutors and judges do, turns a blind eye and profits from his books.

It doesn't take a rocket scientist to figure that out if the primary motivations of psychopaths are domination, manipulation, and control, then a system entirely based on domination, manipulation, and control will not only attract but also breed psychopaths. The domination, manipulation and control are only *but for* the concept of government.

What else can be the result of a system based on anti-social personality flaws? When the foundation of society is psychopathic, is it really a surprise psychopaths dominate it and rise to the top? If autonomy were respected, there would be no government regardless of how badly people wanted a particular road. When you start with violence, then you get the natural results: robbery, wars and economic destruction.

It's tough to listen to radio hosts complaining about the institutional corruption and brutality of governments-that no matter who you vote for, things just get worse. It always seems to be a surprise to these people...or is it? I mean really, you're surprised governments are violent? I just can't believe my cat killed my bird, and then he went for my fish! You will not believe this: I lit the fuse on that bomb and-get this dude-it *exploded*! I didn't see *that* coming.

Here's a gun; now go out and dominate strangers. That's marketed as a moral way to interact with others. And anarchists are the crazy ones!

Let's examine the bureaucrats and those whose lives are heavily dependent on the government concept. This quote from Étienne de la Boétie is very informative:

> "The fact is that the tyrant is never truly loved, nor does he love. Friendship is a sacred word, a holy thing; it is never developed except between persons of character, and never takes root except through mutual respect; it flourishes not so much by kindnesses as by sincerity. What makes one friend sure of another is the knowledge of his integrity: as guarantees he has his friend's fine nature, his honor, and his constancy. **There can be no friendship where there is cruelty, where there is disloyalty, where there is injustice. And in places where the wicked gather there is conspiracy only, not companionship: these have no affection for one another; fear alone holds them together; they are not friends, they are merely accomplices**." *The Politics of Obedience: The Discourse of Voluntary Servitude* (emphasis mine).

This fear, as we've seen, also holds together and strengthens groupthink.

So we see the evidence shows that the government concept, a hierarchy of aggression and manipulation, creates and attracts psychopaths. Let's examine the psychopaths a bit more.

Studies have shown that the brain of a psychopath is different: the frontal lobe doesn't work and register most positive emotions, such as empathy. This has led to theories that psychopaths are born that way. However, there is also plenty of evidence indicating psychopaths are created, and I've only touched on a little of that evidence.

186

There is evidence the brain and nervous system can create new patterns, but what about shutting down connections? Can continued trauma and abuse shut off neural pathways, thereby shutting down-even permanently-such emotional responses as empathy? Yes, constant trauma and disassociation can shut down these connections.

While this is all just words to describe the same behavior, there seems to be two schools of thought on classification: 1. the psychopath and 2. the sociopath. The difference seems to be that while the behaviors are the same, the root cause of the behavior and any treatment, if any, distinguishes the two. Some "experts" believe the sociopath can be treated while the psychopath cannot; the psychopath is born without empathy while the sociopath is created.

For my purposes I really don't care, because the most important issue to me is to not let someone with such anti-social behavior have a platform that allows, encourages and protects such behavior. To me, it's more important to address the tools of mass destruction of societies than to determine if anti-social behavior has a genetic component or not.

If we remove the tools-the *mechanisms* that attract and create the exact type of behavior governments are supposed to be protecting us from-then the damage inflicted by these predators is greatly diminished.

What we can prove is that the government concept causes the behavior we generally call psychopathic or anti-social. It's a platform for predators to thrive and do damage on a global scale.

Summary:

As we've seen, the concept of government-violent domination under the guise of protection and setting up a caste system-*causes* severe psychological damage to the abuser and the abused.

It creates a trauma bond, created known as the Stockholm Syndrome. It damages people psychologically when they pretend one group is in control of the other. The damage is made worse when personal responsibility is removed from the abuser.

Because of groupthink and fear, we have people refusing to stand apart from the crowd. Call it pluralistic ignorance or bystander apathy, it doesn't matter. The fact is people are paralyzed with fear of doing the right thing, of sticking to their principles because they value the opinion of the group more than their own perceptions of right and wrong.

What it comes down to is their perceptions of right and wrong are dictated not by what the crowd *actually* believes, but rather by what they *assume* the crowd believes. It's a self-paralyzing fear; it's probably completely self-inflicted. And thanks to Solomon Asch, we know we can never really know for sure unless each person is privately and anonymously interviewed.

This fundamental human flaw is shown in the Bible: "Pilate said unto him, What is truth? And when he had said this, he went out again unto the Jews..." John 18:38. Pilate lets the crowd dictate what should be done instead of sticking to his own judgment of the facts.

187

Many psychological aspects are at work here; these experiments explain how and why the system is self-perpetuating. It doesn't matter whether it is by design or the unintended consequence, what matters are the predictable and inevitable results: serious psychological damage with a paralyzing fear of change.

> "It is true, such men may stir, whenever they please; but it will be only to their own just ruin and perdition: for till the mischief be grown general, and the ill designs of the rulers become visible, or their attempts sensible to the greater part, the people, who are more disposed to suffer than right themselves by resistance, are not apt to stir. The examples of particular injustice, or oppression of here and there an unfortunate man, moves them not." *Second Treatise on Civil Government*, John Locke, section 230 (1690)

(Many will notice how liberal Thomas Jefferson paraphrased Locke in the *Declaration of Independence* of July 4, 1776.) Political analysts, tyrants and their supporters have practiced this system of human farming for centuries. As technology improves, so does their manipulation and control of the masses. On the other hand, as technology improves, truth can be spread faster too.

The fear is on both sides though, as explained above. Those carrying out the actual threats and coercion fear being out of a job. If a cop is fired, then he's back on the lowest rung of the pecking order and he could lose his pension. Worse, now if they attack someone their victim may fight back and kill them as they deserve.

The same psychological issues keeping the current system in place will aid in maintaining the voluntary society that replaces it. Resistance to new ideas will prevent another government from being erected or imposed.

The story of the naked emperor tells us how to break the spell. All it took was for one child to state the obvious. If we can be as brave as the child, to put the truth above what we think others believe, we can break the spell.

Intense inner conflict results from people's tendency to exaggerate other people's thoughts and belief's. It's been called the "illusion of transparency." We don't know other people's thoughts, and researchers have found people tend to overstate how other people will judge them.

The child was able to point out the truth because he apparently didn't think or care about how other people would judge him-he just pointed out the obvious. Everyone else already knew the emperor was naked, but they were just too afraid to act accordingly. We need to recognize and point out the truth regardless of any perceived judgment from others. Who knows who we'll inspire or what change we'll influence? We'll never know if we don't speak up.

So it comes down to fear. We know politicians are criminals, the facts have been laid before you. And yet, most do nothing about it. Why? So we can continue living a safe life? Because we care so much what our neighbors may think? Do you conduct yourself based on what others think?

An aspect of this fear and immobilization that cannot be overlooked is explained with Plato's allegory of the cave from *The Republic*. Plato describes a false reality where prisoners have spent their entire lives in a cave where they have to stare at a wall that is lit by a fire behind them so all they see are shadows against the wall. The prisoners think these shadows are real and have no idea they are looking at mere shadows and hearing echoes:

> "And now, I said (Plato), let me show in a figure how far our nature is enlightened or unenlightened: -Behold! human beings living in a underground cave, which has a mouth open towards the light and reaching all along the cave; here they have been from their childhood, and have their legs and necks chained so that they cannot move, and can only see before them, being prevented by the chains from turning round their heads. Above and behind them a fire is blazing at a distance, and between the fire and the prisoners there is a raised way; and you will see, if you look, a low wall built along the way, like the screen which marionette players have in front of them, over which they show the puppets.

> "And do you see, I said, men passing along the wall carrying all sorts of vessels, and statues and figures of animals made of wood and stone and various materials, which appear over the wall? Some of them are talking, others silent.

> "- You have shown me a strange image, and they are strange prisoners.

> "Like ourselves, I replied; and they see only their own shadows, or the shadows of one another, which the fire throws on the opposite wall of the cave?

> "And now look again, and see what will naturally follow if the prisoners are released and disabused of their error. At first, when any of them is liberated and compelled suddenly to stand up and turn his neck round and walk and look towards the light, he will suffer sharp pains; the **glare will distress him**, and he will be unable to see the realities of which in his former state he had seen the shadows; and then conceive someone saying to him, that what he saw before was an illusion, but that now, when he is approaching nearer to being and his eye is turned towards more real existence, he has a clearer vision, -what will be his reply? And you may further imagine that his instructor is pointing to the objects as they pass and requiring him to name them, will he not be

perplexed? **Will he not fancy that the shadows which he formerly saw are truer than the objects which are now shown to him**?" (Emphasis added)

Put this into real-life contexts, such as speaking to a lifelong bureaucrat or someone on a jury. Imagine a juror in a tax evasion or drug possession prosecution who, like Martin Jenkins, a lawyer with the New Hampshire labor board, believe "...the laws are universal, it's the law." Then they see us in court asking for facts to prove it, and despite watching the prosecutor fail, fall back on their perception that has served them so well.

This is why it's so important to have some overlap with the people we're communicating with. Their perceptions must be close to the facts we're presenting for most to be able to make any sense of what we're talking about.

If you doubt the power of what I've presented, including basic social pressure, then you can verify this easily for yourself. Call into a political talk show and tell them that there are no states and citizens-that they're all fictions-and that what we refer to as government should be abolished. Send me the audio.

That uneasy feeling you get when you imagine yourself making the call-there's your evidence.

Fear is also generated by the constant contradictory messages. When people with guns are giving conflicting messages, there's stress because we may not know what to do to avoid punishment. An example is the jury system.

The Bushel's Case (1670) (Court of Common Pleas) was the decision establishing the principle that judges may not coerce juries to convict. http://en.wikipedia.org/wiki/Bushel%27s_Case.

Look at the contradiction here; the Honorable John Vaughan apparently overlooked the obvious. It appears that it's perfectly fine to coerce a man to show up at a particular room in a certain building at a set time, and there's no problem coercing that man to make a decision. But *which* decision to make, *then* coercion is not permitted for some reason. Isn't that an arbitrary place to draw the line?

Get your ass in here or I'll have you shot.
No need for guns, mate; I'll be there.
Now you sit there until I say you can leave.
Why are you forcing me to be here?
Because you need to hear this and make a decision with these other eleven farm animals.
I see. What decision do you want me to make?
Excuse me; do I look like a barbarian to you, I can't force you to make a certain decision; only a psycho would do that.
So forcing me to make a *certain* decision is psychopathic, but forcing me to make a decision is not?
Yes, that's our justice system.

Nice formula:
Forcing a particular decision=psycho
Forcing a decision=justice

This just doesn't make any sense to me, and if you look at the justice system you'll see this is exactly what's happening. It reminds of a line from the movie *This is Spinal Tap*: "It's just such a fine line between stupid and clever." That's the same fine line that politicians ride all the time. Sounds like the theme to my radio show.

The line in the sand limiting violence to get their way is wherever the politician thinks it needs to be to ensure compliance with their will. They know very well there is a line they usually cannot cross without having a PR nightmare on their hands-that, or an actual overthrow. Nicolae Ceausescu found that out in 1989.

Their principle comes down to this: violence is moral to get what you want, but at a certain point it overwhelms one's opinions, and even the most conditioned victim cannot deny the observable facts. When your PR cannot manage the victims' perceptions of your violence, you've gone too far.

While there are many examples of this, unfortunately there are not enough yet. How else could the psychopaths get away with dropping those two bombs on Japanese cities? Sorry, I don't buy the PR that tries to justify mass murder. Go sell that crap to those still claiming to be Republicans.

Examples typically do not implicate entire gangs. They usually scapegoat their expendable, useful idiots, such as Lynndie England, involved with the torture in the Abu Ghraib prison in Iraq.

There is also the Rampart scandal in Los Angeles:
http://en.wikipedia.org/wiki/Rampart_scandal.

It seems to be the way the smarter criminals avoid responsibility. The Mafia, when carrying out a big-name hit, will very quickly hit their own assassin. This is what is claimed to have happened with the hit on Joseph Columbo in 1971, and of course with one of the most famous patsies, Lee Harvey Oswald.

To get over this fear, we need to have an open mind and be willing to look at the facts; to separate the facts from the fictions. We all live by certain perceptions; most, or all, are fictions. But they at least sometimes serve some useful purpose. Some fictions we live with every day, such as corporations. We only act as if they are real because there's a purpose. It makes for easier organization, cooperation and identification: Yeah, he's the owner, I'm just a peon worker. We're aware of the fiction, though, most of the time anyway.

The fictional concept of property works the same way. However useful a concept it may be, it's still a man-made concept; property and ownership do not exist naturally. While a tremendously useful fiction, at the same time it's been equally, if not more so, disastrous. One need only look at the Middle East to see this in action every day. There are some pretty persistent fictions going on there: not only the fictions of property and states, but three groups of people who believe god gave them the land. Also look at the blood-soaked history of the British Empire.

While I doubt society can effectively and peacefully function without the fiction of property, I don't think we need to discard it. The fictional concept of *states* is what needs to be removed and we need to be aware that property itself, like rights, are only fictions. With the fiction of states, the government concept is: that which is *immoral* for individuals to do, is magically *moral* when done by individuals ostensibly on behalf of the collective (fictitious state/city).

The collective is a fiction. Look at written history. American history, such as the years 1765-1783, is written from the standpoint of wealthy white slave owners. It gives the impression that a few exceptional men defeated the largest military body in the world, on their own. It doesn't mention the other wars George was fighting in the Caribbean, Europe, and India at that time. Nor do you read about the imprisonment of the Quakers, estate confiscation, slave rebellions and the horrible slaughter of the American natives.

Social evolution involves moving past fictions that no longer serve a useful purpose. Just as important, it's realizing they are just fictions; this is particularly relevant when resolving property disputes.

We have to be able to identify contradictory messages. We're bombarded with them, but it's just a matter of comparing the facts to the rhetoric. Here is a gem:

> "It [13th amendment] introduced no novel doctrine with respect of services always treated as exceptional, and certainly was not intended to interdict enforcement of those duties which individuals owe to the state, such as services in the army, militia, on the jury, etc. The great purpose in view was liberty under the protection of effective government, not the destruction of the latter by depriving it of essential powers." *Butler v. Perry*, 240 U.S. 328 (1916).

Here they are being honest; an essential power of government is forcing people to perform certain services. Slavery is fine as long as you, the tyrant, simply declare the service exceptional!

Isn't "liberty under the protection of effective government" impossible if by effective government is meant forcing people to provide services and support? What liberty is there when forced into temporary slavery at the whim of politicians? These brilliant legal minds didn't see the problem here? Well, when you need to force people to pay you for your services, then I guess the issue is kind of cloudy.

I think they had to realize that the problem with forcing people to pay for services, including protecting liberty, was that it violates one's liberty. So it's easy to say, "We do not respect your liberty nearly as much as we want your property. Sure, we'll protect your liberty, just pay us, and what's left we'll protect. And by protect we mean having courts you can pay more money to, and spend endless hours on paperwork, and deal with lawyers who will imprison you for addressing them by their first name."

Such nonsense is not limited to the American politicians; this is from the Canadian Supreme court:

> "The principles of fundamental justice contemplate an accusatorial and adversarial system of criminal justice which is founded on respect for the autonomy and dignity of the person." *R. v. Swain*, [1991] 1 S.C.R. 933.

How is the Canadian government supported? Last I checked support was the same as everywhere else; it's compulsory-pay or go to jail. So much for autonomy in Canada. Judges won't speak to the media, for good reason: no one wants to be asked a question why a system that is allegedly founded on autonomy and dignity of the person is coercively supported. Respect for autonomy and dignity while being coerced to pay-how does that work now?

Normal people who respect autonomy do not use coercion, they use reason.

It's the same with the PR in the Constitution Act of 1982. This is from the part called the *"Canadian Charter Of Rights And Freedoms"* that states:

> "Everyone has the following fundamental freedoms:
> (b) freedom of thought, belief, opinion and expression, including freedom of the press and other means of communication."

Yeah, believe what you want, but don't act on it. Act as if you believe in being a free, autonomous man/woman and, depending on where you are, there will be a man with a gun teaching you otherwise.

Doesn't matter if you're in Canada or not, autonomy is not something psychopaths tolerate very well. So they use fear to keep those really interested in liberty from doing more than merely speaking about it in free speech zones.

Because deep down, whether you want to admit it or not, you know, as you've always known, the people calling themselves government are ruthless killers, thieves and liars. How do I know this? From the look of horror on people's faces when I suggest we stop paying taxes. While it may not last for more than a second before the ego jumps in to the rescue, it's there and we know why. Must be time to kill the messenger again?

There is that paralyzing fear of possibly standing apart from the pack. The assumption that one will do something they think the pack doesn't agree with, coupled with the fear of what our neighbors (cops etc.) will do to us for taking a stand. I think it's safe to presume, based on observable facts, that as more of your friends and family stop paying taxes your fear will diminish and you will be emboldened to start doing what you know is morally correct: stop paying taxes and stop cooperating with our would-be owners.

As we've seen, most people know that using force is wrong and that politicians are all crooks; that if we operated in the same manner, others would see us as criminals. And if we operated as politicians do, then we would be criminals.

Fear and groupthink explain why political psychopaths get such compliance, and lay psychopaths not so much. Let's do a comparison between a president and Charles Manson.

Manson is in prison because Vincent Bugliosi claimed he got his followers, upper middle class kids, to kill strangers who posed no threat to them. Part of the shock people felt was that seemingly normal kids killed strangers on Manson's orders. Why would young men and women, with no history of violence or mental disease, commit brutal acts of violence against strangers on nothing more than an order from Charles Manson? Knowing what I know now, I'm surprised anyone was shocked or even surprised by the incident, since it happens every day, just on a much larger scale.

I'd go so far to write that Charlie probably had really good role models growing up-people calling themselves president, senator, general etc. After all, Charles Manson was born in 1934 and was a child during World War II and the Korean and Vietnam wars. Vietnam is a good example where young men, eighteen and nineteen years old, were sent thousands of miles away to kill, on orders, perfect strangers who were never a threat to them. This raises a serious question: Wasn't Manson convicted of doing the same thing Richard Nixon was doing, only on a much smaller scale? Maybe the Vietnam War would have been stopped had Nixon used a Beatles' song as his war cry.

Why is it okay when Nixon did it, but criminal when Manson did it? If Manson is a monster for ordering the deaths of seven innocent people, then what is Nixon for not only ordering the deaths of hundreds of thousands of Vietnamese, but complicit in the death of tens of thousands of American men? What about Truman for ordering the extermination of thousands of innocent children?

The only difference I see is the mind control involved. Manson's mind control was limited to a handful of people while Nixon's, or the mind control supporting Nixon, was global.

It's just another example where monsters like Nixon can wreak havoc with impunity while people are shocked when someone does the same thing on a small scale. Many people didn't like what Nixon was doing, but did nothing about it. They went about their lives silently supporting the war machine. Would the same people have sat by helplessly watching Manson and his family commit brutal acts of murder? If serial killers were committing crimes because the community was paying them, doesn't it make sense to stop paying them?

American presidents have thousands of middle-class kids killing people who pose no threat to the people in North America. What's the difference if killing for a country, for a god, or for some other pretended authority?

194

Replication. One of the most important elements of the scientific model is the principle or theory must be predictive. This includes being able to replicate results. My website http://marcstevens.net has many examples where people I have never met, in places I've never been, have replicated what I've done. I mention this in *Adventures*; the difference is now the duplicated results are far wider than just part of North America. We've seen the same results, reactions and excuses in Canada, Europe, Australia and New Zealand.

We can accurately predict that if you ask a barrister acting as magistrate in Melbourne, Australia who they represent, you'll trigger the same rage as when you ask a traffic court judge in Brooklyn, New York or in Toronto, Canada.

We also know that if you ask a cop on the witness stand, "Factually what is the state?" the judge and prosecutor will jump out of their chairs objecting. Even better, watch the psychos flip out when you ask the cop, "Do you have personal firsthand knowledge the constitution and code apply to me?"

The rage is predictable because that's the natural result of the hierarchy due to the government concept. The hierarchy creates a facade of legitimacy; it covers the violence of those higher on the pecking order. This hierarchy diminishes empathy while building a fragile, though massive ego. It's built up of grandiose views of oneself (honorable etc.), so when the facade is challenged, even with just questions, then rage is triggered because the PR cannot stand on its own. Rage is the only way to cope with a challenge to the judge's model of the world.

That's why fits of anger are so predictable. It doesn't matter what the geographic location is as long as there is a hierarchy maintained by violence, but covered up with lies so people accept it, then there will be violent reactions when you challenge those lies. It's a very simple formulaic sequence:

- Violent hierarchy
- Flimsy political PR as cover
- Simple challenges to political lies
- Violent reactions

If you doubt this, (and that's good), then you can try it for yourself. Go to court and ask a judge whom he represents when he's presiding over traffic proceedings. Ask him what the nature of his/her relationship is to the prosecutor or the cop who filed the ticket. That feeling of dread you may have just thinking about asking a lawyer such a question is evidence of the above; that apprehension is probably based on your own personal experience with governments. You already know their true violent nature, even if you still can't publicly admit that all governments should be abolished.

You can get your own independent evidence/verification of the model by replicating the results yourself. Those interested in the truth can get verification from the many calls I've posted on my website and can just ask bureaucrats some simple questions themselves.

Chapter Two

The Economics of Control
The Economic case against the government concept

But for the concept of government could there be such economic disasters such as the 2008 housing crash? *But for* the concept of government would there be large-scale inflation? We'll see the answer is yes to both. Central banking, the monopoly of a medium of exchange is only possible when there's a gang called government forcing the markets to use it.

Have you ever noticed something peculiar about government services? Did you realize there are some services, though by monopoly, where payment is not compulsory? But that does not mean the service is not also supported by compulsory taxation.

Look at municipal fluoride, I mean, water service. If you don't pay, they shut the water off; it's as simple as that. They don't take your house and put you in prison for not paying for water. Think about it in terms of what is most important to the life of a human being (Homo sapiens). Except for oxygen, water ($H2O$) is the most important element to sustain our lives. Power is another one; don't pay the electric bill and the service is shut off. People pay their electric bill because they actually want the service, not because they fear men with guns showing up in the middle of the night to kill their dog.

We hear lots of talk about a free market, but is there one? Maybe on a very small scale, thanks to things like Bitcoin. But there is no large-scale, continent-wide, free market. I could be wrong. I just don't see the evidence of this free market, at least not the one always mentioned in the mainstream media.

So an important question is:

Freedom to do what?

How many people see the contradiction in the phrase *free country*? Do you know many people who can actually identify that as a public relations fiction? Consider yourself lucky if you know more than a handful; trust me, you're among an enlightened group of people and a soon-to-change minority. Even fewer will be able to tell you *why* it's public relations fiction; it has to do with more than just taxes.

People who identify themselves as a Citizen of the United States and of a State, such as Arizona or Florida, believe they live in both a State and a Country. To be more accurate, they live in a city within a county within a particular State that is one of the united States called the United States of America. They believe they live in a free country where they enjoy far

196

more freedoms than people from other countries, such as China or the People's Republic of China.

But is that true; is it a rational belief based on evidence? Most would agree it is, but let's actually look at the facts. Facts are very inconvenient for people who believe this way; just look at the mainstream news.

First, we'll examine the alleged freedoms of a Citizen of the United States living in California. We should always identify what we're talking about. Freedom is defined as:

"Liberty; absence of restraint." *Ballentine's Law Dictionary*, page 499.

Notice it says the "absence of restraint." Freedom, unlike what statists will tell you, is not doing whatever you want regardless of the life, liberty and property of others; that would be a type of restraint on someone else's freedom or liberty. This of course, in my opinion, is the basis of Andrew J. Galambos' definition: "...the societal condition that exists when every individual has full (i.e. 100%) control over his own property."

It's easy to see using this definition of freedom that it does not exist where there is government. No one has full control over their own property, and yes, your body falls into the category of property. Aside from the fact those who act as government don't think we little people own anything, we're certainly not free to use our property (even our bodies) without permission from those wonderful people calling themselves government.

Keep in mind, we're examining whether there is freedom and what Citizens are free to do, not the justifications for laws and statutes. There are many political excuses for restraint, or the killing of freedom, but they are irrelevant to this issue. As stated, there's no freedom in California because there is government; government comes from "govern", which means:

"To direct and control; to regulate; to influence; *to restrain*; to manage." *Ballentine's Law Dictionary*, page 530 (emphasis mine).

So what are Citizens free to do in California as opposed to China? Let's look at the initial similarities. Both California and China have people acting as governments, so there is no freedom in either area because there is restraint and every individual does not have 100% control over their lives and property. We're looking at the degree of restraint, not the degree of freedom and liberty.

Let's look at some of the things we as mankind do to live and survive. We need to eat and drink to live, so we generally work to get money to buy food. Some still have farms and produce their own; some go hunting and fishing. We go to school to help develop skills that are marketable. We get married, buy a house and maybe have children. We also like to entertain and be entertained, as well as relax and take vacations from the grind.

197

The question is: are we free to engage in the activities necessary to sustain our lives and those of our families? Unless you're brain-dead, the answer is no, we're not free. As we'll see, not any more free than others in those other countries.

Yes, there are degrees of restraint, but not freedom; freedom is all or nothing. This is why you get the silly excuse of being "more free" than someone else. But that's the same as arguing your prison is better than the other because you may get raped fewer times per week. Restraint is restraint, and any restraint negates freedom. Yes, I would prefer 10% restraint over 90%, but neither is freedom.

Let's first look at marriage. In California, as with every so-called state, each couple wanting to get married has to first get and pay for permission from a bureaucrat, i.e., a license:

> "(a) Before entering a marriage, or declaring a marriage pursuant to Section 425, the parties shall first obtain a marriage license from a county clerk." *California Family Code* § 350.

> "The person solemnizing the marriage shall return the marriage license, endorsed as required in Section 422, to the county recorder of the county in which the license was issued within 10 days after the ceremony." *California Family Code* § 423.

I thought Americans were free; how so if we need permission to get married? Whoever performs the ceremony needs a license/permission to perform marriage ceremonies. And keep in mind, a license is a tax and is permission to do something you have no right to do and is a crime if done without the license. It's a crime to get married in the United States; the psychopaths made it a crime to get married. Look at this definition of license:

> "A license is a right or permission to carry on a business or to do an act which, without such license, would be illegal." *Sea Lar Trading Co., Inc. v. Michael*, 433 N.Y.S.2d 403, 406.

Some may argue, "Oh, Marc, there are different kinds of licenses-you can't lump all licenses into this particular definition!" That's reasonable, but wrong nonetheless. If you look at the Arizona constitution, there's only one "grant of authority" to issue licenses given:

> "Authority to provide for levy and collection of license and other taxes. The law-making power shall have authority to provide for the levy and collection of license, franchise, gross revenue, excise, income, collateral and direct inheritance, legacy, and succession taxes, also graduated income taxes, graduated collateral and direct inheritance taxes, graduated

198

legacy and succession taxes, stamp, registration, production, or other specific taxes." *Arizona constitution*, article nine § 12.

Let's look briefly at what a crime is supposed to be. Does anyone think *anything* can be a crime? Doesn't the word lose meaning as it becomes more vague? And that's the model of Legal Land: the psychopaths who run the show keep things as vague as possible. Criminals avoid specifics; that's why terrorism comes down to non-compliance with a politician. When you are dealing with someone who insists on abstractions and refuses to be specific, you can be assured you're dealing with a criminal. At the least you're interacting with someone who doesn't have a clue.

The following is from *Black's Law Dictionary*; it's not as vague as lawyers would have you believe:

> "**CRIME**…Crimes are those wrongs which the government notices as injurious to the public, and punishes in what is called a "criminal proceeding," in its own name. 1 Bish.Crim.Law, § 43; In re Jacoby, 74 Ohio App. 147, 57 N.E.2d 932, 934, 935. A crime may be defined to be any act done in violation of those duties which an individual owes to the community, and for the breach of which the law has provided that the offender shall make satisfaction to the public…The distinction between a *crime* and a *tort* or civil injury is that the former is a breach and violation of the public right and of duties due to the whole community considered as such, and in its social and aggregate capacity; whereas the latter is an infringement or privation of the civil rights of individuals merely…A crime, as opposed to a civil injury, is the violation of a right, considered in reference to the evil tendency of such violation, as regards the community at large." *Black's Law Dictionary*, Rev. 4th Ed., 445.

Let's see if standing in a building with family and trading vows of commitment to another falls within the above definitions for a crime…

How is the act of trading vows "injurious to the public?" I can't see how any injury is caused to the public (though with my parents the government may have been on to something!). However, the attorneys who wrote this were careful to use the word "notices." Even if governments could notice anything, don't hold your breath expecting an answer to the question of what kind of injury is allegedly caused. Any time there is no causation, there is no crime.

Is the act of trading vows a "violation of those duties which an individual owes to the community"? What duties? Do we have a duty to not get married that is somehow owed to the community? Notice here the word community is used, not state. This is because statists think they are synonymous. If there is such a duty then how and why was it created? Does it exist naturally, or is it man-made?

199

Is the act of trading vows, "the violation of a right, considered in reference to the evil tendency of such violation, as regards the community at large?" Again, what right and is the trading of vows evil? Keep in mind that this is limited to only the act of trading marriage vows, not to anything taking place after. Those things are covered by other laws, such as the sodomy and cohabitation laws.

Can ordinary people called a legislature make anything they want to be a crime? Yes, but in name only, and it remains their delusion. People can call a cat a dog; it doesn't change anything except a perception. Remember, the public relations regarding the establishment of governments: "to protect and maintain individual rights." This means a real crime has to include the violation of a legal right. As stated, what the psychopaths called legislators are doing is continuously making the word crime mean less and less. Doing so ensures the prisons are always full. The ritual of creating laws-or the more regal sounding "legislation"-is all about perceptions. And we all know how important perceptions are.

> *Give me your money bloody peasant!*
> No, bug off foul cretin.
> *It's my opinion your money is now mine, give it here!*
> Your opinion? Are you drunk? No way mate, bug off.
> *It's not my opinion, it's, it's... it's legislation!*
> Well then, that's different; here you go. We'll have to work to repeal *that* legislation.

This is factually identical to how things work now. People will complain and spend a good part of their lives to vote in their guy/lady to change legislation. An example is the 2012 elections in the US to get a Republican in to change previous opinions or legislation.

We usually support our family by working, by providing services or products to others, generally called the market. Are we free to work and support our selves and family? Of course not; we need permission or armed troops called police will stop us.

This permission takes the form of a license. Why would it be a crime to cut hair without a license? I'm serious. Those outside the United States, the Land of the Free, might be unaware that you need a license to *wash* other people's hair, (see section 1602 of title 9 of the Texas code). You even need permission to *braid* someone's hair, (see Texas state statutes, Title 9, Sec. 1602.002).

In Texas you can be killed by the economic police if you shampoo hair without permission. So I have to wonder, not only when I hear people talking about the free market in the United States, but also when statists claim the Great Depression was caused by the free market, just where is this so-called free market anyway?

A free market is a market without violent restraint and control. The mere presence of people called government proves there's restraint and therefore, no free market. Even if you accept the lie that licenses are necessary for protection, it does not negate the fact there is no free market.

200

Look at what the California psychopaths wrote into their code about vocations; knowing they have men with guns on the payroll really makes this section come alive:

> "The Legislature finds and declares that: (c) The criminal sanction for unlicensed activity should be swift, effective, appropriate, and create a strong incentive to obtain a license." *California Business and Professions Code* § 145.

Read through that part, you'll see these people are willing to kill us for some pretty trivial things. It is certainly evidence of the pay-or-go-to-jail method that characterizes them as psychopaths doesn't it? Create strong incentive to obtain a license indeed.

Point out the obvious-that the means of government are opposed to the stated end-and a big fallacy used by politicians and mass media will rear its ugly, though popular head. They dismiss the idea as being "out of step with the mainstream." (The appeal to popularity fallacy, *argumentum ad populum*.) Everything new is out of step with the mainstream. That does not determine whether an idea has merit or not.

Here the violent status quo is defended by the same people who also tend to speak out in opposition to government corruption and waste. When you mention abolishing government and basing society on voluntary interactions and not violence, rather than commenting on the merits of the idea itself, attention is diverted to what the host/politician alleges is out of step with the mainstream...as if anyone can intelligently speak on behalf of millions of individual men, women and children.

And that is one of the most compelling reasons to have a voluntary society--to respect the autonomy of every man and woman-because we can really only speak for ourselves. How the hell would I know what is best for someone in Ireland or China? Other than that he/she should be left alone to make their own decisions, it's none of my business.

The "out of step with the mainstream" is just as bad a principle as the limits the Roman church put on technological advances. Whatever views the mainstream (impossible to quantify anyway) does not hold are invalid. Should such an abstraction govern the broadcasting of ideas and concepts? The internet was not mainstream until about 1998; should all research and development have been quashed in 1979 because it was not in step with the mainstream? Abolition of slavery was not in step with the mainstream until well after the War for Independence. You get the point.

Even if addressed directly, the idea is dismissed as utopian and impossible. No facts are offered to support these opinions. It comes down to this: Roads cannot be built without killing people, and ideas to the contrary are utopian and out of step with the mainstream.

But statists can still embrace a voluntary society. So cheer up as you watch governments collapsing around you. There's a place for all in a free society. You can still pay others to dominate you as you crave; you just won't have the option to pay others to dominate me and others who value autonomy and liberty.

The economic damage caused by the government concept is probably incalculable. We know when measured in Federal Reserve Notes it's in the trillions per year. The aggression goes by many different names; the two most popular euphemisms are regulations and taxation. There's direct damage caused by that robbery, and also secondary damage. And it is robbery in the lay sense.

I spoke with a tax agent in Washington, and after we had already determined she had no evidence proving the laws applied to me, I asked her a very direct question: If you forcibly take my property, what's the difference between you and a robber? There was a pause, and she feebly stated, "We have a legal sanction." No you don't, we already established you have no evidence the laws apply to me just because I'm physically in Washington. Do you have any such evidence? She agreed she didn't. Then you're nothing more than a common robber if you forcibly take my property. The facts tell the story.

Taxation and regulation are prettied up, usually with the term "reasonable" and the political justification that it's for protection. We already know they're not here to protect; that alone negates any claim the aggression is reasonable.

We don't focus on whether the standard (policy/rule/regulation/statute/law) proposed by a politician is reasonable; it avoids step one: it's not reasonable to coerce people to pay you.

Logic dictates we start with the foundation: how is the politician supported? Aggressive force and threats of force. The foundation is psychopathic. Logically, there's no reason to focus on anything else. When you start with a psychopathic base, then it's easy to see how the resulting damaged is caused.

The harm caused by the credit system from just 2004-2008 when the bubble burst is still being done, it hasn't stopped. Yes, the politicians had hearings with the executives of Goldman Sachs and there seemed to be genuine outrage at Wall Street and they deserved it. But how did the evil Wall St. bankers accomplish such economic disaster while reaping billions in profits? Could they have done that *but for* willing partners and accomplices? Please...

How popular would paper, loaned at interest, be as money in a free market? Could the Federal Reserve and the banking system have been able to pull off the housing bubble in a free market? Could there even be a housing bubble in a free market? I don't think so.

If the Federal Reserve was not forced on the market, but instead introduced as any other service/product, then they would have had to perform. Even if it took hold, there would be competition and it could have been discarded after the first bubble and crash.

Without government forcing people to use only credit as money, the Federal Reserve and Goldman Sachs could not have pulled it off. History shows neither the government nor the banks could convince the market that credit is better than silver and gold. So, starting in 1934, the market was forced to surrender their gold and by 1971 the market was forced to only use credit, represented by pieces of paper, as a medium of exchange.

But the outrage at the banks and governments really hasn't mattered because enough people are still paying taxes and cooperating with people calling themselves governments. If people were really outraged, the entire credit/debt system would have finally collapsed, and the heads of the big banks and the Federal Reserve would have been thrown in prison with congress and the president. The credit/debt system has been in the process of collapsing for decades; it's really picking up steam now and getting near its end.

A big clue that something is not in your best interest is when it's *forced* on you (Captain Obvious again). As shown, there are many fictions at work to divert our attention away from this simple fact.

But more and more people are not focusing on the fictions, and that is a real problem for the economic/political masters of the world. People are seeing that the credit system, like electronics (printers), has a built-in self-destruct button. It's designed to be able to go only for so long until it implodes; it's called interest. It's bad because it takes down entire economies. Many have already collapsed, but because of its rationale, the government concept survived the collapse. The economic/political structure that brought about the economic destruction just continues with a new fiat system.

This is why we already saw Chinese officials and others talking about a world currency; one currency instead of many as if the problem with credit/debit is because it's printed up with too many different icons. Right, the problem is too many tyrants issuing their own credit/debt, not the coerced use of credit (created out of thin air) on an unwilling market. The ones who profit from the current structure naturally never address the obvious fact: a debt system forced on an unwilling market may be the cause of the problem.

Some people in the media claim it's a failure of capitalism; they don't address the coercive nature of the system. Though to be fair some get closer to the source of the problem and address corporatism or fascism.

But rather than capitalism, let's focus on free trade. Any attributes consistent with free trade are great. Capitalism has also been intertwined with statism. There are so many phonies; do you think that those behind the big corporations and those who profit from them want free trade-a market that cannot be controlled by a few? If the criminal cartel dropped their guns and threats, do you think all those people, whose wealth is measured in FRN's want to see competing mediums of exchange? Why would they; who would want to watch their credit system collapse around them?

Government is a tool to keep the economic structures in place. The feudal land barons of the Eastern Seaboard of North America in the eighteenth century continued in the same manner after the War of Independence as before ("loyalists" lost their feudal estates to those who supported independence). The slavery of non-white Europeans continued unabated as did the slaughter of the American Indians.

Credit systems have a history of collapsing, so these days more and more people are looking to operate without the Federal Reserve System. As shown later, they are using alternatives, and that is unacceptable to politicians and their masters. Because when people take responsibility for their lives, it makes governments irrelevant. And that is one of the psychopaths' deepest fears. The psychopaths really have no weapon against irrelevance. This is dramatized in the movie "*V for Vendetta*" when the desperate fascist dictator says, "I want everyone to remember why they need us!"

We must keep in mind how awful being irrelevant can feel. Feeling irrelevant is pretty horrible; life tends to lose all meaning and you can lose your drive and inspiration. When speaking with a bureaucrat, this has to cross their minds; it's no wonder they take challenges personally. This must affect politicians, as they tend to be narcissists and can't stand when people don't buy into their inflated sense of relevance/importance. This personality flaw can be used against bureaucrats to help get problems with them resolved, as we'll later see.

We don't want to alienate bureaucrats when building a free market. We need city engineers and accountants and people who know the sewer systems. We need to always point out that it's not the service that's the problem; it's the manner in which it's paid for.

Bureaucrats probably feel the same way as those in the horseshoeing business felt when the automobile started taking off: they felt threatened that they would not be able to continue to earn a living. Technology and society was evolving and leaving them behind. They probably fought it and denied the obvious benefits of the new technology.

I'll just spend a little time on how crazy the credit system is and why it's so dangerous. Take the so-called "loans" that were described as "toxic" by the media so many times. Do you recall any media source showing the facts about these alleged loans? Think Fox Business channel will show the market there is no actual loan? Don't hold your breath. If you point out the facts, those with a vested interest in the system will attack you and call you a conspiracy theorist or nut.

Max Keiser got close; he referred to them as "phony assets." I've not heard him or anyone else on a mainstream TV or radio show tell the truth: there's no loan. Their sponsors would not like anyone attacking the economic and political structure they rely on. (I heard George Noory being disingenuous when Dr. Judy Wood was on his show. He stated that as hosts, they didn't have to believe everything the guest presented, but to put it on the air and let the audience decide. Really? I'm proof that's not true for *Coast to Coast*.)

There is no loan, it's just paper for paper. When you go to a bank for a loan, you are not borrowing money or an existing asset of the bank, you are borrowing credit. Credit is a fiction, an abstraction:

> "**credit**…The antonym of cash on delivery; the trust or confidence which is reposed by the seller in the buyer when the time of payment is extended without security."
> *Ballentine's Law Dictionary*, page 287.

When you sign the credit card or loan application, the bank accepts it as credit-a trust or confidence of payment by you. The bank then gives you more paper in exchange for the credit created by your signature. It's really no different than giving you a ten for two fives and calling the ten a loan. It's credit for credit, paper for paper. If there is something given, it's the opportunity to participate in their credit (Ponzi scheme) system, a system we're already forced to use. Remember, competition with the credit system, the economic structure of the world, is such a threat to the status quo that it's considered non-terror terrorism.

Even without being terrorism, it's still considered a crime that can get you more than a decade in jail. This is just one more example where free trade is considered a crime; as if we needed more evidence government is not about protecting freedom.

One problem is people don't seem to know or care about the fact that credit, like everything else, is subject to the law of supply and demand. Even in totalitarian states, when there is hyperinflation (hyper credit), prices skyrocket. No amount of force has ever been able to stop it. Even with price controls, the effect will be seen-maybe not always with milk prices, but it will appear.

And never lose sight of the fact that credit and debt are synonyms, it just depends on which side of the deal you're on. Debt is legally defined as "that which is owing to a person under any form or obligation or promise..." *Ballentine's Law Dictionary*, page 311. Above I cite where it is defined as "the antonym of cash". Credit (FRN's etc.) regardless of appearances, is the opposite of cash.

Sadly, most people never question why they are being forced to use credit/debt as money. And if you point out this fact, people attack you as if you're the one personally causing the economic destruction in the world. All they seem to be interested in is if they can pass the paper on to someone else. Many people, thanks to all the gold dealers' ads on the big TV and radio stations, are admitting there is a problem with the almost incalculable debt, but still deny the dollar can or will collapse. It's as if simple math doesn't make sense to them, or that math and economics are mutually exclusive subjects.

Each FRN, or any bank-issued national currency, is "loaned" to governments *at interest*. It cannot be paid in full because of the interest. This is the simplest explanation why the debt is always increasing. Even if governments wanted to pay it off, it's not possible because the interest makes it more than what you "borrowed." This interest may also be the basis for a lien against all the property/possessions you acquire with your use of FRNs. This is suggested by a politician and recorded in the Congressional Record:

> "The money will be worth 100 cents on the dollar, because it is backed by the credit of the Nation. It will represent a mortgage on all the homes and other property of all the people in the Nation." *Congressional Record – House*, March 9, 1933, page 83.

http://www.scribd.com/doc/72347568/Congressional-Record-March-9-1933-73-Cong-First-Sess-re-HR1491-Bank-Conservation-Act-pp-76-83

This is where you can see that politicians are not the ones in control; they are just useful idiots, higher up on the pecking order than cops, but still just useful goons nonetheless.

An historical example of this happened when Andrew "American Hitler" Jackson essentially shut down the central bank of the day, the Bank of the United States. Nicholas Biddle, the head of the bank followed through with his threats, and started pulling bank notes and currency out of the market, causing a panic.

This is what happens; the banks inflate and deflate the amount of credit/debt in the market. They take advantage of the greed and impulse for quick money by making credit/debt easy to get. This is falsely called a growing economy in the main stream media. When there is trouble, such as in 2008, the banks start deflating. This can also be done if the governments who are borrowing the credit/debt into existence increase taxes and pay back the private banking cartel called the Fed.

If the credit/debt is not put back into the market and the Fed doesn't lend as easily, there is deflation. This is bad when the market is forced to trade with that same credit/debt. Everything is financed except for a few essentials. Think about it: even excluding the 2004-2007 orgy, people use credit/debt to finance most of the things they think they are buying e.g., home, car, electronics, appliances etc. Politicians in Ireland, for example, tried to get public support for more bank bailouts by scaring people, saying there would be no money available through ATMs.

Innovations make things more efficient or produce better products, often at lower prices. The automobile took off when they were affordable for the majority of the market. What would happen to the auto market if there was no credit/debt to trade with? Manufacturers would either go out of business or they'd adapt to the current situation. How might they adapt?

We know there is a market for cars. Would there be as much of a market for new cars? It would probably shift to cars that lasted a lot longer. And they'd have to produce a car the market could afford without financing. Look at the innovation with the Internet. Who the hell wants to pay more than ten FRNs per head to see a movie when you can stay home and stream them for less than ten bucks a month? (I'd prefer to play some blues.)

Can there be a dynamic, thriving economy without the forced use of credit/debt as a medium of exchange? Of course there can be. It's silly to think the only way to have a successful economy is to have a small group of people force the rest of the community to only use credit/debt that the small group "creates" out of nothing. Look at the model in simple terms. I like to use the archetypical, sleazy Hollywood agent when he's pitching a really bad idea:

206

OK, stay with me here, OK, you're gonna love this, seriously, this will sell itself, I'm bringin' it to you first because you know quality when you see it, and I trust you.

We take pieces of paper, but only *you* can create them, OK, and you loan them out to the market and… yeah, I see where you're going there, OK not an issue, OK, we have men with guns and lawyers and cages, to make sure only *your* paper is used see.

Why should the men with guns do what you want? Because you can print up so much of this paper money they'll gladly carry out your orders without any discretion at all; we promise them pensions and other perks, early retirement, a wall of silence and immunity for their crimes. I'm telling you this foolproof!

Trying to pay off the debt would cause such deflation, as we've seen already, that the economy (based on the FRN) would grind to a halt. People wouldn't have any credit/debt to trade with. Maybe when that happens, the masses, when they see their kids starving, will finally give up their addiction to credit, break their emotional bond to government, and start acting like responsible adults and trade freely with the rest of the community. Maybe then people will stop asking for permission to live their own lives.

(As of 2013, this has not happened yet, and gas is almost at record price levels. It's averaging $3.75 USD a gallon, having risen about a dollar a gallon in less than two months. It's risen faster recently than it did at the beginning of 2013. The last couple of years, there has been an established pattern of spikes.)

In a free market, there's no army of men stopping competitors from offering their system of credit/debt to the market. Anyone who wanted to loan their credit at interest to the market could, not only an exclusive, unaccountable and largely unknown group of people.

This doesn't mean people should be forcibly stopped from doing so. If someone thinks credit, loaned at interest, is a good service, then they should be free to convince the market their service is better than others.

It's no proof to point out that the system has worked since at least 1913. Many things have appeared to have worked for many years; that's no proof it's rational and beneficial to society. Slavery has worked for thousands of years; is that something we want to continue? China's communist government has worked for more than sixty years. See how the premise is ridiculous?

What the government and banks did, with the help of an uninformed but very willing market, was to flood the market with credit/debt. This was in part accomplished with increasing housing sales through what was later called "toxic assets." Governments and banks encouraged home ownership and urged banks to give credit to those who could not pay them back. This is easy to do because we're talking about credit-something created out of thin air-just numbers in a computer.

I do not excuse the market that helped make it possible. Just as the market allows governments to exist, the market took the bait, again, and assisted the banks in expanding the amount of their credit through the giving of pretended "loans." It's no surprise the Federal Reserve System stopped reporting the M1 numbers in 2006.

The increase in readily available credit drove people to "buy" homes they otherwise could not afford; 100%+ loans were given out. This helped drive the flip craze, whereby you buy a beat-up house entirely on credit, use more credit to make improvements, and then sell within thirty days or before payments come due. Because the prices were going up almost monthly, the sap who bought the property figured he'd be able to rent it out or sell for a nice profit the next month. And they were correct for the most part...for a while. In southern California housing prices were going up by as much as $5000 a month.

The anticipation of an easy windfall in real estate, just as any high-risk gamble, is very much like a drug. There is a rush, just like cops get when getting ready to bust into a house in the middle of the night with machine guns drawn. When gambling, it's this rush that drives the addict.

Even if the market could accept there had to be a crash, the housing bubble had to burst eventually. The lure of such easy money (credit) together with such ever increasing risk of the market crashing, made it even more of a rush.

Someone in my family timed their purchase and sale almost perfectly. They got a house in southern California for about $175,000 in 2003. By 2007 they were able to sell for almost $400,000. Now, well after the bubble burst, the house is again valued at the same $175,000 and I remember them telling me that the buyer, from Orange county, thought it was a great deal. How's that working out for you?

When the credit, existing only on paper and computers, is so easy to get and there is so much of it, the perceived value always goes down. Just because it's not tangible like gold or oil doesn't mean supply and demand do not come into play. And there is nothing any group of people, even those called government, can do to stop this.

That's why the cost of gold and oil priced in FRNs skyrocketed. It's no coincidence that when all that credit started making its way through the market, including the stock market, commodities measured in FRNs went up. Gold averaged $319/oz. in 2003, shot to $409 in 2004, and then went into outer space in 2011, averaging $1,400 and $1700+ in 2012. Remember, this is generally only for prices as measured in FRNs, not commodities compared to other commodities. If you measure the price of oil in silver, the price actually went down.

With real estate, the so-called bundled up "loans," or toxic assets, were then resold to investors, such as customers of Goldman Sachs. Goldman Sachs knowingly sold its own customers pretended loans. Executives even admitted to congress during the dog and pony show hearings that they knew the derivatives (bundled toxic non-loans) were "shitty."

https://www.youtube.com/watch?v=whlzFWwVv98.

I'm sure if they were asked if there were legitimate loans made they still wouldn't admit the loans themselves weren't even real.

It's another castle made of sand. And it was all made possible because the market unwittingly allowed it; we cooperated with people called governments and accepted an abstract system of credit instead of mediums of exchange dictated by a free market.

Instead of going out of business and spending the rest of their lives in prison, Goldman Sachs executives were bailed out by Bush and his cronies, including former Goldman Sachs CEO, Hank Paulsen.

But look at the so-called bailout. The Federal Reserve System just created more of what caused the bubble: more credit/debt. They then loaned it to the criminal cartel called the US government, who then gave it to Goldman Sachs and other banks. This was followed up by another "stimulus" with Barack Obama, and what is called "quantitative easing" by the Federal Reserve front men, such as "Helicopter Ben" Bernanke. Quantitative easing (QE) is just a euphemism for an increase in credit/debt, i.e., inflation of the money supply. The credit is then used to buy stocks and treasuries.

Following "QE1" and then "QE2," "QE3" was unleashed in 2013. In other words, more credit/debt was created as governments and banks spent faster than computers could create more. And people still don't see Greece as a model of what is going to happen everywhere credit/debt is forcibly imposed as a medium of exchange? The suicide rate increased at alarming speed:

http://www.youtube.com/watch?v=VD_phmSldow.

George W. Bush said Americans are addicted to oil. Americans are also addicted to credit and getting something for nothing; immediate gratification is America's real drug of choice. Of course this is not discouraged-why would government, the owners of the people, discourage debt slavery?

When people are not paying their mortgages, they are also not paying property taxes, so the amount of extorted funds starts dropping. But governments never stop spending the stolen money (credit). This causes their deficits to skyrocket and now we're seeing large cities (corporations) declare bankruptcy. Why don't they just leave us alone and get real jobs? Just get out of the way.

Governments and apologists in the media blamed the crash on the free market saying there was not enough coercive control (regulation) over the banks. Instead of dismissing such nonsense, people seemed to buy into it. Oh, you've got a meth problem? No worries, it's your health-nut brother's fault. Here's more meth to help you recover.

Just as there was a housing bubble, there is a student loan bubble on the horizon. It works like the housing bubble: credit is made available to people who graduate from compulsory government high school to go to college, another government business. These bubbles work in the same manner as in health care, or pretty much any business where the ability to pay is separated from the actual payment by the buyer.

Students get easy credit to attend government schools. Because the flood of easy credit insulates students from the actual payment, prices always go up. They have to. Just like the housing debacle, students get credit for more than just tuition and books. They get credit for food, lodging and cars. With higher demand for college made possible by easy credit, prices go up. As the economy gets worse from the increased credit and government aggression, there is more of a push for college. You now hear a bachelor's degree is not enough; the competition for jobs is so great you need at least a master's degree. Demand keeps going up, so prices continue to go up. No amount of political rules can change or stop it.

A master's degree costs an average of twenty-seven thousand dollars a year, for six years. That's about $162,000 not including the interest. When there are so many people unemployed in the market, the price of labor, like with other commodities, goes down. People are racking up incredible amounts of debt to get college degrees, to then enter a market flooded with other college graduates looking for jobs, and the pay offered is going down. Right now (in 2013) many employers, due to increased costs of business, are cutting salaries and benefits such as health insurance.

Just like the housing bubble bursting, when enough people can't pay back their loans, the student loan bubble will burst and there will be another contraction of credit. Then there will be another panic, such as in 2008, when most cannot afford to pay the grossly increased prices, and colleges will not have the credit to continue to operate. What could happen is governments could extort more to subsidize their indoctrination camps.

All can see what a vicious circle it is. Of course, government apologists will lie by insisting, as they always do, that it's a failure of the free market; there just wasn't enough coercion (regulations and oversight). Their suggested fix is more government, because trillions of dollars a year just isn't enough. Funny that they never explain how more aggression and violence helps the market.

When we look at just taxation, we see tremendous obstacles to bringing services and products to the market. I'm still shocked anyone can start a business in California because there are so many taxes and regulations. And governments are the tool of the super wealthy to limit competition. We know regulations are not for the protection of life, liberty and property because support for governments is coerced.

So what are the regulations/licenses and other taxes for? To keep the elite-big business-at the top of the food chain.

Big business and governments have always been interconnected. An example is the FDA in the US. All the FDA does, along with other governments, is give a stamp of approval to new chemicals to poison people. As mentioned earlier, they also attack peaceful people engaging in the nefarious act of selling milk to people on a voluntary basis. When was the last time Bayer was raided by masked maniacs with machine guns and badges?

What the chemical companies get from their psychopathic partners, or tools, is immunity from the damage their products cause the population. People, because they are conditioned to believe governments are there to protect them from the evil, greedy corporations, think the chemicals are safe and those who suggest a natural diet with fruits, vegetables and only some animal products are quacks and weirdoes. They hear that a diet of processed "foods" is actually better than natural, whole foods; that pills are the way to health, not a good diet and proper exercise.

Once the FDA gives a chemical/pill/vaccine the rubber stamp, then it is legally considered safe. So if you're damaged, or killed by their product, you cannot hold them accountable.

According to the federal government, there are **two million** serious adverse drug reactions and **one hundred thousand** deaths yearly. How many from raw milk, you might ask? It's astounding-an almost incomprehensible **two** deaths from drinking raw milk from 1998-2011. That's two deaths reported in thirteen years; a horrific .15 deaths a year. No wonder men with machine guns are raiding the Amish!

From 1998-2011, approximately 1.3 million people died from prescription drugs while two died from drinking raw milk. So the only logical thing to do is to arm the troops and go into health food stores with machine guns drawn.

http://www.fda.gov/Drugs/DevelopmentApprovalProcess/Develo pmentResources/DrugInteractionsLabeling/ucm114848.htm
http://www.cdc.gov/foodsafety/rawmilk/raw-milk-questions-and-answers.html

The credit system underlies the entire economy; it affects everything. When we factor in government aggression/intervention, the damage is beyond calculation.

Wow, I really hope we can qualify for this house Honey.

Yeah, our first house...it's a dream come true. I hope we qualify.

So why do we have to qualify, Mr. Banker?

The bank wants to see that you're a good credit risk before we lend you money.

OK, does the bank actually lend money or credit?

The bank actually lends you credit, we create the credit from your signatures.

So we actually fund the alleged loan?

Yes.

And we give you this credit, you created from <u>our</u> signatures, back with interest?

Yes.

And if we don't pay you back the credit with interest, you take the house? And you get the house despite having done nothing more than create credit with our signatures?

Yes.

I'm sorry, we're confused; where's the risk for the bank again?

The same government that forces us to use credit/debt as money are the same people who will take the house from us and give it to the bank if we cannot pay it back, plus interest, for something created by our signatures. Can we really create credit out of thin air, though?

Wow, that's some business plan! Can we also provide that service to the market?
Silly anarchist; that would be a unique form of domestic terrorism.

In addition to the immeasurable cost to society just with the "legal" requirements and hoops to jump through, there is the problem with corruption-good ol' palm greasing and graft. This doesn't even take into account the conflicts of interest where politicians influence the market for their own profit. There are so many examples of this it would take the rest of my natural life just to scratch the surface.

An example is from Arizona with Jan Brewer, pretended governor of the State of Arizona. Jan is reported as having financial connections to CCA, Corrections Corporation of America. A law she signed in 2010 created the new crime of being in the State of Arizona while not being a US citizen. With the stroke of a pen, thousands more criminals were created. And where will they put them? In one of the CCA prisons. The more people they lock up, the more money Jan Brewer and her associates can make.

Mark Ciavarella and Michael Conahan are former judges who were convicted of racketeering in Feb. 2011. We reported this on the radio show. They were getting kickbacks from a detention facility, a detention facility they were sending children to. They made millions from this scam.

Think the prosecutors care about these judges' records? The prosecutors are doing the same thing. It may not be as blatant, but it's still the same process. If any of the parents of the children who were victimized by these two predators filed a civil cause of action against Ciavarella and Conahan, state attorneys would jump to their rescue arguing absolute immunity, and a fellow judge would allow it and throw out the complaint. And it's doubtful they bothered to investigate the other state actors who aided these two black-robed criminals.

We only need to look at one agency to get an idea of how much is routinely stolen from us: the Pentagon. The day before 9/11, Donald Rumsfeld reported that $2.3 trillion was unaccounted for. $2.3 TRILLION! This doesn't take into account the pallets-yes, *pallets-of billions* that disappeared in the Middle East after 9/11. These people got away with saying they "lost" three hundred sixty-three *tons* of physical paper credit, and not one of them was prosecuted for it. Yet, we are terrorized and our families traumatized if we don't pay a few hundred in blood money or grow a garden on our property.

The "waste" is a direct and unavoidable effect of the system itself; it cannot be stopped. It's the natural result of unaccountable domination. It is not possible *but for* the government concept.

There is a political theme: if someone doesn't pay his "fair share," then everyone else has to pay more to make up for it. If we apply this same theme to all the government waste, it amounts to double or triple taxation if not more. How does one go about doing such an accounting when it runs into the trillions?

Look at the lives politicians lead. They have mansions, limousines, planes etc. They have easy access to the media, who can't wait to hang on every word. There is one radio show in Washington, D.C. that only has senators on as guests. Why would anyone tune in just to hear more lies?

We can also apply the *but for* standard regarding the economy to further prove the damage caused by the government concept. *But for* the government concept, would people pay to drop bombs on people who pose no threat to them? *But for* the government concept, would people use pieces of paper for their transactions or tolerate only one provider of such paper? *But for* the government concept, could depressions be engineered through the expansion and contraction of a single monetary system?

And most important: *But for* the concept of government there could be no large-scale wars.

End of part 1 indictment

Part Two

Dealing with the Psychopaths

Unlike *Adventures*, this book extensively covers dealing with psychopaths such as tax agents, prosecutors and judges. There are no magic formulas. We're really just taking the bureaucrat's accusations and asking them to verify them: are they arbitrary or based on facts?

We already know psychopaths don't like to be challenged. Consider how crazy things can be in the bankruptcy courts. An attorney files a complaint in the bankruptcy court against almost every person and company the insolvent company has paid money to. This is done to recover as much money as possible so there is not as much for the court to discharge. It's a dirty tactic, and unfortunately, someone I work with was caught up in one.

Like the IRS, the attorney's complaint is almost devoid of any supporting facts, just allegations. One defendant, a friend of mine, filed a motion to dismiss for a lack of standing and failure to present any facts. This was based on basic rules of pleading and numerous court opinions such as *Bell Atl. Corp. v. Twombly.*, 550 U.S. 544, 127 S.Ct. 1955, 1964-65 (2007), which states a plaintiff must allege "more than labels and conclusions" or "a formulaic recitation of the elements of a cause of action."

Not surprisingly, the attorney assigned by the court responded by writing there was no requirement to present facts, but even the judge disagreed and quoted the same case above in his order granting the motion to dismiss. He also granted leave to file an amended complaint and you guessed it, the amended complaint also failed to present any facts. They did not even use the defendant's name in the complaint.

Again a motion to dismiss was filed and the attorney responded with basically this, "...there is no pleading requirement that the Trustee allege any wrongdoing against Defendant."

Amazing isn't it? I guess an opinion such as, "A plaintiff must allege personal injury fairly traceable to the defendant's allegedly unlawful conduct and likely to be redressed by the requested relief." *Allen v. Wright*, 468 U.S. 737, 751 (1984) just doesn't apply.

This aversion to witnesses and evidence is S.O.P. (standard operating procedure), with politicians and their henchmen. I can't tell you how many times tax agents have told me they don't need witnesses and evidence. You can make them change their minds just by agreeing with them; all you have to do is re-state their claim: So your assessment is arbitrary? This makes them drop their line about not needing witnesses and evidence; suddenly they're falling over themselves claiming they do have evidence. Of course, there are absolutely no facts connecting you to

214

their sacred writ, so when you question that, suddenly we're "arguing" with them.

These people are pathological liars; almost every statement out of their mouths is a lie. When do two wrongs make a right? When done by those claiming to be government. If the government has a consistent pattern of errors and crimes, then it's considered justice and due process, to wit:

> "But the Court went on to uphold the statute, based upon the historical prevalence and acceptance of similar laws. Id., at 510-511. This case is ultimately a reminder that the Federal Constitution does not prohibit everything that is intensely undesirable." *Bennis v. Michigan*, 517 U.S. 1163 (1996).

This is more proof that when you call yourself a government you set aside any principle of right and wrong in favor of what dead white lawyers have said. It's fine to look to others for guidance when making a decision, just measure it against your own principles of right and wrong.

As we've seen, these people have a really bad track record when it comes to being logical and consistent. What follows is one of thousands of examples of lawyers directly contradicting themselves and other lawyers (and these are supposed to the best in the business). Remember, precision and consistency is not a part of the legal profession:

> "A tax in its essential characteristics is not a debt, nor in the nature of a debt...It is not founded on contract or agreement... Taxes...are not contracts either express or implied...A privilege tax involves contract obligations. The acceptance of the privilege implies a promise to pay the statutory equivalent therefore, and the obligation may be enforced by ordinary remedies for the enforcement of ordinary contract obligations...The ideas involved in a privilege tax are these: The state offers a privilege on condition of being compensated therefore. The acceptance of such offer creates a contract. The law operating upon the acts of the parties raises the implied promise to pay the required compensation. The full consummation of the transaction involves the exchange of equivalents, the same as in any other case of an executed contract." *State v. Chicago & N.W. Ry. Co.*, 108 N.W. 594, 608, 128 Wis. 449.

So one court claims a tax is a debt:

> "The assessment is given the force of a judgment, and if the amount assessed is not paid when due, administrative officials may seize the debtor's property to satisfy the debt." *Bull v. United States*, 295 U.S. 247, 259; 55 S. Ct. 695; 79 L. Ed. 1421 (1935).

215

while another one claims: "A tax in its essential characteristics is not a debt, nor in the nature of a debt." It gets better when you keep reading; apparently these lawyers were going for the laughs because there is no shame when they contradict themselves in the same opinion.

On one page they claim, "Taxes...are not contracts either express or implied..." and a page or two later...wait for it...they write, "The state offers a privilege on condition of being compensated therefore. The acceptance of such offer creates a contract."

When is a tax a contract and not a contract at the same time? Answer: When a lawyer wants to profit from it. Spinning lies for a criminal cartel must be hard work. Then again, these lawyers don't seem to even put in any effort to make it look good. I can imagine if a clerk noticed the obvious and tried to point it out:

> Sir, on page three, you wrote taxes are not debts, and then on page five you wrote they are, how do we reconcile that contradiction? *Just use enough legal words to confuse the reader.*

Didn't these brilliant legal scholars read the part where they stated "Taxes...are not contracts either express or implied" before they justified taxation as a contract? Who are they trying to kid here?

Still not laughing when these lawyers talk about the "science of law?" Then the above opinion should help. Science is about accuracy and precision so things can not only be explained but also predicted.

These scholars also miss the incredibly perverse nature of these so-called contracts. A group of people use threats, duress and coercion to get people to comply with their demands: "If you do this activity without our permission, then we'll attack you." To avoid the attack, the people comply and pay the aggressors. Then apologists for the aggressors call the act of avoiding the attack evidence of a contract and jurisdiction.

This perversion is not by any means new; it's a standard piece of political public relations:

> "...it has been argued that the word "contract," in its broadest sense, would comprehend the political relations between the government and its citizens, would extend to offices held within a State, for State purposes, and to many of those laws concerning civil institutions, which must change with circumstances and be modified by ordinary legislation, which deeply concern the public, and which, to preserve good government, the public judgment must control." *Dartmouth College v. Woodward*, 17 U.S. 627, 4 Wheat. 518 (1819).

Pay or get shot or jailed is a way of describing a contract. So when Al Capone's men threatened a club owner saying he can only buy Al's beer, that was a contract. It was a privilege to sell Al's beer as opposed to Bugs Moran's swill.

When they bother to cover up their contradictions, they play word games-they just redefine the words used. Below is a citation that those who think they have a right to travel may not want to read, it's long but it's important enough to include so much:

"In City of Chicago v. Collins [175 Ill. 45, 51 N.E. 910], the court held that a city wheel tax ordinance was unconstitutional, and the use of the streets was a "right" and not a "privilege." The court stated: "A license, therefore, implying a privilege, cannot possibly exist with reference to something which is a right, free and open to all, as is the right of the citizen to ride and drive over the street of the city without charge and without toll, provided he does so in a reasonable manner." In Harder's Fireproof Storage & Van Co. v. City of Chicago [235 Ill. 58, 85 N.E. 253], however, the court redefined the "use of the streets", as a "privilege" on the ground that the legislature had acted on the subject by authorizing municipalities to exact a tax for the use of the streets. It was urged therein, on the basis of the Collins case, that the use of the streets was a right rather than a taxable privilege, hence, a statute empowering the municipality to exact a fee for revenue purposes was unconstitutional. This contention was similar to that urged by plaintiff herein with reference to the use of cigarettes. The court rejected that argument and distinguished the Collins case on the ground that it was decided before there was a statute authorizing the city to impose the license tax. The court stated: "the use of the streets was a common right, which was free and open to all without charge and without toll, and upon this right the city had no power to impose a license tax; but by the enactment of clause 96 [of the Cities and Villages Act,] the use of the public streets, which before its enactment was a common right, became by virtue of the legislative act, a privilege, and subject to a license tax * * *." In reinterpreting the concept of privilege as applied in the Collins case, the court further stated: "Clearly, therefore, the court in the Collins case did not mean to say that nothing can be subject to license if it be lawful to do the thing without legal authority. *There are a great many things which had been done or enjoyed as a matter of right, and which later, by legislative act, were made the subject of license taxation.*" (Emphasis added)...In other jurisdictions it has also been held that the legislative power to tax privileges is not limited to those privileges which the legislature alone authorizes, and which it can entirely abolish, but extends to inherent rights; 61 C.J. 242; Beals v. State, 139 Wis. 544, 121 N.W. 347, and that the term "privilege" in taxing statutes is synonymous with "right"." State ex rel. Froectert Grain & Malting Co. v. Tax Comm., 221 Wis. 225, 265 N.W. 672, 272 N.W. 52, 104 A.L.R. 1478...For the right to use the streets and the highways, and the right to make inter vivos gifts which are effective at death, all of which have been sustained as taxable privileges in Illinois, were regarded as common rights open to all persons prior to legislative action thereon." *Johnson v. Halpin*, 108 N.E.2d 429, 436, 413 Ill. 257. (emphasis in original)

http://scholar.google.com/scholar_case?case=7129450847307313212&hl=en&as_sdt=2&as_vis=1&oi=scholarr

Dangerous place to visit, especially if you believe you have a right to life. A good reason to not play with the word "right" or focus on what the laws/statutes say, but to stick with the evidence the code applies at all.

This raises an interesting issue though: what if you don't believe in the concept of rights? After all, there's a world of difference between "life, liberty and property" and an alleged right to "life, liberty and property," isn't there? I can certainly prove I have "life, liberty and property" with verifiable facts, but what about rights to such? What kind of facts would I have to bring forth to prove I have rights?

Rights are advertised as the basis for governments and obviously their court system. When being investigated, the resolution of the matter is done in courts where there is supposed to be an adversary system. By their own admissions, there is no separating rights from the adversary system; it cannot be invoked in your favor unless there's evidence your rights were violated:

> "The Court has found unfit for adjudication any cause that "is not in any sense adversary," that "does not assume the **'honest and actual antagonistic assertion of rights'** to be adjudicated – a safeguard essential to the integrity of the judicial process, and one which we have held to be indispensible to adjudication of constitutional questions by this Court." United States v. Johnson, 319 U.S. 302, 305. *Poe v. Ullman*, 367 U.S. 497 (1961) 367 U.S. 497, 505 (emphasis mine).

While government apologists would dismiss this because it is in the context of a civil action, not criminal, the fact is the court systems in the US, Canada, England, Australia,and New Zealand are advertised as adversarial in both contexts. So when the court is discussing the principles of the adversarial system and causes, it's obvious it applies to any adversary proceeding, civil and criminal.

It's interesting to note the double standard; bureaucrats may cite court opinions where the subject matter/facts are completely different, but I'm an idiot for doing that, even for an issue of law. As with any court citation, I already know there are conflicting opinions; it's just to show the contradiction between what the psychopaths are doing and what their laws say.

What is important here is the principle that any cause (a crime is a cause of action) or case, "that is not in any real sense adversary" is "unfit for adjudication…" This is basic common sense; rare among politicians, but utilized when it makes for good PR. It is "unfit for adjudication" if there is no "actual antagonistic assertion of rights by one individual against another..."

This is what we can use to show that any complaint-regardless of the statute/regulation/ordinance claimed to be violated-that doesn't allege the violation of a legal right/breach of a know legal duty, is "unfit for adjudication" because it "is not in any real sense adversary." Even if it did, there could be no facts proving where, when, why and how the alleged duty was created.

We get the stupidest things in response to this when we file a motion to dismiss based on there being no case and no real adversary. This is because to be adversarial there has to be an antagonistic assertion of rights, not just a disagreement. Some lawyer from Kentucky named Billy N. Rilely, a Livingston county attorney, provided this gem:

> "The defendant claims that "The complaint is unfit for adjudication," due to it being non-adversarial. The defendant is charged with violating the criminal and traffic laws of this Commonwealth. He faces jail time and/or fines. This is certainly adversarial. The fact that the Defendant is vehemently arguing his case is proof of the adversarial nature of this action."

What legally makes a proceeding adversarial is an "actual antagonistic assertion of rights by one individual against another," not whether a prosecutor wants you in jail and you "vehemently" defend yourself. If I filed such garbage I'd have to sanction myself.

You'll notice he conveniently-as prosecutors do-failed to include why the Supreme Court considers it non-adversarial. Billy never addresses what we presented showing the complaint was not adversarial. His job is not to administer justice and seek the truth, it's to punish people for non-compliance.

According to Billy, had there been no defense, the complaint would not have been adversarial.

The more vague the proceedings are, the less effectively you can defend yourself. Just as with any common criminal or magician, their target must be kept in the dark, disclosing as little as possible, lest the victim figure out what's really going on.

A common tactic by traffic court psychopaths is to not disclose what kind of proceedings you're stuck in. When a judge is resistant to disclosing if the proceedings are civil or criminal, you can not only ask what the burden of proof is, but also if the proceedings are adversarial. If they say they are adversarial, then ask if you're an adversary and what facts the prosecutor has presented to prove that.

If yes, you can also ask: Whose rights am I accused of violating? It's always fun when the judge claims "the state" when there is no such allegation on the ticket or indictment. I ask why he's making such a broad assumption for what is supposed to be an adversary. So would that be the same state you have an oath of allegiance to, Sir?

219

Incredibly, some of these predators have established a pattern of denying that their system-supposedly the best the world has ever seen-is adversarial. Apparently, when the caption is *State vs. Marc* it doesn't mean there are two adversaries. I thought the "versus" part between the names was a dead giveaway. It's supposed to be adversarial though:

> "We hold only that, when the process shifts from investigatory to accusatory-when its focus is on the accused and its purpose is to elicit a confession-our adversary system begins to operate, and, under the circumstances here, the accused must be permitted to consult with his lawyer." *Escobedo v. Illinois*, 378 U.S. 478, 492 (1964).

> "Not only these precedents, but also reason and reflection, require us to recognize that, in our adversary system of criminal justice, any person haled into court, who is too poor to hire a lawyer, cannot be assured a fair trial unless counsel is provided for him." *Gideon v. Wainwright*, 372 U.S. 335, 344 (1963).

> "The very premise of our adversary system of criminal justice is that partisan advocacy on both sides of a case will best promote the ultimate objective that the guilty be convicted and the innocent go free." *Herring v. New York*, 422 U.S. 853, 862 (1975).

> "The Court elaborated: "[I]f counsel entirely fails to subject the prosecution's case to meaningful adversarial testing, then there has been a denial of Sixth Amendment rights that makes the adversary process itself presumptively unreliable." Id., at 659; see Bell v. Cone, 535 U. S. 685, 696-697 (2002)." *Florida, Petitioner v. Joe Elton Nixon*, Florida murder case. See also *The Adversary System is Dead; Long Live Our Adversary System, Mary Sue Backus.*

Forget about the burden of proof for your supposed adversary; there isn't one. The burden is solely on you-the victim of an attack by a group of lawyers-to prove your innocence. Combine that with the judges' vicious snarl: "I'm not here to answer *your* questions!" and only the brain-dead among us will fail to see the system is rigged.

I've been asked by dozens of bureaucrats what facts I relied on proving the code did not apply to a client. Their PR says the system is supposed to be adversarial, but they are actually operating an inquisitorial system where the burden is on us to prove their opinions are incorrect. It's a good thing they are so full of crap or we wouldn't stand a chance against them. They don't want to openly admit they are acting inquisitorially because then they'd have a problem explaining why we're not presumed innocent.

Despite overwhelming PR regarding the courts being adversarial, Melinda Lasaster, a former prosecutor, on 22 Oct. 2012 in a San Diego courtroom, openly denied that the California and American court systems are adversarial. Jonathan Lapin, ostensibly an officer of the adversarial court system, just sat there mute, not a word of objection to correct Melinda. And why would he correct a judge? Melinda, with that crazy denial, wiped away not only Jonathan's entire burden of proof, but also any pretense of the presumption of innocence.

She not only denied it was adversarial, she refused to take mandatory judicial notice of it. We provided the support by a supreme court opinion (*Poe v. Ullman*, 367 U.S. 497) and she still denied it. It's mandatory by their sacred writ; you remember, the law we're all supposed to obey: section 451 of the California evidence code.

Why? Why would an adult deny something so well established? When I've mentioned it to experienced lawyers/litigators, they've laughed in disbelief. They can't believe that anyone with even a basic understanding of the courts would not freely acknowledge something so obvious.

Everyone I related this story to admitted Lasater was dead wrong, except for those with any meaningful oversight of her. Those who could correct her mistake have not seen anything wrong with what she did. There's a shock. The court of appeals judges refused to intervene, claiming that on a petition for a writ of mandate we failed to show "an abuse of discretion." Yes, I know; mandate is only appropriate to compel a judge to perform a mandatory function; they used a straw man argument to cover up for Melinda.

With these predators, the PR and the actual practice are two different animals. Those familiar with bureaucrats and politicians already know this.

When a judge, a seasoned litigator and veteran of the courts openly denies the obvious, then no rational adult will conclude the lawyer has forgotten this basic principle. No, it was deliberate. Melinda Lasater knew what she was doing and purposely aided the prosecutor. It's the result of extreme prejudice against the accused; there is no other rational explanation.

Can these judges claim ignorance? Of course they can, but they would have to then try to explain away the evidence, and no rational man/woman would believe such nonsense. The evidence is the request for judicial notice; all the information (as if it's needed) is in the request. It's also in the demurrer or motion to dismiss.

The entire basis of the adversary system-what makes it the "best" in the world-is there are two parties where the one who makes the accusation bears the burden of proof. The judge, unlike in an inquisitorial system, is supposed to be a fair, impartial and independent decision maker.

So, when a judge denies the system is adversarial, the prosecutor doesn't object, and your objection is arbitrarily denied, then you have all the evidence you need to prove they are working together. Put that with the fact that the judge is forcing you to answer the prosecutor's complaint/indictment, and we've got irrefutable proof of collusion. And, dare I write it, that's pretty strong circumstantial evidence of conspiracy. That's a lot more evidence than the worst conspiracy theorists (prosecutors) out there who regularly attack us.

Was it worse when we consider Melinda did this in front of another experienced litigator? The facts don't bear it out, at least not to me. I think she was comfortable doing it, because assisting prosecutors is a regular part of the job for these former prosecutors.

Jonathan and his boss, Jan Goldsmith, both refused to communicate with me when I asked if they agree the court system is adversarial. Lawyers are taught the court system is adversarial, they do know the PR. They all know the system is advertised as being adversarial. But as with most advertising, it's a fabrication, a lie; things really change after the sale. (I'm thinking of things such as when fast food is advertised and the way it actually looks.)

> American justice: the greatest system; an adversary system with a presumption of innocence and competent proof by accusers beyond a reasonable doubt. [*]

*Until you're actually in the courtroom. Anyone who beats their chest about the wonderful American system is going to have a dreadful case of buyer's remorse when they are the target of government wrath.

It's too bad I have to discuss the disconnect between the sales pitch and the actual service; the rhetoric doesn't match the practical application. Many have no real experience with these psychopaths and their circuses called courts. Those who have been there know first-hand how vicious and callous current and former prosecutors are.

Melinda apparently is very comfortable denying the obvious, because the other lawyers in the court are either too afraid to correct her, or they just don't care because they recognize the huge advantage she's giving them. And there are the favors mentioned earlier. Melinda probably had judges give her such passes when she was a prosecutor; it's just a part of a system with a psychopathic foundation. Such people don't tolerate challenges well.

Denying that the system is adversarial is tantamount to denying we need water to live. It takes all the PR used to convince people to pay taxes and support the system, and throws it out the window. We've had judges say the law doesn't matter in "their" courts. Anyone who doubts the courts are run by criminals only needs to get a parking ticket and engage the system themselves.

The refusal to inform us of the true nature of the proceedings is a denial of notice, which severely diminishes our ability to defend ourselves. Look at the common sense public relations to prove this:

> "No principle is more vital to the administration of justice than that no man shall be condemned in his person or property without notice, and an opportunity to make his defense." *Boswell's Lessee v. Otis*, 50 U.S. 9 How. 336 336 (1850).

"The fundamental requisite of due process of law is the opportunity to be heard." Grannis v. Ordean, 234 U. S. 385, 234 U. S. 394 (1914). The hearing must be "at a meaningful time and in a meaningful manner." Armstrong v. Manzo, 380 U. S. 545, 380 U. S. 552 (1965)." *Goldberg v. Kelly*, 397 U.S. 254 (1970).

Proper notice, which includes honest disclosure, is necessary for an effective defense, and that's precisely why the psychopaths who force us into their proceedings don't want to answer questions. So it's no wonder they refuse to answer questions and try to blind you with legal opinions and argument. Most people will start focusing on such obvious distraction and not point out the prosecutor is full of crap. Most are so intimidated by the whole process, and with good reason, that they forget the prosecutor bears the entire burden of proof. We need only to hold them to it. Even the courts agree prosecutors are limited to the evidence:

"By going outside the evidence, the prosecutor "violated a fundamental rule, known to every lawyer, that **argument is limited to the facts in evidence.**" United States ex rel. Shaw v. De Robertis, 755 F.2d 1279, 1281 (7th Cir.1985)" http://scholar.google.com/scholar_case? case=4255090692203884911&hl=en&as_sdt=2&as_vis=1&oi=s cholarr (Emphasis mine) United States v. Fearns, 501 F.2d 486, 489 (7th Cir.1974) http://scholar.google.com/scholar_case? case=16739033554289172005&hl=en&as_sdt=2,3&as_vis=1 UNITED STATES of America, Plaintiff-Appellee, v. Norman Harrington WILSON, a/k/a Stormin Norman, Defendant-Appellant. UNITED STATES of America, Plaintiff-Appellee, v. William David WILSON, a/k/a Pudgie, Defendant-Appellant. UNITED STATES of America, Plaintiff-Appellee, v. William Correy TALLEY, a/k/a Rat Rat, Defendant-Appellant. United States v. Handman, 447 F.2d 853, 856 (7th Cir. 1971); see United States v. Jackson, 485 F.2d 300, 303 (7th Cir. 1973); United States v. Grooms, 454 F.2d 1308, 1312 (7th Cir. 1972) United States Court of Appeals for the Fourth Circuit January 29, 1998 48 Fed. R. Evid. Serv. 883; 135 F.3d 291. http://scholar.google.com/scholar_case? case=7432500091684799666&hl=en&as_sdt=2,3&as_vis=1

"The personal opinion of a prosecutor is not an issue for the jury. Greenberg v. United States, 280 F.2d 472, 474-475 (1st Cir. 1960); Hall v. United States, 419 F.2d 582, 586 (5th Cir. 1969). See Dunn v. United States, 307 F.2d 883, 885-886 (5th Cir. 1962); see also this court's opinion in United States v.

D'Antonio, 362 F.2d 151, 155 (7th Cir. 1966)." *United States v. Handman*, 447 F.2d 853, 856 (7th Cir. 1971).
https://bulk.resource.org/courts.gov/c/F2/447/447.F2d.8 53.18736.html

Going outside the evidence is misconduct. When I call prosecutors asking for evidence, I'm building a case for misconduct. Given they are usually so arrogant, it's easy to do.

When a prosecutor argues there is a case or cause against us, they have to go by the facts in evidence. With a traffic complaint, what facts are there to support his argument that there is jurisdiction, that the laws apply, or that he represents a true adversary against us? When we examine these fundamental issues, it becomes clear why judges (former prosecutors) get so upset.

But just to take a minor tangent, let's re-read what the court said, "a fundamental rule, known to every lawyer, [is] that **argument is limited to the facts in evidence.**" I can't tell you how many vile *ad hominen* attacks have been hurled at me over the years because I think this is a valid principle.

Another legal principle is: the **argument/opinion, is limited/supported by facts in evidence**. This is another legal principle ignored by critics and political psychopaths who claim that the argument the court has jurisdiction does not depend on evidence; rather it's an issue of law. Yeah, if by issue of law they mean an *arbitrary* issue of law, then that's correct. There's no valid opinion without supporting facts/evidence, that's the way rational people operate.

Let's examine the complaints/indictments these psychopaths are so fond of using against us to destroy our lives. I've said this before and I'll write it again to be perfectly clear:

A complaint is not a case; the two words are *not* synonymous.

Assuming the two are the same thing has cost people billions, if not trillions over the course of hundreds of years. The complaint is how a case or cause of action is presented to a court. You only need to look at a traffic ticket or complaint to know this is true.

Think of a complaint as a book report; it's not the book and no amount of threats from a man in a robe can change that. If you weren't taught this in government indoctrination camps (AKA schools) then it's for a good reason. You can't continue to run a confidence game when your targets know too much and are asking questions.

No one would mistake a police report as evidence of a real crime, so no one should mistake a complaint for a case or cause of action. A complaint is not evidence of anything except that a complaint was written. The complaint against O.J. Simpson was not evidence of any crimes. The complaint *describes* the evidence; it's not evidence. While this is self-evident with real crimes such as murder and robbery, this seems to be lost on those criminals running traffic courts and tax proceedings. The complaint is at best a report of allegations and alleged evidence.

If you search long enough, you'll see this common sense occasionally comes out in court opinions. This is a fairly recent example; again, it's just common sense:

> "We risk stating the **obvious** here: **a complaint is merely an accusation of conduct and not**, of course, **proof that the conduct alleged occurred**. The prosecution did not introduce evidence that Bailey misused the SEC rules — rather, **the prosecution offered only the complaint, which is far from evidence of anything**. Admitting the complaint may have permitted the jurors to succumb to the simplistic reasoning that if the defendant was accused of the conduct, it probably or actually occurred. **Such inferences are impermissible**.
>
> The government barely addresses this issue but instead leans heavily on the purpose for which the evidence was offered, i.e., "to prove that defendant acted intentionally, knowing that his actions were wrong." There is some logic to the argument that evidence that Bailey had previously been accused of violating Rule S-8 shows that he was on notice of the type of prohibited conduct. **But this is not enough**. The prosecution was still required to prove that the evidence was sufficient to support a finding that Bailey committed the act charged in the complaint. **This a mere complaint cannot do**." *U.S. v. Bailey*, 696 F.3d 794, 801 (2012) (emphasis mine).
> http://scholar.google.com/scholar_case?case=6323800857722081749&hl=en&as_sdt=2&as_vis=1&oi=scholarr

If such "simplistic reasoning" is impermissible for the jury, then it's impermissible for the judge too. Yet judges do it every day and explode into fits of rage when you call them on it, especially on the issue of jurisdiction. It's standard for judges to accept prosecutors' (and cops') complaints as evidence. I've had judges tell me in court that the ticket was evidence. They could not explain how or what it was evidence of, but they were certain it was evidence.

Accusations in a complaint do not magically become evidence when a judge reads them and then back to mere allegations when the jury does. I had a judge Garcia in Mesa, Arizona, finally admit that the complaint was not evidence. When I again asked what evidence there was proving jurisdiction, he just smiled and told me to appeal it.

Imagine what would happen if the former prosecutors held the current prosecutors to this basic truth, "the prosecution offered only the complaint, which is far from evidence of anything." It would be radical. Prosecutors would have to do their so-called jobs. It would also mean they would not be permitted to prosecute anyone until they put up some actual evidence. But they don't. Prosecutors are given a pass, a generous favor from on high. (About four feet high by my estimation.)

We can see these favors between former and current prosecutors in court all the time: prosecutors regularly admit to me they don't have to prove their codes apply, because the judge will not impose that burden on them. When that current prosecutor moves up the pecking order and gets the robe, it's natural for him to give his fellow prosecutors the same pass on jurisdiction, which is an element of the code violation.

There may even be facts described in the complaint, just as there may be facts presented at a hearing/trial, but that doesn't mean there is any *evidence* supporting the accusations. Here in this part of North America, when someone cites an irrelevant fact, we ask, "What does that have to do with the price of tea in China?" So I'll point out the obvious truth:

Facts do not always equal evidence.

So when an agent claims they have jurisdiction over you because you live in Melbourne, that fact in and of itself isn't evidence the code applies, giving the bureaucrat jurisdiction over you. Their willingness to aggress against you comes from his/her claim of jurisdiction-because you are in range of their guns, not because your physical location *magically* makes the code applicable.

Anyone who looks at this issue critically will come to the same conclusion: the act of jurisdiction depends almost entirely on a willingness to initiate force against someone. If you disagree, try to imagine how this so-called jurisdiction could exist without the use or threat of aggressive force. Without the force, claims of jurisdiction are neutered.

There is no logical, factual connection between my physical location and the whims of men/women called legislators. They only have the circular logic: their code applies in a certain area because the code says so.

The same principle is true with complaints. A cop may allege I violated the code. But the allegation is not evidence despite their constant conflating of facts and opinions. It's a standard way bureaucrats operate.

A pretrial and trial are conducted so relevant evidence to support the allegations in the complaint can be presented and examined. Can you imagine these predators trying to prove tax evasion beyond a reasonable doubt using only the indictment?

> Ladies and gentlemen of the jury, we have the indictment against the defendant; that is the evidence that the code applied to the defendant and the court has jurisdiction. We don't need to present anything else to prove this filthy degenerate did not pay his fair share and is guilty beyond a reasonable doubt.

Most will see how silly the above statement is. But this happens in prosecutions; the content may be slightly different, but the underlying *process* is the same.

Prosecutors and former prosecutors, at least prior to the jury deliberating, believe the indictment is evidence the code applies. Ask them and they'll tell you. If you ask for the facts the code applies, they will tell you the complaint is the evidence. We know it's ridiculous, but they get away with it because the psychopaths use guns to get their way.

Just by accident I found the following on a US department of justice website:

> "An indictment merely alleges that crimes have been committed and the defendants are presumed innocent until proven guilty beyond a reasonable doubt."
> http://www.justice.gov/opa/pr/2013/February/13-tax-247.html

This is the public relations, the BS they want people to believe. You'll find this on most of their press releases. But as I've shown, this is not what happens if you are a victim of the legal system. Once in court, if you believe this and expect prosecutors to present evidence the code applies beyond a reasonable doubt, you're in for a rude awakening. You'll see the prosecutors insisting their indictment is evidence, and any objections to this are frivolous.

Norman Smith, a federal prosecutor in Illinois, told me on 28 March 2013, that he was certain "beyond question" the constitution and code applied to a client. Over the course of about thirty minutes he was unable to articulate one specific fact he relied on to prove that argument. In response to my asking for evidence, he dodged answering by saying the "question is nonsense." To many US attorneys, asking for proof of their claims is "nonsense." Norman predictably claimed it was "frivolous."

But why so certain Norm? I'm certain beyond question that it's not because he has evidence. He can be so certain, and present an argument clearly not limited to facts in evidence, because after several decades of prosecuting people, no judge has kept him to his burden of proof. Looks like decades of collusion to me.

For some reason he didn't like it when I said that being certain "beyond question" and working as a prosecutor for thirty years, twenty-three of those with taxes, was not evidence the code applied. Why do so many of these attorneys feel the need to give me their resume when I ask for evidence?

Contrary to the schizophrenic belief of politicians, the so-called "judicial power" does not extend to every complaint, but only to cases. I wrote schizophrenic because they certainly don't believe the judicial power extends to complaints filed against *them*. Want to see the unlimited jurisdiction of the courts instantly shrink? File a complaint against them. All of a sudden these state attorneys remember that judges are supposed to presume there is no jurisdiction until the plaintiff proves otherwise with competent proof.

I worked with someone in Texas where an attorney was forced on all the defendants. My client brought up the issue of standing and the lack of a case. This attorney, ostensibly on behalf of the defendants, responded by telling him the "city" would not have filed the complaint if they didn't have standing. (My guess this guy routinely settles and loses trials.)

I'm just not that trusting of aggressive people. Lawyers give lawyers free passes at the expense of their clients; that doesn't seem like a smart way to defend against an accusation. Looks more like a way to keep lawyers busy racking up billable hours. Great strategy: give the prosecution a pass. It shows there's a lack of critical thought. The question, "Is this in my best interest?" doesn't seem to be asked and investigated.

What a case is was covered in *Adventures in Legal Land* and I won't go into much detail here. Suffice to say, there is injury, damage and redressability.

So when you do go into court, remember we're dealing with violent predators who lie incessantly. Also remember what some claim was said by Holmes:

> "This is a court of law, young man, not a court of justice." Oliver Wendell Holmes, Jr., attributed.

Ollie knew what he was talking about here.

Writing petitions, motions and other responses to bureaucrats

Most jurisdictions do not have hard and fast rules for formatting paperwork in the trial courts. However, there are some rules to remember, especially in places like California where they are *fanatical* about rules. Fanatical only in the sense that the rules help mask the open theft of your property. Appellate courts are different; though there are some similar rules for briefs, they do vary considerably and you should know the rules for formatting briefs before you spend the time and money putting one together.

This is what I've always used as a caption and have rarely had any issues getting motions accepted:

Marc Stevens
P.O. Box 31258
Mesa, Arizona 85275

Phoenix Justice Court

STATE OF ARIZONA aka Psycho cop badge #666	) Docket #12345678
alleged plaintiff,	)
	) **Motion to dismiss**
vs.	)
Marc Stevens,	)
alleged defendant	)
	)

I put the cop's name and badge number after STATE because the cop is acting as the STATE when he is out writing tickets. I know this because many former and current prosecutors have told me so. It's not true; the cop is a cop, he's not acting on behalf of any state.

Under the docket number, I put the title of the motion, which is whatever I'm asking the judge to do, e.g., dismiss, vacate, reconsider, quit and get a real job, etc. Above the name of the court, you'll need to have more space so the clerk can date-stamp the motion.

After the caption, I mention what the motion is for and the general grounds, e.g., "...should be dismissed because there is no evidence proving jurisdiction. Grounds are further set forth below."

Each issue should be numbered so it's easier to read and reference. Most courts require everything but quotations to be double-spaced:

"1. Plaintiff lacks standing. The foundation for standing is article II § 2 of the Arizona constitution: "governments...are established to protect and maintain individual rights." Standing is required because "courts only adjudicate justiciable controversies." *United States v. Interstate Commerce Commission...*

2. Lack of jurisdiction. "Standing represents a jurisdictional requirement which remains open to review at all stages of the litigation." *National Organization for Women, Inc., v. Scheidler*, 510 US 249. As with standing, the foundation of the court's jurisdiction is article II § 2 of the Arizona constitution: "governments...are established to protect and maintain individual rights."

After laying out each point without any unnecessary details and argument, I end with a conclusion and request for dismissal or whatever I'm requesting. Specific issues are provided throughout the rest of this book.

Since many prosecutors have been willing to speak to me and clients, I like to call them before submitting the motion. I've been doing that for years with the IRS. I call and ask prosecutors for the facts and witnesses with personal knowledge that the constitution and code are applicable. When they can't answer or refuse to, I put that in the motion as support. With Jonathan Lapin, Delilah in San Diego was able to use his childish response, "I'm not going to go there," in the motion and quote him in court.

The motion then serves as a guide for when we're in court. The issues are there and it's still the prosecutor's burden to present the facts. We can ask the prosecutor what facts he relies on to prove the code applies, there is an adversary etc.

Some judges will insist that if we file a motion to dismiss, then we have the burden to prove the grounds of the motion. This happened to Peter in Montana. This is actually correct; the burden when we file a motion is on the one who filed the motion.

This does not mean we stop asking the prosecutor questions though; that's how I show the prosecutor has no evidence to prove the code applies and there is jurisdiction. All he has is the complaint, and we already know that's not evidence.

If I've called the prosecutor and he's admitted to not having evidence the code is applicable, I can ask him if he still agrees he has no evidence. The beauty of sticking to the facts is that if they lie, then they still are on the hook for those phantom facts.

I walk the prosecutor through the motion one issue at a time and see if he/she has any disagreements. If they do, then they can present their evidence. If there is disagreement, then they have to articulate it; they have to show exactly why it doesn't have merit or apply. Do not allow the lawyers to be vague when they respond; always ask for a clarification.

Challenge what is presented. This is a common theme. We don't take a burden upon ourselves; we just challenge the opinions/claims/accusations being hurled at us by the psychopaths. There's no need to look beyond the opinions and assume things such as "we're all corporations" and other theories.

We already know, and can easily confirm by asking, that politicians and their henchmen use their constitutions and codes/laws/statutes/regulations/bylaws,etc. as the basis of their attacks against us. So it makes sense to challenge that basis, the foundation of their aggression.

Regardless of how bad things may look even to the bureaucrat, they plow forward with their comforting delusion it's all OK because the code permits it. All the violence is justified by the magic words: The Code authorizes [fill in egregious act of violence here]. I asked a tax agent in Washington how her taking my property by force was different from stealing, and her answer was they had legal authority.

The basis of a tax agent's jurisdiction will be the constitution and code; the same for a cop giving you a traffic ticket. A prosecutor will claim the traffic court has jurisdiction because of the code, just as psychopaths in the federal courts use 18 USC 3231 as evidence of jurisdiction. We know this because they tell us; it's in their paperwork. Our starting point is what the bureaucrat is presenting; we just want them to verify their claims/opinions.

It's logical, and therefore very effective, to challenge the facts the code is applicable. We do this because they tell us that the prosecutor has this burden, and the burden has to be met with competent evidence. Only the feeble minded and the psychopaths will try to convince you that opinions are competent evidence. (You can tell the difference between the two because the feeble minded will probably not use violence to convince you of your error.)

Prosecutors claim there's a case against us. We know that's not true, so we present what a case is, i.e., the violation of a legal right and damage. They will then conflate opinions with facts, such as equating a complaint with a case. You have to see it in person to believe it: grown men and women with advanced university degrees angrily insisting that a complaint is the same as a case, that a complaint is actually evidence, and

231

that their allegations are facts. It's just another reason why their system must be supported by a foundation of lies and violence.

I just ask them if they believe a complaint and a case are the same thing, or ask them to cite the elements of their case in the complaint. It falls apart easily, because it's stupid to claim that a complaint is a case.

You can even read from the constitution where it says the judicial power shall extend to all cases and then say, "Objection: is it your position the jurisdiction extends to all complaints?" Then you're bound to hear the only thing the prosecutor can respond with: a weak personal attack. You can also say:

> So mere allegations are evidence in this court? That's the standard here? So I can just claim the opposite-the laws don't apply-and that's good enough for you? If not, can you please clarify why you maintain a double standard in favor of the prosecutor?

If I take any position when responding to a letter from a tax agency, tit's to stick with pointing out there's no evidence. We already know they are going to disagree with just about everything we present, so be prepared to use that denial in your favor, if possible.

So when they reflexively contradict me when I say there's no evidence, then *the burden stays on them*. They still have to present the evidence and witnesses they rely on. If they claim I'm an idiot, and that there are facts proving the code is applicable, they still have to present those facts. Calling me an idiot does not magically make the facts appear or negate their burden of proof.

> *Your Honor, this is nonsense! Marc is a moron, of course I have evidence.*
> Okay…would you like to tell us?
> *Your honor, this is nonsense, of course I have evidence!*
> Yes, of course. Would you care to tell us?
> YOUR HONOR, THIS IS NONSENSE, OF COURSE I HAVE EVIDENCE!

Keep the burden on them well enough and they will really get upset and start accusing you of "debating" or arguing. I like it when they also make straw man arguments, such as asking if I think I can do whatever I want since I don't think the laws apply to me. Honest people with evidence let the evidence do the talking for them; they have no reason to engage in stupid evasion tactics.

When they do that, I always correct them. I say, "No, my position is that you don't have any evidence proving your laws apply to me."

Stick to questioning the evidence; it cuts through all personal attacks and other logical fallacies.

> *Marc, you're an idiot!*

I'll grant you that; but what facts do you rely on proving the constitution applies to me and you have jurisdiction?

You know you're doing a good job of holding them to their burden of proof if they're doing everything they can to take the focus off themselves. Everything but being responsive and providing the facts, that is.

Everyone should prove this for themselves. Just take a bureaucrat's or a politician's opinion and ask them for the facts they rely on to prove it. First get them to commit that the opinion is not arbitrary, then ask for specific facts. They'll always deny it's arbitrary, so you're setting them up for a shot to their credibility when they cannot give you any facts.

I mentioned to Craig Jones, a prosecutor in Mesa, Arizona, that they must be stealing lots of money to pay for the big new court building. He said he didn't think it was stealing. Really, Craig? Check your facts big man. Simple question: Are people forced to pay for the support of the Mesa city government? Yes, that's a fact. Well, that's what most people over the age of five call *stealing*.

When you do this, then the silly word games these predators play become obvious. I pointed this out to a lawyer in Wyoming named Teresa Tyhbo. I asked for the facts and she could only offer that if you are in the state the law applies. So I asked:

> "What makes you think that that's true though? What makes you think that just because someone's physically in Wyoming the laws apply to them; where do you get that?"

Her response...after a predictable, long pause:

> "Uh, that is just how it works Sir. I don't understand why you are asking me this question. That is how state law works. You're in my state my law applies."
> http://marcstevens.net/cos/cos20130301.html

And that's more evidence why these psychopaths have to use aggression, threats of force, and jail to get people to interact with and comply with them. They have no evidence, just silly platitudes, "Uh, that is just how it works."

This example with Teresa is only one of many, and typical of what you'll hear when you ask for facts that the laws apply. It makes no sense to bring your own positions and put a burden on yourself when the bureaucrats have no evidence proving jurisdiction. Does this make sense to you?

> The prosecutor has the burden of proof to prove everything beyond a reasonable doubt, and they have no evidence to do that. I know, I'll argue I'm not a corporation.

If it does, then good luck with that. Pretty much everything about the allegations bureaucrats make is complete fiction; they are engaged in reification. It makes no sense to go beyond what they're alleging.

Some things may be unspoken, such as jurisdiction. Typically a cop will not come out and claim, "Stop or I'll shoot, I have jurisdiction here, you filthy peasant!" But it certainly is implied. And when you ask if they have jurisdiction they will automatically respond they do, "Uh, yeah, didn't you see this gun? It's not for show, mate."

So when you're doing an appeal and you have all these errors, which ones do you use? Go for the ones where the burden of proof is lowest, and where each error on its own will result in the complete dismissal of the complaint or conviction.

With jurisdiction, we're striking at the root: if there's no jurisdiction, then nothing else matters. It's the foundation of their attacks. The violence is covered up with it, and what's really important here is that bureaucrats still admit they have to have jurisdiction. They will tell you that without jurisdiction, their actions are not legal.

So, for the time being, they still agree they need jurisdiction for their actions to be valid. Until they throw away all pretense of legitimacy, we challenge their weakest points. We just hammer away at the opinion that there is evidence of jurisdiction.

Application is far more effective to challenge than interpretation.

Who cares what a statute/law is supposed to mean on any given day when there's no evidence it's applicable in any way to you? A statute means whatever the tyrant *du jour* wants it to mean. What a law means depends on how badly he wants your property and how many witnesses he has. His sensitivity to shame plays a part too.

We follow a logical progression; that's why most bureaucrats and prosecutors can't seem to follow it. The first step to proving a code violation is proving the code itself is applicable to the one under attack. This includes jurisdiction, which is supposed to be pretty important. Logically, the code has to be applicable before it can be violated.

Then, and only then, may we move to step two: reading the code and properly determining if it's appropriate given the facts alleged.

Facts typically don't depend on the whim of a psycho with a title. Funny thing about facts, they tend not to be transient in nature like opinions. Some facts cannot be spun and don't change, at least not in my experience. That is where challenging *application* of a law or statute is so effective. What a law is factually cannot really be effectively spun. A political law, as shown in *Adventures in Legal Land*, is an opinion backed by a gun. It is more commonly referred to as the will of the legislature or parliament. Most agree it is some kind of rule.

When talking with a bureaucrat who insists the law applies to you, it's very effective to ask, "Are you an expert in the application and interpretation of law?" Very few people have actually admitted to being an expert. A big reason is because people know there are millions of laws, and to be an expert would generally require having read them, let alone having studied them. Given the average life span is about seventy-two years, the six-hundred years required to read all the laws is kind of a deal breaker. Even congressmen admit they don't read the laws they vote on. This doesn't include all the court opinions interpreting and re-interpreting the laws.

This is why attorneys usually specialize; no one can really be an expert in the law, and no one really tries...except for the ones with black robes, of course. You have criminal law, corporate, consumer, labor, etc.

I've had a few people claim they were experts; some took it back though. When they do claim to be experts, challenge them. Ask them about their training and which law school they graduated from. If they say they do not have to be a law school graduate to be an expert, then ask them what kind of training does qualify them. Don't worry-when you ask some probing questions on the application of law, they will probably refuse to answer and claim they are not attorneys and qualified to answer such questions. Keep from laughing at this point and just get them to admit they are not qualified, by their own admission, to make any claims the laws apply to you.

The constitution/law cannot be proven to apply to you unless we know what it is first. But even knowing that the law is a rule, opinion, or whim of the insane does not prove it's obligatory or applicable in any way; what facts connect you to the law?

This has proven to be very, very effective. I've posted many dismissals on the website, including tax assessments, that have been kicked out because we just stuck to asking for the facts the code applies.

So many bureaucrats just want to focus narrowly on a particular statute-say a labor or tax law-and not focus on the entire code. And with good reason: they know they're out of their league. It tends to help them to focus just on the text of a particular section of the code, e.g.,if you are doing business in Toronto, then the code mandates you must file this form. But they still get stuck in a circular loop. What makes you think the code applies to me if I'm in Toronto? Well, we have this code that says...

If there's no evidence you're subject to the will of the individuals called the legislature, then there's no logical reason to bring up whether you may be subject to any individual section of their code; that would be putting the cart before the horse.

Some prosecutors have wanted me to believe that their laws apply when we violate them. Talk about a non-sequitur! That may be the mother of all non-sequiturs presented here. I've had prosecutors tell me this, "The laws apply to everyone who commits a crime." Don't try to make sense of that; it's only going to frustrate you or satisfy the weak-minded.

> *Well Marc, you're not subject to the laws governing fishing because you don't fish.*
> Great, the law doesn't apply; I'll go fishing then.
> *Then the laws would apply to you.*
> Why?
> *Because there are laws about fishing.*

They weren't applicable a moment ago, but now they are, just because I decided to fish?
Yes.
What evidence is there the law applies though?
Fishing.
What makes you think that is true?
Fishing.
But what...
Fishing.

I had a tax agent tell me on 22 February 2013 that the code applied because my client did not file a return. The stupidity of that statement is off the charts. It would be cute and understandable if said by a five year old, but not by an adult. I think they use stupidity as strategery to avoid responsibility. You can hear the call here:
http://marcstevens.net/articles/facts-i-dont-understand-the-question.html.
Application goes right to the root of their attack; everything hinges on the applicability of the law, the code and the constitution. If they don't have facts proving the code applies, then nothing else matters because there is no jurisdiction to even look at me.

Marc you don't have a permit to build that shed in your yard.
Why would I need a permit?
Because the city code mandates that you have one.
So what? Do you have jurisdiction over me and my property?
Of course we do; I'm code compliance.
What facts do you have proving the code is applicable to me?
You didn't get a permit to build that shed.
The code applies because I didn't get a permit, why would I get a permit though?
Because the code requires it.
What facts do you rely on to prove the code applies to me though?
You didn't get a permit.
Could someone *please* call a psychiatrist?

Lawyers use the term "strict liability statute" to explain away victimless crimes or offenses. Traffic violations fall into this category. Unlike real crimes and some so-called crimes such as tax evasion, there is no willfulness element to strict liability code violations. You are ordered by politicians to either to do or not do something, and there's no recognized excuse. Either you possessed certain plants or you didn't. That's the only question in their minds.

So if the predators forbid X and you do X, there's no legal defense, *unless* there's no evidence the code applies to you. Prosecutors put the cart before the horse and hope the jury is too distracted or stupid to notice there's no horse.

Here the effectiveness of challenging applicability really shines. Prosecutors claim that to get a conviction they only have to prove beyond a reasonable doubt you committed the prohibited act. We already know this is untrue from both a logical position and because bureaucrats insist their code is applicable-that we were obligated not to do the prohibited act. A good way to get a bureaucrat angry is to suggest there's no evidence their sacred laws apply to you. But you cannot violate a rule that doesn't apply to you regardless of the violence from the judge and police. There just isn't a single fact to support the argument that if you're physically in Arizona, then the laws of the "state" apply to you.

It's illogical to claim otherwise. Growing poppies in your garden, for example, is only a crime because there is a code/law saying it's a crime. Cops and prosecutors will agree if you ask them.

This is why prosecutors never answer the following question:

How do you prove a code violation without first proving the code applies beyond a reasonable doubt?

Hanging up in anger or asking me if I'm on drugs are not answers. They can't answer because they must know that if they are claiming the code applies, it's the only reason there's an alleged violation at all, and they bear the burden of proving it with facts. Did they miss the part about all those violent predators on the streets called "law enforcement officers?"

Cops enforce the will of other predators called legislators, and I have never met one who actually questioned if there was evidence it applied to those they are aggressing against. The cops, prosecutors, judges, and, unfortunately, their victims all just assume it. Raise the issue and they will mock you for questioning their assumption, which is a mass delusion.

They allege their laws apply, so to borrow an old, but very good principle:

"semper necessitas probandi incumbit ei qui agit...the burden of proof always lies upon him who alleges." *Ballentine's Law Dictionary*, page 1159.

We should go into court with that printed on our shirts. It should be a footer on every document we file with them. People usually run into trouble trying to resolve a problem with a bureaucrat when they stray from this principle. If you want to drive a bureaucrat crazy, then just stick to keeping the burden on them where it belongs.

So, to those prosecutors, cops and tax agents out there: If you don't want to be burdened with having to provide evidence to support your allegations, then (big clue) don't make allegations until after you have credible evidence.

Norman Smith told me, in response to the above question, that he proves the code is applicable by proving the code was violated. Doesn't that include proving the code applies? What evidence do you rely on to prove the code applies Norm? He then contradicts himself, saying that he doesn't have to prove it, and then states that he can, but still refuses to be specific about those alleged facts. The credibility is strong with this one!

I had one tax agent tell me she did not like feeling like she was being backed into a corner with my questions. Really? Easy solution, lady: leave people alone and only make accusations when you have evidence.

My "method." I've been attacked because of my "method" in dealing with bureaucratic attacks, particularly in court. These attacks have come from both statists and liberty activists. The method is to question fictions those attacking me are putting forth. I just question the allegations being made against me; that's really all there is to it. So critics can flame away for all I care. As far as I can tell, asking questions is a pretty effective way to get to the truth.

I accept no sacred cows and neither should you, especially when a bureaucrat is attacking you. If a lawyer, with or without a robe, claims to be fair and independent, then challenge that when it's at odds with the facts. The facts tell the story, and they are easily verified. Remember, the formula I use for courts and most administrative proceedings is:

A forces B to answer C.

These are the only facts needed to completely destroy the perception you're getting a fair trial from a fair, impartial, and independent decision-maker. It's no more difficult than that; the facts will always tell a different story from the public relations the bureaucrats are peddling.

Because of these facts, we can confidently stick to asking the lawyer pretending to be a judge to prove he/she is independent and know they will not be able to do so. If there's no independent decision maker, then we've got a solid, substantive due process violation, and we're only getting started. We know they're lying or engaged in reification too; we just ask questions to bring that into the open. Tear down the facade.

In court, a former prosecutor with a robe is forcing me to answer a current prosecutor's complaint. The facts, clear for all to see and independently verify, destroy the argument/lie the judge is somehow independent. The violence inherent in the system will provide such contradictions for us to exploit.

The facts prove beyond any doubt the judge is acting against me on the prosecutor's behalf. Anyone who claims the judge is not facilitating the attack/prosecution has a dubious grasp of reality. Even prosecutors admit they could not prosecute anyone without judges forcing participation. This includes threatening to have men with guns use deadly force to get us into that building.

The facts prove beyond any doubt the judge's aggression and threats make the prosecution possible; the conflict is blatant. So I ask questions to expose this obvious contradiction.

Critics think this will automatically upset judges and ensure I'm going to prison every time. As usual, there's no evidence. And even if it does upset a lawyer, should we give them a free pass? What's accomplished by questioning this sacred cow?

I believe much is accomplished. It proves the lawyer is not professional and interested in justice at all; he/she is a crook. Any intention of dealing honestly and in good faith is gone with just one question. That looks pretty effective; one question can gut the judge's pretense of fairness and independence. Sounds like a great system. No wonder they like to snarl, "I'm not here to answer your questions!" Sure, why would the Great Oz let anyone look behind the curtain?

Questioning a former prosecutor on his or her relationship to the current prosecutor will not generate rage from honest, stable adults. The relationship is obvious, but covered in layers of public relations, distractions ,and engineered fear. The threat of contempt is usually sufficient to keep even liberty activists from asking such questions. Instead of exposing the charade, some liberty activists will give these violent lawyers a free pass. I don't.

But Marc, if the judge doesn't force you to respond to the complaint, the prosecutor cannot try his case. I agree, but that in no way negates the fact the judge is acting on behalf of the prosecutor. And it doesn't change anything to claim: "that's the way the system works," and other such political platitudes. When the judge forces us to defend against the prosecutor's complaint, they are not independent. If they are not independent, there is going to be bias.

These psychopaths are taking control of your life; for the sake of your safety it makes sense to challenge them every single step of the way. If your position is, "I don't want to upset the judge," then you're not putting together a very effective defense, especially if you're not accused of hurting anyone. The judge is an active participant in your prosecution; he's the gatekeeper enabling the whole thing, and it seems silly to me to just ignore this when we're supposed to have a fair trial:

> "A defendant has a right to "fundamental fairness" as a matter of both substantive and procedural due process. See, e.g., United States v. Lilly, 983 F.2d 300, 309 (1st Cir. 1992) (A sub-stantive due-process violation "occurs when government conduct violates 'fundamental fairness' and is 'shocking to the universal sense of justice.'") (Quoting Kinsella v. United States ex rel. Singleton, 361 U.S. 234, 246 (1960) https://bulk.resource.org/courts.gov/c/US/361/361.US.234 .22.html); Marshall v. Jerrico, Inc., 446 U.S. 238, 242 (1980) (The right to procedural due process "en-titles a person to an impartial and disinterested tribunal in both civil and criminal cases," one that "preserves both the appearance and reality of fairness, 'generating the feeling, so important to a popular government, that justice has been done.'") (Quoting JointAnti-Fascist Refugee Comm. v. McGrath, 341 U.S. 123, 172 (1951) (Frankfurter, J., concurring)) http://supreme.justia.com/cases/federal/us/341/123/case. html *Villalpando v. Reagan*, 1 CA-CV 04-0775, Arizona Court of Appeals.

Even more specific is this opinion regarding a fair trial:

> "Due process entitles a person to an impartial and disinterested tribunal in both civil and criminal cases. Every litigant is entitled to nothing less than the cold neutrality of an impartial judge. Miller Dollarhide, P.C. v. Tal, 2007 OK 58 ¶17, 163 P3d 548, 554." *Casey v. Casey*, 2011 OK 46.

If you miss the impact of those two sentences, then read them again; then read them to a critic. If we're "entitled to nothing less than the cold neutrality of an impartial judge," then why ignore the fact the judge is acting on behalf of the prosecution? Where is the wisdom in ignoring such a blatant contradiction?

Pointing this out by objecting and asking questions is stupid, but ignoring a serious denial of due process is a smart strategy? Seems logical to me that if the public relations says I'm entitled to a cold, neutral and impartial judge, and the facts prove the judge isn't, then I'm going to object and point that out.

I'm telling you from personal first-hand experience: just because a judge gets upset does not mean you are automatically going to jail for contempt, or that the complaint won't get kicked out. You can do everything right, including getting a judge to actually spell out the reasonable doubt, and still get convicted. Talk to Larken Rose to confirm it. You can also listen to the archives of the **No State Project** where people have called about going to court, asking about the conflict of interest and they didn't go to jail.

Lawyers are an integral part of the system that's attacking you; they use your fear and anxiety to their advantage, not yours, and they avoid doing any more work than they have to. It's foolish to think the fear people have of judges is not there on purpose to benefit the lawyers. What kind of defense do they tend to do?

> Whatever we do to defend against these baseless charges, let's always focus on not upsetting the judge. That's the most important part of your defense. Whatever challenge, however effective at showing the proceedings are a sham, we'll avoid that and play it safe. Yes, we're going to play it safe, not effective, with your life in the balance, not mine. I'll just get back into one of my BMWs while you're getting thrown into a cage.

That seems to be a common theme, even with some lawyers claiming to be anarchists. Instead of actively exposing these psychopaths, they hide and cower like children: let's not get daddy mad.

And they know damn well the judges are anti-social, because they openly admit they don't want to get judges pissed off by asking relevant questions regarding jurisdiction. Jack Pointer of Oklahoma City is only one of many lawyers who have told me they won't raise the issues I do. Not because they aren't effective, but because they don't want to piss off the judge. I've been told pissing off a judge can ruin their career. Nice system: ask a relevant question and have your career destroyed.

I've been attacked by lawyers claiming with absolute certainty that if you ask a judge whom he represents you will anger them and you'll go to prison. There is no evidence to prove this and I've done it many times and haven't been thrown in jail. And if it's a very serious, substantive due process violation, then why not use that to get the bogus charges tossed out? It seems if asking questions is enough to get you thrown in prison "for the rest of [your] life," then that's pretty good grounds to establish you can't get a fair trial.

Not standing up for the truth and principles of right and wrong is why there is such organized tyranny: so an effective defense has to include more of that? I'm delusional and the lawyers are not? So just keep using the same *process* and things will be alright?

Because we fail to stand up to these parasites, they can conduct mock trials; so we better play it safe and continue not standing up to them? And if anyone suggests just questioning the process, we'll play up our authority and experience and publicly denounce those people as delusional. Yeah, that's the ticket.

You think these lawyers would at least suggest making the challenges on paper or telephonically. It hardly needs mentioning lawyers are a part of the courts, and they are not at the top of the hierarchy. They benefit from this violent system, so it's no surprise they won't question it. They would like to climb the pecking order, and pointing out these contradictions is not going to get them very far.

We always have to keep in mind the psychological issues discussed earlier when we are looking at how to deal with these bureaucrats. There is just as much, if not more, social pressure on lawyers to conform and keep their mouths shut. Principles? They stay at home, they have no business in court.

The psychopath circus. I've taken to calling courts what they really are: a **psychopath circus**. It certainly helps keep me focused on what is really going on so I can be more effective. This goes for administrative hearings as well.

All the factors are there: their force/threats, incessant lying, callous disregard for others, massive egos and a complete lack of empathy. Anyone who has dealt with these predators knows they do not tolerate questioning well at all.

These people claim to be independent of the very people they work with, and say it with a straight face. I've had IRS agents say they are independent of the IRS because they work in a different department.

Vin James in England (Vin does the **No State Project UK** radio show) spoke with a woman named Downey who got irritated when asked what facts she relied on proving she was actually independent of the "Crown" she admittedly had an oath to. Here's an excerpt from that psychopath circus:

241

Recorder Downey: *I am independent of both the crown and the police, that is a fact.*
Vin: It's based on facts?
Recorder Downey: *Yes.*
Vin: Right, can you tell me what those facts are to prove that you are actually independent?
Recorder Downey: *No, I have told that I am; I have taken an oath; I am independent of the crown. I have dealt with that matter so we are moving on to the next submission. All right?*

Clearly Ms. Downey has an issue with being upfront and honest. She admits to taking an oath of allegiance to the Crown but is magically independent of the Crown? How? The familiar: because she said so.

Normal people would stop just from the embarrassment of looking like a moron. But these people do not have normal personalities. They don't care, and their grandiose view of themselves doesn't allow for it.

This woman just would not stop either; it kept going like this with some other issues. It's an example of how strong perceptions are over the facts right in front of you. Downey's ego could not permit the processing of the sheer stupidity coming out of her mouth.

Knowing we're dealing with psychopaths, we can and should anticipate their actions/responses and we won't be surprised when they lie without a hint of shame. Based on experience, I just assume that everything out of their mouths is going to be a lie. This is why I constantly object and ask for clarifications when they say stupid things like Downey did with Vin. Even if the bureaucrat won't get off the stupid train, I can usually use their statements against them. We can and should make it a credibility issue.

If a bureaucrat says "the law applies because the law says so," then such nonsense should be thrown back in his/her face until they back off for a lack of evidence.

When dealing with psychopaths, the constant lying can always be used against them, so that's why we should always stick to the facts. It's usually not effective to take a position, but if we do take one, then it's that we don't see any facts that the code is applicable. If we ask questions about facts and jurisdiction and we get an admission such as: "I don't have any jurisdiction here" and the bureaucrat lies about what he said, then the burden still stays on them where it belongs:

Alrighty then, you didn't say that? Whatever. So, the facts you rely on proving the code applies to me are what now?

The "similar" game. This cruel game is played extensively by politicians and bureaucrats. The crux of this game is that when confronted by someone who sticks to the facts, bureaucrats will label a question or observation as an argument, and then claim a "similar argument" was raised before and rejected by the courts as frivolous.

For example, I call people at the Franchise Tax Board (FTB) in California and ask for admissible evidence and witnesses with personal knowledge my client is a taxpayer. I'm told there's no evidence and no witnesses. You can hear a call with Carol and others on my website. My position the assessment should be abated is there are no facts to support the assessment.

Someone doing business as the FTB will send a form letter with this:

> "Without substantiation, appellant now claims that he is not a "taxpayer" and, therefore, is outside the scope of the Revenue and Taxation Code. This argument defies the known facts in this case, is unfounded and lacks arguable merit (*Appeal of Michael E. Meyers*, 2001-SBE-001; and *United States v. Studley...* 783 F.2d 934)...your Board stated that the assertion that an appellant is not a "taxpayer" **as defined by statute** is a frivolous argument...When discussing a **similar argument** in the *Appeal of Michael E. Meyers...*" (emphasis mine).

Notice there's no mention of the "known facts." How could there be with a form letter though? The beauty of the internet is years ago if a claim like this was made you had to go to a law library or contact a government agency such as the California State Board of Equalization (SBE) to verify what's being claimed. Now, all we have to do is a search for "Appeal of Michael E. Meyers, 2001-SBE-001" and you can download a PDF copy of such public relations nonsense; on-demand public relations. http://www.boe.ca.gov/legal/legalop01.htm

The SBE has a form letter they use with the initial appeal paperwork packet they send you when you appeal decisions of the FTB. This is a gem of political spin. The SBE sticks the word "may" into the text, as if that permits them to assert *anything* they want and then use "may" as a pass if called on it. They continue the similar game:

> "We note that you may make many of the same arguments that have been presented in previous income tax appeals before this Board...Additionally, you are advised that this Board has addressed arguments similar to those you may have raised in your appeal in the *Appeal of Michael E. Meyers* (2001-SBE-001) [other citations omitted]..."

Then the threat, "if the board finds...your position on appeal is frivolous or groundless, the Board may impose up to a $5,000 penalty..."

When you get the actual text, you'll see Mr. Meyers, as reported by the SBE, did not claim there was no evidence and witnesses without personal knowledge. From experience, I can tell you that what is presented is not always what's reported. The SBE, not exactly known as a bastion of truth, reported the following about Mr. Meyers; notice these are issues of law, not fact:

"Appellant states that because he is a "Citizen" of California, he is not a "resident" of California...appellant states that California's income tax laws apply to a "resident" but not a "Citizen."...Appellant also contends "he was never paid any 'compensation'..."

The arguments-issues of law, not fact-presented are:

1.   He did not receive "due process" from respondent or this Board.
2.   Respondent's brief "is not germane to the case" and should be stricken.
3.   The normal presumption that respondent's assessment is correct was successfully rebutted by appellant.
4.   The California income tax law does not apply to his "remuneration" because (a) he is a "Citizen" of the California Republic and thus not a "resident" or "individual" as those terms are used in the tax law (so the code sections relying on those terms "cannot apply to him") and (b) "he was never paid any 'compensation'" because the "money paid to him was 'remuneration' as set forth in the law."
5.   He was at risk of criminal penalties for perjury if he signed a return that showed any income subject to California income tax.
6.   Only income from "sources" specified in Internal Revenue Code (IRC) section 861, and its implementing regulations...are subject to California income tax.
7.   The United States Supreme Court, in United States v. Burke (1992) 504 US 229, supports appellant's definitions of income stated above.
8.   The Internal Revenue Service (IRS) has accepted and acknowledged the validity of the premise of the same arguments and reasoning as presented in the appellant's Treasury Regulation section 1.861 argument.

The form letter later has: "At the federal level, a position similar to appellant's argument was addressed in United States v. Romero, (9th Cir. 1981) 640 F.2d 1014." What was Mr. Romero's *reported* position? As reported, it was again issues of law; interpretation, not fact:

"Romero also alleges bias and error on the part of the trial judge based upon the judge's comments and instructions concerning the legal meaning of the terms "income" and "person" in 26 U.S.C. §§ 61 and 7203. We find this allegation to be frivolous...Romero's proclaimed belief that he was not a "person" and that the wages he earned as a carpenter were not "income" is fatuous as well as obviously incorrect... Romero received a fair trial. He based his defense on his proclaimed belief that the wages he earned were not taxable income and that he was not a person within the meaning of the income tax laws."

So in the legal minds of the people who are the FTB, the word "similar" is what the courts would describe as "overly broad." Normal people would call them illiterate or liars.

I've had two people at the SBE admit: "We use form letters regardless of the issues raised". I asked several times and they refused to put their "policy" in writing. So this policy is only by word of mouth?

So, I decided to play the similar game myself and saw I could easily trump the court cases cited by the FTB and other tax goons with supreme court cases.

In 2001, a case called *Gitlitz v. Commissioner*, 531 U.S. 206 was decided. It was an income tax case dealing with income "which passes through to shareholders and increases their bases in an S corporation's stock." The attorneys calling themselves the Supreme Court ruled against the IRS:

> "Instead the Commissioner asserts that discharge of indebtedness is unique because it requires no economic outlay on the taxpayer's part, but can identify no statutory language that makes this distinction relevant. **On the contrary, the statute makes clear** that §108(a)'s exclusion does not alter the character of discharge of indebtedness as an item of income. Specifically, §108(e) presumes that such discharge is always "income," and that the only question for §108 purposes is whether it is includible in gross income. **The Commissioner's contentions that, notwithstanding the statute's plain language**, excluded discharge of indebtedness is not income and, specifically, that it is not "tax-exempt income" under §1366(a)(1)(A) **do not alter the conclusion reached here**...The judgment of the Court of Appeals [in favor of the IRS], accordingly, is reversed." (Emphasis mine).

The supreme court ruled against the IRS writing things such as: "Implicit in the Commissioner's labeling of such income as "tax-deferred," however, **is the erroneous assumption** that §1366(a)(1)(A) does not include "tax-deferred" income." (Emphasis mine)

This case shares the same similarity to my client's case as the Romero case did; they're both income tax cases. But hey, that's the same asinine standard used by the FTB, right? So I will use this opinion when they play the similar game. It usually leads to asking them if they have an objective standard of proof.

They haven't bought it yet. Apparently their strategy only has merit when they use it-one of many times we can demonstrate a double standard.

Remember: almost always, a court opinion cited by a politician is meant to divert attention away from their lack of facts and case, and will be non-responsive and irrelevant. If my position is there are no facts, then any contrary position, to be responsive, will point out the alleged facts.

Citing a court case over an issue of facts is a dodge-the old red herring. Don't fall for it. They are conflating opinions with facts, hoping you won't notice or your attorney will be too timid to object.

Citing previous court opinions is to settle issues of law, not fact. Every case is fact specific. The legal definition of precedent is:

> **"precedent.** A decision or determination of a **point of law** made by a court in a case to be followed by a court of the same rank or of a lower rank in a subsequent case presenting the same **legal problem**, although different parties are involved in the subsequent case. 20 Am J2d Cts § 183." *Ballentine's Law Dictionary*, page 975. (Emphasis mine)

> **"stare decisis**...The doctrine or principle that decisions should stand as precedents for guidance in cases arising in the future. A strong judicial policy that the determination of a **point of law** by a court will generally be followed by a court of the same or a lower rank in a subsequent case which presents the same **legal problem**, although different parties are involved in the subsequent case. 20 Am J2d Cts § 183." *Ballentine's Law Dictionary*, page 1209. (Emphasis mine)

Res judicata, on the other hand, refers only to cases involving the same parties:

> **"res judicata**...The principle that an existing final judgment rendered upon the merits, without fraud or collusion, by a court of competent jurisdiction, is conclusive of rights, questions, and **facts in issue**, as to the parties and their privies, in all other actions in the same or any other judicial tribunal of concurrent jurisdiction. 30A Am J Rev ed Judgm § 324." *Ballentine's Law Dictionary*, page 1105. (Emphasis mine)

Ever hear the latin maxim of law *res judicata facit ex albo nigrum, ex nigro album, ex curvo rectum, ex recto curvum*? (Well, the "rectum" part certainly explains why politicians love the principle of *res judicata* so much.) I'm sure Jonathan Swift was very familiar with this term, which means:

> "When anything has been adjudicated, it makes white black, black white, curved straight and straight curved." *Ballentine's Law Dictionary*, page 1105. Also in *Bouvier's Law Dictionary* on page 2161.

Do you need anything else to convince you lawyers/politicians are delusional psychos? What is the basis for such nonsense? This is a maxim of the English common law; it's been around a really long time. Doesn't it seem as if these lawyers have a god complex? I'm sure you already knew that; it's always nice to have more evidence of it.

246

They do not usually admit that they, the "honorable" lawyers, are wrong. The Oregon tax court, referencing the above maxim wrote:

> "Under our system, the authority to construe the law is delegated to the judicial branch. See Marbury v. Madison, 5 US 137, 2 L Ed 60, 1 Cranch 137 (US Dist Col, (1803)). Consequently no other individual, group, or institution is authorized to declare that the courts are wrong." *Clark v. ODOR,* TC 4426 2000. http://www.publications.ojd.state.or.us/docs/TC4426.htm

This lawyer also lays out a false choice: "If the public does not agree with the results of final court decisions, they must resort to the ballot box to change the laws." Not true; there is always door number three: non-violent, non-cooperation.

It seems the Asch experiment on conformity may explain why back-robed lawyers love their opinions/precedent so much. This may be part of the reason why you get such nonsense as the following from the *Bennis* case:

> "whether the reason for [the challenged forfeiture scheme] be artificial or real, it is too firmly fixed in the punitive and remedial jurisprudence of the country to be now displaced,". *Bennis v. Michigan,* 516 U.S. 442 (1996).

Or in lay terms we can all understand: We've been doing it wrong for so many years it makes no sense to start doing the right thing now. It's the Bob and Doug McKenzie method: no brakes, so guess there's "No point in steering now."

Children have a better sense of right and wrong than these exalted attorneys. What's important to them is what dead lawyers have written or "*held,*" not right and wrong. Children can grasp the simple concept it's wrong to punish someone admittedly innocent, but these brilliant legal scholars can't. Couldn't the same thing have been said to justify slavery?

> "...whether the reason for [opposition to slavery] be artificial or real, it is too firmly fixed in the punitive and remedial jurisprudence of the country to be now displaced..."

Those supreme attorneys' comedy routine doesn't end there; they continue dishing out the laughs in the name of precedent:

> "In Calero-Toledo v. Pearson Yacht Leasing Co., 416 U.S. 663 (1974), the most recent decision on point, the Court reviewed the same cases discussed above, and concluded that "the innocence of the owner of property subject to forfeiture has almost uniformly been rejected as a defense." Id., at 683." *Bennis v. Michigan,* 516 U.S. 442 (1996).

Well, these other lawyers have noticed that other lawyers, mostly dead now, are saying: Innocence is not a defense to the theft of your property. Keep in mind, this is a due process issue:

> "We hold that the Michigan court order did not offend the Due Process Clause of the Fourteenth Amendment or the Takings Clause of the Fifth Amendment." *Bennis v. Michigan*, 516 U.S. 442 (1996).

Now you know that due process, from the Magna Carta, is more about appearances than justice or the protection of life, liberty, and property. Punishing the innocent is part of due process. It's the greatest system of justice in the world.

The eagle and the fasces are not the only holdovers from the Romans; the institutional, dogmatic reliance on what the elders did and tradition are very much alive with these lawyers.

Let's put this idea of precedent into another context and see how rational it is. Imagine a mechanic insisting that every future problem with a car's engine is the same as the first problem he fixed:

> *Well Madam, the problem with your car was the engine appeared blown and had to be rebuilt.*
> That's crazy; it's brand new. I came in here for an oil change.
> *Are you a certified mechanic? Do you in fact have an associate's degree in Automotive Repair?*
> Well, no, but...
> *Then please leave the technical problems to a licensed professional!*
> But I don't understand; I drove the car in here, how could the engine be blown?
> *It's simple; it's just a matter of "res judicata facit ex albo nigrum, ex nigro album, ex curvo rectum, ex recto curvum."*
> What the hell does that mean?
> *Yeah, I thought you'd be unfamiliar with it. Trust me, it explains why you owe me five grand. If you don't like it, you can post a bond equal to twice the bill and appeal to my boss.*

I see a similarity between what the lawyers do and what the church in Europe did for centuries to stifle scientific investigation and knowledge. They already "know" how things are and how they work, so they don't permit any questioning or investigation.

Poor coping skills. One important thing to remember when dealing with bureaucrats is you're speaking to a child in an adult body. Watch five-year-old children playing with each other; what happens when one doesn't think things are going his way? The child will throw a fit, they'll get upset. Ask a judge whom he represents at a traffic trial and you'll see him instantly become a child again.

It's helpful to look at it as we're coming to the table in a spirit of good faith to resolve this problem. There is obviously a lack of understanding, the agent doesn't fully understand what they are trying to accomplish and why. But telling them they don't understand is not going to be accepted cheerfully, so we have to get around that.

I do that by telling them I don't really understand why they're asserting jurisdiction over me and making demands on me to perform. This opens the door to asking questions. It's the same as when I go into court ready to plead guilty; I just don't understand, I have some questions first.

By asking them questions, the agent is going to start to realize they are the ones who don't understand what they're doing; they cannot explain in plain English where, when, why and how they acquired jurisdiction over me.

It's easier for me to just accept their opinion that I'm a babbling idiot who needs to be spoon-fed their position, than to just insist they don't understand and have erroneously assessed me. Please educate me, Mr. Bureaucrat; help me to understand how you acquired jurisdiction over me because of some code. Exactly why does your code apply just because I'm physically in Vancouver? How does that work?

When there is hostility in court, such as the judge yelling at us, "You are charged with violating the code by growing poppies in your yard. What about that don't you understand!" Then we can just answer, "I don't see any evidence from the prosecution proving the constitution and code apply to me and there is jurisdiction. Have him provide the specific facts and I can have a better understanding of all this."

Please Mr. Bureaucrat, help me, help you. http://www.youtube.com/watch?v=hZM_x-P_AVk.

Presumptions. Presumptions, or rather assumptions or opinions, are the facade of a bureaucratic attack. Some politician either declares you "owe taxes" or it's spit out of a computer. Either way, the rest of the attack is pretty much automated. Regardless, it is still just *vox et preterea nihil* "Voice and nothing more; that is, nothing but wind." *Ballentine's Law Dictionary*, page 1354.

Consider the computer system the California Franchise Tax Board uses; it's much the same as any other taxing agency. The computer is not programmed to make factual distinctions between so-called "taxpayers" and non-taxpayers as even their law clearly does, "They [the revenue laws] relate to taxpayers, and not to non-taxpayers. The latter are without their scope." *Economy Plumbing & Heating Co., Inc., Et Al. v. the United States*, 470 F.2d 585.

To the computer, everyone's a taxpayer. If challenged, even on factual grounds, the retort is automatic, "The argument appellant is not a taxpayer within meaning of statute is frivolous." Never mind you made no argument at all; you just observed there are no facts.

It's extremely difficult for any politician or bureaucrat to accept the idea that not every man, woman and child is a so-called taxpayer. This is

249

obviously a control issue: we have jurisdiction over all taxpayers, so everyone is a taxpayer because everyone is subject to our authority. If you're in range of their guns, then you're a resident/taxpayer within their jurisdiction.

They either believe or act as if they do believe that *man* is synonymous with *taxpayer* and subject to them. They believe they have control over everyone. This belief is stronger than their devotion to sacred writ because that's how it's been done for so long. The Asch Conformity Experiment helps explain why bureaucrats are so reluctant to go against established procedure, even when it conflicts with sacred writ. These lawyers are more concerned with doing things the same as the rest of the gang, treating everyone equally bad. They know their choosing the wrong line: but the social pressure to conform and their perceptions are far more powerful than any facts or principles of right or wrong.

Isn't that the definition of "due process?" Governments may do whatever can be declared to conform to the opinions of dead lawyers. One is led to believe that when that stupid black robe is put on the judge leaves behind basic concepts of right and wrong. Have these lawyers ever heard it's wrong to kill, steal and deceive?

Let's make this easy: Is it right to take someone's property by force, especially when they have injured no one? No. See how easy that is when you strip out all the lawyerese?

Since 1996, I've only had two tax agents and one judge admit there were non-taxpayers. Of course, they refused to even consider my client may not be one, despite admitting there was no evidence he was a taxpayer. Can't imagine why the high level of alcoholism and drug use with politicians…

The point is, when we're labeled a taxpayer it's just that, a label, an opinion, accusation, assumption or presumption that you are irrefutably a taxpayer. The average bureaucrat will disagree when you correctly identify that their accusation you're a taxpayer is an accusation; nonetheless, it is. Use of this one word presumes you are subject to their laws and jurisdiction, same as accusing you of being a resident. If used in court you would be well advised to object on grounds it assumes facts not in evidence and is speculation.

The word taxpayer is a sacred cow to tyrants though, or in legal terms an "irrebuttable presumption" immune from collateral attack:

> "**collateral attack.** Attempting to impeach or challenging the integrity of a judgment, decree, or order in an action…" *Ballentine's Law Dictionary, 3rd Ed*, page 215.

For some reason, bureaucrats always think I intend violence when I mention a collateral attack. You would think that bureaucrats are taught that when they use the word taxpayer, whomever they say it to or about magically becomes one. They certainly act as if they believe in magic. Why else would they always ask: "What evidence do you have that you're not a taxpayer?"

Go ahead, suggest to a politician there's no evidence you're a taxpayer and they will mock you. In fact, all you have to do is ask them if there's evidence, and they'll start smirking and thinking of a derogatory comeback.

Their henchmen at the taxing agencies, just like your friends are likely to do, will laugh and call you crazy. And don't think calmly asking them to put up the facts proving you're a taxpayer will stop their mocking; because if they have any guts and give it a little thought, it will only ramp up their derision. And why? They'll claim it's so obvious; "everyone knows" you're a taxpayer. Then it'll be easy to prove, won't it? Making a statist think will usually result in them getting upset.

Hopefully you're skeptical. So try it yourself. What facts would someone have to put forth to prove you are a taxpayer? Let's start with a short list:

1. One has to be within the state.
2. One must be a Citizen, resident or some other relationship to the state.
3. Prove the laws are binding on you.
4. They would have to prove you received taxable income.

Think that's an easy task? Not one man or woman has been able to do so since I started addressing this topic in the late 90's. I've done hundreds of radio shows, mostly mainstream, and no one--not the hosts and not the callers--even tried to prove a taxpayer exists. I don't need to go through each of the four elements above here, as that is done throughout this part of the book.

With taxing agencies, it's not always necessary to prove presence within the state. For example, the United States government psychopaths admit no limits on their jurisdiction. Some of the states of the United States require residency in the state or state sources. The fact is, there usually has to be a so-called state somewhere in the mix. They'll claim you are within the jurisdiction of a state, United States, province or commonwealth.

Here's an example right from the mouth of a psychopath. They're just pointing out the obvious, a city, is a corporation or legal fiction:

Cupertino Office of the City Clerk (Exhibits 13m and 13n).

CITY POSITION:
The City of Cupertino is a municipal corporation duly organized pursuant to Article XI of the California Constitution with the power to regulate public health, safety and welfare. *See* Cal. Const. art XI § 7. In addition, pursuant to Sections 50022.1 et seq. of the California Government Code, it has enacted its own municipal code. Appellant owns property within the jurisdictional boundaries of the City (See Exhibit), and is therefore subject to its local codes. *See* Cal. Gov't. Code §§ 57325, 57375. Ordinances passed by the City have the force of law. *See Monterey Club v. Superior Court of Los Angeles* (1941) 48 Cal.App. 2d 131, 147. Violations of City ordinances may be misdemeanors, infractions, or redressed by civil penalty. Gov't. Code § 36900. In addition, cities may impose administrative fines or penalties for violations of ordinances. Gov't. Code § 53069.4.

It's a corporation when talking about themselves, but a geographic area when addressing us, their cattle.

[handwritten annotations: "← NOT a ↗" and "So I can't be within it"]

251

I asked Jeff Wilson of the Chelan county planning board in Washington what he meant by state. I'd been asking for facts the code applies to my client, and he kept responding with statements about being in the state and subject to state authority:

> Jeff, what do you mean by state? What are you trying to convey to me with that word?
> *The state of Washington.*
> What do you mean by the state of Washington?
> *I'm not going to get into this with you. I've already answered you.*
> No, you haven't. What do you mean when you say state of Washington?
> *I'm not going to argue with you.*

Looks like Jeff likes to use words without referents, and when you call him on it, all he can do is lie by saying I'm arguing. When bureaucrats like Jeff are heavily engaged in reification, asking him/her questions will help stop the process, and they may not like it. Remember, no one likes to realize that most of what they say is unsupported garbage, so expect them to get a bit emotional about it.

Jeff's job rests on a foundation of violence and lies, and apparently most people prefer to stay ignorant of that truth. I'm betting it would take lots of medication to dull the pain from such a situation.

Model for effectively dealing with the psychopaths

Always attack the factual basis; keep the burden on the ones making the accusations. Hammer away at their arguments, demanding they provide the evidence to support them. You must meet them at their map of the world though; work with their expectations and perceptions. We know they are contradictory; we all work with conflicting generalizations. You need to know them in advance so you can exploit them. This is the basic model to work from:

- Find out who has authority to stop attack
- Ask what grounds are to stop attack–lack of witnesses, evidence
- Have them walk you through the process of stopping an attack
- Ask if opinions are irrefutable
- Do they hold an objective standard of proof?
- Separate facts from opinions
- Who did the assessment?
- Is there jurisdiction? Applicability of law

252

- Find out if there are witnesses with personal knowledge
- Get them to admit there are witnesses & admissible evidence
- Ask about admissibility–information coerced
- Identify the witnesses with personal knowledge
- What evidence is relied on- who determined admissible, their qualifications
- Can income be proven taxable with just facts?
- Is your intent to administer justice?
- Logical check

After you're really familiar with the process and have engaged others in this, then you can do pretty well with just:

1. Find who has authority to drop attack
2. What are grounds to drop, a lack of evidence?
3. What facts the code applies (jurisdiction)?
4. Are there witnesses with personal knowledge the code applies?

These four steps are a logical, very effective way to resolve problems with bureaucrats. Each step leads to the next. I usually don't get to step four because it's not possible for the psychopaths to get past step three. Step four is usually just to make my point that there is no evidence of jurisdiction, so it's best to just drop the attack against my client. Inability to provide evidence is proof that the agent is speculating.

It's very effective at getting more leverage over a prosecutor or any political predator attacking you. We've just proven the argument/opinion is speculation; there's no evidence and no witnesses to prove jurisdiction. It's also where we get our evidence of misconduct. So keep track of their non-responsive answers and evasions–the dates and times. They will all go into a motion to dismiss for prosecutorial misconduct and malicious prosecution. It also can be used for a complaint to the bar and against those higher on the political pecking order, such as the city council and county commissioners.

Who can drop the attack? When you call or visit a bureaucrat in an effort to limit the damage they intend on doing to you, the first thing you need to do is get to an agent who's able to stop the attack. It serves no purpose to start with an agent who cannot stop it. This doesn't matter where the attack is occurring, be it the United States or Australia. It helps to ask if they have the authority to stop an assessment or whatever you're being threatened with. They all seem to like being an authority. Be

253

warned (and this may be a shock): bureaucrats don't always tell the truth. It's usually a shock when they do let a bit of truth get out.

I spoke with a tax agent in Minnesota and asked him if he was the one who did an assessment against JT. He said he was and that he had authority to abate the assessment. I asked him if anyone else was responsible for the accusation that JT was a taxpayer and had taxable income, and he said he was the only one. Excellent, he's my guy. I wrote it all down. (I think it's a good idea to tell them I'm writing their statements down).

I asked if the assessment was based on facts or just pulled out of thin air. He said it was based on facts. I tend to throw in the last part to gently pressure him into taking the untenable position that his accusation is based on facts.

Since he said it was based on facts, I asked if he could prove the income was taxable with just those facts and no citations to the law. That's when I got the famous long pause–then he snaps at me he's not going to answer the question. I ask why not, and he accuses me of trying to "trap" him. (I get accused all the time of trying to trap them and "twist" their words. Yes, I'm the one playing wordsmith.)

I assure him that I'm only trying to resolve the matter by asking questions. In anger, he refuses to answer and states he's not the one who did the assessment. I remind him that he said he was; that I wrote down his answers. He tells me I'm a liar and can twist his words any way I'd like, and he repeats that he didn't do the assessment. This is why it's important to have a witness and record everything. It's also why they will usually refuse to be recorded. It's all right for everything we say to be recorded, but not their lies.

I told him I was writing his answers down as we spoke, but there was no budging him. He denied there was a recording being done at his end. In the end though, they dropped their attack and left JT alone.

If you're not talking to an agent who can stop the attack, you're probably wasting your time. That's why I usually ask this first: Do you have the authority to drop this assessment? Once the agent admits they have the authority to stop an attack, you want them to walk you through the process of actually vacating or abating the assessment. You want them to spend some time on this: get details, ask questions, and focus on getting them comfortable talking about it.

It's always a good thing to get them to talk about it because it's probably an issue they seldom talk about, if ever. We go to the gatekeeper. In court this is easy; we know the prosecutor can withdraw, though even then the former prosecutor with the robe has the ultimate say in what is thrown out.

This is not the case though with administrative attacks. They may even lie and say there is no one at the agency who can drop the attack. So ask, "So if there's no evidence of jurisdiction, you're supposed to continue despite it being misconduct and malfeasance?" They tend to want us to go through their appeal process. Sure, they make the decisions and if you want to appeal you foot the bill.

This is why I've been going up the pecking order and letting them know what's happening. But even having the boss on the phone won't always help. I had George Copadias, the commissioner of the NHES, lie to me saying he couldn't stop a complaint from one of his own employees. I asked, "You are the commissioner though right? Your general counsel admits there is no evidence and as commissioner you can't do anything to stop a complaint issued without evidence of jurisdiction?" He wouldn't budge.

Such lies are common. I had a city manager in the Toronto area tell me the same thing–that he has no oversight of his *own* employee.

Grounds to drop an attack. After the bureaucrat has admitted to having authority to stop an attack, ask questions to find out what grounds are acceptable to him/her to stop the attack. You can keep things simple and don't really worry about learning all their procedures. I'll ask them about the grounds and suggest, "If the assessment was erroneous, would that be grounds to abate it?" They'll usually agree; if not, I ask, "Would you proceed against someone if the assessment is erroneous?

They'll usually say they wouldn't, even if reluctantly. Then I can ask: If the assessment was arbitrary–not based on facts–would that be grounds to abate it? They'll usually agree that if the assessment is arbitrary then, that would be grounds to abate it.

When they agree to something like this, always have them repeat it back to you. This is not only to make sure everyone is on the same page, but you also want "assessment is arbitrary" repeated often; let this sink in and be the focus of the rest of the conversation.

Another factor is if there is no evidence of jurisdiction. They fight this, but when I point out I just want to understand how things work in general, they will usually confirm that a lack of evidence proving jurisdiction is grounds to stop an attack.

If they fight me, I just ask, "You wouldn't proceed without jurisdiction would you? Wouldn't that be illegal?" They will usually agree, but always add, "But we do have jurisdiction." That's fine, we're just laying the groundwork; we just need to understand your process.

We're only looking to hold them to their opinions/grounds to drop an attack. We're setting them up to contradict themselves. If they don't drop it, then we have their own statements to use against them to not only get it dropped, but as proof of misconduct and bad faith. Their statements have much more weight than ours do. Don't fight it, don't try to change it, just use their dishonesty to your advantage.

Walk through the process. Once we have agreement that they have authority to drop an attack and their acceptable grounds, ask them about the process: "How does that work when you're presented with an erroneous assessment?"

Don't let them off the hook here; this is where they may try to convince you that another office or department has to do that. They may even claim there has to be a hearing or court proceeding. Remind them of their answer they have authority to stop the attack.

They also resist by claiming the assessment is not erroneous. Again, we just want to understand the process.

Are their opinions irrefutable? Once you have their assent on the grounds to abate an assessment, it's important to ask if their opinions against you are irrefutable. This is easier to do after we ask what the grounds are to abate or stop the attack, because they've already admitted their opinions can be wrong, even if not directly.

They need to admit the possibility that the opinion I'm a taxpayer could be erroneous; if they won't, then I have to ask questions to put some cracks in their colossal ego, to shatter some credibility. If they say it's impossible for it to be incorrect, then I ask if they are experts in the interpretation and application of the constitution. This is usually enough to at least sow some seeds of doubt in their opinions. It's pretty rare to get a bureaucrat who claims there's no possibility their opinions could be wrong.

Asking them why their opinion could not possibly be wrong is a good way to get them to back off; they won't be able to tell you anything.

If they are adamant, then I bring up the fact that they already agreed the attack could be abated if not based on facts. Also, if they are particularly nasty, then I ask them to put it in writing since the courts still reject irrefutable presumptions. I'm not going to accomplish much else, so it's better to move on. I've asked them to put it in writing under penalty of perjury, but not one has ever done it. Can't imagine why.

I've only had three agents tell me they were experts-one took it back; one yelled at me and hung up on me when I asked a follow-up question; and one was an attorney with the California Franchise Tax board. When I asked her what facts she relied on proving the constitution applied to my client, all she could offer was "It's an operation of law." That's political-speak for: "I have no clue." She said as much to me when I pointed out that was an opinion, not facts. She admitted she was having trouble understanding me, and I told her there is a disconnect with the communication because I was asking for facts and she was giving me opinions.

Think about her response for a moment: "It's an operation of law." What the hell is that supposed to mean? If it means anything beyond: "Because I said so," I'm more than doubtful. If you get this line, ask them to explain it. But first tell them it's not responsive to the question. Help me to understand: what exactly are you trying to convey to me when you say "it's an operation of law"?

I'd love to use that as a defense:

Sorry love, there's no tax due.
And why is that?
Uh, an operation of law, that's why.
Brilliant! You have a way with words, Marc.

Let me see your license and registration, sir.
Not required, mate.
Really? Why aren't you required? (Tasers are coming out.)
Operation of law, mate. G'day.
G'day, mate!

When they acknowledge their opinions are not irrefutable, you can then ask them questions such as being an expert as shown above. I usually start with, "Since you're so certain the code is applicable, what facts do you rely on proving it applies to me at all?" This makes any qualifications really unnecessary though. It's not relevant if they've been to Cambridge or Yale and on the job for twenty-five years; if there are no facts, then no amount of rhetoric can overcome it.

In a Mesa court recently, I was pointing out that the cop had no evidence the code applied to me and could not prove jurisdiction. I had to sit through a lawyer's list of accomplishments, law school, thirty years as a judge, forty, as a lawyer etc., before I could point out that his impressive resume is irrelevant to the cop's complete lack of evidence. Do I really need to point out that being a judge for thirty years is not evidence the code applies to me? Nice appeal to authority, though; only the cop seemed impressed.

Any questions about their qualifications to interpret and apply the constitution and code are usually met with anger, "How dare you question me?!" Well, that's what they probably mean when they start telling me they're not going to waste their time with my frivolous arguments. We're peeling back the onion of PR and it stinks worse with every unanswered question. The closer we get to exposing their baseless opinions, the more anger we tend to get. Expect it, embrace it, and take it as a signal that as long as we've been calm and professional, we're getting closer to our goal.

It's the same as when a lawyer objects when you ask his/her witness, "What is the plaintiff state, factually?" This is right where we've been leading them. I'm the puppet master here; I stay in control. Yes, judges can have us thrown into cages and even killed, but when they deny a cross-examination or take the testimony of a witness they've declared incompetent, I was in control. Knowing they are psychopaths, it's easy for me to lead them to do it. That was always the point.

The questions I'm asking are deliberate; they're framed in a way leading to a certain conclusion. This can be replicated because they're so rigid in their behavior, so thoroughly dishonest, that whether it's in New York, Toronto, London, Melbourne,or Dunedin, it doesn't matter. It's because of the hierarchy they are a part of; they're all trying to keep the same thing hidden: the gun under all that paperwork.

If I'm asking about their qualifications to make such legal determinations against me and they refuse to discuss the matter, the least I've done is establish bad faith. What if they just lie about what we spoke about? That's easy; go back to the question they refused to answer.

Great, you're qualified. So you're an expert in the interpretation and application of the constitution and code?
Of course, look at this loaded gun, mate.
Great, so you're qualified to determine, with facts, the constitution and code are applicable to me?
Yes, I'm an expert; I just told you that. I also have this nifty badge and Taser.
Excellent. What is the constitution and what facts connect it to me?
[Cue the rants of frivolous argument.]

There's no magic formula or method, we're just asking for the facts their sacred cows rest on. We need to recognize them as sacred cows though and stick to the facts and not let them distract from or evade the questions. We can get them to admit they are not irrefutable; most will if asked. If I'm speaking to a lawyer, they tend to understand that irrefutable presumptions violate due process:

> "Statutes creating permanent irrebuttable presumptions have long been disfavored under the Due Process Clauses of the Fifth and Fourteenth Amendments…In holding that this irrefutable assumption was so arbitrary and unreasonable as to deprive the taxpayer of his property without due process of law, the Court stated that it had 'held more than once that a statute creating a presumption which operates to deny a fair opportunity to rebut it violates the due process clause of the Fourteenth Amendment.' [citations omitted]." *Vlandis v. Kline*, 412 U.S. 441 (1973).

While this specifically addresses statutes/codes/laws, the principle still applies to the opinions/arguments of a cop or other bureaucrat. If the sacred writ cannot have "permanent irrebuttable presumptions" then those lower on the pecking order may not either.

When a tyrant has sent a threatening form letter (I'll use a tax assessment as an example here), I like to call immediately and start a factual timeline. This helps later if we file complaints against those higher up the food chain. They usually have a contact number on the letter, unless you're dealing with the Canadian Revenue Agency-good luck contacting them. It took over a year to get a contact number for the legal department. For the British Columbia branch it's (604) 666-8610.

A factual timeline is necessary if the matter is not dropped right away. This way, if it proceeds to any kind of hearing and you have to present your case, you're not just mimicking the tyrants and putting forth arguments and opinions.

When I put forth my grounds for the assessment to be dropped, e.g., there are no witnesses with personal knowledge and no admissible evidence my client is a taxpayer with taxable income, I can support it with facts. I can write that on September 7, 2011, I spoke to agent Bryant and he told me there are no witnesses. You have your position and supporting facts. Even though they have the burden of proof, you don't want to be without facts to use against them. Get them on the defense.

If you're talking to an agent, they'll tend to snarl, "Why don't you think your client's a taxpayer?" If you've done your homework, you'll be able to answer:

> I spoke to agent Murphy this morning and he was unable to confirm if there were witnesses with personal knowledge and evidence. Murphy also admitted he wasn't qualified to determine my client is a taxpayer. It's just speculation.

Notice the weak link is directly from a tax agent, so you can pit one bureaucrat against another if there's hostility to dropping the attack. Be aware though, some bureaucrats are so desperate to take your money, they will say what their agent said is irrelevant. Again, this is because bureaucrats want reality to conform to their opinions, not the other way around. Reification is a helluva drug.

Even if they claim the agent's statements are irrelevant, the burden of proof stays on them where it belongs. If the first agent is disregarded, then the question of facts proving the code is applicable is still on the table and needs to be addressed.

I had a tax refund claim denied on grounds it was based on a frivolous argument. I called and wrote the agent demanding her to disclose the actual frivolous argument. Several months later, the agency finally revised the denial by striking out the grounds for the denial. The supervisor, Susanne Small, also told me there was no frivolous argument and that was put in by mistake. Making it even more effective were 20+ statements of fact supporting our actual position, and there were no witnesses and no evidence my client was a taxpayer. Now they're admitting evidentiary challenges are not frivolous, and they have to point out which facts, if any, they disagree with and the facts they rely on. I'm not holding my breath waiting for an answer though.

If they're giving me a hassle because they don't want to take responsibility for their assessment or drop it, then I use the traffic ticket analogy to help them understand. The assessment is like a traffic ticket, and the tax agent is like the cop who did the stop and wrote the ticket. If the cop does not show up for trial, it doesn't matter how much the judge thinks I'm guilty; no witness, no case, and the ticket is kicked out. The same thing with a competent witness: no competent/credible witness is the same as no witness.

Bureaucrats never like taking responsibility and answering questions, so even if they start talking to you about the assessment, they'll tend to back off if they were not the one making the accusation. If they're not the one who made the accusation/assessment, then ask them if they can get you the name and contact information for the agent who did.

If they question why you need to speak to the assessing agent, tell them you just want to be able to verify the accusation is accurate before you cut them a check or file a return. If they are convinced the assessment is based on facts, then they should have no trouble disclosing them.

What's incredible is there are people, in and out of government, who believe the agent who did the assessment is *irrelevant* to whether it's accurate or not. These people are apparently not familiar with a word known as *speculation*. It's why they need guns.

If you have no agent's name, then how can the accuracy of the assessment be verified? They have no name, they've had no personal contact with my client before, and yet they can be so absolutely certain the opinions are true, that any challenge is automatically frivolous.

Does the word 'credibility' ever enter the picture? It's like with Saul Goodman from *Breaking Bad*: "Let's just say I know a guy who knows a guy...who knows another guy." This is a standard of proof, that's credible? To the psychopaths it is, at least when they're attacking us.

They have no idea of the thought process the accusing agent went through to determine my client is a taxpayer with taxable income, but even evidentiary challenges are frivolous. It's nice to be omnipotent, isn't it?

Yet when they understand what the word irrefutable means, they're less reluctant admitting their opinions are not irrefutable. Once they admit they can be challenged, they're admitting the possibility their assessment or opinion is wrong. This is keeping in line with their model of the world: they believe their administrative process and court proceedings are fair and provide justice. I just set up a double bind and get them to admit the opinion could be wrong. The conflicting generalizations are:

1. Any challenge to a bureaucrat's opinion is frivolous—the opinions are irrefutable.
2. Their admin process and court proceedings are fair.

While they usually don't drop the frivolous mantra, they will begrudgingly admit their opinions are not irrefutable. Their map of the world has their system as being very relevant; they can't maintain that belief while also holding their opinions are irrefutable.

We know both statements are demonstrably false, but that doesn't matter. What matters is what is true to the bureaucrat. That's why we can put them in a double bind; they believe and act as if their two generalizations are true. It's just that most people don't ask them if their opinions are irrefutable.

When it comes to tax matters, most tend to accept the opinion and challenge only the amount claimed. Because they're not used to such questions, they get pretty uncomfortable and answer the only way they can and still maintain any confidence in their administrative processes and court systems.

This doesn't mean the bureaucrat will be consistent-they can't be. But you are operating within their model of the world, so your chances are much better of getting a resolution. A good example is Daniel with the FTB, he agrees that a lack of evidence is grounds to stop an assessment, then a few minutes later laughs, "There doesn't need to be evidence."

It's important with a double bind situation that you use the stronger generalization to meet your objective. You know the agent has to drop one of them to get out of the situation you helped create; you want it to be one that will get you closer to your goal of getting the attack stopped.

In my experience, the issue of the agent's authority is more emotionally rooted than the irrefutable opinions. Apparently the idea of having authority has much deeper roots into the false personality than the concept the opinions are irrefutable. This can work to my advantage when working to have the agent exercise their authority to vacate an assessment.

Experience proves it's fruitless to debate or disagree with an agent when they claim to have authority. If you push against them, then they will just push back. Most of the time, when an agent mentions their authority, it's just a red herring to distract anyway. With tax agents, when things get too uncomfortable, they usually start pointing the finger at another department with authority. I had a Mr. Weed tell me that IRS Collections was "not allowed to discuss facts…"

An example is when I challenge a traffic ticket on grounds there's no cause of action-there's no standing to complain. A lawyer for the state will respond stating that the police have statutory authority to write traffic tickets and enforce the traffic laws. It's pointless to disagree with that, so I don't. I just point out that it's not relevant to the discussion whether the ticket presents a valid cause of action or not.

It comes down to this: "What does your authority to write tickets have to do with whether a valid cause of action is presented to the court?"

The STATE: serving up red herrings since history has been recorded.

"Yes Mr. Psychopath, you have authority to write tickets, but is there evidence of jurisdiction over me?" At best, they are conflating authority with jurisdiction. Even if we assume they are the same, there is still no evidence the code applies...and where do they get their authority? Ostensibly from their magic code. And how does that apply to me?

The same principle is at play with tax assessments (really not much different than a traffic ticket). The agent claims authority to issue assessments if someone doesn't file a return. Is the presumption of correctness based on the agent's authority? Even the courts aren't so bad as to claim something that silly:

> "Once this minimal evidentiary showing has been made, the Commissioner's deficiency determination is then accorded its usual presumption of correctness. Subsequently, the burden shifts to the taxpayer to prove that the deficiency determination is arbitrary or erroneous. Adamson v. Commissioner, 745 F.2d 541, 547 (9th Cir.1984); Stonehill, 702 F.2d at 1294; Anastasato v. Commissioner, 794 F.2d 884, 887 (3rd Cir.1986)." *Sattar Nadjmechi, v. Commissioner of Internal Revenue*, 77 F.3d 489.

Even the courts-just gangs of lawyers with no voluntary support-give lip service to an evidentiary burden, not basing assessments on mere authority.

What I write in my motion to dismiss, in *anticipation* of the authority claim, is, "The limitation on the courts' jurisdiction, being adversarial systems, not inquisitorial, are limited to only cases. This limitation on the courts' jurisdiction cannot be enlarged by claims of police authority." Yes, let's give them a pass: you have the authority to write tickets, but that does not mean tickets are automatically valid and also present a valid cause of action for a court to then acquire jurisdiction.

With tax agents, it works to my advantage to keep stressing his/her authority to vacate an assessment. I can ask if their authority to vacate means the assessment is not irrefutable. This will usually get an admission that the opinion/assessment is not irrefutable. How could he have authority to abate if the opinions are irrefutable?

It's also a non-sequitur, meaning it doesn't follow. There just isn't any connection between the authority to do something and the merit of any work done. Just because a man/woman has a license to practice medicine doesn't mean they will always do quality work. Imagine someone like Marcia Clark, one of the prosecutors against O.J. Simpson saying:

> Your Honor, why are you insisting I present facts and witnesses to prove Mr. Simpson's guilt?
> Lance Ito: *Because this is a trial; this is where you present evidence to support your accusations of guilt.*
> That's frivolous Your Honor, I have authority to prosecute crimes; I have a bar card same as you.
> Ito: *Oh, that's right, you are a county attorney, sorry for that. Send the jury home.*

Sometimes it takes an extreme example to convince people their map of the world is not as accurate as they think. The principle is the same though: just as a prosecutor still has to produce facts, irrespective of their authority to prosecute crimes, a tax agent must still meet a minimum evidentiary burden, and a cop still has to present a valid cause of action for a court to acquire jurisdiction. Jurisdiction is not based on perceived authority, at least not as advertised.

I wouldn't be surprised to hear of a cop refusing to take the stand for cross-examination for a traffic ticket on grounds he has authority to write tickets. And traffic court judges would buy it, seeing nothing wrong with it. Some of the worst offenders with robes are the traffic court psychos; they just make it up as they go without a hint of shame.

My friend Stan appealed a traffic court judgment. He was not permitted to cross-examine the cop, and not permitted to put on a defense. On appeal, a superior court judge in Phoenix affirmed, writing that there is no right of cross-examination in a traffic proceeding. In other words, justice, fairness, and things such as due process don't apply in traffic proceedings. (No mention was made of the denial of a defense.) And before you think he can appeal it, how about no. Only place to appeal would be the supremes in D.C. and anyone familiar with the big boys in D.C. know they don't review such minor traffic issues.

These people will write anything when they're certain it will not be published or scrutinized in any way. If the judge was bold enough to write there was no right of cross, why did he stop there? Why was there no mention of the denial of a defense? Was his baseness not without its limits? Probably not, he probably just felt it was implied.

> Sir, I'd like to put on my defense now.
> *You have no right of defense in a traffic proceeding. Pay my clerk on your way out.*

There's a lot of truth right there. You have to expect this level of dishonesty though.

Do they hold an objective standard of proof? This is important to know, especially if you're in a hearing or in court for a trial. Any serious investigation will begin with this. I typically don't get an answer though, and it's no surprise why not: bureaucrats are governed by opinions, not facts. When there's a conflict between the two, they will always go with their opinions. It's always subjective with bureaucrats; everything is based on their opinion or argument.

If they ask what you mean by an objective standard of proof, then I usually ask if they've ever done any kind of investigation. I think we've already determined they're not qualified to make a proper determination.

You can also ask, "Don't you hold objective standards of fact finding to determine what is correct? How do you determine if something is right or wrong; do you look at the facts after an open investigation or just start with an opinion and only look at facts that tend to support it?" You really want to know if they look at the facts and then form an opinion, or do they have their opinion first and make the facts conform to the opinion.

Keep in mind, bureaucrats do not typically engage in open investigation into the facts. When I try to engage them, they will usually use the excuse/evasion: "Well, we're not in court, Marc." I have to then ask if they're interested in an accurate determination. They typically will admit they do not want to collect more than what may be owed, though they believe you owe something. The admission they want to collect only the proper amount leads to asking, if there is nothing owed, would they drop the attack?

Another evasion is to ask if I'm a lawyer. Because, in a search for the truth, nothing is more important than membership in a labor union.

So despite the rhetoric, my experience shows tax agents or anyone involved in taxes and traffic proceedings are not regularly involved in open investigations because in the regular course of business they do not accept opposition. Opposition is just not part of their map of the world-they're always right. The political opinion you're a taxpayer is put on a pedestal, worshipped and protected against blasphemy. After all, it's the key to their salaries and pensions.

So any opposition is always frivolous and, with complicit, rubber-stamping lawyers in robes, they don't have to hold objective standards of proof or care about such trivial things as evidence.

We know bureaucrats do it backwards: facts conforming to opinion. We just want to get an admission from them to use later. That is how we set up a double bind. When we ask these questions, the bureaucrat is not going to want to be upfront, but they really want to appear fair. With the psychopath it's about appearances.

They will not want to admit they start and end with an irrefutable opinion, especially when you're in the context of a due process hearing. It's one thing to come into a hearing holding an irrefutable opinion; it's another to broadcast it to everyone present. Remember, this is about the appearance of justice, putting on the false pretense of legitimacy.

But in their world they're always right, so the same double bind described earlier is created with the two conflicting generalizations:

1. Their legal opinions are irrefutable; *all* challenges are automatically frivolous.
2. They are administering justice and due process with their hearings and trials.

If their opinions are irrefutable and all challenges are frivolous, then that moots their administrative and court proceedings. It's obvious you can't have a fair hearing if the issues are decided in advance.

Until you engage them yourself, it's hard to believe it's so incredibly difficult to get these people to just admit the possibility their opinions against you could be wrong. The hearing officers themselves hold the same opinion before walking in the door. In most cases there's no facade covering up the sham.

I'm not even asking initially for a final determination, just to admit the possibility that the opinion is not accurate. They refuse because that opens the door to investigation, the point of the administrative process or hearing. How is it that the opinion of an unknown agent cannot possibly be wrong? Why are they so absolutely certain?

So I put them in a bind by asking: What's the point of the hearing if the opinion is irrefutable? This is usually sufficient to break the generalization that the opinions cannot be refuted. Then they will state it is my opportunity to present evidence the assessment is wrong. They will try to limit the hearing to only the amount of the reported income though; the opinions are strictly off limits.

Some of the agents cling so desperately to their generalization they will admit some truth. Really, it's happened a handful of times. I've had agents, such as IRS appeals officers, admit the "Collection Due Process Hearing" is not a hearing in any legal sense. I'd love to have their lawyers in the hearing when they make such admissions-the same lawyers who claim in court it is a hearing in the legal sense. What they freely admit is the hearing is in no way evidentiary. If not evidentiary, then what's the point?

An example is Eric Fineman of the IRS on 28 July 2011, when he stated that the opinion my client is a taxpayer with taxable income was irrefutable. He reversed himself when I asked how my client could get a fair hearing if the opinions were irrefutable.

I had already put Mr. Fineman in a double bind earlier when I asked the questions about a conflict of interest. When he got upset and accused me of attacking him, I pointed out that I was not accusing him of a conflict of interest; I just wanted him to explain how it was not a conflict of interest to represent the same agency bringing the claim against my client.

I was just pointing out the obvious. Politicians use words as if they change reality. They don't just *act* as if they believe their opinions are real, they seem to believe it too.

Mr. Fineman thinks, just like judges in court, when the word "independent" is placed in front of IRS appeals, that in and of itself magically makes them independent. That's reification in action. If the IRS is bringing the claim, and he is acting on behalf of the IRS and is part of the IRS, then there is a conflict of interest. The wordsmithing does not change the fact he is acting on behalf of the party making the accusations against my client.

This is because not all language represents reality and experience. Our language can be abstract. And as with the schizophrenic, politicians cannot always distinguish between fact and fiction; they have a difficult time comprehending when their language veers off the concrete and into the abstract.

How does one who's a part of the IRS act independently of the IRS while working as part of the IRS? It's no wonder I can't get an answer to this question. I may as well ask a schizophrenic how he knows the voices in his head are real. I like how Gregory Bateson described schizophrenia: it's like looking at a framed picture on the wall and not being able to see the frame; you can't tell where the art-the abstract-starts and finishes and where the real world starts. The abstract and concrete lines are blurred, some more than others. You'll notice this when talking with a bureaucrat.

This is exactly what's going on when a judge claims he's a fair, independent and impartial decision-maker when he represents the state and the state is the plaintiff in a traffic proceeding. I've witnessed this with judges, hearing officers, and IRS agents. I think they actually believe there's no conflict of interest because the voices in their head keep telling them they are independent, and the law gives them authority to conduct the hearings. It's not a question of authority though; it's one of a conflict of interest.

Now you'll understand why I don't have to quote statutes and codes about a conflict of interest. Most people know there can't be a fair hearing if there's a conflict of interest. I'm relying on the bureaucrats' map of the world. They believe they are the good guys, they and their systems are fair and provide justice.

They will tell me they are fair, impartial, and independent. I just need to look at the facts and I can bring out the contradiction with several simple questions.

That's why politicians go through so much trouble setting up these systems, to try to get around this glaring problem. The bureaucrat will usually agree there can't be a fair hearing if there is a conflict of interest. The few times they have not agreed have been in England mostly. But just as in North America, the voices in the bureaucrat's head just can't help them explain exactly how someone can get a fair trial when there is a conflict of interest.

Do you think an IRS agent would agree to have *you* make a decision regarding the dispute you have with them? And why not? The reason is critical to moving towards a resolution. Go ahead and suggest it: tell them you're independent when making the decision and have authority to do so. I've also suggested to tax agents we submit the matter to a hearing with a private mediator or arbitrator. Would you be surprised they've never wanted to do it?

They recoil in horror when we suggest a truly independent decision-maker. They're not interested in honest investigation into the facts, only confirming their irrefutable assumptions.

When we speak in the abstract, bureaucrats notice it, but not when they do. They couldn't function in their jobs too well if they did. We need to help them out. By making such a suggestion, we are separating abstract from concrete; we're demonstrating-so they can understand, the lack of substance to the word "independent" in that context. They can see things more like we do when they suggest they are independent even though they represent the party making the claim. We're making more overlap in our maps of the world and seeing things in the same way. They already know it's silly to have a party to a dispute make a decision; they just need to see it in the context of their job.

If they mock the suggestion that you be the decision-maker, then ask them *why*. They'll desperately hang on to their generalization they are independent because they are authorized, but that doesn't explain how they are independent when in the exact same situation you certainly couldn't be. Who the hell authorized you to do this to me? Really? The same state attacking me?

This is called turnabout, and it's very effective at making a point. That is part of the model when resolving conflicts with bureaucrats: when they do or say something ridiculous, adopt it as your own and throw it back at them. Since they're having trouble separating fact from fiction, give them an example to help them out.

Separate opinions from facts. It should be obvious why separating the authority of the agent from the correctness of the assessment/opinion is necessary and so effective at getting closer to a resolution. We're keeping the agent's model of the world fairly intact because we're not questioning his authority, although we've gotten him to admit the assessment can be vacated for a lack of evidence.

Just as important, we're focused on the assessment/opinion and its merits. This is where you need to be, asking questions about facts to support the assessment that we already know don't exist. "Beat your chest about authority all you want, but where are the facts, sir?" And despite popular opinion, authority does not equal jurisdiction. Both rest on the same fictional foundation.

What I like to do now at this point is to ask the agent if the income can be proven to be taxable with only the facts before them, no citations to the law. I've had agents admit that whether income is taxable or not is strictly an issue of fact, "Marc, it's a fact your client has taxable income, it is not a matter of opinion." This tends to freak out some people, they don't know how to challenge this, especially when the agent has a 1099 or other tax report regarding income.

I think it's a great place to have the agent though; you have tremendous leverage here. I don't argue with them, I don't take a contrary position. All I have to do is ask them if they can demonstrate exactly how those facts prove the income is taxable. Then I just sit back and wait for the stuttering and lame excuses about how it's not their job to go through all the requirements of the tax code. I point out two things:

1. I didn't ask you to demonstrate anything, only if you could.
2. I didn't ask anything about the tax code, only the facts proving the income is taxable.

It's now becoming clear to the agent that any determination that income is *taxable* involves applying the constitution and laws. You'd think that would be obvious. This is why it's so important to get them to admit there is a factual difference between income and taxable income. You have to establish there must be more facts beyond just the reported income to prove it's taxable. This is a pretty strong position to be in. We already know there's no factual connection between me and the constitution and laws, so the agent, even if they honestly want to, can't make a valid assessment.

When we have the agent admit there has to be more facts beyond the reported income, I can usually get them to admit there are no facts just by asking them: What facts, beyond the 1099, do you rely on?

But if I've set it up properly, they've already admitted the 1099 or other report is the sole basis of the assessment. I just have to remind them they've already admitted this, I just want them to affirm there are no facts to prove the income is actually taxable. And they have the authority to abate an assessment that is not supported by facts.

Have them admit-contradicting their earlier statement-that there are no factual differences between income and taxable income, it's just a matter of opinion. It's an opinion based entirely on the application of law that the agent is not qualified to do-and they'll admit they're not qualified. Here you have inconsistent testimony from someone admittedly not qualified to make such determinations of law. That's a strong position for them isn't it?

> Let me get this straight, there are factual differences between income and taxable income, but you don't want to talk about what they are?

267

That's not my job.

But do you know what those factual differences are? You are insisting I have taxable income.

I'm not going to give you all those details!

I didn't ask that, only yes or no, if you know what the differences are. Do you?

Well, whether the income is taxable is based on the code.

So income and taxable income are factually identical now?

Yes.

But you said whether I have taxable income is an issue of fact, now it's an issue of opinion?

Yes.

But you're not qualified to make such legal determinations of law?

Correct, that's what examination does.

So, let me see if I'm following you correctly: taxable income is an issue of fact, but income and taxable income are not factually identical. You refuse to discuss what those factual differences are, so whether I have taxable income is an issue of law you're not qualified to make?

Correct.

Are you drunk, stoned or just plain stupid?

It's easy to see how little regard bureaucrats have for those they attack. I've actually had the above conversations before; though I've been less offensive than the last line was. I've asked if they thought I was mentally handicapped though: Have I given you the impression I'm retarded? Really? Then stop acting as if I am and treat me like an adult. This tends to bring them back down to earth; puts them off their arrogant perch.

I had a lawyer from the Idaho attorney general's office named Bill von Tagen tell me he didn't think there was any reason to try to resolve anything without going to court. My position was there was no evidence the code applied so the matter should be dropped. He said I could look up the definition of taxpayer in the code and relay that to my client. I asked: "Who are you responding to?" Bill stated me, and he repeated back my question: Are there any witnesses with personal first-hand knowledge my client is a taxpayer?

I asked: "What does that have to do with the definition in the code?" He yelled back: "I'm trying to answer your damn question!" I pointed out he didn't need to talk to me like that, so he barked back: "I'll talk to you any way I want!"

Predictably, Billy never did provide any evidence the code applied though.

When the agents throw an employer or vendor under the bus to divert attention away from themselves, you want to have them clarify that the only witnesses the IRS has you're a taxpayer is the vendor who issued the 1099 under threat, duress and coercion. You back them into a corner with their own lies; have them clarify that the IRS only relies on the

268

vendor and has no other competent witnesses, including the agent who did the assessment. If they don't want to take responsibility, that's fine; it can always be used against them, especially since they have to insist their opinions are correct. When you insist you're correct about something, such a statement implies it's supported by facts and competent witnesses. It's a bad spot for a bureaucrat to be in.

If the agent insists the employer is the only witness, then the next logical question would be, "So you have evidence the employer has personal first-hand knowledge the constitution and code apply to me?" If they don't have personal knowledge, then it's all speculation. This may be hard to believe, but I have never been given any evidence an employer had personal knowledge the code applies to a client.

This is also where an affidavit from the vendor is really effective. If the IRS agent has gone on record that the vendor is the only witness that you're a taxpayer, you can show the agent the affidavit from the vendor stating that the information was given to the IRS under threat, duress, and coercion, and the vendor is not acting as a witness against you that you're a taxpayer. They are also not qualified to make such determinations of tax law. After all, they're only doing what the Man has coerced them to do under threat of jail.

They'll usually get very upset and state that the information was not given under threat, duress and coercion. This is a *factual* dispute and far more effective to use than a legal dispute. They'll also now claim the IRS agent who did the assessment is a witness that you're a taxpayer. But now they have to provide a name-something they hate doing-and tax court judges will not allow even that much discovery.

Without a name (and in some cases they don't know), how do you determine if that opinion/assessment is valid? What was the process used to determine someone is a taxpayer and income is taxable? And why is the rule requiring personal knowledge almost never applied to government witnesses?

The agent, who is now relying on the unknown agent's opinion, has no way of knowing if the agent had any personal knowledge of any facts proving my client is a taxpayer and the income is taxable. Sounds like a strong witness doesn't it? No wonder you can't get a name out of these people. Despite this complete lack of knowledge, the agents insist the opinion is correct. Based on what? Why are they so absolutely certain that they are unable to admit there is a possibility of error? If the opinion is so infallible, then why not name the agent who did the assessment?

Not only are they certain the unknown agent is correct, they are equally convinced that the client, **the one who actually has personal knowledge**, is so absolutely wrong that any opposition or investigation is automatically frivolous.

I've asked them how and why they are so convinced when they've had no contact with the unknown agent and have no personal knowledge of the process the agent used to reach his opinions. They cannot answer. Instead they try to persuade me by bringing up the financial reports and making their own assessments. You'll usually get that deer-in-the-headlights look when you ask that question.

I then ask if they are witnesses against my client with personal first-hand knowledge he/she is a taxpayer and the income is taxable. I also ask if they're experts in the interpretation and application of the constitution and laws. They answer no, so I can ask, "If you're not an expert, and you have no personal knowledge, then how do you know with such certainty that any challenge is frivolous? If they have no personal knowledge what makes you think they are witnesses?"

By relying on the testimony of an unknown witness, I don't think it even qualifies as hearsay. Hearsay is what was said at least in someone's presence. With the IRS, you don't get to know the name of the agent and they freely admit to not having any contact. The IRS agents state they cannot even contact the department. Again, it's speculation at our expense.

I finally got through to an agent in the substitute for return unit in Holtsville, Long Island [(631) 654-6279, (631) 447-4984)] . When I asked about the agent who did the return, they claimed it was by the computer. It's Skynet all over again, like with the California FTB. Everyone is put into the computer with the irrefutable presumption they're a taxpayer and there's no challenge.

There's a pattern with bureaucrats that's very easy to identify: Don't challenge their actions/determinations. There are exceptions, but not too many when in the area of taxes. With the FTB, it's SOP; they only permit challenge to the employer who provided the information to them under threat, duress and coercion. They will not permit any challenges to their arguments and actions.

Knowing bureaucrats are engaged in some serious reification-believing their opinions are real-we have to demonstrate, gently if we can, this is not true.

I spoke with Dasha with the FTB and asked if the opinion my client had taxable income was irrefutable; she answered it was. Nice admission. I then asked if the opinion the income was taxable can be proven without using or citing the law. Dasha insisted it could. Remember, this a person who thinks her opinions are real.

I asked her if she could demonstrate how she proves the income is taxable without using the law. She predictably hung up the phone. The question is very effective and I didn't ask her to demonstrate, only if she could. She thought about it and, while I speculate here, she knew she couldn't and did the easiest thing she could: she slammed the phone down. Problem solved, she'll never have contact with this schmuck from Long Island again.

What you want to do is ask if the opinion can be proven using just the facts without any citation to the law. My observation is that the agents are so arrogant-they answer yes without giving the question any real thought. Then again, if they were capable of any real thought, they wouldn't be bureaucrats. Knowing how they are, we can then use that to our advantage.

Separating the facts from the opinions is a necessary and effective way to prove that all the agents rely on are their opinions, usually the opinions of a computer or unknown IRS agent. Yes, there may be a report of income, given under threat, duress, and coercion, but who determined the income was taxable and why? Who determined you're a taxpayer and based on what facts? It hinges on being a taxpayer with taxable income, which requires being subject to the constitution and laws. If there is no factual connection to the constitution and laws, then it's not possible to be a taxpayer with taxable income.

You can even have them admit this in advance:

> Would an assessment be valid if based on nothing more than political opinions and information given under threat, duress and coercion?

They do admit that no, such an assessment would not be valid. Even the supremes agree information given under threat, duress, and coercion is inadmissible:

> "The Due Process Clauses of both the state and federal Constitutions preclude admitting an involuntary confession into evidence." *State v. McClain*, 285 Neb. 537, 2013 .

Apparently the shock of the truth prevents them from exercising their authority and throwing out what they admit is not a valid assessment.

> *Your client is absolutely a taxpayer with taxable income.*
> Based on what facts?
> *He received taxable income.*
> Based on what facts?
> *He's a taxpayer.*
> Based on what facts?
> *This report we threatened the employer to send us. Why else would they have sent it to us if he wasn't a taxpayer?*
> To avoid going to jail.
> *That's frivolous, and a $5,000 fine. Any more questions jackass?*

So you have the report of income, at best only evidence of a financial transaction. And then you have the opinion, from the tax agents that the client is a taxpayer and the income is taxable. I spoke to a Chuck with the FTB the day after speaking with Dasha. Chuck also insisted the opinions were irrefutable. I asked him if there was any chance the opinions were wrong; he stated, "they cannot be wrong." Yes, seasoned scientists allow for error and continued improvement, but tax agents are omnipotent, and absolutely never wrong. The higher the throne of arrogance, the harder the fall to reality.

I asked if he was an expert in the interpretation and application of California law. He said he wasn't and before I could question him again, he said it was their "assumption" the income was taxable. He tells me it's just an assumption and yet he still asks me why I think the FTB is wrong? How removed from reality do you have to be to think your "assumptions...cannot be wrong"?

FTB – experts in nothing and never wrong

How many people have lost their homes on these assumptions? Look at the economic destruction the governments in California have done with their assumptions.

With normal people-the admission that their position is nothing more than an "assumption" would be enough to slam the brakes on and stop things. Psychopaths don't think like that though; normal people would (should) be saying, "Whoa, wait a minute here, let's examine this. Let's make sure this is correct." The psychopath's enormous ego prevents him/her from seeing any fallibility with his/her assumptions. Our concrete evidence is always frivolous while assumptions from their unknown agents are irrefutable.

Psychopaths just plow ahead as long as they can maintain their perception of authority. It also helps when the majority of the people continue cooperating with them. It doesn't matter to the psychopath that the people around him/her are lying yes-men like the crowd with the naked emperor. What matters is getting what they want in that moment. So it's no wonder psychopaths have no regard for others around them; who respects a yes-man? All it does is reinforce their anti-social behavior; the yes-men are nothing more than a means to an end. Why not use them if they are going to put aside all concepts of right and wrong and go along to get along?

Tax agents cannot process the fact there is a huge gap in their procedure: they get a report of financial transactions by threats and coercion. And from that they'll assume one is a taxpayer and the reported income is taxable. They'll even ask, ostensibly innocently, "Why would the company send us a 1099 if you aren't a taxpayer and the income was not taxable?" When I answer, "To avoid going to jail, being fined, having their business shut down," most agents can't accept it. This is very much like the subject in the Bruner & Postman study:

> "I can't make the suit out, whatever it is. It didn't even look like a card that time. I don't know what color it is now or whether it's a spade or heart. I'm not even sure now what a spade looks like! My God!"

They either refuse or cannot process the facts; the facts conflict with their map of the world, their perceptions. They see a world where people send information to the tax agencies voluntarily and with a big smile on their faces; they make valid determinations someone is a taxpayer and then cheerfully send information to the IRS and other tax agencies. It's their happy place-how they avoid the horrors of their system.

Some seem to believe the tax agents do not make assessments, the people and the employers are by making the compulsory financial reports. I've been told there are no tax agents acting as witnesses against my clients. I had an "Ed" at the FTB tell me no one there could verify my client was a taxpayer with taxable income.

272

There are apologists for the IRS who, in an effort to denounce me, have claimed the tax agents who do assessments are not relevant to whether the assessment is correct; that whether the agent is qualified to make legal determinations I'm a taxpayer is irrelevant. That's a lot of stupidity to take in.

Tax agents have a difficult time processing observable facts; they conflict with their model of the world. I have not spoken with one tax agent who could accept the plain truth: people only send the information to the tax agencies out of fear; they are coerced. I had a Canadian tax agent also tell me that forcing people to file returns under threat of jail was not violence and coercion. At that point, the person is either being dishonest or is plain stupid. Either way we're discrediting the agent.

Bureaucrats like to say the employer is "required," as if that's somehow different than coerced/forced. It doesn't matter that people are regularly sent to jail, such as the late Richard Simkanin, but they have to ignore their own laws such as 26 USC § 7202:

> "§ 7202. Willful failure to collect or pay over tax
> Any person required under this title to collect, **account for**, and pay over any tax imposed by this title who willfully fails to collect or truthfully account for and pay over such tax shall, in addition to other penalties provided by law, **be guilty of a felony** and, upon conviction thereof, shall be **fined not more than $10,000, or imprisoned not more than 5 years, or both**, together with the costs of prosecution." (emphasis mine).

> § 7203. Willful failure to file return, supply information, or pay tax

> "Any person required under this title to pay any estimated tax or tax, or required by this title or by regulations made under authority thereof to make a return, keep any records, **or supply any information**, who willfully fails to pay such estimated tax or tax, make such return, **keep such records, or supply such information**, at the time or times required by law or regulations, shall, in addition to other penalties provided by law, be guilty of a misdemeanor and, upon conviction thereof, shall be fined not more than $25,000 ($100,000 in the case of a corporation), or imprisoned not more than 1 year, or both, together with the costs of prosecution. In the case of any person with respect to whom there is a failure to pay any estimated tax, this section shall not apply to such person with respect to such failure if there is no addition to tax under section 6654 or 6655 with respect to such failure. In the case of a willful violation of any provision of section 6050I, the first sentence of this section shall be applied by substituting "felony" for "misdemeanor" and "5 years" for "1 year"." (emphasis mine)

And from California, § 19701 of the *Revenue & Taxation code*:

Any person who does any of the following **is liable for a penalty** of not more than five thousand dollars ($5,000):

(a) With or without intent to evade any requirement of Part 10 (commencing with Section 17001), Part 11 (commencing with Section 23001), or this part or any lawful requirement of the Franchise Tax Board, repeatedly over a period of two years or more, **fails to file any return or to supply any information required**, or who, with or without that intent, makes, renders, signs, or verifies any false or fraudulent return or statement, or supplies any false or fraudulent information, resulting in an estimated delinquent tax liability of at least fifteen thousand dollars ($15,000)... That person is also **guilty of a misdemeanor and shall upon conviction be fined not to exceed five thousand dollars ($5,000) or be imprisoned not to exceed one year, or both**..."(emphasis mine).

Looks like threat, duress and coercion to me. As if anyone needs me to point out that governments are supported by theft-you pay or you go to jail. Yet, because such facts are harsh when you're the agent who lives by that theft, the agents will delete this part of the experience. They have to if they are to continue functioning as they do.

This is a great example of schizophrenic communication; it's no wonder tax agents always accuse me of arguing with them and trying to trap them. How does the agent process the conflicting information, exactly how do they convince themselves there's no coercion involved when it's a felony not to do as ordered?

This is deleted from the experience to conform to their map of the world and explains why they think they're being attacked when we question them. Paranoia is a part of schizophrenic behavior.

I've been told numerous times people don't go to jail or suffer any consequences for not making reports. Really? And I've also heard there's no such thing as the Mafia and the US government never conducted chemical and biological warfare experiments on entire North American populations. Check those facts again. Also, the constant threat is what makes the act coercive and wrong. Carrying out that threat is a separate wrongful act.

So this FTB Chuck had a really hard time using the 1099 as the basis of the opinions when the company had an officer sign a statement the 1099 was only issued to avoid going to jail, not because they thought my client was a taxpayer.

Chuck was upset and claimed I had refused to tell him why I thought the assessment was wrong. So I again told him by his own admission it was just an assumption and there were no witnesses with personal knowledge my client was a taxpayer. Even the company stated they were not witnesses or qualified to determine my client is a taxpayer and the income was taxable. Why would I have to prove an assumption is wrong? Isn't the fact it's an *assumption* enough to prove that? To the rational minded yes.

It's fairly easy to determine if there are any witnesses with personal knowledge my client is taxpayer; just ask. This is even easier if you get the statement from the issuer of the 1099 or other tax document because that narrows things down in advance. What will typically happen is they'll discover the omnipotent unknown tax agent. This is the guy who secretly determines everyone is a taxpayer, but no one knows the identity of this godlike agent, and he or she is never wrong: "Let's just say I know a guy, who knows a guy…who knows another guy."

Of course, if they continue insisting they have a competent, qualified witness, then you can print out a statement from your own unknown witness. When they start ranting about how that's ridiculous, then thank them for finally taking on a more objective standard of proof. This is where the gun in the room is exposed; you make it a contest of opinions. Why is the bureaucrat's opinion from an unknown agent irrefutable, but mine is not?

They have claimed that once the computer, not an agent, spits out the assessment, it is "presumptively correct" and it's up to us to show it is incorrect. But, even if we give them a pass on this, they will not consider anything other than the *amount* reported. They will resist any challenge to their actions/opinions. Any attempt to separate the argument from the evidence is resisted.

This is where they may get crafty and can subtly threaten you or the employer with false reporting, as if the employer hasn't been threatened enough already. The issue regarding whether you're a taxpayer and have taxable income may not be addressed.

> *This is from our computer. It says you are a taxpayer. It's irrefutable.*
> This is from my computer. It says I'm not a taxpayer. It's irrefutable.
> *Well, my father can kick your father's ass!*

Of course the game is rigged. Why would these parasites have it otherwise?

Speaking with an IRS lawyer regarding a summons for books and records, I told her the agent who issued the summons already stated there were no witnesses my client was a taxpayer. She agreed, stating there was a minimal burden for the summons. I accepted that and asked if the summons may be arbitrary and still be issued in good faith. She said no, that it wasn't arbitrary.

Using the fact she was a lawyer to my advantage, I asked, "Then you would agree if it's not arbitrary, by definition there has to be a qualified witness proving my client is taxpayer with taxable income." She quickly changed her position and stated the IRS agent was the witness. She even agreed the IRS agent was the sole witness my client was a taxpayer, not the ones who issued the 1099.

So if they file in court, this agent is going to have to claim, under penalty of perjury, she is a witness even though she claimed she was not one. Oops. *Strong* witness.

When you get them to make such admissions or see how ridiculous their positions are, this is where they will usually try to deflect attention away from themselves. Bureaucrats love to accuse us of arguing as a way of diverting attention. They'll also accuse us of "debating" and "going around in circles."

This is one of the reasons why just asking questions and not taking a position is so important if you want to be more effective in resolving problems with bureaucrats. You can point out you are not arguing, you're just asking questions. If there is any contradiction, it's from them contradicting themselves. If I do have an opposing view, it's that I don't see any witnesses with personal knowledge and evidence my client is a taxpayer with taxable income. I'll then state that if you disagree, please answer yes or no if there are witnesses with personal knowledge and evidence. If not, then we are not arguing, the bureaucrat is just contradicting and being non-responsive. I've even quoted the Monty Python routine when talking with tax agents:

> "An argument is a collected series of statements to establish a definite proposition…An argument is an intellectual process. Contradiction is just the automatic gainsaying of anything the other person says."

> "No it isn't."

> "Yes it is."
> http://www.youtube.com/watch?v=hnTmBjk-M0c

Talking with the IRS is like being at the Argument Clinic; they automatically contradict you, very much like a child does to a parent. I don't think there's any actual thought involved either; it's completely reflexive and anyone who has ever dealt with the average bureaucrat can confirm this. They not only immediately contradict you, but when you ask a question they then accuse you of arguing. There are times out of sheer frustration I've asked them what they mean by arguing. It's not always easy to stay focused when dealing with such people.

I'd actually prefer the guy at the Argument Clinic over dealing with tax agents; tax agents contradict themselves and still accuse me of arguing with them. Since I'm just asking questions, I can ask them: How can I be arguing when I'm only asking questions? I had a lawyer in Phoenix come unglued and accuse me of arguing, so I tried not to laugh when I asked with a hint of sarcasm, "I'm sorry, was I arguing? I thought I asked you for evidence." She actually backed off.

If I take a contrary position, it's always the same thing: there are no witnesses and no evidence to support the opinion/assessment. That's why I tell them if they disagree, then tell me yes or no:

276

1. Are there any witnesses with personal, first-hand knowledge my client is a taxpayer with taxable income?
2. Is there any admissible evidence my client is a taxpayer with taxable income?

Yes, my position may be incorrect; I always allow for that. Here, the contrary position is:

1. There are witnesses with personal, first-hand knowledge my client is a taxpayer with taxable income.
2. There is admissible evidence my client is a taxpayer with taxable income.

And that's why they don't usually answer these questions. They probably know they cannot provide any witnesses and evidence, so it's better not to lie about it. Better to just avoid it as much as possible.

We already know the IRS will say one of two things here; usually they refuse to discuss the issue. If they say yes, then I always ask them to disclose the name of the agent they rely on. Most of the time, the agents adamantly refuse any such disclosure. Even tax court judges, long held as a standard of excellence and integrity, refuse to permit any real discovery against the IRS, including the names of agents who do assessments.

In the tax court case with Kimberly Clark, the assigned psycho with the magic robe, Michael B. Thornton, ruled that asking for witnesses and the admissible evidence relied on "could not advance the case and could only lead to frivolous arguments." For such blatant dishonesty and disregard for the truth, Mike was elected the chief liar of the tax court.

It's no shock this Thornton guy was a tax attorney for the treasury department and congressional taxing committee (ways and means) before becoming a tax court judge. Thornton was also given a Meritorious Service Award in 1998 by the United States treasury department. I won't be surprised if he's given a few more awards for all his hard work rubber-stamping all those IRS assessments.

Talk about a conflict of interest. The guy works for the treasury and gets service awards, so what do you do? You put him in a position to make decisions for you in your favor. It's not like they take their rules seriously, such as the canons, Here is canon 3 from the federal judicial code: "(1) A judge shall disqualify himself or herself in a proceeding in which the judge's impartiality might reasonably be questioned..."

I think the fact he worked for the treasury and was given multiple awards is sufficient grounds to question his impartiality. Not to mention the IRS are the ones actually stealing the money used to cover his salary, pension and many other perks.

His expectations-his generalizations conditioned from decades representing the treasury-may be a psychological block preventing him from processing any conflicting information. This man does not look at the facts and does not process from a standpoint of right and wrong. It is always: IRS is right, those who disagree are wrong. Everything, facts and opinions, must then conform to this. That's why he decided the name of

277

the agent who did the assessment "could not advance the case..." This is science speaking, not any of my paranoid, bitter, conspiracy theory madness.

Try to find a logical reason why the agent who did the assessment "could not advance the case." What coherent reason could there be? Mike doesn't explain that, of course.

The only reason is that Mike's just as corrupt as any other gangster. Well, stupidity would also explain how a witness who did a presumptively correct assessment is somehow not relevant to determining if the assessment is valid. In the minds of these psychopaths, issues of fact, competency and credibility, have nothing to do with advancing a case. How can such idiocy be reconciled with reality? That's easy, as stated: Because they have already made up their minds it's absolutely, irrefutably correct-so correct that any examination into the assessment is frivolous.

> *This assessment is presumptively correct.*
> Based on what? There are no witnesses with personal knowledge and we don't know who did the assessment.
> *It's based on the law.*
> But not witnesses, not evidence.
> *Your point?*
> What's the point of a trial if witnesses and evidence are not relevant?
> *So we can say you had your day in court. We're not animals, you know.*
> Check your facts again.

Think all those years of serving the treasury and those wonderful awards had nothing to do with Thornton's refusing basic discovery, including the agent's name that did the assessment?

> Disclosure of admissible evidence "could only lead to frivolous arguments." Michael B. Thornton, legal scholar, tax court judge appointed by Bill Clinton, and apparently also a super-genius.

And who can argue with such logic? The name of the agent who did the assessment "could only lead to frivolous arguments." Apparently Michael is also clairvoyant and mystic. It must be the robe.

Seriously though, how could the name of the agent who did the assessment not be a legitimate issue for disclosure? And to think Lance Ito, who presided over the O.J. trial, caught hell for some of his rulings.

> *Your Honor, we'd like the prosecution to disclose the witnesses and forensic evidence proving O.J. is guilty of murdering these two people.*
> Denied. Such disclosure "could not advance the case and could only lead to frivolous arguments."

This Michael Thornton has to know the name of the agent is a legitimate subject of discovery; it's fundamental stuff. Based on years of personal experience, I'm thinking he knows how damaging to the presumption of correctness any investigation is and he just can't resist rubber-stamping everything as he eyes those service awards on his wall.

Thornton doesn't stop delivering the laughs there either, he keeps them coming. In an order of judgment, he not only ignores the fact there are no witnesses proving the victim is a taxpayer, but to justify his nonsense the agent who did the assessment is irrelevant, and claims the review is *de novo*. *De novo* is legalese for new, over again. In other words, it's a new assessment based only on what is presented in the tax court. But Thornton and the IRS still maintain the "presumption of correctness" for the original assessment.

If there is *de novo* review, then the assessment is supposed to be set aside, but Thornton adamantly refused on grounds the request was frivolous. A is A and not A at the same time. So while setting aside the old assessment is supposed to be a matter of procedure with *de novo* review, Thornton goes for the laughs and maintains a presumption of correctness anyway. All the while he is an accomplice to the IRS's refusal to disclose the agent's name who did the assessment.

Whatever your view of the world is, there is just no making sense or justifying in any way refusing to strike the original, presumptively correct assessment, during *de novo* review. Sorry, either one is doing hits of acid or they're really bad liars and spin doctors.

In the real world, there is no partial pregnancy, just as there is no presumptively correct assessment with *de novo* review. These facts are not changed based on how we feel about the IRS. We could give a pass that *de novo* review doesn't wipe out the original assessment, but that means the agent who did the assessment is relevant.

Even if we give Thornton another pass on the presumption, it still doesn't arise unless there are facts, and it doesn't excuse the refusal to disclose the agent who did the assessment. If the assessment is so absolutely correct, then it will withstand vigorous investigation and questioning.

And there you have the reason why (former) treasury lawyer Thornton protected "his precious" the way he did.

Sometimes they claim the employer is the witness. This is easily countered with statements from the employer though. But we can really use this to our advantage. Like most of the gibberish they spew, we can embrace it and exploit it to get closer to our objective.

The IRS has forced employers into the tax court to testify. We had someone from payroll testify in court about the forms sent to the IRS. It was pretty embarrassing for them to testify they only did the 1099 out of fear, not because they thought the victim was a taxpayer with taxable income.

He also testified to not being qualified to make such legal determinations. All the IRS has is information provided under threat, duress and coercion by men/woman unqualified to determine anyone is a taxpayer with taxable income. They also have no one at the IRS who can verify the victim is a taxpayer.

They ask: Why would the employer send the 1099 if Mr. Victim of IRS abuse is not a taxpayer? That is their actual standard of proof; asking why the 1099 was issued if the victim was not a taxpayer. The fact it's always done to avoid jail is, of course, irrelevant and frivolous.

None of this deterred Thornton though. And even when the IRS employee testified under oath he wasn't qualified to make such legal determinations, Thornton did not let the lack of qualified witnesses stand in his way of a cruel joke; he just brushed off the lack of a qualified witness as a "frivolous argument."

What it came down to is this:

- There was a presumption of correctness for an assessment by an unknown agent;
- The agent was irrelevant because it was *de novo* review;
- No qualified witnesses testified the victim was a taxpayer with taxable income;
- All information given under threat, duress and coercion was considered admissible;
- Michael B. Thornton drew his own opinion the victim was a taxpayer;
- Thornton refuses to be questioned regarding his opinions;
- Any disagreement with Thornton and the unknown agent is frivolous.

Because nothing says credibility like an unknown witness and no evidence. It's why the rules about witnesses having first-hand knowledge are some of the most ignored in the courts. Any time any kind of objective standard threatens to creep into a prosecution you can be sure psychopaths like Thornton are ever vigilant, making sure they don't get in to ruin the IRS's position. These judges then ensure that the perpetrator of anything fair is severely punished. Tax court psychopaths like Thornton routinely impose fines for challenging the IRS in the tens of thousands, and it doesn't matter if you can technically appeal it. You have to pay the fines first.

Who did the assessment? It's obvious why you want the tax agents to identify the witnesses relied on for the assessment, or the agent making the assessment. The accusation is their opinion-who else do you ask to verify it's true? It's an issue of reliability, competency and credibility. None of these exist with a tax assessment. You either take it on faith or they have guns to persuade you.

This isn't limited to taxes, it applies to any bureaucrat or agency attacking you. It all comes down to the same thing: A is accusing B of XYZ. Is the accusation based on facts? Who's making the accusation? Why do they think they have jurisdiction over me?

The common sense parts of rules of evidence are the ones where witnesses must have personal, first-hand knowledge of the facts. In the United States the qualifications for a witness are at rule 602 of the federal rules of evidence:

> "A witness may not testify to a matter unless evidence is introduced sufficient to support a finding that the witness has personal knowledge of the matter. Evidence to prove personal knowledge may, but need not, consist of the witness' own testimony."

California:

> "(a) Subject to Section 801, the testimony of a witness concerning a particular matter is inadmissible unless he has personal knowledge of the matter. Against the objection of a party, such personal knowledge must be shown before the witness may testify concerning the matter." Evidence Code § 702.

Even with hearsay exceptions-in England, hearsay is generally acceptable in civil proceedings-you typically know who the witness is. It's usually only explicitly military tribunals that permit hearsay from *unidentified* witnesses.

I wouldn't mind hearsay so much if I were able to at least challenge the witness. The foundation of a tax assessment is built on opinions with no evidentiary support. As long as I can question the agent who did the assessment, it's very easy to get them to admit they're not qualified or there are no facts. But when there is no identified witness, then what? I've asked tax agents:

So you don't know the agent who did the assessment?
No, I don't.
But you're absolutely certain his opinions are correct?
Yes.
So much so, that any disagreement is frivolous?
Yes.
How can you be so certain about an opinion made by someone you've had no contact with and you have no idea how and why they came up with the opinion? Would you accept such speculation from me?

You just turn it back on them, like that. You don't have to disagree with them, just use their standard of proof. Ask them,

"So the opinions of unidentified witnesses are irrefutable, that's your standard?"

Wow, *strong* position! Great, I have a friend who said there is no tax due. Remember the objective standard of proof question? This is putting

281

the agent into a double bind. They already know unidentified witnesses are not permitted; most of us understand this as children. The bureaucrat's other generalization is they are never wrong. Once the computer says you're a taxpayer and the income is taxable, that's the end of the discussion. The double bind consists of the two conflicting generalizations:

1. Opinions from unidentified witnesses are not permitted.
2. Opinion you're a taxpayer is irrefutable.

But if you throw their standard back at them, they will laugh and not accept it. All you have to do is ask them why. Now we're on the same page as the bureaucrat.

This same principle can be used in traffic court where you call someone randomly out of the audience to testify on your behalf (after the cop has been declared incompetent and the testimony is not stricken). The judge and prosecutors freak out and state unqualified witnesses may not testify. Yeah, no kidding Sherlock. So now you'll strike the testimony of a cop you declared unqualified?

With the double bind he should drop the nonsense about relying on unqualified and unidentified witnesses. If in court or at the agent's office or even on the phone, doing this would make anyone feel like a fool. And they damn well should if they're pretending to rely on an unidentified or unqualified witness. If you think the opinions of unidentified witnesses are reliable, even irrefutable, then you probably deserve to be made to look like a fool. It's the only natural outcome; so we exploit it.

A good reason for personal knowledge is to separate facts from mere speculation. And now we know why the rule for personal knowledge is one of the most ignored principles of evidence. Almost everything the bureaucrat has is speculation and lies.

Applicability of the law. For those unfamiliar with my work, you may think this is a no-brainer; the laws apply to everyone or "it goes without saying." You wouldn't think so, but this is one of the most effective challenges to a bureaucrat attack-it's the basis of jurisdiction. And it doesn't matter who makes the attack; it crosses all imaginary political boundaries. We've even had success reported in Israel.

I spoke with Ann Walker, a prosecutor in Toronto, and asked what facts she relied on to prove the bylaws of the City of Toronto applied to my client. She answered, "The bylaws your client violated." If you do this yourself, you'll get similar non-responsive circular logic:

The evidence the code is applicable is the code itself.

That's breathtakingly stupid, and if you're not careful a part of you will die every time a bureaucrat says it. But it's the basis of how and why politicians think their will applies to everyone in the world. I asked the Canadian tax agent Brian Parrot, to confirm his position: "So the code applies because the code says so?" Without a hint of shame, he said, "Yes." He accused me of "going in circles." Canadians seem to have a really keen sense of irony.

Unless we're talking about the United States government, then political psychopaths typically admit their laws do not apply outside their fictions, be it called a state, city, province, county or borough.

When you get a traffic ticket, doesn't the judge always, as a matter of unquestioned procedure, just assume the laws of the state he represents apply to you? Of course they do, that's obvious. Judges and prosecutors will say that you are in the state so the laws apply to you. It's the "**because I said so**" legal standard.

With the US government psychopaths, they claim their laws apply everywhere and to everyone all over the earth, whether a citizen, resident or not, and regardless if you have ever set foot in their particular part of North America. Facts to prove it, you ask? That's hilarious.

Seriously, what facts do the criminals calling themselves the US government rely on to prove their laws apply to anyone, especially to those outside North America who are not citizens and have no interaction/relationship at all to the cartel?

Because *they say so*; that's it. It's only because they have plenty of henchmen on the payroll that anyone takes them seriously. Remember, it's not very effective to talk about facts to people with machine guns.

Ask them what facts they rely on and you'll get the same responses I do: platitudes, rhetoric and personal attacks. Then they do what they can to deflect the attention away from themselves.

A common tactic of politicians and bureaucrats, especially those attacking you, is *gaslighting* (it's also referred to as the Jedi mind trick by the more sophisticated). Gaslighting refers to the tactic of deflecting attention away from the truth by making the victim think he's crazy and imagining things. It's a more intelligent variation of the kill the messenger routine.

Social pressure and the psychological need to conform to the crowd make this a particularly brutal way of deflecting attention away from the real criminals in the room. What do you think they are doing when I ask them for witnesses and they claim it's a frivolous argument rejected by all the courts? It's a pathetic attempt at using social pressure to marginalize me, to make me think I'm the only one who thinks that's reasonable.

If we just look at the facts, and only accept the evidence and not consensus, then such tactics will not affect us or deflect our attention. Who cares what the crowd may think; what do the facts tell us?

Studies show most people will tend to back off though. Remember the conformity experiments. Another common tactic used in the media is: "Do you know how outside the mainstream thinking that is?" It's the same process, different content. Not relevant. What facts do you rely on? Sometimes my patience is thin and I'll point out the tactic first: "That's a deflection technique; stick to the issue, not appeals to popularity." What facts... I have even had to tell them to stop the lawyer tricks and treat me like an adult-be professional and stop treating me like a child.

I asked that attorney acting as a deputy attorney general in Idaho, Bill von Tagen, about the facts, if any, supporting the opinion my client was subject to the laws of the state of Idaho. He snaps back: "I'm not going to debate the tax laws with you!" After all this time, it still rendered me speechless for a moment; I had to process how stupid a comment this was and contain myself when I answered him. I had to stay calm and remind him I asked about the facts-I'm not debating anything.

I spoke with someone with a very large insurance company. This woman did not keep her word to me; she had promised to put in writing the 1099 they issued was not a voluntary act, but was coerced. When I pointed out she had agreed by reading her own email back to her, she yelled, "Stop yelling at me!" Again, I have to take a breath, wait a moment and ask her, *"Are you on another call? I'm* not yelling. Who are you responding to?" (Kind of my own gaslighting there I guess.)

It's very common for prosecutors to do this when challenged in court. Ask them to produce evidence they have a client, a so-called state, and even if you've never seen this in court, you can probably guess the lawyer's response: mockery and utter disgust at the thought of having to prove something so seemingly easy. How dare I even think to ask him/her to prove something? "Sir, Sir! Do not start with me, just do not start with me," says the psychopath Phillip Mangone.

Bureaucrats have accused *me* of wasting everyone's time, as if I had any power or authority to have forced everyone to be there that day.

If it's so easy to prove there were states, then they would just put up the facts, not act like spoiled brats.

Circular reasoning. Politicians and bureaucrats usually engage in circular reasoning; it's SOP. Because you hear it so much, combined with the fear we have when tax agents intrude into our lives, it can sound convincing.

An example is when you talk about the facts proving the law is applicable. In a tax context, tax agents and apologists will respond with:

> "Yes, the law creates the obligation. How[?], Like this:
> TITLE 26, Subtitle A. CHAPTER 1, Subchapter A, PART 1,
> § 1. Tax imposed
> There is hereby imposed…a tax determined in accordance with the following"

This is a real response from YouTube comments to one of my videos. It's the same when someone says the Bible is true because the Bible says so. Apparently these people don't know the difference between an issue of fact and an issue of law.

Another great example is when discussing income and taxable income. A typical exchange can go like this (it's hard not to laugh):

> *Why is my money taxable?*
> Because a 1099 was issued.

284

Why was the 1099 issued?
Because you have taxable income.

When tax agents talk like this, it's tough to take seriously. Tax agents may actually be pretending to not notice how silly their reasoning is. It's hard to believe this passes as an intelligent exchange. The following is also very common and is the same process as the one above (you'd think they were going for the laughs):

You're a taxpayer because you received taxable income.
Why is the income taxable?
Because you're a taxpayer.
How did I become a taxpayer?
You received taxable income.

Tax agents believe this is an intelligent conversation; that they are like Newton discussing calculus. People usually laugh when I share these conversations. Sometimes it's a nervous laugh as they may be seeing for the first time how lame the justification for taxation really is.

I don't ask that anyone take my word on this though; as with most of what I present, you can call a tax agent and get the same responses. It's usually easy to get an agent engaged in circular reasoning because all they have are opinions and platitudes. Another good one is:

- You must have a driver's license because you're a resident of the State
- You are a resident of the State because you have a driver's license

The same people who will condescendingly snap at you, "You really believe governments should be abolished?" will repeat the nonsense above as if they're some kind of legal scholar. Even when you repeat it back to them with a hint of sarcasm, they act as if it's a sound position: Let me get this straight, I'm a taxpayer because I received taxable income, and the income is taxable because I'm a taxpayer? *You got it, are you paying by check or cash?*

They're so confident they're willing to take your home away from you and threaten prosecution. That's confidence, and you really need it when someone else's life is at stake.

This further highlights the violence inherent in the system. Their legal opinions are not the basis of their confidence, it's the willingness to use force against you. Having no empathy and responsibility for your actions really motivates these people.

I went through the 1099 routine recently. When I asked for the facts the constitution and code were applicable, the agent, Charlie, told me there was a 1099 with information about income. I repeated the questions and he said the code mandated the 1099 was a taxable event. Again, Charlie, what facts do you rely on the code is applicable at all? Charlie stuck to his guns that the code made the 1099 a taxable event. And the 1099 is a taxable event because...? And we're right back with the code.

So look at what is going on: the code is a written threat from politicians; provide the information or go to jail. Then the information is, by the same code, considered a taxable event. When you ask for the facts the code is applicable, all they can tell you is they have the 1099 they coerced the vender to give them. This is considered evidence.

What comes first? Let's inject some logic here. You would think the code is applicable first, and then the income is taxable. No, they put the cart before the horse: you have income and that's evidence in and of itself the code is applicable. They are arguing the code is applicable when you have income. Let that sink in.

It's the same thing as a judge claiming he has jurisdiction because you're standing in the courtroom. Of course, they deny that when you ask them: "If I never set foot in the courtroom then you'd never acquire jurisdiction, and any warrants or judgments against me would be void because I never set foot in your court?"

This is why it's so important not to focus on a specific section of the code or any particular statute or ordinance. Focus on the code itself, the *constitution and the code*, not just the tax sections. When I ask about applicability, they stutter and spit out circular nonsense, such as "the code is applicable because it's the code." I've been using the below image in written communications with bureaucrats:

Of course, we can always back them into a corner by asking, "So the code is only applicable by getting a 1099 or other tax document? The only way for the constitution and code to apply to me is if there is a 1099 issued against me?" They will deny that and we've knocked down another of their supporting pillars of jurisdiction. I keep asking them for the facts proving the constitution and code are applicable.

If you keep asking for the facts, the circular reasoning will probably lead back to the logical fallacy of the appeal to authority. When you point out that a prosecutor has failed to present facts proving jurisdiction, the prosecutor will appeal to their authority, their partner in crime, the trial judge.

What the trial judge does for the prosecutor is appeal to another former prosecutor. Edward Lodge, facilitating the prosecution against Mike in Idaho, did this in an order denying a motion to dismiss for lack of jurisdiction: "The court [me, Edward Lodge] has jurisdiction and the laws apply to the Defendant. *See United States v. Marks*, 530 F.3rd 799, 810."

Edward, instead of pointing out evidence the prosecutor was supposed to present (ironically the lawyers in *Marks* agree), appeals to his authority: more judges like himself (though a little *more* honorable).

When we examine the lawyers' opinion in the *Marks* appeal, note that the facts of *Marks* have nothing to do with the prosecution Edward is presiding over. The lawyers just cite more opinions from other judges; from *Marks*: "See United States v. Williams, 341 U.S. 58, 65-66" and "United States v. Studley, 783 F.2d 934, 937".

Now we see a new legal standard, the turtle standard, and its related the circular logic above: It's turtles all the way down (http://en.wikipedia.org/wiki/Turtles_all_the_way_down). Instead of turtles though, we have opinions of lawyers, so it's opinion, argument and speculation all the way down:

United States v. Fitzpatrick, CR-10-089-N-EJL

United States v. Marks, 530 F.3rd 799, 810

United States v. Studley, 783 F.2d 934

United States v. Warren, 610 F.2d 680

United States v. Williams, 341 U.S. 58, 65-66

When you get to the bottom of the lawyer opinions, all you get are more opinions about the code: "The District Court had jurisdiction of offenses against the laws of the United States. 18 U.S.C. § 3231." *Williams* at page 66. But that's just the opinion of a lawyer named Stanley Forman Reed in 1951. It's not evidence proving the code applies to someone today, over sixty years later. Nothing Stanley said in 1951 has anything to do with what Lori Hendrickson is trying to prove in an Idaho court in 2012.

So you start with the code and you end with the code. And the psychopaths are willing to kill you over the code, regardless of their circular reasoning, fallacious appeals to authority and turtles.

It's imperative that the ones who carry out the orders and inflict damage on us don't think about the applicability of the code. They have to ignore this gaping hole in the evidence, so it's never a part of the training and can't ever be. After all, some may be interested in truth and justice and they need to be neutralized or weeded out. You get enough lawyers and bureaucrats with OCD and the whole system would collapse because they could never establish jurisdiction over anyone.

> Let's see, step one, prove the constitution and code apply to
> victim A...Hmmm, I'm not seeing anything.
> *It's okay, there are tons of judges who say it's OK.*
> I need facts.
> *These lawyers said it's OK.*
> I need facts.
> *Do you also need a job?*
> Got it, the courts have ruled on this.

I spoke with a federal prosecutor in Idaho, Rafael M. Gonzalez Jr., who said he did not understand what I meant about proving the code was applicable beyond a reasonable doubt. He agreed you cannot prove elements of a crime by citing an opinion, but the concept of proving with evidence that the code is applicable to someone accused of a code violation seemed to be completely foreign to him. And it was. I didn't ask him how many people he has prosecuted, but he's admittedly never even tried to prove the code was applicable to the people he claimed violated the code.

It's interesting that when he admitted the obvious-citing an opinion is not proving an element of the crime-he then adamantly disagreed with me when I mentioned we were in agreement on that. He did not want to be on record as agreeing with me on anything. I got the impression he had found my website during the call. He started saying there are differences in opinion about facts, opinions-lots of legalese to make it seem as though he weren't in agreement. I said we were off to such a good start, but here you go and lawyer up on me.

I asked a Mr. Brennan with the IRS for facts the code was applicable. He said he didn't understand, that I was being too vague and not giving him any facts. I was a bit bewildered. I got this funny feeling in my head and told him, "I'm asking *you* for the facts, why would I answer for you?"

You're guilty of murder, Marc.
Really, what facts do you rely on to prove that?
Uh, um…I don't understand. You're being too vague, you're not giving me any facts.
[speechless]

Now, I'm sure not all are being genuine, that some are feigning ignorance. While I think Mr. Gonzalez was being genuine with me, there are those who know they are at the bottom of a deep hole and just use it to avoid the issue. Mr. Gonzalez declined to permit me to record him saying he did not understand what I meant about proving the code was applicable. (Maybe he thought it would not show him in his best light.)

This is a mind-boggling level of ignorance, and it's only one part of the picture. I've spoken to lawyers and bureaucrats who have been at the job for three decades and it never dawned on them to try to prove the code they are using to destroy people's lives is applicable in any way. I'm getting writer's block just thinking about it.

"I'm here for a paycheck; critical thought and questioning things? I ain't no Tesla there buddy." Said most bureaucrats.

It's no surprise the victims are not questioning this issue either. It's part of our conditioning; we're told it's the law and we have to obey. There's little or no critical thought; such questioning is discouraged. And when one does, just like the bucket of crabs, the others have to try to drag the inquisitive one back down.

288

Maybe that's why Gonzales insisted I was the one who was confusing facts and opinions, as if I was the one citing *United States v. Marks*, 530 F.3rd 799 as a substitute for facts.

Jurisdiction. Keeping in mind you're dealing with a narcissistic control freak, you shouldn't be surprised by the anger generated when you question their opinion/argument of jurisdiction. Jurisdiction should be the main focus of our challenge. Without jurisdiction, even if there is a valid case, the wrong bureaucrat is addressing you.

The thought that a bureaucrat may not have jurisdiction is fairly repugnant to them; you'd think you were calling their mother a whore. (Actually, I don't think they're as offended by a personal attack to their mother as a challenge to their precious jurisdiction.) So if you want a bureaucrat to end a conversation with you, just ask:

Can you confirm there is evidence proving jurisdiction over me? *Why, you insolent bastard! I'd like your head on a plate!*

There are two definitions I like that address, in a legal sense, what jurisdiction is:

"**jurisdiction**...The power to hear, determine, and adjudicate...the power or authority of administrative or executive agencies, even to the power of the state." *Ballentine's Law Dictionary*, page 690.

"Jurisdiction is essentially the authority conferred by Congress to decide a given type of case one way or the other. The Fair v. Kohler Die Co., 228 U. S. 22, 228 U. S. 25 (1913)." *Hagans v. Lavine*, 415 U.S. 528 (1974).

The purpose of any challenge is to uncover the evidence proving where, when, why and how this alleged "power or authority" was acquired over me. Is it the individual agent, each individual agent making up the agency, the agency as an abstraction (corporate person), or whatever the agent is claiming at the time?

If there are no facts, then the claim of jurisdiction is arbitrary. It's reasonable to know who or what has this alleged power or authority over us. It's the first step to proving there is any jurisdiction over us.

I stand on my previous assertion that when it's based entirely on violence-as it is-facts are unnecessary. Facts are not an issue when dealing with psychopaths who think they have a right to control your life, liberty and property. After all, we're just farm animals to them. It is not for the cows to challenge the farmer. This, together with more than a decade of personal experience and investigation, is another reason I'm so confident they have no evidence.

Lawyers like to say the court has jurisdiction over us, while tax agents claim the IRS or CRA does. This opens the door for questions to find out what they mean by court or CRA. I ask them directly what they mean by the word; what facts or idea are you intending to convey to me when you use the word *court*?

In California, tax agents with the Franchise Tax Board have told me directly the FTB is separate from the employees who comprise it; they are not the FTB, they only work for the FTB. That's some serious reification there. The best they can do when asked what they mean by the FTB is just go circular; it's the board or the agency:

> So a figment of your imagination has jurisdiction over me?
> *No, of course not.*
> Then can you put in concrete terms what you mean by the board?

The point of the questions is to bring out that there are no facts, just aggression. Bureaucrats don't like it when I point out their assessment or summons is arbitrary. They get defensive and snap back, "It's not arbitrary!" So by definition it's based on competent witnesses and evidence? Good, let's talk about the facts you rely on.

Daryl Wright of the New York state tax department on 7 March 2013 was pretty confident his assertion of jurisdiction was not arbitrary. He said it was based on facts. When I asked what the facts were, he was unable to tell me. His reification process got interrupted though, and he then said, "we believe" there is jurisdiction.

Yeah, I know that's your belief, but are there any facts? I asked if there were any witnesses with personal knowledge the code was applicable and there was jurisdiction. His answer was: "I'm not going to answer that." Checkmate. I just proved their belief was irrational and not based on any evidence and credible witnesses. It also proved bad faith.

I have only spoken with a few bureaucrats who admitted, off the record of course, it was based on their say-so and aggression. This includes one IRS lawyer who claimed that an agent named Chadwell, who admittedly didn't know how to do a hearing, did a proper hearing with no due process violations. It didn't matter there was *no hearing* though; it was still a proper due process hearing. No hearing took place (the agent didn't know how) and this lawyer lied about it as easily as giving the time.

I asked him if he read the transcript; he said yes. "Did you read where the agent admitted to not knowing how to do a hearing as she had never done one?" He agreed he did read that.

> Can you please explain how she was able to pull off such an amazing feat-not conduct a hearing while conducting a hearing and still not violating any due process requirements? And all without having ever conducted a hearing before?
> *As I said, she conducted a fair hearing that conformed to the due process requirements.*
> Yeah, you said that. How is that possible when she didn't conduct a hearing?
> *As I said, she conducted a fair hearing that conformed to the due process requirements.*

Is your jurisdiction based on your job? Do you still have this power over me when you punch out? Do I have to be within the state to be subject to federal law? Do I have to be a taxpayer? What is the limit, if any, of what you can make me do? These are all good questions regarding jurisdiction, and you'd be lucky to get an agent with any degree of good faith and honesty who would answer them.

Because if we just look at the facts, all we have are (usually) two people where one is claiming to have jurisdiction (power and/or authority) over the other. All the rest is PR. What facts does the one asserting jurisdiction rely on? So I ask, "Beyond your opinion, what facts do you rely on that prove where, when, why, and how this alleged jurisdiction was acquired? Please help me understand, because I'd really like to be able to avoid it from now on."

Remember, the model is to always start with the verifiable facts before us. When those are clear, then we can frame our questions to the psychopaths looking to put something over on us. The questions are geared towards making it obvious there are no facts other than violence and threats of violence. That's all jurisdiction amounts to when you stop the reification.

This is where we exploit the nature of the psychopaths and narcissists, their "inflated sense of their own importance". A few basic factual inquiries will rip the "mask of ultra-confidence" right off their smirking face.

Sir, do you believe you have jurisdiction over me?
Yes, I do.
Are you absolutely certain; is there any possibility you're not correct?
Yes, I'm certain. There's no possibility I'm wrong. I'm a lawyer; look at my fine robe and little Masonic hammer.
And you would not proceed against me if you believed you didn't have jurisdiction?
Of course not; I'm not an animal.
What do you mean by jurisdiction? Do mean control over me?
Well, I don't agree with your verbiage there.
But you do agree by jurisdiction you mean you have power to order me around, don't you?
Of course, I have authority to issue orders you must obey or I can have you incarcerated.
So I'm your slave? Exactly how did you acquire ownership of me?
You're not saying it right. I don't think you're my slave…
You treat me as your slave, you order me around and will put me in jail, right?
But you're making it sound… no, you're not my slave, but I have jurisdiction and can order you to comply…
If you can order me around and put me in jail, how am I not your slave?

So far, I haven't met any bureaucrats who have been willing to openly admit that I, or a client, are their personal slave.

It can be used to set up a nice double bind though. We can exploit the bureaucrat's grandiose view of himself as the ultimate good guy who's never wrong by asking them to explain what they mean when they claim jurisdiction over us. It can be that simple. After they've insisted they had jurisdiction over me, when asked what evidence they have to prove it, many will ask me: "What do you mean by jurisdiction, Marc?"

We know the facts prove that it's slavery. We need to ask them questions so they can start to see through their reification; show the disconnect between the facts and the opinions. A nice way to cut through the nonsense and expose the gun in the room is:

> Excepting aggression and threats of violence, please explain to me exactly what you mean by your claim you have jurisdiction over me?

In other words, "Beyond just your say-so, what facts, if any, do you rely on proving you have this alleged jurisdiction over me?" I see no benefit to allowing the gun in the room to remain hidden. That's only making it easier for the attacker to put his scam over on us. It also intimidates anyone watching-they may just timidly accept the attack. Keep their feet to the fire and the burden right where it belongs. I'm subject to your personal jurisdiction? I'm your slave? No? Then what facts has the prosecutor presented proving the code applies and you have jurisdiction over me? If it's not aggression, then what is it?

A bureaucrat is attacking you; they are uninvited and didn't ask for your permission or cooperation. They deserve no special courtesy and no free pass. If they think they're in control and are laboring under the delusion that I've consented and I'm not really their slave, then they need to present evidence, not just rehash their insulting political platitudes. Exactly how are you different than a common criminal?

I'd love to call a bureaucrat and ask, "How can we avoid your jurisdiction?" Aside from moving out of range of your guns, how does one escape your control? A good thing to remind the psychopaths is:

Don't confuse your willingness to kill me as jurisdiction.

Aren't they the same thing in the real world? I would ask them, "Is your jurisdiction just aggression? If not, then exactly what is it?" All these questions are designed to prove there is a master-slave relationship at work; the judge is acting as if we are his/her property. Because they don't want their slaves to revolt or just ignore them, they use reification, as mentioned earlier. Bureaucrats use jurisdiction, power and authority in a desperate attempt to cover up our slavery.

Any claims of jurisdiction are dependent on the laws of the state, province, or commonwealth being applicable and binding on you. Even on our modern plantations, the masters and their useful idiots with guns still rely on the PR that the law is applicable. That is what's covering up their violence so many would otherwise object to. In my experience, they will cling desperately to the nonsense that their law applies to us and gives them jurisdiction. So desperate to look good, they will say some of the stupidest things to justify their continued aggression. We can use all of them to discredit them.

Because the psychopath attacking you believes he has jurisdiction because of the PR that you are within his state and subject to his laws, it's very effective to challenge these fictions. It's not just effective, it's necessary if you're serious about being left alone and minimizing the damage these predators are trying to inflict on you.

As far as I can tell, the fetal position is not an effective strategy.

If the basis of the attack against you is the code and you don't challenge them on the facts proving the code is applicable, then you're effectively dropping on the floor and curling up into a ball.

If you're being attacked by the tax people, then ask if they would have jurisdiction if their laws weren't applicable; they'll eventually admit they wouldn't. This tends to freak them out. They get very upset at the idea that their law may not apply to someone. They'll probably accuse you of arguing the law with them.

They'll just have to get over the fact you've presented no argument that they don't have jurisdiction. (The very thought that their sacred laws may not apply to you is almost more than a bureaucrat can handle.) Again, as with everything else presented here, if you doubt this is *predictive* and *replicable*, then do it yourself and get your own independent evidence. When you do, please call the show about it.

After the psychopath calms down and stops insisting that the laws apply to you, they'll probably agree there is no jurisdiction if there is no evidence the laws apply to you. It's a hypothetical; get over it. I'm just trying to understand so I can defend myself here.

I only want to understand the basis for the bureaucrat's attack. We need a base to start from; we need some agreement and understanding how they work if we're going to be able to resolve a conflict with them. By asking them in this manner, it's not necessary to know what their codes and procedures are before calling them.

I've never read the provincial legislation in Ontario and don't plan on ever doing so. Life is too short and precious. But I was still able to confront Brian Parrot with the Orangeville, Ontario treasury and have him demonstrate his complete inability to provide any proof those laws apply to my client. This is despite the fact the client and the property they want to tax are located in Orangeville.

I set the stage, asked the question and let the bureaucrat make a fool of himself. I asked, "What evidence do you rely on proving the provincial laws apply just because I'm physically in Canada?"

The excruciating minutia of the ramblings of the insane (provincial legislation, acts of parliament and congress etc.) are not necessary to know because they are irrelevant without evidence they apply at all. Don't let them skip step one and jump to what the code says! Application comes first, if there's evidence the code applies, then and only then is it logical to discuss what a particular section says.

Anyone claiming to be defending you who doesn't challenge the foundation of the attack against you is not really defending you. And if they criticize attacking the foundation of the attack, then they are actually advocating for those attacking you.

A friend in Australia sent me a court opinion from the U.S. that backs up what I've said about jurisdiction, that it really is just a willingness to kill someone. Yes, it conflicts with many other court opinions, but it's nice to see even a little bit of honesty from these liars. This gem was written by Holmes:

> "While, ordinarily, **jurisdiction over a person is based on the power of the sovereign to seize and imprison him**, it is one of the decencies of civilization that, when the power exists and has been asserted at the beginning of a cause, the necessity of maintaining the **physical power** is dispensed with. Jurisdiction is power..." *Michigan Trust Co. v. Ferry*, 228 U.S. 346 (1913) (emphasis mine).

In other words: once your victim has been coerced and terrorized into submission, then you maintain your domination through threats of violence as civilized people are known to do. Holmes, you keep using that word, *civilized*; I do not think it means what you think it means.

But even if a bureaucrat is bold enough to make such a statement as Holmes above, they still claim their jurisdiction comes from the constitution. The "power" to throw us into prison is allegedly from where? Four pieces of paper from 1787, the constitution. Any claim of jurisdiction is still defeated by asking for the evidence the constitution applies. One day I will have one of those professional parasites publicly admit, in plain terms, their jurisdiction is based on a gun, like Mao said.

Logical check. Given the gross dishonesty of bureaucrats-pathological lying being one of the defining flaws with psychopaths-we have to ensure we're on the same page. We want to minimize their predictable lies that we are misquoting them or taking them out of context so it's more difficult to keep up their facades. We do this to give them as little wiggle room as possible; I'm not going to let them BS their way out of this exchange.

When we're engaging them, whether in person or on the phone, I always keep track of the admissions I need to use against them. So I write them down and make a point of telling them. I tell them to please bear with me; I want to write this down so I don't misquote you:

> Marc: "You're saying that it applies because the provincial legislation says it does; because she is the owner, it applies?"
> Canadian tax agent Raheel: "*That's correct, yes.*"

It doesn't matter if this agent from Ontario later lies and claims he didn't say the above; the burden still stays on him to provide the facts that the provincial legislation applies to my client. By keeping track like this it is much easier to impress on the bureaucrat that I know what I'm doing. The more they contradict themselves and are unable to provide the facts they said they have, the more leverage we can use to have them drop the attack. They know I'm keeping track of their lies.

Speaking with a Marie Maple of the IRS on 11 April 2013, I told her I was not arguing, that I had not taken a position, I was just asking if there was evidence proving jurisdiction. She said, "I don't need any evidence." I said, "I have to write that down." So I slowly write it out, saying each word: "I...don't...need...any...evidence." just to let the idiocy of the statement sink in. She hung up fast.

I show that I'm much more difficult to deal with because I ask for facts and stay on point. It's easier to go after someone who'll pay an attorney and curl into a ball crying, "Please just do whatever we need to do to avoid jail." They use threats of jail as leverage. I use their lack of evidence, their compulsive lying, and their circular logic against them.

So as we walk the agent through the model, we keep track of their answers. Most will admit that a lack of evidence is grounds to drop the attack. But when it comes to actually doing it, they tend to act as if we're asking them to slit their own throat. (Because to a sadist, it probably is like a part of them is dying if they have to drop an attack against a peaceful victim.)

Bureaucrats tend to be so arrogant, have such an inflated view of themselves, that they see everyone else as not just inferior, but impossibly stupid. As mentioned, this inflated view of themselves is a direct cause of people accepting the government concept. If people see such marginal, borderline personalities as an authority, then the natural result is for the psychopath to look upon them with utter disdain. If you've dealt with bureaucrats you know the disdain of which I write.

They always seem so surprised when I read back their words, they just can't believe there was a logical reason for the questions I asked. What surprises me is that so many people are still so timid about defending themselves when bureaucrats attack them. Even those familiar with my work, who've heard the recordings and know the psychopaths have no evidence, can still be intimidated.

Keeping this record is also very helpful with written follow-ups, such as with the IRS. I can quote the agent's own statements to whoever is reviewing or has the authority to stop the attack. The agent's statements carry much more weight than mine.

These written timelines of fact can also be used for complaints of misconduct.

When in a court or administrative proceeding, it's adversarial. The plaintiff is supposed to be the victim in a controversy. But with government, it's backwards: the plaintiff is the aggressor and you're the victim. With bureaucrats, you're a defendant because of the actions of the bureaucrats.

With real crimes, when the government charges you, it's because your actions caused a certain harmful result. With *mala prohibita* laws, there's only a problem because of the actions of the politicians. That is, your action is wrong only because you did or did not do something a politician demanded of you (your action is not harmful in and of itself).

If we look at a tax evasion prosecution, the minimum needed to be proven beyond a reasonable doubt with facts and credible witnesses are the following:

1. The code is applicable to me (this includes jurisdiction).
2. The code created an obligation to pay taxes.
3. I believed I had a legitimate obligation to pay taxes.
4. I willfully refused to pay taxes.

Each one leads to the next–they depend on each other. If you doubt what the elements are, then you can just ask them some questions; they'll usually tell you. I've asked many prosecutors if applicability of the code is an element of the crime, and they've agreed. Just ask them. We can usually use what they say against them.

At this point in the book, you should be able to see how impossible it really is to get a valid conviction, as there are no facts for any of the four elements. Even apologists for the IRS and other tax agencies will agree these are elements of a code violation such as tax evasion.

With Mike in Idaho's retrial, the lawyer acting as judge, the psychopath Larry Burns, threatened Mike repeatedly. Larry didn't want Mike to question what facts proved the code was applicable. The applicability of the code is so serious a problem to the prosecution it apparently scares the crap out of them in court. Why else would a judge threaten Mike with punishment for challenging an element of the crimes? Why would a man put another man into a cage for asking a question?

I think the circumstantial evidence is very strong here: the fair, impartial, independent decision-maker is threatening punishment for challenging an element of a crime that's supposed to be proven beyond a reasonable doubt by the prosecution. If the judge refuses to let you challenge an element of the crime, that's not fair. It's strong evidence the judge is biased and has already determined your guilt; he's not presuming innocence. That's evidence the game is rigged against you.

On cross you can and should be challenging the witness on competency and credibility–no sacred cows. This includes challenging them on their opinion that law applies. A good way to do that is to include a line of questions starting with, "**Did any of your testimony relate to any of the elements of the alleged code violation?**"

This opens the door to further challenge the testimony. We should use a whiteboard, especially if the charges are serious and there's a jury. We only need to reach one to hang the jury and get a mistrial. Have the cop or other witness walk you through the elements and what he/she testified to during direct examination.

We can, with the elements on the whiteboard, walk the judge and prosecutor through, e.g., what facts does the prosecutor have to prove the code is applicable? What facts has the prosecutor presented proving the code created an obligation?

Could this be considered dumbing things down? Sure, but we have to because it makes it more difficult for them to ignore everything. This makes it much more difficult to make their coercion and lies look legitimate; and that is the point, that's our goal.

For a cop in a traffic trial, the above question is particularly effective since the cop is the one writing the ticket and accusing us of violating the law. He/she may also be the one prosecuting us, so there's no legitimate objection to such questions. Imagine a lawyer objecting to such a question. What grounds could they have that does not work in our favor to have the cop impeached as a witness?

If you do get affirmative answers, now the door is open for the cop to explain, if he can, what facts he has testified to already, proving the code is applicable. Do not underestimate how powerful this can be; this is going to be based on his/her testimony during direct examination. Our point is to bring out that the witness has not testified, and cannot testify, about facts that the code is applicable. We're just using his testimony on cross against him to prove he has not testified to an element of the crime.

It's much better to get the cop to say he has no facts instead of us saying it. We don't really count; the judge and jury couldn't care less what we have to say.

> Let's use this whiteboard to get your position clear, Mr. Supercop. Just so even the simpleminded like me can understand: you charged me with violating a section of the code? And you're certain the Arizona code applies to me? And you have proven here today the code does apply to me? And you agree you cannot prove the code was violated unless you've proven the code applies to me?

This usually elicits an objection though, and the prosecutor will argue against his own witness. It's something you may need to see in person to believe.

Utilizing bureaucrats' rigid behavior. Keep in mind that the more rigid people are in their behaviors, the easier it can be to influence and predict their behavior. Most people get intimidated when they are around bureaucrats and see how domineering and arrogant they are. But any rigid behavior, if you're familiar with the context, can be influenced to reach your goal. That's why the double bind can be so effective.

Rigid behavior is very predictable. If you know bureaucrats will always contradict you, then you know how to get what you need. If you can anticipate a response, then you can formulate a double bind. This is why you don't need to bring your own opinion to the table if you can help it.

We also know the politician's contradictions are always reflexive. There's no thought involved so they don't know until it's too late and they've been backed into the corner they put themselves in. Judges are usually too arrogant to admit that a non-lawyer played them while on their wooden throne. It's not necessary to me that they admit it, I just want to be left alone.

An example is when I purposely ask a cop questions requiring a legal opinion. The prosecutors impeach him as incompetent to give legal opinions. Then I ask the judge to strike the cop's legal opinions, including the one on the ticket. The judge now knows he was played and is sometimes blind with rage trying to figure out how I did it.

With the IRS, I already know there are no facts proving I'm a taxpayer with taxable income. Knowing the agent will contradict me, I can ask: Do you agree there are no facts proving I'm a taxpayer? He reflexively disagrees, not realizing he's taking an affirmative position there are facts. This is not a winnable position for the tax agent. Relying on their hubris-after all, they are Americans-I can ask if there is a factual difference between a taxpayer and non-taxpayer. They will always say yes, there are. Great! Then I ask:

> Do you know what they are?
> *I'm not going to go through every little detail regarding that!*
> I didn't ask you to; I just asked if you knew what the factual differences were-do you?

Then they seem to start thinking about it and realize they dug themselves a pretty deep hole, courtesy of my leading questions and their excessive arrogance. Another example is:

> Do you have jurisdiction over me?
> *Of course; I'm with the IRS.*
> Can you confirm there's evidence proving you have jurisdiction over me?
> *Look, your client received income and didn't file a return. We're not going anywhere with this.*

This is where most discussions get derailed. The bureaucrat desperately wants to stop talking about observable facts and wants to be back in the secure world of fictions. The fictions are safer; those wonderful people with black robes they steal money for are always willing to rubber-stamp their abuses. Lawyers love fictions-fictions are easier to endlessly twist into any way to make them appear to be right.

I ask about the factual differences and they will not answer, usually saying it's a waste of time. So, bring them back to their previous answers: are you convinced there are sufficient facts to prove the income is taxable? They want and are compelled to say yes because it makes them look good; but it's just another lie. They know they just committed to there being facts, and are anticipating more questions they cannot answer truthfully without contradicting themselves. This is a pretty bad position to be in.

I'm pressing the obvious: there are no facts. What they rely on are opinions/abstractions-opinions that they will admit they are not qualified to make. It's the same as asking if there are factual differences between income and taxable income. I have not spoken with an agent who wants to admit they are factually identical. The worst part of this is being put into a position regarding the process the bureaucrat used to come to the conclusion the law applies to my client or me.

The agent didn't go through any real process where facts were collected, examined and the law then applied. All they do is assume the law applies. That's a fairly common generalization, it's accepted without question. It's a habit, just like my dropping into a half squat when snatching. It's just accepted like religious concepts, a sacred cow you don't dare investigate. Those who discourage investigation probably know it's because they have accepted the concept blindly and can't show any proof.

When I establish the income cannot be proven to be taxable without the application of the constitution and laws, then the focus shifts to what facts the agent relied on to establish a connection between the client and the constitution and law.

Are there witnesses with personal knowledge? Asking for witnesses and evidence, as shown, is effective for several reasons. Another is so you can get tax agents to drop this one-size-fits-all defense-the old "just call it frivolous" dodge.

I spoke with Roseanne Novetti, an IRS employee in Holtsville, New York. She was one of the only ones who claimed I made a frivolous argument and actually tried to identify it.

She claimed that my pointing out there were no witnesses my client is a taxpayer was a frivolous argument. I had to ask, "Do you know what the courts mean when they use the word frivolous?" She paused and said, "When someone doesn't file a return, that's frivolous." I was almost speechless. I stated that was silly and told her to give me a straight answer. She said, "I'd have to look that up." I told her I'd help her out, and read her:

> **"frivolous.** So clearly and palpably bad and insufficient as to require no argument or illustration to show the character as indicative of bad faith upon a bare inspection...Strong v Sproul, 53 NY 497, 499." *Ballentine's Law Dictionary*, page 503.

I told Roseanne the mere fact she would have to identify the witnesses in question was proof that the argument was not frivolous. It may lack merit, but it certainly isn't frivolous: "not all unsuccessful claims are frivolous." *Neitzke v. Williams*, 490 U.S. 319 (1989).

Claiming it's frivolous is a stupid attempt to avoid any discussion of the facts. It's a quick fix to avoid any evidentiary process whatsoever. At no time in the process is there opportunity to investigate the factual basis. While some have lied to me, most agents admit the truth when asked:

There is no evidentiary procedure to determine whether or not one is a taxpayer with taxable income.

Well, why the hell not?! This cuts through all the PR regarding their administrative hearings, doesn't it? The point of the hearing is to put the agent's actions under scrutiny, to see if there are facts to support their opinions. But, especially with taxes, challenge to the agent's actions is not allowed.

If you engage them you'll experience the same hostility to investigation into the facts supporting their sacred cows, i.e., taxpayer, resident, citizen etc.

False choices in court. In traffic court, especially with parking tickets, they only give you two options: pay the fine or request a hearing. If you file a demurrer or motion to dismiss, they generally don't rule on the demurrer. You can call and ask if the hearing is regarding the demurrer, and they'll tell you: "No, we took the demurrer to be a request for hearing." They're changing reality with mere words.

> *Listen here, jerky, why didn't you pay your ticket?*
> Oh that... I took the ticket to be a thank you note.
> *A thank you note? Thanks for what?*
> How about thanks for not striking you down as the criminal you are and ostracizing your family?

They deny reality as if that changes it. Even if *they* don't believe it, they expect everyone else to act as if they do. My observation convinces me the lower on the political pecking order they are, the more they actually believe the nonsense they spew.

You'll see this in traffic court when you hand them a written, unsigned plea of no contest or guilty. It's tangible evidence but it will not make a bit of difference to them. You put the document right on the bench or in his hands and then ask some questions. When you get to the one about whom the judge represents, he flips out, starts screaming, enters a plea of not guilty and throws you out.

I've asked why he's pleading for me (as if he were my attorney), especially when the rules don't permit it. The rules only allow a judge to plea not guilty when a defendant refuses or a plea cannot be ascertained. For some reason they feel compelled to feign compliance with that rule and they will lie, saying that I refused to plea.

> "If a defendant refuses to enter a plea or if a defendant organization fails to appear, the court must enter a plea of not guilty." *Federal Rules of Criminal Procedure*, 11(a)(4).

> "If a defendant refuses to plead or stands mute, or if the court refuses to accept a plea of guilty, a plea of not guilty shall be entered." 3:9-2. Pleas, *New Jersey Rules of Criminal Procedure*'

"If the defendant refuses to answer the accusatory pleading, by demurrer or plea, a plea of not guilty must be entered." *California penal code* § 1024.

Yes, staying at least somewhat consistent with reality isn't a priority, but faked compliance with a procedural rule is. I need to ask one of these judges if they really think people believe their nonsense about refusing to plea. No one paying attention could take a word of it seriously. Then again, as I've mentioned to several traffic court judges-people are not in court because they think the judge is some kind of sage; they are there to avoid going to jail.

Why does an adult man/woman insist, usually in a fit of rage, that I'm refusing to plea when there's a proposed plea of guilty in their hands? It's evidence of the judge's dishonesty and misconduct. It's grounds to reverse and possibly get the ticket dismissed.

This is more evidence the opinions come first and are considered irrefutable. The evidence comes after and future events must conform to the opinion. It's all backwards with bureaucrats.

Now you know why I go in with an unsigned written plea; it makes it really difficult for the judge to maintain I'm refusing to plea. Them there facts is tough to ignore; the people in the peanut gallery are seeing the judge's credibility crumbling here. Even after I point to the written evidence proving I'm not refusing to plea, they continue ranting I'm refusing to plea.

This almost complete denial of observable facts is how bureaucrats and politicians behave and interact with others. They all tend to work with the same fictions and generalizations, so they can communicate fairly well. But when you file a demurrer in a traffic proceeding, despite a demurrer/motion to dismiss being a basic, preliminary type of pleading, the clerks and judges act in the only way they can: they deny it is a demurrer; instead it's a request for a hearing on the merits of the ticket.

If you question a judge on it, they will make up lame excuses (they are not the best at making things up off the cuff). This is why you'll hear a judge's and prosecutor's defense to a motion to dismiss based on no case and jurisdiction consisting of nothing more than some empty words such as:

"That doesn't apply here in this court."

That's a direct quote. They actually say it with a straight face; well, usually contorted with anger.

You can predictably cause them to fly into a psychotic rage by following up with, "Can you cite the legal authority exempting this particular court from these provisions of law?" Notice this question is yes or no; I'm not even looking for the citation yet.

When they can't, it doesn't matter, use it your advantage; apparently "That doesn't apply" is a legitimate defense in their little court. You can now feel confident using their defense as your defense. After all, they've already proven that in their court, legal defenses need no support.

So, if they ask you how you plea to the ticket, you can confidently state:

> I'm going to rely on the same legal principle you and the prosecutor rely on, those laws don't apply to me.
> *Based on what?*
> Do you prefer that I calmly tell you "nothing," or scream it at you like a madman?
> *Scream it like a madman, of course.*

It's always more effective to demonstrate an absurdity than to just point it out verbally by an objection. It's an easy way to prove the judge knows he's wrong, just call him on his BS. It's as easy as I've just shown above. You still make your objection though to preserve the issue for appeal if you have to.

This is an effective method to prove they're making things up as they go and have a double standard. Another issue is when a judge has declared a cop incompetent and then refuses to strike the cop's testimony. If you're permitted a defense, you stand up, turn around, and pick someone randomly out of the peanut gallery to testify on your behalf. Then calmly stand your ground during the storm.

You can expect both prosecutors (former and current) to come unglued and start yelling. Pay attention to what they will be yelling though. In their anger, some truth will come out: **the witness is not qualified or competent to testify**. Really, you think so? And why is that?

Is this deliberately setting up the judge to look like a fool? Of course it is. But if the judge only did the right thing and struck the cop's testimony, then he would not have laid the groundwork for me to make a fool of him. This is only possible because the judge is so used to playing everyone else for a fool. Who else would declare a witness incompetent and then still accept the testimony? It's as if he's begging to have someone finally call him on his nonsense.

We're only taking advantage of the fact the judge is putting up a facade of legitimacy. If he/she gets up on their wooden throne with even the slightest interest in doing the right thing, then I could not make a fool of him. But until that time, we should not back away from any opportunity to expose them for the criminals they are.

And we can do this with the IRS and other taxing agents as well. Use their standards against them. It may dawn on them that all they have are opinions and threats of force. After all, if they refuse to accept opinions from my unnamed witnesses, it becomes clear that the only real difference between the IRS and me is the gun the IRS uses to get compliance.

Why is your unknown witness credible at all? Why are you so certain? How do you know this is accurate-because it came out of a computer? So it's kind of like everything being true on the internet? How and why does someone gain credibility with you? What has to happen before someone loses credibility? These are all valid, relevant questions to ask anyone making decisions affecting my life and doing it based on the opinion of someone else.

Of course, there is the old standby: "How do you know that's true?" It's hard to go wrong with that one.

The unsigned plea of guilty is also a tool to really put the prosecutor on the spot. You go into the arraignment, and when the judge asks how you plea, you hand him a copy of the unsigned plea of guilty and say, "I intend on pleading guilty. What evidence has the prosecutor provided that proves the constitution and code apply to me and there's jurisdiction over me?"

This is basically telling the prosecutor to put up or shut up. Put your cards on the table or fold and leave me alone. If he has evidence proving the constitution applies to me, and the judge is supposed to be presuming innocence, then I don't see how this can proceed without his evidence.

This only takes advantage of what we know about the system being used against us, e.g., presumption of innocence, being informed so we can defend ourselves, and the prosecution has the burden of proof.

They tend to lie and say that such evidence is for trial. It's a lie because if the judge thinks he has jurisdiction to force a plea, then the only one he could have gotten evidence from is the prosecutor. So just disclose what you're required to have already disclosed. Also, jurisdiction may be raised at any time, even on appeal.

My intention to plead guilty moots the point of having a trial. I want to make this easy for everyone. Just provide the evidence you gave the judge to convince this psychopath he has jurisdiction over me, and I can sign my guilty plea.

If you want to expose the prosecutor and prove misconduct in open court, then this is a pretty good way to go. They have no business filing a complaint or indictment that can cause us to be put in jail, unless they have evidence. And if they refuse and the judge permits it, then use that evidence against the prosecutor, not just with a complaint to the bar. Object and let them know the issue will not be dropped.

> Objection, you're permitting this man to proceed without evidence of jurisdiction, and you're not presuming innocence. If you force me into a trial I will not drop it. I will raise it at pretrial; it'll be part of my *voir dire*, my opening statement; I will object throughout direct examination, all through my cross, my close and it'll be part of my jury instructions. And if you threaten me not to raise the issue, then I'll tell the jury you threatened me.

Yes, the judge will probably threaten contempt for telling a jury that I wanted to plead guilty. All the prosecutor had to do was provide the evidence relied on proving the code applies to me, but he couldn't and the judge refuses to presume me innocent. But the jury needs to hear it and see the judge threaten me for it. I would let the jury know that every step of the way I tried to plead guilty and he was unable to provide evidence of jurisdiction.

Agent qualifications. This is important in and out of court, and bureaucrats can't stand being challenged this way. Tax agents in particular hate this. I spoke with one agent who insisted my client was a taxpayer. I asked if he was an expert in the interpretation and application of the constitution and federal law. He would not answer responsively; he stated the law was being properly applied and if I disagreed to take it to tax court.

I said that's not an answer to the question, but since you're convinced the law is being properly applied, are you an expert in the interpretation and application of the constitution and federal law? He still refused. I made it even easier: Are you qualified to interpret and apply the constitution and federal law? Again, he adamantly refused to discuss his qualifications to accuse my client of being a taxpayer with taxable income.

There is no separating the constitution and federal law with being a taxpayer with taxable income. It's the be-all, end-all of jurisdiction and any legal arguments. All of their PR relies on the constitution and the law. If one is going to put forth opinions I'm a taxpayer with taxable income, then unless they admit the constitution and law are irrelevant to being a taxpayer with taxable income, there has to be facts connecting me to both. The minimum needed to be qualified to apply the constitution and law to anyone is to know what the constitution and law are factually.

But I almost never get that far; they always refuse to discuss their qualifications. I tell agents their refusal to discuss qualifications can only lead us to believe they are not qualified to make such determinations. You'd think that would bother someone though, especially those who snap at me about being an agent for thirty years. I'd say it also smacks of bad faith.

When you rely on violent domination, you don't have to worry about being qualified and having evidence.

On cross-examination with a cop in traffic court, the current and former prosecutors will try desperately to convince you that cross-examination is limited to only what happened at the traffic stop. Like most assertions from these criminals, it's a lie. And you should tell them it's a lie and you will be filing complaints for misconduct against them. It's no wonder they don't want video cameras in traffic courts.

First, the judge and prosecutor want to ignore the fact the ticket was written at the stop, so it is fair game and open to challenge.

Second, it's well established that any witness is subject to challenges to competency and credibility on cross-examination. It's called impeaching the witness; it's part of every evidence code I've read. These are just a few examples:

> "Any party, including the party that called the witness, may attack the witness's credibility." Rule 607, *Federal Rules of Evidence*.

> "22(1) A witness may be cross-examined with regard to previous statements made by the witness in writing, or reduced to writing, and relative to the matter in question,

without the writing being shown to the witness." Alberta, Canada RSA 2000, evidence code.

If someone is going to act like a witness by accusing you of something, then they'd better be prepared to show they have personal knowledge: "Are you speculating or do you have personal knowledge of this?"

Such questions raise issues that cannot be answered though; there is no evidence the constitutions and law apply, so there can't be personal knowledge of it. But the agents need to look as though they have evidence, so they lie about having facts and personal knowledge.

With prosecutors it's not just misconduct, it's a malicious prosecution. To knowingly bring a complaint and prosecute when there is no evidence of jurisdiction is malicious.

I spoke to Scott Young, a prosecutor in Napa, California. The first time he insisted that evidence the code was applicable was in the complaint and police report. I told him I'd seen both and was certain such evidence was not described, and asked if he sure that was the position he wanted take. He saw where I was going with it, and tried to get away from the question by stating some other prosecutor had filed the complaint.

Here's a clue: it doesn't matter who filed the complaint, the lawyer prosecuting still has the burden of proof. After that other lawyer didn't call back, I spoke with Scott again on 27 March 2013. He was adamant about not being specific about the facts relied on to prove an element of the code violations and jurisdiction. He stuck to his guns and said he would present these mysterious facts in court. This is code for: in court the judge will protect me, we prosecutors stick together.

So I mentioned to him that it's not only a part of discovery, but to knowingly prosecute without such evidence is misconduct. Scott couldn't care less; he didn't back off at all. He doesn't need evidence or good faith.

It's all about the qualifications. An IRS agent told me: "I don't know anything" when I asked for evidence of jurisdiction. Normal people would have stopped the proceedings; this was an IRS agent though.

She dug her heels in and refused to release the withholding order we were calling about. When I asked if she could confirm there was evidence of jurisdiction, she said, "I have no idea." I was at least able to convince her we needed to speak to someone who knew what they were doing.

I asked the supervisor, Ms. Hutcherson, about the evidence and she went in circles, stating she was not going to argue with me and hung up the phone.

Regardless of the accusation, if the bureaucrat is not qualified and has no personal knowledge of any facts, then it's pointless to go any further investigating or questioning them. We're deconstructing the accusations against us, so it's perfectly logical to question them regarding their qualifications.

Presumptions. The presumption of correctness has to be examined; what better way to demonstrate an institutional bias in favor of the government than this? Here is the law, or rather the argument/opinion:

> "The Commissioner is required to produce "some evidentiary foundation linking the taxpayer to the alleged income-producing activity" before the deficiency determination will be accorded its usual presumption of correctness. Id.; Blohm v. Commissioner, 994 F.2d 1542, 1549 (11th Cir.1993). This evidentiary showing required by the Commissioner is minimal in nature. Weimerskirch, 596 F.2d at 361; United States v. Stonehill, 702 F.2d 1288, 1293 (9th Cir.1983), cert. denied, 465 U.S. 1079 (1984).
>
> "Once this minimal evidentiary showing has been made, the Commissioner's deficiency determination is then accorded its usual presumption of correctness. Subsequently, the burden shifts to the taxpayer to prove that the deficiency determination is arbitrary or erroneous. Adamson v. Commissioner, 745 F.2d 541, 547 (9th Cir.1984); Stonehill, 702 F.2d at 1294; Anastasato v. Commissioner, 794 F.2d 884, 887 (3rd Cir.1986)." *Sattar Nadjmechi, v. Commissioner of Internal Revenue,* 77 F.3d 489. http://law.justia.com/cases/federal/appellate-courts/F3/77/489/638512/

Why should the opinions of an unknown employee be presumed correct? The facts I've gathered prove the agents in Collections and IRS attorneys have no contact with the employees doing the assessments. IRS lawyers have told me even when they file lawsuits they have not had any contact with the assessing agents. There's no investigation despite it being a part of their rules. They rely on a presumption of correctness, a presumption the opinions of unknown agents are correct. Did you get that? A presumption the opinions are correct. Is it me? Do I just not understand what speculation is?

The agents in Collections will tell you they are not qualified to do assessments. After all, they don't do that, the agents in Audit or the mysterious "Substitute for Return" and "Reconsideration" units do that.

Call the IRS and ask for the contact information and names of the agents who did the assessments or substitute for returns, and they will tell you they cannot get that information. There are no direct contact numbers. There is an alleged SFR unit in Fresno, California, but there is no contact information. They'll tell you, as "K.O. Justice" told me, they have to put in an order for the files, but only if the matter is in court. We all know that they still don't disclose the names when it is in court.

The worst I've encountered is the Canada Revenue Agency. I have never been able to get contact information about the agents. They will do nothing but misdirect you, and if they give you any contact information, it will likely be incorrect and get you nowhere. The bureaucrats in Colorado give them a run for their money though; it took me months to get a human on the phone (and she was like a robot).

If I get anything, it's statements the agents are not qualified to do assessments, which is great, but I can't do anything with it because no one knows what department has authority to vacate/abate assessments. They tell me I have to contact the Legal Department, but no one knows how to contact this elusive group of Canadian legal experts.

The agents are unknown and there's no contacting them to question them. Their opinions are presumed correct. *Why*? What kind of standard of proof is that? I'm expected to prove the agent wrong, and they expect facts from me. Nice double standard! It wouldn't be so bad if they didn't mindlessly label everything "frivolous."

Even when we get the agents in court, such as with Bruce Gilbert in Wyoming, the judges either refuse to let them be questioned, or if they are, they are declared incompetent to make legal determinations. If every agent is either unknown or incompetent, then why do these judges continue rubber-stamping their assessments as presumptively correct?

The assessment (including proposed assessments, substitute for returns, and notice of deficiency) is nothing more than the opinions of an unnamed agent and information given under threat, duress and coercion. If I'm in error on this, no one has been willing or able to step forward and correct it.

While there are those who claim the agent who did the presumptively correct assessment is not relevant to whether the assessment is correct, there are those of us who think it's pretty important. You may be surprised to see this includes lawyers:

> "Yet, under our adversary system of justice, cross-examination has always been considered a most effective way to ascertain truth." Watkins v. Sowders, 449 U.S. 341, 349 http://supreme.justia.com/us/449/341/case.html "As Professor Wigmore put it, "[cross-examination] is beyond any doubt the greatest legal engine ever invented for the discovery of truth." 5 J. Wigmore, Evidence § 1367 (Chadbourn rev.1974)."

It's really no surprise then, if confrontation is the "most effective way to ascertain the truth," why those with an interest in the taxing system would not want the agents doing assessments to be questioned. Why use the "greatest legal engine ever invented for the discovery of the truth" when you're stealing people's property? They know there's no actual evidence, so they resist investigation. Just as George Bush did regarding 9/11. Bush knew there was no evidence to support the official conspiracy theory.

When you're a criminal you don't want the truth to come out; it tends to put a damper on your mojo, making it really hard to continue convincing people they should keep paying you. It's pretty obvious that cross-examination is intended only for criminals who work for the gangs called governments. It's great when it suits them, not us. Do you think the courts would give you a presumption of correctness? Even when they are required to, the lawyers in black have consistently refused.

The rules governing demurrers and motions to dismiss mandate that when a defendant files a motion to dismiss, the judge must accept all well-pleaded facts favorably to the plaintiff for the purpose of the motion or demurrer:

> "a court must accept as true all facts which are well pleaded in the complaint, and it must view such facts in the light most favorable to the plaintiff. 'It is axiomatic that a motion to dismiss an action for failure to state a claim upon which relief can be granted admits the facts alleged in the complaint, but challenges plaintiff's rights to relief based upon those facts. Thus, in deciding such a motion, the court views the allegations of the complaint in the light most favorable to the plaintiff, accepting as true all facts well pleaded.' Ward v. Hudnell, 5 Cir., 1966, 366 F.2d 247, 249." *Madison, v. Gerstein,* 410 F.2d 99.

> "the allegations of the complaint must be regarded as true." Carruth v. Fritch, 36 Cal.2d 426, 224 P.2d 702, and 4) "A demurrer admits all of the facts well pleaded however improbable." *Hitson v. Dwyer,* 61 Cal.App.2d 803, 143 P.2d 952; also *Mock v. Santa Monica Hospital,* 187 Cal. App. 2d 57.

This rule is adamantly resisted when the defendant is the government though, especially if you file a complaint against the IRS or other tax agency. You can present your facts:

1. I called IRS agent Eric Fineman on 4 July 2008 and asked him if there were witnesses with personal first-hand knowledge I'm a taxpayer with taxable income.
2. IRS agent Eric Fineman told me there were no witnesses and evidence to prove I'm a taxpayer.
3. I asked agent Fineman if he knew the agent who did the assessment against me and he said he did not.
4. I asked IRS agent Eric Fineman if he was qualified to determine if I was a taxpayer with taxable income and he said he was not.

Every single judge-federal or state-I've had experience with has refused to "view the allegations in the light most favorable to the plaintiff." There's only one way to take these facts: there are no witnesses and evidence proving I'm a taxpayer. It's obvious that without witnesses and evidence the tax thieves cannot prevail under any circumstances. That means the complaint is clearly an exception to the anti-injunctive tax acts:

> "We recognized that "[t]he ban on prepayment judicial review found in the state Constitution must yield, of course, to the

requirements of the federal Constitution." (P. 213.) Since the federal courts permitted prepayment relief in "those situations in which it is clear that '"under no circumstances" can the government prevail'" (p. 214; see Enochs v. Williams Packing Co. (1962) 370 U.S. 1, 7 [8 L.Ed.2d 292, 296-297, 82 S.Ct. 1125]), we adopted that same standard for state prepayment suits asserting federal constitutional issues." *Calfarm Ins. Co. v. Deukmejian*, 48 Cal.3d 805, 258 Cal.Rptr. 161; 771 P.2d 1247 (1989).

They have even refused to take mandatory judicial notice of this. I've not heard any good faith reason why these judges all refuse to take the facts favorable to the plaintiff or to take notice there's an exception to the anti-injunctive tax act.

You'll notice this opinion about presumptions assumes there has been a valid determination one is a taxpayer first:

> ""some evidentiary foundation linking the taxpayer to the alleged income-producing activity" before the deficiency determination will be accorded its usual presumption of correctness." *Sattar.*

I'm not familiar with any citation where the determination that one is a taxpayer must be based on a minimum of evidence as the court above points out. In fact, one judge in the tax court in Buffalo, New York, when confronted with this lack of a proper determination by a qualified witness and evidence, responded with: "We're all taxpayers." That's some serious clarity of thought there. Not. That's some pre-judgment there. What are the facts in evidence proving I'm a taxpayer?

This legal opinion that one is a taxpayer, which apparently no one is qualified to make, is just thrown around as if it's as self-evident as your gender. And I'm not saying there has to be a case citation or lawyer opinion about such a determination; I'm just pointing out the lack of relevance there seems to be about this opinion.

It's just common sense that one must be a taxpayer before they can have taxable income. The minimum facts would have to include a factual connection to the constitution and laws. Alleging there is no need to factually connect someone to the constitution and law means the constitution and laws are not relevant to whether you're a taxpayer with taxable income. So if the laws don't make you a taxpayer with taxable income, what's the basis of the opinion? What do they think makes you a taxpayer if not the constitution and laws?

In the real world there has to be a connection, as even the tax agents still claim their authority and jurisdiction to tax us is the constitution and laws. In their world though, only their opinion is required to make you a taxpayer.

This is why I've asked if taxpayer and non-taxpayers were factually identical, or if taxpayer is synonymous with man, woman and child. To show how silly this all that is, ask the agent to prove you're a taxpayer using just facts. It'll become apparent really fast you're a taxpayer on nothing more than the say-so of the agent.

Politicians only give lip service to supporting facts. I'll use an IRS complaint to enforce an administrative summons as an example. All you get are legal opinions you're a taxpayer; no facts connecting you to the constitution and laws and no allegations of any wrongdoing. Even the lawyers called the Supreme Court agree opinions alone are not sufficient:

> "a complaint must contain a "short and plain statement of the claim showing that the pleader is entitled to relief." "[D]etailed factual allegations" are not required, Twombly, 550 U. S., at 555, but the Rule does call for **sufficient factual matter**, accepted as true, to "state a claim to relief that is plausible on its face," id., at 570. A claim has facial plausibility when the pleaded factual content allows the court to draw the reasonable inference that the defendant is liable for the misconduct alleged. Id., at 556. Two working principles underlie Twombly. First, the tenet that a court must accept a complaint's allegations as true **is inapplicable to threadbare recitals of a cause of action's elements, supported by mere conclusory statements**. Id., at 555. Second, determining whether a complaint states a plausible claim is context-specific, requiring the reviewing court to draw on its experience and common sense. Id., at 556. A court considering a motion to dismiss may begin by identifying allegations that, **because they are mere conclusions, are not entitled to the assumption of truth. While legal conclusions can provide the complaint's framework, they must be supported by factual allegations**. When there are well-pleaded factual allegations, a court should assume their veracity and then determine whether they plausibly give rise to an entitlement to relief." *Ashcroft, et al. v. Iqbal et al.*, 556 U.S. 662, 129 S.Ct. 1937 (2008) (emphasis added).

If you look at an IRS complaint, there are never any facts to suggest you're a taxpayer; it's just an opinion with no factual support, that even the supreme lawyers above agree must be presented. A good example is from Rick Watson, a lawyer with the Department of Justice in Washington, DC. Rick wrote:

> "On the dates and in the amounts set forth below, a duly authorized delegate of the Secretary of the Treasury made timely assessments for unpaid federal income taxes, interest, penalties and other statutory additions accruing thereto, against [name omitted] for the following tax types and periods..."

The "duly authorized delegate" who did the assessments is unknown. Even if we had a name, this statement contains no facts proving my client's a taxpayer with taxable income. Even though the complaint fails to meet the standard for a federal complaint, who do you think the court will side with? I think we all know the courts are not afraid of my client.

Maybe in Rick's world a "timely assessment" is synonymous with "accurate assessment"? The supposed legal standard is the opinion "must be supported by factual allegations", and the IRS and their apologists just don't believe in facts or that the rules apply to them. And they're right. They can count on their buddies in the black robes to rubber-stamp anything they put forth.

I've spoken with a former IRS lawyer named John McClain. He quit after discovering some tax court judges ruled in favor of the IRS 100% of the time. He investigated the records because he thought it was odd that inexperienced attorneys like him were always kicking the snot out of lawyers with decades of experience. He told me that overall, the tax court judges ruled in favor of the IRS 98% of the time. And this was in the mid-1950's. It's only gotten worse since then. Now you not only lose, they also punish you up to twenty-five thousand dollars.

I have not found one IRS agent who was qualified to do assessments; they tell me this themselves. Yet, any challenge is frivolous and their assessments are almost always upheld. And not just upheld, but with cruel sanctions against the victim who decided to challenge. You can be sanctioned tens of thousands of dollars for filing a petition deemed frivolous by former IRS lawyers.

In all these years, I've only had one agent claim he was an expert in the interpretation and application of the constitution and federal law, and he hung up on me when I asked him about his qualifications. They must think hanging up the phone is a way of meeting a burden of proof. Maybe that's why they don't want their agents identified and appearing in court. You can't refuse to speak when on the witness stand and still have your testimony stand. Well, according to the rules anyway.

When you're dealing with judges and other bureaucrats/politicians, keep in mind this man/woman sought out a position of dominance and irresponsibility. Not a stable adult if you ask me. There's plenty of evidence to support a finding that the judge forcing you to defend against the prosecutor's or cop's complaint is a psychopath or garden-variety narcissist. As already shown, evidence proves this beyond a reasonable doubt: 67-91 percent exhibit psychopathic behavior. While this usually doesn't make going to court any more of a picnic, this type of personality can be dealt with easier when we understand what makes them tick. Below is a medical description of a narcissist:

> "Narcissistic personality disorder is a mental disorder in which people have an inflated sense of their own importance and a deep need for admiration. Those with narcissistic personality disorder believe that they're superior to others

and have little regard for other people's feelings. But behind this mask of ultra-confidence lies a fragile self-esteem, vulnerable to the slightest criticism."
http://www.mayoclinic.com/health/narcissistic-personality-disorder/DS00652/DSECTION=sympto

Here is a list of the traits of a typical narcissist:

1. "Has a grandiose sense of self-importance (e.g., exaggerates achievements and talents, expects to be recognized as superior without commensurate achievements)
2. Is preoccupied with fantasies of unlimited success, power, brilliance, beauty, or ideal love
3. Believes that he or she is "special" and unique and can only be understood by, or should associate with, other special or high-status people (or institutions)
4. Requires excessive admiration
5. Has a sense of entitlement, i.e., unreasonable expectations of especially favorable treatment or automatic compliance with his or her expectations
6. Is interpersonally exploitative, i.e., takes advantage of others to achieve his or her own ends
7. Lacks empathy: is unwilling to recognize or identify with the feelings and needs of others
8. Is often envious of others or believes others are envious of him or her
9. Shows arrogant, haughty behaviors or attitudes"
http://en.wikipedia.org/wiki/Narcissistic_personality_disorder

You'll easily recognize these are the basic traits and requirements to be a politician and bureaucrat. Why else would a judge become enraged when you refer to him/her by their first name? Add pathological lying and a lack of empathy and you have a psychopath.

And they are the clues to dealing with them on and off the bench e.g., "behind this mask of ultra-confidence lies a fragile self-esteem, vulnerable to the slightest criticism". I had federal judge Franks in St. Paul, Minnesota, permit me to speak on a friend's behalf because I took advantage of his narcissism. I stated that as a judge, he had the authority to disregard a rule of court in the interest of justice, and that my lack of membership in a mere labor union should not be used as an excuse to not permit me to assist a friend.

It took a few minutes, but as I predicted, he just couldn't stand my referring to his precious bar association as a "mere labor union" and he started engaging me about it. Well, as my wife can attest, if you extend me an invitation to talk I run with it, and that's exactly what I did. I spoke on my friend's behalf for the next twenty to thirty minutes, including demanding that IRS counsel point out each element of a cause of action in his complaint. Of course, Danny refused because he knew there was no cause of action set forth in the complaint.

My crack about the bar being a labor union was taken as a personal offence against his belief the bar is some kind of "special or high status... institution". And here I am, a non-member, standing there not exalting him with Your Honor, calling an IRS lawyer Danny, and using their special language, i.e., cause of action, standing, etc.

Another trait of this personality disorder is being prone to fits of rage:

> "People with this personality type may be extremely sensitive to failure, defeat or criticism and, when confronted by a failure to fulfill their high opinion of themselves, can easily become enraged..." *Merck Manual of Medical Information*, page 427.

This is where having media reps at hearings is so valuable. Judges have an insatiable need to be perceived as honorable people; they crave and demand our admiration. If I refer to him by his first name in a full courtroom and he knows there are members of the media present, he/she is probably not going to start screaming and frothing at the mouth the way they typically do. Experience proves these lawyers are not nearly as violent and threatening when there's media present, even if only for my radio show.

That is some heavy-duty leverage we can use against these flawed personalities. It's why they sometimes shake with fury when you ask them whom they represent in the proceedings. This is a serious double bind the lawyer is in. He desperately needs the adulation of the audience, but his fragile ego and facade of legitimacy are being attacked by some jerk from Long Island who doesn't have the common decency to address him/her as Your Honor.

I've seen first-hand the rage of lawyers when I call them on their groundless decisions. I can turn around and use their silly "it doesn't apply" line on them and their precious ticket; when they catch up to what I'm doing, their anger breaks into screaming fits for security and threats of contempt when they realize I've played them. They don't like it when their double standards are exposed.

Imagine if they demand you refer to them as Your Honor and you come back with:

> "Okay, then *you*...shall refer to me as Your Highness."

Yes, good Knight of the Rueful Figure, I have my own delusions of grandeur and shall not be outdone by one as low on the political pecking order as yourself, ye scoundrel.

It should go without saying that we have to be very careful with how we provoke the black-robed, psychopathic former prosecutors. But imagine the outrage of the public if congress wanted to pass laws making it a jailable crime to address a politician by his/her first name or to wear a hat. Such unwritten laws are already in the United States under the broad banner of contempt.

313

Yes, for those not aware, having a hat on is a criminal offence. My friend Pete Eyre went to jail for not taking off his hat. New Hampshire, long the "Live Free or Die" state, is now the "Take off the damn hat or go to jail" state.

When dealing with tax agents though, it's not quite as volatile a situation. I'm usually on the phone and there usually aren't armed goons around like in courts.

I had a court clerk tell me that she was offended by what I was saying about the courts. I said, "Really? What offends me is the fact you are helping the judge steal millions of dollars from a peaceful community and you don't even know what a cause of action is; maybe if you did, then you could direct your anger towards the judge and stop being his accomplice". Nice priorities there. My pointing the theft out-not the theft itself-was what offended her.

It's a cross-examination. What I'm doing is basically cross-examining the agents; I'm just not in court. This has caused some sharp criticism from some who were just starting to realize they have no evidence: "We're not in court, Marc!" Just answer the question and we can resolve this. In or out of court, you're supposed to have evidence.

The purpose of a cross-examination is to subject the testimony (accusations) to scrutiny, to see if the accuser is competent and credible. Do they have personal knowledge of the matter? I like to ask: "Can you confirm there are facts proving the code is applicable to my client?" On 5 March 2013, I had John Scott, a cop in Sheffield, England finally admit, "I have absolutely no idea." No idea? Well, mate, here's a gun and a car; start giving out tickets.

While this would be devastating when admitted on the stand in front of a jury, it's still damaging when done on the phone during pretrial. Such an admission technically makes whatever the cop has to say about my client irrelevant. And that is pretty damn effective when working to stop an attack.

If a prosecutor insists on using such a witness, I can always object on grounds the witness and prosecutor know the witness is not qualified. That is misconduct and malicious prosecution. Plus, I can be certain that on cross-examination in court, when I ask the cop about his previous statement, the prosecutor will launch out of his/her chair objecting on relevance.

Yes, you need to get used to the reality that the competency and credibility of a prosecution witness is never a relevant issue to prosecutors; just expect it and use it against them.

When psychopaths are attacking you, they couldn't care less that it's based on witnesses who have no idea what they are talking about. As long as they are saying what the prosecutor wants, then it's no problem.

Always looking to the future, when we speak with tax agents or other bureaucrats, we create a record to use against them later if the agent doesn't do the right thing and drop the attack when it's clear they have no evidence. For a worst-case scenario, we'll be well prepared for court later if we stick to the facts and record their bad faith and inability to produce any empirical evidence. You're building your appeal or case against them. They'll hang themselves; relevant questions about the facts is usually all the rope they need.

When speaking with them, part of the objective is to show the agent is not a credible or competent witness against us. This way, we can give them a scapegoat; the cop just doesn't know what he's talking about or the prosecutor wasn't prepared properly.

Inability to prove willfulness in tax prosecutions. What about failure to file a tax return or pay taxes i.e., tax evasion? If you look at the code, there is a *mens rea* element, willfulness. You have to believe you have a legitimate obligation to file and then knowingly refuse to do so. Is this possible with taxes though? I don't see any evidence of it, and I'm not talking about being able to understand the code to determine you're required to pay and file a return.

This so-called "crime" hinges on beliefs. A prosecutor must provide facts proving beyond a reasonable doubt you knew you were obligated to pay taxes and you made the conscious decision not to pay. What facts do prosecutors rely on to prove, beyond a reasonable doubt, you believed you are obligated to pay taxes? I've heard them admit they only have circumstantial evidence to prove it. This usually consists of prior filing and paying taxes or in not reporting transactions to the tax agencies.

Do those circumstances prove beyond a reasonable doubt you believed there was a legitimate obligation? Absolutely not; there is not only plenty of doubt, I don't think it's possible to prove such a thing.

As far as I can tell, the only facts are threats of jail if you don't pay. Does a threat-an act of coercion-constitute evidence proving beyond a reasonable doubt you believed you're obligated to pay taxes? This is the case a prosecutor brings against you when you strip out the legalese: We threatened you will jail if you don't pay, therefore, you knew you were required and you didn't pay. That's crazy; it's not logical at all and is a mother of a non sequitur.

> You knew you were obligated to pay, and you willfully chose not to.
> What facts prove I believed there's a legitimate obligation?
> *What part of* pay or go to jail *don't you understand?* See, you understand.
> The same way slaves *knew* they were obligated to pick cotton?

Tax evasion is non-compliance with a threat of jail. That's about all you can distill it down to. Without political fluff and legalese it's you didn't comply with their threat of jail and economic punishment.

Yes, they play up the laws, court decisions and any past examples of you paying taxes as "evidence" you knew you were required to do so. But that isn't evidence you believed there was a legitimate obligation; it's the cart before the horse again and an assumption. It doesn't take into account *why* someone paid. As I mention to agents, taxes are paid out of fear, not because I see any facts creating an obligation to pay. The laws and court decisions, as we already know, are not facts. They are PR covering up the facts: the ever-present gun in the room.

A question for agents, especially when being investigated by the criminal investigation division, is: Does the singular fact you threatened to put me in jail constitute evidence I'm required to pay? Can nothing more than a threat of jail and other punishment be considered evidence an obligation was created? As a rational adult, I don't think so, and tax agents and lawyers don't think so either. Ask them and they'll tell you.

It's why we get excuses from them that there are no threats, that I'm being "dramatic" claiming taxes are compulsory or coercive in nature. I've been told it's "hyperbole" that taxes are taken under threat of jail. They know that threats of violence don't create obligations or the belief that one has an obligation, yet they prosecute people all the time for willful failure to file tax returns and pay taxes.

They'll claim the code "requires" me to file a return, and that there is no coercion:

> Is there a threat of jail if I don't file?
> *Yes, but that's not making anything compulsory or coercive.*
> You don't consider a threat of jail coercive?
> *No, it's required or you go to jail.*
> There's no coercion involved with taxation?
> *No.*
> So it's voluntary. If I choose not to pay there are no consequences?
> *No, not at all...I'm not explaining it as well as my boss does. You have to pay; it's required. If you don't pay, we can take your house and put you in jail.*
> Okay. So how is that not coercive again?

If you talk to the average victim of governments about not paying taxes, they'll point out that you'll go to jail like Wesley Snipes if you don't comply. So you get more circular reasoning: you pay taxes or go to jail; you go to jail if you don't pay taxes. But why do I have to pay? Because if you don't you'll go to jail and they'll take your stuff. An appeal to force, or *argumentum ad baculum*
http://en.wikipedia.org/wiki/Argumentum_ad_baculum.

Most people seem very close to understanding that there are no facts obligating us to pay taxes, there's only a threat of violence. That's why they bring up Wesley Snipes. They just don't realize the implications of what they're saying.

Unless you are anti-social and irrational, threats of violence do not create obligations. In the mind of a victim, they are paying or complying out of fear of going to jail. Does that fear caused by the threat constitute a rational belief one is obligated to pay taxes? I don't see it.

There's no merit to the tax apologist's opinion, "It doesn't matter if you did it out of fear; we all know the law requires us to pay taxes."

First, it's just an opinion; there are no facts proving what someone believed or not. Let's put this to rest right now: "we all know" is not proof of anything, it's an excuse to cover for a lack of evidence; it's the logical fallacy of appealing to popularity or *argumentum ad populum*. I can do the same thing: "We all know lawyers are [insert any random insult]." I wish that all I needed to do was say, "We all know there's no evidence the laws apply," and the attack would be dropped.

Second, if done out of fear, it has everything to do with whether someone believed they were obligated or not. It's easy to find out:

> *Did you file a tax return because there were facts proving you were required?*
> Hell no. Are you drunk? I did it for the same reason anyone does: to keep those maniacs from putting me in jail.

Remember, no one has standing to testify to another's state of mind. I've had tax agents and their lawyers agree. If you say you pay out of fear of going to jail, then that's the end of the discussion. You can point to the code and to Wesley Snipes as your support. I've had critics tell me: "Your argument is frivolous. You have to pay taxes or you go to jail." They've unwittingly supported my position.

"We all know the law requires us to pay taxes." Really? And the facts to support that are...? I've spoken with many agents and none of them have been able to tell me. Yes, lawyers and other critics will bash me on the internets, but they never present any facts, just opinions the code applies. But what are the facts that *prove* the code applies? Oh yeah, Wesley Snipes went to jail.

Can anyone prove beyond a reasonable doubt you willfully failed to file a return and pay taxes? No, they can't. They have to prove beyond a reasonable doubt the code created an obligation.

> *You know you are required to pay taxes, but you didn't!*
> No, I only knew I had to pay to avoid going to jail. Got any evidence to oppose that, mate?
> *You know you are required to pay taxes, but you didn't!*

There are people who have convinced themselves they are the same thing. Only a psychopath would equate a threat with an obligation. Welcome to the mind of the average prosecutor though.

(These are the same psychopaths who also claim a question is an argument or a debate, so it's no surprise.) Many have tried to convince me they are same thing. There are those, such as Charlie and Suzanne Small with the Franchise Tax Board in California. Both thought they could convince me there's no coercion involved with taxation. A good response to such nonsense would be to quote a line from Jack Nicholson, "Sell crazy somewhere else, we're all stocked up here."

The line above is really all that is necessary to defeat a charge of tax evasion or failure to file. Just saying, "I did it under threat, duress and coercion to avoid going to jail" defeats the willful element. "You threatened me, jackass" should also suffice, but we're not dealing with rational adults here.

317

So why are people investigated and put on trial? I think one of the reasons is to instill more fear into the masses. Threats are not as effective if you're not seen carrying them out. When those within your scope of influence see the Feds destroying your life, they'll cower in fear and be more compliant.

You're not filing your return; didn't you hear what they're doing to Jack? They took everything and are prosecuting him; he's looking at five years in prison. He can't even afford a lawyer. If you don't file, they'll put you in prison too.
What facts are there that I'm required to file?
The fact they'll put you in prison; isn't that enough evidence for you?

Governments and their accomplices/apologists don't seem to understand a very simple truth: acts of violence/aggression negate the need for facts. It's one or the other: you have facts proving an obligation was created or you have violence and threats. I'm not aware of any middle ground there. If I'm truly obligated to do something, then it's not created by aggression.

They should just be upfront like psychopaths of old and say:

Stop asking us for facts; we carry machine guns.

They should update their form letters and put at the top: Pay your taxes-remember Wesley Snipes. But I guess that's bad PR.

It wouldn't matter if they changed the code to make it a strict liability offence so *mens rea* or willfulness is not an element. A threat of violence does not create obligations. If there's no obligation to act or not act, then there's no crime or cause of action. Even prosecutors and judges admit this. They don't always admit the code has to be proven to be applicable, but they do agree (wait, this is crazy) the code has to create an obligation or liability. Yes, let that sink in for a moment. I've developed sort of a tolerance to such nonsense.

You're obligated to file a return.
And why is that?
Because I'll put you in jail, take all your stuff and terrorize your friends and family if you don't.

In a tax evasion prosecution, they will freely admit, and it may be in the jury instructions, that one of the three elements the prosecution must prove is that the code created a liability. Now, you may be thinking: how is that even remotely possible if they don't *first* prove the code applies? Welcome to Legal Land.

This gigantic hole in the evidence is just assumed by the fair, impartial and independent former prosecutor. My proof of this is the fact that the judge will instruct the jury that the code, not proven to apply at all during the "trial," actually does apply because he said so. The jury must accept the law as the judge instructs them. Can't prove an element of your case? That's easy; just have the judge give instructions to the jury as if you did prove it.

The code is not applicable to us at all; it's just the threats of those called government. When you're in the trenches with these agents, nothing else is necessary to prove that the code is just PR. They are going to aggress against you regardless of their written law.

Yes, some people may claim they happily pay taxes and believe it is their civic duty. How credible is that though? The fact is they are still coerced regardless of their claim, just as a victim is happy to give a mugger his wallet to avoid getting shot in the head. Until the coercion is taken away there's no credibility to claims people happily pay taxes and think there's a legitimate obligation.

Constant lying. This takes some getting used to, it is still tough for me to deal with it every day. The evidence, if you deal with bureaucrats for any amount of time, proves lying is an integral part of their communication. This should not be a surprise since violence and lies are the foundation of the government concept. Police dishonesty is so prevalent it's an accepted part of the job:

> "As I read about the disbelief expressed by some prosecutors... I thought of Claude Rains's classic response, in Casablanca on being told there was gambling in Rick's place: "I'm shocked—shocked!" For anyone who has practiced criminal law in the state or Federal courts, the disclosures about rampant police perjury cannot possibly come as a surprise. "Testilying"—as the police call it—has long been an open secret among prosecutors, defense lawyers, and judges."
> http://en.wikipedia.org/wiki/Police_perjury

This is not just the police; if you have to speak to any bureaucrat of any level, you need to be prepared to handle someone lying right to your face, who knows they're lying, knows you don't buy it for a second and just doesn't give a damn about it. That's not a good place to be if you want to stay professional and non-confrontational. You have to remember bureaucrats just don't care; it's not in the nature of a psychopath to give a damn about anyone other than themselves. It's even more so when they are acting as a government.

I spoke a second time with Chris Lianos with the New Hampshire Employment Security agency and he was insulted when I asked again about who made the determination my client was obligated to register with him. The day before, someone at the office said he was responsible for the determination. He did not want to admit sole responsibility, so he said Celine Allen, a supervisor, assisted him.

When I asked him to confirm this, he backed off and said it was done by the agency. How surprising: a bureaucrat getting vaguer. He's trying to convince me the agency, the NHES, made the claim. I used an analogy

319

to demonstrate it was a really stupid thing to say: it was the same as saying that a traffic ticket was written by the police department, not an individual cop. Chris didn't seem to like that. He admitted: "I don't have any jurisdiction here." I told him I was writing that down, and then asked him if he didn't have jurisdiction, why did he send my client letters in the first place?

What does a bureaucrat do when confronted with such a tough question? Drop the attack? Ask for time to investigate? No, Chris did what bureaucrats do so well: he lied and said he never said he didn't have jurisdiction. I point out that's exactly what he said; I wrote it down and Bill also heard him. He gets madder, says he doesn't want to deal with my "crap" and asks me, "Marc, do you talk English?"

He also stated we were not accomplishing anything. I countered that I thought we accomplished quite a bit, we have you on record admitting you don't have jurisdiction. So in that situation, I was able to get valuable testimony from the lead agent.

So what do you do when the agent is lying to your face? It's easy to handle. It's all about challenging fictions, the only difference is the agent is aware of this one. The model to follow is, always go from the vague to the specific. Lying does not get them off the hook, they still have to present facts.

Just call them on it, "Are you changing your mind? You *do* have jurisdiction over me, as opposed to what you said just a moment ago?" And if someone claims they have jurisdiction over me, I follow up with the standard, "Excepting your opinion, do you rely on any evidence to prove you have jurisdiction?"

The difficult part is staying professional and not calling them a liar outright. We have to stay calm and professional even when the agent lies. I've called a few bureaucrats on it saying, "Sir you're lying," but it usually doesn't help unless you're in public in front of others.

You catch them with their hands in the cookie jar, and they congruently deny it. It's quite a sight for a normal, honest adult to behold. I had a problem with it because I would take it personally that the agents assumed I was so stupid I could not keep track and know when they're lying. They will change their story from one sentence to the next as if you can't follow. If you call them on it, they resort to personal attacks: "this is crap," and other distractions. It's always to get the attention away from their lack of evidence and credibility. Remember, psychopaths have poor coping skills; they hate being exposed.

It's not that they think we're all so stupid; some do, but I think it's more that they don't care and they don't have to. We can't hold them responsible and they know it. They sought out a job of violent domination and no personal responsibility.

Even when I tell the bureaucrat on the phone I'm writing down their statements to make sure I have them correct, they will still claim they didn't say what they said two minutes earlier. I've asked them to confirm statements: "Sir, just to quote you accurately, you said you have no jurisdiction over my client?" "That's correct."

A few minutes later, or less, the same bureaucrat, realizing how damaging the admission is, will accuse me of lying or twisting their words. It doesn't matter I probably have a witness to the statement on the line with me. Yes, with bureaucrats quoting them directly is "twisting [their] words."

A well-worn pattern is to deflect attention away from themselves; they can't stand taking any responsibility for anything they may be confronted with. It's the pattern of the criminal.

Evidence of this is when they consistently refuse to give a name of the individual man/woman making the claim. Why? Because if it's the Canadian Revenue Agency instead of Wendi, then there's a facade of authority. Who am I to question the Agency? But if it's just Wendi the accountant who works in another office, the assessment *may* be wrong.

They may also gaslight you, "What are you *talking* about?" I don't know what you mean; this is just how it's done. Are you interested in actually helping your client, or making things worse if this escalates? Do you want your client to go to prison? Then I advise you to have them speak to a *real* lawyer."

The diversion is useful to them both as a delay and a fear tactic. It really wears on you, at least for me after doing it for a few hours; and I expect it. You wouldn't think so, but dealing with psychopaths can be a real drag. A call that should be over in five minutes may take twenty, because you have to keep asking questions to get them to be specific and the questions are not anything they commonly hear: What are you trying to convey to me when you use the words Canadian Revenue Agency? And that's without some lawyer objecting to every question.

Even if you found the name of the agent and had them in court or administrative hearing for a cross-examination, their lawyers will be objecting incessantly. Because the facts connecting you to their laws couldn't possibly be relevant, could they?

The same holds true for the witness's qualifications to interpret and apply the constitution and laws, and their personal knowledge of the same. In my strange world, facts are important, not the opinions of those who want to take my stuff. You need to stay on point whenever they gaslight you when you challenge their sacred cows.

Don't discuss the merits. Jurisdiction is step one, then you determine if there's a valid cause of action. If you get past those, then discussion of the merits is appropriate. But until then, the merits are irrelevant.

It's my experience that it's more effective to stick to being a bit vague, like politicians, when challenging them. Bureaucrats are always accusing us of violating their laws, statutes, ordinances, codes, rules and regulations, so keep your focus on that instead of the specific behavior they are you accusing of. There are two reasons: it keeps the attention on the application of the laws, and there is less opportunity to work some distracting guilt on you, the victim of the politician's attack.

It's always a *code violation*, not possession or driving on a suspended license. They accuse us of violating the code, so stick with that.

> What facts do you rely on proving the code applies to me?
> *Oh, so you must think you're different, that it's okay to use the roads and not pay taxes?*
> What facts do you rely on proving the code applies to me?
> *Why do you think you don't have to pay your fair share like the rest of us?*
> What facts do you rely on proving the code applies to me?
> *We all have to pay more to cover what you're not paying!*
> Is that the evidentiary standard you're using? What facts do you rely on proving the code applies to me?

It's more effective to challenge the legal opinion that the laws apply to me, than to discuss whether or not I was growing certain plants in my garden or giving advice without permission from a psychopathic cult.

There seems to be a personality trait we have to proclaim our innocence: we didn't do what we were accused of, and the whole world needs to stop so we can explain. Don't get off track like that. Liberty activists may claim the law is unconstitutional, and never challenge the applicability of the law in the first place. They may claim the law or drug war is immoral because there are no victims, but they don't challenge the bureaucrat on the evidence supporting their argument that the laws apply at all. Strike at the root; don't hack away at the branches.

For example, I worked with a doctor who was involved in a bankruptcy proceeding; he was accused of fraud-only accused. There were no facts; his name was not even mentioned in the complaint, except maybe in the caption at one point.

When we did telephonic hearings regarding the motion to dismiss based on the complete lack of facts to support the "conclusory statements," I had to keep reminding him not to say a word about the merits of the allegations. We were to stick to the one relevant issue: the lack of facts. We don't discuss anything about the accuracy of the accusations until the attorney presents the facts they were based on, if any. The doctor was constantly berated by the other defendants' lawyers that he has to settle because "these guys are serious." Oh, that changes everything-the lawyers are serious! I didn't go to law school, so I'm not familiar with such a sophisticated legal standard. I've inadvertently said it sarcastically many times in response to bureaucrats:

> *Marc, you must file this statement that you're not practicing law without a license.*
> Are you serious?
> *Yes, always.*
> Oh, that changes everything; where do I sign?

All this time I had no idea I may have been engaging these professional parasites in a legitimate legal discussion.

The attorney eventually dropped the complaint against the doctor because there were no facts, just baseless accusations. Had the doctor starting talking about not being a fraud, he would probably have had to submit to discovery and trial. All of the other defendants who tried to scare him into making a deal wound up paying tens of thousands of dollars while the good doctor paid me about a thousand to see it through to a voluntary dismissal from the serious lawyer acting as receiver.

From my standpoint, being serious, or even being really pissed off, is no substitute for facts. A stern look doesn't equal the facts necessary to establish a cause of action. I'm no Latin scholar, but I'm not fooled for a moment that *injuria et damnum* translates to *serious lawyer*. I'm only familiar with two burdens of proof, i.e., "beyond a reasonable doubt" and "by a preponderance of evidence"; I've not read where "serious lawyer" was a legal standard. What if all the lawyers are serious? Who prevails then?

Well, I've good news and bad news for you.
OK, what's going on?
Well, the good news is there's no evidence against you.
How could there possibly be bad news then?
Well, the plaintiff's lawyer is really serious.
Oh, that is bad. Whatever I have to pay you to avoid jail, let's do that. Wait, can I pay you to be more serious?

Keep this perspective: a lack of evidence speaks much louder than your protests of innocence. Your protests of innocence, while they may be accurate, are not facts, just more opinions. They may be based on facts, but you don't have the burden of proof, so why pick it up when you don't need to? There may be times when it's necessary, but real criminal trials are rare compared to prosecutions for violations of statutes, politician-created offences i.e., *mala prohibita*.

Let's update that earlier quote:

Your lack of evidence is so loud I can't hear a word you're saying.

If we're interested in truth, then we ignore the opinions and platitudes, at least until the facts are presented. We're only interested in what story the facts tell, then we can compare them to the one presented by the bureaucrat. When a politician claims we violated their law, it makes sense to focus on that accusation and its basis, not on our actual actions or inaction.

You cannot violate a statute/law/regulation that doesn't apply to you. This is pretty basic stuff, and bureaucrats don't want us to focus on it because there are no facts to prove their PR and distractions apply to us.

In court, lawyers routinely give prosecutors a free pass on this essential element. The only excuse I've ever been given to not challenge the applicability of the laws is because it "will piss off the judge." Who said it was a government of laws, and not of men?

Well, we can challenge the applicability of the laws and demolish probable cause and jurisdiction.
Great, let's do that.
Yeah, I'm really conflicted here; even though you did give me a ten thousand dollar retainer, I can't do that.
Why the hell not? I'm looking at ten years in prison, not you!
There is a chance it could piss off the judge.
Ah, true, use the 10k to make a deal; anything to stay out of jail and not piss off the judge. And please also waive my right to sue and get back my property that was stolen in the raid.

Is that brilliant strategy taught in law school or something firms teach lawyers? Get people to pay thousands of dollars so that, despite the cops having no evidence of jurisdiction, you just make a deal to avoid prison? I'm guessing the word lawyer comes from the Greek word eunuch.

When someone is *lying right to your face,* you can and should call them on it. They may not even be aware that they are relying on fictions. Call them on it. Challenge the fictions. Ask for the facts. They are dangerous people, but that doesn't mean we should not defend ourselves and have them verify their allegations. Not challenging them only enriches the lawyer cult.

I've had agents lie to me, fully aware that I know they are lying and it doesn't faze them. It's hard for normal people to wrap their mind around it. It's similar to watching a comedian knowing he's bombing, knows the audience wants him to stop and he just keeps going as if he's the new George Carlin.

It has to take years to develop a personality where you care nothing about what other people think.

You do realize everyone is aware you're lying right now?
Yeah. So what?
They all know you're lying; you're not fooling anyone.
What's your point?

It appears that the best system of justice in the world is predicated not on fairness and objective standards of proof and cross-examination, but instead on not pissing off lawyers. How is that different from all the rest?

The US, greatest system of justice in the world, as long as you don't piss off the judge.

It's a system of "justice" where innocent people are sent to prison because they dare to question sacred cows that cause an unstable lawyer to come unglued? Sounds like a great system. The science of law? What's one of the principles of this science of law? Don't piss off the judge by challenging the prosecutor's assertion of jurisdiction.

They always avoid the tough questions. Ask them for evidence the laws of the state apply, and they won't answer. They may ask: "Are you a resident of the State of Victoria?" Then a good response would be: "Please answer my question: what evidence do you have proving the laws of the state apply to me?"

They ask me that all the time, as if they are being nice by asking me to give them information to use against my own clients. I'm asking for facts to support the opinions they already hold against my client, and instead of just providing the evidence, they ask me questions:

> *Marc, we can resolve this right now. Did your client work last year?*
> Not relevant. You've already decided my client is within your jurisdiction and the laws apply. Unless that opinion is arbitrary, it must be based on facts. What are those facts?
> *Don't you want to help your client and get this resolved?*
> Yes, what facts do you rely on proving my client is subject to the laws of the state?

Don't feel the need to fill in the blanks for them. They're the ones with the burden of proof. No free passes.

The principle that you should never talk to the police applies to all attacks by bureaucrats too; it can only be used against you. The one initiating the attack has the burden of proof and we should exploit this because I have yet to interact with a psychopath claiming to be a state or government admit their accusation is arbitrary. There was one, but she quickly changed her position because she was confused by the question. Even politicians recognize good faith and arbitrary don't go together very well. It's bad to the appearance of justice and due process.

They've already made decisions, formed opinions and initiated the contact. They don't even like being called aggressors; it makes them look bad, it's bad PR. Chris Lianos with the New Hampshire Employment Security office got very upset when I said he was the aggressor, not my client. I had to ask who initiated contact; who threatened field agents? Despite this, he still didn't want to be viewed as an aggressor. That can be used to your advantage.

The principle about getting your facts straight before making an accusation is not one taught to would-be bureaucrats. It's always: make the attack first, no need to bother with facts. After all, there are former state prosecutors to cover for you and threaten contempt for anyone asking for evidence.

They think we have to prove our innocence; they act as if they have no burden of proof. Almost every day I have a bureaucrat ask me why the laws would not apply. How about because you have no evidence proving they do? Because your argument they do apply is groundless.

There's no need to argue though; accept it and move on using it to your advantage. From experience, they don't like it at all when I mention, "I'm proving my client's innocence by having you admit your opinions have no supporting facts." A bureaucrat will ask, "Where are you going with this, Marc?" I'm happy to tell them that I'm asking about the facts they rely on because they don't rely on any. Yes, they initially get indignant at this suggestion, but they usually will admit they have no facts.

325

I can't tell you how many times I've asked for facts the laws apply only to have a bureaucrat smugly ask me, "What facts do you have proving the code doesn't apply?" One day, rather than correct them by saying the burden is on the one making the accusation, I will fire back, "Because they are the ramblings of the insane; is that sufficient for you?"

Again, if it's so easy to prove the laws apply, then why would a judge get pissed off and threaten contempt? Why would lawyers be so afraid of challenging an essential element of a crime? Yes, they have an oath to support the laws, but does that really explain it all?

By keeping the prosecutor's feet to the fire to produce facts that the laws apply, it becomes clear to everyone not completely corrupt that there's no evidence. It's just an opinion, and even judges will tell you elements of crimes may not be based on opinions, but must be proven beyond a reasonable doubt with facts from witnesses with personal knowledge.

I don't let bureaucrats and lawyers get away with trying to use opinions as evidence. It makes no sense when your life is in the balance. It doesn't matter if there are at least three state agents claiming their laws apply to you; opinions can't magically become facts because more people say them.

And they pull this crap with juries too: despite no evidence and no witnesses the code applies, a judge, like the psychopath Larry Burns, will assume it for the jury. You can object and submit your own proposed jury instructions, but they will ignore you. Here are some jury instructions that judges have completely denied and refused to give to a jury. Not one part is untrue or irrelevant:

Mr. Smith is accused of violating the laws of the state of Montana; the plaintiff city, a municipal corporation, a fiction, is a political subdivision of the state.

The prosecutor, who is acting as a proxy for a corporation, a fiction, must prove every element of this code violation beyond a reasonable doubt and may not make arguments outside the facts in evidence. You as the jury may not substitute your opinions for the prosecutor's evidence. If the prosecutor has made any arguments outside the facts in evidence, it's misconduct.

The applicability of the laws is an essential element of the alleged crime and necessary to prove jurisdiction. You may not just assume this for the prosecutor, even if it seems obvious. No element of the alleged crime may be taken lightly and assumed.

Like the other elements, the prosecutor must prove this beyond a reasonable doubt with competent, relevant evidence from witnesses with personal first-hand knowledge of the facts.

The first step to proving the laws were violated is proving the laws apply. This isn't done with allegations and circular logic, or as the prosecutor has previously asserted, "You're in my state, my laws apply."

If the prosecutor didn't provide facts in evidence, from a witness proven at trial to have personal knowledge the laws applied, then an essential element of the alleged violation was not proven beyond a reasonable doubt. Arguing the laws apply does not constitute evidence. If that's all the prosecution has, then your only choice is to acquit.

While the prosecutor has elicited testimony regarding Smith's physical presence, this does not mean Smith is within the plaintiff city, a municipal corporation. It only means that a corporation-people such as the prosecutor-may have jurisdiction over Smith, but that must be proven with evidence by a competent witness. The prosecutor has the burden of proving Smith is within the jurisdiction of a corporation, a fiction. You have to decide if the prosecutor did that, and be able to identify the facts in evidence from a witness with personal knowledge.

If the prosecutor has not presented facts in evidence, from a witness proven to have personal knowledge the laws apply, and that Smith is actually subject to the jurisdiction of the plaintiff corporation, then your only choice today is acquittal.

Would such jury instructions be prejudicial to a prosecutor? They would be only if he's engaged in misconduct and malicious prosecution. The judge would only be pointing out the prosecutor's burden of proof. The judge would be giving honest and fair instructions for a change. If the prosecutor wants to prosecute someone, then they're supposed to have evidence and witnesses; otherwise it's just argument and speculation.

So it doesn't matter if three, three thousand, or three hundred million people are of the opinion that the laws apply to me. What facts do they rely on? Looks like they play legal alchemy. It's not just two wrongs making a right, but, when you get a bunch of people calling themselves a government, then opinions magically become facts. What kind of formula is required to turn mere opinions, or dictum, into irrefutable facts though? Does it depend on the location, the politician? What I can prove is the following, as anyone who has been to court can attest to:

1 opinion = irrefutable fact if lawyer has a black robe
2 opinions = irrefutable fact if lawyer lacks a black robe

When a prosecutor accuses another of violating a statute, the first thing for them to prove is the court or agency has jurisdiction over the accused. To prove that, there has to be evidence proving two things: presence within the state and the laws apply. Evidence of this is overwhelming, as even the US constitution explicitly mandates the federal courts only have jurisdiction involving cases and controversies "arising under this Constitution, the Laws of the United States, and Treaties..."Article III § 2.

Whoever is making the accusation needs to have jurisdiction in the first place, whether a cop, a building inspector or a tax agent.

If an agent from the Canadian Revenue Agency claims a man is required to file a return as mandated by law, then an appropriate question is: "Can you confirm that there is evidence proving you have jurisdiction over me?" Another is: "What evidence do you rely on proving the laws are applicable to me just because I'm physically in Canada?"

I went through this with Brian Parrot, a bureaucrat in Orangeville, Ontario on 6 March 2013. His response to my question about evidence the code applied and jurisdiction was that the "provincial legislation" applied to all property within the province. I asked, "How do you know that's true? What is that based on?" Brian referred to the code again. It's that simple to show there's no evidence.

Putting words on a piece of paper does not create an obligation on someone just because someone declares it. Writing that your laws apply to me and putting it in fancy books doesn't mean they apply. Those are not facts, in case you missed that. There's a great scene in the US version of the show *The Office*, where Michael Scott walks into the office and says...no, I got that wrong; he *declares*, "I DECLARE BANKRUPTCY!" https://www.youtube.com/watch?v=xuuv0syoHnM.

And that sums up the factual basis politicians rely on to prove their laws/statutes apply to us. To that, Oscar of *The Office* would say, "You can't just [declare something] and expect anything to happen."

> *We wrote down our opinions and they apply to everyone.*
> You can't just write things down and say they apply to anyone just because you say so.
> *We didn't just say it; we wrote them down, we called them laws, and judges declared it.*
> "Still...that's...it's not anything," as Oscar would also say.

If it's not sufficient for Michael Scott, then it's not for the rest of us. When discussing the applicability of the laws, it comes down to nothing more than someone's say-so. Even a declaration from a bureaucrat that his/her laws apply and they have jurisdiction is still nothing more than a declaration.

Angel Hallman from Chelan, Washington thought there was evidence of jurisdiction on nothing more than, "We do because we've adopted the code."

There's even a maxim covering this type of nonsense:

> "**vox et preterea nihil**...Voice and nothing more; that is, nothing but wind. See Mitchell v Hazen, 4 Conn 495."
> *Ballentine's Law Dictionary*, page 1354.

Politicians have been around long enough that there are ancient maxims covering their usual gibberish. Remember this maxim when you hear government apologists insisting that the law applies because it's the law, and the argument that there is jurisdiction doesn't require supporting evidence.

> Do you hold an objective standard of proof?
> *Of course I do. I declare something, and my goons make it happen.*
> *You will be objectively imprisoned or killed in the process if you don't comply. Objective enough there for you, mate? Your skull*

split open, or your confession-there's your objective standard of proof, jackass.

You know you've got the bureaucrat on the ropes when they feign confidence like the tax agents mentioned earlier. They'll start insisting their declaration the laws apply is a statement of fact: "It's not my opinion, it's a fact!" Really? Why, because you said so? It's nice, because they unwittingly take the law out of the equation for you. All I do from there is to continue asking for the facts connecting me to the laws.

I did a short article on this with a call from a bureaucrat on 2 Aug. 2012 http://marcstevens.net/cos/cos20120802.html. Debby insisted the code was binding and was the basis of why they could proceed against my client even if the assessment was not correct. I know it's hard to believe; I have to hear this stuff for myself to believe it.

I asked her what facts she relied on to prove the code applied at all and her response was, "Because the code applies, that's the code." I pointed out that was circular reasoning and not a responsive answer. I also could not resist saying, "The bible is true because the bible says so" as an example of the faulty logic she just tried to pass off as evidence. She was not happy about that at all and predictably hung up on us.

Let's separate the facts from your say-so, all right? This is where you may run up against a case of reification. The task is to gently help the bureaucrat see and understand the difference; an analogy usually helps. The church analogy is a good one: you compare the state to a church. Just because some religious leader draws lines on a map and says all of Toronto is a parish of the church doesn't mean you're a member of the church because you live in that area. I have a short video of this analogy here:

https://www.youtube.com/watch?v=-WFg5O3vB1s.

Objecting. I encourage incessant objections in court and administrative hearings; but not for all the same reasons prosecutors do it. Prosecutors object because they want to cover up the truth; I object to uncover it. We're both objecting because we know there's a lack of evidence; I want that exposed, the prosecutor wants it to stay hidden.

When we're in court we should be objecting to everything the prosecutor is trying to get away with. When they say they're representing a fiction such as a city, borough, state, or province, object and demand proof. We want the facts they rely on to prove their statements.

So my goal in objecting is opposite to the prosecutor's incessant objections. Yes, I do want to frustrate the lawyers and get them upset; why should forcing me to participate in their charade be easy for them? If you don't want to deal with me because it's so difficult and annoying to proceed, then the solution is to leave me alone. Normal people don't use coercion against people who have not used or threatened to use coercion against them.

Cops and prosecutors are the ones starting these circuses; if they don't want to be challenged on every single thing they say, then they should really consider getting real work. They should provide their services to the market on a voluntary basis and stop forcing us to pay them. I suggest objecting even when prosecutors say they are ready to proceed:

> *Yes, Your Honor, the prosecution is ready to proceed.*

> *Objection*, the prosecution is not ready to proceed. Rick Brown has already admitted he has no evidence the code is applicable to me; he can't establish jurisdiction, let alone prove anything else beyond a reasonable doubt.

> *Your Honor the state is ready to...*

> *Objection*, this lawyer has no facts proving he has a client; he will not even discuss what he means when he uses the word state. Knowingly bringing a complaint without evidence of jurisdiction is prosecutorial misconduct.

Objecting to the prosecutor's complete lack of evidence proving the code is applicable (notwithstanding the common political opinion it's not necessary to prove it) must be constant so it's always on everyone's mind and expected.

Whenever the prosecutor starts to talk, the jury is not focused so much on what they are going to say as waiting for me to object. Is it distracting? Of course, that's the point. We're distracting the jury from the irrelevant nonsense and platitudes this lawyer is spewing.

In the above scenario, it will be obvious to everyone in the room the judge is relieving the prosecutor of his/her burden of proof. No one denies the burden is on the prosecutor. But when it comes to a sacred cow of politics such as the applicability of the law, the burden can get thrown out the window. Threats of violence are then used to try to take everyone's attention away from it.

I can't even imagine a lawyer trying to convince twelve people they don't have to prove the code is applicable; that in a trial they may instead just assume it, even though it's an element of the alleged crime. I can't see anyone sitting still for that:

> Ladies and gentlemen of the jury, the honorable judge did not coerce you here today to mess around with silly things the defendant is bringing up. You were all coerced here today for a very serious issue: did the defendant disobey our beloved rulers? Yes. I have no facts to prove it, but of course the code is applicable; it's so obvious I don't need facts to prove it. And more important, the defendant has no evidence the code is not applicable. Yes, the applicability of the code is an element of these crimes, but we can just assume it applies because that's the way the system works. How else would

the roads get built? Do you want feces in your cheese? No, me neither. So you must convict.

If the jury sees us standing up to the lawyers and questioning jurisdiction, jurors may start getting ideas and challenging the jurisdiction *over them*. And why not-it's about time, isn't it? Why shouldn't jurors be asking for evidence of jurisdiction? Would the judge treat them in the same callous, condescending manner as they do to defendants? I'd like to see jurors asking to see the prosecutor's evidence there is jurisdiction. If they don't have it, then trying to seat a jury is premature at best.

That would make it very difficult to stack a jury biased in favor of the prosecution. If they seat a jury after treating them like me, e.g., screaming and threatening contempt, that should make for a hostile jury. And they'll be seeing more evidence proving these two lawyers are working together. They may not be willing to overlook the prosecutor's lack of evidence as easily as the judges do.

It would be a judge's nightmare to have jurors asking why he/she has not held the prosecutor to their burden of proof:

> Excuse me Edward, why do you permit this to continue despite Lori's refusal to present any facts proving jurisdiction? Isn't the prosecutor supposed to have the burden of proof here?
> *Shut up, peasant; I order you to be quiet!*
> It looks like you are aiding the prosecution; you're not even trying to be impartial here. Why? Are the twelve of us supposed to just sit here and allow this?

I think this is reasonable, since prosecutors avoid proving jurisdiction when defendants ask. They certainly don't want to see a jury pool asking for their facts proving jurisdiction. The last thing a prosecutor and judge want in a jury is one capable of critical thought and demanding to see facts proving the code is applicable. Because it's obvious that if there is no jurisdiction over the defendant, then it follows there is no jurisdiction over the people making up a jury. I would love to see a juror say to a prosecutor:

> This lawyer (pointing to judge) coerced us to be here today because of you. The judge let you off the hook, but we won't. What facts do you rely on proving jurisdiction?
> *Your Honor, this man is hostile. We'll pass on him.*
> [Next juror stands] This lawyer (pointing to judge) coerced us to be here today because of you. The judge let you off the hook, but we won't. What facts do you rely on proving jurisdiction?

It would only take one potential juror taking the defendant's lead for the lawyers to have a "mutiny" on their hands. If the judge gets upset

331

(they almost always do-big surprise when most exhibit psychopathic behavior), then it would only make the situation worse for them.

We've exposed the gun in the room, and now the bandwagon effect takes over and the lawyers lose their control. Even if the jurors are forced to participate, the prosecutor's lack of facts is the central issue it should be. If that happened, I would mention it every chance I had. In my opening statement I would tell them what they probably already know: they could acquit now because the prosecutor cannot prove two elements of the alleged statutory violations.

The jurors would know that everything called a trial from that point is irrelevant and a complete waste of time to anyone interested in justice. The prosecutors cannot prove the first point- jurisdiction-i.e., applicability of their code. So they could stand up and say," We've already heard enough, we're acquitting the defendant. There are no facts to even begin to put on a trial. Have a nice day."

I would tell the jurors no amount of coercion and screaming from the judge can change their verdict of acquittal. Once they acquit, the proceedings are over, end of discussion. A juror could say, after I brought it up, "If you guys retaliate, then we're going to challenge applicability of the law and call each of you (prosecutors and judge) as witnesses. We're also going to tell the media how you conduct yourselves."

Is objecting constantly going to make the jury think their time is being wasted? I sure hope so, and I'll keep pointing out the cause: the two lawyers (judge and prosecutor) are working together and forcing the jury to be there.

Nothing is relevant if there are no facts the code is applicable because that's essential to proving the lawyer with the black dress has jurisdiction. It's the first step in any court or administrative proceeding. Therefore, if there's no evidence of jurisdiction, nothing else from the prosecution is relevant. This includes discovery and witnesses "testilying." I don't care what office they work for, what title they hold or how many other people they have prosecuted before me. If they don't have evidence supporting their argument the code is applicable, then you cannot begin to prove jurisdiction over me.

I would object every time a prosecutor is referred to as the state's attorney on grounds it assumes facts the lawyer is incapable of presenting. It would probably also be wise to object to a lawyer being referred to as the prosecution because there is no evidence of jurisdiction and there is no valid cause of action before the court. It's the same as referring to me as a defendant. I'm not a defendant unless there is a cause of action against me in a court with jurisdiction and the parties are true adversaries.

It has to bewilder a juror to hear who they were told is the defendant, objecting every time the lawyers refer to them as the defendant. And the grounds are well versed by now: it assumes facts not in evidence. The prosecutor has no facts proving the code is applicable and that there is jurisdiction over me. It's not even proper to call these twelve people a jury until that lawyer presents facts.

Does this distract from the actual statutory violations alleged? That depends, doesn't it? It's actually putting the focus directly on them.

> *Your Honor the defendant has violated one of our codes.*
> Objection, I'm not the defendant, as there is no evidence of jurisdiction; I'm just a guy that this lawyer (judge) coerced to participate here today, same as you unfortunate twelve victims.
> *What do you mean you object?*
> Just what I said: there are no facts proving the code is applicable, there is no valid cause of action. Do I need to continue?

"But Marc, you have no respect for lawyers who do that, why would you do that? You're just trying to distract the jury from your impudent disobedience to our political law." Lawyers do not object incessantly to bring out the truth though, so that's not a fair comparison and complaint. Second, I cannot violate a law when there is no evidence it applies to me.

How many times have agents and prosecutors admitted the obvious to me, that they have no facts the code is applicable? I would have to be as crazy as my critics claim to back off such a strong issue. Why would I? Because it may piss off some lawyer? That's not a good reason when my freedom is on the line. Who doesn't see the merit in making such objections? The best these lawyers can come up with, if they dare address it at all, is the circular garbage: the code is applicable because it's the code. And let's not forget the turtle argument.

All we typically get is the gaslight tactic and silly personal attacks. I had an agent at the Canadian Revenue Agency say, "We've got one of *those*" right before she put me on hold and the call dropped.

So if they want to set a hearing..."*Objection*, this lawyer has failed to present any facts proving jurisdiction." You get the idea. I don't doubt they'll talk about it outside of the courtroom. I know they do from personal experience.

> You believe that guy today? He objected to everything.
> *Really, did he ever have any grounds?*
> No, he just kept repeating that Lori had no facts to prove the code was applicable to him.
> *Wow, Lori provided those facts though, right?*
> No. What, are you siding with this lunatic?
> *No, no, of course not. What a nut, making such objections. I hope the bastard gets the chair!*

Definitely learn your objections, they are absolutely necessary to stop the proceedings and you have to use the word "objection" to preserve the issues for appeal.

The main ones you'll be using the most are, relevance, non-responsive, assumes facts not in evidence, outside the pleadings, lacks foundation, leading the witness, argumentative, calls for speculation, and counsel is testifying. A list of objections is here:

http://en.wikipedia.org/wiki/List_of_objections_%28law%29

For me, if something is not fair, then I'll object on those grounds even if not found in any legal book. Also, I have objected on grounds the prosecutor is lying and using a logical fallacy.

While we should be objecting often, do not interrupt the judge when he/she is speaking. Let them finish then object.

If an objection is denied without response from the prosecution, or the judge doesn't provide grounds, then object and ask for grounds, "If you have grounds, then you'd disclose them."

Those who have been to traffic or tax court know judges reflexively deny motions without any grounds. They already know you lose, so everything has to conform to the pre-judgment.

Go from vague to specific. An easy way to get to the truth, especially when dealing with bureaucrats, is to follow a simple model: get the vague, false opinion, and ask them questions that get more and more specific:

Vague –> specific

Politicians and bureaucrats have to stay vague; the vaguer they are, the guiltier you look. The opposite then is: the more specific they are, the more innocent you look/are. "Taxpayer" is a good example. As with any legal opinion, it's very vague and conveys no real information, certainly no facts. Remember, opinions don't give you any facts or specific information, e.g., murder, extortion, taxpayer, taxable income, etc. Legal or political opinions are purposely vague.

Look at murder: if a bureaucrat accuses you of murder, people will look at you with contempt, but usually want an explanation. What if the bureaucrat cannot give any facts, just the opinion you're a murderer? It's the same with the taxpayer accusation/opinion: since there are no facts. The one making the accusation is going to start losing credibility, and they'll see it for what it is, an opinion and nothing more.

But, if they say they found George dead in your house with your knife stuck in his chest, then you're starting to match the opinion. Get more specific, and we learn you were two hundred miles away at the time, so then you don't look guilty anymore. If it turns out there was an email from you to a friend down the street about getting rid of George... you get the idea.

The problem with taxpayer, as opposed to so many other legal opinions, is that people tend to fill in the factual gaps because it's a familiar opinion they can relate to. So instead of being as vague as any other opinion, it appears to be more solid and is given as much credibility as statements of fact.

It doesn't really matter what the fiction or lie is, it will usually be very vague and most likely an example of reification and PR. The applicability of the law and presence within the state are good ones. Lawyers don't challenge such fictions, so cops, prosecutors, and judges are not very good at handling such confrontations. About the best they can do is revert to childlike behavior. Take away a child's toy and they cry. Take away a judge's perception as a fair, honest legal authority, and you get screams of anger and threats of contempt. Ask a bureaucrat for the facts they rely on proving they have jurisdiction, and they yell and hang up the phone, as if that's a substitute for evidence.

I always start with a vague position/opinion that's helpful to the bureaucrat. This way they will easily commit to it e.g., "Am I entitled to a fair trial?" This helps them; like most of their PR it makes them look good because it's vague. We know it's false because of the underlying facts, but the judge or other predator is acting as if it's true. It's always more effective to pick an opinion you know is false; there are many to choose from when dealing with governments.

If a tax agent insists they have jurisdiction over me, I take the vague statement and ask questions geared towards having him be more specific. It helps to also get the admission that if there are no facts proving there is jurisdiction, they would exercise their authority and vacate the assessment. Just asking if they can confirm there's evidence of jurisdiction is usually enough to get them to realize they've said too much: "My attorneys advised me not to speak to you!"

If you want to end a conversation with one of these parasites, then just ask them: "Can you confirm there's evidence of jurisdiction over me?"

If they throw you a curve ball, remember that you need responsive answers, and each answer should be getting more and more specific. If not, the answer is probably not responsive. A big one is when judges claim something such as case or cause of action requirements don't apply. That's pretty vague and is just his opinion. To follow the simple model, just ask him what facts and legal support he relies on to support his opinion. Challenge them: "It doesn't apply, really? How do you know that? Why is that true?"

Never take their word for anything, always verify. I've been able to expose bureaucrats lying many times just by asking logical follow-up questions. One commissioner in New Hampshire told me he could not discuss evidence because the matter had already been set for a hearing. (Apparently, he had never heard of discovery.) I was able to prove he was lying by asking: "What's the date?" It doesn't take much to destroy the credibility of those who have none and are only acting as if they do.

Asking if they would proceed absent evidence of jurisdiction, though just a general statement, presupposes they may not always have jurisdiction. They will usually say they would not proceed without jurisdiction, but then insist in this situation that they certainly have it. This is a good place to be before proceeding to whether there is evidence of jurisdiction. The agent is insisting there is evidence of jurisdiction, and we know they don't have it. Well, excepting physical violence, there's no evidence they have it.

What if they claim they personally don't need jurisdiction, that the agency or court has jurisdiction? Again, following the model of vague to specific, I just ask what they mean by agency and what facts they rely on the agency or court acquired jurisdiction over me. The agents will continue following their model, staying vague/general; we need to keep them on point and get them to be more specific. We have to break their pattern of being vague.

When I asked Kimberly Clarke about the factual differences between income and taxable income, she responded by telling me I could read the code. That's misdirection and non-responsive-a predator desperately trying to stay vague. As if anyone hearing that conversation can't see through her facade. If you haven't heard this classic example of stupid lawyer tricks, it's at http://marcstevens.net/cos/cos20101215.html.

I like asking if the agency exists separate and apart from the individual men and women who comprise it. It's the same with the word government. Asking about the government is also a good way to challenge the opinion the laws of a particular government apply to us. While this may bring out claims about society picking representatives to pass laws, it doesn't establish any kind of factual connection between the laws and us.

The line, "If you don't want to abide by our laws, you can move" is not a substitute for a factual connection. It's a political platitude from those who are too afraid to think for themselves, those who lack the courage to let the facts speak, no matter what they say. They are submitting to social pressure, their own largely exaggerated perception of what they think the herd believes, and just don't want to stand apart.

If they think the laws apply to everyone, if that is their argument, then they need to put up the evidence they rely on, not the other way around. Statists and statist apologists make arguments that I'm someone different from the herd: "What makes you so special?" If I respond at all, then I tell them it's not an isolated thing here guys; political laws don't apply to anyone, not even to the politicians. Go into court any day of the week for traffic or taxes and you'll see it first-hand. So stop with the silly arguments or appeals to emotion and stick to the facts.

The burden of proof stuff is not something I made up; it's part of the sacred writ, the law. An old maxim is:

> "**semper necessitas probandi incumbit ei qui agit**...The burden of proof always lies upon him who alleges."
> *Ballentine's Law Dictionary*, page 1159.

It's one of the few rational principles in politics. To be sure, there are those who have a vested interest in the systematic enslavement of mankind who will try convincing us that if you get a letter from the tax people you're required to pay taxes, that *they* are not alleging or accusing you of anything.

> Why are you accusing me of being a taxpayer owing taxes?
> *I'm not accusing you of anything.*
> So you're not saying I owe taxes?
> *Of course you owe taxes.*
> But you're not accusing me of anything?

No, I'm not.
Well, I'm glad you cleared that up.

It's as if they know they bear the burden when making an accusation/allegation and believe they can shift that burden by just denying their allegation is an allegation. You see why I describe bureaucrats as children?

I had a Jennifer from the Colorado department of revenue tell me the "department" made the claim against my client. I asked if she could be more specific, not be so vague. She was robotic; it was like she was reading from a script:

> *Sir, as I told you, you'll have put your questions in writing.*
> Will you be responsive and specific?
> *Sir, as I told you, you'll have put your questions in writing.*
> Why are you refusing to be specific?
> *Sir, as I told you, you'll have put your questions in writing.*

I've had agents get upset with me and snap: "I'm not accusing your client of anything!" Great, then who is? I'd prefer to speak to them as they have the burden. When your accusations are baseless, you have to hide behind a wall of vague fictions and cowardly evade specific facts.

When we engage bureaucrats to resolve problems they started, stopping their reification process is all we're really doing. And from my experience it's very effective.

Our line of questions is constructed with the objective of stopping the attacker from engaging in the process of acting as though abstract concepts are real. Prosecutors are as bad as any, if not worse than the average bureaucrat. After all, they see wrongdoing and conspiracy all around them. Their paranoia is probably a close second to the average psychologist or psychiatrist.

Despite claims to the contrary, the questions follow a logical line of reasoning. We know we're starting from a fiction, how do we get our witness to admit it's a fiction though? Will they admit it? Yes, I have plenty of recordings where they admit there are no facts or they don't understand the question and they are not qualified. It does help to baby step them if you want to keep them on the phone long enough to make the admission though.

It's why we're asking if they have authority to stop the attack and what the grounds might be, i.e., a lack of facts. A follow-up question can be to ask them if the assessment (opinion/accusation) is arbitrary. This locks them into an untenable position because there are no facts.

The next logical step is to ask for the facts their code is applicable or "Can you confirm there is evidence proving jurisdiction over me?" That slams the brakes on their reification process. We're bringing the deleted parts of their experience back into consciousness/awareness. The violence negating the need for evidence is coming back to haunt them. With questions about the facts, they cannot hide behind their platitudes and PR. With each question their violence is becoming more and more obvious.

337

This is not going to be comfortable for anyone; there's a very good reason why parts of our experience are deleted from our map of the world.

I had a Vanessa from the Idaho tax commission tell me she could not comprehend the question about evidence proving the code was applicable. I can only think this is just a lame diversion attempt to get more time to think about a question she cannot answer. It's so far outside her known world, she freezes when asked such a simple question.

The "I don't understand the question" or from the prosecutor, "I don't think the witness understands the question" are dodges to avoid the question. I say call them on it. During the 22 January 2013 circus with some tax agents, the hearing officer pulled that crap. All Betty was doing was protecting the witness by saying the witness doesn't understand the question. You object, "*Objection*; let the witness tell me he doesn't understand." They would not permit him. So I said that anyone literate in the English language can understand the question. It riled Betty up and she warned me about being abusive. I said what is abusive is a hearing officer blocking my cross-examination.

The witness is either illiterate or a liar. So I objected and said they're lying, they're deliberately stopping my cross-examination under the guise the witness doesn't understand. If that's the case, then they're not qualified to apply the sacred writ.

Sticking to the facts is not easy when most of society is engaged in mass reification. Their maps of the world are not built on personal observations and investigation, but instead on political PR, platitudes, procedure and policy. For example, why else would republicans complain about socialism when it involves being forced to buy medical insurance, but not when forced to buy auto insurance? It's perfectly fine for governments to use violence against us to pay for services from private companies when it's something they're conditioned as Republicans to see as acceptable. They seem to have no problem with being forced to pay for Medicare, but Obamacare they do.

Republicans also don't seem to have a problem with public schools, colleges, the military, police and courts. Because they're conditioned to believe those are "conservative" beliefs. Socialism, the taking of property of one and giving it to another, is good when you take the property and give it to the military and people running the University of California, but somehow not good when taken and given to hospitals.

By sticking to the facts, we separate fact from fiction and get closer to a resolution.

Government: 100% fiction, fear and coercion.

Why do I need a license; because you say so?
No, that's ridiculous; it's the law, that's why!
Oh, I need a license because someone else said so?
You're an idiot, Marc.

The above is a typical exchange we could all have with bureaucrats who think their constitutions, codes and laws apply to us. They typically

338

don't want to say the truth so openly; owing taxes or being required to get a license is not something cops think is based just on their say-so. They'll give us orders, such as pulling over or stopping us and asking questions. But I'm sure most agents and cops will not say we're required to pay taxes and get licenses because they said so. In my experience they default to the abstract; they just deflect the attention away by saying, "It's the law."

As shown above, that's exactly what is meant by the words: "it's the law." We're looking at the facts, the deep structure of the sentence. These three magical words obscure the facts that are deleted from the sentence; they have to be to get compliance and enforcement. I think most normal adults would not attack peaceful people on only the say-so of some stranger.

A group of men and women I have never met or heard of said you have to do this or I am supposed to take your house.

This is exactly the same as saying the law requires you to do something. Of course, it doesn't pack the same punch as "it's the law," and that's why it's used. It's why I get such ridiculous statements from bureaucrats when asking about the facts the code is applicable: "Everyone pays the council tax" is not a responsive answer when asking for the facts the code is applicable.

But, even if just felt on an unconscious level, the deep structure of "it's the law" is starting to make its long-lost appearance. And it's not going to be a warm and fuzzy feeling either. It's going to be pretty uncomfortable, as evidenced by their sudden inability to put together a clear sentence. Their lack of coherency doesn't stop them from calling me an idiot though. They never seem to lose that ability.

I think there could be a mathematical formula regarding the lack of evidence to angry personal attacks. As the amount of relevant facts drops, the degree of anger and insults rises. It's an inverse ratio.

It's also the same as when a politician or bureaucrat claims the constitution is the basis of his authority to control your life and property:

These four pieces of paper give me the right to take your house.
What facts do you rely on proving they have anything to do with me?
These four pieces of paper give me the right to take your house!

What we're doing when challenging their assertions is to, as gently as possible, have them stop the reification process. We interrupt the pattern by asking questions, taking their abstract concepts and having them tell us what concepts/ideas they are trying to convey to us with the words they're using. That is all I'm doing when asking judge questions such as, "Who do you represent?"

The reification pattern and good acting is what has convinced this lawyer they are fair, impartial and independent decision-makers. It's also what has convinced those around them.

The question angers them because it's the same as an actor who has long forgotten they're playing a role and is faced with finding out right in front of their adoring audience. As long as a judge/magistrate continues forcing me to answer another lawyer's complaint, then they are not fair, impartial and independent and I refuse to stand there and allow them to continue acting as if those were not easily verifiable facts.

We've all heard the justification, "That's the system, jackass." I know that's the system, and it conflicts with the PR. That's the point of asking who the judge represents. It's just a platitude though. You may as well justify the obvious conflict of interest with, "It is what it is."

I had a Canadian bureaucrat actually say that to me when I pointed out his response the "law applies because the law says so" is circular. I had to ask, "Are you really resorting to platitudes?"

The conflict of interest with the judge is easy to show, but also goes very deep. I'll also point out that a conflict of interest is about a relationship to a party, it's certainly not limited to only direct monetary benefits. An example is where a judge is sleeping with the prosecutor. While there may be money involved, that's not the only reason why there may be a conflict of interest. Who would argue there isn't a problem in such a situation just because there is no direct financial interest?

The conflict of interest here has everything to do with the relationship every single judge has to the other players involved. This relationship, as already shown above (A forces B to answer C), has a tremendous impact on a man/woman's behavior. As such, there is no reform; the only way to get rid of it is the abolition of what we call government.

Most people still follow the model of getting a job with security, benefits,and a nice pension. Cops and firemen, like the military, can generally retire starting at twenty years service. A nice pension is certainly motive to disregard other people's autonomy; in many cases, it's motive for murder. Retiring by forty-five? Yeah, that's certainly an incentive to look the other way when your associates are abusing peaceful people. When you add in the social pressure, then it's no wonder we see so few whistleblowers.

However, the word retirement, when used in a political context, is pretty misleading. In many cases, it only means the employee has just changed positions within the agency and is getting a salary and collecting a pension. It's called "double-dipping" if you've never heard of it. It's also been called "Public Pension Piracy."

The primary source of the pensions and benefits are taxes: the forcible taking of property from an unwilling community. The cop or judge is also thinking of his family here; they're as important as anyone else's. What is going to be their overriding interest-freedom and autonomy of the individual or the well-being of their families and pensions? That's a no-brainer. Add in the prestige, power, fear and worship that comes with such positions, and it's clearly understood why they don't, or won't tolerate challenges to the rationale of their system. Calling such lawyers by their first name appears to undermine the facade they want to maintain. There's just no prestige when you address someone as Bert. Perceptions are powerful, one hell of a drug it seems.

340

It's no wonder bureaucrats don't care about the people they are damaging. Most are probably just hanging on in quiet desperation until they can retire. Aside from the psychological elements, the economic benefits are tremendous. That's one hell of a carrot dangling there-pretty potent when combined as they are.

Do the taxes collected from the courts--usually called fines, costs and fees--go into the general treasury fund? And if they do, are the funds used for salaries, benefits and pension funds? It's reasonable to assume they all go into the general fund so there's a direct financial incentive to arrest, prosecute, convict and imprison people. Again, the United States criminal cartels called government imprison more per capita than any other cartel. The PR is about the "Land of the Free," which has the highest incarceration rate.

It would be silly to think the actors involved don't know that taxes and fines pay their salaries, benefits and pensions. It's self-evident that those who profit and so heavily depend on taxation would be opposed to stopping it. They're certainly going to be the system's biggest cheerleaders; their map of the world is an obedience-based model.

From a behavioral standpoint, violent domination with no accountability drastically affects behavior. That is beyond dispute; those who need more evidence need only call a judge by his first name to get all the facts they need to put this to rest. What about the fact we are forced to pay a judge's salary, benefits and pension? Does this have an effect on a man/woman's behavior? What do the facts tell us?

While politicians in California have thousands of funds with the intent of showing there is no direct conflict of interest regarding where traffic fines are dispersed, there is no disputing the judges, like the cops and prosecutors, are paid by *first* forcibly taking the funds from the men and women of each community. Remember, monetary compensation is only one aspect of a conflict of interest, and it's not essential to there being a conflict of interest.

In proving a conflict of interest, it's immaterial where the collected fines go because judges, as well as his support staff, are all paid from the same exact source: *an unwilling community*, in exactly the same manner: *under threat, duress and coercion*. Saying the judge is independent because he is part of a "different branch" of the government is tantamount to saying a catcher on a baseball team is independent of the team because he plays a different position than the first baseman. I'm crying foul here!

While the fines are important and certainly can prove a conflict of interest, as evidence for a conflict all we need are the original sources, not the secondary ones. One thing with politicians though, there's no shortage of evidence against them.

Here are the facts:

- Men and women (group A) forcibly take money from those in society (group B).
- Group A uses the money to forcibly take even more money from those in group B.

- Group A attacks group B and pays group A to settle disputes they create or cause.
- Group A claims they are fair, impartial and **independent of themselves** (incongruent).
- Group B points these facts out and group A chants frivolous and throws group B in a cage.

If you're part of group A, and your livelihood and retirement are dependent on group B being obedient, then how fair and impartial are you able to be if they are before you for disobedience? The fact your whole life is based on others quite beneath you being obedient, you're not going to take disobedience lightly. You're already prejudiced before the poor victim comes into "your" courtroom.

Federal judges in the US owe their positions to the same people (Congress) who create and inflict laws on everyone. Is it not reasonable to expect they are somewhat biased in their favor? Does anyone seriously think they have no allegiance to the congress? That they will not be prejudiced against us when we're accused of disobeying the will of the same congress who put people who put them in office?

If you're a judge, then your entire professional and social life is based on the taking of property by force; you live by a system of slavery—it's normal to you. Why would you fight against it? If you're involved in a college football program such as the one at USC in Southern California, then you live in a certain culture. While you may never have direct contact with the violence enabling your lifestyle, given your investment in such a culture, how willing are you going to be to listen to anyone talking about the coercion supporting your football programs?

If we put ourselves into their shoes for a few moments (I don't recommend doing this for long, as psychopathic behavior is started this way) we'll see why there's so much hostility when we challenge their opinions. These are not just mere opinions or casually held ideas. They are deeply rooted, the foundation of their personalities-*borderline personalities*. If we're not obedient that's perceived as a threat to them; it's a threat to their perceptions and therefore to them personally. Obedience is a way of life, giving and taking orders. Of course you're going to take offence when you don't get the obedience you think you're entitled to.

For those who expect and demand obedience, those black swans that come in daring to question you are not going to be the highlight of your day.

A free, voluntary society means the end of college sports as we know them. Sports relying on taxes to pay for stadiums will have to change how they're funded. How many want to see that? What is more important though?

This also explains why cops react the way they do. If they think you're not being obedient to them, they start using violence to get you to be obedient, such as using a Taser. A Taser is not for police safety, that's another lie. Tasers are for obedience. There's a continuum of force that police are taught http://en.wikipedia.org/wiki/Use_of_force_continuum. After ordering you to do something and you don't do it, they'll use more force to get your compliance. If you continue not complying, they increase the force until deadly force is used. Suddenly a "routine" traffic stop doesn't seem too routine if one asks questions instead of blindly obeying.

If you really want to put a cop or other bureaucrat into a horrendous double bind, then ask them if they consider you their own personal slave. Just put all your cards on the table when they claim jurisdiction. (It's better to do this on the phone so they can't tase or shoot you in an effort to get out of the double bind). They'd certainly like to give you the beating you deserve for asking such questions.

An easy way to turn an adult into a raging, almost incoherent child is to ask, "What evidence do you rely on proving you acquired jurisdiction over me? (Yes, I have over a decade of experience doing that, and can tell you with absolute certainty it only takes a few seconds.)

Can someone whose life-whose whole worldview-is based on obedience, such as a cop, judge or juror, be fair and impartial with someone who is being accused of disobedience? Well, observation and the studies shown above give us a bleak 67-91% (Milgram) of the time they won't or can't be fair. With nine percent possibly being fair the deck is stacked against us.

The model governing their thoughts and behavior is one of unquestioning subjection and obedience. Taking the Bruner & Postman study into account, are they even able to process non-violent non-cooperation as anything other than criminal acts deserving punishment? Their perceptions govern how the facts are processed, so this is going to severely limit a fair disposition of the facts.

I have seen too many times where judges, not just in traffic court but also federal courts, reflexively assume the prosecution's burden of proof while the mythical presumption of innocence is not even given a token mention.

The allegory of the cave shows how people respond to facts that challenge life-long perceptions. I've posted plenty of IRS calls as evidence of this extreme emotional response. Just like with those in the Bruner & Postman study, there will be distress caused by the inability to process the facts; we're pulling them out of their cave:

> "...when any of them is liberated and compelled suddenly to stand up and turn his neck round and walk and look towards the light, he will suffer sharp pains; the glare will distress him, and he will be unable to see the realities of which in his former state he had seen the shadows..." Plato, *Allegory of the Cave*.

When we add in the social pressure to go along with the crowd, even knowing they are dead wrong, there is an immobilizing fear. This explains why a judge like John McDonald in Toronto, Canada, can admit there is no valid cause of action against Keith and that the ticket should be thrown out, but he's not going to do it. He'll leave that to someone else. So even when the facts can be processed, and the politician admits they're wrong, social pressure still dictates action.

In a typical prosecution, all but the defendant may be living lives based on the idea of obedience, not autonomy. Each lawyer involved is certainly steeped in such conditioning. Being a lawyer is about ever-changing rules. The jury is comprised of obedient slaves, many too frightened to stand up to the former prosecutor with the black dress.

When you add group think, it doesn't look good for anyone attacked for non-compliance. The prosecutor, defense lawyer, judge and jury may all be incapable of accepting the concept of liberty and personal autonomy. Social pressure may certainly make it impossible for one to break away from the pack because the obedience model is held by the overwhelming majority. Unfortunately, this model is also held by the most violent one in the room: the lawyer with the robe. To drag these people out of their cave of ignorance, we need to baby step them and overlap their models of the world:

> "And suppose once more, that he is reluctantly dragged up a steep and rugged ascent, and held fast until he's forced into the presence of the sun himself, is he not likely to be pained and irritated? When he approaches the light his eyes will be dazzled, and he will not be able to see anything at all of what are now called realities." Plato, *Allegory of the Cave*.

If everyone but me in that courtroom has a perception that blind obedience is a virtue, that will control their behavior and decisions. The fact I'm not accused of hurting anyone, there is no evidence the code is applicable and there are no competent witnesses are not going to be strong issues with such a brainwashed group. All they know is I was not obedient, end of discussion.

That's one hell of a conflict of interest there if you ask me. They are interested in obedience and blind compliance (strict liability, for the lawyers reading), not in administering justice. And whom are we supposed to be obedient to? Group A of course, the psychopaths who think their opinions are binding law on everyone within range of their guns. When a politician or bureaucrat claims you're subject to their jurisdiction, ask them.

> "Do you rely on any facts to support that, or am I to rely on just the authority of your say-so?"

When you call someone on such obvious nonsense, expect angry, though witty retorts, "I'm not going to debate the code with you!" or "I don't appreciate you badgering and arguing with me!"

Non-compliance is only a problem if someone hurts or is threatening to hurt someone (*Primum non nocere*), but that's non-compliance with a basic principle of social behavior understood by five-year-olds, not disobedience to a group of psychopaths. That's a pretty big difference where I'm from. The facts tell us this distinction is lost on governments and their compliant slaves and accomplices.

All this should be taken into account when discussing a conflict of interest. Certainly, what has happened before you entered the picture is more important than what happens after. It makes no sense to ignore a judge's model of the world; seems important for anyone who is going to be making decisions that directly affect your life. This is consistent with the actual written standard.

The bias or prejudice required to mandate a judge's recusal is supposed to arise from an "extrajudicial source." The bias must be to a point to prevent a fair trial/hearing: "they require recusal only when they evidence such deep seated favoritism or antagonism as would make fair judgment impossible." *Liteky v. United States*, 510 U.S. 540 (1994).

Using this standard, the evidence shows that 67-91% of the time, a judge is so conditioned, and holds a rigid view of the world dominated by obedience, how could they be fair to anyone charged with disobedience (all victimless crimes are about disobedience)?

We have evidence that judges, bureaucrats and other politicians believe their laws apply to everyone with no showing of any evidence at all. It's just assumed as if self-evident. Funny thing about a self-evident truth, it can still be proven easily, no need to resort to hostility because someone dared asked for proof. Such emotional outbursts and threats of violence are not a standard of proof as far as I'm aware.

Not only that, but almost every time you challenge jurisdiction it's not the prosecutor who stands up and starts presenting their facts, not even close. It's the judge insisting he/she has jurisdiction over us on behalf of the prosecutor. If not the prosecutor's behalf, then on whose behalf? Only the prosecutor has the burden to prove jurisdiction. So when a judge insists he/she has jurisdiction when the prosecutor stands mute, they are acting for the prosecution. Kind of obvious, isn't it? The threats of violence tend to keep people from pointing out the obvious.

Their perception of blind obedience to men and women called government was instilled long before they became a judge. Lots of judges are former prosecutors, so the bias against people like me who are charged with disobedience is from an extrajudicial source. It's reasonable that anyone whose view of the world is to respect individual autonomy, to do no harm, is not going to be attracted to a position of violent domination. A good example of an extrajudicial source of bias is tax court judge Thornton; his bias arose from all his years as a treasury attorney.

Traffic court judges and prosecutors are notorious for thinking and acting as though they have jurisdiction over everyone they set their sights on. We know physical location is not a factor because of the warrants they routinely issue, yet they do it anyway.

These are people who think they are independent of the rest of the government, despite overwhelming evidence to the contrary. That's their perception of the world because their map of the world was created through years of conditioning in government schools and then working as a government. The facts prove the prosecutor, judge and cop are paid in the same manner from the same victims. We pay and enable all of them to punish us for disobedience to their will. They are paid in the same manner, and yet they want rational adults to believe that because they

345

claim the judge and prosecutor are in different branches of the same government, they are independent of each other.

A look at the facts shows the judge forces us to defend against the prosecutor's complaint. If we have a choice between platitudes and facts, it's better to stick with the facts. Even if the only thing we accomplish is making the prosecutor's job so difficult they start to shake.

If your model of the world is based on obedience and subservience, then you may not be able to process real liberty and peaceful cooperation. Look at the military: it's not about cooperation, it's about giving and taking orders. It's all coercion. This allows them to give lip service to the concept of liberty. But when the facts are before them, it conflicts so sharply with their map of the world that they cannot be tolerated or processed in any meaningful way. That, or there is difficulty with the concept, and that is not going to help a judge or jury be fair and impartial. There's too much baggage, including this basic fact:

One group is forcibly taking money from the defendant to pay the judge, prosecutor and jury.

Apologists and honest critics will point out that judges pay taxes also, so they may hate the IRS as much as any of us; they may actually be biased against the IRS and taxing system. Yes, they might; but, I've not seen evidence of that. But I for one don't want anyone ruling against someone because of bias against them; it should always be based on the facts.

While it's true there are judges who rule against the tax agents, they are not holding the tax agents to their burden of proof on jurisdiction. They are still skipping the foundation and forcing people to address the merits. And yes, the tax people don't always read the code or add/subtract correctly, so it's hardly an issue of judicial bias when they rarely rule against the tax bureaucrats.

I'm certain if there was a judge treating the prosecutors in tax proceedings the same as they treat us (denying all motions without grounds), we'd hear about it. However, the judge is a product of the taxing system; it contributes to his map of the world. They are also higher on that pecking order, the hierarchy, and that affects their behavior towards those of us lower on the scale.

Plus, while some judges may not like taxes, that's not the same as seeing taxation for what it is: theft.

> Whee, look at me, I'm a judge! I'm untouchable; I can do pretty much whatever I want. All those peons to pay my salary, pension and the benefits. Can I really hate on a system that has me set for the rest of my life?

What about when an ostensibly private individual or group files a complaint against you? It's easy to see when it's a government or state attacking you, as the judge is clearly on the same team. Is there a conflict of interest when it is not a government attack though? The facts are very similar. Just as with a government attack, the judge is forcing you to participate in the proceedings.

While some would argue you are not actually forced to participate in a civil proceeding as you are in a government attack against you, that ignores the facts. If a complaint is filed against you, the judge does not force you to defend against the complaint, but you will have a judgment issued against you. Then the judge, on behalf of the plaintiff, will start threatening you with violence to enforce his/her judgment. If you ignore that, the judge will order armed men to enforce the judgment, including the forcible taking of your property and putting you in jail for contempt.

This violence, on behalf of the plaintiff, is why most people respond at all to complaints. You have a supposed independent third party who will threaten violence against you and possibly destroy you economically if you don't respond.

There are many blatant examples of where a judge openly and notoriously acts on behalf of a private party, but that's not what I'm talking about though. An example took place in Utah during a hearing for a motion for summary judgment. This should have been denied without a hearing, as there were facts in dispute, but since the plaintiff is a bank, the judge was bending over backwards to help. There was no illusion of impartiality and no shame.

Despite the well-established rule the burden of proof on jurisdiction is always on the plaintiff, the judge assumes jurisdiction and asks the defendant why he believes the court does not have jurisdiction. It was pointed out that the plaintiff had the burden of proof and had presented no facts and had also failed to present evidence of presence within the state and a valid cause of action. These words were wasted, as the lawyer with the robe was all too happy to assume jurisdiction on behalf of the bank's lawyer. Remember, the law means nothing to them if it gets in the way of their agenda. This is supposed to be the law:

> "If a plaintiff's allegations of jurisdictional facts are challenged by the defendant, the plaintiff bears the burden of supporting the allegations by competent proof. McNutt v. General Motors Acceptance Corp., 298 U.S. 178, 188, 189 S., 56 S.Ct. 780, 784, 785; KVOS, Inc. v. Associated Press, 299 U.S. 269, 278, 57 S.Ct 197, 200. Gibbs v. Buck, 307 U.S. 66, 72, 59 S.Ct. 725, 729." *Thomson v. Gaskill*, 315 U.S. 442, 446.

So assuming jurisdiction for a plaintiff is an obvious conflict of interest and bias, and is an inherent element of the system that cannot be reformed. It's the natural result of a system based on violence and layers of lies.

The fact the judge is going to initiate physical violence against someone who has done no harm to him/her seems enough to show a conflict of interest. Yes, it may be argued that if I take my time and money and participate, then violence may not be used; I may even get the complaint thrown out. True, but only true in the sense if I just give my wallet to a criminal he may not beat the crap out of me or kill me. It does not negate the violence inherent in the situation. Also, it doesn't make the threat of contempt go away, does it?

> Let me get this straight, you're forcing me to defend against this complaint?
> *How dare you accuse me of that! You don't have to do anything; you're free to ignore it.*
> Free? So if I do, then you'll form an opinion against me?
> *Yes, but my opinions are called a judgment.*
> And then you order me to comply with your opinion?
> *Yes, my judgment.*
> And what happens if I don't comply with your opinion?
> *I will find you in contempt and throw your insolent ass in jail.*
> OK, and this is all on behalf of the guy who filed the complaint?
> *Yes, what's your point?*

This is easier when we start with facts we can observe and easily verify, that even die-hard politicians do not dare try to spin. When in court or administrative hearing for non-compliance to a bureaucrat, what are the generally universal facts? We have one man forcing another man to answer/defend against a complaint filed by another man. Just the fact one man is forcing you to answer or defend against the complaint is evidence beyond all doubt of a conflict of interest. How can you expect the man to be fair when he is forcing you to answer?

You can't; so stop having faith in a criminal system and go by the facts before you.

Prejudgments and presumptions. Has the judge or hearing officer already decided or assumed the laws in question are applicable to me? What about the presumption of innocence? Doesn't he have to presume the statute is not applicable until competent evidence is presented and challenged before he can make such a decision? If it's a statutory crime, where the act is only a crime because of a statute, it stands to reason the statute must be applicable, and as an element of the crime, that may not be assumed.

There's plenty of evidence proving this, such as this statement from a prosecutor in Tennessee, "it is well settled law that many offenses are "malum prohibitium"; that is, they are wrong because they are prohibited by statute." Kristen L. Corn, staff attorney, City of Franklin, Tenn.

This also ties directly into jurisdiction. There's no separating the law from jurisdiction. It seems obvious that if the laws are applicable, then there is jurisdiction. I don't think the two are separated in any meaningful way with most people, especially those who profit from the current structure.

The applicability of the law should be one of the first fictions questioned. Everything stems from this. I mean *everything*. If there's no evidence the code is applicable, then that's the end of the story. That's why any challenge is resisted so much by those higher on the pecking order. I've spoken with agents in England regarding the council tax about this. I get the same question: What make you think the laws don't apply to your client? Because I'm not seeing where you have any facts to prove it, mate. This tends to bewilder agents. It's just too outside their view of the world. The law not applicable? Impossible, must not think like that.

Despite being the foundation for all their aggression against us, this is given a pass, and why would an attorney challenge this? All attorneys have an oath of office to protect, defend, and preserve the constitution and uphold the laws of the state. Even if taken from a purely economic standpoint, attorneys wouldn't challenge other attorneys on this point, as it would be impossible to put anyone on trial; there's no evidence the laws apply to anyone. And it's fairly easy to see there's more money putting on a trial than getting a complaint thrown out for a lack of jurisdiction.

Let's be rational adults here, money is a pretty big motivator. It's a motive for killing family, it's a top motive for killing in general. So it makes perfect sense lawyers would be unwilling to bite the hand that feeds them. Hey I have an idea, let's make it so we can't justify $50,000+ retainers!

Lawyers have a huge economic incentive to keep the courts busy with trials. This is not rocket science. Even if they don't take most complaints to trial, the threat of trial is essential to leveraging victims into settling.

To prove, with facts, the law is applicable, we have to start with what the law is, and then we can discuss any potential connection. Anyone who has brought this up has encountered the emotional response from those who are still conditioned to believe the law just applies to everyone. You can't even get to step one with most people, and almost every bureaucrat I've been involved with has refused to discuss it. It doesn't matter how simple you make it, they will refuse and act like children.

You cannot connect the dots between the law and me without knowing what the law is. The most common answer is, "You're here." (There's that advanced college degree at work again.) OK, please tell me what the law is and the facts connecting it to me *right here*. It all comes down to their say-so, their collective delusion. And I write delusion, because no matter how many times they fail to present any facts, they continue acting as if they believe they exist.

Even without establishing what the constitution is, there is no evidence and no politician/bureaucrat has ever produced a single fact proving the constitution and laws apply to me just because I am physically in Arizona.

I had a Debra Nostdahl of the IRS on 17 April 2013 insist there was jurisdiction after she had just told me minutes earlier, "There's no evidence the code applies." I asked her why she was so absolutely certain there was jurisdiction when she admittedly had no evidence. She suggested she could get the evidence. The fact she didn't respond is more evidence of bad faith.

Tax agents think they have an easy out when you challenge the applicability of the law; they routinely claim they are not qualified to do assessments, only the predators in Audit and Examination are. You just remind them you're not asking about the actual assessment, it's about them (Collections) thinking they have jurisdiction. If they snap back they do, you just remind them they already admitted to not being qualified to make such determinations. So now you're qualified? So I may ask the following questions:

> Would you attempt collections absent evidence of jurisdiction?
> *No, of course not, but we do have jurisdiction.*
> Is that an arbitrary opinion-is it based on facts-or did you pull it out of thin air?
> *It's not arbitrary, and this sounds like a frivolous argument.*
> I've not taken a position yet, there is no argument, just a question. When you claim, "we have jurisdiction," what do you mean by "we"?

They really hate answering such questions, where they have to explain the platitudes and PR they routinely use to cover up their crimes. I like to ask, "Do you personally have jurisdiction over me?" Unless they are the more aggressive types like cops, they will usually answer no. As shown, they will deflect attention from them to an abstraction, i.e., the agency or department they work for.

Also on conflict of interest, the cops, prosecutors and judges are all doing the same thing to us: they are applying their laws to us. The PR is that the executive branch applies the laws and the judicial branch interprets the laws. This is not what is happening though, as a few moments of lucid thought bear out.

When judges claim they have jurisdiction, they are applying the constitution and code to me; the code ostensibly gives them jurisdiction and authority over me. How is that different from what the cops are doing? Each player-cop, prosecutor and judge-uses the same basis to justify their aggression against me. If they are all claiming to have the same starting point (the code), how can they be independent and not have the same interests?

Again, the facts are clear and irrefutable. The formula is **A forces B to answer C**.

A is the judge, B is the so-called defendant; and C is the cop/prosecutor. The only way to correct this is to take the force, the violence, out of the equation. It's the very real gun in the room, and it proves beyond any doubt that the former prosecutors are working with the current prosecutors.

Because of these facts, any rhetoric is defeated:

> *I assure you I am independent!*
> You're forcing me to answer this lawyer's complaint, right?
> *Well, yes, what's your point?*
> If you're forcing me to answer his complaint, how are you independent?

We can always go back to these irrefutable facts to expose what's going on, to prove they are lying about everything they claim: that they are fair, impartial, independent decision-makers. It's all we need to show such political rhetoric is non-responsive. Look how they try to avoid the obvious. This was presented by a lawyer in Toronto in Dec. 2012 (I cannot confirm the citation though; it looks like he was paraphrasing the court):

> "That the prosecutor and the police witness are paid by the same municipal government, albeit through different legislative authorities, is of no moment in a consideration of entitlement to fair trial." *Provincial Court Judges Assn of B.C. v. B.C.* (Attorney General), 2012] BCI No. 1443.

What does this lawyer mean "is of no moment"? Oh, that gaping chest wound? It's of no moment, mate. See, if I waive my hands like this, it goes away.

A fair trial includes a fair, impartial and independent decision-maker. How is writing "is of no moment" changing the fact that judges force us to participate on behalf of the prosecutors and are paid from the same stolen money as the prosecutors?

> *You're charged with tax evasion, violating section 7201. How do you plea?*
> Your charge is of no moment, mate.
> *Brilliant defense! We're in the presence of genius everyone.*

Opening and closing statements. The opening is where each side tells the jury or judge what they plan on proving during the trial. The close is to summarize what was proven. Technically, only what is being presented at trial, or happened in the trial, should be in the opening and closing statements.

If a prosecutor goes outside the evidence, you need to object every single time. Dave in Massachusetts had a lawyer representing him for a tax prosecution. The prosecutor lied during the close, and Dave's lawyer didn't object. When asked why he didn't object, the lawyer said he didn't like objecting during opening and closing arguments. I think that's just wrong. A free pass for lying to a jury? Don't ignore such misconduct.

The prosecutor's closing argument is the last the jury will hear before going to deliberate. It's imperative to object whenever a prosecutor goes outside the evidence, whether on opening, closing argument ,or at an arraignment-more so when they are lying in front of a jury. Every single time the prosecutor starts to speculate there should be an objection.

As I've already shown, most of what is coming from the prosecutor is speculation, fictions and outright lies. I can't think of any reason not to object.

You can really have the prosecutor demonstrate his lack of evidence by using the proposed plea of guilty. I think this is like checkmating them.

While this is something we already do at arraignment, it would be effective for the jury to see it.

After the jury is seated and the judge asks if everyone is ready to proceed, I would say:

> No, I'm not ready, I'm still willing to plead guilty right now and avoid this trial if the prosecutor can just produce the evidence the code applies to me and there's jurisdiction. [Addressing jury directly] Maybe the jury needs to know I've repeatedly tried to plead guilty and the prosecutor has refused to bring forth evidence the code applies to me. All I'm asking for is evidence they're supposed to have anyway; and they've refused every step of the way, including providing me with the evidence in discovery.

Maybe the prosecutor would be screaming for a mistrial before I got done saying this. I would still use this in my opening and closing statements so the jury can see it's an easy acquittal because the prosecutor cannot meet his/her burden of proof.

In an opening, I would lay out what has already happened-how the prosecutor has refused to provide evidence and the names of witnesses with firsthand knowledge the code applies-and predict they will continue doing the same; how every step of the way the prosecutor will refuse to provide any evidence, including attacking his own witnesses when I cross-examine them. I'd include how the judge will overrule my objections to the witnesses, but sustain the same objection when made by the prosecutor.

We need to stick to the key issue: the lack of evidence and witnesses the code applies. In the opening, we just lay out what's going to happen: the prosecutor will present no witnesses with personal knowledge the code applies and no evidence.

Our close is to just summarize what has already happened. As predicted, the prosecutor was unable to provide any evidence the code applies and he attacked his own witnesses when I questioned them on their evidence.

If we use a whiteboard, then it should make for a short, focused summary of the trial. Don't bore the jury or judge any further, just stick to the same tactic we've been using throughout: hammering away at the prosecutor's lack of evidence and witnesses with personal knowledge.

This way, we are not only speaking in terms they can understand, we also don't get into problems with the judge, as people do when they mention jury nullification.

The jury is then better able to understand why we are objecting when the judge is giving jury instructions that assume the prosecutor's burden of proof. This is important because it may be the last time we get to make such statements to the jury before they deliberate.

When a judge gives a jury instruction such as "the law requires everyone to file tax returns" we object on grounds there was no evidence the law applied. While the objection probably won't be sustained, it may be what's needed to reach that one juror necessary to hang the jury and stop a conviction.

Handling common responses. Dealing with bureaucrats is no picnic; it's more draining than manual labor. After all, we're dealing with psychopaths who just don't care.

Most responses tend to be non-responsive evasions; they keep using the same ones, so they are easy to recognize and deal with. So much of this is just to get into a dialogue with them, get them to engage us in the process. Their arguments cannot withstand any scrutiny and fall apart with just a few questions; so our focus needs to be on having them speak and be as responsive and specific as possible.

Just as we use a model to communicate, so do professional psychopaths. The tactic they use is usually more important than the content of their statements. It's not that we have to worry about responding to dozens of different answers an agent or lawyer will put forth, only whether the answer is responsive or non-responsive. There are many ways they can be non-responsive: deflection, evasion, distraction, shoot the messenger, gaslighting, and other popular fallacies such as straw man.

Unless the answer is responsive, then the content, if any, is usually irrelevant. At worst, we have to be able to stay calm while being threatened or yelled at to be able to determine if they are being responsive. What's important is the process at play:

- Asking questions,
- not taking a position; and
- only accepting responsive answers.

We're guiding the conversation, taking their vague opinions and asking for the facts, having them get more and more specific until they admit they have no facts or it's clear that they have none. This will also show they are not acting in good faith with us.

We need to keep in mind they will tend to always agree with their fictions. This is helpful in leading them into a situation where they cannot continue answering direct questions on the facts. It doesn't do any good and we accomplish nothing if they don't talk to us. People always ask me, "What do I do if they refuse to speak to me?" If that's the case, then there is not much that can be done. In court it's a serious error to not inform someone of the nature and cause of the charges and proceedings, but I would not want that to be the only error. It rarely is, because with such rigid lawyers they will usually deny cross-examination. We also follow up calls with a letter/fax asking for the evidence. The lack of response can be used against them.

With the IRS or other agencies making allegations, the refusal to communicate may be construed as bad faith, and we can presume, if we're asking for facts, that there are no facts. That can be very effective. If someone is acting in good faith, then they will openly communicate the evidence they rely on and not avoid our questions.

I'm not aware of too many situations where all agents and supervisors are completely non-responsive and don't answer anything. When they refuse to answer a question, we need to examine the question to see if it's a proper question or not. Sometimes it's a great question and we can follow up with one that makes the judge look bad and his ego won't permit him to keep his mouth shut. A lawyer makes a decision and I ask, "What facts and law do you rely on to support that decision?" The lawyer snaps back, "I'm not here to answer your questions." An example of my response is, "Let the record reflect you have no grounds, you just make arbitrary decisions." "So you make it up as you go?" is also a good response.

When a tax agent refuses to answer any questions, then I do like I do in court when intending on pleading guilty: I tell the agent I'm happy to file a return with them, provided the allegation or assessment isn't arbitrary. That's usually sufficient to get them to open up and start talking. I say, This is not an arbitrary assessment is it?" When they insist it isn't, I ask them, "So it's based on facts?" Now, like the judges, I have them talking about the issues.

This is why intending on pleading guilty or settling with them is so effective; they drop their defenses thinking you want to settle things. I've got to open communication with them, but I can't if they think I'm there to argue or challenge them. So I offer to settle: "So there are facts, Mr. Wagner, because you wouldn't come after me arbitrarily would you? No, so this is based on evidence and witnesses with personal knowledge?" I've told them that we're happy to participate in an audit: "This isn't arbitrary, is it?" With the IRS, they claim they have jurisdiction to investigate if someone is "potentially a taxpayer."

Really? "So you're convinced there are sufficient facts proving you have jurisdiction over me, even as a potential taxpayer?" It makes sense to me to be cooperative and do it on their terms. They will tell me they would not arbitrarily audit someone, there has to be jurisdiction. While that admission is easy for them to make because it makes them look good, it's not possible to follow up. That's why they will employ diversion tactics.

Because bureaucrats and politicians are governed by public relations covering up their violence, there are never any facts to support their opinions and accusations. They rely on fictions and fear; knowing that, we can predict their evasions fairly easily. We can also respond appropriately if we're being attacked by them and want to limit the damage these predators intend on causing.

I spoke to an IRS supervisor on 6 August 2012; she was in Collections. As I've mentioned, IRS agents will actually admit to not being qualified to do or verify assessments; only the Audit department and Substitute for Return (SFR) units are qualified. This time, the supervisor made an admission I'd not heard before. When asked about the facts she relied on that the code was applicable to my client, she responded with: "We don't have anything to do with the code." Wow, that's a great admission!

I followed up by asking for a clarification-that there were no facts proving the code is applicable. And the response? "Sir, I'm not going to argue with you." Literate people know asking questions is not arguing. All I do is point out I'm not arguing, just asking a question: "So unless you're admitting there are no facts, what facts to do you rely on proving the code is applicable?" Stay on point and let them know you are not being fooled by their silly answers or lawyer tricks.

This agent knew she was knee-deep in crap and went into hysterical mode; she got angry and accused me of arguing and talking in circles. She stated I should go to the IRS website and answer the questions about having to pay taxes. She thought their website would be helpful in determining if my client was required to file. I said those questions are appropriate when there is evidence the code is applicable. I also mentioned that someone at the IRS had already made the determination; I just wanted the facts, if any, the determination was based on.

She hung up on me. You'll find that when you inject logic and rational thought into the situation, the bureaucrats run and hide. It's really the only weapon they have when you disrupt their reification process on the phone.

Sometimes it's best to just ignore the arguing retort and just repeat the question:

> What facts do you rely on proving the code is applicable to me?
> *Sir, I'm not going to argue with you!*
> Is the code applicable to me?
> *Of course it is.*
> Okay, but you rely on no facts to prove the code is applicable to me?

There are many times where all I have to do is not engage them in their little game and can get some more answers from them by keeping them on point. By accusing them of not having any facts, I can get them to defend themselves and answer that they do have facts. We all know there are no facts, but they will say there are so they don't look bad. Then they are in trouble again and at the least I've established bad faith because they are refusing to discuss the facts they say they rely on.

Legal advice. A common dodge in court is when we ask: Is there a valid cause of action here? and the judge will say, "I can't give you legal advice." They give legal advice all the time to fellow state lawyers, but ask a question that challenges their facade of legitimacy and all of a sudden they clam up. What's interesting is they tend to actually give legal advice when you challenge them, e.g., "I suggest you get yourself a lawyer" or, if I'm working with someone the judge will say, "I'm advising you to get a *real* lawyer" as if I'm holding myself out as a lawyer, fake or otherwise.

Normal people who understand English will immediately recognize the above question is not one seeking advice, just clarification. Advice is: "an opinion or recommendation offered as a guide to action, conduct..." http://dictionary.reference.com/browse/advice. To be asking for legal advice I would have to ask, "If there is no valid cause of action here, then should I request a dismissal?"

The lawyer is using a pathetic evasion to get the pressure off of him. They want the attention off this issue because they know, or are reckless in not knowing, there is no case or cause of action. While most people would see through this tactic, lawyers tend to reinforce it with an increasingly angry tone. It's probably to let everyone know they're serious.

If anyone did pick up on the evasion, the judge's anger is usually sufficient to get most people to back off. That's where most people choke; they don't realize the bureaucrat is just evading a difficult question.

Sticking to this issue, just as with most of their fictions, is very effective. To get them to engage me on this issue I just ask, "Are you convinced there's a valid cause of action before you?" Saying yes supports their facade of legitimacy, so they usually can't help themselves and they say yes. Great, that's dialogue and a commitment to a transparent lie. The follow-up is familiar by now: how many elements in a cause of action and where are they pled in this complaint?

In one proceeding in a Medford, Oregon court, a lawyer was confronted on this issue and he got very upset. Knowing he was cornered on his BS, he tried to deflect the attention away from himself and attempted to mislead my client (Norman) by stating Norman was not willing to participate. Norman stated that wasn't true, that since the judge was insisting there was a valid cause of action, he just wanted to know how many elements there were and where in the complaint they were presented. The judge lost patience and lied saying Norman was not interested in proceeding. He reset the hearing for another day. Predictably, the cop didn't show up at the next hearing.

I may be unwilling to participate, but that has nothing to do with whether there is a valid cause of action or not. The fact I'm *forced* to participate is evidence I don't want to have anything to do with this psychopathic lawyer; and it's no defense for the lack of a cause of action before the court.

> Sir, where is the evidence of a valid cause of action?
> *Judge: Do you wish to participate in this hearing?*
> Not relevant, where's the evidence of a valid cause of action?
> *Judge: You do not want to participate so I'll reset this for another date.*
> *Prosecutor: Objection Your Honor, there may be no facts proving the laws apply, but that's not relevant. The defendant does not want to participate in this hearing.*
> *Judge: You're right; apparently this jerk is not aware of this particular legal standard we all learned in law school: if the defendant is unwilling to participate, then the prosecution is relieved of their burden of proof. I'll reset this for another date.*

Beyond a reasonable doubt, unless the defendant is unwilling to participate.

At arraignment, when we want to discuss the motion to dismiss, which is based on a lack of jurisdiction, their evasion is straight to the point: *"We're not here to argue motions."* This is usually a very easy way to get a discussion going, *"Objection,* you're convinced the prosecutor has presented evidence proving jurisdiction?" Either a yes or no is going to open a can of worms for this lawyer. If yes, then I can challenge them before proceeding, "What are those facts, where are they in the complaint?" If no, "Then I want this dismissed for a lack of jurisdiction. They usually yell, "Denied!" You're proceeding against me knowing there is no jurisdiction? I'm getting the idea the relationship you have with the police and prosecution is pretty tight.

I can place an unsigned plea of guilty on their wooden throne and tell them, "I intend on pleading guilty" (this moots any evasion about not arguing motions at arraignment); "what facts did the cop/prosecutor provide proving the code is applicable and you have jurisdiction over me? Just show me the facts the cop has presented and this can end right now. If there are facts proving the code applies to me I'll plead guilty and pay the fine today, your move." I can't make it any easier for them...if there was evidence, of course.

If he/she refuses, I can say, "Objection, you want me to plead when there's no evidence of jurisdiction?" One of the most repugnant ideas for a judge to consider when his own pseudonym (the state) is attacking you is a lack of jurisdiction. It's as bad as the very suggestion their sacred writ doesn't apply to you.

They can't stand this question: Are there facts proving the laws of the plaintiff state are applicable in any way? It's offensive because as Rick Brown, a cop in Whitefield, New Hampshire stated, "You're implying there are people the laws do not apply to."

Rick said it was "ludicrous" to even imply the laws did not apply to everyone. He admittedly had no facts, but the implication was still ludicrous. You would think I was implying gravity didn't apply to me.

Rick seemed repulsed by the logical conclusion of his own lack of evidence. Adults accept the facts and act accordingly; children get upset because the world doesn't conform to their opinions. When it doesn't-when the spoon doesn't bend-all they have is anger. Psychopaths just ignore the lack of evidence, and continue attacking as if nothing out of the ordinary has happened.

This is how the conversation went with Rick Brown:

> So let me get this straight: you insist the code applies to Bill; I ask you for the facts proving the code is applicable; you don't understand the question; I ask again for the facts proving the code is applicable; you tell me you don't have any facts, and I'm the one being ludicrous?
> *Yes, that's right.*

Okay then.

Despite his admitted lack of evidence, Rick still went into court and did what he usually does. He repeated his arguments knowing he had no evidence. Not only did the judge allow him to get away with it, twelve people still convicted Bill. The judge and jury all knew Rick admittedly had no evidence proving the code was applicable, yet were somehow convinced the code was violated beyond a reasonable doubt. It brings up the question prosecutors don't want to answer:

How do you prove a code was violated without first proving the code is applicable?

Their map of the world doesn't allow for the possibility their laws don't apply to everyone, at least the ones they're attacking. We've all heard them say the law or code allows them to do X to us. Without the law as a justification or cover for their attacks, they are just violent psychopaths and they seem to know it. Not much fun being a psychopath for hire; most people tend to frown on overtly psychopathic behavior. Most people will still rally behind psychopaths who wrap themselves in flags though.

I'm not here to answer your questions. This one is also said in anger with a healthy dose of arrogance. This is a little tricky when in court, because the judge may be technically correct depending on what you're asking them and when. The burden of proof for jurisdiction is always on the one who filed the complaint-the one trying to invoke the court's jurisdiction. It's not on the judge; his/her burden or obligation is just to make sure sufficient evidence is presented to prove jurisdiction.

I'll remind the judge the question is really to the prosecutor who should be there to prosecute his complaint.

I like to also respond with, "Are you here in good faith to administer justice openly and honestly?" That's usually enough of an attack on his ego to get him to start talking, at least to answer yes. Good, then I intend on pleading guilty, I just have a few questions. Then I start asking them.

But he's not technically correct if I ask the judge if I'm presumed innocent, and follow up with asking if he's under the assumption the laws of the plaintiff state apply to me. We can only defend against what is disclosed. A fair hearing, justice and due process, require notice and opportunity to defend.

How can I defend myself adequately if the judge refuses to say whether he's presuming the laws are applicable? And how silly it is to refuse such a thing when the facts make it clear the judge absolutely presumes the laws of the plaintiff state apply to me? He's forcing me to answer the prosecutor's complaint. Is he withholding evidence, or pretending there's evidence and just refusing to disclose it? I think those are serious offenses. We may also get the mother of arraignment lies: "Jurisdiction is a trial issue."

If we accept the judge's statement, then it makes sense to use that against the prosecutor, "Oh, you're not here to answer my questions? No problem, it's not your complaint. Where's the prosecutor? He's 'got some splainin to do.'"

It makes no sense to disagree with the lawyer with the robe, use his statement to your advantage. If the prosecutor or cop is not there to prosecute, then there's nothing but the complaint for any judge to go by. In a typical complaint, there's nothing about jurisdiction and applicability of the laws. So the judge is in a real bind if I mention there are no facts to establish jurisdiction. He/she can disagree with me; they're like children, so they will disagree. They may continue to be obstinate and refuse to answer whether there are facts:

> Well, you're standing there mute, mate. Neither you nor the prosecutor has anything of substance to offer, the prosecutor isn't here, and you're not answering questions. I see no grounds for this to continue.

Unfortunately, arrogance and a lack of evidence go a long way with lawyers. A lack of evidence isn't always grounds to get them to drop attacks. As arrogant as they are, they still usually respond when I mention there are no facts to prove jurisdiction, "I assure you I have jurisdiction!" Great, I've got your *argument*; what *facts* do you rely on, tough guy?

Yes, because we can all rely on the assurances of a man who forces us to answer some cop's complaint. Very trustworthy, and that's not taking into account how his pension is paid. They like giving assurances.

I got this garbage after waiting three months for the facts proving the California constitution and code applied to my clients: "I want to assure you that the FTB has authority to assess, enforce, and collect state income taxes." Three months for a non-responsive form letter. Nice assurance though.

So if a lawyer shouts at you, "I'm not here to answer your questions!" fire right back at him: They're not for you, jackass; they're for the one who filed the complaint. But if they're not here and you're insisting there is evidence of jurisdiction, then I want those facts disclosed to me; otherwise, you're not permitting me to defend myself.

Talk about hubris! A lawyer forces you to his courtroom, insists on behalf of other lawyers that they have jurisdiction and when asked about the facts to prove it, can only respond with, "I'm not here to answer your questions!"

So the lawyer is insisting there is jurisdiction and still doesn't want to answer questions about the facts they rely on proving jurisdiction, then I politely ask if he/she is withholding evidence from me so I cannot defend myself. Withholding evidence is generally seen as not only a violation of due process, but considered a crime. Ask a judge, "Is withholding evidence (or covering up a lack of evidence) a regular part of the process with you?"

You can also ask, "Can you confirm the prosecutor has presented facts proving the code applies and you have jurisdiction over me?" Always start vague and go for the throat by getting more specific.

Always say, *objection* first though, just to cover yourself because you may need to appeal and it usually stops the process.

Withholding evidence is generally considered obstruction of justice. While judges have conveniently given themselves absolute immunity, given their professional and social connections and networks, it's doubtful we'll ever see a judge indicted for withholding facts on behalf of a prosecutor. See how that works? If judges, mostly former prosecutors, are aiding prosecutors as a matter of standard procedure, why would a prosecutor then try to indict them? While they gave themselves immunity, such criminal actions are still grounds for dismissal of a complaint, and that's our main objective anyway.

Mike Nifong, as a prosecutor, withheld evidence and falsely accused some college students. Nifong was disbarred by the North Carolina State Bar only because his victims had the money to fight him. He was also held in contempt and spent a whole day in jail. He was sued by his victims and filed for bankruptcy.

Make no mistake: when a judge refuses to disclose facts proving jurisdiction-especially when his assumption of jurisdiction negates his obligation to presume innocence-it's a crime and they should be accused of it every single time. Examples are § 139 of the Canadian Criminal Code; elsewhere in the realm it's generally referred to as "perverting the course of justice." Australia has used the following that has been quoted by Canadian courts:

> "the most that can usefully be said is that the notion of "pervert(ing)" the course of justice involves no more than an adverse interference with the proper administration of justice." Meissner v R [1995] HCA 41; (1995) 130 ALR 547 (1995); 69 ALJR 693; (1005) 184 CLR 132 (16 August 1995). http://www.austlii.edu.au/au/cases/cth/HCA/1995/41.html

From New Jersey is NJSA 2C:29-1 "Obstructing administration of law or other governmental function". And as shown judges, can obstruct justice; Sammy Kent is one example:
http://en.wikipedia.org/wiki/Samuel_B._Kent.

Not only should such objections be made, we should automatically file to change the judge, and also file a complaint about them to several agencies. Not that they will go anywhere; we know they probably won't, but file them anyway because the abuses should not be hidden and no one wants to have complaints against them. It may also be taken into account when raises are due or promotions. And if it makes the bureaucrat the object of office jokes, then that works too. Maybe the social pressure will get them to change their anti-social behavior for the better. It may help those who work with the judge decide to blow the whistle on them.

And I don't mean complaints just from the victim, I'd like to see dozens, if not hundreds from those who listen to the show and file their own complaints. I think judges and other bureaucrats in Melbourne, Australia would be just a little concerned that people from California, Alberta, England and New Zealand were also filing complaints about their conduct:

> I heard from the victim of judge Wilson and a witness on the No State Project that judge Wilson assumed jurisdiction on behalf of the prosecutor. I know enough law to know that's the burden of the prosecution. That judge Wilson, while arrogantly insisting there was jurisdiction, refused to disclose the facts, if any, the prosecution had given him. Such insolence is shocking, even to my American sensibilities, that judge Wilson would pervert the course of justice and so brazenly aid the prosecution.

"Hey, Bert's getting complaints from Long Island now. What the hell did you do to get a complaint from Long Island?"

I also suggest we make YouTube videos about our complaints. This way friends and family who search for their dad who's a judge will get our videos.

And when we file our complaints, I would present the facts proving they are exhibiting psychopathic behaviors. With judges, it's easy. We just need to show the callous disregard for others and the incessant lying.

Making up fake straw men. Another tactical favorite of bureaucrats is addressing an issue you didn't raise. They just make them up. An example is: The prosecutor has admitted he has no facts proving the laws of the plaintiff state are applicable to me. The judge responds with: "The laws of the state are presumptively constitutional." A good reply to that is: "Who are you responding to?" They really hate when you ask that question.

It's not correct to classify it as a straw man fallacy because it's not clever enough. It's not just a superficial misrepresentation, it's a complete fabrication, or red herring. They're two different issues entirely; one is an issue of fact, the other an issue of law. You always know you've got them on the ropes when they refuse to address the actual issue you're raising. So the smart thing to do is to keep hitting them, keep asking for the facts.

I've encountered this many times, even when as a guest on radio shows. What state apologists may do is attack my motive when they are confronted with a lack of evidence: "I think Marc just wants to sell books." This is just a childish variation on the *ad hominem* fallacy. Okay, let's say my only motive and intent is to sell books. Now tell me, "What evidence do you rely on the people calling themselves governments have any voluntary support?"

But the same can be said of politicians and judges, can't it? The judge denied my motion because he's only interested in making money,

361

protecting his pension and courting favors from the cops and prosecutors. Now that may be true, and there's certainly evidence proving that. But looking at motive doesn't relieve any of us of our burden of showing whether what I present has merit any more than a close investigation of the judge's denial of a motion. We can set motive aside and still judge the action/information presented.

An example is where a judge denies a motion for judicial notice. Melinda Lasater in San Diego denied that the California court system is adversarial. We can prove her decision is wrong, and do so independently of her actual motive. While motive may be important, it's not relevant to establish the merit of a position, information or argument. Intent is much more important and the intent is to subvert any chance of justice in the court.

Is there evidence proving Melinda's intent was not to administer justice as a fair, impartial and independent decision-maker? The fact she forced the defendant to participate in the proceedings on behalf of the cops and prosecutor proves that beyond any doubt. The denial of something as well-established and known as the court system being adversarial, as opposed to inquisitorial, is certainly very strong circumstantial evidence her motive and intent was to aid the prosecutors.

What other rational explanation is there for a former prosecutor denying the obvious? When you consider that to have a true adversarial proceeding there must be an antagonistic assertion of rights, and the prosecution didn't and couldn't do that, then the motive and intent become clear. If Melinda admits the obvious-the system is supposedly adversarial-then she opens herself up to the fact the prosecution has not presented an antagonistic assertion of rights. That means the complaint is not fit for adjudication and must be dismissed.

So judges-mostly former prosecutors-just deny the whole demurrer or motion and don't give any grounds. This enables them and the prosecutors to continue with their little show. Most people are not going to question what's happening, and if someone does, then the judge can blow it off and flippantly tell you to appeal it (which costs the average man/woman a week's paycheck). If you persist, then men with guns come to the rescue, as the lawyer must resort to threats of violence to get the attention away from what's happening. Is this taught in law school?

> Professor, I have a question. What if a litigant calls us on our arbitrary ruling?
> *You do the only logical thing you can: you answer by threatening the bastard with contempt. Have the police stand right next to them to remind them who's boss.*

What's happening is a disconnect in the communication. This is done either by design or ignorantly. There's an easy way to identify a disconnect in communication. Kids use this when saying, "Yeah, well my brother can beat up your brother."

They must break the line of communication or it will be revealed there's no evidence to support the opinions against you. Questions have a way of uncovering the truth. So you get *ad hominem* attacks and other logical fallacies until they feel it's necessary to pull the intimidation card.

I pay my fair share Marc, who'll build the roads without taxes? This is clearly an emotional reach to create guilt and play on the human emotion of getting something for nothing. I don't entertain such distraction and evasions: Not relevant for our purposes. What facts do you rely on proving jurisdiction? Is your opinion arbitrary, yes or no?

Just stick to the point like a broken record, even if just discussing these things among friends or on the internet. It's not rude or unprofessional; not responding to you and constantly evading the issue is unprofessional.

There are no facts, that's why their main tool is violence. Still, they persist with such evasions: Marc doesn't your client live in Toronto? Can you confirm there's evidence proving jurisdiction? Is it your opinion your laws apply to me just because I'm physically in Toronto?

What are you an anarchist!? I like this one. It's really tempting to engage them when they ask: "Are you advocating anarchy? Without laws, there would be anarchy and chaos." I am inclined to say, "Hell yes, of course I am, it's called being *normal*, and anarchy means no rulers, not no rules and chaos." But that's not relevant on a call to an agent, at least not until the attack is dropped.

You know the pattern now. All I'm advocating here is a responsive answer to my question: What facts do you rely on proving the laws apply to my client? I can always correct them later that anarchy is not chaos. What's relevant at the moment is the evidence.

Anything other than the facts is non-responsive, which amounts to anything they say; there are no facts. Their anarchy question, just as "who will build the roads?!" is just a diversion from their lack of anything of substance to support their claims.

"But you live here!?" This is very common; I put a question mark there because it always seems to me the bureaucrat doesn't really believe it either. To politicians, their henchmen and apologists, it's as if the applicability of the code is as evident and provable as 1+1=2. Just so long as no one asks them to prove it.

Okay, please explain how and why the code is applicable because I live in this area. *What facts to do you rely on to prove that the code applies because I live in this area*? If they respond, then the best they can do is "because the people said so." They're engaging in reification (the people) and not identifying any facts connecting the code to me.

The only thing they have to "prove" their codes apply to us is "someone said so." If you press the issue-and you very well should if you want to get to the truth-all they can offer is, "*Because we said so.*" This gun right here tells me you'll comply with my every whim you little jerk.

I mentioned this in *Adventures,* so suffice to say here, if anyone claims the constitution and code is applicable because "Uh, dude, you live here," -then ask what the constitution is.

You can go another route by asking them: "How do you know that's true?" We're always going from vague to the specific: so it's logical to ask your accusers how they know the constitution and code apply to you because of your physical location. After the predicable stuttering and stammering, they'll probably come back to the code itself. Now we've come full circle (yes, pun intended).

Even if we went by the document or the code itself, where does it say it's applicable to everyone within a certain area? An area defined in the code itself? Even if the code had that in there, it's circular and not evidence it applies to anyone. The best that can be shown are the opinions of lawyers, such as in court opinions. An example was shown earlier from California:

> "The term resident is defined to ensure that every person who is physically present in California for other than a transitory purpose and thereby receives the benefits and protections of its laws and government, contributes to the support of the state (*Whittel v. Franchise Tax Board* (1964) 231 Cal.App.2d 278, 285)." FTB PASS 2190 (REV 02-2008).

This is another great example where you just say someone is a resident and the code magically applies to them. When you examine the actual opinion, you'll notice some sleight of hand and see why it's more effective to challenge the facts the code is applicable than get bogged down in statutory construction and interpretation. The opinion for resident from the code cited in *Whittel* is: "Every individual who is in this State for other than a temporary or transitory purpose." On the FTB form, they use "present in California" as if synonymous with "in this State." That's misleading at best.

There is also the situation in Maine where someone who lives in Russia has a warrant issued against her. A lawyer in Maine, Bruce Malonee, filled out a paper, called it a warrant and declares he has jurisdiction over a woman in Russia. So the claim of physical presence in Maine or the state is still not a valid argument that the code applies even at the state level. As mentioned, the US Congress acknowledges no boundaries of their jurisdiction. Looks like Bruce has federal aspirations-he's thinking like a real Fed.

As I did with a lawyer in Washington on 8 March 2013 who insisted the code applied because of geographic location, you don't need to say much to prove there's no evidence of jurisdiction:

> Marc: "Tell me exactly why the code is applicable because of geography."
> Susan Hinkle: "Well it just is."

This is a professional litigator with an advanced degree. She claimed the agent is not trained in the law and could not answer complex legal questions. It didn't faze her in the least when I said it was an issue of fact, not law.

She didn't agree with me that if an agent is insisting they have jurisdiction they should be able to present the facts the alleged jurisdiction is based on. To me, that's a statement of the bad faith inherent in every act of political aggression. This woman essentially endorsed arbitrarily proceeding against peaceful people. This callous or flippant disregard for the autonomy of others is why I describe them as psychopaths. It's not just lacking evidence, it's knowing you lack evidence and not caring. Even worse, they ratchet up the attack when it comes out publicly you have no evidence.

As of this writing, Susan's boss (her husband) and the Chelan county commissioners have ignored this misconduct. They could not care less that there's no evidence of jurisdiction. The bar association has strongly encouraged them to respond to my complaint. (They have since dropped the complaint, finding no wrongdoing.)

Why would someone, knowing they have no evidence of jurisdiction, *increase* their aggression against a peaceful man or woman? A callous disregard for others, pathological lying, no shame or guilt for the damage they are causing to others, inflated ego... **They are psychopaths**.

I spoke with a lawyer with the NHES named Lon Seal, and he had some typical responses you may hear. When I raised the issue that the lead agent admitted there were no facts proving the New Hampshire constitution and code were applicable to my client, he could not understand. He had an issue with the basic question, "What facts do you rely on proving the const. and code are applicable to me?" He stated several times he did not understand why the laws of a state would not apply to someone within that state.

I said, "You keep mixing things up, that's why you don't seem to understand. I'm talking about individual men and women, and you keep throwing in fictions." It unnecessarily complicates things, making it impossible to have a rational and productive conversation. But that's the goal lawyers have in mind; they stay in the abstract. It's much safer because it's what they know; they escape responsibility for their actions.

They sometimes try to put the burden on me, asking me to give me an example of where there code would not apply. Don't be tricked into answering just because you can prove a negative. If they pull this one, just remind them the one making the accusation bears the burden of proving it, not the other way around. So I say, "Wrong answer, what facts do you rely on? Unless you're ready to admit what we both already know-the opinion was pulled out of thin air-then what are your facts?"

This reveals the mind control, the conditioning we've all endured. They view the law as omnipotent, magically applying to everyone as a given. Lon Seal told me that himself. He claimed the "applicability of the law is a given" and they "don't have to prove the code is applicable." He also stated, "They [laws] apply as a matter of law...you don't need facts to prove it." Try to process the depth of such stupidity.

A man with a doctorate degree believes: **the laws "apply as a matter of law."** Does anyone think this man engages in much critical thought? One has to be trained not to question such nonsense in order to do their jobs. There doesn't seem to be any evidence lawyers and government apologists/employees are trained in critical thought and being rational. If they're taught critical thought, then why don't they practice it? And if they are taught it, why do they resist being open and honest? Why are they always so hostile when questioned?

> *How dare you accuse my profession of not engaging in critical thought, we're as open to investigation into the truth as anyone.*
> Really? What facts do you rely on that your code is applicable to me?
> *That's a given, I don't have any facts and it's silly to even ask the question. The laws apply as a matter of law.*
> That's circular; what facts do you rely on the code is applicable to me though?
> *You're implying the code may not apply to everyone; that's ludicrous.*
> You're right, excellent critical analysis.

It seems incredible that people, presumably trained in cross-examination (admittedly critical to fact-finding), would be so oblivious to using such techniques when it comes to jurisdiction. This is the power of the government concept and the resulting social pressure to not point out the obvious.

What would really shake them up is to have a judge tell them it's not a given, they need to provide facts. An example of this happened in a motor vehicle hearing in San Diego when a cop named Samson was asked what facts he relied on proving the code was applicable. He objected claiming the facts the code applies were irrelevant and had nothing to do with why they were there that day. I was pretty surprised when the hearing officer corrected him and told him that had everything to do with why they were there. The cop did not give a responsive answer and the hearing officer overruled the objection, but it was still a nice change from the usual rubber-stamp of every stupid thing cops/prosecutors say.

A prosecutor named Clark Askins from Texas told me he believed the applicability of the code "goes without saying." So I asked if the applicability of the code was an essential element of a code violation and he agreed. He also agreed that, as an element of the violation, it had to be proven beyond a reasonable doubt.

So it doesn't go without saying, it has to be proven beyond a reasonable doubt by facts from a competent witness, someone who has personal knowledge of the matter. He said he understood, though he thought all the other elements the cop testifies to prove the applicability of the code. I asked him, "What testimony proves the code is applicable? All he had was that the cop "observed a violation."

So I reminded him that was circular and he disagreed asserting my argument was circular. But you're the one claiming that the fact the code is applicable is the cop's *accusation* that the code was violated. So the cop's claim he saw you violate the code is now somehow evidence proving beyond a reasonable doubt the code is applicable? It comes down to this principle which plays out every day if we're paying attention and questioning:

The code is applicable when we accuse you of violating it.

It's reification in action again. Their laws apply because they said so: *vox et preterea nihil*. We can break the pattern by asking, "How do you know it's true that the code is applicable when you accuse me of violating it?"

The idiocy is hard to wrap your mind around though. Using their "logic," how would they prove the law applies when there's no accusation it was violated? If the law is applicable when it's violated, and there is no accusation yet, then how can they prove it applies at all?

I've asked many bureaucrats and politicians this question: What evidence do you rely on to prove your code applies to me just because I'm physically in Keene, New Hampshire? I've gotten no responses.

You have a driver's license. This is common; Samson from the example above used this when Delilah asked him what facts he relied on proving the code was applicable. Samson objected to the question on grounds it had nothing to do with the hearing. While the hearing officer denied his objection, Samson answered the question with, "You have a driver's license." The hearing officer accepted this example of putting the cart before the horse. It's the same as saying the code is applicable because you have a social security or insurance number. Another example is if you filed a tax return.

There are obvious examples of how silly this is when we look at so-called US copyright violations by people in Australia who are neither US citizens nor have a social security number.

It's also not an answer to the question when asking for facts the constitution and code are applicable. What does a driver's license have to do with a written instrument no one bothered to sign? So you have to object or remind them they're putting the cart before the horse: Was the constitution and code applicable to me before I got the license? Getting the license was to avoid going to jail, and the social security (or insurance) number was either mandatory or effectively mandatory because it's not possible to function in today's world without it.

So you can cut through the nonsense and just ask if they know how and why the constitution and code become binding on someone. Usually just asking what the constitution is factually is enough to get the agent to back off their opinion; they'll often claim to not be qualified. Good, now we're on the same page.

I had a Montana lawyer/prosecutor tell me, "The code applies to all who commit a crime." Sorry, Ms. Prosecutor, I'm kind of stuck on linear thinking with these things. When does the code become applicable, before, during or after the alleged crime is committed? The same logic can be applied to other contexts:

> *You owe taxes, Marc.*
> What facts do you have the code is applicable to me?
> *You owe taxes because you didn't pay when due.*
> Pardon me? What does that mean?
> *The law requires you to pay taxes when due.*
> But what facts do you rely on the code applies at all?
> *You didn't pay the taxes when due.*
> What facts prove the code applies at all?
> *Wesley Snipes went to jail.*

It's rather pernicious to coerce someone to do something, such as get a driver's license, and then try to use that as evidence against them. So the fact you forced me to do this proves the law is applicable, is that your thought process?

The driver's license argument *presupposes* the foundation argument: If you're physically in California, then the constitution and laws apply. That's why they argue that if you want to drive a car, then you have to get a license because the code, (that already applies to you because you're physically in California), requires it.

If someone hits you with this fallacy, just ask them if the laws of the state would apply if you didn't have a driver's license. You'll find that this silly argument will be eliminated in a true Socratic way.

That's just semantics. This used to be a popular criticism; I don't get it much anymore. It was always very common with radio show hosts that hated what I was presenting. This is just an arrogant way of trying to dismiss a lack of evidence. You ask about evidence proving you're a taxpayer and because they can't answer they beat their chests saying, "That's just semantics!"

It really is one of the least intelligent evasions they use.

All I do is ask them what they mean by that. What do you mean that's just semantics; do you realize I'm asking for facts? Of course, asking, "Who the hell are you responding to?" also works nicely. It's a metaphorical bitch-slap to their arrogant face.

Probably the best thing to do is just tell them to stop trying to look like a scholar and just answer the question. To get them to stop playing word games, just ask them what they are trying to convey to you when they use certain words such as law or resident.

The birth certificate. Is a birth certificate evidence of citizenship or that the constitution and code apply to you? It's another case of putting the cart before the horse and presumes there are citizens, body politics and states.

Factually, it's not much different than a constitution; it's just a piece of paper. In many places, the certificate is compulsory: you get it for your child or you go to jail. If anything, it records a birth and is evidence your parents did what they were coerced to do.

As previously stated, there has to be a pre-existing state for there to be citizenship. But as with the claim that geographic location means the code applies, all we need to do is ask, "Why do you believe that; what makes you think a piece of paper my parents were forced to submit means the code applies to me?"

The only answer you'll get, if any, is, "Because it's in the code" or some other circular nonsense.

What should not be overlooked is that these people are claiming the law applies to us the moment we're born. This ties in with the nonsense that the law applies if you are physically in the area politicians call the state.

Again, are you a member of the Catholic church because you're born within a parish? Some church official draws lines on a map, and if you're born within those boundaries you're magically a member of the church? Does that sound rational to you?

Our objective and tactic. Keep the objective clear when we're being attacked by these psychopaths: it's to be left alone. This is damage control; it's our main *objective*. Our *tactic* though is to constantly point out the lack of evidence; all the governments (men and women) have are opinions backed by guns. That is done, as discussed extensively already, by looking at the facts, comparing them with the opinions and then asking questions for the psychopaths to answer designed to bring out their contradictions. The words don't match the actions.

Even if we're activists who may be using the courts to make a point, to publicize abuse, to demonstrate the criminal basis of the concept of government and the gross evil it enables, our overall objective is to be left alone. Isn't that the end of activism, to be left alone to live our lives?

We still go into court and show how it's all based on lies and aggression. Why focus on a narrow part of the abuse when we can focus on the main issue, one that most already agree to: using coercion to provide services is wrong. The abuse comes from the anti-social behavior caused by the government concept. The government concept, the subject of this indictment, is the cause and should not be ignored when we're in court.

Those who go into court or into an administrative proceeding with the goal of teaching a jury or government apologists are usually not going to prevail. It makes no sense to me to engage in a contest of opinions, and *that's exactly what you're doing when you make legal arguments*. Break this down and really think about it: You're trying to convince aggressive strangers that your opinions are better than theirs. That's even worse when you're dealing with a herd mentality and intense social pressure to conform.

In situations where bureaucrats are making the decision, you really don't want to be in a contest of opinions because we all know who's going to prevail there. Anyone who has engaged bureaucrats knows they don't care about your opinions; don't try to change that. We don't want to engage them in the reification process, we need to stop it, and asking questions is effective precisely because it stops their reification. We're jamming a big monkey wrench into the works.

When you walk into court, there is a singular focus: the lack of facts to back up their opinions. That's it; let that be the game plan and you'll be very effective. It's much more effective because it's not a clash of the abstract. All you're doing is pointing out something the jury is able to see and understand, e.g.,

Do you have facts proving the code is applicable to me?
Objection, relevance!
Sustained!

It's the objective against the subjective, and not subjective against subjective. That's what happened in Mike's first tax evasion trial in Sept. 2012. We're not all going to have twenty-seven witnesses all declared to have no relevant testimony. It's certainly easier to convince a jury the prosecutor presented no evidence to prove an element of the code violation than it is to convince them the opinions they brought to the court with them are wrong. Their opinions are probably the same as the judge and they're not going to want to disagree with a judge.

We're meeting the jury at their map of the world; know your audience. They probably have as difficult a time wrapping their minds around the reality the constitution and code don't apply as the agents I speak with. On 14 January 2013, I asked Steven with the California Franchise Tax Board if there were facts that the code applied to my client, and he said after I asked him three times:

"I don't know how to answer that question."

But juries will understand when the cop or tax agent admits the applicability of the code is an element of the charge. They'll understand that as an element of the alleged code violation, it must be proven beyond a reasonable doubt. If Steven is in front of a jury, do you think this so-called tax expert would still be considered a credible witness if that was his answer to a question for the facts? You just follow up with:

You have no evidence that the code applies; so your opinion the code applies is arbitrary?

Maybe he'll want to rethink his other answer. It doesn't matter, there are no facts and that'll be obvious. This is where his lawyers will jump in to the rescue and in the process discredit their own witness to our advantage.

When they refuse to answer a question about specific facts relied on, then asking the above question will help back them into a corner. If they testify the opinion is not arbitrary, then they must provide the facts for their testimony to be consistent and credible. Don't let them off the hook here.

If you're lucky enough to get a jury, then you have to play to your audience and use the path of least resistance. They aren't there to hear about, and they don't care about, your political opinions. If you want to make the point the system is criminal, then let the criminals demonstrate that for you. Does this mean you may anger the judge and prosecutor? It could-you're dealing with criminals-they're psychopaths and they don't have adult coping skills. That's the reality of the situation. The fact you may be afraid to ask questions because you don't want to upset the judge is because you know you're dealing with a callous criminal.

But if you want the jury, who were coerced by this predator to be there, to believe the judge is a criminal and not being fair, then a fit of rage from the one in the robe is going to prove it, not you telling them that. Let the jury see the former and current prosecutors working together to cover up the lack of facts proving each element of the code violation. Every time the judge bails out the prosecutor and his witness, object and get discussion in front of the jury.

Objecting every step of the way and demanding facts and not getting them is going to have an impact, at least more of an impact than trying to teach them something even as obvious as there are no states. People watching will question why the lawyers keep objecting to questions on the evidence. We can bring it up in a closing argument, reminding the jury that every time we asked for facts the code was applicable, there was an objection. No one testified the code was applicable, and if they are permitted to say it does apply, we won't be able to cross-examine them about it. Prosecutors need the applicability of the law to be assumed by the jury; they'll practically tell the jury that and the judge will too in his instructions.

People can grasp all this. Jurors don't care and won't pay attention to drawn out legal discourses about the name in all CAPS and other irrelevant and meritless points.

I have never seen a cop or prosecutor mention anything about the name in all CAPS, so why bring it up? Even if you bring it up on cross-examination, they can just give an innocent answer that it's procedural. The jury will probably buy it. Why take the chance when all you need to do is challenge the opinions they are already using against us.

What are you going to do, try arguing with the witness, even an expert whose job is to testify? And when the judge sustains the prosecutor's objection on relevance or for being argumentative, then you're stuck trying to convince the jury on close. Again, you've already lost the jury; they likely are going to side with the judge that the issue is irrelevant.

It puts a burden on us during cross-examination: we have to try to get a cop or tax agent to agree to it, and I don't see that happening. So we stick to what we did throughout the psychopath circus: point out the lack

371

of facts and the objection sustained the witness could not testify. We stick to what the jury can already relate to: for tax evasion or willful failure to file, we bring out the threat, duress and coercion to negate any assumptions of willfulness.

That's already part of their experience and they can identify with it. It's a common bond the jury will have with a defendant in a tax evasion charge. We all pay out of fear, not because we believe we're required.

I had someone at a private company agree very easily with this recently. Her company was served with a wage garnishment, and I asked if we could look past the terminology; did she agree she was being threatened to take my client's money and send it to the franchise tax board or was she required to do it? She agreed it was to avoid the threats of punishment, not that they were required: "I know that to be the fact." She assured me: "This is not an idle threat." She related some examples where they have been punished by tax agencies in the past.

We need to stick with what the jury, mainstream people for the most part, are able to identify with. This is common sense; we do the same with bureaucrats as already mentioned. It's why I always ask them if a lack of evidence is grounds to dismiss. Once it's clear what my audience will accept as grounds to dismiss or acquit, then I know what I need to do. I need to show there's no evidence. It's not guaranteed of course; we're dealing with dishonest, callous individuals. But it's going to be more effective than taking a burden on myself and trying to teach the jury or bureaucrat something new they probably can't relate to.

Every time we take a burden of proof on ourselves we're taking the burden from our attackers. We're diverting attention away from their greatest weakness. That doesn't sound like a good tactic and should be avoided. Their attack is based on diverting attention away from their lack of evidence, be it threats or legal gibberish such as citizen, city, constitution, required by law etc. So don't let them utilize their silly diversion tactics; don't ignore the gun in the room and don't let the jury either.

In court, prosecutors try diverting attention away from the coercion and focus on the roads built with tax money. So we counter by bringing the focus on how the money was acquired because that's evidence of why we're paying, to avoid the punishment:

> Yes, the prosecution is correct, the money the IRS coerces from us does go to build roads, and just as the cotton industry didn't require coerced labor to thrive, we don't need to be terrorized, robbed, prosecuted and caged to build roads. And because we pay to avoid the threatened punishment, we are no more required to pay them as slaves were *required* to pick cotton. They picked cotton to avoid being punished, same as why we all pay taxes.

Don't confuse their coercion with being required.

They may even quote a dead lawyer that taxes are what we pay for civilized society. Well, I believe as you do, civilized people do not threaten people to provide services. Civilized people don't confuse threats with being required.

And they don't dare try to tell you that there are no threats involved. They'll say things like: "Oh, but no one likes to pay, but we're all required to pay our fair share."

Oh, nobody likes slavery, but cotton doesn't pick itself. And what nice clothes that cotton makes. Just like all those great roads and drone wars, indefinite detention and a total surveillance state.

The typical tactic of lawyers is to disrupt the flow and progression of questions. One of their favorites, because it also drives you nuts, is the nefarious: "Objection, asked and answered!" This almost never means you're repeating a question already asked where a responsive answer was given-oh no. And this is a big clue you're dealing with a weasel hell-bent on keeping the truth from coming out. When they pull this crap they're laying their cards on the table so everyone knows they're dealing with a troll.

An example of this ridiculous evasion and protection of a witness is from a 22 January 2013 hearing in New Hampshire. It's beyond stupid-but it's very effective at derailing a cross-examination and making you want to claw your eyes out. It went like this: Chris Lianos is the witness; he's a field agent for the New Hampshire Employment Security bureaucracy, a state agency. This was supposed to be a hearing on his determinations made while on the job:

Marc Stevens: "Do you work for the state?"
Betty Thomas: "Objection, asked and answered."

It's hard to stay calm when they won't allow an answer to such a question. That's the purpose of such an objection. I protested of course, saying the question hadn't been asked so it couldn't have been answered. Like you, I could see what was really going on and objected that Betty, the hearing officer, was again protecting the witness from having to say exactly what the "State of New Hampshire" really is. They know full well that the state is not the ground, and because it's their only fact that you're in the state, they have to always avoid any discussion of what the state is factually. Otherwise it would go like this:

Do you work for the state?
Yes I do.
Do you know what the state is that you work for?
Of course, I'm not an idiot like the people we tax.
Good, factually what is the state?

373

It'll be obvious he's not going to say the ground, he knows better. It's why almost every single cop I've asked on cross has not been permitted to answer what the state is factually.

I've even asked them to tell me what the answer allegedly was so I could move on to the next question. Their response? Betty just said move on to your next question. No, what was the answer to this question? She just repeated, "Move on to your next question." In hindsight, as I've even done before, it's probably best to call them out on how unfair they are being and refuse to participate any further. The client and I did tell them it was a circus and they were fooling no one into thinking this so-called hearing was fair.

It's usually best to demand that the alleged answer be given, and point out they are deliberately misstating the truth. If they're recording or there's a court reporter, we can just ask for the question and answer to be read back. That'll make the psychopath regret the objection.

And why worry about answering a question a second time anyway? What, and save five seconds it would take to say yes or no again? Because not getting an answer is the objective when saying, "asked and answered." You'd think this phantom answer took the witness six hours to deliver they resist it so much.

Betty even claimed that what the state is "is not relevant" to proving Bill is in the state and subject to the state code. Such mind-numbing stupidity is by design though, to derail your cross and get you upset. It's tough, but we need to recognize it and call them on it and do so very calmly.

Betty Thomas is a typical psychopath; throughout the circus, she was robotic, maintained no emotion, and went through the motions regardless of the damage she could be causing Bill. Betty just didn't care, even when caught in her devious tactics and lies.

When we go into these hearings or any problem resolution with a bureaucrat, we have to know and prepare to interact with a cold-blooded psychopath, someone who doesn't care. It should never come as a surprise they are non-responsive and lie incessantly.

Dealing with such people can seem surreal because we can't make sense of how someone can be so callous when dealing with other people. We can't understand how someone publicly caught in their lies just continues to lie without any hint of embarrassment. We think there should be shame or embarrassment, something to govern their behavior that would indicate "hey jackass, they're not buying this crap, try something else." But that's not there. They don't care, and we can't change it; we have to be aware and communicate better with them.

That is one of the toughest parts when dealing with them: they're intentionally trying to get under your skin. It serves two purposes: 1. They avoid having to provide facts, and 2. It makes us look like the bad guys.

It's a good thing they pretend to administer justice and feel a need to make things look good or we wouldn't have a chance.

They stop conflating political and geographic. When they get into trouble because I'm just asking for the evidence, some will stop conflating the political with the geographic. But it doesn't help them any to try saying you're within the territorial jurisdiction of the state as some kind of evidence there's jurisdiction. Some prosecutors and judges try to make a distinction between the state and the territorial jurisdiction of the state:

> ""It is a general rule of criminal law that the crime must be committed within the territorial jurisdiction of the sovereignty seeking to try the offense in order to give that sovereign jurisdiction." *Ito v. United States*, 64 F.2d 73." Memorandum written by Nicholas Cort, New Hampshire deputy attorney general, January 2013.

What are the limits of the "territorial jurisdiction"? Does it extend beyond the state? And how does physical location make the code applicable and why? What is that based on? What evidence do these people (the sovereignty) rely on proving they have any jurisdiction over me? "First base!"

The offense is always a violation of the state law and has to be committed within the state. So we get caught in the circular loop again. Where do the psychopaths get their jurisdiction? It's from the constitution and code; so the obvious question is still: What facts do you rely the constitution and code apply to me and you have jurisdiction over me?

Using whiteboards. This is a great visual aid. Even the lowest traffic courts tend to have whiteboards or just the easel available. If you're being attacked and they don't have them, it should not be a problem to bring your own to the court. This is an excellent way to continually show the prosecutor's lack of evidence proving the essential elements of the code violations they're alleging. It should be present the whole trial. Remember, we're sticking to what the jury can relate to: the prosecutor proving each element beyond a reasonable doubt, and hammering away at it incessantly with objections.

I would start in my opening by showing the jury the elements that must be proven. In a tax evasion prosecution, at least in the United States, there are four essential elements:

1. The constitution and code are applicable to me;
2. The constitution and code created a legitimate tax liability;
3. I believed there was a legitimate liability and obligation to pay;
4. I chose to not pay the legitimate liability.

We know from experience the psychopaths don't like us focusing on the first one; they will violently insist that the code's applicable and may be assumed. Many of us have been threatened with contempt if we dare challenge this element of the alleged code violation.

When they call a witness, I object on grounds the witness lacks personal knowledge of the four elements (Rule 602-type rules). If there's an issue, then, standing by the whiteboard and pointing to the four elements, I would demand the prosecutor inform everyone what evidence they rely on proving personal knowledge. If this is denied and they have made no connection, then I would tell the jury each time is happens:

> Members of the jury, we can see the prosecutor has no evidence the witness has personal knowledge as required by the rules. You may want to ask the judge why such important rules don't apply here today. If your life were on the line, you'd probably think it would be a good idea for the judge to have all of us go by the rules of evidence. Not doing so is at minimum misconduct.

Every question the prosecutor asks I would object: Objection, relevance; there's no connection to any of the four elements of the alleged code violations. This follows the above by demanding the prosecutor show the relevance to the jury-how does the question relate to the four elements of the code violation? Which element of the crime is this question about?

I would start my cross-examination by asking if the witness has any testimony proving any of the four elements. Sir, can you please tell me which of the elements of the code violation you have testified to? Larry Burns did not permit this question to be answered when Mike in Idaho asked the IRS expert witness on cross-examination. You may have to rephrase the question and instead ask if any testimony relates to any of the elements. Then you ask which ones and how they relate: Did any of your testimony relate to the constitution and code applying to me? How did your testimony that I received money from Acme prove the code applies to me?

If we ask the witness if he's testified and *proven an element beyond a reasonable doubt*, then there may be a reasonable objection. There's no reasonable objection when asking the witness which of the elements they are testifying to. Can you see now why prosecutors refuse to be specific in pretrial about which witnesses are relied on for which elements of the code violation? If they are so confident they have sufficient evidence to prove every element beyond a reasonable doubt, then why refuse to be specific?

And it's no defense for the prosecutor to claim they are presenting circumstantial evidence; the testimony/facts must still relate to the elements of the code violation or else it's not relevant. If the testimony/facts are not relevant, then they are not evidence:

> "**evidence.** The means by which any matter of fact, the truth of which is submitted to investigation, may be established or disproved. That which demonstrates, makes clear, or ascertains the truth of the very fact or point in issue, either on the one side or the other. Lynch v. Rosenberger, 121 Kan 601, 249 P 682..." *Ballentine's Law Dictionary*, page 424.

Show the connection/relevance to at least one element of the code violation, or the witness may not testify. It's pretty simple.

During the entire direct and cross-examination (the trial), the jury should hear nothing but incessant objections the witnesses have no personal knowledge and no relevant testimony to the four elements. If the trial were fair and not a psychopath circus, you would not have to object so often. But it is and we should make it impossible for them to make it look fair.

We keep track of how many elements have been testified to, like the scoreboard in a baseball game. I encourage the jurors to also keep track in my opening statement:

> Members of the jury, there are going to be lots of objections this week: and the prosecutors are going to do whatever they can to divert your attention away from their lack of evidence, while I'll be objecting to keep the focus on their lack of evidence. You can negate and neutralize their lawyer tricks though. An easy way to do it is to keep track. Just write down these four elements, and as we go along you can write down which witness testified to what elements the prosecutor must prove beyond a reasonable doubt.

Knowing the witnesses lack personal knowledge yet still putting them on the stand is prosecutorial misconduct. And the judge not applying the rules and permitting it is denying a fair trial and perverting the course of justice.

This would make it more difficult for the judge to even require closing statements, let alone pass anything off to the jury for a decision. Sir, the jury and I have kept track through this entire circus; not one witness testified to these four elements, so there's no reason to continue. If there is hostility, I would object and again put the burden on the prosecution to be specific about which witness testified to each of the four elements.

This way, the jury, before closing arguments, will again see the prosecutor refuse to connect any of the witnesses and their testimony to the elements of the alleged crime.

This also applies to objections about the prosecutor's exhibits. The exhibits must be relevant to be admitted and considered.

During my close, I use my board with the four elements showing how I kept score. I just review what happened throughout the trial. This is important because the jury can relate to all of it; we're not covering any new ground and they're familiar with the process by now. They will hear the judge say the burden of proof is on the prosecutor to prove every element beyond a reasonable doubt. If any jurors have been keeping track, there shouldn't be any points for the prosecutor.

It will tough for the prosecutor to paint me as some kind of radical when all I've done is hold them to their burden of proof. Smart prosecutors know it's very bad for them to ignore their weaknesses, such as not having direct evidence proving willfulness. So they spin the irrelevant testimony and exhibits that their corrupt partner, the judge, let in despite the rules. Ignoring a weakness seems to magnify whatever the weakness is, so they will really spew the legalese and platitudes.

During the prosecutor's first close, I would be objecting on grounds their arguments are not based on any relevant testimony from a witness with personal knowledge: *Objection*, misconduct; the prosecutor's argument is outside the facts in evidence.

We have to anticipate this on close because we're probably going to go first. The prosecutor can have two closing arguments: the first and then a rebuttal. Because the prosecutor is the one with the burden of proof, they are the ones the jury gets to hear last before deliberations. This doesn't mean we can't object though; if they go beyond the evidence. We must object for the jury to hear and to preserve the issue if we have to appeal.

Because we anticipate this, we can have a very effective, straightforward closing argument addressing the most important issue the jury can relate to: the prosecutor's lack of evidence for each element. They've watched the prosecutor desperately try to avoid the issue:

Ladies and gentlemen, it is going to be very easy for you to quickly vote for acquittal today. We've all seen and heard these lawyers try to divert your attention away from their lack of evidence proving each element of this alleged code violation; they're on our scorecards [pointing to the whiteboard]:

1. The constitution and code are applicable to me;
2. The constitution and code created a legitimate tax liability;
3. I believed there was a legitimate liability and obligation to pay;
4. I chose to not pay the legitimate liability.

We've seen that every time a witness was called by the prosecutor, I objected on grounds the witness had no personal first-hand knowledge of any of these four elements, and every time the judge refused to apply rule 602 and allowed the witnesses to testify anyway. The prosecutor, aided by the judge, couldn't show evidence of personal knowledge. So, on direct examination there was no testimony relevant to the elements of the alleged code violation.

During my cross, you saw me ask each witness if they had personal knowledge of any of these four elements of the alleged code violations. Predictably, the prosecutor and judge would not allow the question. Why would they do that with such a simple question? Do you have evidence? Objection!

You all saw how both the judge and the prosecutor agree that the witnesses lack personal knowledge of the matters; legally they should not have been permitted to testify because nothing they said was relevant.

These four elements determine the relevance of the testimony and exhibits. The prosecutor could not show relevance, and resisted any connection of the testimony and exhibits to these four elements of the alleged code violation. Maybe they think we're stupid, deaf and blind, or have a serious short-term memory problem.

Now these lawyers will try to spin all the irrelevant fluff they presented, thinking you're not smart enough to know what went on here during this pretended trial, not smart enough to keep a simple score of which witnesses testified to which four elements the prosecutor must prove beyond a reasonable doubt. And if you ask them, they'll resist you too, because they have no evidence. Facts? Where? Relevant evidence and witnesses with personal knowledge? Where are they? If they had relevant testimony, then they would have demonstrated a clear connection to each element of the code violations.

Instead, they resisted every time I objected and demanded a connection between the testimony and these four elements. Don't forget the prosecutor's own actions in this court, relentlessly avoiding any proof their witnesses have personal knowledge of these four elements. It's as shameful and insufficient as accusing you of murder, and then refusing to identify the victim and how they were killed.

Look at my scoreboard, everyone; if you've been keeping track, then you'll agree that there's no reason to deliberate. All that's required is reasonable doubt on one of these four elements; we have reasonable doubt with all four, not just one. Ask them about it; they cannot address this without lying to you again.

The prosecutor has proven something beyond a reasonable doubt though: they have no witnesses with personal knowledge of the four elements of the code violation. There's no doubt they failed to present any relevant testimony and exhibits. It's also beyond doubt that the prosecutor knew he had no evidence to prove the code applies and that he had no witnesses with personal knowledge. The technical terms for this are prosecutorial misconduct and malicious prosecution.

You were all forced to be here, and the prosecutor has wasted your time by showing you no witnesses with personal knowledge and no proof of any of the elements of the code violation beyond a reasonable doubt.

Now don't be surprised when they spew political platitudes about needing to build the roads and how we may not like paying taxes but it's our responsibility. It's all they've got, because they have no evidence.

And when they try using logical fallacies such as appeals to emotion and authority, then just look at our scorecards and remember they had no witnesses with personal knowledge of the four elements of the code violation they accused me of. It's about evidence not political platitudes about the roads and libraries.

You should be very aware that as they do their close they will not mention these elements of the code violation, they won't tell you which witness testified to each element.

The prosecutor would have to try to rebut all that or just ignore it. But what can they say? They cannot always convince all twelve people that they presented testimony from witnesses with personal knowledge. The twelve watched the prosecutor utterly fail to make a connection throughout the entire trial, and not just failing to show relevance, but fighting to not have to show any. When they refuse to demonstrate the relevance and the witness's personal knowledge, it's damaging to their presentation. Failing to prove relevance should be fatal to their case.

I've done this recently with Betty Thomas. She insisted her questions were relevant, despite my objections and demand that she demonstrate a connection proving the constitution and code were applicable. All she could do was just deny the objection and tell me I could appeal her decision. If the question is relevant, then the connection can be demonstrated.

I can guarantee that if a prosecutor objected to *my* question on relevance, I'd have to show the relevance or else the objection would be sustained, and rightfully so. That 's why I focus on building a foundation for my questions, because objections on relevance are very common when prosecutors know the questions are "devastating to [their] case."

And if I went through this in front of a jury, and the prosecutor lied in their closing arguments that they did present relevant testimony, then I would object on grounds the prosecutor is lying and is engaging in further misconduct. This keeps the focus on our main issue: the prosecutor's lack of evidence. The jury sees an unrelenting attack on the prosecutor's lack of evidence, and will have dozens of objections from the prosecutors themselves as proof they lacked qualified witnesses.

In my rebuttal I could go back to the scorecard and remind everyone the prosecutor could not prove the witness has personal knowledge of the matters and no relevant testimony for any of the elements of the code violation:

> Regardless of how the judge rules on my objection, we can all see from the scoreboard that the prosecution has failed to present any witnesses with personal knowledge; we don't need the judge to agree with us to remember what we've all seen here today.

Not only is this a rock-solid issue the jury can easily relate to, I think they would be so tired of it being brought up they'd be itching for the opportunity to acquit so the psychopath circus could finally end. It's effective because the jury has watched the prosecutor object to their own witnesses and fail to show any relevance of their witnesses' testimony. When asked to show a connection, they could not, and they also see the judge allow them to get away with it.

How many times do I need to object and ask the prosecutor to connect the question to an element of the code violation-which they can't do-before the jury is convinced beyond a reasonable doubt there is no relevant evidence/testimony? Since every question must be relevant to an element of the code violation on direct examination, I'd object to every question. The jury will see the prosecutor unable and unwilling to show relevance and should be convinced after only a few questions.

I'm guessing that most people have not had such experiences in court. They have not seen prosecutors objecting to their own witnesses, so it's difficult to relate to. It happens every time with me though. It seemed odd at first, to see prosecutors objecting to the competency of their own witnesses. Then you realize what's really happening.

An example of a scoreboard is:

	The constitution and code are applicable to me	The constitution and code created a legitimate obligation	I believed the const. and code created a legitimate obligation	I could pay but I chose not to
witness 1?				
witness 2?				
witness 3?				
Evidence?				
Evidence?				

This is a very effective way to make it as easy as possible for everyone in court to follow and understand. I'm certain that judges and prosecutors will be objecting to this. After all, it is devastating to their case, which consists of baseless opinions, platitudes and logical fallacies.

Jury Servitude

A fair trial is supposed to include a decision by an impartial jury; this has long been the hallmark of the American and English court systems. But, as with the presumption of innocence, is this also a fiction? What do the facts tell us?

No one is invited to be a juror; everyone acting as a juror has been forced to do so. You get a jury summons and there is always a threat from the presiding judge: you show up or you'll go to jail and pay a fine. Of course, they use political words to cover up their violence, such as if you fail to appear, you must appear and show cause why you failed. In the real world, this means: Do as I say or go to jail. Same facts, different words. It doesn't matter what words are used, the same concept is being conveyed.

The evidence proves beyond any doubt that forcing people to do things will cause adverse behaviors-violence begets violence. It's an easy formula.

Who is this contempt going to be directed at? How or will it manifest itself? I can't know for sure. If your life is on the line though, why take a chance? If they are promising a fair trial, then make them prove it's fair.

It's easy to see and understand that forcing twelve people to listen to lawyers arguing for a few days is going to cause general feelings of contempt. So I've long recommended questioning prospective jurors during the *voir dire* regarding any prejudice or contempt the man/woman may have as a result of being forced to be a juror. I would ask point blank:

Do you have any bias against me because the judge forced you to be here under threat of jail?

381

Think about this; it's reasonable to conclude that people forced to appear on a jury may harbor ill feelings about being forced away from their friends, family, their job and their television. It's a no-brainer. Slavery doesn't make for the best system of justice, does it?

Let's first examine if the juror has a moral or other issue with being forced to perform. Maybe I'm wrong, but I'm fairly certain most people don't like being slaves, even for a good cause or just a few days. Though I can hear statists now:

> I don't mind being a slave if it means just one life is saved.

If a juror is questioned about harboring prejudice or contempt because the judge is forcing them to be jurors-always under threat of jail-then there's a real problem to be addressed. How truthful will they be? Would they lie to serve on the jury? Maybe they don't want to tell the truth because they rightfully fear the judge can throw them in jail for contempt. This goes directly to whether the juror holds any bias or prejudice, so it's a relevant question.

I doubt the lawyers benefiting from this slavery are going to sit still and quietly watch a juror be questioned about the gun in the room. The last thing a prosecutor wants in a tax proceeding is a juror who may think beyond what the lawyers tell them. They're going to come unglued with such questions. But it'll be like a cross-examination, they won't permit a *voir dire* of prospective jurors. I imagine that would be considered a pretty bad error, at least in those parts where they claim a defendant is entitled to a fair trial with an impartial jury. The courts have been pretty consistent with the PR about juries being impartial; there are many citations holding the denial of a proper *voir dire* to be a reversible error, with no showing of prejudice or harm. In lay terms, like a denial of cross, it's a pretty bad error to make:

> "In Whitlock v. Salmon, 104 Nev. 24, 25, 752 P.2d 210, 211 (1988), we held that while a "trial judge may reasonably restrict the right of supplemental attorney-conducted voir dire. . . he may not prohibit the right altogether."" *Leone v. Goodman*, 105 Nev. 221, 221 (1989).

> "There we concluded that, in a criminal prosecution, denial on voir dire of the right to pose questions such as that here proffered ["defendant's right on voir dire to disclose prejudices resulting from prospective jurors' experiences as victims of crimes similar to that for which the defendant stands trial"] constitutes reversible error. See United States v. Poole (Appeal of Finkley), 450 F.2d 1082." *U.S. v. James Poole et al. Appeal of Willie Thomas*, 450 F.2d 1084.

> "Denial of proper question during voir dire is always reversible error and will not be subject to harm analysis. Penry v. State (Cr.App. 1995) 903 S.W.2d 715, rehearing

overruled , certiorari denied 116 S.Ct. 480, 516 U.S. 977, 133 L.Ed.2d 408, rehearing denied 116 S.Ct. 759, 516 U.S. 1069."

"A broad latitude should be allowed to a litigant during voir dire examination. This will enable the litigant to discover any bias or prejudice by the potential jurors so that peremptory challenges may be intelligently exercised. Lubbock Bus Co. v. Pearson,277 S.W.2d 186, 190 (Tex.Civ.App.-San Antonio 1955, writ ref'd n.r.e.). Although we recognize that voir dire examination is largely within the sound discretion of the trial judge, Loesch, 538 S.W.2d at 440, a court abuses its discretion when its denial of the right to ask a proper question prevents determination of whether grounds exist to challenge for cause or denies intelligent use of peremptory challenges... Respondents contend that the trial court's refusal to allow the questions was harmless error. We disagree. The trial court's actions, which resulted in the denial of the Babcocks' constitutional right to trial by a fair and impartial jury, was harmful. Texas & Pac. Ry. v. Van Zandt, 159 Tex. 178, 182, 317 S.W.2d 528, 531 (1958). Therefore, we hold that the trial court's refusal to allow questions during voir dire addressing the alleged "liability insurance crisis" and "lawsuit crisis" was an abuse of discretion and was reasonably calculated to cause and probably did cause the rendition of an improper judgment." *Babcock v. Northwest Memorial Hosp.*, 767 S.W.2d 705 (1989).

Michael A. Caddell, Houston, Texas attorney in 2004 cited Babcock: "this court held that a trial court's refusal to permit a *voir dire* question intended "to discover any bias or prejudice by the potential jurors" is a reversible error." And from the federal court in the United States:

"Indeed, it has been characterized as an essential component of an impartial jury trial as long ago as by Coke and Blackstone, 3 and as recently as by the Supreme Court in 1965 in Swain v. Alabama, 380 U.S. 202, 85 S.Ct. 824, 13 L.Ed.2d 759 (1965). "The function of the challenge is not only to eliminate extremes of partiality, on both sides, but to assure the parties that the jurors before whom they try the case will **decide on the basis of the evidence placed before them and not otherwise.**"4 Id. at 219, 85 S.Ct. at 835...While the conduct of a voir dire examination is a matter within the broad discretion of the trial judge, Ristaino v. Ross, 424 U.S. 589, 594, 96 S.Ct. 1017, 47 L.Ed.2d 258 (1976); Ham v. South Carolina, 409 U.S. 524, 93 S.Ct. 848, 35 L.Ed.2d 46 (1973); Aldridge v. United States, 283 U.S. 308, 51 S.Ct. 470, 75 L.Ed. 1054 (1931), the exercise of that discretion is limited by "**the essential demands of fairness.**" Aldridge, supra, at 310, 51 S.Ct. 470. A voir dire that has the effect of impairing the defendant's ability to exercise intelligently his challenges is ground for reversal, irrespective of prejudice. Swain v. Alabama, supra, 380 U.S. at 219, 85 S.Ct. 824; United States v. Lewin, 467 F.2d 1132 (7th Cir. 1972)." *U.S. v Rucker*, 557 F.2d 1046.

"nonetheless the challenge is "**one of the most important of the rights secured to the accused**," Pointer v. United States, 151 U. S. 396, 151 U. S. 408. The denial or impairment of the right is reversible error **without a showing of prejudice**, Lewis v. United States, supra; Harrison v. United States, 163 U. S. 140; cf. Gulf, Colorado & Santa Fe R. Co. v. Shane, 157 U. S. 348." *Swain v. Alabama*, 380 U.S. 202 (1965) (emphasis mine).

There it is-not my words-this is the supreme court saying it's "one of the most important...rights" in a criminal proceeding. I think we can safely say that if you dare exercise it though, judges will fly into a fit of rage. (Something like this may get us our first on-the-bench fatality--it may be enough to cause a heart attack or a stroke. I've been waiting for reports of spontaneous nosebleeds. We could start a dead pool-see who gets a judge to rage hard enough to give himself a heart attack.) First, ask the jurors if they have any bias or prejudice against you, and if the judge doesn't allow it, object and ask him why, addressing him by his first name:

Why is grandpa dead, mommy?
Someone called him Frank, dear. His little black heart just couldn't take it.

When you don't have to show prejudice, you've got a pretty bad error. You don't have to prove there would have been a different outcome to the trial, only that it happened. This is as bad an error as a denial of cross-examination and defense. And I demonstrate how we can easily use the judge's own rigid behavior and prejudgments to commit all three.

Knowing how bad an error it is, we've got to exploit this to our benefit. Based on experience, we know judges will not permit such questions; I've seen it many times where the judge will not permit anything that makes the prosecution look bad. So it makes sense to really hammer this point and manipulate the judge into committing a reversible error by denying a proper *voir dire*.

One double bind we can put the judge in is based on the alleged impartiality of the jury: How can there be a fair and impartial jury if they're only there because they were coerced under threat of jail? They are not there out of any primary interest to administer justice; they're there to avoid going to jail.

You can make excuses about forcing the accused to participate in the trial, but what about the jury? Juries are not accused of any crimes. And make no mistake, the courts have no problem with slavery; this is another example:

384

"The trinoda necessitas was an obligation falling on all freemen, or at least on all free householders. Vinogradoff, English Society in the Eleventh Century, p. 82. From Colonial days to the present time conscripted labor has been much relied on for the construction and maintenance of roads." *Butler v. Perry*, 240 U.S. 328, 331 (1916).

There are those all-important roads again, always used to justify slavery, genocide, economic destruction, etc.

Those comprising the courts have no problem with slavery as long as it is a type of slavery accepted by dead white lawyers for the building of roads and the military. As long as the slavery was considered by the legal cult as "exceptional," then the slavery was not only moral, but necessary for the existence of governments themselves: "The great purpose in view was liberty under the protection of effective government, not the destruction of the latter by depriving it of essential powers." *Perry* at 333.

And they don't stop there; James Clark McReynolds and his fellow psychopaths go so far as to declare what they really think of us:

> "**There is no merit in the claim that a man's labor is property**, the taking of which without compensation by the state for building and maintenance of public roads violates the due process clause of the Fourteenth Amendment." *Perry* at 333 (Emphasis mine).

Re-read that first sentence a few times and really let it sink in. If our labor is not ours, then whose is it? And if it does belong to those called government, how and why did they acquire it, especially if their own labor is not theirs? If our labor is not ours, then why should anyone be paid for what they think is their labor? I saw online a quote where someone claimed this McReynolds (he wrote the *Perry* opinion) was "a man of stern morality and firm conservative convictions".

http://en.wikipedia.org/wiki/James_Clark_McReynolds.

I'd say that slavery's cheerleaders have questionable morals at best.

This is another example where custom-not principles of right and wrong, and not reason and critical analysis-is given as a flimsy excuse for mass injustice. But that's the government concept at work; we cannot expect anything else.

I'm not aware of any studies ever done on psychological issues caused by being forced to be on a jury. How many innocent people have been convicted because of contempt directed at the accused? What about conviction based on social pressure to conform and obedience to authority? They may have felt it was the only thing they could do to avoid the wrath of the judge. It's a matter of obedience to authority, and the statistics are against us.

How can we ignore the coercion, especially when we know there's usually some kind of trauma involved? While some may accuse me of having confirmation bias myself-that all I tend to see is violence and coercion when examining government actions-how is that different from what we can all observe and verify so easily? If I have any confirmation bias, then it's certainly a bias heavily in favor of the facts before me, not political PR.

Even the supreme courts recognize innocent people are convicted:

> "He requires the guiding hand of counsel at every step in the proceedings against him. Without it, though he be not guilty, he faces the danger of conviction because he does not know how to establish his innocence." *Powell v. Alabama,* 287 U.S. 45, 69 (1932).

There are probably many legitimate variables as to why innocent people are convicted, and this is just one. What sets it apart from what lawyers would reference is that it's an error that's accompanied by childish rage from the judge because it's a collateral attack on the pretense of legitimacy of the courts.

Let's now examine the other side: the juror has no (conscious) moral or other issue with being forced to perform. In other words, the juror appears to honestly have no problem with the use of force to ostensibly administer justice. This is truly someone put into a schizophrenic double bind, and I would use the *voir dire* to bring this out. Why should I make this easy for people who want to make decisions about my life? Gregory Bateson wrote:

> "The organism is then faced with the dilemma either of being wrong in the primary context or of being right for the wrong reasons or in the wrong way. This is the so-called double bind. We are investigating the hypothesis that schizophrenic communication is learned and be-comes habitual as a result of continual traumata of this kind. That is all there is to it." *Ecology,* page 182.

The prospective juror already knows they're being coerced, but tends to delete the coercion from their experience because it contradicts the PR that the courts and juries are administering justice. Questioning the juror on any prejudices that could influence their decision, such as those caused by being treated as the judge's slave, will bring the deleted portions of the experience back into consciousness. That brings about the double bind.

This isn't a comfortable place for the juror and judge to be in. I'm also sure the prosecutor is not going to like the ginormous monkey wrench I just put into the works; prosecutors tend to like stacking the jury with those in favor of the government. They want people who are law-abiding and obedient to authority; that if there's an issue with the law you comply until the law's changed. They don't like losing jurors who will act as their rubber stamp and improve their conviction rate.

The potential juror can just lie and say they have no problem being forced to act as a juror. You can challenge him/her on this, "So you don't mind being the judge's bitch, I mean slave?" I would ask them point-blank if they're okay with slavery. I'm sure lawyers and state apologists would object to that question, but can they articulate factual difference between being forced to be a juror and an overt form of slavery? The grounds for the objection are only because they may not like the question, not because it's an improper question. Unorthodox or unusual, yes, but not improper or irrelevant, as it attempts to uncover any prejudice they may have. As far as I know, not liking a question is not legal grounds for an objection.

The essence of slavery is being forced to perform, the legal definition includes: "Involuntary servitude…" *Ballentine's Law Dictionary*, page 1186; and involuntary servitude is self-explanatory, but for state apologists it's defined as "Compulsory labor…" *Ballentine's Law Dictionary*, page 665. The interwebs also has:

> "Slavery is a system under which people are treated as property and are forced to work… Forced labor is when an individual is forced to work against their will, under threat of violence or other punishment, with restrictions on their freedom." http://en.wikipedia.org/wiki/Slavery

"When an individual is forced to work against their will, under threat of violence or other punishment," that is factually identical to the process of getting people to act as jurors. Yes, the lawyers will not hesitate to add the legal justification for the slavery of their fellow man:

> "Slavery implies involuntary servitude-a state of bondage; the ownership of mankind as a chattel, or at least the control of the labor and services of one man for the benefit of another, and the absence of a legal right to the disposal of his own person, property and services." *Plessy v Ferguson*, 163 US 537, 542.

The facts are clear: people are not invited to be jurors; they're coerced under threat of jail and other punishments. They may be given a token payment, but being forced to perform is slavery.

Let me also point out a glaring inconsistency with these lawyers. I'll re-quote the *Perry* opinion and then the part from *Plessy*:

> "**There is no merit in the claim that a man's labor is property**, the taking of which without compensation by the state for building and maintenance of public roads violates the due process clause of the Fourteenth Amendment." *Perry* at 333 (Emphasis mine).

> "Slavery implies involuntary servitude -- a state of bondage; the ownership of mankind as a chattel, or at least **the control of the labor and services of one man for the benefit of another**, and the absence of a legal right to the disposal of his own person, property

and services." *Plessy v Ferguson*, 163 US 537, 542. (Emphasis mine).

What I glean from this is: slavery is involuntary servitude-the control of the labor and services of one man for the benefit of another-except when done by men and woman called government. Slavery by government is the privilege of citizenship and residency, which isn't slavery because they said so.

Slavery is something openly supported by people pretending to be government. This is nothing new. Make no mistake, the religiously revered United States constitution and its apologists were still supporting it well after even the English statists moved on to only covert slavery:

> "The state of slavery is of such a nature, that it is incapable of now being introduced by Courts of Justice upon mere reasoning or inferences from any principles, natural or political; it must take its rise from positive law; the origin of it can in no country or age be traced back to any other source: immemorial usage preserves the memory of positive law long after all traces of the occasion; reason, authority, and time of its introduction are lost; and in a case so odious as the condition of slaves must be taken strictly, the power claimed by this return was never in use here; no master ever was allowed here to take a slave by force to be sold abroad because he had deserted from his service, or for any other reason whatever; we cannot say the cause set forth by this return is allowed or approved of by the laws of this kingdom, therefore the man must be discharged." *Somerset v Stewart*, (1772) 98 ER 499.

That was some clear thinking from English courts in the 1700's, excepting, of course, taking a man and forcing him to labor in the military and to build roads. This is ostensibly from the greatest American legal minds of the nineteenth century:

> "The Constitution of the United States recognises slaves [people] as property, and pledges the Federal Government to protect it." *Scott v. Sandford*, 60 U.S. 19 How. 393, 395 (1856).

The constitution somehow protects slavery-people as property. It's still used for that purpose today; just look at any tax prosecution if you doubt this. If you're under attack, even for something as heinous as selling raw milk, what's the justification? The constitution-a pledge to protect slave owners. Every single restriction on your life, liberty and property is justified by some pieces of paper no one bothered to sign.

Actually, the constitution does not protect slavery; it's the psychopaths who use it as justification that are in the business of protecting slavery.

The courts have explicitly stated the constitution was not to protect the people, the Citizens. The only protection is for the slave owners and the system of slavery; our modern society where the few control the many by force. That's the government concept in action. This is the "supreme law of the land" everyone. The sacred writ-the law itself-is and always has been about protecting slavery. You can kill the messenger, but that doesn't change anything.

It's truly disgusting reading what these people, the architects of the law itself, believed; how they spoke of and treated fellow men, women and children. Here's the law in all its glory everyone:

> "The plaintiff himself [Dred Scott] acquired no title to freedom by being taken by his owner to Rock Island, in Illinois, and brought back to Missouri." *Scott v. Sandford*, 60 U.S. 393, 396 (1856).

> "On the contrary, they [Africans] were at that time considered as a subordinate and inferior class of beings who had been subjugated by the dominant race, and, whether emancipated or not, yet remained subject to their authority, and had no rights or privileges but such as those who held the power and the Government might choose to grant them." *Scott* at page 404-405

> "The unhappy black race were separated from the white by indelible marks, and laws long before established, and were never thought of or spoken of except as property, and when the claims of the owner or the profit of the trader were supposed to need protection." *Scott* at page 410.

Dred Scott had an owner, an *owner*! The law is about slavery, not right and wrong or protecting the innocent. Notice here you can interchange dominance with authority.

What made Scott a slave was the fact he wasn't free to act for himself; he was compelled to work for another or suffer severe consequences. That's the basis of slavery, being forced to perform. While this was prior to the Civil War, the constitution and laws are still used to enslave us today and it doesn't change what its original purpose is.

So a juror is, at best, a temporary slave to the judge to perform as the judge orders him to do. The so-called nobility of serving as a juror, while subjective nonsense, are empty words meant only to divert attention away from the fact governments operate by violence, not respect and cooperation. Can justice prevail on a foundation of slavery? No, says anyone capable of any measure of rational thought.

Whether we like it or not, the facts tell a familiar story of slavery.

Being a temporary slave to a lawyer has to have a psychological effect; it has to cause something in the attitudes and behavior of the ones subjected to the situation. Many feel at least some contempt or ill feelings from being threatened and coerced into servitude by a lawyer in a dress.

389

What about a juror though, could a scientific experiment be done to see? Does it even need to be done? This is pretty basic stuff. I don't think any experiments need to be done to prove people don't like being forced to do things.

A similar question regarding the effects of coercion was asked by Leon Festinger and James M. Carlsmith in 1959 concerning cognitive dissonance theory: "What happens to a person's private opinion if he is forced to do or say something contrary to that opinion?" *Cognitive Consequences of Forced Compliance*, Leon Festinger & James M. Carlsmith (1959), First published in Journal of Abnormal and Social Psychology, 58, 203-210. http://psychclassics.yorku.ca/Festinger/

One of the factors/variables missing from the experiments is: *judges use real coercion to get compliance*; judges routinely throw people in jail and fine them. One lawyer in a fit of rage jailed forty-six people when a cell phone went off. http://news.cnet.com/8301-10784_3-9824710-7.html. The threat of jail causes deep anxiety and stress, dare I write *trauma*? The juror worries about his family: Who will take care of them if this crazy lawyer puts him in jail? Will the rent/mortgage be paid if a fine must be paid instead? So the real violence will likely amplify the results seen in any experiment.

With a jury summons, the threat of violence is typically deleted from the conscious experience; people usually just want to come up with a good excuse not to miss work. What's important to keep in mind is that doesn't mean the deleted portions will not affect someone's behavior. The underlying violence is still there and will affect the jurors' perspectives. And we know how important perceptions are and how they govern actions.

Judges and prosecutors are going to have their hands full when such questioning becomes widespread. I'm looking forward to the day when people stop being so obedient to these bureaucrats. When they show up to court pissed off because some lawyer they've never met is threatening them, and do what judge and prosecutors can't stand: they start asking questions and looking at the situation critically. Not only that, they can stand together as a group against these psychopaths in robes and demand answers.

After all, I'm pretty certain most people don't think that as jurors they can question the almighty judge. It's certainly a new concept as far as I know. Once they realize he/she is just some lawyer, a former prosecutor on a wooden throne and can very well be questioned, then it's an issue of *should* this violent lawyer be questioned? And why not? Unless as a juror you're just a slave, there to do what you are told, then it stands to reason that since you took a man/woman away from their family and normal life for the day, these lawyers can answer a few questions. If the lawyers get angry, then one could ask:

> Excuse me, do you think we are your slaves for the day, your property to just follow your orders?

No, of course not, it's a civic responsibility to serve on a jury; it's a privilege.
We're not slaves? Then stop treating us as slaves. Why did you coerce our participation?

Just put the cards on the table; stop dancing around the gun in the room and making it easier for them to get away with treating us like farm animals. You want my participation; you'd better start treating me better.
You want me to make decisions? Then treat me as if you actually believe I can make such important decisions. Treating me as your slave is not instilling any defendants with any confidence in your system.
All I'm suggesting is critical thought and questions instead of blind obedience and faith. What can judges and prosecutors do when potential jurors challenge the rationale of their system? Threaten them some more? That could cause the jurors' anger to be directed at the prosecutor and the judge, not at the defendant where they want it.
They could just excuse them from participating. This could have the encouraging result of a prosecution stymied from sitting a jury. A contemporary example where a jury could not be empaneled happened in Montana in December 2010. In what was declared a "mutiny", a judge could not sit a jury in a proceeding involving a non-crime. Despite this, the defense attorney made a plea deal. Why take a plea, or even talk about a plea, when they can't seat a jury? Nice defense; the smart move would have been to fire the lawyer.

The results of Festinger's theory of cognitive dissonance theory experiment are summed up as:

> "Festinger (1957) has proposed a theory concerning cognitive dissonance. Two derivations from this theory are tested here. These are:
>
> 1. If a person is induced to do or say something which is contrary to his private opinion, there will be a tendency for him to change his opinion so as to bring it into correspondence with what he has done or said.
> 2. The larger the pressure used to elicit the [p. 210] overt behavior (beyond the minimum needed to elicit it) the weaker will be the above-mentioned tendency.
>
> A laboratory experiment was designed to test these derivations. Subjects were subjected to a boring experience and then paid to tell someone that the experience had been interesting and enjoyable. The amount of money paid the subject was varied. The private opinions of the subjects concerning the experience were then determined.
>
> The results strongly corroborate the theory that was tested." http://psychclassics.yorku.ca/Festinger/

391

The Asch conformity experiment has a direct connection and is relevant here. As shown, people are more likely to engage in giving wrong answers when social pressure is applied. With a jury you have twelve people forced to listen to lawyers and then make a decision based on what the most violent lawyer in the room orders them to do. It's obvious there's social pressure to conform to the judge's instructions.

Each juror is not only going to have the pressure from the lawyer who coerced them to be there, there's also pressure from the other jurors. It's reasonable to question the potential juror regarding these issues. The fact the judge has threatened to throw them in jail does not have to remain in consciousness to cause a direct effect on someone's behavior. By definition, the deleted experiences and parts of experiences are not in consciousness. Just as you may not remember a traumatic childhood experience with a birthday clown, you still have an automatic phobic response every time you see a clown today.

We can apply the *but for* standard/test here. The jury would not be here *but for* the coercion of the judge. The jury would not have believed the law applied to me *but for* the instructions from the authority figure forcing their participation. That doesn't look like a formula for justice to me.

While experiment results show that the more pressure used beyond the minimum to get the overt change in behavior, I believe that may not always be true in a real setting, such as when questioning a juror right in front of the slave master. When in such a situation, when the very real risk of armed men forcibly throwing you into a cage is imminent and certain, then the greater the dissonance created, the greater chance people will change their opinion. Though it could also be argued the actual pressure "beyond the minimum" depends on other factors and is somewhat subjective, the amount of fear involved is going to affect compliance. Can we doubt for a moment that terrorizing someone is going to increase compliance? Let's look at some examples.

The extreme would be having a deputy point his gun directly at the juror's head to deliver the judge's honorable threat. There would be no doubt this is way beyond the minimum pressure needed, but as it is almost the maximum that could be applied, we're certain compliance would be 100%. (Well, let's say 98-100% to allow for those in Keene who would not back down that easily.) From here we can then dial down the actual violence and see compliance dropping somewhat. The violence is always there though.

It could be argued the minimum required is for the judge to start yelling and threatening contempt to bring about the desired response as opposed to having armed men actually start manhandling the potential juror. Having them fly into a rage actually makes my case for me; he's demonstrating the true nature of the proceedings and why the potential jurors are there.

The results of the Stanford Prison Experiment cannot be ignored. Most, if not all, of the psychological experiments mentioned earlier are relevant with every trial. Each one is grounds enough to seriously challenge every single man/woman forced into jury servitude. There's no rational basis to object to questioning a potential juror and any prejudice they may have from being forced into servitude by the judge.

If you have a right to a fair trial with an impartial jury, and you're entitled to question potential jurors on any prejudice they may have that could prevent that, then every juror should be questioned about their involuntary servitude.

Therein lies the double bind to be exploited:

A fair and impartial jury of people coerced to participate.

Sounds like a great system of justice, doesn't it? How can people who are forced to participate be impartial?

The jurors aren't blind and stupid; they can see the judge is forcing this trial on behalf of the prosecutor, and that they are on the same team. The social dynamics will only be ignored by those who benefit from the situation, are too damned scared to say anything, or can't even process the information. If the jurors' perception is the American or English court system is the best and fairest in the world, that perception will win out over contradictory facts before them. They may not be able to process facts contradicting their perceptions. Even if they can, they won't want to be the first one to speak up. They don't want to stand apart from the team.

Proceedings like the one where Larken Rose was convicted resemble what happened to Kitty Genovese much more than actual trials http://en.wikipedia.org/wiki/Murder_of_Kitty_Genovese. Jurors just sit there as the lawyers crucify the victim.

A juror is being forced into a situation by someone who has no personally accountability whatsoever to his victims. In the Stanford Prison experiment, the pretend prisoners dramatically changed their behavior to conform to the will of the pretend prison guards. This is significant because what are the jurors going to be thinking when the defendant objects to what the judge may be doing?

For example, I start questioning a potential juror about possible prejudice towards me because the judge is forcing jurors to be there. While some jurors will not even be able to process the facts, some will just go along with the judge and conform to his decisions. We only need one to hang a jury though.

What are jurors going to think when I question the cop or prosecutor while pointing to judge: What is the nature of your relationship to this lawyer? We know that most will see this as a threat to the judge and want to conform to the judge. This can result in tremendous social pressure from other jurors if one or more questions the underlying fairness of the trial itself.

Any issues regarding a fair trial will be deleted from the experience, and only keeping the judge happy will be important. There will probably be deindividuation with the jurors, just as there was with the pretend prisoners and guards in the Stanford Prison experiment. This really throws a cloud over whether political trials can actually be fair.

It's clear these issues will be far more pronounced with trials of people who are not accused of hurting others, such as tax and drug possession prosecutions. Such prosecutions are about compliance, not wrongdoing. If the juror has no issues with forced compliance, then that's a strong bias against the defendant; they already think the defendant should have complied. The whole trial comes down to whether the defendant complied, not whether he was required to and injured someone as a result. The concept of causation is completely foreign to such prosecutions.

If there was any interest in justice with political courts, then the main question in every single prosecution would be: Did the defendant cause the damage to the plaintiff? Of course, this is already a legal requirement, it's just ignored in the interest of money and control. It can't be stated openly in a drug, traffic or tax prosecution because someone on the jury might stand up and ask why they are all there wasting their time since the defendant has not been accused of causing anything.

The 1949 Bruner & Postman study, the Stanford Prison, Milgram, and Asch conformity experiments should scare the crap out of anyone in a political witch hunt, such as Larken had to endure.

Jurors, like the rest of us, are scared of the IRS; it's more accurate to say we're terrified of the IRS. They operate by threats and coercion same as the judge, that's how they get compliance. There is a very real, though possibly deleted from experience, caste system at work in the court. The defendant is at the bottom, but the jurors are only one step higher. In one sense, they are actually lower: the defendant may be permitted to send an attorney to conduct the trial, a juror has to be there or they go to jail.

All these expectations and generalizations are brought into the jury box; there's no way to avoid them and the hierarchy at play. One is: you pay taxes or go to jail. That's why people pay; there is no discussion about facts making one a taxpayer and other issues of evidence. People tend to only know the obvious: pay or go to jail.

Regardless of the evidence or what transpires at trial, the expectation-pay or go to jail-will dictate the decision of the juror, not the evidence. To the jurors, the only thing the IRS has to prove is the defendant did not file the return or pay the taxes, nothing else is necessary because we all understand at some level: you pay or go to jail. The juror's expectations are easily met.

This explains why the judge in Larken's inquisition could say in front of the jury that Larken was sincere in his beliefs he didn't owe taxes or was required to file. The judge admitted that the crux of the charge-willfulness-was negated. The jury still convicted, most likely because they could not process the information because it contradicted their generalization about taxes: But he made money; everyone *knows* if you make money you have to pay taxes.

To these and most jurors (general population), the evidence proving one is a taxpayer with taxable income is not relevant; the only question is: did he file a return and pay like everyone else? The evidence is: despite the judge telling the jury there was no evidence to convict for willful failure to file, the jury still convicted on nothing other than Larken didn't file. Whether he was required to file and believed he was required could not have been a part of their decision to vote guilty.

There is also a line of nonsense that because people such as Wesley Snipes have been convicted of tax evasion that's somehow evidence everyone is required to file. It doesn't matter to such people that others are also acquitted, such as Joe Banister and Vernice Kuglin. So convictions and acquittals are only evidence twelve people agreed to convict or acquit, really nothing more.

I go through this practically every day with IRS agents. They just can't seem to understand how one can get money/income/federal reserve notes and not be a taxpayer with taxable income. They will ask me to tell them why my client is not a taxpayer and doesn't have taxable income.

So I'll go through the process again and tell them: You told me there are no witnesses with personal knowledge and no admissible evidence Jack is a taxpayer with taxable income. They appear to not be able to understand; some have asked me, "What do you mean by witnesses?" These people are making accusations against us and destroying the lives of peaceful people-and they admittedly don't know what the word witness means. Breathtaking!

And this doesn't even take into account that even the courts acknowledge the lack of credibility of eyewitness identifications, referring to them as "notoriously unreliable," *Watkins v. Sowders*, 449 U.S. 341, 350. How much more so for agents who admittedly have never met us?

You'd never know this when speaking to IRS agents and their lawyers, who think their opinions are so absolutely correct that evidentiary challenges are frivolous arguments. Apparently, evidentiary questions are so frivolous they're magically arguments.

And given that only a few tax agents have ever agreed to being experts in the interpretation and application of the constitution and laws, you have some really lousy witnesses.

More important though, what if a potential juror is being honest that they have no issue with being forced to perform (slavery) and are biased in favor of the prosecution. Can they objectively and impartially act as jurors where the accused does have a problem with being forced to perform?

That's a prejudice against the poor accused. If the juror believes slavery is fine, and he/she has no problem with the use or threat of force, and the defendant is being prosecuted because of non-compliance, then the bias is clear. The juror's perceptions are going to govern, not the facts, regardless of how contradictory the evidence may be. This may not be true of all the potential jurors, but it will be for a large percentage of them.

When we add in the fear of angering the judge, who's already used threats of violence against each juror, the pressure to conform is ramped up considerably.

So either way the juror responds i.e., has a problem with slavery or doesn't, it could result in a prejudice against a defendant. And what juror is going to want to direct his disdain at the judge because the judge forced them to be on the jury? The judge, not the defendant, can jail the jury for contempt. The disdain will be directed at the defendant. It goes to whether the juror can be fair and impartial.

So it's obvious why it's so important and relevant to question every potential juror on any prejudice they may have resulting from the judge forcing them to perform. I'm suggesting this to people who are in jail waiting for trial. We know when they call from jail the calls are monitored. So I'm very open and know that prosecutors are hearing me talk about this challenge knowing they will either speak to the judge before the trial or make an objection prior to the *voir dire*.

I actually want the judge to start yelling and get violent so I can just stand there and let this psycho make my case for me. At the least, like with cross-examination, the judge and prosecutor will be waiting, no, they'll be itching to stop me from questioning potential jurors. We all know it's supposed to be an automatic reversal on appeal or interlocutory appeal before trial. I really doubt any judge, even with foreknowledge of what I'm doing, is going to sit there calmly and permit me to make an issue of the force they're using against the jury. I think the technical phrase is "gumming up the works."

Why ignore the gun in the room? So the judge can sit there on his wooden throne and continue getting away with it? There's no merit to giving this violent lawyer a free pass.

And that's the nature of using these automatic reversible errors to our advantage. We purposely engage the judge in a manner where his only choices are to throw the complaint out or commit unforgivable sins. If they were honest and interested in administering justice, then I could not do this. It stems directly from the contradictory nature of how courts operate; all I do is exploit it. I'm not the one threatening the jury with jail, that's the lawyer with the black robe; he's the "honorable" one, not me.

If we, as the accused, ask such leading questions, then we are like the little boy who first says the emperor is naked. This could give the jurors the courage necessary to stand up for the truth, to refuse to comply with the lawyers.

In addition to being forced to participate, who pays the jury and how? The same people attacking you are paying the jury and getting them meals. This has to invoke some trauma-type bond with the attackers. While not all aspire to getting jury duty as Stanley from *The Office* does (https://www.youtube.com/watch?v=-3zY5SMpfaI) it doesn't change how it's all funded.

How is the money acquired to then give to the jury? Taxes, of course. The entire psychopath circus is on a foundation of violence and money stolen from us. And if you're in the unfortunate position of being the subject of a tax prosecution, then how can bias be avoided when the jury is getting a free lunch from the same people who are stealing from everyone and claiming you're not paying your fair share?

Look at what taxes pay for: the privilege of participating in the greatest justice system in the world. Prosecutors tell jurors-and I imagine they believe them-that being forced to be on a jury is a sacred responsibility, that as Americans we're lucky to have such a wonderful system. And the most attractive part to Americans? All the "free" food. Sometimes jurors also get put up in a hotel for trial-hey, "free" cable! That means "free" porn for everyone. How could jurors not be biased against someone not paying their fare share when they are accepting such benefits?

Let's not ignore the other things learned from the other psychological studies above; they're just as applicable in the setting of a court with a jury, the conformity studies in particular. It's comforting to know people will knowingly do/say the wrong thing to be part of the herd. No amount of jingoism is going to magically stop this behavior. You coerce people to make a decision and that has an immediate impact on their behavior, put them in a group and there is going to be tremendous pressure to conform.

It's more proof a decision is based on fear, not facts. It's a decision that may have a tremendous impact on your life though. And I've already seen judges not permit any discussion of these psychological factors during a *voir dire*. But if there are factors that adversely affect someone's ability to make a fair judgment, then that's appropriate and relevant to question and bring out.

When we see judges routinely refuse any such questioning, we have more evidence of the callous disregard for life characterizing the control freaks that like to be called "Your Honor". We can't be surprised when a man with no respect for human life refuses to permit questions that would stop the jury selection process.

The *voir dire* is supposed to be the process to see if the potential jurors can be impartial and base their decision on the facts, not emotion or fear. Despite this, judges will block every attempt to properly question jurors. Again, while it's an automatic reversible error technically, that doesn't mean a conviction will get reversed while we're getting gang-raped in prison. Because nothing says honorable more than having a peaceful man sit in prison while you decide the obvious: denial of *voir dire* is reversible without showing prejudice.

Deep emotional stress, social pressure and plain fear are the only legitimate explanations why juries just sit in their chairs as lawyers and their prize witnesses do their best to strain patience and credibility. Why else would twelve adults continue to participate in such an obvious sham as Mike's tax evasion prosecution in September 2012?

Mike reported to me that when he asked the lead tax agent investigating him for tax evasion what facts he relied on proving the code was applicable to him, the agent essentially stated:

> *Ladies and gentlemen of the jury, my evidence the code applies to Mike is the testimony of the previous twenty-seven unqualified witnesses.*

None of the previous twenty-seven witnesses provided any facts. Mike wasn't permitted to cross-examine any of the witnesses against him on the facts the code was applicable, and here the last witness claims his evidence that the code is applicable, is the non-testimony of the previous witnesses.

You would think one man/woman would at least put their hand up and say, "Excuse, me did I just hear you right? That's all you have to offer? Are you kidding me? Your facts are what the previous witnesses didn't testify to? You forced me to be away from my family all week for this? And you think Mike's the criminal? It's no surprise you had to coerce us all to be here. I'll tell you this: you've motivated me to stop filing and paying taxes."

I would expect them to stand up and say, "That's all I need to hear; acquitted of all charges, good day to you, sir." *Where do think you're going?* "I said good day!" http://www.youtube.com/watch?v=Y0Rjn6W9jYk.

This is evidence of fear. Juries are not making decisions based on the facts, or here, the complete lack of facts. It's beyond dispute every single jury verdict is under threat, duress and coercion. No rational adult can watch lawyers trot out twenty-eight witnesses (each coerced to testify) who aren't permitted to testify to essential elements of the crimes and just let it go, unless they're afraid of the judge. Yes, there's also social pressure as they may think they are the only one who is seeing the lack of evidence. That's just more fear.

We see the same psychological reasons why people pay taxes at play with the jury. Why would all their conditioning and perceptions suddenly stop when they're jurors? It's not a reasonable assumption that someone will drop their perceptions when forced onto a jury. So what do we do? We have to exploit the jurors' perceptions to our advantage:

> Are you intimidated by the judge?
> *No.*
> Then why did you comply with his threat to be here today?

There are too many contradictions going on, we need to make the jury aware of them, and do it often. The judge will tell the jury they must look at the facts and decide what's true based on evidence proving the charges beyond a reasonable doubt. That's one thing we can focus on.

In Mike's prosecution, every time a witness wasn't permitted to testify on the applicability of the code and Mike believed he was required to pay taxes, Mike could then point that out each time. You can tell the jury:

> This is witness twenty-five and the twenty-fifth witness not qualified, according to the prosecution and the judge, to testify that the code is applicable to me and I believed I was required to pay taxes. We can pretty much guarantee the prosecutor will continue calling witnesses they know have no facts to prove these two elements of the crime.

Prosecutions are adversary proceedings, and lawyers use the jury to take responsibility for conviction away from themselves. The government certainly wants twelve people who share their opinions and see the world the way they do; that's why they stack the jury and force people to participate.

Just as you can't have a free society that's based on violence and slavery, you can't have a justice system based on violence. This is sometimes admitted by the supreme lawyers:

> "It is not the province of the court to decide upon the justice or injustice, the policy or impolicy, of these laws. The decision of that question belonged to the political or lawmaking power, to those who formed the sovereignty and framed the Constitution. The duty of the court is to interpret the instrument they have framed with the best lights we can obtain on the subject, and to administer it as we find it, according to its true intent and meaning when it was adopted." *Scott v. Sandford* at page 404-405.

I need to take a minor tangent here as I have to point out just how these lawyers spin things to meet their ends. They seem to have forgotten a very well-known opinion regarding judicial review:

> "If an act of the legislature, repugnant to the constitution, is void, does it, notwithstanding its invalidity, bind the courts and oblige them to give it effect? Or, in other words, though it be not law, does it constitute a rule as operative as if it was a law? This would be to overthrow in fact what was established in theory; and would seem, at first view, an absurdity too gross to be insisted on. It shall, however, receive a more attentive consideration." *Marbury v Madison*, 5 US 137, 177-178.

The only sense I can make of this apparent contradiction is so an injustice may be interpreted as consistent with the constitution. More likely, it's so the cowardly psychopaths who wrote the Dredd Scott opinion could avoid making a rational decision.

***Voir dire* the judge**. I've examined asking potential jurors, but what about asking the judge if he/she has any moral issue with forcing people, not accused of a crime, to perform or go to jail? We're supposed to be informed of the nature and cause of the charges and proceedings; this includes what kind of people are making decisions affecting my life.

Like the jury, judges are supposed to be fair and impartial. If a jury is subject to a *voir dire*, then why not judges? Legally, once the judge's impartiality is made an issue, the judge is required to give disclosure. Most of the proceedings I help people with do not involve juries anyway; it's just the judge-lawyer for the state-who's making the decisions.

I wouldn't let the judge off the hook; confront him/her and ask why they feel the need to threaten dozens of people to participate. Ask them if they believe such use of force will affect the decision to convict or acquit.

I would ask:

How does a man who threatens people into involuntary servitude intend on administering justice?

When we ask if we're entitled to a fair trial before a fair, impartial, and independent decision-maker, they always say yes. So a relevant question is, how are we to know this violent stranger is really impartial unless we ask some questions?

Other questions to ask a judge are if he/she was a prosecutor for the plaintiff state and if he/she has an interest in the prison system. Do they get any grant money (such as the Byrne Grant) from the Feds regarding the drug war?

Be prepared for a judge to get upset with such questions. You can't expect anything less from a professional predator.

Vincent Bugliosi, the Manson prosecutor, makes a very candid admission in his book *Outrage: The Five Reasons Why O.J. Simpson Got Away With Murder*, when discussing the prosecution's handling of a witness, Mark Furhman, being caught lying in a trial:

> "Surely they must have known that lying is not only common in criminal as well as civil trials, it's routine and expected. The late Francis L. Wellman, a distinguished member of the New York Bar, once observed: "Scarcely a trial is conducted in which perjury does not appear in a more or less flagrant form." Perjury is so common that instead of being surprised by it, seasoned prosecutors expect it." Page 220.

He also admits:

> "As any seasoned criminal trial lawyer will attest, most juries see through the transparent fiction of the presumption of innocence...If the jury knows the presumption of innocence is a legal fiction, yet the judge intones the presumption to them in a very sober manner, and with the straightest of countenances, could it be there he thereby loses a speck of credibility in their eyes?" page 35.

> "One day a defendant is going to stand up in court and tell the judge, "Your Honor, if I am legally presumed to be innocent, why have I been arrested for this crime, why has a criminal complaint been filed against me, and why am I now here in court being tried?" page 35.

Mr. Bugliosi hasn't heard my discourses, apparently. I know, what a shock. Bugliosi does generalize the presumption of innocence extends beyond the judge and jury. I'm not aware of any law or legal principle claiming the presumption extends to the police or prosecutors; it doesn't. So if someone did make the above statement, a judge could just respond with the obvious: Sir, only the jury and I are required to presume you innocent, not the police and prosecutors. But, as I've written before, this doesn't get the judge out of his bind.

The judge has to explain how he can presume you innocent at the same time he is assuming the codes apply to you. I don't know a way out of that, so good luck because either the code is presumed not to apply or they assume it does without evidence from the prosecutor.

As far as losing "credibility in [the] eyes" of a jury, yes, the judge deserves to lose credibility and really deserves none. And why should they? What has the judge done up to the point of empaneling a jury deserving of any credibility? What do to the facts tell us? Has the judge treated any of the jurors as autonomous adults, with respect and professionalism?

Is one juror there because they were asked to participate? Did the judge treat them as equals, just as honorable as himself; did he treat them with the same respect he thinks he deserves? No, he forced each one to be there. Jurors are threatened with jail if they don't show up. Yeah, they're permitted to make an excuse once, but bottom line is: show up at this time, we're not asking, we're ordering you; if you don't, we have men with guns to put you into jail or kill you in the process. Thank you in advance for your service, ladies and gentlemen.

Imagine if those same twelve people decided to turn the tables on the violent prosecutors (former and current) by forcing them to participate in some kind of trial: *It's for the common good, mate, now sit down and shut up or we'll put you in this cage until you realize this is a privilege for us to force you to do this.*

This is another reason why there should be a voluntary society. Maybe if prosecutors and judges knew people could just walk away they wouldn't be as wasteful and long-winded and bring frivolous complaints. It would motivate everyone involved in administering justice to do so openly and efficiently, and to actually focus on justice itself, not just prosecuting as a way to climb a psychopathic pecking order. People in the community, people who want a safe community and don't want resources wasted, including their time, would not tolerate prosecutions against people growing plants in their homes.

Politicians claim people want government to protect them and keep their communities safe. They also claim society wants government; that society would collapse without them, the sky would fall. Oh really? Then why is support compulsory? Why is jury service, in the greatest justice system in the world, always compulsory? Why would people who allegedly want the greatest system of justice to protect them have to be threatened and forced to participate?

It stands to reason that people forced to sit on a jury are going to be harboring some anger or contempt, silent or otherwise. We can only speculate on where that anger is directed. But it's reasonable to conclude that anger may influence the decision being made. While I would certainly sympathize with a juror refusing to convict someone accused of drug possession because he's mad at the Man for forcing him there, it should trouble you when you realize it could also be a contributing factor in another decision against someone not accused of hurting anyone.

This doesn't mean I oppose a jury system; quite the contrary-twelve or more people of different backgrounds and perspectives examining the facts is a great thing. It's scientific, the basis of peer-reviewed studies. The issue is the violence used to put the system in place and maintain it.

Statists would argue, "It's the best we can do" or "It's the best system available." First of all, *no*. Second, let's consider for a moment how subjective such an assessment is. Then consider that there's no evidence there isn't a better system available.

While my belief a voluntary system is better is subjective, there is certainly objective evidence proving the compulsory system is destructive and contrary to the stated end of government. With a voluntary system, the means are consistent with the end-that's already more evidence it's better than a compulsory system.

With a voluntary society there are far fewer fictions for the people to accept.

People don't need to be forced; there are too many examples of spontaneous order proving otherwise. Isn't the fact people don't want to pay for something an indication they don't want it? Isn't it at least a reasonable presumption? They apparently value their money more than the service.

Regarding the judges, what does this need to threaten people tell you about their nature, and the nature of the proceedings? Why doesn't anyone cooperate with him; why does he have to use violence? If he/she is *honorable*, then they'll be happy to openly discuss the nature of their system, the stated goal of which is to administer justice.

Can you imagine the response from a judge when asked, "Why can't you just ask people to cooperate with you, why do you need to threaten them and force them to participate? Are people so unwilling to work with you they have to be coerced? Don't you think when you force people they may take that out on me?"

I expect the judge to stay true to his violent nature and fly into a psychotic rage when confronted with such questions. I can then stand there and let him make the case against their system for me. Rational people, those interested in justice and problem resolution, will have no trouble answering such questions. This is another empirical basis proving politicians and bureaucrats are interested in neither.

As with everything else presented in this book and on my radio show, this does not require input from me for you to know this. If you're unfamiliar with the legal system, then a little independent investigation will produce the same results. Very little research is required to know the legal system, as a part of government, is based on violence. A search on the interwebs will show pictures of jury summons with the threats on them. Here are a few examples:

> "Every resident of Sacramento County who is qualified to serve and who does not have a legal hardship or excuse must appear for jury service when summoned. Willful failure to appear is contempt of court. Contempt of court is punishable

by fine of up to $1,500.00 and/or five days in the county jail."
http://www.saccourt.ca.gov/jury/general.aspx

"A jury summons is not an invitation," writes Ontario Superior Court Justice Casey Hill in a stern judgment released last week. "Nor is it a mere option to volunteer to be a juror. It cannot simply be ignored. It is a court order with consequences for disobedience." Michele Mandel, who also wrote "And truth be told, you can hardly blame people for not rushing to fulfill the privilege of being on a jury -- not when it's akin to slave labour."
http://cnews.canoe.ca/CNEWS/Canada/2011/03/09/1754 7096.html

Mandel likens it to slavery because there is little or no pay; she seems to have missed the whole coercive nature of the system. See how so much of our experience is deleted from consciousness?

Notice how upfront Casey Hill is about the nature of being a juror. A man who makes threats without any responsibility to the people he's threatening can afford to be so direct. Do you think Casey has the guts to walk up to someone's home in his black robe, knock on the door and order them to come to the court with him immediately or he'll personally force them into a cage? That's the difference between *perceived* authority and ability.

Of course, the typical response from government apologists will be to attack the messenger and say, "If you don't like the court system, move to Somalia." But we know that's not a response to the facts; jury duty is involuntary servitude, temporary slavery. That's why you're ordered to participate and not invited. Invitations are for those who are free to say no.

And this doesn't require us to get a jury summons in the mail in order to ask these questions. We should ask judges these questions in writing. And if you're sending it to a judge in another state, there's little risk of retaliation.

I think it's very effective to ask jurors if they bring their own sense of right and wrong with them to the court or will they rely on what the judge tells them. If they do have their own sense of right and wrong, what is the standard and will they apply that to me? I would ask what they'd do if that conflicts with the judge's orders and instructions. I could also ask, "What would you do if your standard of right and wrong conflicted with what a politician says is legal or illegal?"

I know this will upset the prosecutors; that's part of the point. Judges will accuse me of jury nullification and may threaten me with contempt if I continue mentioning it during the trial. His display of anger can be used against him, especially if the potential juror's standard of right and wrong is not based on the initiation of force. In such a situation, I would ask:

Do you respect people who resort to force and threats of force, such as these lawyers, the prosecutor and judge? Is that the type of person whose judgment you trust?

If the judge is being patient and is permitting such questions, I would be very direct and ask,

"Do you like being used as a tool of the politicians?"

And yes, that is meant to be a serious question. If your first impression is fear, fear of contempt, then you already know why it's an effective question, as well as relevant. These people are predators, they are fully intent on changing the course of our lives; it's not an issue for them, but I'd like to be the one dictating the course of my life, not some narcissistic control freak.

If you cannot see how important this is, then I can't make it any clearer. When someone orders you to perform, they are not just treating you as a farm animal, but directing the course of your life. They are demonstrating their callous disregard for you and do not deserve a pass. Don't even look at it from their standpoint; we owe it to ourselves to dictate our own lives, not some cowardly psychopath who doesn't have the guts to use violence with us one on one. If you ever doubt the importance of this, ask the bureaucrat what'll happen if you don't comply.

I cannot overemphasize this point enough; it's clear and convincing evidence of how little concern they have for human life. This point is demonstrated in the movie *And Justice for All* with Al Pacino. When one lawyer forgets about a court proceeding, he blows it off as "nickel and dime", nothing important. It didn't matter that a man went to prison and subsequently hanged himself:

"If he's not in jail this week, he'll be there next week! Appeal it!"
"I CAN'T APPEAL IT, HE'S DEAD! HE'S DEAD! HALF HOUR AFTER THEY PUT HIM IN THE LOCKUP, HE HANGED HIMSELF!"

This scenario is played out *ad nauseum* on television cop shows where a suspect is not aiding in his prosecution. The solution? Let's see if a few days in the tank will change his mind. So instead of getting things like evidence, throw him into a cage.

I had one particular anti-social slacker laughing at me as he left me in a cage in Mesa, Arizona; Jimmy thought it was hilarious how they may allegedly cage you for twenty-four hours without charging you with a crime. Like a high school jackass, he put his hands up and flashed his fingers, two on one hand, four on the other while repeating twenty-four over and over. I think it's safe to assume his parents were more than disappointed in how he turned out.

What do the facts tell you about the juror who claims to not have a problem being a tool for the judge? Look at the verifiable facts, not patriotic platitudes and about civic duty and other PR.

Politicians force their will on each individual man, woman and child in society. They use the money stolen from us to pay for more enforcers to arrest and prosecute us. They use the same enforcers to coerce the jurors, under threat of jail, to comply with their persecution of peaceful, non-violent people. Sounds like the jurors are the tools of the predators called governments. If these facts tell you anything other than the juror is a slave to psychopath lawyers, then please present the facts that would lead you to that conclusion.

Other relevant questions are, "What do you think of the legal profession? Politicians? Do you think people, not accused of hurting anyone should be punished just because politicians said so?" I can ask if they know they're being forced to participate in an attack against me where I'm not accused of hurting anyone, just not complying with the opinions of politicians.

Of course their opinion of politicians is relevant; the whole proceeding is based on the written will of politicians. How could the personal opinion of potential jurors not be relevant?

What about any personal or familial relationships the juror may have with governments? It seems reasonable to ask such questions when you're being punished for disobedience to a politician's will. Does the juror believe all laws should be blindly complied with, that if we don't like a law we should ask the politicians to ignore the billions of dollars such prosecutions bring in and repeal their cash cow? Are they for blind obedience or not? Does their model of the world require subjection and following orders, because that would certainly mean they are probably going to frown on my disobedience. What kind of response will they have when I continue attacking the opinion I was supposed to be obedient to an unknown parasite anyway?

The fact they showed up is evidence of their map of the world is based on obedience. Such a juror believes in being obedient to lawyers and other control freaks incapable of providing services to willing customers. This is going to make it statistically impossible for some, and extremely difficult for others, to be fair.

Are you involved with the military? Any family members? Do you work for the government, have any employment/involvement with government work and/or contracts? Do you now or have you ever lived in a military town or have family members who do/have? Do they receive government benefits; are they reliant to any degree on the system of robbery called taxation? There's a big one.

I don't see how it's going to be possible to find people who are not getting some kind of government benefit when you factor in social security, unemployment and mortgages.

Because it's reasonable that being dependent on the tax system would tend to bias someone, it's a relevant line of questioning to potential jurors. It's also a good way to get a prosecutor out of his chair with a silly objection.

A good strategy is to frame not only relevant questions, but questions where we are fairly certain the judge, in a fit of anger and prejudice, will not permit. This way we can bait them into committing a reversible error. And for those who may think it's wrong to intentionally ask a lawyer a question calculated to enrage him/her, put it into context before you go off half-cocked: don't compare asking a question to coercing dozens of people to be in your courtroom.

A good question to a juror in a tax prosecution would be, "Is 'everybody should pay his fair share' a standard of proof for you as a juror?" Judges have shamelessly refused this question. No grounds given, of course, and that will only help prove the judge's bias against us.

We're always just sticking to the facts, attacking the fictions, revealing the contradictions and exposing the gun in the room.

Anyone whose model of the world is based on blind obedience to authority is going to be prejudiced against someone who does not blindly obey. Their perceptions, together with social pressure, will inhibit them from being impartial.

This cannot be ignored when we are attacked and are able to have a jury trial.

Part Three - Solutions

Making the psychopaths irrelevant

The object is to make the psychopaths called government irrelevant. There are varying means, but they should all have as their main objective making these gangs irrelevant, where people feel no need to comply or even pay attention.

Most, if not all, of the many solutions to ending the current psychopathic foundation of society and bringing about a voluntary society involve some risk. It's irrational to not recognize the concept of government is antithetical to a free market; they're opposites. We're dealing with a system of psychopathic men and women; there are going to be risks involved. Driving to a football game has risks too, but that doesn't seem to stop many people.

There's an obvious truth that's being ignored: building a free society has risks involved and it will not build itself. Those people who refuse to cooperate with you, who refuse to deal with you on a voluntary basis as equals, they are the problem whatever they call themselves. They tend to cloak their violence against us with the government concept, as already explained. They have no regard for our autonomy, they lie incessantly and they only care about power over us. They are by nature very dangerous people. Of course there's a risk when we call them on their lies and refuse to comply and enable them to control us.

If you believe all human interaction should be voluntary, and you want a free, voluntary society, then you need to start putting those beliefs into action. Endless debates on the virtues of voluntaryism vs. statism are useless without action. The really important part of the **A3** symbol is the last part: agora, anarchy, and **action**. It's the same as just sitting around talking about how much you enjoy playing guitar, but never picking one up and playing.

There's just no way around it: building a free society/market involves non-violent, non-cooperation with those acting as governments. This means non-compliance with tax laws. If you're not willing to trade without permission, then you should probably re-evaluate your beliefs because you really don't believe them. Without practical application, all voluntaryist/anarchist/agorist writing and discussions are as empty as the promises politicians make every two years when they want another few years to farm us.

There are legitimate concerns; no one wants their family to be deprived of the basic necessities of life. That's why we should at least start with baby steps and support each other. Those psychopaths relying on your cooperation know you don't want to see your kids go without; they count on it.

What does that teach our children though? Where is the line, where do we stop cooperating? This is different for each of us. For some it's when the dairy police raid with guns drawn, for others it's when the politicians threaten the internet.

When I look around at what's happening, all the economic problems, I can't help but place the ultimate responsibility on all of us for allowing this small minority of predators to get away with treating us as chattel. The only way a small number can control a vastly superior majority is because the majority allows it.

Fear. This may be the biggest stumbling block. I have suggested taking combat and/or boxing lessons as a way of acting in the face of fear. This doesn't mean using violence to intimidate bureaucrats; but it's well-known that martial arts and boxing has a positive effect on one's confidence and ability in negotiating difficult situations. They're very effective in developing coping skills to stand up for yourself despite fear. Courage is not being without fear; it's acting despite it.

Nothing discussed in this book has any relevance if you can't overcome your fear of being a free, autonomous adult. Life has risks; get over it. The time for lip service is long over; philosophy is great, but useless if not put into action. Think of the philosophers who rail about the evils of taxation and acting consistently with your beliefs, and they advocate paying taxes. Great philosophy.

Freedom has to mean more than some empty political slogan. We all have our line in the sand, some further out than others, of how much we'll risk. This is why we talk about taking baby steps. For example, instead of not paying a vehicle license tax, you can turn the plate upside down. What's important is we take steps to living free, not ask for permission from people called government, and expose them for the criminals they are.

See an NLP practitioner for help. There are probably times in your life when you do act or have acted in spite of being afraid. You have the resources within you; you may just need some help having those resources available again at the conscious level and in different contexts. An NLP practitioner will be able to help with that.

So again, so much of this comes down to fear. We know politicians are criminals; the facts have been laid before you. And yet, many do nothing about it. Why? So we can continue living a safe life? Because we care so much about our neighbors and what they may think? Do we really live our lives and conduct ourselves based on what they think? That's a god even atheists worship.

Networking. We need to build networks with others who are working to build a voluntary society. As long as there's reporting to government agencies, such as tax info and business licenses, we're at risk for an attack. We need to build networks with those who want to do business without permission and making such reports to the psychos. Anything we can do to eliminate the paper trail will lower the risk.

It's important to keep in mind that even when there are no financial reports given to the tax agencies, if you have a business or professional license, assessments will be based on that. Tax agencies use a formula to get an average income for each profession. If you have a license, they will "guess" you made the average and attack you. Yes, they have told me it's a guess because there is no return filed.

Of course, there are risks and drawbacks to not getting a license; you have to do your own risk/benefit analysis. With some professions, you may not be able to get insurance without having the license, so insuring your business may not be possible the traditional way.

This has to do with living without asking permission. If we believe in freedom, then we don't ask for permission to use our own property and to interact with others; this includes trading freely. Yeoman from Austin is a great example; he's the one with the contraband turkey. Yeoman didn't go begging for permission.

Yeoman provides his community with valuable products; no one's forced to buy his poultry. If they don't like the product, they're free to not buy. The market dictates whether Yeoman stays in business; if he doesn't deliver what they want he'd have no business. He has no veil to hide behind and is open and honest with his customers. If he screws up, then he's responsible. That's what being an adult means. The same cannot be said for the people called the department of health who attacked him.

Barter, electronic currency. There are members of the US government that have described alternative mediums of exchange as domestic terrorism. This was clear after the conviction of Bernard von NotHaus in 2011 for selling silver freely to the market. Yes, convicted for selling silver coins. Governments hate free trade and there will always be a risk of attack by some bureaucrat as we work building a free market and a society without a political hierarchy.

There's also a risk of being attacked just by having a spike in sales; does that mean you don't work to increase your sales because you fear an attack by the tax thieves? No, this is why it helps to build a network to trade with that is not going to weasel out and drop a dime on you to the psychopaths in DC, London, Canberra or wherever they carry out operations.

Barter is also good because not only is the value of used commodities pretty subjective, but it can also be anonymous. Being anonymous protects us from thieving third parties.

Trading up. I heard about this from a video about a guy in Canada, Kyle McDonald. Kyle used the internet and made fourteen trades, starting with one red paperclip, to getting a house.

https://www.youtube.com/watch?v=BE8b02EdZvw.

It was based on a game called Bigger and Better, where the idea is to keep making trades for things you think are better than what you already got.

Given technology, this is a really effective method of trading. I have lots of online resources on the website that have helped facilitate trades. The radio show has also helped.

Bitcoin and other forms of electronic mediums make it possible to send value instantly to anyone, anywhere in the world over the internet, and it's stateless and anonymous. Just imagine where Bitcoin and other electronic mediums will be in ten years, remember the internet in 1990.

Bitcoin takes the banking-government cartel right out of the picture, and they hate it. They can't tax it, though I'm sure the psychopaths in D.C. and London are going to try.

If you're not familiar with Bitcoin yet, do a search and find out. It is a viable alternative to the credit/debt system.

Radio. This is still an amazing tool; we can not only educate people on the true nature of government, we can also help people limit damage done by an attack, and reach more of the market. This is done in several ways.

As mentioned on the show, you can get equipment and start your own radio station. There's risk involved, but there are precautions you can take. The Man will know exactly where you're transmitting from, so make sure you are not stepping on someone else's signal.

Some "illegal" stations have gotten so big, the man doesn't hassle them anymore. An example is radio free Berkeley in California.

We can get local entrepreneurs and vendors to promote the radio station in return for airtime.

Affidavit of fear. This was started in April 2011. Most politicians and bureaucrats are far removed from the actual violence keeping their system in place. Being removed, it's much easier for them to carry out orders leading to the theft of our property; after all, it's just a name on a piece of paper.

In my experience, it's very uncomfortable for bureaucrats to have the truth presented that they have no voluntary support. When confronted, they get offended and try to justify it with such nonsense as: "We agreed to be forced."

If we comply with a bureaucrat, then we send the affidavit of fear to let them know it's done only out of fear. If we file a tax return, it's not because we think we're obligated; we're doing it because we're afraid, even terrorized, and we don't want to be attacked and jailed. Ironically, the main objection to submitting an affidavit of fear is people are terrified of the IRS taking their home and destroying their lives. It reminds me of an old joke about the three dentists, where the one Russian one says to fill a cavity in Russia costs $5,000. The other dentists are shocked and ask why it's so much. The Russian says, In Soviet Russia, you have to go through the ass; no one will open their mouth.

If we're interested in the truth, and strive to govern our lives by it, then we shouldn't make it easy for politicians to farm us. I know it bothers them; they think they're the good guys, just doing their jobs. I say make them aware of the violent nature of their jobs. I told one IRS agent recently that the IRS earns every bit of contempt Americans have for them. They steal our property with no regard for right and wrong and not a bit of empathy, especially when they have utterly failed to provide any evidence to prove their accusations. In fact, it seems the less they can prove, the more effort they put in stealing our property.

The other reason we file an affidavit of fear is admissibility. Financial reports and licenses are the be-all and end-all of tax assessments. If there's a license or financial report given to the IRS, then there's an irrefutable presumption you're a taxpayer with taxable income. Irrefutable presumptions are supposedly illegal though, *Vlandis v. Kline*, 412 US 441.

Tax agencies and their accomplices in the courts do it anyway and even sanction you up to $25,000 for daring to question the presumption you're a taxpayer with taxable income. Can you believe people are sanctioned $25,000 for questioning an opinion? Does that also remind you of the inquisition? Don't dare question the opinion of an unknown tax agent.

As to admissibility, testimony/information given under threat, duress and coercion is considered inadmissible. Tax agency attorneys have affirmed this many times. They just don't think it's threat, duress and coercion when done by people called government. Although I'm sure an American tax lawyer would probably agree it's threat, duress and coercion when done by the Chinese government.

It's not a question of whether the information is correct; it's coerced and generally unreliable. When a business provides financial information to governments, they are only doing so because they have been terrorized into compliance; they don't want to be attacked. They usually have no idea if the financial reports are actually required to be sent; they're only doing it to avoid being put in jail or out of business.

Whether the information is correct is not relevant. Trading with others is not evidence the constitution and laws apply and the psychopaths have jurisdiction over us.

Agora Hour. This was also started in April 2011. The idea is for local businesses to have at least one hour a week where they would broadcast the radio show and not collect sales tax or display a business license if they had one.

We encourage people to donate the sales tax equivalent to the Civil Disobedience Evolution Fund http://cdevolution.org/ . This is a fund established to help those engaged in non-violent, non-cooperation who are attacked by politicians. Instead of paying to fund attacks, we can donate to a fund helping to minimize the damage caused by the attacks.

Here we really work together to build the agora, the business sets an example of non-violent, non-cooperation and encourages their customers, voluntaryists and statists alike, to do the same; to empower others by their example. They get promotion on the **No State Project** and they promote the show during the week.

This will continue to grow; as we add more and more Agora Hours we can expand to an Agora Day, then to an Agora Week, and the Agora Month. Think about a business trading with the community and not collecting sales tax or displaying a license for an entire month. This can progress to the Agora Year, which could mean the collapse of city governments.

I would imagine that along the way, city governments would be getting pretty worried about their cushy jobs and would want to have some compromise to get people to comply.

411

Bureaucrat insurance. This is where an established insurance business will be helpful, though there is nothing stopping people from setting up their own funds. The idea is to have a business that insures your life, liberty and property from attack by politicians such as the IRS and DEA.

If one is attacked, then there's an insurance settlement to cover the damage. This should include taking care of your family if you're attacked and put into a cage; all or part of your family's living expenses are covered. So if you are put in jail for not paying tribute or filing a tax return, then the insurance will cover that.

This can also be similar to the CD Evolution Fund mentioned earlier. Instead of paying taxes, one may contribute to an insurance fund covering political attacks.

With an established insurance business, there is the added benefit of insurance payments being tax-free. Yes, governments will have a problem with it; the object is to get enough of the market involved the insurance companies will push back.

The benefit of the show and the Liberty Radio Network http://lrn.fm, we can use the radio to promote the insurance, whether by established insurance companies or local funds.

This lowers the risk involved in non-violent, non-cooperation. In my experience, most people cower before governments out of fear of having their property taken; this diminishes that fear considerably. This is an insurance that appeals even to statists; they know their property is at constant risk of being taken by politicians. At some point, the market will come to an inevitable conclusion: Why are we paying insurance to protect us against governments, when governments are supposed to be protecting us? The market will see the futility in paying governments, and they'll see how much more effective the market is in protecting their property.

Insurance companies can start to lower their rates by encouraging the market not to pay taxes. I also think insurance companies would intervene and try to stop the bureaucrats from stealing your property. After all, they would have a big financial interest in you being left alone. Let them convince the bureaucrat to go after a non-insured victim. That drives up the demand for insurance. Companies can advertise their track records: Insure with Acme, we stopped 95% of political attacks last year alone.

And let's not forget that governments are themselves insured. They may self-insure, but they usually then have insurance companies underwrite their policies. So using insurance companies could help provide leverage over bureaucrats.

Media reps. We've been doing this for years and it's very effective. If you or someone you know is going to court or other type of hearing, bring a media rep. This is where support and community are so important.

What a media rep does is tell the bailiff or clerk they are from the media doing a series of shows on judicial misconduct and want the judge to know they're observing. Make sure to dress and act professionally. If there is enough time, you can request permission to record the proceedings. Judges don't like to be on display though and will usually refuse.

Having media reps are effective at putting judges on better behavior. In my experience, judges are less likely to fly into screaming rages when they know the media is there watching them. What I do and recommend is ask questions to then get the judge to contradict himself. Contradicting himself is bad enough when it's just in front of us, the unwashed masses, but it's got to be frustrating for them to know there are reporters taking notes. They probably know they can't just start screaming without it being reported.

And we don't have to tell them what media we're from; it's none of their business what part of the media we're from. Let them stay in the dark and wonder about it. And the way things work on the interwebs, a local story can go viral easily. So don't tell them who you're with, let them sweat it out thinking the New York Times or NBC is there.

It's also good to point out there will be more reporters later and they probably won't announce their presence. Have them tell the judge they don't want the media to affect the way he conducts trials. This way the judge may assume the media could be there at any time.

And this does not have to be limited to only times someone we know is being attacked; you can go into any court, preferably traffic, and do this. Between hearings you can ask questions. I'd ask:

> Media: Excuse me; that was a civil traffic case?
> Judge: *Yes, it was a complaint for not having a seatbelt.*
> Media: OK, I didn't get too much information regarding that. Could you tell me if that civil case was in the nature of a contract dispute or tort?
> Judge: *Excuse me; what did you just say?*
> Media: Was that civil case in the nature of a contract dispute or tort?

You can also ask questions regarding the conflict of interest:

> Media: If I have a traffic ticket against me, and I opted for a trial, am I entitled to a fair trial?
> Judge: *Yes, of course.*
> Media: Can I get a fair trial if there's a conflict of interest?
> Judge: *No, you couldn't.*
> Media: Who do you represent in such proceedings?
> Judge: *Excuse me; what the hell did you just say? Get me the police!*

While this tends to enrage judges, because we're there from the media, they usually don't start yelling, they have more self-control. I think they're like those sharks at the zoo that are behind the glass; they see tourists and are thinking "The moment this glass is gone you're lunch!"

They'll desperately try to avoid the question; they usually do. What's he going to do though, threaten reporters with contempt for asking a question? He's making a story of judicial misconduct pretty easy to write.

He's probably only going to avoid the question and ask you to sit down or to leave. You can play stupid and ask: Since I'm doing a series of shows on judicial misconduct, would not answering such basic questions be considered misconduct? You can tell him you'll put that in writing if he needs time to ~~spin~~ formulate an answer.

If they refuse to answer, then that would also be a good time to remind them there will be more reporters regularly observing and reporting his courtroom antics. You can be bold and include: Apparently you have something to hide.

He has to be thinking the question is going to be part of the report; what if more people start asking him? They have to leave the court and talk to friends and family about it later. I'm pretty sure it has an effect on them.

And it was pointed out to me that any of us, as defendants, can tell the bailiff we're media reps. There's no reason why we have to have someone else doing it, the effect should be the same.

Jury activism. As mentioned earlier, we need to start questioning potential jurors regarding the threatened violence to each juror by judges. I imagine that if this can be a regular and expected part of *voir dire*, then the prosecutors and prosecutors would take notice.

They legally have to permit the questioning of prospective jurors and provide a fair trial with an impartial jury. Why make it easy for them to persecute us?

What if we make it impossible for them to maintain a perception of fairness? It's actually pretty easy to do; it's my objective when there isn't a jury.

This isn't for real crimes; as much as I know the system is violent and supports human farming, I'm only suggesting this for those proceedings where they want to punish non-compliance to the will of a politician or they're attacking someone truly innocent of a *mala in se* charge. I see this as a way for politicians to focus on doing things closer to the way described by their PR. This way, as more people stop accepting the program, governments out of necessity will have no choice but to eliminate programs not consistent with their PR. Before the actual dissolution of governments, there will probably only be a skeleton of what we have now; there will only be police, courts and military left.

This has the potential of really disrupting their scam. The amount of violence has to either be ramped up, or they won't be able to prosecute nearly as many people. And less people will be willing to take a deal when they know they can ask jurors these questions.

Increasing the violence will only make the situation worse because they have to have juries for most crimes. This approach can really disrupt their prosecutions of *mala prohibita* laws.

Prospective jurors may start questioning judges and prosecutors on their own and really gum up the works. Some have expressed concern

414

that if people did this, it could just get them excluded from being a juror and then the prosecution could stack the jury with pro-government drones and secure convictions. While this is possible, I don't think it's very probable because it doesn't take into account the other jurors hearing this as well as the defendant who should be inspired to pick up the ball and run with it. If the defendant realizes what's happening, then he can start asking each potential juror the same thing. After all, it's in his best interest to make sure he has an impartial jury. His lawyer certainly won't do it, because lawyers have an allegiance to the judges and they tend to be babies who don't want to upset the judge. Grow a spine already.

From my experience, judges are their own worst enemies because they lack adult coping skills and just fly into fits of blind rage. Even when they know in advance we want to use their anger against them, they still come unglued. They're stuck in a pattern; violence is the only way they can cope. Some people jump when they see a spider, judges rage when asked questions.

Since judges sit on a throne of lies, they view everything as a threat; even simple questions. They know they're criminals; their black robes can only hide so much shame.

And that is exactly why they shun the media. You would think narcissists that demand public adulation would also be like Joe Arpaio who seems to love the media. And yes, people who cage you for not standing when they enter a room are narcissists demanding reverence and adulation. Anyone who rages because someone calls them by their first name is unstable at best. Not the first one you want to invite to parties, I'd bet.

So imagine how openly violent these black-robed lawyers are going to get in front of dozens of people they rely on for their perception of legitimacy. What effect is it going to have when each one is now questioning why this lawyer is threatening them and forcing them into temporary slavery? How much violence can he exhibit and threaten before he has a roomful of people who will deliberately not comply and refuse to hand them and the persecutor convictions against peaceful people?

It has to dawn on them these fits of anger are going to affect the jury's decision. It definitely won't be lost on the defendant, nor should it be.

Like I mentioned in *Adventures*, if you don't have the decency to ask me for permission, then don't expect my compliance. We need to tell these violent lawyers: If you're going to force me into slavery, then I'll be kicking and screaming every step of the way.

Word should get out as well as videos; soon some judges will develop public reputations for being psychos. I don't mean just a few anarchists like me talking about them; I mean the average man/woman in the community. I can talk about Harold Reeb being crazed, but only his unfortunate victims will probably know whom I'm talking about. The same with Robin Allen, a man with a serious anger problem. I worked with Todd in the valley who did some work at Robin's house; Todd said he was just as angry at home.

This can include the flyers given out at the courts mentioned below.

Constant challenges. While it may seem that bureaucrats and politicians don't care about anything but violent domination and their next victim, I think it's a mistake to think they are all immune from criticism and enlightenment. Psychopaths have a bloated sense of grandiosity about themselves; they don't like being questioned and certainly hate being criticized, though they probably hate being questioned more.

Lots of the lower level grunts think they're the good guys administering justice and providing services to a willing community. Some seem genuinely surprised when you start talking about the violent nature of their jobs.

This is also a way to convince those who are on the fence about government. There are plenty of low-to no-risk, ways to challenge bureaucrats on their positions; we don't have to be in court at the whim of a lawyer who can't stand up to some simple questions.

I think we need to whittle away at the lower level bureaucrats, the ones carrying out the violence for the pigs who run the farm. This is in effect engaging the nine to thirty-three percent that are not apathetic psychopaths.

We should engage them by challenging their perceptions; get them to question their positions. Are they really on some moral high ground, or are they engaged in criminal activity? They can and do wake up to the fact they've been duped like everyone else. Yes, I know there are always more useful idiots who'll be happy to replace a cop or TSA agent who quits and gets a real job, but that's a narrow way to look at it. Before someone quits, it's obvious they are going to be talking to others at the office; we know this happens. With whistleblower cases there is usually a history of speaking with family, friends and coworkers before they go public. This is where they are particularly important and influential.

There's no doubt a cop or other agent may have more influence about the nature of government than me or other voluntaryists who have never been government employees. At least in his scope of influence he/she will be. I think of radio/TV show hosts who practically worship police and they'd have a difficult time attacking a former cop, especially when the cop has personal, first-hand knowledge of the facts.

I've encountered lots of refusals to answer simple questions, e.g., is the court's jurisdiction unlimited? While I may not get answers all the time, I think it's safe to assume that even in those cases the agents are thinking about the questions and the issues raised. I know from speaking with agents they do think about these things after talking with me. I've had them tell me they were at the website and they know I raise difficult questions. Some have admitted it was the first time they even examined the morality of what they were doing.

Far too often, and it's by design, the enforcers are not familiar with what led to the decision or judgment to attack someone. They're automatons and admittedly exercise no discretion of their own. On Feb 8, 2012, Paul from Utah Administrative Services told me it's not his job to determine if the decision is right or wrong, just to enforce it. When I asked him if he took a standard of right and wrong with him to work, he declined to respond.

So the last thing those who are really behind governments want are their henchmen actually thinking about what they're doing. If the grunts are questioning the moral ground their jobs rest on, they're not as likely to just carry out the orders. There are many historical examples of this. William Doniphan, a general with the Missouri State Guard, was ordered to execute Joseph Smith and several others in 1838.

http://en.wikipedia.org/wiki/Alexander_William_Doniphan.

He refused on grounds it would be cold-blooded murder.

There are contemporary examples as well. Don't we see this already when cops pull over other cops or their family? When there's a personal connection to the victim, the bureaucrat tends to have some empathy and isn't so quick to continue the attack. They can tell the victim hasn't hurt anyone and it's no big deal if a fee is not paid or a code isn't complied with. They go back to the same standard we all tend to hold, that aggression is wrong. The victim broke into his/her circle of empathy, as small as it may be when on the job.

Empathy is stronger than a sense of self-preservation.

We need to work to correct what causes the apathy towards the victims; the bureaucrat doesn't look at us as their victims, or even as victims of the system. Remember what contributes to the anti-social behavior discussed in the psychology section, the Lord of the Flies effect mentioned by Philip Zimbardo:

- The power of anonymity, of loss of personal identity,
- To dis-inhibit repressed actions; violence and sexuality
- Behaving in any way permissible in new situations
- Transfer from cognitive to situational control of behavior

The bureaucrats, the ones doing the collections and making the system turn, need to hear from us and see us. They need to see we are real and just as important, and lose at least some of their feeling of anonymity. This is going to weaken their ability to just carry out orders they know are wrong.

Empathy is stronger than, and overcomes, delusions of omnipotence. It's just not as easy to put aside your principles of right and wrong if you can feel something for your victim.

Being anonymous was a contributing factor to the abuse dished out in the Milgram Experiment. Most of the psychological elements contributing to the anti-social behavior can be reversed. Some rapport is sometimes all that's needed to turn a situation around. I've used my history of growing up on Long Island to some advantage when speaking to IRS agents at the Holtsville, New York office. I grew up only a few miles from their fortress of hate.

This is why asking questions can be so effective, especially when you start with some common ground and the man/woman you're speaking with thinks they are coming to an understanding on their own. If the process starts with reification, then questioning people to expose the fictions will start to break the pattern leading to a willingness to kill innocent people.

It's the difference between a "judgment" and just the "opinion of a lawyer," and that's a big difference. They're the same thing-only most people are not nearly as willing to blindly carry out the opinions of some lawyer. It's the same with a tax summons, such as with the IRS. It's an order from an accountant, just some guy who, if we can get a name, is using a false one. Why is he ordering me around? Why not just ask me?

If he takes you to court and gets a judgment, then it's still nothing more than the opinion of a lawyer.

A good reason to constantly challenge them is because we know it makes their job more difficult. I see no virtue in making their jobs easier. I'm not talking about being abusive or unprofessional in any way, just asking them questions. Just help me understand where you're coming from, Mr. Politician. You think your constitution and laws apply for no other reason than I was born in a hospital located in New York? What evidence do you rely on to prove that?

We can go to their offices, to their city council meetings or just call them on the phone.

Constant complaints. Part of networking and supporting each other includes letting the psychopaths know we're watching and reporting their crimes. They need to know we're not alone standing up to the machine that's grinding away at us.

It should come as no surprise when a judge in San Diego prepares for the afternoon slaughter, there's also a reporter for the **No State Project** observing them. They can expect complaints from people in Sidney, Australia and London for the crimes they are committing against peaceful people in California.

This works against the hierarchy they need in place; we need to show that we do care what happens to other people, even if they're not from the same geographical area and tribe.

Complaints should be against each cop and lawyer involved with traffic or drug complaints. It's tough with tax agents because we generally won't be able to get contact information or a true name, but we can still file complaints with what we do get.

Can they accuse us of so-called "paper terrorism"? Sure, that's a tactic that has been used before, but it's usually associated with the filing of liens and lawsuits against government agents. At the least, if an agency did that, it would be bringing attention to a serious issue: the lack of facts proving their codes are applicable.

The complaints would generally be based on a judge assuming the prosecutor's burden on jurisdiction and refusing to presume innocence. Any attention given to this standard criminal tactic of lawyers is a good thing. Another would be to ask why the judge ruled that the witness (cop who wrote the ticket) is incompetent but took the testimony anyway. I'm pretty certain no lawyer wants that crap examined away from his wooden

418

throne.

They commit the same crimes with pretty much every complaint they prosecute, so our complaints are easy to write up from a template. Another benefit to looking at the facts and putting them into action: you can easily predict their behaviors. We can get complaints filed with their agency, judicial conduct commission or bar association within a day or two.

And we should be complaining about their psychopathic behavior. I suggest using the word psychopath in the complaint. Being described as a psychopath will not sit well with their grandiose view of themselves; they're not going to like a flood of complaints about how they launched into a screaming rage because someone asked them whom they represent. Psychopaths fear being exposed as psychopaths, so we should call them on it when filing complaints:

> Mr. Richard Bohlander, acting as a judge, started out professionally. His victim addressed him as Richard and he immediately became enraged and started screaming. He threatened the victim with incarceration. Richard exhibited psychopathic behavior; he appears to lack adult coping skills and must resort to violence whereas a normal adult would have politely asked to have been addressed differently.

> If this type of behavior is common, then it's no surprise the legal profession is in such disrepute. I certainly would not want to interact with such violent individuals.

What we can do with the complaints is also include the pattern from the other lawyers. To prove this is not an isolated incident, we can document the tactic in Australia, Canada, England, New Zealand and the US. Every new judge just gets added to the growing list of criminals who assume the prosecutor's burden and refuse to presume innocence.

Compiling such a record would also provide valuable information regarding how the complaints are handled. To prove that regardless of the jurisdiction, lawyers work together to rape and pillage us, and their support staff knows what's going on and turns a blind eye to the pattern of crimes these lawyers are committing. Because we already know judges will not publicly address the issues with the media, they are cowards and will resist any independent investigation into their practices.

Is a goal here to erode public confidence in the political system? Yes, and the best way to do that is to just lay the facts out for people to see for themselves. People can call prosecutors and ask them why judges habitually assume their burden on jurisdiction. When those lawyers refuse to discuss the matter, they lose credibility and there's less confidence in the system. And there are historical examples were many people have lost confidence in the political system. A recent one is the Marc Dutroux affair in Belgium. http://www.nytimes.com/1996/10/21/world/275000-in-belgium-protest-handling-of-child-sex-scandal.html there is a BBC documentary also http://www.youtube.com/watch?v=0uCoqldzLJs.

We can even help diminish the bureaucrats' confidence in their system-at least make it look less attractive. Why should they enjoy going to work? Why should they go into that courtroom with anything less than dread? Oy vey, here we go again; how many complaints is this morning's session going to bring? If we can use non-violent techniques to make them dread going to work and make it less appealing, then we should. Word can spread so those considering it may decide to offer their services/products to the market on a voluntary basis:

Don't bother mate, unless you enjoy being compared to Hitler every day.

Because of social pressure, support staff seeing these psychopaths at work every day may be too afraid to openly discuss it. But the complaints can serve as the kid pointing out the emperor really has no clothes. It only has to start with office chatter and it takes off from there. That alone could make it unbearable for some of them and they'll be looking for other employment.

Given the grandiose view they have of themselves, they probably don't take well to the little people calling them on their anti-social personalities.

They have families and friends just like we do; their kids will not like going to school and hearing other kids talking about mom or dad being a nut. Did you see Katy's dad on YouTube? He was acting like a spoiled child and screaming at people who just asked a question.

It may be really effective to focus on one small criminal organization with such constant challenges. Imagine those doing business as the Keene, New Hampshire government getting calls every day asking for evidence their laws apply just because we're physically in Keene. We could flood them with requests for evidence and follow up with complaints.

We should also be bringing the complaints to the insurance companies who hold the liability policies for these criminal syndicates. While there are exceptions, governments have liability policies covering damages caused by agents, including judges.

It's going to be easier to convince insurance investigators that the judges and prosecutors are crooks than to convince associates of the judges. Insurance companies can conduct under-oath investigations; if the judges and prosecutors don't cooperate, the insurance company can drop the policy.

This may be the only way we can get judges and prosecutors into a hearing where they can be questioned.

Flyers. This has long been a tool for education and disrupting government operations. One example I started doing again is giving out flyers to people entering courts in Arizona. I point out the judges and clerks are lying that civil penalties must be paid the day of the judgment, and provide a copy of the relevant text from the code.

This way, not only do victims of the system learn about it and can challenge it, but employees of the court can see it. Let them see flyers where we put a judge's face on there with a prosecutor and show how they work together to steal from people. I see it as a type of public safety announcement to warn people just how dangerous these lawyers are and how they operate. It gives people another tool to defend themselves and call these predators on their many crimes.

An example is Melinda Lasater and Jonathan Lapin in San Diego. Melinda denied the California court system was adversarial. Was it the result of bias in favor of Jonathan or incompetence? Jonathan, a prosecutor, didn't object or do anything to correct Melinda. Tough for a lawyer to claim they didn't know the court system is adversarial. It's something we learn in high school here in the United States.

I called as a member of the press to find out if the city attorneys thought the California system is adversarial or not. That's pretty basic stuff right? Wrong; not when you realize that requires an antagonistic assertion of rights and you're prosecuting people without one.

The city attorney's office in San Diego refuses to answer the question. And with good reason: they know I will ask follow-up questions they really don't want to answer.

But if we give people flyers with the information, they can ask the questions in court. No, the lawyers don't have to answer, but that will only tend to prove my point that those calling themselves government are criminals.

They get away with their robbery in part because people don't challenge them on their lies. It's a matter of routine for both sides. I get calls from people all the time who are surprised when I talk about asking for evidence that the prosecutor has to prove jurisdiction and people ask me: "I can ask that?" Yes, of course; why not? Why would you give them a pass on something so important?

On the flyer it's easy to set forth the conflict of interest with the formula: A forces B to answer C. That, with the three questions: (am I entitled to a fair trial; can I get a fair trial if there is a conflict of interest; who do you, the judge, represent?) are going to enable people to ask judges a few questions that undermine the facade of legitimacy and make it tougher for these lawyers to ram everyone through their system.

We can also point out that the judge will not presume you innocent; they will instead insist the code (an element of the violation) applies, thereby assuming jurisdiction for the prosecutor. Anyone can watch this play out in court if they have the impudence to challenge His Majesty's jurisdiction.

Others who are on the fence will get a preview of what they can expect from the psychopath in the robe. They'll also see others doing it and we can witness the bandwagon effect take over. If coordinated, we can have press there and keep track of what the judge is doing. We can record how the judge refused to presume innocence and assumed jurisdiction with ten people. That evidence can then be reported online and be part of another flyer. It can also be used as the basis for a group complaint against the lawyer.

If we can have media reps regularly at the courts also giving out flyers, then there is certainly going to be social pressure on the judges.

They'll be informed that there are flyers being given out with their names on them outlining not only their crimes, but with information people can use to undermine their facade of legitimacy. We also tell them the press is there observing, and that has to make them think twice about yelling and denying everything without explanation. If carried out, I don't see them doing business as usual; no, I see them trying to stop us from giving out the flyers.

> *This is ridiculous; I can't get anything done here today!*
> Why is that Your Honor?
> *Everyone is trying to plead guilty.*
> And this is a problem how?
> *Because, you little jerk, they're asking me whom I represent!*
> I still don't see why that's a problem.
> *Oh, you don't? Because first they ask if they're entitled to a fair trial and I have to say yes. Then they ask if they can get a fair trial if there's a conflict of interest.*
> Yeah, so?
> *I have to say no, I'm supposed to be a judge, a fair, impartial and independent decision-maker.*
> So what's the problem?
> *Because they follow up asking whom do I represent in the proceedings!*
> I'm not following you here; what's the problem?
> *You're an idiot.*

Real change happens at the local level and this is an excellent way to do just that. Just because the bureaucrats don't care about right and wrong doesn't mean their victims (us) don't. If they want to be liars and claim when their law says thirty days that it actually means one day, then I'm sure the people forced to be there do know the difference and can challenge them once they have the truth in their hands.

If they roll their eyes when I walk in and get that feeling of dread because I'm there again, it's going to be a hundred times worse when their victims refuse to be intimidated into paying the same day. I'd like to be there when each person tells the judge and clerks they're not paying a dime that day, that regardless of their threats, they're walking out and taking the thirty days. They can also tell them they will include the threat as part of their appeal. They can tell these judges and clerks their dishonesty will be an issue on appeal they can try to justify.

We can also give out flyers at city council meetings. This should lead to more people challenging these local predators, to constantly ask them difficult questions. Good examples are:

> If you believe your services are valuable and that we want them, then why is support coerced?

> What makes you think you represent us when you force us to pay for your services?

Given the fact that you coerce support, what facts do you rely on proving you represent us?

We always need a common ground though. This is very important, whether questioning a bureaucrat or someone we know. We can start with, "Do you believe in initiating violence or using threats of violence against peaceful people?" Most will answer no, they don't.

"So you're not a violent person by nature?"

"Are you aware you have no voluntary support that we're all forced to support and pay you?"

These questions focus on the real problem: the coercive manner in which services are provided. They may claim the community has voted. That is only a distraction because we do not have a choice in whether there is government or not. Having a dozen or more people asking these questions at every meeting for weeks on end would really bother them. Imagine asking a city council member the above questions, and then asking:

Why do you need to use violence to provide your services?

So you don't need to use violence? Don't you think most, if not all of the problems associated with government would stop if you didn't start from a foundation of violence and irresponsibility? You guys could stop the police from aggressing against us anytime you wanted to.

I believe that if we continually raise the moral problem with the government concept, that even those engaged in carrying it out will help bring about some meaningful change. This is also why it's important for them to see us at their meetings so they have an idea of what the community thinks about what they are doing.

And the question that guts their whole facade of legitimacy, the one they don't even have to answer publicly for everyone to know the answer:

If I did things like you, and I forced people to give me money, would you consider me a criminal?

Surveillance. We already know politicians and their henchmen don't like being recorded, especially when confronted by domestic terrorists asking them simple questions such as evidence they represent those they are coercing. Ademo Freeman
http://www.copblock.org/tag/ademo-freeman/
is only one example of someone who was thrown into a cage for recording a cop. We live in a total surveillance state; everything we do is recorded and stored. The massive NSA building going up in Bluffdale, Utah is only one of many such facilities, and they are not just spying on Americans, it's everyone. Ademo was convicted for recording a phone call to a police station where every call is already recorded. Anyone with half a brain

knows calling the government means the line is not secure.

The people need to know there is no reform, this is a psychopathic system controlled by psychopaths and can't be any other way when it begins with coercion. When people are willing to kill you and take all your stuff under the guise of providing roads, then there is no option other than complete abolition.

With total surveillance comes total control and the drones are already here. The asinine "I'm not doing anything wrong, I've got nothing to hide" is costing us all. As whistleblower William Binney has stated: we don't get to decide what's right and wrong. The psychopaths who are spying on us are doing that. Not doing anything wrong? How deluded must one be to use that line despite all the evidence innocent people are prosecuted and killed every day by these anti-social parasites? Who said you have to do something wrong to be prosecuted? Kids selling lemonade have been charged as criminals.

When a group of people coerces you to pay them, what evidence is there that they have your best interests when spying on everyone? If you still think there's merit to the concept of government at this point in this book, then do yourself and your family a favor: try finding evidence proving people who coerce your support represent you, that they are your servants who only want to protect you.

Surveillance on the psychopaths should include the other methods set forth above. The cameras and audio recorders should be turned on those calling themselves government. When we file complaints we should follow up on the phone and ask questions, put them on the spot to explain themselves. They don't deserve a pass and if people don't see and hear these predators for what they are, just imagine what our world will look like with ten more years of technological advances.

If they have the "authority" to spy on us and collect data, then where did they get it? According to the PR, the authority and power of the government, at least in so-called democracies/republics, is ostensibly delegated from the people. So unless every individual man and woman has the authority or right to spy on everyone else, then the collective does not have it to then delegate to the psychopaths called government.

When you keep your focus on the coercive support, nothing those called government do survives any investigation and scrutiny.

The goal of all this questioning and recording is to destroy the remaining credibility the concept of government still has. We need to incessantly point out that none of us believes it is justified to kill people to provide services; that none of us wants aggression used against us.

Non-compliance. The most obvious reason we still have governments, is because there is compliance. The slave owners cannot control us without our compliance. So, solutions have to include non-compliance. We just have to reverse the program: we enable them to rule over us by our compliance; by stopping our compliance they can't rule over us.

Flyers, complaints, radio appearances and education have as their goals getting people to understand the government concept is a castle made of sand. It's childish at best and is the cause of immense trauma and damage worldwide. Once they know what they are dealing with and there is no evidence we owe them anything, then we can move on with our lives and stop complying with them.

What critical mass will make it impossible for governments to continue functioning? I don't know, but I'm sure it's going to be easier to put a gang like the Keene city government out of business than the US cartel in DC.

"No one rules when no one obeys." Lao-Tzu

Final Thoughts

The reason this indictment is about the concept that created the war/slavery system is because if governments collapsed tomorrow, psychopaths would be able to just create more of the same systems. Getting to a voluntary society has to include the destruction of the concepts themselves; the rationale for the psychopathic system itself is what needs to be permanently discredited. As long as a certain percentage of the world's population still see merit in the concept, then a voluntary society is not going to come about, at least not on a large scale.

This is shown in instances where there are police strikes and there is a reported increase in crime. Those in the media claim that without police, there is anarchy. These are not examples of a voluntary society because there is still a political structure in place, just no police for a while, it's worth noting several facts regarding these alleged increases in crime.

The hierarchy of the society is still in place; the vertical structure is still there. It's silly to think there is anarchy or a voluntary society just because there's a police strike; the *rulers* are still there, just a few less enforcers. The statist rationale/perceptions are still there along with the taxing and other political structures. The people still have these concepts governing their behaviors. So while changing the context to a degree will affect behavior, it will only change it a degree.

Until people see not only the fallacy of the concept, but also realize there is no authority out there to take care them, that we're responsible for ourselves, we won't have a voluntary society. The current violent society is held in place by two things: 1) violence used to provide services is OK when the label government is used, and 2) fear of non-compliance with psychopaths called government.

Both elements must be dealt with if we are to have a free, voluntary society. If we want to rid this world of human farming and war, we have to address these two factors. If half the population of California rejects the program, sees right through it as the insanity it is, but they continue complying out of fear, then it doesn't change anything.

For all we know, more than half the population may already reject the concept. But they are obviously cooperating; there is overwhelming evidence of that. While we may not know what they believe, we do know

425

they are still complying and acting as if they do believe in the concept.

We want a system that doesn't enable, attract, create and immunize psychopaths. The government concept permits exactly that. A voluntary society, where personal autonomy is honored; where there's no such thing as an authority to dictate the actions of others; where are all are free to live their lives on their own terms, is the most rational concept we have, at least I think so.

I don't think a society based on coercion and irresponsibility is one anyone would publicly agree to. I doubt anyone, even those who have a vested interest in such a society, would explicitly advocate such, but that's exactly what government apologetics is all about. If they do agree with that, then an appropriate response I've used before is: "Are you also anti-social in your private life?"

Let them chew on that for a while.

It's my hope that more people will realize there are no governments, just gangs of killers, thieves and liars; that if we need protection from anyone, it's from those claiming authority to rule us.

I want to live in a world where most people accept the following creed:

Reject authority – Embrace Autonomy

Alphabetical Index

429

432

Made in the USA
Monee, IL
24 February 2021

61231663R00240